Dictionary of Literary Biography • Volume Forty-four

American Screenwriters
Second Series

Dictionary of Literary Biography

Dictionary of Literary Biography • Volume Forty-four

American Screenwriters

Second Series

Edited by
Randall Clark

A Bruccoli Clark Book
Gale Research Company • Book Tower • Detroit, Michigan 48226

Manufactured by Edwards Brothers, Inc.
Ann Arbor, Michigan
Printed in the United States of America

Library of Congress Cataloging-in-Publication Data
Main entry under title:

American screenwriters.

(Dictionary of literary biography; v. 44)
"A Bruccoli Clark book."
Includes index.
1. Screen writers—United States—Biography—
Dictionaries. I. Clark, Randall. II. Series.
PN1998.A2A586 1986 812'.03'09 [B] 85-31221
ISBN 0-8103-1722-2

Contents

Contents

Plan of the Series

. . . Almost the most prodigious asset of a country, and perhaps its most precious possession, is its native literary product—when that product is fine and noble and enduring.

Mark Twain*

The advisory board, the editors, and the publisher of the *Dictionary of Literary Biography* are joined in endorsing Mark Twain's declaration. The literature of a nation provides an inexhaustible resource of permanent worth. It is our expectation that this endeavor will make literature and its creators better understood and more accessible to students and the literate public, while satisfying the standards of teachers and scholars.

To meet these requirements, *literary biography* has been construed in terms of the author's achievement. The most important thing about a writer is his writing. Accordingly, the entries in *DLB* are career biographies, tracing the development of the author's canon and the evolution of his reputation.

The publication plan for *DLB* resulted from two years of preparation. The project was proposed to Bruccoli Clark by Frederick G. Ruffner, president of the Gale Research Company, in November 1975. After specimen entries were prepared and typeset, an advisory board was formed to refine the entry format and develop the series rationale. In meetings held during 1976, the publisher, series editors, and advisory board approved the scheme for a comprehensive biographical dictionary of persons who contributed to North American literature. Editorial work on the first volume began in January 1977, and it was published in 1978.

In order to make *DLB* more than a reference tool and to compile volumes that individually have claim to status as literary history, it was decided to organize volumes by topic or period or genre. Each of these freestanding volumes provides a biographical-bibliographical guide and overview for a particular area of literature. We are convinced that this organization—as opposed to a single alphabet method—constitutes a valuable innovation in the presentation of reference material. The volume plan necessarily requires many decisions for the placement and treatment of authors who might properly be included in two or three volumes. In some instances a major figure will be included in separate volumes, but with different entries emphasizing the aspect of his career appropriate to each volume. Ernest Hemingway, for example, is represented in *American Writers in Paris, 1920-1939* by an entry focusing on his expatriate apprenticeship; he is also in *American Novelists, 1910-1945* with an entry surveying his entire career. Each volume includes a cumulative index of subject authors. The final *DLB* volume will be a comprehensive index to the entire series.

With volume ten in 1982 it was decided to enlarge the scope of *DLB* beyond the literature of the United States. By the end of 1985 twenty-one volumes treating British literature had been published, and volumes for Commonwealth and Modern European literature were in progress. The series has been further augmented by the *DLB Yearbooks* (since 1981) which update published entries and add new entries to keep the *DLB* current with contemporary activity. There have also been occasional *DLB Documentary Series* volumes which provide biographical and critical background source materials for figures whose work is judged to have particular interest for students. One of these companion volumes is entirely devoted to Tennessee Williams.

The purpose of *DLB* is not only to provide reliable information in a convenient format but also to place the figures in the larger perspective of literary history and to offer appraisals of their accomplishments by qualified scholars.

We define literature as the *intellectual commerce of a nation:* not merely as belles lettres, but as that ample and complex process by which ideas are generated, shaped, and transmitted. *DLB* entries are not limited to "creative writers" but extend to other figures who in this time and in this way influenced the mind of a people. Thus the series encompasses historians, journalists, publishers, and screenwriters. By this means readers of *DLB* may be aided to perceive literature not as cult scripture in the keeping of cultural high priests, but as at the center of a nation's life.

*From an unpublished section of Mark Twain's autobiography, copyright © by the Mark Twain Company.

DLB includes the major writers appropriate to each volume and those standing in the ranks immediately behind them. Scholarly and critical counsel has been sought in deciding which minor figures to include and how full their entries should be. Wherever possible, useful references will be made to figures who do not warrant separate entries.

Each *DLB* volume has a volume editor responsible for planning the volume, selecting the figures for inclusion, and assigning the entries. Volume editors are also responsible for preparing, where appropriate, appendices surveying the major periodicals and literary and intellectual movements for their volumes, as well as lists of further readings. Work on the series as a whole is coordinated at the Bruccoli Clark editorial center in Columbia, South Carolina, where the editorial staff is responsible for the accuracy of the published volumes.

One feature that distinguishes *DLB* is the illustration policy—its concern with the iconography of literature. Just as an author is influenced by his surroundings, so is the reader's understanding of the author enhanced by a knowledge of his environment. Therefore *DLB* volumes include not only drawings, paintings, and photographs of authors, often depicting them at various stages in their careers, but also illustrations of their families and places where they lived. Title pages are regularly reproduced in facsimile along with dust jackets for modern authors. The dust jackets are a special feature of *DLB* because they often document better than anything else the way in which an author's work was launched in its own time. Specimens of the writers' manuscripts are included when feasible.

A supplement to *DLB*—tentatively titled *A Guide, Chronology, and Glossary for American Literature*—will outline the history of literature in North America and trace the influences that shaped it. This volume will provide a framework for the study of American literature by means of chronological tables, literary affiliation charts, glossarial entries, and concise surveys of the major movements. It has been planned to stand on its own as a vade mecum, providing a ready-reference guide to the study of American literature as well as a companion to the *DLB* volumes for American literature.

Samuel Johnson rightly decreed that "The chief glory of every people arises from its authors." The purpose of the *Dictionary of Literary Biography* is to compile literary history in the surest way available to us—by accurate and comprehensive treatment of the lives and work of those who contributed to it.

The *DLB* Advisory Board

Foreword

American Screenwriters, Second Series, is published as a companion volume to *DLB 26: American Screenwriters.* It contains career studies and biographies of sixty-four additional screenwriters. As with the first volume, the screenwriters here are a representative sample of the hundreds who have written films in the past seventy years. Because the book is a study of screenwriters, only authors who wrote primarily for the screen—or who wrote for other media but had noteworthy film achievements—are included. Thus, novelists such as Calder Willingham and Richard Matheson, who had lengthy film careers, are included. Performers who wrote their own material—Mae West, W. C. Fields, Charlie Chaplin—are also included. Finally, "American screenwriters" are defined as authors who worked in America for most of their careers. Writers like Charles Bennett, Ernest Vajda, and Walter Reisch, who immigrated to the United States where they had substantial film careers, are considered to be Americans.

In order to understand the art and craft of the screenwriter it is necessary to know both the history and the unique restrictions of his medium. Scriptwriting did not emerge as a distinct literary form until the late 1930s. The earliest American movies, one-reel shorts, were almost entirely improvised and required no screenplays. As silent films became more sophisticated, full scripts were required, but dialogue and exposition were still by necessity kept very brief because they were presented on title cards. Therefore silent-movie scripts, on the whole, were sketchier and less elaborate than those later written for sound films (though there were some noteworthy exceptions: Erich von Stroheim's original script for *Greed,* written in 1923, was over 600 pages long). The development of sound film resulted in a demand for writers who could provide dialogue; most of these writers had backgrounds in other media, usually the theater, and were invited to Hollywood where their writing experience was needed. By the end of the 1930s those dialogue writers were being replaced by a new kind of screenwriter, one who spent his entire career writing movies and who understood the special demands of the screen.

Those demands have remained largely the same since the 1930s. Possibly the strictest requirement is that of length: a standard screenplay should be no more than 140 pages, no fewer than 100; this length translates roughly into 90 to 120 minutes. And much of every page is blank space or given over to description, as can be seen in this excerpt from Ernest Lehman's script for *North by Northwest:*

> THORNHILL
> Yes?
>
> FIRST MAN
> (with a faint foreign accent)
> The car is waiting outside. You will walk between us saying nothing.
>
> THORNHILL
> What are you talking about?
>
> SECOND MAN
> (taking arm)
> Let's go.

One hundred twenty pages of a script, then, contain many fewer words than 100 pages of a novel, and the writer has to make good use of limited space. Plot must be developed and paced very carefully. Usually a script is divided roughly into three sections of unequal length. The first twenty-five percent of the script establishes problems and builds toward a conflict. Section two, which should be nearly one half of the movie, depicts the conflict and ends with the protagonist facing a threat. Section three, the final twenty-five percent of the film, shows the protagonist overcoming his crisis and presents a resolution.

The screenwriter must present a proper mixture of dialogue and visual image; he must be sure to show, and not just to tell. The inherent requirements for the motion picture can be a help as well as a restriction, as can be seen in this excerpt from another Ernest Lehman script, this time for *The Sound of Music:*

> We are floating in utter silence over a scene of spectacular and unearthly beauty. As far as the eye can see are majestic mountain peaks, lush green meadows, deep blue lakes, the silver ribbon of a winding river. Isolated locales are selected by the camera and photographed with such stylized beauty that the world below, however real, will be seen as a lovely never-

never land where stories such as ours can happen, and where people sometimes express their deepest emotions in song. As we glide in silence over the countryside, we see an occasional fair, animals grazing in the meadows, houses nestling in the hills, the steeples of churches, a castle surrounded by water. And now something is subtly happening to us as we gaze down at the enchanted world. Faint sounds are beginning to drift up and penetrate our awareness . . . the tinkle of cowbells . . . the approaching and receding song of a swiftly passing flock of birds . . . the call of a goatherd echoing from one mountain side to another. And with this, we are aware that the ground seems to be rising. The treetops are getting closer. Our speed seems to be increasing. Without knowing it, we have started to approach a mountain. A musical note is heard, the first prolonged musical note that leads to "The Sound of Music." Faster and faster we skim the treetops. And then suddenly we clear the trees and reveal: Maria on her mountain-top.

It is a soft and verdant place with a magnificent panorama of the surrounding countryside. Dressed as a postulant, but bareheaded, gazing about at all this breathtaking beauty, is Maria.

This rather lengthy passage can be shown on film in a matter of seconds, with no need for any spoken words.

A script goes through several different stages as it is written. Like any other author, the screenwriter begins with an idea, though it may be (and until the 1960s, probably was) a concept assigned to him rather than one of his own creation. He writes a brief story outline; ten pages is standard. He then writes a treatment, a descriptive scene-by-scene breakdown of the plot; this is usually forty to fifty pages long and contains little, if any, dialogue. Finally the treatment is turned into a full script, complete with dialogue and directions for actors and camera.

One must understand several terms in order to comprehend a screenwriter's film credits. "Scenario" means the same thing as "screenplay" and was used primarily during the silent-film era. "Continuity" refers to title cards used to present expository material to the audience in a silent picture. "Titles" is used when the author wrote both continuity and dialogue cards for silents or for early sound films that were released in a silent format. "Dialogue" and "additional dialogue" credits indicate that the writer had nothing to do with the film's plot but merely provided the actors with words to speak. The "additional dialogue" credit was common, particularly in comedies, throughout the 1950s. Writers Guild regulations now prohibit its use, though it still appears in some independent productions. "Story" or "screen story" credit is given to writers who created the film's plot but did not write the full screenplay. "Story and screenplay" originally was used to show the writer had written an original plot and a full script (in the days when adaptations were common) but since the 1970s has been used primarily when the author was basing his work very loosely on another source, usually so loosely that he had created an entirely new plot. "Adaptation" means that the author provided an outline showing how work could be adapted to film but did not write a screenplay from that outline.

The filmographies in this volume represent only official screen credit. Uncredited contributions are discussed in the text.

—Randall Clark

Acknowledgments

This book was produced by BC Research. Karen L. Rood is senior editor for the *Dictionary of Literary Biography* series. Ellen Rosenberg Kovner was the in-house editor.

Art supervisor is Patricia M. Flanagan. Copyediting supervisor is Patricia Coate. Production coordinator is Kimberly Casey. Typesetting supervisor is Laura Ingram. The production staff includes Rowena Betts, Matt Brook, Kathleen M. Flanagan, Joyce Fowler, Pamela Haynes, Judith K. Ingle, Vickie Lowers, Beatrice McClain, Judith McCray, George Stone Saussy, Joycelyn R. Smith, James Adam Sutton, and Lucia Tarbox. Jean W. Ross is permissions editor. Joseph Caldwell, photography editor, did photographic copy work for the volume.

No record of screenwriters' careers is complete without visual evidence of their most memorable films. Muriel Hamilton of Hampton Books, Newberry, South Carolina, and Fred Zentner of Cinema Bookshop, London, generously gave of their time and energy to help assemble movie stills and other illustrative materials for this volume. To them the editors would like to express their deepest gratitude.

Walter W. Ross and Jennifer Castillo did the library research with the assistance of the staff at the Thomas Cooper Library of the University of South Carolina: Lynn Barron, Daniel Boice, Connie Crider, Kathy Eckman, Michael Freeman, Gary Geer, David L. Haggard, Jens Holley, Marcia Martin, Dana Rabon, Jean Rhyne, Jan Squire, Ellen Tillett, and Virginia Weathers.

American Screenwriters
Second Series

Dictionary of Literary Biography

Woody Allen
(1 December 1935-   )

Alan S. Horowitz

MOTION PICTURES: *What's New Pussycat?*
(United Artists, 1965), screenplay;
What's Up, Tiger Lily? (American International,
1966), screenplay by Allen, Frank Buxton,
Len Maxwell, Louise Lasser, and Mickey
Rose;
Take the Money and Run (Palomar, 1969), screen
story and screenplay by Allen and Rose;
Bananas (United Artists, 1971), screenplay by Allen
and Rose;
Everything You Always Wanted to Know About Sex*
(*but were afraid to ask) (United Artists, 1972),
screenplay;
Play It Again, Sam (Paramount, 1972), screenplay;
Sleeper (United Artists, 1973), screenplay by Allen
and Marshall Brickman;
Love and Death (United Artists, 1975), screenplay;
Annie Hall (United Artists, 1977), screenplay by Al-
len and Brickman;
Interiors (United Artists, 1978), screenplay;
Manhattan (United Artists, 1979), screenplay by Al-
len and Brickman;
Stardust Memories (United Artists, 1980), screen-
play;
A Midsummer Night's Sex Comedy (Warner Bros.,
1982), screenplay;
Zelig (Orion, 1983), screenplay;
Broadway Danny Rose (Orion, 1984), screenplay;
The Purple Rose of Cairo (Orion, 1985), screenplay.

PLAY PRODUCTIONS: *From A to Z*, by Allen and
Herbert Farjeon, Hermione Gingold, and
others, New York, Plymouth Theatre, 20
April 1960;
Don't Drink the Water, New York, Morosco Theatre,
17 November 1966;

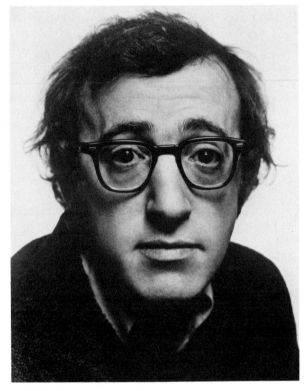

Woody Allen

Play It Again, Sam, New York, Broadhurst Theatre,
12 February 1969;
The Floating Light Bulb, New York, Vivian Beaumont Theatre, 27 April 1981.

BOOKS: *Don't Drink the Water* (New York: French,
1967);
Play It Again, Sam (New York: Random House,
1969);

3

Getting Even (New York: Random House, 1971; London: W. H. Allen, 1973);

Death: A Comedy in One Act (New York: French, 1975);

God: A Comedy in One Act (New York: French, 1975);

Without Feathers (New York: Random House, 1975);

Four Screenplays: Sleeper, Love and Death, Bananas, Annie Hall (New York: Random House, 1978);

Non-being and Somethingness, illustrated by Stuart Hample (New York: Random House, 1978);

Side Effects (New York: Random House, 1980);

The Floating Light Bulb (New York: Random House, 1982);

Four Films of Woody Allen (New York: Random House, 1982; London: Faber & Faber, 1983).

RADIO: *God* (National Radio Theatre of Chicago, 1978).

RECORDINGS: *Play It Again, Sam* (Paramount, 1972);

Woody Allen, Stand-up Comic; 1964-1968 (United Artists Records, 1978).

Woody Allen is one of the most prominent and important figures in contemporary film comedy. As his career has progressed, he has evolved from stand-up comic to talented writer and director, to sophisticated filmmaker. Born Allen Stewart Konigsberg, the son of Martin Konigsberg and Nettie Cherry, Allen was brought up in the Flatbush section of Brooklyn. His early interests included magic and card tricks, the clarinet (he still plays), sports, and movies. The influence of the cinema can be seen in his early films which spoof familiar movie genres like the gangster and spy films and the documentary. His later work is heavily influenced by Ingmar Bergman. He began writing early, and from the time he was in the first grade his papers were read aloud at school because of their excellence. While at Midwood High School (1949 to 1953) he started sending jokes to columnists such as Earl Wilson and Walter Winchell, who used them by claiming they were the witty remarks of a star or public personality. At this time he changed his name to Woody Allen, a nickname his father said the neighborhood kids gave him because he always brought the stick to play stickball.

Allen attended New York University, was expelled for poor grades, and later enrolled at City College of New York, only to leave quickly. His decision to attend college seemed motivated solely by a desire to please his parents. He left home at

eighteen when he married Harlene Rosen; they were divorced in 1960. His first job was writing jokes for a public relations agency, producing fifty jokes a day. Subsequently, he entered NBC's writers' development program where he received his first and possibly only formal training in comedy writing. The network sent him to Hollywood to help salvage the failing *Colgate Comedy Hour,* but after a few months he returned to New York and started writing for several comedians and television shows, including *Your Show of Shows,* starring Sid Caesar.

Dissatisfied with how others used his material, Allen decided to perform his jokes himself. He was encouraged by Jack Rollins and Charles Joffe, who, beginning in 1958, became his agents, managers, and confidants, and later, producers of most of his films. Allen cites Mort Sahl and Bob Hope as the strongest influences on him as a stand-up comic. Allen's stage personality is very similar to Sahl's, though Sahl's material is more biting and political. The influence of Bob Hope is more subtle and difficult to detect. It is perhaps Hope's timing, his plays on words (which Allen uses in his films), and his wisecracking that can be seen in Allen's work.

After returning to New York from Hollywood, Allen became increasingly involved with writing for television, earning as much as seventeen hundred dollars per week. He gave up this position for a seventy-five-dollar-a-week job as a stand-up comic at Greenwich Village's Blue Angel nightclub, eventually performing in several clubs around New York. He was married again, this time to actress Louise Lasser (they were divorced in the late 1960s), who later collaborated with him on the screenplay for *What's Up, Tiger Lily?* and appeared in several of his films.

In 1964 producer Charles K. Feldman came to the Blue Angel to see Allen's act and offered him a job as screenwriter for his film *What's New Pussycat?* (1965). The film centered on psychiatrist Fritz Fassbender (Peter Sellers) and his patient Michael Jones (Peter O'Toole). Jones has a nearly maniacal desire to marry and be faithful to his fiancée, Carol Werner (Romy Schneider); throughout their long courtship, however, he has been consistently unfaithful. Beautiful women constantly pursue Jones, causing him great anxiety, while the unhappily married Fassbender can only envy Jones's "problem." Allen also appears in the film, bringing much of his self-effacing stage character to the part of Victor Shakapoplis, another patient of Fassbender. Fassbender and Shakapoplis want to break out of their rut and roam free, while

Jones, who is already free, seeks conventionality and regimentation. This conflict between security and freedom, and its related problem of freedom versus commitment, recurs in later Allen films.

Although *What's New Pussycat?* was a great financial success, Allen was not entirely pleased with the finished film, and he began looking for a project over which he would have more creative control. He acquired the Japanese-made spy film *Kagi no Kagi* (1964), reedited it, and dubbed in a sound track written and performed by himself, Lasser, Mickey Rose, Frank Buxton, and Len Maxwell, changing the film to a spy spoof about a search for an egg salad recipe. What resulted was *What's Up, Tiger Lily?* (1966), a fast-paced, nearly plotless collection of jokes and puns. It was a financial success and artistically unusual enough to help establish Allen as a comic talent. He was hired to appear in another spy spoof, *Casino Royale* (1967), in which

he played James Bond's bumbling nephew Jimmy Bond. He also wrote some material for the film, none of which seems to have been used.

After writing two successful Broadway plays, *Don't Drink the Water* (produced in 1966) and *Play It Again, Sam* (produced in 1969), Allen again turned his attention to film. Coauthored with Mickey Rose, *Take the Money and Run* (1969) was the first film Allen wrote, directed, and starred in, and it was the first of his films to center on the character he had earlier developed. *Take the Money and Run* parodies cinema verité, using blackouts and interviews to study the life of bumbling thief Virgil Starkwell (Allen), who is aggressive but inept in his attempts to become a heroic criminal. By focusing on this incompetent, whose intentions are so far removed from his accomplishments, the film pokes fun at the idea of the cinema accurately depicting life, and Allen comments on how motion

Woody Allen and Louise Lasser, 1966

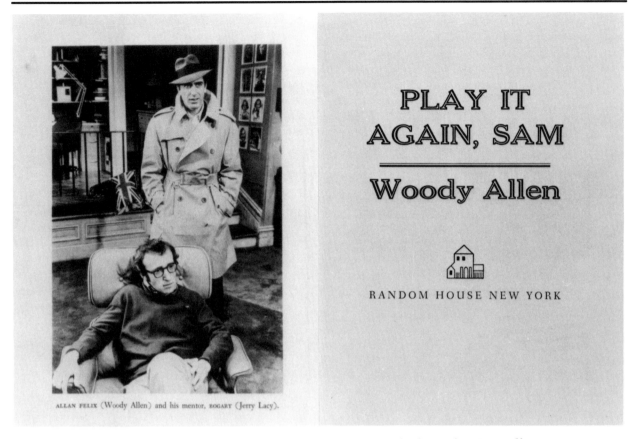

Frontispiece and title page for the play version of Allen's parody of Humphrey Bogart films

pictures may affect an audience's perceptions.

Take the Money and Run introduces a character type which appears regularly in Allen's films—the inferior woman who never equals the protagonist in wit, talent, or intelligence. Despite Virgil Starkwell's shortcomings, his wife, the pretty but unintelligent Louise (Janet Margolin), is deficient when compared to him. This inequality between characters is a flaw in this and later Allen films. The focus is on the relationships between the main characters, but all the characters are written as inferior to the protagonist so that the films' central relationships can never be developed fully; instead these relationships merely serve as a background for jokes.

In his next film, *Bananas* (1971), Allen plays Fielding Melish, a products tester introduced to revolutionary politics by protester Nancy (Louise Lasser), who is obtaining signatures on a petition against the dictatorship in the banana republic of San Marcos. To get to know Nancy better, Melish feigns an interest in her cause; when she leaves him, he travels to San Marcos on his own. Eventually involved in the country's revolution, he becomes

the nation's new leader and returns, disguised, to the United States in search of foreign aid. He is branded a subversive, placed on trial, and set free, winning back Nancy (who did not see through his disguise) because he is now a real-life leader of a revolution. *Bananas* exemplifies Allen's concern with the outsider who wishes to be accepted. Melish is an American in a Latin American country. After he joins the rebels, he must work at being accepted by them. When Melish is tried for treason, the judge suspends his fifteen-year sentence on the condition that he agrees never to move into the judge's neighborhood.

Play It Again, Sam (1972) is based on Allen's highly successful play and is written in a more cohesive, linear manner than his earlier films. It is also his only screenplay, except *What's New Pussycat?*, that he did not direct; the film was directed by Herbert Ross. Allan Felix (Allen) is going through a difficult period following his divorce. Not happy as he is, Felix longs to be more like his hero Humphrey Bogart. Sporadically, Bogart (played by Jerry Lacy) appears to give Felix advice. Felix's friends Dick and Linda Christie (Tony Roberts and

Diane Keaton) offer him emotional support, and Felix falls in love with Linda. As Linda becomes alienated from her insensitive husband, she also falls in love with Felix. At the film's conclusion, a parody of the final scene of *Casablanca*, Felix graciously gives up Linda, who returns to Dick. Felix is content to be himself, and he has learned the difference between illusion and reality.

Everything You Always Wanted to Know About Sex* (*but were afraid to ask) (1972) is an oddity among Allen's films. Consisting of several separate skits, the film was loosely based on a nonfiction bestseller by doctor David Reuben. Each skit is intended to answer specific questions about sexuality, so that, for example, the question "What Is a Transvestite?" is followed by a skit about a man who succumbs to his desire to try on women's clothing. Other skits include an inept court jester (Allen) who lusts for his queen (Lynn Redgrave) and gives her an aphrodisiac; a psychiatrist (Gene Wilder) who ruins his life when he falls in love with a sheep; a look at what happens in the male body during lovemaking; and three separate parodies, one of game

shows ("What's My Perversion?"), one of horror films, in which a mad scientist creates two huge breasts, and the story of a frigid wife, done in the style of a European art film. The segmented nature of the movie made it almost impossible for it to be entirely successful, and it was not; some of the skits simply do not work. It remains Allen's most uneven film.

Sleeper (1973) was the last of Allen's slapstick, antic-filled movies. He plays Miles Monroe, a Greenwich Village health food restaurant owner who enters the hospital for a minor ulcer operation and awakes two hundred years later to find that he has been placed in cold storage. The civilization he knew has been destroyed and replaced by a dictatorial government that has spawned an opposition revolutionary movement. Monroe is a threat to the government; his knowledge of the past as it truly was contradicts the lies that have been told the populace. Much of the film shows Monroe fleeing the government and seeking out the rebels. He meets the pleasure-loving Luna (Diane Keaton), who tries to remain apolitical but eventually be-

Woody Allen (center) in his futuristic film Sleeper

Woody Allen directing a scene in Love and Death, *the film that marked a turning point in his cinematic style*

comes a fugitive with him. Monroe is caught by the government, but Luna joins the rebels and they rescue him. When Monroe and Luna realize that the rebel leader is no better than the current government (a situation that also existed in *Bananas*), they abandon the rebellion and try to live a life apart from both forces.

While *Sleeper* was Allen's most cohesive original screenplay up to that time, it is also apparent that he was writing for himself as star. Beginning with *Take the Money and Run*, all his comedy scripts center around the Allen character, but *Sleeper* differs from previous films by relying more on Allen the slapstick comedian than the stand-up comic. Allen has said, "I believe in *Sleeper* I came out aggressively a little bit," and in fact, he relies more on visual humor, usually stemming from futuristic, sometimes malfunctioning devices, than on the spoken word.

Allen's next work was *Love and Death* (1975), the beginning of his exploration of more serious themes which reappear with great frequency in his later films. The film takes place in Czarist Russia. Boris (Allen) has had a crush on his cousin Sonia (Diane Keaton) since childhood, but she does not

respond. When Russia goes to war against Napoleon, Boris is forced by his family to fight. Through luck, he emerges as a hero. He marries Sonia, and they are happy until she decides that she and Boris should kill Napoleon. Boris is captured and executed but returns as a spirit and finds the still-living Sonia happy. The film ends with Boris and the Angel of Death frolicking by a lakeside.

Although the story sounds tragic, *Love and Death* is a comedy. The dead Boris appears at the beginning, joking about death and setting the story in flashback. By letting the audience know what Boris's fate will be, Allen makes the film lighter and more amenable to humor. (Similarly, *Annie Hall*, 1977, opens with Allen joking and then exclaiming, "Annie and I broke up. I still can't get my mind around that.") Besides the opening voice-over, the film has other literary and theatrical devices which Allen has used in many of his films. Frequently he speaks directly to the audience in an absurdist fashion. The film is filled with allusions to Russian literature and to the films of Ingmar Bergman, one of Allen's favorite filmmakers. Finally, Allen's discussion of death leads him to examine the rationale behind death, which brings him to explore the existence and nature of God.

Allen followed *Love and Death* with *Annie Hall*, his most successful film and winner of the Academy Award for best picture, best director, and best screenplay. What makes this the most satisfying of all Allen's films is the balance he brought to the central relationship between Annie Hall (Diane Keaton) and Alvy Singer (Allen). Annie is Allen's only character to develop during a film and Alvy loses her because of inherent shortcomings in his character. The Alvy-Annie relationship dominates the Allen-versus-the-world conflicts that play an important part in his earlier films.

Much, though not all, of *Annie Hall* is autobiographical, and the plot is superficially simple. Alvy and Annie meet, court, move in together, and break up. Through it all, Annie grows and matures, while Alvy advances only professionally; personally he stagnates. Annie's maturation and Alvy's inability to commit himself to a relationship eventually destroy the romance. The film ends as it began, with Alvy telling a joke, resigned to the notion that he will continue to suffer through unsatisfactory relationships.

Following *Annie Hall* was *Interiors* (1978), Allen's only noncomedy script and his only film in which he does not appear as an actor. The film owes much to Ingmar Bergman in its tone, concerns, and atmosphere. *Interiors* focuses on a family

Diane Keaton and Woody Allen in his Academy Award-winning film Annie Hall

of neurotic, repressed individuals. Eve (Geraldine Page) is an interior decorator who has "created" her husband Arthur (E. G. Marshall) by supporting him through law school and who lives through him and their three daughters. The daughters, Flyn (Kristin Griffith), Joey (Marybeth Hurt), and Renata (Diane Keaton), are like Chekhov's *Three Sisters:* Chekhov's women talk about "going to Moscow" but never go anywhere. Allen's women talk of becoming artists and achieving self-fulfillment, yet manage only to wallow in their own despair. Arthur leaves Eve and marries vivacious and lively Pearl (Maureen Stapleton). The family, particularly Eve, cannot accept this, and Eve commits suicide.

Allen has said in interviews that "laughter submerges everything else" and that he has no trouble making people laugh. It seems that *Interiors*

was an attempt to confront serious questions without the technique of comedy that comes easily for him. But his conscious avoidance of laughter gives the film a stilted, unnatural quality, and his dialogue is unrealistic, filled with psychological jargon. The daughters speak of "the state of my well being," the "preoccupation of my own mortality," and Joey declares, "at the center of a sick psyche is a sick spirit." The effect is to give an unintended sameness to the three daughters. Though their personalities differ, they share the same artistic aspirations, and all suffer from guilt, disappointments, broken dreams, repressed emotions, and an inability to relate to people. *Interiors* represents an unsuccessful attempt at moving in a new direction.

Allen's interest in addressing serious topics through a comic veneer, which began in *Love and*

Lobby poster for Allen's 1979 movie, one of his more serious films (courtesy of Dale Campbell, The Nickelodeon, Columbia, S.C.)

Woody Allen

Death, is continued in *Manhattan* (1979). Allen plays Isaac Davis, a television writer unhappy with his work and determined to do some "serious writing" on a novel. Davis's inability to complete his book—the film's opening scene finds him struggling over the first paragraph—is paralleled by his inability to develop a lasting sexual relationship. His wife Jill (Meryl Streep) has announced she is a lesbian and has left him. He is having an affair with seventeen-year-old Tracy (Mariel Hemingway) but will not commit himself to her. His friend Yale (Michael Murphy) is having an affair with Mary Wilke (Diane Keaton) but drops her out of guilt, and Davis takes up with Mary. Mary is intelligent, attractive, but hopelessly neurotic, and Davis leaves her and goes back to Tracy. She is departing for six months of study in London, and the film ends with nothing resolved, though Davis has learned one thing from Tracy—he must learn to trust people.

Much of *Manhattan* is spent on what is by now familiar material, and the film is interesting mainly for the developments that can be seen in Allen's standard characterization. No longer is he inept, struggling with mechanical objects, and being rebuffed by women. Davis says that meeting women is "no problem," and when complimented by Mary on his humor, he comments, "I don't need you to tell me that. I've been making good money off it." Here is a self-assured character, financially and socially successful.

This self-assuredness reaches a culmination in *Stardust Memories* (1980). Here Allen plays Sandy Bates, a filmmaker who is attending a convention of film buffs who have met to honor him. He puts up with constant assaults by his public, including listening to insipid, pseudointellectual comments, signing autographs, and having scripts shoved at him. Though a celebrity, Bates would like nothing better than to be left alone, quite a contrast to Virgil Starkwell in *Take the Money and Run*, who spent most of his energies trying to become famous.

Stardust Memories is highly fragmented and filled with symbols; Bates's memories, his fantasies, and scenes from his films are all interspersed with the narrative. There is much autobiographical content and the film owes a debt to Fellini's *8 1/2*. Here, more than in any of Allen's other scripts, the distinction between life and film is blurred. It is difficult for the audience to distinguish between "real" scenes and the scenes from Bates's films. The picture's conclusion carries this one step further, as all the actors step out of their characters and revert to their true identities.

Stardust Memories was neither a financial nor a critical success for Allen, with both critics and viewers complaining that the film was bitter and self-indulgent. *A Midsummer Night's Sex Comedy* (1982) was considerably lighter in tone. As the title indicates, the film was inspired partly by Shakespeare's *A Midsummer Night's Dream*, but the Ingmar Bergman film *Smiles of a Summer Night* (1955) was a major influence.

Set at the turn of the century, the film takes place during one weekend at the country home of eccentric inventor Andrew (Allen) and his wife, Adrian (Mary Steenburgen). Their guests for the weekend are Andrew's closest friend, Maxwell (Tony Roberts), a doctor; Maxwell's nurse Dulcy (Julie Hagerty); Andrew's former lover Ariel (Mia Farrow); and her fiancé, Leopold (Jose Ferrer), a pompous intellectual. The relationships of the couples become scrambled: Andrew, unhappy with his frigid wife, yearns for Ariel; Maxwell, tired of his womanizing ways, decides he is in love with Ariel and wants to marry her and settle down; Leopold turns his attentions to Dulcy. When Maxwell admits to Andrew that he and Adrian had an affair, Andrew is furious, but Adrian is so relieved of her guilt that she is no longer frigid. Andrew decides he does not really love Ariel, and she agrees to marry Maxwell. Leopold dies in a tryst with Dulcy, but his spirit flees into the woods, urging others to be happy.

Critical response to *A Midsummer Night's Sex*

Lobby poster for Allen's 1982 film, which parodies Shakespeare's comedy (courtesy of Dale Campbell, The Nickelodeon, Columbia, S.C.)

Comedy was mixed, but Allen's next film, *Zelig*, became one of the most acclaimed films of 1983. The film is about Leonard Zelig (Allen), a man so desperate to be liked that he develops the ability to become identical to anyone around him. Once Zelig's abilities are discovered, he becomes one of the best-known figures of the 1920s. Like *Stardust Memories*, *Zelig* is a bitter commentary on the nature of fame; Zelig's adoring public quickly turns on him when it is revealed that he committed bigamy while living out his many guises. Done in a mock-documentary style, the film consists largely of interviews, newsreel footage, and scenes of Zelig with his psychiatrist (Mia Farrow).

Broadway Danny Rose, Allen's 1984 film, was in many ways a return to his earlier comedies, relying more on slapstick humor than any of the other post-*Sleeper* films. Danny Rose (Allen) is a New York talent agent who handles only the worst acts in the business. He has finally landed an important engagement for one client, singer Tony Canova (Nick Apollo Forte), but Canova will not perform unless his mistress Tina (Mia Farrow) is in the audience. Rose goes to find Tina but inadvertently offends some of her criminal friends, and they set out to kill him. Later, at Tina's urging, Canova leaves Rose for another agent. *Broadway Danny Rose* is not an entirely successful film. The first part of the movie contains much slapstick humor, particularly in the pursuit of Rose by the gangsters and in Rose's untalented clients; later the screenplay changes tone somewhat abruptly with a warmer, more sentimental scene depicting Rose and his clients during their Thanksgiving dinner. It finally concludes with the kind of upbeat moral present in *A Midsummer Night's Sex Comedy* and *Zelig*. Tina feels guilty for causing Rose to lose his best client; he rejects, then accepts her apologies and says they can be friends. The film earned Allen an Academy Award nomination for best director.

Broadway Danny Rose was followed by *The Purple Rose of Cairo* (1985), Allen's first film since *Interiors* in which he did not appear as an actor. The picture's theme is one that Allen had first examined in *Take the Money and Run*: the relationship between movies and real life. During the 1930s, a woman (Mia Farrow) finds escape from her unhappy life by constantly going to the movies. One day, a character (Jeff Daniels) in the film she is watching comes to life. As the character explores the real world movie producers panic, because this could be the end of motion pictures.

With a body of works that is both critically and commercially successful, Allen has remained unique among contemporary filmmakers. In his substantial and important body of comedic work, Allen expresses views of love, life, death, and the world that are unquestionably his own.

Interviews:
Frank Rich, "An Interview with Woody," *Time*, 113 (30 April 1979): 68-69;
R. F. Moss, Interview with Woody Allen, *Saturday Review*, 7 (November 1980): 40-44.

References:
John Dart, "Woody Allen, Theologian," *Christian Century*, 19 (22 June 1979): 585-589;
Michael Dempsey, "The Autobiography of Woody Allen," *Film Comment* (May 1979): 9-16;
Seymour Fisher and Rhoda Lee Fisher, "Schlemiel Children," *Psychology Today*, 14 (September 1980): 64-73;
Natalie Gittelson, "The Maturing of Woody Allen," *New York Times Magazine*, 22 April 1979, pp. 30-32, 102-107;
Richard Grenier, "Woody Allen in the Limelight," *Commentary*, 68 (July 1979): 65-67;
Pauline Kael, "The Current Cinema," *New Yorker*, 49 (31 December 1973): 47-49;
Eric Lax, *On Being Funny: Woody Allen and Comedy* (New York: Charterhouse, 1977);
Leonard Maltin, "Take Woody Allen—Please!," *Film Comment*, 10 (March 1974): 42-45;
Larry McMurtry, "Woody Allen, Neighborhood Filmmaker," *American Film*, 4 (September 1979): 6;
Frank Rich, "Woody Allen Wipes the Smile Off His Face," *Esquire*, 87 (May 1977): 72-76;
Richard Schickel, "Woody Allen Comes of Age," *Time*, 113 (30 April 1979): 62-65;
George W. S. Trow, "A Film About a Very Funny Man," *Film Comment*, 13 (May-June 1977): 32-33;
Maurice Yacowar, *Loser Take All: The Comic Art of Woody Allen* (New York: Ungar, 1979).

S. N. Behrman

(9 June 1893-9 September 1973)

Christopher Adcock

See also the Behrman entry in *DLB 7, Twentieth-Century American Dramatists.*

MOTION PICTURES: *Liliom* (Fox, 1930), screenplay and dialogue by Behrman and Sonya Levien;

Sea Wolf (Fox, 1930), dialogue;

Lightnin' (Fox, 1930), screenplay, adaptation, and dialogue by Behrman and Levien;

The Brat (Fox, 1931), screenplay by Behrman, Levien, and Maude Fulton;

Daddy Long Legs (Fox, 1931), screenplay by Behrman and Levien;

Surrender (Fox, 1931), screenplay by Behrman and Levien;

Rebecca of Sunnybrook Farm (Fox, 1932), screenplay by Behrman and Levien;

Tess of the Storm Country (Fox, 1932), screenplay by Behrman, Levien, and Rupert Hughes;

My Lips Betray (Fox, 1933), dialogue;

As Husbands Go (Fox, 1933), screenplay by Behrman and Levien;

Hallelujah, I'm a Bum! (United Artists, 1933), screenplay;

Queen Christina (M-G-M, 1933), dialogue;

Anna Karenina (M-G-M, 1935), dialogue;

A Tale of Two Cities (M-G-M, 1935), screenplay by Behrman and W. P. Lipscomb;

Parnell (M-G-M, 1937), screenplay by Behrman and John Van Druten;

Conquest (M-G-M, 1937), screenplay by Behrman, Salka Viertel, and Samuel Hoffenstein;

The Cowboy and the Lady (United Artists, 1938), screenplay by Behrman and Levien;

Waterloo Bridge (M-G-M, 1940), screenplay by Behrman, George Froeschel, and Hans Rambeau;

Two-Faced Woman (M-G-M, 1941), screenplay by Behrman, Viertel, and George Oppenheimer;

Quo Vadis (M-G-M, 1951), screenplay by Behrman, Levien, and John Lee Mahin;

Me and the Colonel (Columbia, 1958), screenplay by Behrman and Froeschel, adapted from Behrman's play *Jacobowsky and the Colonel;*

S. N. Behrman (courtesy of the Billy Rose Theatre Collection, The New York Public Library at Lincoln Center, Astor, Lenox and Tilden Foundations)

Stowaway in the Sky (United Artists, 1962), narration.

PLAY PRODUCTIONS: *Bedside Manners,* by Behrman and J. Kenyon Nicholson, New York, Threshold Theatre, 1923;

A Night's Work, by Behrman and Nicholson, Peekskill, N.Y., Grand Theatre, 7 June 1924;

The Man Who Forgot, by Behrman and Owen Davis, adapted from Behrman's "The Scant Pint," Atlantic City, Apollo Theatre, 25 October 1926;

The Second Man, New York, Guild Theatre, 11 April 1927;

Love Is Like That, by Behrman and Nicholson, New

York, Cort Theatre, 18 April 1927;

Serena Blandish; or The Difficulty of Getting Married, New York, Morosco Theatre, 23 January 1929;

Meteor, New York, Guild Theatre, 23 December 1929;

Brief Moment, New York, Belasco Theatre, 9 November 1931;

Biography, New York, Guild Theatre, 12 December 1932;

Love Story, Philadelphia, Walnut Street Theatre, 13 December 1933;

Rain from Heaven, New York, John Golden Theatre, 24 December 1934;

End of Summer, New York, Guild Theatre, 17 February 1936;

Amphitryon 38, New York, Shubert Theatre, 1 November 1937;

Wine of Choice, New York, Guild Theatre, 21 February 1938;

No Time for Comedy, New York, Ethel Barrymore Theatre, 17 April 1939;

The Talley Method, New York, Henry Miller's Theatre, 24 February 1941;

The Pirate, New York, Martin Beck Theatre, 25 November 1942;

Jacobowsky and the Colonel, New York, Martin Beck Theatre, 14 March 1944;

Dunnigan's Daughter, New York, John Golden Theatre, 26 December 1945;

I Know My Love, New York, Shubert Theatre, 2 November 1949;

Let Me Hear the Melody, Philadelphia, Walnut Street Theatre, 12 March 1951;

Jane, New York, Coronet Theatre, 1 February 1952;

Fanny, by Behrman and Joshua Logan, New York, Majestic Theatre, 4 November 1954;

The Cold Wind and the Warm, New York, Morosco Theatre, 8 December 1958;

Lord Pengo, New York, Royale Theatre, 19 November 1962;

But for Whom Charlie, New York, ANTA Washington Square Theatre, 12 March 1964.

BOOKS: *Bedside Manners*, by Behrman and J. Kenyon Nicholson (New York: French, 1924; London: French, 1924);

A Night's Work, by Behrman and Nicholson (New York: French, 1926);

The Second Man (Garden City: Doubleday, Page, 1927; London: Heinemann, 1927);

Meteor (New York: Brentano's, 1930);

Brief Moment (New York: Farrar & Rinehart, 1931);

Biography (New York: Farrar & Rinehart, 1933; London: Secker, 1934);

Serena Blandish; or The Difficulty of Getting Married (New York: Farrar & Rinehart, 1934);

Three Plays (New York: Farrar & Rinehart, 1934);

Rain from Heaven (New York: Random House, 1935);

End of Summer (New York: Random House, 1936);

Amphitryon 38, adapted from Jean Giraudoux's play (New York: Random House, 1938);

Wine of Choice (New York: Random House, 1938; London: Hamilton, 1939);

No Time for Comedy (New York: Random House, 1939; London: Hamilton, 1939);

The Talley Method (New York: Random House, 1941);

The Pirate, adapted from Ludwig Fulda's play (New York: Random House, 1943);

Jacobowsky and the Colonel, based on Franz Werfel's unproduced play (New York: Random House, 1944);

Dunnigan's Daughter (New York: Random House, 1946);

I Know My Love, adapted from Marcel Archad's *Auprès de ma blonde* (New York: French, 1952);

4 Plays (New York: Random House, 1952);

Jane, based on W. Somerset Maugham's short story (New York: Random House, 1952);

Duveen (New York: Random House, 1952; London: Hamilton, 1952);

The Worcester Account (New York: Random House, 1954; London: Hamilton, 1954);

Fanny, by Behrman and Joshua Logan, adapted from Marcel Pagnol's trilogy, *Marius, Fanny,* and *César* (New York: Random House, 1955);

The Cold Wind and the Warm (New York: Random House, 1959; London: French, 1960);

Portrait of Max: An Intimate Memoir of Sir Max Beerbohm (New York: Random House, 1960); republished as *Conversation with Max* (London: Hamilton, 1960);

Lord Pengo (New York: Random House, 1963; London: French, 1963);

But for Whom Charlie (New York: Random House, 1964);

The Suspended Drawing Room (New York: Stein & Day, 1965; London: Hamilton, 1966);

The Burning Glass (Boston: Little, Brown, 1968; London: Hamilton, 1968);

People in a Diary: A Memoir (Boston: Little, Brown, 1972); republished as *Tribulations and Laughter* (London: Hamilton, 1972).

PERIODICAL PUBLICATIONS: "Query: What

Greta Garbo and John Gilbert as the Swedish queen and her Spanish lover in the 1933 version of Queen Christina

Makes Comedy High?," *New York Times,* 30 March 1952, II: 13;

"Rest But Not In Peace," *Esquire,* 49 (February 1958): 41-42;

"At 75, S. N. Behrman, Speaking as a Survivor, Not a Contemporary, Talks of Many Things. . . ," *New York Times Magazine,* 2 June 1968, pp. 28-29, 90-94, 96, 100;

"Thornton Wilder: America's Universal Man," *Reader's Digest,* 104 (May 1974): 132-136.

S. N. Behrman in many ways typifies the American screenwriter of the early sound film era. He was brought to Hollywood following a career as a playwright, worked mostly as an adapter of plays and novels to the screen, wrote nearly all of his scripts with a collaborator, and stayed in motion pictures strictly for the financial reward. Behrman displayed considerable artistic integrity and had the ability to adapt faithfully from works as diverse as *Rebecca of Sunnybrook Farm* and *Anna Karenina.*

Samuel Nathaniel Behrman was born in Worcester, Massachusetts, in 1893, the son of Zelda Feingold and Joseph Behrman. No official record of his birthdate exists, and years later he arbitrarily selected his own birthday: 9 June. Behrman grew up in the Jewish section of Worcester, where his father was a Talmudic scholar who taught Hebrew to neighborhood children. Behrman's childhood experiences provided the basis for his play *The Cold Wind and the Warm* (produced in 1958) and his memoirs *The Worcester Account* (1954).

As a child, Behrman was befriended by Daniel Asher, a local intellectual who became his mentor, and it was Asher who introduced Behrman to the theater, taking him to see a melodrama titled *Devil's Island* when Behrman was eleven years old. At fifteen, without his parents' knowledge, Behrman took a trip to New York and was impressed by the theater district. This trip seems to have left him determined to become active on the stage; after graduating from high school, he toured the vaudeville circuit performing in a skit he had written. His health was not good during these years, and he eventually returned home. He enrolled in Clark College and became an assistant to the Board of Publications but was suspended several times for failure to attend physical education classes. He finally transferred to Harvard at Asher's suggestion. While at Harvard, he worked in theater productions and wrote plays and sold his first short story to the *Parisienne* in 1915 for fifteen dollars. Behrman graduated with a bachelor's degree from Harvard in 1916 and received his master's degree from Columbia University in 1918. He spent two years working at the *New York Times*, first writing classified advertisements, then book reviews. He later wrote book reviews for the *New Republic* and worked as a publicist for a Texas oil man.

In the early 1920s Behrman met another aspiring playwright, J. Kenyon Nicholson, and they began collaborating on plays and short stories; two of their one-act plays, *Bedside Manners* and *A Night's Work*, were produced in little theaters in New York City, in 1923 and 1924, respectively, and a third, *Love Is Like That*, was previewed in Indianapolis in 1926 and opened in New York in 1927. *The Man Who Forgot* (produced in 1926), written with Owen Davis, was a failure in Atlantic City. Behrman's first success, and the play that launched him on his long career as playwright, was *The Second Man* (produced in 1927), which he adapted from his own short story. Alfred Lunt and Lynn Fontanne opened in the play, and Behrman later said the production "changed all my circumstances for the rest of my life." It was an immediate critical success, and Behrman was established as a master of sophisticated comedy, a genre in which he continued to work for the remainder of his career as a playwright. Also in 1927 Behrman began his long association with Harold Ross of the *New Yorker*, and it was Ross who gave Behrman the opportunity to flourish as a nondramatic writer by employing him to produce essays for the magazine over the years.

After he established himself as a playwright, Behrman became one of many writers asked to come to Hollywood to help provide dialogue for the then new talking pictures. In 1930 he accepted an offer from Fox studios. Undoubtedly, Behrman made the move to Hollywood primarily for financial reasons—the Depression was just beginning and he was paid $1,250 a week, an enormous sum at the time—but it was also a way of coping with two personal problems that had left him with little interest in playwriting. His most recent play, *Meteor* (produced in 1929), had been a failure, and Daniel

Asher, the person who had done the most to encourage Behrman in his career, had recently committed suicide. Initially Behrman was somewhat cynical about Hollywood; in his 1932 play *Biography*, a character hopes that in the future "men won't have to prostitute themselves in Hollywood." Still, he was grateful for the money that screenwriting provided—without it, he admitted, "I would have been dead of malnutrition long ago"— and eventually he became less defensive about Hollywood in interviews.

His first script for Fox was *Liliom* (1930), and like nearly all of his work at that studio, it was written in collaboration with Sonya Levien although they received separate credits. Adapted from a play by Ferenc Molnár, the film was directed by Frank Borzage. Liliom (Charles Farrell) is an egotistical and amoral carnival barker, cruel to Julie (Rose Hobart), a carnival worker who loves him. Liliom is arrested after committing a payroll theft, but he kills himself rather than face prison. In heaven, he is told he can return to Earth after ten years in purgatory; when he returns, he finds Julie still loves him.

Behrman's theater background proved valuable to him in Hollywood, where he was recognized for his abilities to adapt literary works and to produce clever dialogue. After working on *Liliom*, Behrman wrote the dialogue for the film version of Jack London's *Sea Wolf* (1930). He and Levien were credited with screenplay, adaptation, and dialogue for *Lightnin'* (1930), based on a play by Winchell Smith and Frank Bacon. The movie was a vehicle for Will Rogers's standard folksy character.

Although almost all of his screenplays were adaptations of other people's work, Behrman's scripts still contain certain recurring themes. In particular, his early work at Fox studios shows some of the same motifs that mark his plays: the plots frequently stem from the conflict between two highly different characters, with one sometimes serving to civilize the other. This dynamic is evident in *The Brat* (1931), which Behrman, Levien, and Maude Fulton adapted from Fulton's play. Novelist MacMullan Forester (Allan Dinehart) meets a street urchin (Sally O'Neil) and on a whim decides to try to make her into a society lady. John Ford directed.

After *The Brat*, Behrman and Levien adapted three novels to the screen: Jean Webster's *Daddy Long Legs*, Pierre Benoit's *Axelle* (filmed as *Surrender*), and Kate D. Wiggins's *Rebecca of Sunnybrook Farm*. *Daddy Long Legs* (1931) is about an orphan (Janet Gaynor) whose school tuition is secretly paid by a playboy (Warner Baxter); they begin a long

Greta Garbo and Charles Boyer as Napoleon and his Polish mistress in Conquest

correspondence by mail and fall in love. *Surrender* (1931) takes place in a World War I German prison camp run by Count Reichendorf (C. Aubrey Smith); problems ensue when Reichendorf's niece Axelle (Leila Hyams) takes an interest in a prisoner, French Sergeant Dumaine (Baxter).

By this point, Behrman was sufficiently established as a screenwriter to be entrusted with screenplay assignments for some of Fox studio's biggest stars; *Tess of the Storm Country* (1932) was written expressly for Janet Gaynor and Charles Farrell, "America's favorite lovebirds." Behrman collaborated on the screenplay with Levien and Rupert Hughes, working from a novel by Grace Miller White and the dramatization of the novel by Hughes. Tess (Gaynor) moves from a New England fishing village to Rock Bayou, where she encoun-

ters an almost unending series of problems: her father (Dudley Digges) is framed for murder; she adopts a baby, and the townspeople believe it to be her own illegitimate child; she prevents the baby's true unmarried mother from committing suicide; and she falls in love with Frederick Garfield (Farrell), whose disapproving father (Claude Gillingwater) controls the town. Following this motion picture, Behrman worked on *My Lips Betray* (1933), his only film at Fox not written with Levien. Set in the mythical European country Ruthania, this romantic comedy is about poor Lilli Wieler (Lilian Harvey), who becomes a successful singer after she claims to be the king's favorite; anxious to meet her, the king (John Boles) disguises himself as a songwriter and falls in love with her. The movie was based on the play *Der Komet* by Attila Orbuk.

As Husbands Go (1933) was Behrman's last film at Fox and his last collaboration with Levien for many years. (They were reunited with *The Cowboy and the Lady*, 1938.) Rachel Crothers's play provided the basis for this comedy about two American couples returning to the United States after living in Paris.

Leaving Fox, Behrman worked briefly for United Artists, where he wrote *Hallelujah, I'm a Bum!* (1933) for Al Jolson. Taken from a story by Ben Hecht, the movie is about Bumper (Jolson), the unofficial mayor of Central Park, who is befriended by the mayor of New York City (Frank Morgan) after Bumper finds $1,000 belonging to the mayor's girl friend (Madge Evans). Bumper and his friend Acorn (Edgar Connor) are given jobs but then are tried in a Central Park kangaroo court for deserting the other bums. They are found not guilty by reason of insanity.

Behrman next went to work at M-G-M, where he remained until 1951. His first projects at that studio were two pictures starring Greta Garbo: *Queen Christina* (1933) and *Anna Karenina* (1935). *Queen Christina* begins with young Christina (Garbo) ascending to the throne after her father is killed in battle. Fleeing a marriage arranged for

political purposes, she disguises herself as a young man and travels the country. She meets and falls in love with Spanish ambassador Don Antonio (John Gilbert), reveals her true identity to him, and finally renounces the throne in order to marry him. Well directed by Rouben Mamoulian, *Queen Christina* provided Garbo with one of her most notable film roles.

Based on Tolstoy's novel, *Anna Karenina* is the story of a married woman who takes a lover. (Garbo had also starred in an earlier film version, *Love*, in 1927.) Unhappy with her unfeeling husband Karenin (Basil Rathbone), Anna begins an affair with Count Vronsky (Fredric March). When the affair is discovered, she kills herself by leaping in front of a moving train. Because of censorship problems with the production code, the movie had to be toned down and the romance between Anna and Vronsky was somewhat milder than might be expected. It is still an effective and highly moving film, one whose critical reputation has grown over the years. Behrman is credited only with adapting the novel to the screen; Salka Viertel, Behrman's collaborator on *Queen Christina*, wrote the final screenplay with Clemence Dane. Clarence Brown directed.

Clark Gable as Parnell in M-G-M's disastrous 1937 biographical film about the Irish political leader

His adaptation of *A Tale of Two Cities* (1935) was Behrman's favorite of his own screenplays; W. P. Lipscomb collaborated. This third film version of Charles Dickens's novel was in many ways the best. Lavishly produced by David O. Selznick and directed by Jack Conway (Val Lewton and Jacques Tourneur also directed some sequences), the large and impressive cast was headed by Ronald Colman, who played Sidney Carton.

Shortly after his work on *A Tale of Two Cities* was finished, Behrman married Elsa Heifetz, sister of violinist Jascha Heifetz. They had one son, David Arthur Behrman.

Conquest (1937) reunited most of the creative team that had worked on *Anna Karenina:* writers Behrman and Viertel, director Brown, and star Garbo. The movie depicted the romance between

Napoleon Bonaparte (Charles Boyer) and his mistress Countess Marie Walewska (Garbo). As with *Anna Karenina*, the production code interfered and the romance between the two characters had to be muted; the screenplay emphasizes Napoleon's lust for power at the expense of his relationship with Walewska and their child.

Although Behrman wrote screenplays for some of the leading motion picture stars of his day, he did not always attempt to tailor his material to the star, as can be seen with *Parnell* (1937), which Behrman and John Van Druten adapted from a play by Elsie T. Schauffler. Clark Gable starred as Charles Stewart Parnell, the Irish political leader who led the fight in the British House of Commons for Irish self-government. The screenplay took considerable liberties with the facts when present-

Robert Taylor and Vivien Leigh in the 1940 version of Waterloo Bridge, *based on Robert E. Sherwood's play*

Scene from the first sound version of the epic film Quo Vadis

ing the romance between Parnell and Katie O'Shea (Myrna Loy), who was married to one of Parnell's political enemies. Audiences did not wish to see Gable in this period film, and the movie was a great financial failure.

The Cowboy and the Lady (1938) reunited Behrman with Sonya Levien; this United Artists production was also the only one of Behrman's films of this period not made at M-G-M. This romantic comedy was probably Behrman's best variation of his rough-hewn man-civilizing-woman theme. The cowboy (Gary Cooper) is an uneducated rodeo rider who falls in love with a maid (Merle Oberon), not realizing she is really a wealthy heiress who has run away from home. Both characters are changed for the better after their meeting; he becomes more mannerly and she less snobbish.

Waterloo Bridge (1940) was Behrman's next credit, and it was an important one—M-G-M had great hopes for this film, Vivien Leigh's first since her success in *Gone With the Wind* (1939) the year before. They were not disappointed in this moving adaptation of Robert Sherwood's play about a soldier (Robert Taylor) and a ballerina (Leigh) who meet in London during the war and fall in love. They quarrel and separate when he finds out that she has been driven to prostitution. The movie was a great success with both audiences and critics, and it remains one of Behrman's best-remembered motion pictures.

From the career highpoint of *Waterloo Bridge*, Behrman next reached his low: *Two-Faced Woman* (1941). Greta Garbo stars as a woman who fears she will lose her boyfriend (Melvyn Douglas) and plots to keep him by passing herself off as her more worldly twin sister. The movie was intended to be not just a sophisticated comedy but also an effort to give Garbo a more American, less European image. It failed on both accounts. Critics were almost unanimous in their negative reviews, and the movie's lighthearted treatment of adultery earned it a condemnation from the Legion of Decency, along with complaints from other censorship groups. *Two-Faced Woman* inflicted damage to the careers of nearly everyone associated with it; it marked Garbo's retirement, began a long, unproductive period for director George Cukor, and was Behrman's last produced screenplay for a decade.

Behrman busied himself with the theater and other projects until beginning work on his next film, *Quo Vadis*, in 1951. It was written in collaboration with Levien—their last work together—and veteran screenwriter John Lee Mahin, adapted from a novel by Henryk Sienkiewicz and directed by Mervyn LeRoy, with whom Behrman had worked on *Waterloo Bridge*. Set in ancient Rome, the film depicts the persecution of Christians under the Emperor Nero (Peter Ustinov), centering on Roman soldier Marcus Vinicius (Robert Taylor), who falls in love with Christian Lygia (Deborah Kerr). *Quo Vadis* was one of the first and best of the many historical epics of the 1950s; it was nominated for an Academy Award for best picture of 1951.

Quo Vadis was Behrman's last script for M-G-M. His final screenplay, *Me and the Colonel* (1958), was an adaptation of his own play, which was taken from *Jacobowsky and the Colonel* (1944), which Behrman, in turn, had based on an unproduced work by Franz Werfel. It is about a Polish Jew (Danny Kaye) who is forced to escape from the Nazis with a colonel (Curt Jurgens), who is loyal to Poland but who is also an anti-Semite. *Fanny* (1961) was produced by Warner Bros., and Julius Epstein wrote the screen adaptation of Behrman's 1954 play about a young French woman who becomes pregnant, marries a much older man, and is finally reunited with her baby's father. Joshua Logan, who had collaborated with Behrman on the play, directed the film version.

Behrman's last film work was providing the narrative for *Stowaway in the Sky* (1962), a French film about a boy and his eccentric inventor uncle who travel the country in a balloon. The following year, Behrman suffered a debilitating stroke and was only able to work infrequently. He completed his final play, *But for Whom Charlie*, in 1964. After that, he devoted his time to writing books and contributing regularly to the *New Yorker*. Behrman died of heart failure in 1973.

Reference:

Charles Affron, "Uncensored Garbo," in *Film Theory and Criticism*, edited by Gerald Mast and Marshall Cohen (New York & London: Oxford University Press, 1974), pp. 730-740.

Papers:
The bulk of Behrman's plays are deposited at the Wisconsin Center for Theatre Research, Wisconsin State Historical Society, Madison. *Lord Pengo* and *Duveen* manuscripts and pertinent correspondence are deposited at the Humanities Research Center, University of Texas at Austin. *But for Whom Charlie*, nonfiction manuscripts, and correspondence remain with the Behrman Estate in New York.

Charles Bennett
(2 August 1899-)

Kevin Mace
Oklahoma State University

MOTION PICTURES: *Blackmail* (British International Pictures, 1929), screenplay adapted by Bennett, Alfred Hitchcock, and Benn W. Levy from Bennett's play;

The Last Hour (Universal, 1930), screenplay;

Deadlock (George King, 1931), screenplay by Bennett and Billie Bristow;

Number Please (George King, 1931), screenplay by Bennett and Bristow;

Two-way Street (Nettlefold, 1931), screenplay by Bennett and Bristow;

Partners Please (Producers Distributing Corp., 1932), screenplay;

The Man Who Knew Too Much (Gaumont-British, 1934), screen story by Bennett, A. R. Rawlinson, and D. B. Wyndham Lewis; refilmed (Paramount, 1956), screen story by Bennett and Lewis;

The Clairvoyant (Gainsborough-British, 1935), screenplay by Bennett, Bryan Edgar Wallace, and Robert Edmunds;

The Thirty-Nine Steps (Gaumont-British, 1935), adaptation;

King of the Damned (Gaumont-British, 1935), screenplay by Bennett, Sidney Gilliatt, and Noel Langley;

Sabotage (Gaumont-British, 1936); released in the United States as *The Woman Alone*, screenplay;

Secret Agent (Gaumont-British, 1936), screenplay;

King Solomon's Mines (Gainsborough, 1937), screenplay by Bennett, Michael Hogan, Rawlinson, Roland Pertwee, and Ralph Spence;

The Girl Was Young (Gaumont-British, 1938), screenplay by Bennett, Edwin Greenwood, and Anthony Armstrong;

The Young In Heart (David Selznick, 1938), screenplay by Bennett and Paul Osborn;

Balalaika (M-G-M, 1939), screenplay by Bennett, Leon Gordon, and Jacques Deval;

Foreign Correspondent (United Artists, 1940), screenplay by Bennett and Joan Harrison;

They Dare Not Love (Columbia, 1941), screenplay by Bennett and Ernest Vajda;

Joan of Paris (20th Century-Fox, 1942), screenplay

Charles Bennett (photograph by Claude Harris)

by Bennett and Ellis St. Joseph;

Reap the Wild Wind (Paramount, 1942), screenplay by Bennett, Jesse L. Lasky, Jr., and Alan LeMay;

Forever and a Day (RKO, 1943), screenplay by Bennett and others;

The Story of Dr. Wassell (Paramount, 1944), screenplay by Bennett and LeMay;

Ivy (Universal, 1947), screenplay;

Unconquered (Paramount, 1947), screenplay by Bennett, Frederic Frank, and Lasky;

The Sign of the Ram (Columbia, 1948), screenplay;

Black Magic (Edward Small, 1949), screenplay;

Madness of the Heart (Two Cities, 1950), screenplay;

Where Danger Lives (RKO, 1950), screenplay;

Kind Lady (M-G-M, 1951), screenplay by Bennett, Edward Chodorov, and Jerry Davis;

The Green Glove (United Artists, 1952), screenplay;

No Escape (United Artists, 1953), screenplay;

Dangerous Mission (RKO, 1954), screenplay by Bennett, Horace McCoy, and W. R. Burnett;

Night of the Demon (Great Britain, 1957); released in the United States as *Curse of the Demon* (RKO, 1957), screenplay by Bennett and Hal E. Chester;

The Story of Mankind (Warner Bros., 1957), screenplay by Bennett and Irwin Allen;

The Big Circus (Allied Artists, 1959), screenplay by Bennett, Allen, and Irving Wallace;

The Lost World (20th Century-Fox, 1960), screenplay by Bennett and Allen;

Voyage to the Bottom of the Sea (20th Century-Fox, 1961), screenplay by Bennett and Allen;

Five Weeks in a Balloon (20th Century-Fox, 1962), screenplay by Bennett, Allen, and Al Gail;

War Gods of the Deep (American International Pictures, 1965), screenplay by Bennett and Louis M. Heyward.

PLAY PRODUCTIONS: *The Return,* London, Everyman Theatre, 30 May 1927;

Midnight, Nottingham, 10 December 1928; retitled *The Last Hour,* London, Comedy Theatre, 20 December 1928;

Blackmail, London, Globe Theatre, 28 February 1928;

After Midnight (one-act play), London, Rudolph Steiner Hall, 23 June 1929;

The Danger Line, London, 1930;

Sensation, London, Lyceum Theatre, October 1931;

Big Business, London, 1932;

Page from a Diary, London, Garrick Theatre, January 1936.

SELECTED TELEVISION: "Secret of the Loch," "Escape from Venice," "The Heat Monster," "The Deadly Dolls," "The Terrible Leprechaun," *Voyage to the Bottom of the Sea* (ABC, 14 September 1964-15 September 1968), teleplays;

"Terror-Go-Round," *Land of the Giants* (ABC, 22 September 1968), teleplay.

PERIODICAL PUBLICATION: "Rank Enthusiasm," *Screen Writer,* 1 (November 1945).

Before retiring in the mid-1960s, Charles Bennett had enjoyed a long and distinguished career as a screenwriter in both England and the United States. Specializing in thrillers, whether working with Alfred Hitchcock in the 1930s and early 1940s or Irwin Allen in the late 1950s and early 1960s, Bennett wrote films that often dealt with political or moral corruption, and his characters were often ordinary and innocent people who found themselves in circumstances beyond their control, demanding great physical courage and a strong and resolute moral will.

Born in Shoreham-on-Sea, Sussex, England, the son of Charles Bennett and Lilian Langrishe, Bennett was privately educated. He spent most of his early life as an actor, making his debut at twelve years old on 23 December 1911 in *The Miracle*. Six years later, he was serving in France during World War I; afterward, he toured with the Compton Comedy Company in 1920, with the Lena Ashwell Players in 1922, and with the Ben Greet Players in 1925. Bennett became notable for his performances as Theseus in a 1927 production of *A Midsummer Night's Dream* and as Aramis in *Cyrano de Bergerac,* produced in the same year. He married Margaret Riddick (Faith Bennett), who was an actress.

In 1927 Bennett turned to playwriting, a career decision that would eventually bring him into contact with Alfred Hitchcock. His first London play was *The Return* (produced in 1927), followed by *The Last Hour* (produced in 1928), *Blackmail* (produced in 1928), *After Midnight* (produced in 1929), and *The Danger Line* (produced in 1930). Other plays he wrote are *Sensation* (produced in 1931), *Big Business* (produced in 1932), and *Page from a Diary* (1936). His most successful play was *Blackmail,* starring Tallulah Bankhead as Alice White, a young woman who kills an artist who tried to rape her after he took her to his studio to sketch her. Complicating matters for Alice and Frank Webber, her policeman boyfriend, is an insidious man who has seen Alice entering the artist's quarters and attempts to use this information to blackmail Alice and Frank.

Directed by actor Raymond Massey, *Blackmail* enjoyed a modest success when it opened at the Globe Theatre in London in February 1928; however, when Hitchcock bought the rights to make Bennett's play into a motion picture, *Blackmail* became a historically important film, because it was the first British talking movie. Although the film was originally meant to be a silent one, and there are stretches in the film that are still silent, dialogue scenes were reshot so that Hitchcock could make use of the sound facilities given to him by his studio,

British International Pictures. While *Blackmail* provided Bennett with his first screen credit, he insists he had no hand in the writing of the film; all the work was done by Hitchcock and Benn W. Levy, with whom he shared credit.

Though he never worked on *Blackmail*, Bennett and Hitchcock became good friends, and as soon as *Blackmail* opened to rave reviews and healthy box office returns, the men planned a second film together, to be based on H. C. McNeile's "Bulldog Drummond" character. In 1934 Michael Balcon, executive in charge of production for Gaumont-British, asked Bennett and Hitchcock to come to work at his studio, bringing their Drummond story with them. Both men accepted Balcon's offer, but the Bulldog Drummond idea became lost in the move. Instead, the first film that Bennett and Hitchcock worked on, as part of a five-picture con-

tract, became one of their most successful pictures, *The Man Who Knew Too Much* (1934).

The Man Who Knew Too Much is based on a story by Bennett and D. B. Wyndham Lewis, while Ivor Montagu was responsible for the story's adaptation; Edwin Greenwood and A. R. Rawlinson wrote the screenplay and Emlyn Williams is credited with additional dialogue. Despite so many hands the film remains fresh and exciting fifty years later. Edna Best and Leslie Banks portray parents who along with their daughter (Nova Pilbeam) are vacationing in Saint Moritz. When a close friend (Pierre Fresnay) is murdered, and it turns out that he is a British secret agent trying to prevent an assassination from occurring in London, the family finds itself ensnarled in a deadly game of intrigue. To keep the parents from going to the authorities, the murderers kidnap the daughter;

John Longden (left) and Anny Ondra in Alfred Hitchcock's Blackmail. *Though this film was based on Charles Bennett's play and he shared screen credit with Hitchcock and Benn W. Levy, Bennett had no part in writing the screenplay.*

Leslie Banks, unidentified actor, Nova Pilbeam, and Peter Lorre in the 1934 version of The Man Who Knew Too Much

however, in London, the mother foils the assassination attempt during the concert at Albert Hall, then rescues her daughter from the kidnappers. What makes the film exciting are the breakneck pace, spectacular, on-location shooting in Saint Moritz, and the engaging performances by Banks, Best, and Pilbeam, plus a delightfully sinister performance by Peter Lorre, as leader of the kidnappers. In 1956 Hitchcock remade *The Man Who Knew Too Much,* and while it is still very much Bennett's and Lewis's story, Hitchcock gave the remake a more American feeling, especially in the characterizations: the parents are an American couple (James Stewart and Doris Day) accidentally involved in international intrigue. The remake proved as successful with critics and audiences as the original did in 1934. The 1934 version of *The Man Who Knew Too Much* proved a critical and financial success, and it helped pave the way for Bennett and Hitchcock's next project, an adaptation of John Buchan's novel *The Thirty-Nine Steps.*

What Bennett admired most about Buchan's novel is the sudden eruption of a sense of terror in the life of an ordinary man falsely accused of murder by the police. Bennett thought the novel lacked character, humor, or any possibilities of audience participation; so Bennett and Hitchcock decided to exploit two aspects of the 1930s scene that are not in Buchan's book: the threat of sabotage from German spies and the audience's demand for comic-romantic elements in the film. Bennett and Hitchcock took care of the first requirement easily

enough: the film tells the story of a young Canadian (Robert Donat) and a beautiful blonde (Madeleine Carroll) who become involved in a deadly game of espionage when they attempt to bring to justice an international ring of spies known as "the thirty-nine steps." Donat and Carroll created a charmingly droll couple who always manage to get into trouble; in fact, a highlight of the film occurs when these characters find themselves handcuffed to each other, and as they wander about the Scottish countryside, fleeing from both the spies and the police, they do their very best to hide their embarrassing predicament from passersby. *The Thirty-Nine Steps* (1935) became a box office success and today is considered one of Hitchcock's best works. The motion picture is also an excellent example of how Hitchcock and his writers scripted his films. The process is an extremely simple, yet efficient one that Hitchcock—and, as long as he was associated with him, Bennett—would continue to use throughout his career.

Hitchcock would begin by selecting a property, in this case *The Thirty-Nine Steps,* and then he, Bennett, and Hitchcock's wife, Alma Reville, would reduce it to a half-page outline. Then they would start asking pertinent questions about the characters in the story, such as "What are their occupations?" and "What is their social position?" From the answers they would create a sixty- or seventy-page outline that plotted the visual action scene by scene with no dialogue. Once the outline was completed, Hitchcock would call in others to write the dialogue; so when Hitchcock was ready to start shooting, he would have a finished, detailed script, broken down shot by shot and sketched into story boards by Hitchcock himself. Bennett followed such a procedure while he wrote two films for Hitchcock in 1935: *Secret Agent* was based on the play by Campbell Dixon, which in turn was based on the Ashenden short stories by W. Somerset Maugham; *Sabotage* was based on Joseph Conrad's novel *The Secret Agent*.

Secret Agent is a strange, murky story about two British agents (John Gielgud and Madeleine Carroll) who pose as a married couple in order to pursue an enemy agent in Switzerland. Bennett tried to make the screenplay a blend of comedy and thriller, but he never really succeeded. While *Secret Agent* is somewhat flawed, *Sabotage* brilliantly succeeds as a dark and somber tale of espionage and murder. It is an elaborately detailed thriller about a young American woman (Sylvia Sidney) who suspects her husband (Oskar Homalka), a movie theater manager in London, is a German spy who uses his theater as a front for enemy spy activities. The film is full of clever touches, and it is rich with moral ambiguity and psychological ambivalence in its characterizations. *Sabotage* is more than just a spy thriller; it is also a moral fable that asks its audience to side with both the helpless young wife and her charming, basically honest husband whose politics eventually lead to tragedy and death.

Still in Britain, Bennett also contributed to the screenplays for *The Clairvoyant* (1935), a film about a fake mentalist (Claude Rains) who foresees an actual disaster; *King of the Damned* (1935), about the inmates of a South Seas prison who rebel against their cruel treatment; and *King Solomon's Mines* (1937), an excellent adaptation of H. Rider Haggard's African adventure novel. The last film that Bennett wrote for Hitchcock in Britain was *Young and Innocent*, retitled *The Girl Was Young* (1938), a charming and humorous thriller about a young woman (Nova Pilbeam) who helps a runaway man falsely accused of murder. Somewhat reminiscent of *The Thirty-Nine Steps* in both plot and characterizations, *The Girl Was Young* contains one of the most unusual scenes in any Hitchcock movie: a nightclub scene which reveals the real murderer, an eye-twitching drummer in blackface.

In 1938 Bennett left for America where he would remain for most of the 1940s. His first American film was *The Young In Heart* (1938), a wacky comedy about a family of con artists. This was fol-

lowed by *Balalaika* (1939), a musical about Russian exiles in Paris.

After the beginning of the war, Bennett wrote mostly propaganda war films such as *They Dare Not Love* (1941), about an Austrian prince (George Brent) who flees his country when the Germans invade and then returns to fight them, and *Joan of Paris* (1942), in which a French resistance fighter (Michele Morgan) turns herself over to the Nazis so her associates can escape. Ernest Vajda collaborated on the screenplay of the former. Bennett's best film of the period was *Foreign Correspondent* (1940), which Hitchcock directed and Bennett wrote with Joan Harrison, Hitchcock's secretary and frequent collaborator. More than a propaganda film, *Foreign Correspondent* is an intricately structured and sharply written story about an innocent man's terrifying journey into and subsequent flight from the sinister world of international espionage. A somewhat naive American journalist (Joel McCrea), sent to cover the European situation in August 1939, discovers a plot to assassinate a Dutch diplomat (Albert Basserman) and falls in love with the daughter (Laraine Day) of an English pacifist (Herbert Marshall), only to discover that her father is the chief enemy spy. Not just anti-Nazi and antiwar, *Foreign Correspondent* is a picaresque story, a romantic melodrama with considerable comic tone. The film received rave critical notices and enjoyed a healthy success at the box office in both the United States and Canada.

Cecil B. De Mille hired Bennett to write three pictures that De Mille produced and directed. *Reap the Wild Wind* (1942) was an attempt to repeat the success *Gone with the Wind* (1939) had had three years before. An epic drama set in Georgia in the 1800s, it centers on the romantic triangle of Loxi Claiborne (Paulette Goddard), salvage ship captain Jack Stuart (John Wayne), and lawyer Stephen Tolliver (Ray Milland). *The Story of Dr. Wassell* (1944) is about a dedicated Navy doctor (Gary Cooper) who saved fighting men in the Pacific during World War II. *Unconquered* (1947) is the lengthy story of early American settlers and their battles with Indians. Also during this period, Bennett was one of many writers who contributed material to *Forever and a Day* (1943). Twenty-one scripters, seven directors, and eighty leading actors took part in this film, which depicts the happenings in one English house over several decades.

For the next several years Bennett devoted his efforts to writing and, occasionally, directing mysteries and thrillers. In *Ivy* (1947), a woman (Joan Fontaine) plans to commit a perfect murder

Madeleine Carroll and Robert Donat in a scene from The Thirty-Nine Steps, *one of Charles Bennett's early adaptations for*
Alfred Hitchcock

by poisoning her victim. John Sturges directed *The Sign of the Ram* (1948), which Bennett wrote for Susan Peters, a young actress making her first picture after being paralyzed in a hunting accident. She plays a wheelchair-bound woman who uses her handicap and her supposed psychic powers to manipulate her family and neighbors. *Black Magic* (1949) is a period melodrama about a magician (Orson Welles, who also directed parts of the film without credit) who becomes involved in a scheme to replace Marie Antoinette with a look-alike.

Bennett made his directorial debut with *Madness of the Heart* (1949), which he adapted from a popular novel by Flora Sandstrom. The film tells the story of a blind girl (Margaret Lockwood) who marries a French aristocrat (Paul Dupuis) and has to cope with a jealous neighbor (Kathleen Byron). Considered a second-rate *Rebecca* (1940), Bennett's

film did not fare well at the box office in England or the United States; it was four more years before Bennett directed his second, and last, film, *No Escape* (1953). A married couple (Lew Ayres and Marjorie Steele) are wrongly accused of murder and try to find the real killer. In between his directorial roles, he wrote three other movies. John Farrow directed *Where Danger Lives* (1950), about a woman (Faith Domergue) who convinces a man (Robert Mitchum) he has killed her wealthy husband (Claude Rains). *Kind Lady* (1951) was a remake of an earlier film about a con man (Maurice Evans) and his associates who move into the home of an elderly woman (Ethel Barrymore) and plan to rob her. *The Green Glove* (1952), set in postwar France, is a tale of stolen jewels and murder.

Dangerous Mission (1954) was Bennett's final crime drama. Louise Graham (Piper Laurie) witnesses a professional killing and flees to Glacier National Park. She is pursued by two men: one, a hired killer (Vincent Price), the other (Victor Mature), a member of the district attorney's office who has come to convince her to testify. Bennett wrote his screenplay with two novelists who were quite familiar with this sort of material, Horace McCoy and W. R. Burnett, but the movie never creates any real suspense and was a box office failure. It was still very important for Bennett's career: he met producer Irwin Allen, for whom Bennett was to write all but two of his remaining screenplays.

Before teaming with Allen to produce a series of fantasy adventure films, Bennett earned one more important screen credit, writing one of the best of the 1950s horror films, *Night of the Demon* (1957). Dr. John Holden (Dana Andrews) comes to London to expose as a fraud the leader of a satanic cult (Niall MacGinnis). But Holden is wrong; Julian Karswell has genuine supernatural powers and

plans to use them to kill Holden. The movie was well received in its initial release and is still considered a classic of the horror genre, but it remains an unpleasant memory for Bennett. He had hoped to direct the film himself but could not find the backing; instead he sold the script to producer Hal E. Chester who rewrote Bennett's screenplay and hired Jacques Tourneur to direct. Furthermore, for its American release, the film's title was changed to *Curse of the Demon* (Bennett did not approve of the American title), and thirteen minutes were cut from the movie. It still remains an impressive picture; aside from his work with Hitchcock, it is Bennett's best-known screenplay.

Although Bennett's collaborations with Allen produced several financial successes and inspired one television series (*Voyage to the Bottom of the Sea*, 1964), their first projects together were not so successful. *The Story of Mankind* (1957) is Bennett's most embarrassing film; very loosely based on Hen-

Madeleine Carroll, John Gielgud, and Peter Lorre in Alfred Hitchcock's Secret Agent, *adapted from the play that Campbell Dixon had based on W. Somerset Maugham's Ashenden stories*

Joel McCrea and Laraine Day in Alfred Hitchcock's Foreign Correspondent, *an anti-Nazi film that is now considered one of the best World War II movies*

drik Van Loon's study of human history, the film is a laughable, childish attempt at costume drama, depicting important historic events. The film suffers from juvenile moralizing and incredible miscasting: Harpo Marx as Isaac Newton, Dennis Hopper as Napoleon. *The Big Circus* (1959) is about a circus beset with many problems, including sabotage by a rival company. It was dismissed by many viewers as a poor imitation of *The Greatest Show on Earth* (1952).

It was when they turned to science fiction that Bennett and Allen enjoyed real financial success. Their adaptation of Sir Arthur Conan Doyle's *The Lost World* (1960) was found by most critics to be inferior to the 1925 silent version, but audiences enjoyed it all the same. An even bigger hit was *Voyage to the Bottom of the Sea* (1961), about the adventures of a submarine crew; more important, it inspired Allen's long-running series for which Bennett was a frequent scripter.

Five Weeks in a Balloon (1962), a tongue-in-cheek version of Jules Verne's novel about a trip by balloon from Europe to Africa, was the last of Bennett's film scripts for Allen, though his final screenplay, *War Gods of the Deep* (1965), continued in the science fiction vein. Based on a poem by Edgar Allen Poe, and directed by Tourneur, it is the story of an underwater city ruled by an insane commander (Vincent Price). Following the release of this film, Bennett retired from screenwriting; he continued to write television scripts for Irwin Allen throughout the 1960s.

The significance of Charles Bennett's career lies chiefly in his association with Alfred Hitchcock, for in many respects both men are responsible for establishing the thriller as an important film genre, one with its own unique and unmistakable identity. Bennett helped create such popular thriller elements as the falsely accused hero, the beautiful and intelligent heroine, the handsome and charming

Dana Andrews (right) in Night of the Demon, *one of the classic horror films*

villain, and the climactic, suspenseful chase that depends as much on the heroine's courage as it does the hero's for its successful outcome. He is also responsible for including romantic-comic elements in the thriller genre: the often strained and bittersweet romance, as in *Blackmail* and *The Man Who Knew Too Much,* and the droll and cynical comedy, as in *The Thirty-Nine Steps* and *Foreign Correspondent.* Finally, Bennett has been a meticulous craftsman striving to create fascinating stories and engaging characters.

References:

Danny Peary, *Cult Movies 2* (New York: Dell, 1983), pp. 108-110;

Donald Spoto, *The Art of Alfred Hitchcock: Fifty Years of His Motion Pictures* (New York: Hopkinson & Blake, 1976);

Spoto, *The Dark Side of Genius: The Life of Alfred Hitchcock* (Boston: Little, Brown, 1983);

John Russell Taylor, *Hitch: The Life and Times of Alfred Hitchcock* (New York: Pantheon Books, 1978).

Robert Benton
(29 September 1932-   )

David Newman
(4 February 1937-   )

Michael Adams

MOTION PICTURES: *Bonnie and Clyde* (Warner Bros.-Seven Arts, 1967), story and screenplay;

There Was a Crooked Man (Warner Bros., 1970), story and screenplay;

What's Up, Doc? (Warner Bros., 1972), screenplay by Benton, Newman, and Buck Henry;

Oh, Calcutta! (Cinemation, 1972), screenplay by Benton, Newman, Kenneth Tynan, Jules Feiffer, Dan Greenburg, and John Lennon;

Bad Company (Paramount, 1972), story and screenplay;

The Crazy American Girl (20th Century-Fox, 1976), screenplay by Newman and Leslie Newman;

The Late Show (Warner Bros., 1977), story and screenplay by Benton;

Superman (Warner Bros., 1978), screenplay by Benton, Newman, Leslie Newman, and Mario Puzo;

Kramer vs. Kramer (Columbia, 1979), screenplay by Benton;

Superman II (Warner Bros., 1981), screenplay by Newman, Leslie Newman, and Puzo;

Jinxed! (M-G-M-United Artists, 1982), screenplay by Newman and Frank Gilroy (as Bert Blessing);

Still of the Night (M-G-M-United Artists, 1982), story by Benton and Newman, screenplay by Benton;

Superman III (Warner Bros., 1983), screenplay by Newman and Leslie Newman;

Sheena (Columbia, 1984), story by Newman, screenplay by Newman and Lorenzo Semple, Jr.;

Places in the Heart (Tri-Star, 1984), screenplay by Benton.

PLAY PRODUCTIONS: *It's a Bird . . . It's a Plane . . . It's Superman*, New York, Alvin Theatre, 3 March 1966, book;

Oh, Calcutta!, New York, Eden Theatre, 6 June 1969, by Benton, Newman, and others.

BOOKS: *The In and Out Book*, by Benton and Harvey Schmidt (New York: Viking, 1959);

Little Brother No More, by Benton (New York: Knopf, 1960);

Esquire's Book of Gambling, by Benton and others (New York: Harper & Row, 1962);

The Worry Book, by Benton and Schmidt (New York: Viking, 1962);

Esquire's World of Humor, by Newman and others (New York: Harper & Row, 1964);

Extremism; A Non Book, by Newman and Benton (New York: Viking, 1964).

PERIODICAL PUBLICATIONS: "The New Sentimentality," *Esquire*, 62 (July 1964): 25-31;

"The Basic Library of Trash," *Esquire*, 63 (February 1965): 78-79, 126-127;

"The Movies Will Save Themselves," *Esquire*, 70 (October 1968): 182-187;

"The Kids of *Bad Company*," *Esquire*, 79 (February 1973): 67;

Benton, *"Bad Company," Action*, 8 (March-April 1973);

Newman, "People We Like: Robert Walker," *Film Comment*, 10 (May-June 1974): 36;

Newman, "David Newman's Guilty Pleasures," *Film Comment*, 14 (November-December 1978): 28-32.

The screenplays of Robert Benton and David Newman offer some support for the screenwriter-as-auteur theory as they display a consistent concern with a handful of themes. Their characters are usually outsiders to some degree, whether they are the actual outlaws of *Bonnie and Clyde* (1967), *There Was a Crooked Man* (1970), and *Bad Company* (1972), the aging detective with an anachronistic set of values of *The Late Show* (1977), or the most perfect person on Earth, who is isolated by his perfection, in *Superman* (1978). These characters are always seeking comradeship or love (sometimes

David Newman and Robert Benton, 1960s

finding them) and often making a journey of discovery. They usually move away from respectability rather than toward it, as in the case of lawman-turned-outlaw Woodward Lopeman in *There Was a Crooked Man*. Other characters assume roles: Bonnie and Clyde become glamorous criminals, and the being from Krypton poses as Clark Kent who is, in reality, Superman.

Robert Benton was born in Dallas and grew up in Waxachie, Texas, where his great-grandfather had served as sheriff. This great-grandfather, as well as two of his uncles, died of gunshot wounds, a possible explanation for Benton's fascination with violence and the American West. In high school, he decided to be a painter. He received his Bachelor of Fine Arts from the University of Texas in 1953 and continued his art studies at Columbia University before spending two years (1954 to 1956) in the U.S. Army. He became an assistant art director at *Esquire* magazine in 1957, art director from 1958 to 1964, and a contributing editor from 1964 to 1972. He married Sally Rendigs in 1964, and they have a son, John Douglas.

David Newman was born in New York. As a child Newman enjoyed watching the comedies of Abbott and Costello. In an article years later, he said that these movies taught him a sense of "comedy and timing" which helped him in his own career. He was an English major at the University of Michigan and received his bachelor's degree in 1958 and master's degree in 1959. At Michigan he studied creative writing with Malcolm Cowley, who was instrumental in helping him obtain an editorial position at *Esquire* in 1960. Like Benton, he was a contributing editor from 1964 to 1972. He married Leslie Harris England in 1958, and they have two children, Nathan and Catherine.

After separately writing several *Esquire* articles, Benton and Newman began collaborating in 1964. Their articles usually focused on popular culture, as in "The Basic Library of Trash," an annotated list of sixty-six books of "no literary distinction." Their most famous *Esquire* article, "The New Sentimentality," published in July 1964, is a satiric look at self-indulgence and nostalgia. Benton and Newman also developed *Esquire*'s annual college issue and the Dubious Achievement Awards. From 1964 to 1974, they also wrote "Man Talk," a monthly column for *Mademoiselle* designed, according to the editors, to tell "the girls . . . how gents felt about the same stuff that was bothering them." In addition to their script and magazine work, Benton and Newman have also collaborated on the Broadway musical *It's a Bird . . . It's a Plane . . . It's Superman* (1966), and they contributed to the revue *Oh, Calcutta!* (1969).

Working together at *Esquire*, Benton and Newman found they talked increasingly about movies, both classic American films like those of Howard Hawks and Alfred Hitchcock, and about the New Wave masterpieces of Jean-Luc Godard and François Truffaut. They gradually realized that they felt "movies are just simply the best things in the world, the most worthy subjects for study, the best examples of genuinely artistic accomplishment today." They knew they wanted to make movies and found the subject of their first script in a brief reference to Bonnie Parker and Clyde Barrow in John Toland's book *The Dillinger Days* (1963). They were particularly inspired by one line: "Not only were they outlaws, but they were outcasts."

After writing the script of *Bonnie and Clyde* (1967), Benton and Newman began the long process of getting it filmed. They first wanted Godard to direct and later, Truffaut, but potential backers were not enthusiastic about combining foreign filmmakers with an American story. Finally, Warren Beatty heard about the script from Truffaut, decided to produce it, and hired director Arthur Penn, with whom he had worked on *Mickey One* (1965). Penn worked with Benton and Newman on revising the screenplay, concerning himself not with dialogue but with unifying the story's various elements. Benton and Newman originally had a ménage à trois consisting of Bonnie, Clyde, and their companion C. W. Moss; in that script Clyde was unable to perform sexually without the presence of a third person. Penn felt this perversity would make the audience unsympathetic to Clyde. Other changes instigated by Penn developed and expanded the film's social context. Eventually, Robert Towne, listed in the credits as "Special Consultant," was called in to prepare the final shooting script. One of his major contributions was to restructure the script so that its elements foreshadowed the conclusion.

Bonnie and Clyde is loosely based on real characters and events but is much more concerned with theme, style, and mood than with being faithful to history. In the film, Bonnie (Faye Dunaway) and Clyde (Warren Beatty) meet by chance as he is about to steal her mother's car. He proves his manhood to Bonnie by robbing a grocery store and stealing a car, actions which sexually excite her. Although she learns that Clyde is incapable of meeting her physical needs, she is still attracted to him because of his promise to take her away from her drab, dead-end life as a waitress and make her into someone important. They begin their journey, stopping to pick up C. W. Moss (Michael J. Pollard), Clyde's brother Buck (Gene Hackman), and Buck's wife Blanche (Estelle Parsons). Together they become legendary bank robbers and killers, who, themselves, are finally killed.

Benton and Newman have said that in writing the script they were strongly influenced by two Truffaut films: "*Shoot the Piano Player* (1963), with its combination of comedy and bleakness, gangsterism and humanity, and *Jules and Jim* (1962), which managed to define the present as it evoked the past." The Truffaut influence is evident in the way *Bonnie and Clyde* combines the elements of the action movie with those of "black" comedy and the love story. The film evokes the bleakness of the Depression era while it captures the restlessness and ethical ambiguities of the 1960s. It also foreshadows the 1970s through Bonnie and Clyde's obsession with becoming celebrities, orchestrating their holdups with a style copied from movies, exulting in their legend as created by newspaper gossip.

Bonnie and Clyde was perhaps the most important and influential American movie of the 1960s. It demonstrated that domestic films could successfully incorporate the styles of foreign films with indigenous American material. By making use of what Benton, Newman, and Penn had learned from Godard, Truffaut, and others, *Bonnie and Clyde* proved that an elliptical style—omitting the traditional transitions between scenes—could work in American movies. Benton and Newman broke another Hollywood tradition by refusing to trumpet their role in the success of *Bonnie and Clyde*, apparently believing that it was more Arthur Penn's film than their own. Nevertheless, their script won awards from the New York Film Critics, the National Society of Film Critics, and the Writers' Guild (best original screenplay and best drama), and was nominated for an Academy Award.

Benton and Newman's next film, *There Was a Crooked Man* (1970), was less successful. They were approached by Kenneth Hyman, head of production at Warner Bros., to write a violent, prison-break Western. Originally titled *Hell*, the movie centers on a conflict between outlaw Paris Pitman (Kirk Douglas) and lawman Woodward Lopeman (Henry Fonda). After hiding half a million dollars in a nest of rattlesnakes, Pitman is arrested by Lopeman and sent to an Arizona prison. Pitman convinces the warden to allow him to escape in exchange for half the loot, but the warden is killed by another prisoner before the break can take place. Lopeman becomes the new warden, and, with Pitman's cooperation, he improves prison conditions. During a governor's tour, Pitman escapes, letting three of his accomplices be killed. While retrieving the money, Pitman is bitten by a snake and dies as Lopeman, who has tracked him, takes the money and heads for Mexico.

Joseph L. Mankiewicz agreed to direct *There Was a Crooked Man* because the Dickensian supporting characters appealed to him. He was not entirely pleased with the screenplay, however, and decided to emphasize the comic elements over the violent ones. His 165-minute rough cut was trimmed to 125 minutes, leaving out nuances of character and plot development. The studio's indifference was equaled by that of the critics and the public. The main problem was that Benton and

Newman failed to make any of the characters appealing or even very interesting. Pitman's amoral cynicism sets the dominant tone, and all the characters are repellent; there is none of the refreshing originality found in so many anti-hero films of the period. In addition, the reasons for Lopeman's transformation from moralistic public servant to outlaw are not clear.

About their next project, Newman comments, "Of all the things we've done, *What's Up, Doc?* (1972) is the project we felt least personally involved with." Director Peter Bogdanovich devised a story loosely based on the classic screwball comedy *Bringing Up Baby* (1938) and had Benton and Newman write a script. They turned out a first draft in a week and a half, did a quick rewrite, and moved on to other projects. Buck Henry was hired to prepare the shooting script.

The film tells the story of Howard Bannister (Ryan O'Neal), a young absentminded professor from Iowa who goes to San Francisco in the hopes of winning a $20,000 fellowship. Along the way, his suitcase full of the igneous rocks which illustrate his theory about the prehistoric origins of music is mixed up with identical suitcases, one filled with

Michael J. Pollard, Gene Hackman, Warren Beatty, and Faye Dunaway in Bonnie and Clyde, *one of the most successful and influential films of the 1960s*

Joseph Mankiewicz directing Kirk Douglas in There Was a Crooked Man, *Benton and Newman's second film*

jewels and stolen government documents, and another owned by eccentric Judy Maxwell (Barbra Streisand). Further confusion is added when Judy has to pretend to be Howard's fiancée Eunice. These mix-ups ultimately result in a frantic chase through the city, ending with all the characters falling into San Francisco Bay. Finally, Howard wins both the fellowship and Judy.

Benton has said that while working on the script, he, Newman, and Bogdanovich watched several Preston Sturges and Ernst Lubitsch films as well as the cartoons Frank Tashlin made for Warner Bros. in the 1930s and 1940s. As its title indicates, *What's Up, Doc?* owes more to Bugs Bunny than to Sturges, Lubitsch, or even Howard Hawks. The emphasis is on physical humor with little wit or sophistication. Despite its flaws, the film was a great financial success and won the Writers' Guild award for comedy writing.

According to Newman, "No matter how much we think screenwriters have been overlooked or the fact that their contribution is so enormous, if we didn't believe the director's stamp on the film is the primary one, we wouldn't have become directors." They had been trying for some time to get backing for scripts which they would direct, but no studio showed interest until Paramount accepted the screenplay for *Bad Company* (1972) with Benton directing.

Bad Company is a Civil War drama about two young men, draft evader Drew Dixon (Barry Brown) and deserter Jake Rumsey (Jeff Bridges) who meet when Rumsey robs Dixon. Later, Dixon joins the group of runaways led by Rumsey, but their tentative friendship ends when Rumsey robs Dixon a second time. Dixon helps a posse trap Rumsey, but after Rumsey convinces Dixon that they are kindred spirits, Dixon helps him escape and they embark on a life of crime.

Bad Company is an amalgam of influences: Hollywood Westerns, the elliptical European style, and the works of Mark Twain, especially *Roughing It* (1871). But it lacks the excitement, depth, and humor of its models. One of the major problems with *Bad Company* is that its intentions are not always clear. According to Benton, "To us, *Bad Company* is a film about friendship, it's a film—in the same way *Bonnie and Clyde* was—about that artificial family you create in your life." The film succeeds in showing how people from disparate backgrounds—the courteous Dixon and the brutish Rumsey—can form an alliance, first from the need to survive and then from a shared experience and recognition of their common humanity. But Benton and Newman fail to make their characters distinctive, with Rumsey emerging as far less sympathetic than he is meant to be. The film also appeared at a time when too many such anti-Westerns were being made, dulling the effect of its originality.

It was now Newman's turn to direct a film, and after several projects fell through, he made *The Crazy American Girl* (1976) which he cowrote with his wife Leslie. Due to legal complications, the film has never been released in the United States, but it was distributed in Europe in 1976. It tells the story of a young woman (Patti D'Arbanville) from Pennsylvania who goes to Paris hoping to become a leading model. Her problem is that she is, in Newman's words, "on shaky emotional ground, but no one realizes it. She is used by everyone who comes in contact with her. No one wants to see that she is about to have a breakdown." *The Crazy American Girl* gradually progresses from being a funny love story to being a sad tale about the exploitation and disintegration of a complex, fragile human being; Newman has said that the film fails to work as well as it should because it does not show enough of what is sympathetic about the characters.

Benton began working on his first solo screenplay, *The Late Show* (1977), while editing *Bad Company*, left it incomplete for two years, and returned to it while Newman was making *The Crazy American Girl*. Inspired by *Ride the High Country* (1962), the Western film about two aging lawmen, *The Late Show* focuses on Ira Wells (Art Carney), a small-time Los Angeles private detective in advanced middle-age. His former partner is murdered, and

Wells sets out to solve the case, meanwhile getting involved with Margo (Lily Tomlin), an eccentric who hires him to find her stolen cat. Together they uncover a nest of corruption and several corpses.

Although *The Late Show* is derived from *The Maltese Falcon* (1941), *The Big Sleep* (1946), and other films of the hard-boiled detective genre, Benton is less concerned with examining evil than with exploring character. Ira Wells is desperately trying to live by a code he has learned from movies: being loyal to his friends, punishing wrongdoers, trying to impose some order on the chaos which threatens to engulf him, making the most of what will probably be his last chance to be a hero. Margo is just as desperate as she searches for something to give some meaning to her life. She finds it in her relationship with a balding, paunchy man with a hearing aid and a perforated ulcer. These two characters are outsiders who, with no substantial ties to the rest of the world, unite in an effort to help each other. The theme of friendship which recurs in Benton and Newman films is at its most poignant in *The Late Show* as a man and a woman from different generations and with different values develop affection and respect for each other without sentimentality. Benton invests his characters and their story with compassion and humor and directs the film with vitality and style. *The Late Show* was the basis for a television series, *Eye to Eye*, in 1985.

Nearly a decade after their work on *It's a Bird . . . It's a Plane . . . It's Superman*, circumstances led Benton and Newman back to the same material. Mario Puzo had written a screenplay based on the Superman character, but the producers were dissatisfied with the result, feeling that he had treated the subject too seriously. Benton and Newman were hired to revise Puzo's work, and they spent three months working to add some levity to it before Benton had to leave for *The Late Show*. Newman and Leslie Newman did several more rewrites, and Tom Mankiewicz (son of Joseph Mankiewicz) polished the script during the film's shooting.

Superman was a mixture of pop-camp, serious adventure, romantic comedy, and epic. Much of the film is devoted to retelling the Superman legend. Sent as an infant from the doomed planet Krypton, young Kal-el is found and adopted by an Earth couple, Jonathan and Martha Kent (Glenn Ford and Phyllis Thaxter). When young Clark Kent (Jeff East) enters his teens, a holographic vision of his Kryptonian father (Marlon Brando) informs him of his past and instructs him in the use of the powers he receives due to the Earth's lighter gravity and yellow sun. Young Kent retreats to his Fortress of Solitude for a period of study, then emerges as Superman (Christopher Reeve). He makes his presence known one night in the city of Metropolis, stopping criminals and saving Lois Lane (Margot Kidder). Finally he battles Lex Luthor (Gene Hackman), who intends to destroy California with an atomic bomb, thus making his useless land in Nevada valuable ocean-front property.

Kramer vs. Kramer (1979), Benton's third directorial effort, was adapted from the novel by Avery Corman, and it is the only adaptation by either Benton or Newman to reach the screen. Benton has said he revises more frequently and extensively those screenplays he is to direct, and he rewrote *Kramer vs. Kramer* twenty times, changing it at least forty percent each time.

The film has the simplest plot of any Benton or Newman endeavor: a wife (Meryl Streep) walks out on her husband (Dustin Hoffman) and young son (Justin Henry) and later attempts to win the boy's custody. The emphasis is on Ted Kramer's attempts to be a better parent while almost sacrificing his advertising career. Benton's theme once again is friendship. Ted and Billy Kramer become more than father and son; they grow to love and respect each other deeply.

Although *Kramer vs. Kramer* won high praise from critics for its sensitivity and humor, it was criticized by some as an antifeminist tract, with Joanna Kramer emerging as an unsympathetic character. This minor controversy did not keep *Kramer vs. Kramer* from earning over $60 million and winning the Academy Award as the best film of 1979. Benton won two Oscars, among several other awards, for his writing and directing.

Following *Superman*, Newman began work on several projects, none of which were produced, so that his next screen credit was for *Superman II* (1981), parts of which had been written and filmed

Robert Benton and David Newman, 1970s

Advertisement for Benton's 1979 movie, which the studio promoted as a family film

during the shooting of *Superman*. In the original film the Newmans had begun a romantic triangle in which Clark Kent loves Lois Lane who loves Superman who is Clark Kent; this triangle formed the basis for *Superman II*, in which Superman reveals his secret identity to Lois, then deprives himself of his powers so that the two of them can lead a normal life together. Meanwhile, three Kryptonian criminals (Terence Stamp, Sarah Douglas, and Jack O'Halloran) have escaped from the "phantom zone" to which they were banished at the beginning of *Superman*. They come to Earth where, like Superman, they gain super powers. The three vow to conquer the planet and seek vengeance on Superman, whose father imprisoned them. When the criminals join forces with Lex Luthor, the now-powerless Superman must regain his powers and battle his enemies. *Superman II*, like its predecessor, was a great financial success and an even greater critical one; most reviewers agreed that the sequel had a consistency of tone that the original had lacked.

Newman next worked on the screenplay for *Jinxed!* (1982), sharing screen credit with Frank D. Gilroy, who wrote the original story as Bert Blessing. Directed by Don Siegel, the film is the story of Las Vegas blackjack dealer Willie (Ken Wahl), who finds himself jinxed by customer Harold (Rip Torn), who never loses and who follows him from job to job. Willie meets Harold's mistreated girlfriend Bonita (Bette Midler), and they plot to kill him. But Willie's romance with Bonita breaks the jinx; he beats Harold in cards. Harold commits suicide moments before Bonita can kill him, leaving her unable to collect on his insurance policy unless she and Willie can make his death look accidental. Finally Willie returns to his job as a dealer, only to have Bonita become his new jinx. *Jinxed!* is Newman's least successful film, a failed attempt to mix comedy with suspense.

Benton's next picture as a director was to have been titled "Stab," from a story he and Newman wrote years earlier, a modern Jack the Ripper tale about a woman who kills men she meets in singles bars. What finally emerged was a film titled *Still of the Night* (1982) with a somewhat different story. A slow-paced, moody thriller very much in the style of Alfred Hitchcock, the film is about a psychiatrist, Sam Rice (Roy Scheider), one of whose patients has just been murdered. Rice meets Brooke Reynolds (Meryl Streep), a coworker of the murdered man with whom she had been having an affair. Rice suspects Reynolds might be the murderer, but he finds himself attracted to her nevertheless and protects her from the police, thereby placing his own life in danger. Finally he learns Reynolds is innocent; the real killer is another coworker (Sara Botsford), jealous that Reynolds had received the promotion to which she aspired. *Still of the Night* is Benton's least successful film, partly because the original ending (and murderer) was changed before the film's release and partly because the film's suspenseful tone and frequent symbolism could not overcome its thin plot.

The Newmans returned to Superman with *Superman III* (1983). Superman's newest enemies are computer genius Gus Gorman (Richard Pryor) and a ruthless tycoon (Robert Vaughn) who wants to corner the market on coffee beans. Gorman is told to reprogram Superman and make him evil; his plot succeeds for a time before Superman reverts to his normal self. *Superman III* was the least rewarding of the Superman films; under Richard Lester's direction, the film was more of a spoof of the character than a tribute. As with *Superman II*, the best scenes were those that centered on romance, in this case, one between Clark Kent and his high school sweetheart Lana Lang (Annette O'Toole).

Sheena (1984), Newman's next film, was also based on a comic book character. Sheena is an American woman who was orphaned in Africa and reared by natives, who taught her mystic powers. She teams with an American reporter (Ted Wass) to combat men who would exploit the jungle's natural resources.

After the failure of *Still of the Night,* Benton wrote one of his most successful screenplays, *Places in the Heart* (1984). Set during the Depression, the movie is the story of a young widow (Sally Field) trying to manage her farm after the death of her husband. It earned Benton an Academy Award for best screenplay and a nomination for best director; Field won the best actress Oscar, and the movie was nominated for best picture.

Having mastered the art of successful collaboration, Benton and Newman are pursuing separate careers in which they carry with them the experience of having worked together as screenwriters. Benton says his collaborative work taught

him "to be open to other ideas," and each brings this ability into his current work. Benton and Newman have produced a body of interesting, original work which displays their passion for the movies—past, present, and future.

References:

Tom Buckley, "The Writing of *Superman:* A Fantastic Story," *New York Times*, 22 December 1978, p. 10c;

John G. Cawelti, ed., *Focus on Bonnie and Clyde* (Englewood Cliffs, N.J.: Prentice-Hall, 1973);

James Childs, "Closet Outlaws," *Film Comment*, 9 (March-April 1973): 17-23;

Childs, "Five Years After *Bonnie and Clyde,*" *Village Voice*, 18 January 1973, pp. 79, 84;

Childs, "Known by the Company They Keep," *Village Voice*, 25 January 1973, pp. 79, 84;

Richard Corliss, "The Hollywood Screenwriter: Take 2," *Film Comment*, 14 (July-August 1978): 33-47;

Corliss, *Talking Pictures: Screenwriters in the American Cinema, 1927-1973* (Woodstock, N.Y.: Overlook Press, 1974), pp. 371-382;

"Dynamic Duo," *Newsweek* (6 November 1967): 84;

Richard Eder, "The Man Who Pulled 'The Late Show' Job," *New York Times*, 11 February 1977, p. 4c;

Stephen Farber, "The Writer in American Films," *Film Quarterly*, 21 (Summer 1968): 2-13;

Kenneth L. Geist, *Pictures Will Talk: The Life and Films of Joseph L. Mankiewicz* (New York: Scribners, 1978), pp. 364-376;

Larry Gross, "Robert Benton & David Newman: What Have They Been Up to Since 'Bonnie and Clyde'— A Lot!," *Millimeter*, 5 (October 1976): 12-15, 16, 57-59;

"Marlowe in Nighttown: Robert Benton and *The Late Show,*" *Film Comment*, 13 (January-February 1977): 6-9;

Stephen M. Silverman, "Life Without Mother," *American Film*, 4 (July-August 1979): 50-55;

Garner Simmons, "The Western: New Directors in New Directions," *Film Reader*, 1 (1975): 65-70;

Colin L. Westerbeck, Jr., "Good Company," *Sight and Sound*, 42 (Autumn 1973): 222-224.

Robert Bloch
(5 April 1917-   )

Tanita C. Kelly

MOTION PICTURES: *The Couch* (Warner Bros., 1962), screenplay;
The Cabinet of Caligari (20th Century-Fox, 1962), screenplay;
Strait-Jacket (Columbia, 1964), story and screenplay;
The Night Walker (Universal, 1964), story and screenplay;
The Psychopath (Paramount, 1966), story and screenplay;
The Deadly Bees (Paramount, 1967), screenplay by Bloch and Anthony Marriott;
Torture Garden (Columbia, 1968), story and screenplay;
The House That Dripped Blood (Cinerama, 1971), story and screenplay;
Asylum (Cinerama, 1972), story and screenplay.

SELECTED BOOKS: *Sea-Kissed* (London: Utopia, 1945);
The Opener of the Way (Sauk City, Wis.: Arkham House, 1945);
The Scarf (New York: Dial Press, 1947; London: New English Library, 1972);
The Kidnapper (New York: Lion, 1954);
Spiderweb (New York: Ace, 1954);
The Will to Kill (New York: Ace, 1954);
Shooting Star (New York: Ace, 1958);
Terror In the Night and Other Stories (New York: Ace, 1958);
Pleasant Dreams—Nightmares (Sauk City, Wis.: Arkham House, 1959; London: Whiting & Wheaton, 1967);
Psycho (New York: Simon & Schuster, 1959; London: Hale, 1960);
The Dead Beat (New York: Simon & Schuster, 1960; London: Hale, 1961);
Blood Runs Cold (New York: Simon & Schuster, 1961; London: Hale, 1963);
Firebug (Evanston, Ill.: Regency, 1961);
More Nightmares (New York: Belmont, 1962);
The Couch (Greenwich, Conn.: Fawcett, 1962; London: Muller, 1962);
Yours Truly, Jack the Ripper: Tales of Horror (New York: Belmont, 1962);

Robert Bloch

Atoms and Evil (Greenwich, Conn.: Fawcett, 1962; London: Muller, 1963);
Terror (New York: Belmont, 1962; London: Transworld, 1969);
Bogey Men; Ten Tales (New York: Pyramid, 1963);
Horror—7 (New York: Belmont, 1963; London: New English Library, 1965);
The Skull of the Marquis de Sade and Other Stories (New York: Pyramid, 1965; London: Robert Hale, 1975);
Tales in a Jugular Vein (New York: Pyramid, 1965; London: Sphere Books, 1970);
Chamber of Horrors (New York: Award, 1966);

The Living Demons (New York: Belmont, 1967; London: Sphere Books, 1970);

Ladies Day/This Crowded Earth (New York: Belmont, 1968);

The Star Stalker (New York: Pyramid, 1968);

Dragons and Nightmares (Baltimore: Mirage Press, 1968);

The Todd Dossier, as Collier Young (New York: Delacorte Press, 1969);

Bloch and Bradbury (New York: Tower, 1969); republished as *Fever Dream and Other Fantasies* (London: Sphere, 1970);

It's All In Your Mind (New York: Modern Library, 1971);

Fear Today, Gone Tomorrow (New York: Award, 1971; London: Tandem, 1971);

Sneak Preview (New York: Paperback Library, 1971);

American Gothic (New York: Simon & Schuster, 1974);

Cold Chills (Garden City: Doubleday, 1977);

The King of Terrors (New York: Mysterious Press, 1977; London: Hale, 1978);

The Best of Robert Bloch (New York: Ballantine, 1977);

Out of the Mouths of Graves (New York: Mysterious Press, 1979);

Such Stuff as Screams Are Made Of (New York: Ballantine, 1979);

There Is A Serpent In Eden (New York: Zebra, 1979);

The Cunning (New York: Zebra, 1981);

Mysteries of the Worm (New York: Zebra, 1981);

The Night of the Ripper (Garden City: Doubleday, 1984).

SELECTED TELEVISION:"Mme. Mystery," *Alfred Hitchcock Presents* (CBS, 1959), script;

"A Good Imagination," "The Devil's Ticket," "The Grim Reaper," "Yours Truly, Jack the Ripper," *Thriller* (NBC, 1961), scripts;

"Man of Mystery," "Till Death Do Us Part," "Waxworks," "The Weird Tailor," *Thriller* (NBC, 1962), scripts;

Off Season (NBC, 1965), teleplay;

The Second Wife (NBC, 1965), teleplay;

"Catspaw," "Mudd's Women," "What Are Little Girls Made Of," "Wolf in the Fold," *Star Trek* (NBC, 1967), scripts;

"Logoda's Heads," *Night Gallery* (NBC, 1971);

The Cat Creature (ABC, 1973);

The Dead Don't Die (ABC, 1975);

The Return of Captain Nemo (CBS, 1978);

"The Boogey Man Will Get You," "Catnip," "A Quiet Funeral," *Darkroom* (ABC, 1981), scripts;

A Home Away from Home (CBS, 1983), teleplay adapted from his story.

RECORDINGS: *Gravely, Robert Bloch* (Alternate World, 1976);

"A Toy for Juliette" and "Yours Truly, Jack the Ripper," in *Blood!: The Life and Future Times of Jack the Ripper* (Alternate World, 1977).

Robert Bloch's forte is psychological horror. During a career as an author that has spanned fifty years, he has concentrated mostly on short stories, teleplays, and occasional novels. For a ten-year period, though, from 1962 to 1972, he was responsible for a series of modest but very effective suspense films.

Bloch, the son of Raphael A. Bloch and Stella Loeb, was born in Chicago, Illinois. An extremely bright child, Bloch skipped grades in a Milwaukee grammar school and at age fifteen was corresponding with veteran fantasy writer H. P. Lovecraft. He made his first professional sale at age seventeen to *Weird Tales* magazine. He has since written over 400 short stories, nonfiction articles, and radio, television, and movie scripts. He has received many awards and honors, including the Screen Writers Guild Award, 1960; the Mystery Writers of America Edgar, 1960; the Third Trieste Science Fiction Film Festival Award, 1965; the Ann Radcliffe Memorial Award for Television, 1966; and the Convention du Cinema Fantastique de Paris Prize in 1973.

Although his earliest works reveal the unmistakable influence of his mentor, Lovecraft, Bloch gradually emerged with a style of his own; he specializes in wry, ironic horror stories in which he juxtaposes horror with humor and employs trick endings. His writing is marked by a gallows humor with a modern flavor in which the skepticism and slang of twentieth-century life are contrasted with archetypal terrors.

During the earliest years of his career, Bloch was mainly a short story writer; his first novel, *The Scarf,* was not published until 1947. He did his first scriptwriting for the radio series *Stay Tuned for Terror* (1944 to 1945), adapting his own short stories (the series was produced with the cooperation of *Weird Tales*) and producing thirty-nine radio plays in all. These plays included dramatizations of two of his best-known short stories: "Yours Truly, Jack the Ripper," which suggests the ripper has stayed eternally young by committing a series of ritual murders.

From 1942 to 1953 Bloch worked as a copywriter at the Gustave Marx Advertising Agency in Milwaukee and he continued producing his own work during this period. In 1953 he moved to Weyauwega, Wisconsin, and resumed writing fulltime. He continued to write novels and stories throughout the 1950s, but it was at the end of the decade that he produced the novel that has remained the cornerstone for his reputation: *Psycho* (1959). The novel is about a schizophrenic multiple murderer and was based on the true case of Ed Gein, a mass murderer in Wisconsin in the 1950s; what particularly intrigued Bloch was the notion that a deranged person could exist without notice in an ordinary community. The novel was purchased by Alfred Hitchcock and made into his famous movie. Bloch was denied the opportunity to write the screenplay when Hitchcock was mistakenly informed that Bloch was unavailable. Still, he became established as a writer of psychological suspense because of the film, and he began to receive many offers to write scripts, first for television, then for films.

Bloch's first teleplays were written for *Alfred Hitchcock Presents* and its expanded version, *The Alfred Hitchcock Hour;* later he wrote for *Thriller, Bus Stop, I Spy, Journey to the Unknown, Star Trek,* and *Night Gallery.* Approximately seventy-five television episodes have either been written by Bloch or adapted from his short stories. On the whole,

Advertisement for the Alfred Hitchcock film based on Bloch's 1959 novel

he was not pleased with his television writing but speaks highly of *Thriller,* for which he wrote eight scripts, saying that, "Almost invariably my first draft teleplay was shot exactly as I wrote it. The director didn't try to change the shots or angles or anything regarding the story."

Compared with his prolific television output, Bloch has been involved with relatively few motion pictures. His first screenplay was *The Couch* (1962), which he wrote from a screen story by Blake Edwards and Owen Crump, who was also the film's producer and director. (Bloch's 1962 novel of the same title is based upon his screenplay.) Like *Psycho* and most of Bloch's subsequent screenplays, the film centers on an insane person set free in a normal world, in this case a rapist (Grant Williams) who is paroled from prison under the condition that he seek psychiatric treatment. He resents the psychiatrist Dr. Janz (Onslow Stevens) but resents even more the psychiatrist's couch, which he sees as a representation of his guilt. Finally he begins committing random murders with an icepick, always warning the police before he kills. The most intriguing aspect of the film is the relationship between the rapist and the psychiatrist's niece (Shirley Knight), who falls in love with him even though she knows he may be suffering from a severe mental aberration.

His 1962 remake of the German Expressionist silent film *The Cabinet of Caligari* (1919) is one of the major disappointments of Bloch's career. Bearing little resemblance to the original, it tells the story of Jane Lindstrom (Glynis Johns), who has a flat tire while driving down a lonely road and seeks

Glynis Johns as Jane Lindstrom in the 1962 version of The Cabinet of Dr. Caligari

help at a mansion. After entering the mansion, she is held prisoner by Dr. Caligari (Dan O'Herlihy); she receives occasional friendly visits from another doctor, Paul (also O'Herlihy), and Mark, a handsome young man (Richard Davalos). Finally, it is revealed that all is a hallucination: Lindstrom is in an asylum, Paul is her doctor, and Mark is her son. Bloch's original screenplay had examined the sexual aspects of his Freudian interpretation, making it clear that Lindstrom was in love with her son; he also suggested that the doctor might be insane himself. His script was drastically altered by the producers before filming, and even now Bloch refuses to view the final product.

Bloch next wrote two films, *Strait-Jacket* and *The Night Walker*, which William Castle produced and directed in 1964. In *Strait-Jacket* Lucy Harbin (Joan Crawford) has been freed from an asylum after murdering her husband with an ax twenty years earlier. After her release a series of similar murders strike the community, and Harbin begins to doubt her sanity until it is revealed that the real killer is her daughter Carol (Diane Baker). Although Bloch has never been entirely satisfied with the film version of any of his screenplays, he cites a scene from *Strait-Jacket* in which the las murder takes place as "the only film segment I have really had any complete enjoyment from."

The Night Walker was based on a previously written but unproduced screenplay, *Witches' Friday* by Elizabeth Kada. Irene Trent's (Barbara Stanwyck) husband thinks she has been unfaithful to him; she has not, but she does have dreams about a mysterious lover (Lloyd Bochner). These dreams become more frequent after her husband is killed in an accident. Finally, it is revealed that her husband was murdered by his attorney (Robert Taylor) and the man she is dreaming of is a private detective hired by her husband to follow her. As filmed, Bloch's script is rather muddled and the meaning of this surprise ending is never clear. *The Night Walker* confused critics and audiences alike, but Bloch's reality versus illusion theme is explored effectively in this film; perhaps viewers should merely perceive and accept the events rather than try to seek a specific meaning or reality.

Bloch next wrote three successive films directed by Freddie Francis and produced by Amicus Films, a new British studio specializing in horror films. In *The Psychopath* (1966), four men who served on an Allied commission during World War II and convicted a war criminal are murdered. The police suspect the criminal's son, Mark Von Sturn (John Standing), but the killer is really his wife

(Margaret Johnson). *The Deadly Bees* (1967) was adapted from the novel *A Taste for Honey* by H. F. Heard. A young woman (Suzanna Leigh) vacationing in England finds that a neighbor (Frank Finlay) is breeding a deadly species of bee. Handicapped by an absurd premise and poor direction, *The Deadly Bees* is Bloch's worst film.

Torture Garden (1968) set the pattern for Bloch's final three screenplays. It is an anthology film, featuring several stories loosely connected by a narrative device. For the film, Bloch adapted four of his own short stories and created a framing sequence set in a carnival sideshow run by Dr. Diablo (Burgess Meredith), who promises his patrons a glimpse of their future. In "Enoch" a young man (Michael Bryant) murders his rich uncle but falls under the influence of his uncle's satanic cats. A woman is engaged to a pianist but killed by his piano in "Mr. Steinway." In "The Man Who Collected Poe" an obsessed collector (Jack Palance) murders to obtain a newly discovered Poe manuscript; Poe is resurrected in the man's home but kills them both by burning down the house. Bloch's fascination with Hollywood can be seen in "Terror Over Hollywood" in which a woman falls in love with a successful actor who is really a robot; with typical Bloch humor, the segment concludes with her becoming a successful actress—after she has also been transformed into a robot.

Torture Garden was successful enough to prompt a series of anthology films, both at Amicus and other studios. Bloch wrote two more such movies for Amicus: *The House That Dripped Blood* (1971) and *Asylum* (1972). *The House That Dripped Blood* contains four stories set in a haunted house in the English countryside which is leased to a variety of tenants, all of whom come to a grisly end. In the first story a horror writer (Denholm Elliot) fears his latest character, a psychotic strangler, is coming to life. "Waxworks" has two men irresistibly drawn to the wax image of a woman who reminds them of a former mutual love; they are murdered by the owner of the waxworks and put on display. A young girl uses voodoo to kill her father (Christopher Lee) in "Sweets to the Sweet." "The Cloak" is a tongue-in-cheek story of a horror film star (Jon Pertwee) who becomes a genuine vampire. This story leads back to the framing device, and to a conclusion, as the police inspector searching for the missing film star goes to the house and becomes the victim of the former occupants.

Aided by Roy Ward Baker's understated direction, *Asylum* became the best of Bloch's anthology films and one of his better movies. The framing device in this film is an extension of, rather than an excuse for, the other stories. Young Dr. Martin (Robert Powell) arrives at the asylum to be interviewed for a job. Dr. Rutherford (Patrick Magee) instructs him to visit the four most severely disturbed inmates to determine which is the asylum's former head; his diagnosis will determine if he gets the position he seeks. The first patient is a woman (Barbara Parkins) who, with her lover (Richard Todd), murdered his wife (Sylvia Sims) and chopped up her corpse, only to have her dismembered limbs attack them. The second is a tailor (Barry Morse) who fashions a suit from a peculiar cloth intended to bring a client's dead son back to life; instead, it animates the tailor's dummy. (Earlier, Bloch had adapted this short story for *Thriller*.) Barbara (Charlotte Rampling) is a schizophrenic woman who believes her other personality to be embodied as a woman named Lucy (Britt Ekland). The final patient (Herbert Lom) makes a ghastly doll which he is able to bring to life. It kills Dr. Rutherford, and Dr. Martin is killed by an inmate who then assumes control of the asylum.

Bloch has done no screenwriting since *Asylum*, but two of his projects for television are noteworthy. The television films *The Cat Creature* (1973) and

The Dead Don't Die (1975) are both deliberate attempts to recreate the "B" horror movies. Furthermore, both films were directed by Curtis Harrington, a director whose previous works, such as *Night Tide* (1961) and *Games* (1967), had shown an affinity for the sort of psychological terror in which Bloch specializes. *The Cat Creature*, an atmospheric story about the spirit of an Egyptian priestess trying to gain control of a powerful amulet, was the better of the two. In *The Dead Don't Die*, which was set in the 1930s, a sailor (George Hamilton) on leave tries to prove his brother was innocent of the crime for which he was executed. His investigation causes him to discover the plot to take over the United States with an army of zombies.

Bloch's screenplays, like his work for other media, are all derived from his formula for success—he gives the audience a mixture of humor, irony, and suspense and systematically catches them off guard. His suggestion that there are no clear-cut definitions, no division between the world of the sane and the insane, of reality and illusion, allows several of his films to work better today than they did upon their initial release. Perhaps the climate of the 1970s and 1980s is more conducive to empathy with the ambiguity of reality.

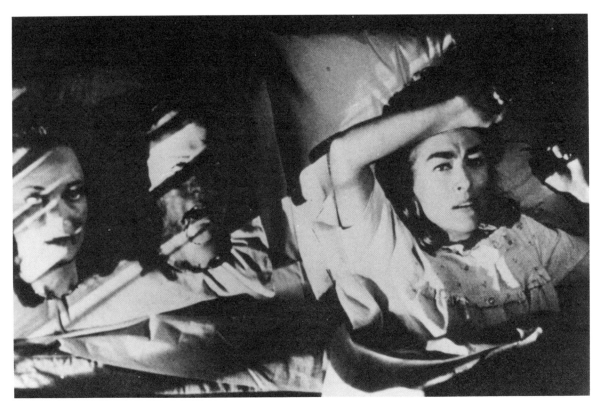

Joan Crawford as a mental patient in Strait-Jacket

References:

Les Daniels, *Living in Fear: A History of Horror in the Mass Media* (New York: Scribners, 1975);

Films and Filming, 18 (February 1872): 26-30;

James Naremore, *Filmguide to Psycho* (Bloomington: Indiana University Press, 1973);

Samuel A. Peoples, "Robert Bloch," *Films in Review* (August-September 1968);

Robert Bloch Fanzine (Los Altos, Cal., 1973);

John Stanley, An Interview with Robert Bloch, *Castle of Frankenstein*, 4 (July 1971): 4-11.

Sydney Boehm
(4 April 1908-   )

Michael Hartman
Oklahoma State University

MOTION PICTURES: *High Wall* (M-G-M, 1948), screenplay by Boehm and Lester Cole;

The Undercover Man (Columbia, 1949), screenplay;

Mystery Street (M-G-M, 1950), screenplay by Boehm and Richard Brooks;

Side Street (M-G-M, 1950), screenplay;

Union Station (Paramount, 1950), screenplay;

Branded (Paramount, 1950), screenplay by Boehm and Cyril Hume;

When Worlds Collide (Paramount, 1951), screenplay;

The Atomic City (Paramount, 1952), screenplay;

The Savage (Paramount, 1952), screenplay;

The Big Heat (Columbia, 1953), screenplay;

Second Chance (RKO, 1953), screenplay by Boehm and Oscar Millard;

Black Tuesday (United Artists, 1954), screenplay;

The Raid (20th Century-Fox, 1954), screenplay;

Secret of the Incas (Paramount, 1954), screenplay by Boehm and Ranald MacDougall;

The Siege at Red River (20th Century-Fox, 1954), screenplay;

Rogue Cop (M-G-M, 1954), screenplay;

Violent Saturday (20th Century-Fox, 1955), screenplay;

The Tall Men (20th Century-Fox, 1955), screenplay by Boehm and Frank Nugent;

Six Bridges to Cross (Universal-International, 1955), screenplay;

Hell on Frisco Bay (Jaguar, 1955), screenplay by Boehm and Martin Rackin;

The Bottom of the Bottle (20th Century-Fox, 1956), screenplay;

The Revolt of Mamie Stover (20th Century-Fox, 1956), screenplay;

Harry Black and the Tiger (20th Century-Fox, 1958), screenplay;

A Nice Little Bank That Should Be Robbed (20th Century-Fox, 1958), screenplay;

Woman Obsessed (20th Century-Fox, 1959), screenplay;

One Foot in Hell (20th Century-Fox, 1960), screenplay by Boehm and Aaron Spelling;

Seven Thieves (20th Century-Fox, 1960), screenplay;

Shock Treatment (Warner Bros., 1964), screenplay;

Sylvia (Paramount, 1964), screenplay;

Rough Night in Jericho (Universal, 1967), screenplay by Boehm and Marvin H. Albert.

Although he sometimes tried his hand at adventure, science fiction, and Westerns, with generally disappointing results, Sydney Boehm excelled at one thing: crime stories. Boehm succeeded in transferring the sometimes grim industrial atmosphere of his youth to his detective and "caper" scripts with eminently believable results.

Boehm was born in Philadelphia and attended Lehigh University in Bethlehem, Pennsylvania, from 1925 to 1929. He worked as a reporter for over fifteen years, first for the *New York Journal-American*, later for an independent news service. The years of newspaper experience were later to be beneficial to his screenwriting career: his best screenplays take a documentary approach and are filled with detail.

Significantly, Boehm did not write his first screenplay until 1948, when the war was over and he was nearly forty years old. The film noir genre flourished during those cynical postwar years, and at forty Boehm lacked the idealism a younger man might have had. His first picture, *High Wall* (1948), a thriller typical of the 1940s, has an air force pilot (Robert Taylor) turning to a psychiatrist (Audrey Totter) to prove he is innocent of murder.

With *The Undercover Man* (1949), his second script, Boehm established the hard-hitting documentary style that was to reappear in his later films. Based loosely on the nonfiction article "Undercover Man: He Trapped Capone," the film is about United States Treasury agents working toward an indictment of a gangland leader. The plethora of factual details Boehm took from the Capone case and the fast pace created by director Joseph Lewis distinguish the film from other similar pictures of the period.

In 1950 Boehm wrote three more crime melodramas: *Side Street, Union Station,* and *Mystery Street.* In *Side Street* courier Joe Norson (Farley Granger) unwittingly steals money belonging to gangsters; then he is pursued by the police for murders he did not commit. Under Anthony Mann's direction, the film has more action than usual for one of Boehm's screenplays; it includes an exhilarating car chase through New York. The picture is primarily concerned with the moral dilemma of an honest man who turns to crime during a weak moment. A blind girl is kidnapped in *Union Station;* a some-

what routine story is made noteworthy by the movie's unusual location—a Chicago train depot—and its excellent, big-city atmosphere. A married man (Marshall Thompson) murders his pregnant mistress (Jan Sterling) in *Mystery Street.* Boehm's documentary approach to a crime may again be seen here as Harvard forensic pathologists unravel a murder from the victim's skeleton. Richard Brooks collaborated on the script, and John Sturges directed.

Following these three films, Boehm turned to other genres, writing two Westerns, *Branded* (1950) and *The Savage* (1952), as well as the science fiction film *When Worlds Collide* (1951). While none of these films was as successful as Boehm's earlier work, neither were they complete failures; *The Savage* and *When Worlds Collide* pleased most viewers. In *Branded* a young drifter (Alan Ladd) agrees to pose as the long-lost son of a dying and wealthy rancher (Charles Bickford); eventually he is conscience-stricken and helps find the rancher's real son. *The Savage*, adapted from a novel by L. L. Foreman, tells of a young white man (Charlton Heston) who tries to rejoin white society after being reared by an Indian tribe.

When adapting Philip Wylie and Edwin Balmer's well-known novel *When Worlds Collide*, Boehm transferred with mixed results his documentary technique to science fiction. The film depicts the selection of a crew to leave Earth in a spaceship when it becomes apparent the planet is going to collide with the giant star Bellus. Most of the film leading to the departure of the ship from Earth is flat; conversation occupies most of the screen time, leaving the viewer wishing for more action. The end of the film—the survivors making a successful landing on another planet—is quite good if one ignores the fact, as Boehm seems to, that most of the human race has been destroyed. Critical reception of the film was poor, but audience response was good, and like many other science fiction movies of the period, its reputation has grown with time.

With *The Atomic City* (1952), the story of a physicist's kidnapped son (Lee Aaker), Boehm returned to more familiar material. As in *Union Station,* the story is coupled with a sort of documentary about atomic research. Boehm was nominated for an Academy Award for his tight plot and well-researched screenplay.

Many critics believe *The Big Heat* (1953) to be Boehm's best work. Based on a novel by William P. McGivern (whose works Boehm also adapted in *Rogue Cop*, 1954, and *Hell on Frisco Bay*, 1955), *The*

Farley Granger and Cathy O'Donnell as the young lovers in Boehm's Side Street

The Times Square tidal wave in When Worlds Collide, *Boehm's adaptation of Philip Wylie and Edwin Balmer's novel*

Big Heat was a milestone in the depiction of crime on film. It is a shocking story, full of corruption and graft among police and city officials; it is a violent story, with some disturbing scenes of violence against women (particularly the scalding of a gangster's mistress [Gloria Grahame]); and it is a daring movie, with the nominal "good guy" Dave Bannion (Glenn Ford) moving dangerously toward vigilantism as he goes outside the corrupted legal system. The violent nature of the film resulted in adverse critical comment at the time of its release, but the seedy characters, menacing settings, and nervous ambience of the movie have remained powerful through the years. This is the seminal picture for the "honest cop" genre, a major influence on such later works as *The Case Against Brooklyn* (1958), *Dirty Harry* (1971), and *Serpico* (1973).

It is no surprise that Boehm turned again to the same theme and the same author to write *Rogue Cop* the following year. In this film the police officer (Robert Taylor) turns to crime and must face the grim consequences when his younger brother (Steve Forrest), an honest policeman, is murdered. Only then does he turn on the criminal syndicate that has corrupted him. While *Rogue Cop* lacks the gripping material and taut suspense of *The Big Heat,* Boehm's script is aided by a strong cast, including George Raft, Janet Leigh, and Anne Francis.

In between *The Big Heat* and *Rogue Cop,* Boehm wrote the melodrama *Second Chance* (1953). A prizefighter (Robert Mitchum) living in Mexico falls in love with a gangster's mistress (Linda Darnell) who is being stalked by a hired killer (Jack

Palace). It is an offbeat film remembered best for having been selected for RKO's experiment in three-dimensional films, and for its unusual climactic battle on cable cars.

Nineteen fifty-four was Boehm's busiest year as a screenwriter; in addition to *Rogue Cop*, four other films were produced from his scripts that year. Among these, only *Black Tuesday* is a crime drama: a convict (Edward G. Robinson) scheduled for execution escapes from prison, takes hostages, and hides out in a deserted warehouse. *The Raid* was a fairly successful combination of period drama and violent crime thriller. Six Confederate soldiers escape from their Northern prison and seek revenge by terrorizing a town in Vermont; only a woman (Anne Bancroft) and a young boy (Tommy Rettig) try to stop them. In *Secret of the Incas,* two men (Robert Young and Charlton Heston) search for an Incan treasure they believe will give them immortality. *The Siege at Red River* is another Civil War story, about a Confederate spy (Van Johnson) who uncovers a Southern traitor, then travels west, where he is caught up in an Indian raid.

With *Violent Saturday* (1955) Boehm returned to the crime film, relying on tough hoodlums as protagonists. Set in an Arizona mining town, the film depicts the robbery of the local bank and the aftermath of that robbery. Unlike most of Boehm's other crime stories, this movie does not seem to have a great deal of sociological insight, relying instead on sordid characters and a great deal of violence.

A series of mediocre screenplays followed *Violent Saturday*. *Hell on Frisco Bay* (1955) was Boehm's third, and least successful, adaptation of a William P. McGivern novel. An ex-policeman (Alan Ladd) is framed for a killing; in trying to clear himself, he uncovers a large crime syndicate. Boehm and Frank Nugent adapted *The Tall Men* (1955) from a novel by respected Western author Clay Fisher. Despite the talent associated with the film—including director Raoul Walsh—it is a forgettable tale of two brothers (Clark Gable and Cameron Mitchell) settling the wilderness.

Boehm continued to adapt novels to the screen, with less than successful results. *The Bottom of the Bottle* (1956), from a novel by Georges Simenon, is about a lawyer (Van Johnson) who helps his alcoholic brother (Joseph Cotten) travel to Mexico. Henry Hathaway directed. William Bradford Huie's novel *The Revolt of Mamie Stover* was considerably toned down for its film version which was produced in 1956. The novel's protagonist—a prostitute—is now a saloon singer (Jane Russell)

Lee Marvin and Gloria Grahame in Boehm's landmark crime film The Big Heat

who travels to Hawaii and decides to lead a better life. *Harry Black and the Tiger* (1958), which Boehm adapted from a novel by David Walker, is a muddled jungle adventure picture.

In *A Nice Little Bank That Should Be Robbed* (1958) Boehm attempted to inject tongue-in-cheek humor into his usual crime plot, but the combination of comedy and caper film never completely works. He had better success with *One Foot in Hell* (1960), possibly his best work in the Western genre. The sheriff (Alan Ladd) of a small town is secretly plotting to avenge his wife's mistreatment by the townspeople.

Seven Thieves (1960), directed by Henry Hathaway, was both written and produced by Boehm; it is in this film that his best talents emerge. An ingenious band of thieves robs the reserve vaults

of a casino on the Riviera. Starring Edward G. Robinson, Rod Steiger, Joan Collins, and Eli Wallach, the story is brilliantly conceived and flawlessly paced; audiences watch each elaborate subterfuge with anticipation and hang on every subtle word and gesture. Boehm's masterful understatement and smooth timing make this film, if not his best, perhaps his most sophisticated.

Only three screenplays followed *Seven Thieves*. *Shock Treatment* (1964) is a somewhat exploitative mystery set in a mental institution. *Sylvia* (1964), adapted from E. V. Cunningham's novel, is the story of a prostitute (Carol Baker) as seen through the eyes of the police detective (George Maharis) investigating her murder. It is a theme Boehm also explored, less explicitly, in *The Revolt of Mamie Stover* and a theme he should have avoided, as both

In the climax to Second Chance, *RKO's first 3-D movie, Robert Mitchum and Linda Darnell are suspended in a broken cable car*

stories are rather unbelievable. *Rough Night in Jericho* (1967) is a clichéd Western about a frontier woman (Jean Simmons), fighting off the ruthless man (Dean Martin) who wants her land. Like most of Boehm's Western scripts, it is routine, unexciting, and predictable.

As a screenwriter, Sydney Boehm mastered one genre and never seemed comfortable when writing in others. In spite of this, Boehm's creative skills cannot be denied. The tense realism of his crime films, their colloquial and fast-paced dialogue, and the believability of the violent and desperate nature of his protagonists mark his work as the epitome of the violent dramas that emerged in the 1960s and 1970s. In these respects and in the documentary nature of his films, Boehm surpasses almost all who have come after him.

Reference:

Carlos Clarens, *Crime Movies: From Griffith to the Godfather and Beyond* (New York: W. W. Norton, 1980).

Richard Brooks
(18 May 1912-)

Jonathan Buchsbaum

MOTION PICTURES: *Men of Texas* (Universal, 1942), additional dialogue;
Sin Town (Universal, 1942), additional dialogue;
Don Winslow of the Coast Guard (Universal, 1943), additional dialogue;
White Savage (Universal, 1943), screenplay;
Cobra Woman (Universal, 1944), screenplay by Brooks and Gene Lewis;
My Best Gal (Republic, 1944), story;
Swell Guy (Universal-International, 1947), screenplay;
Brute Force (Universal-International, 1947), screenplay;
To the Victor (Warner Bros., 1948), screenplay;
Key Largo (Warner Bros., 1948), screenplay by Brooks and John Huston;
Any Number Can Play (M-G-M, 1949), screenplay;
Mystery Street (M-G-M, 1950), screenplay by Brooks and Sydney Boehm;
Storm Warning (Warner Bros., 1950), screenplay by Brooks and Daniel Fuchs;
Crisis (M-G-M, 1950), screenplay;
The Light Touch (M-G-M, 1951), screenplay;
Deadline U.S.A. (20th Century-Fox, 1952), screenplay;
Battle Circus (M-G-M, 1953), screenplay;
The Last Time I Saw Paris (M-G-M, 1954), screenplay by Brooks, Julius J. Epstein, and Philip G. Epstein;

The Blackboard Jungle (M-G-M, 1955), screenplay;
The Last Hunt (M-G-M, 1956), screenplay;
Something of Value (M-G-M, 1957), screenplay;
The Brothers Karamazov (M-G-M, 1958), screenplay;
Cat on a Hot Tin Roof (M-G-M, 1958), screenplay by Brooks and James Poe;
Elmer Gantry (United Artists, 1960), screenplay;
Sweet Bird of Youth (M-G-M, 1962), screenplay;
Lord Jim (Columbia, 1965), screenplay;
The Professionals (Columbia, 1966), screenplay;
In Cold Blood (Columbia, 1967), screenplay;
The Happy Ending (United Artists, 1969), screenplay;
$ (Columbia, 1971), screenplay;
Bite the Bullet (Columbia, 1975), screenplay;
Looking for Mr. Goodbar (Paramount, 1977), screenplay;
Wrong Is Right (Columbia, 1982), screenplay.

BOOKS: *The Brick Foxhole* (New York: Harper, 1945);
The Boiling Point (New York: Harper, 1948);
The Producer (New York: Simon & Schuster, 1951; London: Heinemann, 1952).

PERIODICAL PUBLICATIONS: "Swell Guy," *Screen Writer*, 3 (March 1948): 13-17;
"A Novel Isn't a Movie," *Films in Review*, 3 (February 1952): 55-60;

"On Filming Karamazov," *Films in Review,* 9 (February 1958): 49;

"Dostoevsky, Love—American Cinema," *Films & Filming,* 4 (April 1958): 11;

"Foreword to *Lord Jim,*" *Movie,* 12 (Spring 1965).

Richard Brooks established his reputation in the decades following World War II as one of Hollywood's most prominent screenwriter/directors. His major screenplays are adaptations of works by such literary luminaries as Fëdor Dostoevski, Joseph Conrad, Sinclair Lewis, and Tennessee Williams. Brooks has always tried to remain faithful to the original, but at the same time he insists on imposing his own interpretations. Critics have had mixed responses to these interpretations—sympathetic to the difficulties, caustic about the realizations—but Brooks has generally managed to achieve his own vision, retaining a consistency and

integrity throughout his mature work.

Brooks was born in Philadelphia, the son of factory workers. He studied journalism at Temple University, but when he asked his parents for tuition for his final semester, they requested that he sign a promissory note for the money. Deciding at that point not to return to school, he left Philadelphia in 1930 with one dollar and sixty cents in his pocket, and he traveled around the country for several years, picking up brief journalism jobs in Kansas and Pittsburgh and working odd jobs in New Orleans and Texas. In 1934 he returned to Philadelphia to work for the *Philadelphia Record* and moved to the *Atlantic City Press Union* in 1936. He credits a stranger he met (in a Salvation Army center) on his travels with passing on important advice for his writing: read at least 1,000 words for every word you write. The following year he worked for the *New York World-Telegram* for twenty-one dollars

Richard Brooks

a week. After that, he began writing radio scripts in New York for WNEW. Andrew Love then hired him at the NBC Blue Network where he continued to write original scripts and also served as announcer and commentator.

In 1940 Brooks organized the Mill Pond Theatre in New York City with producer David Loew, intending to present a different play each week. They parted company when Loew wanted to change the format to allow popular plays longer runs. Brooks left New York for Hollywood, where he had a job writing stories for NBC radio. Receiving a weekly salary of twenty-five dollars, Brooks wrote five 2,500-word stories per week for a fifteen-minute program; two of these radio scripts were written in collaboration with Orson Welles.

The job at NBC lasted for nine months, until Brooks was hired by Universal Studios to write dialogue for their "B" films and serials, including *Men of Texas* (1942), *Sin Town* (1942), and *Don Winslow of the Coast Guard* (1943). He was then allowed to write two complete screenplays, both exotic adventures of the sort that Universal specialized in during the 1940s and both starring Maria Montez and Jon Hall, two of the most popular stars of the genre. *White Savage* (1943) is about an island princess (Montez) who wishes to marry a shark hunter (Hall); in *Cobra Woman* (1944) Montez plays twin sisters, one good, the other an evil priestess to an island cult. *Cobra Woman* remains the most popular of the Montez-Hall films. Brooks also met Frank Capra at Universal, where Capra was directing the *Why We Fight* series; he says Capra taught him how to edit a film.

In the spring of 1943 Brooks joined the Marines and served for the rest of the war. His first novel, *The Brick Foxhole* (1945), was written while he was still in the service. Because he did not follow the military procedure of submitting the book to the Marines for clearance, Brooks was almost court-martialed: the book concerns the murder of a civilian homosexual by a group of Marines, and Brooks maintained that he actually witnessed a similar incident. The novel also addresses the frustrations of being denied the opportunity of active duty and the pressures of separation from one's family. *The Brick Foxhole* displays Brooks's tendency to draw on his personal experiences for material and his interest in men under intense pressure. As a self-made man, hostile to compromises, he often submits his characters to tests of their moral fiber.

After the war, Brooks married Harriet Levin on 20 September 1945; they were divorced in the 1950s. He went to work for producer Mark Hel-

linger, who was making films for Universal. Brooks advised Hellinger on the story construction for *The Killers* (1946) and *The Naked City* (1948), and he wrote the screenplay for *Brute Force* (1947), about a group of convicts who, driven to desperation by their cruel warden (Hume Cronyn), decide to escape from prison. Brooks's script and Jules Dassin's direction give the movie a somber, fatalistic tone; during the course of the breakout, nearly everyone is killed.

The collaboration with Hellinger ended in 1948, but the producer seems to have left his mark on Brooks: he continued to make the sort of male-oriented action films that Hellinger specialized in, and in 1951 he published a novel, *The Producer*, based on Hellinger.

Following his work with Hellinger, Brooks wrote three films for Warner Bros. before going to work for M-G-M in 1949. *To the Victor* (1948) is about Nazi collaborators who are placed on trial after the war. In *Storm Warning* (1950) a town is terrorized by the Ku Klux Klan. The script was written in collaboration with Daniel Fuchs, and Brooks's major contribution seems to have been the character of the crusading district attorney (Ronald Reagan) who fights the Klan. The most significant of his films for Warner Bros. was *Key Largo* (1948). Not only was it the best-received of Brooks's early films, but it was the first time he had been on a set during shooting. He says he received valuable advice from writer/director John Huston and cinematographer Karl Freund, although his so-called "Lesson #1: Get to the point" has been a mixed blessing, leading to both tight scripts and an evisceration of subtlety. *Key Largo* also deals with an embittered character challenged by circumstances to make a moral commitment: veteran Frank McCloud (Humphrey Bogart) is forced to save an army buddy's widow and father from gangsters. Brooks and Huston adapted their screenplay from a play by Maxwell Anderson. Claire Trevor won a best supporting actress Oscar for her performance as a gangster's alcoholic moll.

Arthur Freed signed Brooks to a contract at M-G-M, promising him the chance to direct. Despite some conflicts with the studio, Brooks remained there for over a decade. His first script was *Any Number Can Play* (1949), about a casino owner (Clark Gable) torn between his job and personal ethics. Brooks then collaborated with Sydney Boehm on *Mystery Street* (1950), in which a dedicated police officer (Ricardo Montalban) clears a man who has been framed for murder.

Brooks finally received the directorial oppor-

Humphrey Bogart and Edward G. Robinson in Brooks's classic film Key Largo

tunity he had been promised with *Crisis* (1950); Cary Grant, the film's star, had asked M-G-M to let Brooks direct his own script. Critical response to this directorial debut was much the same as it has been to Brooks's subsequent films: the subject matter—an American doctor (Grant) is forced to treat a South American dictator (Jose Ferrer)—is intriguing, but Brooks's handling of it was somewhat stolid. Still, the movie marked the beginning of a long career as director; Brooks has since directed all his screenplays and since 1965 has produced them as well. He also directed, but did not write, three films for M-G-M in the 1950s: *Take the High Ground* (1953), *The Flame and the Flesh* (1954), and *The Catered Affair* (1956). He dismisses these early films as assignments over which he had little control.

Crisis was followed by *The Light Touch* (1951), a minor film about a jewel thief (Stewart Granger) and his disapproving girlfriend (Pier Angeli). Brooks then went to 20th Century-Fox to write and direct *Deadline U.S.A.* (1952), the only one of his films in the 1950s that was not filmed at M-G-M. This is a well-made account of a newspaper editor

(Humphrey Bogart) who, days before the paper is to cease publication, begins investigating a gangster. He refuses to give in to threats and gets his story out in the last edition. *Deadline U.S.A.* is such a well-paced and hard-hitting film that the studio tried unsuccessfully to have Brooks delete some of the editor's more impassioned speeches about journalistic responsibility. It was the first sign of Brooks's later promise as a writer/director.

Unfortunately, this promise was not immediately realized, and Brooks's next two scripts were unexciting, pedestrian efforts. *Battle Circus* (1953) is set in a mobile hospital unit during the Korean war and centers on the romance between Major Jed Webbe (Bogart) and nurse Ruth McCara (June Allyson). Webbe is another study of a character under pressure—he drinks in times of stress—but much of the film is devoted to romance. *The Last Time I Saw Paris* (1954) is an adaptation of F. Scott Fitzgerald's "Babylon Revisited," updated and set in post-World War II France. It is noteworthy mainly as an early indication of Brooks's interest in filming literary works.

After working on eight films for M-G-M,

Brooks finally wrote and directed the first movie on which he had complete control. When several other directors did not want to make *The Blackboard Jungle* (1955), Brooks took over the project and wrote the script from Evan Hunter's novel. Like the films he worked on with Hellinger, *The Blackboard Jungle* combines elements of the documentary with fiction. In a tough, urban high school, where despair marks the attitudes of teachers and students, new teacher Dadier (Glenn Ford) resists renouncing hope. To Brooks, the film revolves around the responses of Dadier to provocations from the juvenile delinquent students; typically, he struggles between his commitment as a teacher and the threat to his domestic life. While other teachers have either left the school or retreated into a shell of quiet desperation, Dadier refuses to accept either of these defeats and eventually wins the trust and respect of the students. The film ends on a

positive note that many critics felt was contrived and unrealistic (and one not present in the novel), but the movie was a popular success.

The two movies that followed *The Blackboard Jungle* were interesting but uneven variations on Brooks's earlier themes of personal and professional commitments. *The Last Hunt* (1956) presents two buffalo hunters in the Old West, one of whom (Robert Taylor) has grown to love killing, while the other (Stewart Granger) has become troubled by it. *Something of Value* (1957), adapted from Robert Ruark's novel about conflicts in Kenya between natives and British settlers, centers on one landowner (Rock Hudson) now separated from his boyhood friend, a native (Sidney Poitier).

Brooks next undertook the task of adapting *The Brothers Karamazov*. For the first time he worked with a text of great complexity that interweaves psychology, metaphysics, and religion with Russian

Teacher Glenn Ford confronts student Sidney Poitier in The Blackboard Jungle

culture. Brooks tried to extract certain universal elements from the novel, and he condensed it considerably. For example, because he deemed it peripheral to the main action of the film, Brooks eliminated the Grand Inquisitor chapter, even though he considered it one of the "most brilliant chapters ever written into a novel." To capture the spirituality of Father Zossima without using the long flashback in the book, Brooks "cast an actor (William Vedder) in the role of Father Zossima who would give, by his very appearance, an immediate and lasting impression of the spiritual qualities required." Such excisions tend to reduce the script to a skeleton outline of the novel.

In defense of his technique, Brooks has often commented on a crucial difference between literature and film which he discovered while working on this film: "The play, the novel, because they are the written or spoken word, deal with the intellect first: the first response is intellectual. If they are put together properly, your second reaction will probably be emotional. I found out in this picture that precisely the opposite happens in film. Because the film deals with images and the first reaction to images is emotional. If the images all add up to something worthwhile, you may get an intellectual response as well." Unfortunately, Dostoevski's writing uses relatively simple situations as mere pretext for exploring intellectual ideas and animating profound questions about the meaning of life. Each of the Karamazov brothers stands for a different set of life choices, and in a sense, the father is only the catalyst for examining these alternatives. To deny the complexity and subtlety of these intellectual systems empties the novel of its essential meaning and transforms the philosophical disquisitions into melodrama.

Brooks tackled Tennessee Williams next in *Cat on a Hot Tin Roof* (1958), which he adapted with James Poe. As with *The Brothers Karamazov*, the plot is less important than the evocation of a milieu and Williams's theme of latent homosexuality. A self-made Southern patriarch, Big Daddy Pollitt (Burl Ives) is about to die of cancer, and the families of the two sons gather for his birthday party. One son, Gooper (Jack Carson), though unappreciated by Big Daddy for his staid conservatism, has sired five children and this progeny could carry on Big Daddy's name. The other son, Brick (Paul Newman), much loved by Big Daddy for his hard living, his former athletic prowess, and his choice of wife, has no children and no concern for his inheritance. Brooks follows these basic details of the play but suppresses the crucial information about why Brick

no longer sleeps with his wife (Elizabeth Taylor). Years before, Brick's best friend, Skipper, had revealed his homosexual feeling for Brick. Brick abandoned Skipper and married Maggie, and Skipper committed suicide. Williams's play implies that Brick's failure to have relations with Maggie stems from his own guilt and fear of his unacknowledged homosexuality. The play ends with no resolution of Brick's and Maggie's sexual problems. Brooks does not approve of passivity and insisted on changing the ending: in his script, Maggie goads Brick into action. Williams objected to this radical transformation of his play, and many critics agreed, but overall the movie was a success and Brooks received Academy Award nominations for his screenplay and his direction.

For his next project, Brooks adapted Sinclair Lewis's *Elmer Gantry* (1960), for which he received an Academy Award as screenwriter. Brooks had met Lewis at the end of the war, and Lewis had mentioned the criticism his novel had received, adding that one could learn from those criticisms. Brooks followed this advice when preparing his script, but as with *The Blackboard Jungle*, he was interested in the personal story of his character. Hence, the film presents only one part of the novel, Gantry's relationship with Sharon Falconer (Jean Simmons), a midwestern fundamentalist evangelist. She inspires Gantry (Burt Lancaster), a fast-talking but unsuccessful salesman, to become a hell-fire and damnation minister. His newfound faith awakens him to the possibility of a domestic life with Sharon, but his very contribution to her growing evangelical success convinces her of her calling and dashes his dream. The film ends with Sharon curing a deaf man and perishing in a fire that destroys the tabernacle. As Gantry walks away from the fire, a man who had been following the rise of Sharon says, "Be seein' you, brother." In the original script Gantry replies, "I'll see you in hell, brother," but Brooks was forced to remove this line, which to him was a crucial moment of self-awareness for Gantry, a recognition of his own status as sinner. Brooks married Jean Simmons on 1 November 1961.

Sweet Bird of Youth (1962), another adaptation of a Tennessee Williams play, followed. Once more faced with material uncongenial to him, Brooks made changes in the main character, Chance Wayne (Paul Newman). Chance has been seeing Heavenly (Shirley Knight), the daughter of the town boss (Ed Begley), who convinces Chance to leave town and try to make it on his own. But Chance has given Heavenly syphilis, and when her

Paul Newman and Elizabeth Taylor in Brooks's film version of Cat on a Hot Tin Roof. *Though Tennessee Williams and many critics objected to the way in which Brooks changed the ending of Williams's play, Brooks's screenplay was nominated for an Academy Award.*

father finds out, he vows to castrate him. For Brooks, passivity and admission of defeat are unacceptable. Therefore, he has Chance drive to Heavenly's house to find her; Chance knows that he is risking castration by coming for her, but this becomes a heroic act. As filmed, Heavenly rides up to see Chance lying beaten on the ground and they drive off together. Brooks wanted to end the film with Chance riding out of town on a garbage scow, but the studio refused to permit such a downbeat ending.

When M-G-M vetoed this conclusion, Brooks left the studio to produce his next film independently. Having thought about filming Joseph Conrad's *Lord Jim* for years, he spent three years

preparing the script. Once more, Brooks strove to assert the ineradicability of hope: "With hope, man can seek the truth about himself, find it, acknowledge it, face it, and *do* something about it, hopefully become a better man. That is the story of Lord Jim. That *ought* to be the story of Everyman." In paring away the particularities of the novel, however, Brooks eliminated certain elements that identify it as a Conrad work and which were presumably part of its appeal to Brooks as a source. He suppressed the novel's complex structure, levels of meaning, and irony in favor of a straightforward unfolding of events and a series of gratuitous battles. The narrator Marlow disappears early in the film to facilitate the smooth flow of events, and Brooks simplifies the characterization of Jim so that the theme becomes what he has called "his second chance," what man will do when given that second chance—will he redeem himself from his initial cowardice? The film received uniformly negative critical comment, with many accusing Brooks of sacrificing the complexity of the story for visual effects.

Lord Jim (1965) was the last of Brooks's adaptations of literary classics, but he continued to draw from the work of others. The following year he wrote *The Professionals* (1966) from Frank O'Rourke's novel *A Mule for the Marquesa* (1964). The professionals are four soldiers of fortune (Burt Lancaster, Lee Marvin, Robert Ryan, and Woody Strode) hired by an unscrupulous Texas businessman (Ralph Bellamy) to rescue his wife (Claudia Cardinale) from the Mexican revolutionary (Jack Palance) who has abducted her. The foursome discover that the wife hates her husband with good reason, and they decide to let her remain in Mexico. Most critics found the movie to be a pleasing, if farfetched, adventure story but took exception to Brooks's occasional attempts at profundity: when one bandit remarks in passing, "I'll be damned!," another asks, "Aren't we all?" Yet another character states that revolution begins as a mistress and ends as a whore. Brooks earned a fourth Academy Award nomination for his script.

Brooks chose one of the most celebrated books of the 1960s for his next film: Truman Capote's *In Cold Blood*, about the brutal murder of a Kansas family. He faced two problems in filming the book—reproducing Capote's detached reconstruction of the crime and compressing the details of the book into the film's 134-minute running time. He shot the movie in black and white, giving it the look of a documentary, and imposed a brisk pace on the dramatic episodes so that the events fit together neatly in a mechanical and causal pattern.

Burt Lancaster as Elmer Gantry in Brooks's film version of Sinclair Lewis's novel

Lee Marvin and Burt Lancaster in The Professionals. *Brooks received his fourth Academy Award nomination for the screenplay.*

Brooks began the film showing the victims and killers Perry Smith (Robert Blake) and Dick Hickock (Scott Wilson) before the murders take place. He then jumped directly to the actions of Smith and Hickock after the murders. The killings are not shown until near the film's end, when Smith tells his story to the police. The problem of compression was solved by a strategy of intercutting scenes to introduce a fantasy or a flashback or simply to change location. The flashbacks generally supply material about Smith's past, just as the fantasies usually hint at his motivation: we are shown his cruel father and the Oedipal fantasies about his mother.

While the book takes no stand on the murders or on Smith's and Hickock's executions, the film emphasizes the psychological scars left on Smith by his upbringing, leaving the impression that Brooks has made a tract against capital punishment. His comments support such an interpretation: "I guess the film must somehow say that this tragedy is to some degree the responsibility of all of us. None of us can turn away from another. It's our problem,

not that of a few people in Kansas." In the film, at the execution, when someone asks a reporter at the scene who the executioner is, he replies, "We, the people." Brooks wants to hold society responsible for both sets of deaths.

In Cold Blood (1967) was perhaps the peak of Brooks's career, earning him the best reviews of any of his films and Academy Award nominations for best director and best screenplay, his last such nominations to date. In 1967 he also was presented the Writers Guild Laurel Award, an award presented for a body of work rather than for an individual film.

Following *In Cold Blood* Brooks's career entered a period of decline, and his next two movies, both from original screenplays, were not successes. *The Happy Ending* (1969) examines the response of a middle-aged woman to the realization that her marriage has become meaningless and empty. Brooks had conceived of the story as a showcase for Jean Simmons, and at that it was successful—she received an Academy Award nomination as best actress—but as a drama, it failed. In the heist film, $ (1971), the victims are professional thieves who have holdings stored in a high security bank in Europe. A caper film with little dialogue, an anomaly in Brooks's career, $ failed critically and commercially.

After these two failures, Brooks wrote one more original script but returned to more familiar territory; *Bite the Bullet* (1975) is a Western adventure very much in the vein of *The Professionals*. The movie is about a cross-country horse race at the beginning of the twentieth century, but the emphasis is less upon action than upon personality. Much of the movie is about the characters' reasons for entering the race. The reasons range from money, fame, and thrill of competition to more personal goals; one contestant (Gene Hackman) simply does not want to see a fine horse mistreated, and another (Candice Bergen) is using the race as a cover for her plan to help her husband escape from jail. Critical response to the film was mixed.

With *Looking for Mr. Goodbar* (1977), Brooks made the biggest gamble of his career, mortgaging

everything he owned to finance the film. His script was adapted from Judith Rossner's novel about a twenty-eight-year-old schoolteacher in New York City who is murdered by a casual pick-up. Brooks embarked on a considerable campaign of firsthand research before writing the script. He visited some 300 singles bars throughout the country and interviewed more than 600 women to glean their reactions to the book. His obsession with the project damaged his marriage; he and Simmons separated in 1977 and later divorced.

Typical of his work, the completed film lacks the ambiguity that was present in the novel. Brooks enlarged considerably the repressive Catholicism of the family of Theresa Dunn (Diane Keaton), giving her a bigoted father (Richard Kiley), a weak-willed mother (Priscilla Pointer), and an unstable sister (Tuesday Weld); another sister (Laurie Prange) emerges as a far more passive character than she is in the novel. Rather than allowing Theresa some complexity, Brooks wants the dichotomy in her "dual personality"—dedicated teacher ver-

Ian Bannen, Gene Hackman, and Richard Brooks on the set of Bite the Bullet

sus sexually liberated woman—to be unmistakable. He even invents heartrending scenes of Theresa teaching young deaf children (normal first graders in the novel).

Not surprisingly, the film became a source of controversy upon its release. Critics attacked Brooks for moralizing about Theresa's life; her murder at the film's end seems to stand as final punishment for her sexual transgressions. And neither critics nor audiences seemed prepared for the movie's frank language and sexual situations. Brooks received threatening mail and telephone calls following the movie's release. He defended his film against all detractors: "I wanted to tell the truth. I wanted to say violent death is painful, rape is painful, the invasion of another person is painful. And I guess it worked. It's one girl fighting for her life, and it was too much for a lot of people."

Five years passed before Brooks made another motion picture, and when it finally appeared *Wrong Is Right* (1982) became one of the least successful films of his career. As the title implies, the movie is a study of moral ambiguity in contemporary society, and it is Brooks's most thorough exploration of this theme. Other Brooks films have presented protagonists who try to separate their personal and professional lives, but such detachment is required of *Wrong Is Right*'s central character, news anchorman Patrick Hale (Sean Connery), and he is not always able to supply it. Covering a story about a Middle-Eastern terrorist group, Hale associates himself with the terrorists, foreign leaders, the President of the United States (George Grizzard), and the president's political rival (Leslie Nielsen). Eventually Hale attempts to buy an atomic bomb from the terrorists and he becomes a pawn in a CIA assassination. *Wrong Is Right* is not entirely without merit, but Brooks's script, adapted from the novel *The Better Angels* (1979) by Charles McCarry, tries to cover too much ground; there are too many targets for his satire to be effective. Audiences stayed away, and the movie disappeared almost immediately after its release. Brooks then began work on "Fever Pitch" about a sportswriter (Ryan O'Neal) who begins an investigation of gambling in America and becomes a gambling addict.

As an individual, Richard Brooks will not tolerate ambiguity of motivation, behavior, or morality; as a screenwriter, he has persisted in making motion pictures that adhere to his moral code. This ethical code results in certain problems in his work; nearly all of his scripts show a penchant for heavy-handed moralizing. Particularly affected are his literary adaptations, where he must alter the material to suit his own views, and his later films, where he shows difficulty relating his possibly anachronistic morality to contemporary issues. Brooks does not seem as much unaware of these problems as he is unconcerned by them. He still follows the rules he set for himself in the 1960s: "In all my films, I try to show this 'feeling of honor'; I don't mean to say a feeling of good or bad, but the desire to follow a certain ideal. This is a feeling that has been disappearing from our society. . . and is yielding to a simple instinct for survival. Needless to say, to live without honor leads the individual inevitably to destroy himself."

Interviews:

Interview with Richard Brooks, *Cahiers du Cinema* (February 1959): 4-23;

Interview with Brooks, *Cinema*, 2 (March-April 1965): 4-5;

Interview with Brooks, *Movie*, 12 (Spring 1965): 2-9;

Interview with Brooks, *Cahiers du Cinema* (May/June 1965): 88-96;

Michel Ciment, Alain Garsault, and Michael Henry, "Nouvel entretien avec Richard Brooks," *Positif*, no. 175 (November 1975): 2-9;

Richard Brooks, James Powers, Jean Simmons, and Marilyn Bergman, "Dialogue on Film," *American Film*, 3 (October 1977): 33-48.

References:

George Bluestone, "Adaptation or Evasion: *Elmer Gantry*," *Film Quarterly*, 14 (Spring 1961): 15-19;

Raymond Durgnat, "Two Christian Films," *Movie*, 12 (Spring 1965): 13-14;

"Gunning for Mr. Goodbar," *Playboy*, 25 (September 1978): 261;

Bernard Kantor, *Directors at Work* (New York: Funk & Wagnall's, 1970), pp. 1-58;

Paul Mayersberg, "Conservative Idealist," *Movie*, 12 (Spring 1965): 10-12;

Edward Murray, "*In Cold Blood*: The Filmic Novel and the Problem of Adaptation," *Film and Literature Quarterly*, 1 (Spring 1973): 132-137;

Louis Seguin, "Richard Brooks, ou la sincérité," *Positif* (June/July 1956): 11-18;

Roger Tailleur, "Brooks Romancier. Le combat permanent," *Positif* (June/July 1956): 19-26.

Niven Busch

(26 April 1903-   )

Dale Winogura

MOTION PICTURES: *Miss Pinkerton* (First National, 1932), screenplay by Busch and Lilyan Hayward;

The Crowd Roars (Warner Bros., 1932), screenplay by Busch, Kubec Glasmon, and John Bright;

College Coach (First National, 1933), story by Busch and Manuel Seff;

The Big Shakedown (First National, 1934), screenplay by Busch and Rian James;

The Man with Two Faces (First National, 1934), screenplay by Busch and Tom Reed;

Babbitt (First National, 1934), adapted by Busch and Reed;

He Was Her Man (Warner Bros., 1934), screenplay by Busch and Tom Buckingham;

In Old Chicago (20th Century-Fox, 1937), story;

Off the Record (Warner Bros., 1938), screenplay by Busch, Lawrence Kimble, and Earl Baldwin;

Angels Wash Their Faces (Warner Bros., 1939), screenplay by Busch, Michael Fessier, and Robert Buckner;

The Westerner (United Artists, 1940), screenplay by Busch and Jo Swerling;

Belle Starr (20th Century-Fox, 1941), story by Busch and Cameron Rogers;

The Postman Always Rings Twice (M-G-M, 1946), screenplay by Busch and Harry Ruskin;

Pursued (Warner Bros., 1947), screenplay;

Moss Rose (20th Century-Fox, 1947), adaptation;

The Capture (RKO, 1950), screenplay;

Distant Drums (United States Pictures, 1951), screenplay by Busch and Martin Rackin;

The Man from the Alamo (Universal, 1953), story by Busch and Oliver Crawford;

Moonlighter (Warner Bros., 1953), screen story and screenplay;

The Treasure of Pancho Villa (RKO, 1955), screenplay.

BOOKS: *Twenty-One Americans: Being Profiles of Some People Famous in Our Time, Together with Silly Pictures of Them Drawn by De Miskey* (Garden City: Doubleday, Doran, 1930);

Niven Busch (photograph by Pete Breinig)

The Carrington Incident (New York: Morrow, 1941; London: Hale, 1942);

They Dream of Home (New York & London: Appleton Century, 1944);

Duel in the Sun (New York: Hampton, 1944; London: W. H. Allen, 1947);

Day of the Conquerors (New York: Harper, 1946);

The Furies (New York: Dial, 1948; London: White Lion, 1974);

The Hate Merchant (New York: Simon & Schuster, 1953; London: W. H. Allen, 1953);

The Actor (New York: Simon & Schuster, 1955; London: Muller, 1955);

California Street (New York: Simon & Schuster/ London: Cape, 1959);

The San Franciscan (New York: Simon & Schuster, 1962; London: Cape, 1962);

The Gentleman from California (New York: Simon & Schuster, 1965);

The Takeover (New York: Simon & Schuster, 1973; London: W. H. Allen, 1974);

Continent's Edge (New York: Simon & Schuster, 1980).

The psychological Western was almost the sole interest of Niven Busch. He helped develop the genre with his novels *Duel in the Sun* (1944) and *The Furies* (1948) and with his screenplays for such films as *The Westerner* (1940) and *Pursued* (1947).

Busch was born in New York City, the son of Christine Fairchild and Briton Niven Busch. He grew up in an upper-class family; his father was a member of the New York Stock Exchange. Busch was educated at Princeton University and graduated in 1924. He became an associate editor at *Time* magazine in 1927 and later held that position at *Newsweek.* From his high school days, he had contributed plays and poems to magazines and he became a regular contributor to the *New Yorker.* In 1931 he devoted his time to free-lance writing and selling fiction to magazines such as *Collier's* and *Liberty.*

Between 1932 and 1934 Busch wrote five screenplays or screen stories for First National studios, most of them dealing with the corrupting influence of money. With Lilyan Hayward, he adapted *Miss Pinkerton* (1932) from a serial by Mary Roberts Rinehart. Lloyd Bacon directed this mystery about the puzzling death of a wealthy recluse. *College Coach* (1933) was a satire about callous football coach Gore (Pat O'Brien) who ruthlessly promotes his team in an attempt to get more spectators and thus, more money. Busch collaborated with Manuel Seff, and William Wellman directed. In *The Big Shakedown* (1934) a gangster (Ricardo Cortez) bootlegs drugs and sells them to pharmacies; a struggling young chemist (Charles Farrell), desperate for money, is glad to make the drugs for him until the chemist's wife takes one of the illegal drugs, miscarries, and nearly dies. Busch and Tom Reed adapted *The Man with Two Faces* (1934) from George S. Kaufman and Alexander Woollcott's play *The Dark Tower* (1933). A cruel man (Ricardo Cortez) who bullies his wife is murdered by a heavily disguised man who turns out to be his brother-in-law (Edward G. Robinson). Busch's final project for First National was an adaptation of Sinclair Lewis's *Babbitt* (1934), again written with Tom Reed.

In addition to his work for First National, Busch's early screenplays also include two James Cagney pictures written for Warner Bros. *The Crowd Roars* (1932) was a fast-paced narrative about professional auto racing. Howard Hawks directed and wrote the original screen story. In *He Was Her Man* (1934), Cagney played Flicker Hayes, a safecracker recently released from prison. He gets revenge on Ralf Harolde and Dan Page, the criminals who sent him to jail, and he is later killed by Dan's gang.

One of Busch's first important film credits was *In Old Chicago* (1937), for which he received an Academy Award nomination for original story. The saga of the O'Leary family, who were responsible for both the growth and destruction of Chicago in the late 1800s, was fiction at its most clever and entertaining. The dramatic friction between two brothers, the attractive but corrupt Dion (Ty-

Alice Brady as Molly O'Leary in one of Busch's first important films, In Old Chicago

Gary Cooper and Walter Brennan in The Westerner

rone Power) and idealistic Jack (Don Ameche), becomes a counterpart to the unstable development of the community and the climactic fire that destroys it. The effective combination of humor, drama, and action, along with the apocalyptic overtones of the climax, show a talent that was to express itself more assertively in the future.

After *In Old Chicago*, Busch wrote two films dealing with urban problems. *Angels Wash Their Faces* (1939) was one of the series of films Warner Bros. made about the Dead End Kids, a gang of slum children; this time a juvenile delinquent (Frankie Thomas) takes up with the kids while his sister (Ann Sheridan) urges him to go straight. Far more lightweight was *Off the Record* (1938). A young boy working for slot machine operators is sent to reform school because of the muckraking articles of journalist Jane Morgan (Joan Blondell). She takes pity on him, arranges his release, and with another reporter, "Breezy" Elliot (Edmond

O'Brien), tries to expose the boy to good influences.

The Westerner (1940) was one of the first mature Westerns, abandoning the one-dimensional characters usually associated with the genre for well-rounded and properly motivated characters. Busch and Jo Swerling provided director William Wyler with an unusually literate script filled with psychological complexities. Though Gary Cooper was the star, the film was more about the incorrigible, ruthless, yet romantic Judge Roy Bean (Walter Brennan, who won an Oscar).

There were some slight psychological elements in *In Old Chicago*, but *The Westerner* brought them into even greater prominence. Though Roy Bean is made to seem cold, heartless, and irresponsible in dispensing hangings to any horse stealer, his relationship with Cooper's character, a saddle tramp who sides with the homesteaders during a range war, brings out much of the infamous judge's humanity, especially when he is talking about the charms and talents of Miss Lily Langtry. Bean's hopeless infatuation with the actress and his obsessive desire to meet her are conveyed with much wit and affection, bringing a complexity to the film that clearly shows Busch's hand. Wyler's direction matches the screenplay, never stressing the psychological aspects too heavily, integrating them into the action naturally. But the Judge is the film's major success, and Busch and Swerling's accomplishment is in making him at once the supporting and the central character.

Another Western, *Belle Starr* (1941), followed *The Westerner*. Busch wrote only the screen story for this film, which like *The Westerner* explored the motivations of its central character, although not as satisfyingly. Belle Starr (Gene Tierney) is presented as a loyal Southerner during the Civil War who is driven to criminal activity after being mistreated by Northern authorities.

Busch then did no screenwriting for several years. For a while he worked as story editor and special assistant to Samuel Goldwyn, producer of *The Westerner*. He also devoted more of his time to writing novels. "After some fifteen years of work at the film-makers bench," he explained, "I felt that I had established myself securely enough as a novelist to get out of Hollywood and locate myself in less hectic surroundings." He also became involved with orchard growing and cattle ranching, his experiences with which were the partial basis for his complicated Western novel *The Furies*. Busch married actress Teresa Wright in 1942. They divorced in 1952 and he has since remarried twice. Busch has six children.

Cecil Kellaway, John Garfield, and Lana Turner in The Postman Always Rings Twice, *based on James M. Cain's classic hard-boiled novel*

Rory Calhoun and Shelley Winters in The Treasure of Pancho Villa, *Busch's last film*

His return to screenwriting in 1946 was marked by two of Busch's finest films. The intervening years had seen the development of the film noir genre, movies filled with moral ambiguity and fatalistic plots. Busch's fascination with the psychology of his characters made him particularly suited to write film noir, and his next projects, *The Postman Always Rings Twice* (1946) and *Pursued* (1947), were two of the most successful motion pictures of the genre.

Based on the novel by James M. Cain, *The Postman Always Rings Twice* is about drifter Frank Chambers (John Garfield), who comes to a small café and is attracted to Cora Smith (Lana Turner), the beautiful wife of the café's elderly owner (Cecil Kellaway). Cora and Frank decide to murder her husband; after they kill him, Cora is arrested. She is freed, but her relationship with Frank is doomed. As they are leaving town, Cora dies in an automobile accident, and Frank is convicted of her murder. *The Postman Always Rings Twice* is faithful to the spirit, if not the letter, of Cain's novel. The screenplay, well directed by Tay Garnett, carefully reinforces the idea that Frank and Cora are doomed from the time they first meet. Busch and

his collaborator, Harry Ruskin, wisely decided to retain the novel's first-person narration by Frank, who gradually realizes that he has condemned himself.

A narrative voice-over also figured prominently in *Pursued* (1947), an unusual and highly successful mixture of the film noir and Western genres, which was publicized as the first psychological Western. Orphan Jeb Rand (Robert Mitchum) is adopted by the Callum family and falls in love with Thorley (Teresa Wright), his adoptive sister. Jeb has suppressed his memories of the affair between his father and Thorley's mother, and as a result he suffers from frequent nightmares. He is cured after he confronts and kills his father's murderer. Under Raoul Walsh's direction, *Pursued* became Busch's most controlled and best-developed work. Particularly noteworthy is the irreconcilable love-hate dichotomy that exists between his characters. The Callums agree to adopt Jeb, but there has long been a feud between the Callums and the Rands, and even after Jeb is adopted, three different members of his family try to kill him. Busch's explanations of amnesia and revenge may seem rather facile on the surface. But the screenplay never spells anything out too clearly; the reasons for every action, even the violent ones, are covered in myriad emotional and character facets.

Perhaps *Pursued* represented the summit of Busch's work; for whatever reason, a falling-off in his work began with *Moss Rose* (1947), a mystery set in turn-of-the-century England. Belle Adair (Peggy Cummins), an ambitious, social-climbing chorus girl, has evidence implicating Sir Alexander Sterling (Victor Mature) in a murder. Her blackmail attempts cause Sterling to bring Belle to live in his luxurious home, where he and his mother plot to murder her. Busch adapted the film from a novel by Joseph Shearing; Jules Furthman and Tom Reed wrote the final screenplay.

The remainder of Busch's screenplays were for Westerns. In 1950 he produced as well as wrote *The Capture*, which was directed by John Sturges. A detective (Lew Ayres) is plagued by the idea that he might have shot an innocent man during a robbery. Guilt-ridden, he flees to Mexico where he decides to try to find the real thief. *Distant Drums* (1951) reunited Busch with Raoul Walsh but with much less success than they had in *Pursued*. Busch's original script was largely rewritten, and the result was a pedestrian film about an Indian uprising in nineteenth-century Florida. *Moonlighter* (1953) was an unimaginative film about a cattle rustler (Fred MacMurray) who encounters a former girlfriend

(Barbara Stanwyck). In *The Treasure of Pancho Villa* (1955) a mercenary (Rory Calhoun) is hired to rob a train to help finance Pancho Villa's Mexican revolution in 1915; after he steals a shipment of gold, a series of double crosses occur. By far the best work of this period was *Man From the Alamo* (1953), about a man (Glenn Ford) who is selected by lot to leave the Alamo and protect nearby settlers. When he reaches the settlement, he finds he has been branded a deserter and his family has been murdered; he must clear himself and find the killers. The film was directed by Budd Boetticher, who has frequently dealt with the heroics of the common man in the American West, and his unpretentious direction provided a perfect complement to Busch's plotting.

Busch has had no screenplays produced since *The Treasure of Pancho Villa*. The market for Westerns, particularly the type in which Busch specialized, dried up in the 1950s, and the few scripts he has written since then have gone unfilmed. Busch now concentrates mainly on writing fiction, and he considers himself to be at the height of his powers as a novelist.

Charlie Chaplin
(16 April 1889-25 December 1977)

Botham Stone

MOTION PICTURES: *Twenty Minutes of Love* (Keystone, 1914), story and screenplay;
Caught in a Cabaret (Keystone, 1914), story and screenplay;
Caught in the Rain (Keystone, 1914), story and screenplay;
A Busy Day (Keystone, 1914), story and screenplay;
The Fatal Mallet (Keystone, 1914), story and screenplay by Charles Chaplin or Mack Sennett;
The Knockout (Keystone, 1914), story and screenplay;
Mabel's Busy Day (Keystone, 1914), story and screenplay;
Mabel's Married Life (Keystone, 1914), story and screenplay;
Laughing Gas (Keystone, 1914), story and screenplay;
The Property Man (Keystone, 1914), story and screenplay;
The Face on the Bar-Room Floor (Keystone, 1914), story and screenplay;
Recreation (Keystone, 1914), story and screenplay;
The Masquerader (Keystone, 1914), story and screenplay;
His New Profession (Keystone, 1914), story and screenplay;
The Rounders (Keystone, 1914), story and screenplay;
The New Janitor (Keystone, 1914), story and screenplay;
Those Love Pangs (Keystone, 1914), story and screenplay;
Dough and Dynamite (Keystone, 1914), story and screenplay;
Gentlemen of Nerve (Keystone, 1914), story and screenplay;
His Musical Career (Keystone, 1914), story and screenplay;
His Trysting Place (Keystone, 1914), story and screenplay;
Getting Acquainted (Keystone, 1914), story and screenplay;
His Prehistoric Past (Keystone, 1914), story and screenplay;
His New Job (Essanay, 1915), story and screenplay;
A Night Out (Essanay, 1915), story and screenplay;
The Champion (Essanay, 1915), story and screenplay;
In the Park (Essanay, 1915), story and screenplay;
A Jitney Elopement (Essanay, 1915), story and screenplay;
The Tramp (Essanay, 1915), story and screenplay;
By the Sea (Essanay, 1915), story and screenplay;
Work (Essanay, 1915), story and screenplay;
A Woman (Essanay, 1915), story and screenplay;
The Bank (Essanay, 1915), story and screenplay;
Shanghaied (Essanay, 1915), story and screenplay;

Charlie Chaplin

A Night in the Show (Essanay, 1915), story and screenplay;

Charles Chaplin's Burlesque on Carmen (Essanay, 1915-1916), story and screenplay;

Police (Essanay, 1916), story by Chaplin and Vincent Bryan; screenplay;

The Floorwalker (Lone Star-Mutual, 1916), story by Chaplin and Bryan; screenplay;

The Fireman (Essanay, 1916), screenplay;

The Vagabond (Lone Star-Mutual, 1916), story by Chaplin and Bryan; screenplay;

One A.M. (Lone Star-Mutual, 1916), story and screenplay;

The Count (Lone Star-Mutual, 1916), story and screenplay;

The Pawnshop (Lone Star-Mutual, 1916), story and screenplay;

Behind the Screen (Lone Star-Mutual, 1916), story and screenplay;

The Rink (Lone Star-Mutual, 1916), story and screenplay;

Easy Street (Lone Star-Mutual, 1917), story and screenplay;

The Cure (Lone Star-Mutual, 1917), story and screenplay;

The Immigrant (Lone Star-Mutual, 1917), story and screenplay;

The Adventurer (Lone Star-Mutual, 1917), story and screenplay;

A Dog's Life (Chaplin-First National, 1918), story and screenplay;

Triple Trouble (Essanay, 1918), story and screenplay;

Shoulder Arms (Chaplin-First National, 1918), story and screenplay;

Charles Chaplin in a Liberty Loan Appeal (The Bond) (Chaplin-Liberty Loan Committee, 1918), screenplay;

Sunnyside (Chaplin-First National, 1919), story and screenplay; rereleased in 1976, with music by Chaplin;

A Day's Pleasure (Chaplin-First National, 1919), story and screenplay; rereleased in 1970, with music by Chaplin;

The Kid (Chaplin-First National, 1921), story and screenplay; rereleased in 1971, with music by Chaplin;

The Idle Class (Chaplin-First National, 1921), story and screenplay; rereleased in 1971, with music by Chaplin;

Pay Day (Chaplin-First National, 1922), story and screenplay;

Nice and Friendly (Accidental Film Corporation, 1922), story and screenplay;

The Pilgrim (Chaplin-First National, 1923), story and screenplay;

A Woman of Paris (Regent-United Artists, 1923), story, screenplay and music;

The Gold Rush (Chaplin-United Artists, 1925), story and screenplay; reedited (Chaplin-United Artists, 1942), story, screenplay, music, and narration;

A Woman of the Sea (Chaplin, 1926), story;

The Circus (Chaplin-United Artists, 1928), story and screenplay;

City Lights (Chaplin-United Artists, 1931), story, screenplay, and music;

Modern Times (Chaplin-United Artists, 1936), story and music;

The Great Dictator (Chaplin-United Artists, 1940), story, screenplay, and music;

Monsieur Verdoux (Chaplin-United Artists, 1947), story, screenplay, and music;

Limelight (Celebrated-United Artists, 1952), story, screenplay, music, songs by Chaplin, Ray-

mond Rasch, and Larry Russell;
A King in New York (Attica-Archevay, 1957), story, screenplay, and music;
The Chaplin Revue (Roy-United Artists, 1959)—includes footage from *A Dog's Life, Shoulder Arms,* and *The Pilgrim,* music and narration;
A Countess from Hong Kong (Universal, 1966), screenplay and music.

BOOKS: *Charlie Chaplin's Own Story* (Indianapolis: Bobbs, Merrill, 1916);
My Wonderful Visit (London: Hurst & Blackett, 1922), republished as *My Trip Abroad* (New York/London: Harper, 1922);
My Autobiography (London: Bodley Head, 1964; New York: Simon & Schuster, 1964):
My Life in Pictures (London: Bodley Head, 1974).

PERIODICAL PUBLICATIONS: "How I Made My Success," *Theatre* (September 1915): 121;
"What People Laugh At," *American Magazine,* 86 (November 1918): 34-35, 134-137;
"In Defense of Myself," *Colliers* (11 November 1922): 18;
"Does the Public Know What It Wants?," *Adelphi* (1 January 1924): 702-710;
"Pantomine and Comedy," *New York Times,* 25 January 1931, VIII: p. 6;
"A Comedian Sees the World," *Woman's Home Companion* (September, October, November, December 1933, January 1934).

Master actor, director, producer, composer, and writer, Charles Spencer Chaplin was born into a theatrical family in East Lane, Walworth, London. His parents were music hall entertainers. Hannah Chaplin sang, danced, and was a mimic; Charles Chaplin, Sr., was a popular comedian, baritone, and sometime composer. He was Hannah's second husband and young Chaplin was brought up with Sydney, the son of her first union. When Chaplin was two, his parents separated, and his mother's career faltered; she eventually became insane. Although Charles, Jr., danced in the street for money and Sydney sold papers, the Chaplins were forced into the poorhouse in 1896. Chaplin and his brother endured the agony of separation from their mother, the indignities of poverty, and, later, neglect and abuse from their alcoholic father and his mistress. Chaplin's experiences influenced his art and his view of human nature; he understood and depicted the common man, the romantic down-and-outer who always hopes for a better day. Hannah Chaplin had given her son an interest in

the eccentricities of individuals by entertaining him with pantomimes of persons they saw. Later, he said of the comedic art: "There is no study in the art of acting that requires such an accurate and sympathetic knowledge of human nature as comedy work." The pain and poverty of Chaplin's childhood made him sensitive to the needs and feelings of others. In his films he realistically portrays the miseries of poverty and the suffering man behind his most famous character, the Tramp.

At age five, Chaplin had stood in for his laryngitis-stricken mother and delivered a song that was well-received by the audience. Eight-year-old Chaplin found employment on the stage as a clog-dancer, a career culminating in his successful roles in the troupe of Fred Karno (Sydney was already a company member), whose clowns perfected pantomime slapstick. Chaplin, who once forced fellow Karno Company member and friend Stan Jefferson (Stan Laurel) out of a leading role to make room for himself, credited his work with Karno with providing him the basis for his comedy. On Chaplin's second American tour with the Karno troupe in 1912, after viewing him in *Mumming Birds,* Mack Sennett offered him a job as a film clown in his Keystone comedies. A year later Chaplin began a screen career that would include every facet of filmmaking.

Chaplin was twenty-four years old when he began with Sennett's company, Keystone. Thirty-five films and one year later, Chaplin began writing and directing the films in which he starred. Because he was the director and the leading actor of his films, Chaplin did not work from a fully developed script until he wrote *Modern Times* in 1936. His talent as a screenwriter was improvisational and collaborative. Rollie Totheroh, his cameraman for thirty years, said that often Chaplin would suggest an idea for a film and others would add to it. Usually, Chaplin composed with the camera, and he revised by careful film editing. He shot thousands more feet of film than he used and said he had taken as much as sixty thousand feet in order to provide the two thousand feet seen by the public.

The comedies that Chaplin made for Keystone were fast-paced and zany, filled with pie-throwing, pratfalls, somersaults, and chases. The tramp character he devised for Sennett was sometimes cruel and amoral, and the character, to some extent, determined the plot of a Chaplin comedy. "All my pictures are built around the idea of getting me into trouble and so giving me the chance to be desperately serious in my attempt to appear as a normal little gentleman. That is why, no matter

Karno's Company hockey team: Chaplin is seated second from left; Stan Laurel is standing on left

how desperate the predicament is, I am always very much in earnest about clutching my cane, straightening my derby hat, and fixing my tie, even though I have just landed on my head."

Chaplin played the role of the tramp so frequently that in the eyes of the public the character and the actor were one: the Tramp was Charlie. Although Chaplin was constantly refining the role and making it more subtle, the character, throughout his career, is indiscriminately referred to as Charlie, the Tramp, or the Little Fella. In most of Chaplin's early films the characters are not named; they are referred to by profession, class, or type.

From his appearance in his first picture, *Making a Living* (1914), Chaplin's films became an instant success with the moviegoing public. Consequently, his pictures netted huge sums for

Sennett. Fearing his popularity might be short-lived, Chaplin was interested in making as much money as he could and threatened to start his own film company when his contract with Keystone ran out in December 1914. Sennett offered more money per film and a bonus, but George Spoon and G. M. "Bronco Billy" Anderson, the movies' first cowboy star, made a more generous offer, and Chaplin signed with their company, Essanay. Essanay offered him the opportunity to be an independent filmmaker and more time to devote to each film. With approximately three weeks to work on each film instead of the one week he had had with Sennett, Chaplin became more of a perfectionist. Although the films he made for Essanay are generically the same as those made for Keystone, the slapstick is more polished, the humor more subtle, and the character of the Tramp more fully developed.

The two films that mark a turning point in Chaplin's career are *The Bank* (1915) and *The Tramp* (1915). In these films the Tramp becomes more sympathetic and is a character with whom everyone can identify. In these films, too, the love interest begins to be an important element, producing the sentimentality and romance that Chaplin thought necessary for good drama. Although his pictures remained episodic and loosely structured, the story often consisting of a series of jokes strung along a plot line, the characters become more credible: real people with strong feelings.

The Tramp, considered to be Chaplin's first masterpiece, affords a rich contrast between the fastidiousness of the genteel tramp and the realities of farm life. After rescuing a farmer's daughter (Edna Purviance), he is given a job on a farm, and hilarious comic episodes are produced by Chaplin's ignorance of rural matters. The comedy is sharpened and made more poignant by the love Charlie feels for the farmer's daughter. Like many of the film love affairs Charlie was to have, this one is doomed to failure—the daughter's fiancé appears. The tramp writes a farewell note, packs his bag, and wanders forlornly down the road, then kicks his feet, straightens his shoulders, and boldly faces a new adventure.

The films Chaplin made for Essanay were huge financial successes; many were critical successes as well. When the contract with Essanay ran out, Chaplin's brother Sydney, now his business manager, negotiated a new contract with the Mutual Corporation—Chaplin received $10,000 a week and a $150,000 bonus upon signing. With Mutual he became even more of a perfectionist, taking eighteen months to complete the twelve two-reelers he had promised to finish within a year. The pictures reflect the extra time and attention Chaplin insisted on giving them. The slapstick is highly sophisticated, combining acrobatics and ballet; the characters are given more depth. Timing becomes perfect.

Chaplin's first important film for the Mutual Corporation was *The Vagabond* (1916), a movie which relies on the use of pathos as an integral part of the comedy. A poor jobless violinist, Charlie, meets a beautiful woman (Purviance) who is a gypsy slave. He rescues her, nurses her, and falls in love, but a young artist comes to paint the young woman, and they fall in love. The portrait is seen by the woman's mother, who comes to get her in a limousine. Charlie gazes wistfully after the car as it

disappears down the road. The two endings Chaplin filmed for this movie reveal the double edge of his comedy; the ending could be either comic or serious. In one of the endings, Charlie jumps into a lake; an ugly hag rescues him, but after one look at her he jumps back in. In the ending Chaplin used, the beautiful woman comes back for him in a limousine.

Easy Street (1917), set in a slum street not unlike his boyhood home on South London's Kennington Road, is Chaplin's best two-reeler. Charlie wanders into a mission where he is converted by the minister's sermon and the beauty of the minister's daughter (Purviance). He becomes a policeman, and much humor comes from his attempt to stop criminals. Although most of the movie is unrestrained comedy, the miseries of poverty, starvation, and deprivation are graphically portrayed. Despite the grimness of some of the scenes, the movie ends happily.

Many of Chaplin's pictures depend on a single object or his surroundings for humor: an escalator in *The Floorwalker* (1916), a fire engine in *The Fireman* (1916), a slippery dance floor in *The Count* (1916). Similarly, *The Cure* (1917), the film he made after *Easy Street*, relies on a place to produce the laughs. It has a simple plot centered on a health spa. The high point of the action occurs when a bellhop pours a supply of liquor into the fountain of medicinal waters. This results in a riotous party as all the patrons lose their inhibitions.

Chaplin said his next film, *The Immigrant* (1917), touched him more than any other film he made because "the end had quite a poetic feeling." In the opening shot, Charlie is hunched over the side of the ship, his shoulder convulsed in what appears to be a fit of seasickness. When he turns around, he is holding a big fish he has caught. Charlie cited this shot as his ideal of the comic: "An idea, going in one direction, meets an opposite idea suddenly." On the ship Charlie befriends two immigrants, a young woman (Purviance) and her mother. When he meets the woman again in a restaurant in America, the mother has died. After a serious moment in which Charlie reveals he loves the woman and shares her loss, there comes a long comic scene in which Charlie tries to avoid paying the bill. The end of the movie turns again to the poignant: the couple walks out into the heavy rain; suddenly Charlie picks the woman up and takes her to the marriage bureau.

With *The Adventurer* (1917), Chaplin's career at Mutual came to an end. He tried to enlist in the armed forces during World War I but was turned down for medical reasons, a fact he did not publicize. Consequently, he was regarded as a slacker for not contributing to the war effort, the first of many accusations that clouded his reputation. That same year, Chaplin rejected Mutual's offer of one million dollars for an additional twelve films and signed instead with First National for one million dollars for eight films each with a minimum length of one thousand feet, and more money for any film running over twenty-three hundred feet. To have full control over his work, Chaplin became his own producer and bore the production costs that Mutual would have paid for him. Toward this end, he also built his own studio. Chaplin was now able to lavish attention on each of his productions. The eight films he made for First National took him a year apiece to complete.

Chaplin's productivity was slowed not only by his increasing perfectionism but also by his private life. In a shotgun wedding, the motivation for which turned out to be a lie, he married teen-aged actress Mildred Harris in October 1918; they were divorced two years later. Despite his domestic problems, Chaplin was able to produce, through what he called "sheer perseverance to the point of madness," two masterpieces in 1918. In the first, *A Dog's Life*, Chaplin shares the stage with a dog, called in the titles "a thoroughbred mongrel," which is also a good description of the Little Fella. They ate food from a stand run by a stolid vendor (Sydney Chaplin). Later Charlie meets Edna (Purviance), a singer in a cafe; thereupon a complex piece of action takes place involving a wallet stolen by crooks, dug up by the dog, stolen again, and dug up again. At the end Charlie and Edna, having settled down on a small farm, gaze lovingly into a bassinet—at the dog and her litter of puppies.

Although he was criticized for not taking part in the war, Chaplin wanted to make a contribution to the war effort. This he did in *Shoulder Arms* (1918), which was joyfully received by both military and civilian audiences. Charlie is a bumbling enlisted man who dreams of being a war hero. In one inventive sketch which ranks as one of the most

Charlie Chaplin, Eric Campbell, and Edna Purviance in The Vagabond, *one of the many silent films Chaplin made with Purviance*

Charlie Chaplin, Edna Purviance, and Kitty Bradbury in The Immigrant, *a film that touched Chaplin more than any of his other films because of the "poetic feeling" of its ending*

famous comic scenes in film history, he disguises himself as a tree trunk.

After *Sunnyside* (1919) and *A Day's Pleasure* (1919), two pleasant but mediocre films, Chaplin produced his first feature-length movie, *The Kid* (1921). The opening title reveals the tone of the movie and Chaplin's theory of comedy: "A comedy with a smile—and perhaps a tear." There is more sentiment in this film than in any of those preceding. In a scenario that reads like a corrective to the grim realities of Chaplin's childhood, Charlie finds an abandoned baby and is forced to rear him. When the child (Jackie Coogan) is five, he is placed in an orphanage (in a scene reminiscent of Chaplin's youth). They are reunited, then separated again before Charlie is united with both the child and the child's mother, who is now a successful opera singer. Like many of the endings to Chaplin's films, this conclusion has been the subject of controversy. Some critics have attacked the happy ending, others have praised it, and others have insisted

it is not truly happy because Charlie has no place in the boy's new world.

In April 1919 Chaplin, Mary Pickford, Douglas Fairbanks, and D. W. Griffith formed United Artists to produce and distribute their films independently, though Chaplin's contract with First National left him unable to work independently until 1923. His last film for First National, *The Pilgrim* (1923), is an irreverent satire on false piety and narrow-mindedness. Charlie, an escaped convict wearing a minister's clothes, arrives in the small town of Devil's Gulch and is mistaken for the new clergyman. He falls in love with his landlady's daughter (Purviance) and decides to reform. The sheriff recognizes Charlie but realizes he is trying to go straight and leads him to the Mexican border where he can escape. Charlie sees a gang of outlaws on the other side of the border and, caught between the criminals and the lawman, runs down the border with one foot in Mexico and the other in the United States. This is the perfect ending for a

Charlie Chaplin and Jackie Coogan peeking around the corner in The Kid, *Chaplin's first feature-length film*

Chaplin comedy, reflecting the unity in polarity of the entire work.

Chaplin called his next film, *A Woman of Paris* (1923), the first silent film "to articulate irony and psychology." It is a completely serious film designed as a vehicle for Purviance and the only film written by Chaplin in which he did not appear. The complicated plot traces two star-crossed lovers, Marie (Purviance) and Jean (Carl Miller). Although it is quite melodramatic, Chaplin's script realistically depicts character and emotion. His observation of human nature and his attention to the details that reveal character are as acute in this serious drama as they are in his comic films.

After the completion of *A Woman of Paris*, in November 1924, thirty-five-year-old Chaplin married sixteen-year-old Lillita McMurphy (who acted under the name Lita Grey), in a second shotgun wedding. It was a bad marriage from the start, but it produced two sons, Charles, Jr. and Sydney, to whom Chaplin was devoted. This marriage ended

in divorce in August 1927, amidst a maelstrom of public scandal.

The film for which Chaplin most wanted to be remembered, *The Gold Rush,* was released in 1925. Most critics agree with Chaplin that it is his finest work. Although the film is episodic in structure, it is unified by setting and theme. The characterization of the Tramp is fully developed; he possesses depth and evokes audience sympathy and interest. At the beginning of the movie he is lonely and isolated, one of many prospectors seeking gold in the Yukon. By the film's end, he has befriended another miner (Mack Swain), and they are wealthy. The highlights of the movie are the Thanksgiving feast and the New Year's Eve party. Starving at Thanksgiving time, Charlie is forced to cook his shoe and eat it as if it were a turkey. The New Year's Eve party occurs after Charlie has gone to town and fallen in love with a saloon girl (Georgia Hale, who had replaced the obviously pregnant Lita Grey). She promises to bring her friends to his New Year's party, but no one comes. Instead, Charlie dreams of a spirited party where he entertains the women by performing a dance with rolls on forks.

Chaplin's next important film, *The Circus* (1928), is a retelling of Leoncavallo's Pagliacci story in a modern circus setting. Charlie falls in love with the bareback rider (Merna Kennedy), stepdaughter of the oppressive owner of the circus (Harry Bergman); but, she is in love with the tightrope walker (Harry Crocker). At the end, the circus moves on and Charlie is left alone, sitting on an empty box in a desolate lot. Although it does not have the richness and depth of *The Gold Rush, The Circus* is a technically competent film with artistic integrity. Reception of *The Circus* was somewhat dampened by the release in 1927 of *The Jazz Singer*, the first talking movie.

The advent of sound films seriously damaged the careers of such great silent film comedians as Buster Keaton and Harold Lloyd, but Chaplin continued to make semi-silent films throughout the 1930s. These had soundtracks with music composed by Chaplin himself and sound effects, but no spoken dialogue; they still relied on pantomime and titles. The first of these, *City Lights* (1931), contains the ideal mixture of the humorous and the pathetic that all of Chaplin's great films have. Running from the police, the Tramp stumbles into a lovely, blind flower girl (Virginia Cherrill). Later, he meets a suicidal millionaire (Harry Myers) and convinces him he should live. The millionaire takes Charlie out for a night on the town, and this produces several comic situations. It also leads the flower girl to believe that Charlie is rich. Eventually he is falsely accused of robbing the millionaire and is sent to jail. When he is released, he meets the flower girl who can now see and recognizes him as her benefactor. In a rare Chaplin closeup, he looks into her eyes pathetically.

The extraordinary success of *City Lights* surprised everyone who thought the public would not patronize a silent film in the age of sound, and it confirmed Chaplin's opinion that the talking picture should be regarded as "a valuable addition to the dramatic art," rather than as a substitute for the silent film. He said he continued to make films without dialogue because pantomime is the "universal means of communication" and "is at the base of any form of drama."

Chaplin's next film, *Modern Times* (1936), is structurally weak and conceptually unsatisfying, although it contains some perfect satire of the modern world. The opening title says the film is the "story of industry, of individual enterprise—humanity crusading in the pursuit of happiness," but that is not what the picture is really about. In fact, it portrays the cruelty of the machine age, what technology has done to man, and what man has done to man as a result of the machine. This theme, however, is not developed consistently, as large sections of the film have nothing to do with it. Charlie works on an assembly line and is driven mad by his work. He loses his job, is mistaken for a participant in a Communist parade, and is arrested. When he is freed, he falls in love with a girl (Paulette Goddard), but the juvenile authorities come to take her

At the incorporation of United Artists, 17 April 1919: (front) founders D. W. Griffith, Mary Pickford, Charlie Chaplin, and Douglas Fairbanks, Sr.; (back) attorneys Albert Banzhaf and Dennis O'Brien

Charlie Chaplin (center) directing the opening shot in The Gold Rush, *generally considered his finest film*

away, and they are forced to flee. Although their situation is dire, the audience last sees them walking down a sunlit road, hand in hand. This is the first film for which Chaplin wrote a full-length screenplay; neither the plot nor the comic routines seem to have improved because of this new procedure. And, in a bow to the ever-strengthening talking movie, Charlie speaks briefly for the first time on film in what he calls "a sort of Katzenjammer French," a gibberish meant to obfuscate the Tramp's English accent. Sometime during or after the production of *Modern Times,* Chaplin and Goddard were allegedly married, perhaps while they were on a five-month tour of the Far East. Gossip of the day suggested Goddard's seemingly illicit affair with Chaplin cost her the role of Scarlett in *Gone With the Wind* (1939).

The Great Dictator (1940), Chaplin's first talking film, is a satire of Adolph Hitler based on an idea by Alexander Korda. Chaplin plays the dual role of a Jewish barber, who is an inept, ordinary person with none of the charm and elegance of the Little Fella, and dictator Adenoid Hynkel, leader of the Double Cross Party and physical double of the barber. Inevitably, the two are mistaken for one another, and the barber is called upon to make a public speech. He describes the way people and nations should behave and treat one another, predicts the return of power to the people, and beseeches his listeners, "Now let us fight . . . to free the world, to do away with national barriers, to do away with greed, with hate and intolerance. Let us fight for a world of reason—a world where science and progress will lead to man's happiness. Soldiers, in the name of democracy, let us unite." This speech was condemned by critics as being didactic, dull, inconsistent, and out of character. Despite this criticism, the motion picture was the greatest popular success of any of Chaplin's films. He also earned Academy Award nominations for his writing and his acting, the first of three times a single individual has been so honored.

The 1940s was a trouble-filled decade for Chaplin. He and Goddard separated in 1941, and she allegedly divorced him in Mexico in 1942. The Internal Revenue Service was investigating him for income tax evasion. His reputation was being assaulted by political conservatives who had objected to the speech in *The Great Dictator* and to the fact that Chaplin had never become an American citizen. His popularity further declined when, in 1941, he argued for the opening of a second front in support of our Soviet ally in the war against Germany, and he mistakenly came to be viewed as a Communist sympathizer. His most painful experience was the paternity suit filed against him by temperamentally volatile, aspiring actress Joan Barry in 1943. Barry won the paternity suit, although a blood test did not prove Chaplin was the

father. Ironically, this coincided with the event in his life that was to bring him the greatest happiness—his marriage to eighteen-year-old Oona O'Neill, the daughter of playwright Eugene O'Neill. This marriage produced eight children.

By the mid-1940s, the public had turned against Chaplin, and his next film, *Monsieur Verdoux* (1947), was unfavorably received by the public and critics alike, with the notable exception of James Agee, who thought it a quite profound analysis of modern business and war. The film was subtitled "A Comedy of Murder," a genre the public was unwilling to accept. It makes a modern-day Bluebeard a sympathetic murderer who supports his crippled wife and their son through wooing, wedding, and killing rich women. The satire is obvious: after Verdoux is captured and tried for murder, he says, "Wars, conflict—it's all business. One murder makes a villain; millions, a hero. Numbers sanctify." There is some comedy in the film, particularly in the scene with one victim (Martha Raye) who is

Virginia Cherrill and Charlie Chaplin in City Lights. *Though the movie was made after the advent of sound, its story is told entirely through pantomime and titles, and the film's extraordinary success confirmed Chaplin's belief that pantomime is the "universal means of communication" and "at the base of any form of drama."*

Lobby poster for Chaplin's satire on Adolf Hitler, the first Chaplin film in which the actors talk

difficult to kill; but, on the whole, the satire is mordant.

After making *Monsieur Verdoux,* Chaplin was comparatively inactive professionally. He was happy domestically with Oona and his growing family, but he continued to be troubled politically. His support of unpopular causes and his associations with leftist artists continued to make him unpopular with such groups as the American Legion, which boycotted his films. The House un-American Activities Committee informed him that he would be called before them as a witness. Chaplin sent a telegram to chairman J. Parnell Thomas saying, "I am not a Communist. I am a peace-monger." During the 1940s and early 1950s Chaplin was also embroiled in several controversies at United Artists which led to his estrangement from Mary Pickford and culminated in his selling his stock in United Artists in 1955.

Limelight (1952) was the last film Chaplin made for United Artists and the last he made in America. Calvero (Chaplin), a washed up music hall

star of the 1890s, makes his comeback after inspiring a young ballet dancer, Terry (Claire Bloom), who has psychosomatic paralysis. By convincing Terry that she should not give up, Calvero convinces himself that he should not. The romantic subplot of the film is in the Chaplin tradition: Calvero loves Terry, who forces herself to love him out of gratitude, but she really loves Neville (Chaplin's son Sydney), a composer. Calvero drops out of her life to release her from any debt of gratitude and dies onstage while performing in a music hall.

In September 1952 Charlie, Oona, and their four children sailed for England. When they were two days at sea, the Attorney General of the United States, James McGraney, issued an order barring Charlie's return to America under a code that denied an alien's entry on grounds of morals or Communist affiliation. Later, the Attorney General issued a statement saying that Chaplin had been "publicly charged" with being a Communist and with "grave moral charges and with making statements that would indicate a leering, sneering atti-

Buster Keaton and Charlie Chaplin in Limelight, *the last film Chaplin made in the United States*

tude toward a country whose hospitality has enriched him." Chaplin, indignant of this treatment, decided not to appeal the decision, but rather to stay in Europe indefinitely. Oona returned briefly to America to see to the transfer of Chaplin's fortune. They eventually settled in the village of Corsair, near Vevey, on Lake Geneva in Switzerland, where he bought the estate of Manoir de Ban.

Understandably, Chaplin felt some rancor about his exile and the events leading up to it, and these feelings clearly color his next film, *A King in New York* (1957), made at Shepperton Studios in England. This work reflects his ambivalent feelings toward America; it portrays the intolerance of McCarthyism, the obsession with political labels, and the commercialism of the nation, while at the same time praising the hospitality and friendliness of Americans and predicting that in the end all will be well. King Shahdov (Chaplin) of Estrovia flees his country because of revolution. In New York City, he befriends Rupert McAbee (Michael Chaplin), who has been accused of being a Communist by schoolmates because he reads Karl Marx. Both Shahdov and Rupert's parents are called before a congressional committee. Shahdov is cleared, but not before he creates comic chaos. As Shahdov prepares to return to his country, a neighbor (Dawn Addams) who befriended him says that the present hysteria in America will pass; Shahdov replies, "Quite so. In the meantime, I'll sit it out in Europe."

In general, critics found the film's plot lifeless and the comedy beneath Chaplin's standards. It was not released in the United States until 1973, at which time Chaplin himself admitted that the movie "started out to be good and then it got complicated and a little heavy-handed." The film has few comic situations, and the ones it does contain are not fully worked. Chaplin was too personally involved in the story; however, through the medium of film he could fantasize clearing himself before the House Un-American Activities Committee and choosing exile freely, two things he could not do in reality.

After this cathartic film, Chaplin worked on his autobiography, an interesting but highly selective account of his life, which was published in 1964. He also spent time composing music for his early silent films and conceiving the film that was to be his last, *A Countess from Hong Kong* (1966). It was intended to be an old-fashioned comedy-romance, but the critics felt that the comedy and romance did not fuse, and the dialogue was stilted and unconvincing. It departed further from Chaplin's earlier films by using established actors—Marlon

Brando and Sophia Loren—with Chaplin taking only a cameo role. The simple plot traces the journey of Ogden Mears (Brando), a rich American diplomat returning home from Hong Kong. He spends a drunken evening in port with a Russian countess, Natascha (Sophia Loren), who decides to sneak aboard Mears's ship. During the rest of the trip, Mears must prevent her from being discovered by the crew.

Although he made no films after *A Countess from Hong Kong*, Chaplin received many honors in the last years of his life. He received a special award at the Cannes Film Festival in 1971. The following year—twenty years after his forced exile—he and Oona made a triumphal return to the United States, where he was honored in New York by the Film Society of Lincoln Center and in Los Angeles by the Academy of Motion Picture Arts and Sciences. In 1972 he was awarded the Venice Film Festival's Golden Lion; and in 1973 he won an Oscar with Raymond Rasch and Larry Russell for best original dramatic score for *Limelight* (belatedly run in Los Angeles). Chaplin's last book, *My Life in Pictures*, was published in 1974. He became a Knight Commander of the British Empire on 2 January 1975. On Christmas Day 1977, Charlie Chaplin died in his sleep at his estate in Switzerland.

Chaplin's place in the history of film is an important one. He drew millions to the new art form in the early part of this century, appealing both to the masses and to the discerning moviegoer. His greatest contributions to the comedy genre include his creation of character and his ability to exhaust all possibilities of a comic situation to evoke as many kinds of laughter as possible. As a screenwriter, he was often banal and melodramatic, but he believed melodrama was an important part of his work, sharpening and deepening the humor. The combination of pathos and comedy was realistic, reflecting the range of human experience, and revealed Chaplin's view of the innate dignity of humanity. There is little doubt that Chaplin's work will endure. Winston Churchill said that Charles Dickens and Charles Chaplin "both quarried in the same rich mine of common life and found there treasures of laughter and drama for the delight of all mankind." This universal quality of Chaplin's work will continue to delight and entertain.

References:

James Agee, *Agee on Film* (New York: McDowell, Obolensky, 1958);

Kevin Brownlow, *The Parade's Gone By* (New York: Knopf, 1968);

Margaret Rutherford, Sophia Loren, and Charlie Chaplin on the set of A Countess from Hong Kong, *Chaplin's last film*

Charles Chaplin, Jr., with N. and M. Rau, *My Father, Charlie Chaplin* (New York: Random House, 1960);

Wes D. Gehring, *Charlie Chaplin: A Bio-Bibliography* (Westport, Conn.: Greenwood, 1983);

Theodore Huff, *Charlie Chaplin* (New York: Henry Schuman, 1951);

Walter Kerr, *The Silent Clowns* (New York: Knopf, 1975);

Roger Manvell, *Chaplin* (Boston: Little, Brown, 1974; London: Hutchinson, 1974);

John McCabe, *Charlie Chaplin* (Garden City: Doubleday, 1978);

Donald W. McCaffrey, ed., *Focus on Chaplin* (Englewood Cliffs N.J.: Prentice-Hall, 1971);

McCaffrey, *4 Great Comedians: Chaplin, Lloyd, Keaton, Langdon* (New York: A. S. Barnes, 1968);

Gerald D. McDonald, Michael Conway, and Mark Ricci, eds., *The Films of Charlie Chaplin* (New York: Bonanza Books, 1965);

Roger Manvell, *Chaplin* (Boston: Little, Brown, 1974; London: Hutchinson, 1974);

R. J. Minney, *Chaplin, The Immortal Tramp* (London: G. Newnes, 1954);

Robert Payne, *The Great God Pan: A Biography of the Tramp Played by Charlie Chaplin* (New York: Hermitage House, 1952); also titled *The Great Charlie* (London: Andre Deutsch, 1952);

Isabel Quigley, *Charlie Chaplin: Early Comedies* (London: Studio Vista, 1968).

Paddy Chayefsky

(29 January 1923-1 August 1981)

Sam Frank

See also the Chayefsky entries in *DLB 7, Twentieth-Century American Dramatists*, and *DLB Yearbook 1981*.

MOTION PICTURES: *True Glory* (U.S. Army, 1945), screenplay by Chayefsky and Garson Kanin;

As Young as You Feel (20th Century-Fox, 1951), screen story;

Marty (United Artists, 1955), screenplay adapted by Chayefsky from his television play;

The Bachelor Party (United Artists, 1957), screenplay adapted by Chayefsky from his television play;

The Goddess (Columbia, 1958), screen story and screenplay;

Middle of the Night (Columbia, 1959), screenplay adapted by Chayefsky from his play;

The Americanization of Emily (M-G-M, 1964), screenplay;

Paint Your Wagon (Paramount, 1969), adaptation;

The Hospital (United Artists, 1971), story and screenplay;

Network (M-G-M/United Artists, 1976), screenplay;

Altered States (Warner Bros., 1980), screenplay as Sidney Aaron, adapted from Chayefsky's novel.

PLAY PRODUCTIONS: *No T. O. For Love*, London Special Services Tour, 1945;

Middle of the Night, New York, ANTA Theatre, 8 February 1956;

The Tenth Man, New York, Booth Theatre, 5 November 1959;

Gideon, New York, Plymouth Theatre, 9 November 1961;

The Passion of Josef D., New York, Ethel Barrymore Theatre, 11 February 1964;

The Latent Heterosexual, Dallas, Dallas Theatre Center, 15 March 1968; London, Aldwych Theatre, 16 September 1968.

BOOKS: *Television Plays* (New York: Simon & Schuster, 1955);

The Bachelor Party (New York: New American Library, 1957);

Middle of the Night (New York: Random House, 1957);

The Goddess (New York: Simon & Schuster, 1958);

The Tenth Man (New York: Random House, 1960);

Gideon (New York: Random House, 1962);

The Passion of Josef D. (New York: Random House, 1964);

The Latent Heterosexual (New York: Random House, 1967);

Altered States (New York & London: Harper & Row, 1978; London: Hutchinson, 1978).

SELECTED TELEVISION: *Holiday Song*, Philco-Goodyear Playhouse (NBC, 14 September 1952);

Paddy Chayefsky

The Reluctant Citizen, Philco-Goodyear Playhouse (NBC, 1952);

Marty, Philco-Goodyear Playhouse (NBC, 24 March 1953);

Printer's Measure, Philco-Goodyear Playhouse (NBC, 26 April 1953);

The Big Deal, Philco-Goodyear Playhouse (NBC, 19 July 1953);

The Bachelor Party, Philco-Goodyear Playhouse (NBC, 11 October 1953);

The Sixth Year, Philco-Goodyear Playhouse (NBC, 20 November 1953);

Catch My Boy on Sunday, Philco-Goodyear Playhouse (NBC, 1953);

The Mother, Philco-Goodyear Playhouse (NBC, 4 April 1954);

Middle of the Night, Philco-Goodyear Playhouse (NBC, 19 September 1954);

The Catered Affair, Philco-Goodyear Playhouse (NBC, 22 May 1955);

The Great American Hoax, 20th Century-Fox Hour (CBS, 15 May 1957).

RADIO: *The Meanest Man in the World, Tommy,* and *Over 21* (Theatre Guild of the Air, 1951-1952), adaptations.

OTHER: "Good Theatre in Television," in *How to Write for Television,* edited by William I. Kaufman (New York: Hastings House, 1955), pp. 44-48.

PERIODICAL PUBLICATIONS: "Not So Little," *New York Times,* 15 July 1956, II: 1;

"Art Films—Dedicated Insanity," *Saturday Review,* 40 (21 December 1957): 16-17;

"The Giant Fan," *Harper's Bazaar,* no. 2967 (February 1959): 122-123, 182-185;

"Has Broadway Had It?," *New York Times,* 23 November 1969, II: 7;

"An Ad Lib for Four Playwrights," by Chayefsky, Israel Horovitz, Arthur Laurents, and Leonard Melfi, *Dramatists Guild Quarterly,* 5 (Winter 1969): 4-19.

Paddy Chayefsky is one of a handful of American screenwriters who first achieved fame during the golden age of television, producing some of his best work for the live dramatic anthology programs. At the time Chayefsky was honing his craft on the *Philco-Goodyear Playhouse,* the movies were concentrating on visual gimmicks such as Cinemascope and Cinerama to lure the public away from television. And yet, there was far more inti-macy and human truth in any one of Chayefsky's scripts for television than in most of the widescreen spectaculars combined. For these dramas Chayefsky drew upon his upbringing in New York: a world of garment workers, cabdrivers, cantors, print-shop compositors, butchers, and callous Casanovas looking for "tomatoes" at Waverly Ballrooms. The characters in his plays were never larger-than-life; they *were* life—mundane people whose problems were universal and who, therefore, touched a deep nerve with the viewing public. The characters were mostly ethnic types, usually Jewish, sometimes Italian.

He was born Sidney Chayefsky, one of three sons of Russian-born immigrants Harry and Gussie Stuchevsky Chayefsky. The household was a traditional Jewish one in the Bronx, supported by Harry's Dellwood Dairy firm in Yonkers, which went bankrupt in 1934. Harry instilled in young Sidney a love for traditional Yiddish theater and the arts and respect for education. The Yiddish theater, especially, would later play a large role in Chayefsky's scripts for television, stage, and movies.

Chayefsky graduated in 1939 from DeWitt Clinton High School, where he had edited the literary yearbook and school paper. He earned a bachelor's degree in social science from City College of New York in 1943. While at college, he played semi-professional football with a Bronx team called the Kingsbridge Trojans. He enlisted in the United States Army, and during his stint as an army machine gunner from 1943 to 1945, he received the nickname "Paddy" from a skeptical lieutenant who thought it odd when this very Jewish young man opted to attend Catholic Mass rather than endure the drudgery of KP duty; he kept the nickname professionally because it was distinctive. Chayefsky earned a Purple Heart after being injured by stepping on a German land mine in 1944.

Chayefsky's first film work came in 1944 when he was approached by director Garson Kanin to collaborate on the script for an Army film called *True Glory* (1945). The following year, while he was recovering in an English army hospital from the land mine explosion, he wrote the book and lyrics for a GI musical comedy called *No T. O. For Love,* which was subsequently produced in London, with Chayefsky in a leading role, and which also was put on a tour of army camps.

After the war, he became an apprentice in his uncle's New York print shop and was given five hundred dollars by Garson Kanin to write a play called "Put Them All Together," which was never produced. However, it did attract the attention of producers Mike Gordon and Jerry Bressler; they gave Chayefsky a Junior Writer's contract in Hollywood. In 1949 he wrote a screen treatment for "The Great American Hoax," a story which was sold to *Good Housekeeping* but never published.

During his stay in Hollywood, Chayefsky met Susan Sackler, whom he married on 24 February 1949. They had one son, Dan. Finding no employment in Hollywood, Chayefsky returned to New York. He worked for a few months as a gag writer for comedian Robert Q. Lewis, while writing plays and trying to find backers for them. He later recalled, "I sold some plays to men who had an uncanny ability not to raise money."

Undeterred, he got the attention of Elia Kazan with a play called "The Man Who Made the Mountain Shake." Kazan's wife, Molly, assisted Chayefsky in writing revisions, but the play—which was retitled "Fifth From Garibaldi"—was never produced. In the early 1950s, Chayefsky began writing radio scripts for *Theatre Guild of the Air* and *Cavalcade of America*. He wrote television episodes for *Danger* and *Manhunt* and contributed the story for the film *As Young as You Feel* (1951), a comedy about a man (Monty Woolley) battling compulsory retirement.

His real opportunity as a writer finally came about in 1952 when Fred Coe, the galvanic producer of *Philco-Goodyear Playhouse,* who had seen

Marilyn Monroe and Albert Dekker in As Young as You Feel, *the film for which Chayefsky received his first Hollywood screen credit*

the *Danger* and *Manhunt* episodes, approached Chayefsky to adapt a short story called "It Happened on the Brooklyn Subway." The story was a minor human interest one about a photographer on a New York subway train whose faith in God is renewed when he reunites a concentration camp survivor with his long-lost wife.

By itself, there was nothing about the story to compel dramatic interest for thirty minutes, let alone an hour, so Chayefsky searched his own Jewish background for a dramatic hook. He had always wanted to write a script with a synagogue as backdrop, and he created *Holiday Song,* about a cantor (Joseph Buloff) who loses his faith in God on the eve of Yom Kippur, the highest of Jewish holy days. On his way to a New York suburb to talk with a rabbi who might rejuvenate his faith, he is seated on the wrong subway train by a security guard. It is during this trip that he talks with a man, a concentration camp survivor, searching for his long-lost wife. On the return trip, he meets a woman on another train—to which he has been guided by the same guard—who turns out to be the man's wife. He reunites the couple. In the end, the cantor's faith is renewed by this experience, and the drama implies that the subway guard, who seemingly guided him in the wrong direction twice, was actually God.

Although *Holiday Song* aired to critical acclaim in 1952 and was aired again in 1954, Chayefsky was unhappy with the play because it was a contrivance of coincidences with little solid backbone, and because he felt that Buloff, though a fine actor, was too strong for the role of the cantor, who he felt should be "a wan little scholar, confused when outside the sheltered confines of his synagogue." He later detailed the structuring of this play and his misgivings about it in a collection of his *Philco-Goodyear Playhouse* scripts.

At his insistence, all of Chayefsky's subsequent work for *Philco-Goodyear* was original, based on his own experiences. The result was that 1953 was a banner year for him, with six television plays produced, including: *Printer's Measure,* a semi-autobiographical drama about a print-shop compositor whose lifelong handicraft is threatened by the greater speed of a linotype machine; *The Bachelor Party,* about an engaged man who goes on one last fling with the guys at his office while having last-minute doubts about getting married; and *The Big Deal,* about a has-been building contractor pursuing one last dream of striking it rich with a land-buying scheme.

In his commentary, Chayefsky discusses in detail the various problems these scripts posed. In the case of *Printer's Measure*, he had to build a drama around what most people would consider a minor trauma, though it was a significant one for the compositor. "*The Bachelor Party*," he writes, "should have told the individual stories of five men who go on a night about town, each of whom resolves something in his own life as a result of the party. . . . However, in the multiple story, you build the body of your script by cutting from one story to the other as the basic line accumulates to its high point. This means there are no such things as first and second-act curtains; one story or another is always moving along. In television, you have to have first and second-act curtains for the reasons that commercials have to be introduced." He was later able to rework *The Bachelor Party* to his satisfaction as a feature film.

The Big Deal was a stage play that had to be reduced to the time and physical limitations of television. "The crisis of *The Big Deal* was too big to be handled properly on television. The relationships between Joe Manx and his wife and daughter needed to be seen more if the positive resolution of the play was to make honest sense. The point of the play was that this man had given the true values of life to his family—warmth, love, respect, dignity—which was a far more successful achievement than material wealth. I didn't have the time to show how he had given all these qualities."

The highlight of 1953, the peak of Chayefsky's television career, and one of the most acclaimed of all live television dramas, was *Marty*. It appealed to many viewers because it dealt with a universal theme: a homely butcher in his thirties named Marty Pilletti (Rod Steiger) who feels that, whatever women are looking for in a man, "I ain't got it." When he meets an equally homely, lonely woman named Clara Davis (Nancy Marchand) at a ballroom on Saturday night, he discovers he is not alone in his inner torment, that others, women included, can feel just as ugly inside as he. "We aren't such dogs as we think we are," he states.

The coup de grace is when Marty's buddies chide him for going out with a "dog," but are unable to find anything better to do themselves that night except talk about what they are going to do. "Hey Angie, what do you feel like doing tonight?" "I don't know, what do you feel like doing?"—a classic exchange. Suddenly Marty has had his fill of this time-killing rhetoric and decides to call the girl regardless of what his friends think:

MARTY: You don't like her. My mother don't like her. She's a dog, and I'm a fat, ugly little man. All I know is I had a good time last night. I'm gonna have a good time tonight. If we have enough good times, I'm going to go down on my knees and beg that girl to marry me. If we make a party again this New Year's, I gotta date for the party. You don't like her, that's too bad.

This emotional outburst focuses the climax, making the audience feel that Marty is speaking for them. The show was live, immediate, compelling. But, for all the rave attention it got at the time, NBC never rebroadcast *Marty*, either live or on kinescope. The public had to wait two years to see it again at the movies in an expanded version.

Both versions of *Marty* were directed by Delbert Mann. The television version has a spare look to it by virtue of economic as well as dramatic necessity. Except for the living room, the sets are simple, creating a desperate, closed-in atmosphere. The 1955 movie version, with Ernest Borgnine and Betsy Blair, by sheer virtue of its larger budget, more expansive script, bigger sets, and location sequences is able to correct the earlier limitations, but at a cost. The simple appearance of the television version is replaced by a more realistic set, but one which looks too elaborate. The Waverly Ballroom, for instance, is overly bright and cheery. There is also the problem of casting: Borgnine seems too gregarious, and Blair too attractive, for their parts. The tension of the television original is lost. Still, the movie—which remains entertaining for all its faults—took the nation by storm, becoming a box office hit and earning Academy Awards for best picture, best director (Mann), and best actor (Borgnine). Chayefsky won his first best screenplay Oscar for the film.

Now that Chayefsky was a proven commodity in both television and the movies, two more of his television plays were adapted for the big screen. Gore Vidal wrote the screenplay for the motion picture based on Chayefsky's 1955 teleplay *The Catered Affair*, and Chayefsky wrote *The Bachelor Party* (1957). Both films expanded these popular plays beyond the restrictive time and set confines of television, and they explored and deepened Chayefsky's characters and their conflicts.

The more artistically successful film, and the less commercially successful, was *The Bachelor Party* (1957), directed by Mann, who had an affinity for Chayefsky's work. As with *Marty*, the film script improves on the television original because there is more leeway to characterize and explore the men, their wives and girlfriends, and the deep-seated

Esther Minciotti, Betsy Blair, and Ernest Borgnine in the film version of Marty, *which earned Chayefsky his first Academy Award for best screenplay*

feelings and motivations of each. Here the realistic ambience is just right; the oppressive atmosphere of the white collar workaday world is captured perfectly. However, it did not attract the public as *Marty* had. *Marty* was a love story about shy, lonely people with an upbeat ending, while *The Bachelor Party* dealt with a more depressing subject and had an ambivalent ending. Here Chayefsky presents people questioning the idea of marriage, of commitment to one person, of going to the same, dull job, day after day, year after year, to support a family. *The Bachelor Party*—disturbing in its stark portrayal of daily reality—was tolerable to the public on television, but downright uncomfortable on screen.

Chayefsky's next film was even more depressing—*The Goddess* (1958). Loosely based on the life of Marilyn Monroe, the film is about Emily Ann Faulkner (Kim Stanley), a small-town girl who becomes the movies' ultimate blonde sex goddess. Faulkner is a shallow, mousy sort of girl, lured by the glamour of Hollywood. And like Monroe, when she achieves stardom, she becomes emotionally dis-

turbed and a problem to all around her: her producer, her director, and her husband (Lloyd Bridges). *The Goddess* was neither a critical nor a popular success. Under John Cromwell's direction, Chayefsky's script, which was written as three separate "acts," emerges as a series of set pieces rather than a cohesive whole. And while it depicts Faulkner's personal problems in great detail, the film offers too little insight into her professional life, so that viewers never see a fully developed picture of "the goddess." Stanley is also badly cast and unconvincing as a sex symbol. It was a financial failure for another reason as well; once again, Chayefsky revealed the reality behind an illusion—in this case, the price Faulkner pays to become a star—in painful detail, and it was more than most audiences found comfortable.

The last of Chayefsky's television-to-movie cycle was also a hit Broadway play. *Middle of the Night* (1959) is about a widowed, middle-aged businessman (Fredric March) who finds love and solace with a secretary (Kim Novak) on the verge of divorce from her callous husband. What plays well

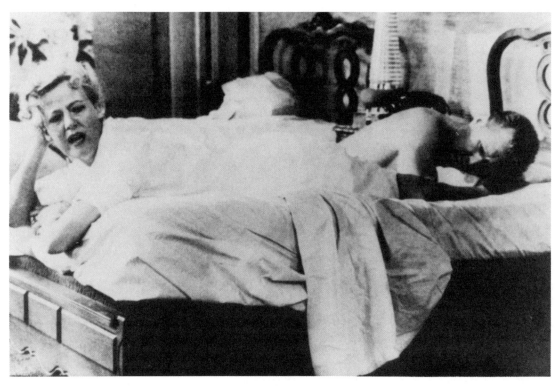

Kim Stanley and Lloyd Bridges in The Goddess, *loosely based on the life of Marilyn Monroe*

on Broadway does not necessarily appeal to a film audience, and though Delbert Mann directed and March was critically praised, the public was not interested in a movie that shattered the salacious clichés of such relationships. Apparently, the sort of intimate and sometimes oppressive dramas Chayefsky excelled at had worn out their welcome. He moved on to new territory and larger themes on the Broadway stage with satirical plays like *The Tenth Man* (produced in 1959) and *Gideon* (produced in 1961), both of which drew on his traditional Jewish background, and both of which had good runs, especially *The Tenth Man,* which ran for nearly two years.

When Chayefsky returned to screen writing, it was with a scathing military satire, *The Americanization of Emily* (1964). Instead of using the realistic dialogue of his earlier work, Chayefsky's new material was characterized by pungent and witty speech. Lieutenant Commander Charlie Madison (James Garner) is a "dog robber" for senile navy Admiral Jessup (Melvyn Douglas), seeing to it that the admiral has every comfort he could wish for, while keeping some for himself. He even persuades motor-pool driver Emily Barham (Julie Andrews) to go to bed with him and to be a bridge partner for the admiral. Emily is attracted to this charming

con-artist but is put off by his seemingly cowardly approach to war. "When the first bullet is fired," he says, "I get out of the way so there isn't a second bullet." He likes the perks of war, but not its pain and hardships.

Meanwhile, Jessup wants Madison's friend Bus Cummings (James Coburn) to make a movie spotlighting the navy's role on D-Day. Madison emphatically does not want to be present at the storming of Normandy beach, but he ends up going and becoming its first casualty—Cummings shoots him in the leg in a fit of anger—and, thereby, its first hero. Madison will have none of it, stating that he will tell the world's press the truth. Jessup is remorseful about the incident, but Cummings and Emily double-talk Madison out of his plan, saying that, in the long run, the public wants patriotic glamour, not mundane truth.

The Americanization of Emily is a refreshingly sardonic commentary on war heroics in general, and on World War II in particular. It never made money, though, and this may have been because the film was too irreverent for mass audience taste in 1964.

Chayefsky's next film, an adaptation of the Lerner and Loewe musical *Paint Your Wagon* (1969), also flopped, but for vastly different reasons. Despite the wartime GI musical he had written, musical comedy was not Chayefsky's forte, and even though the movie is better in spots than most critics would concede, this tale of two gold miners (Clint Eastwood and Lee Marvin) and their mutual wife (Jean Seberg) was far too long at sixty-six minutes. Chayefsky's screenplay was rewritten almost entirely, and he never wrote another musical.

He returned in triumph with his second institutional satire, *The Hospital* (1971), a dark comedy about an ineptly run big-city hospital where a maniac is killing promiscuous interns. The hospital's chief-of-staff, Dr. Herbert Bock (George C. Scott), is incensed over these murders but is also beside himself with rage, impotence, and anger over his son's terrorist "peace" antics. "He wants to love his fellow man by blowing him up with a bomb," Bock sardonically declares.

He finds solace and sex with Barbara Drummond (Diana Rigg), daughter of the patient (Barnard Hughes) who turns out to be the mad killer. In one of the movie's highlights, father Drummond delivers a speech telling of his sadness and anger over the pain and sickness and indifference of American society, as symbolized by the hospital, explaining the killings as vengeance for those sins.

The Hospital was both a critical and commercial success, earning Chayefsky his second Oscar for screenwriting. It succeeded where *The Americanization of Emily* had failed, because the public was ready for a sacred cow to be attacked and because his sardonic mouthpiece, Bock, said a lot of things that needed saying about the decay of American society. Today *The Hospital* seems talky and pretentious, but at the time it was daring.

Despite this success, Chayefsky wrote no more screenplays until 1976, when he unleashed his most furious satire, *Network*, for which he won his third Oscar for screenwriting. This time, he returned to the scene of his first successes, network television, launching an all-out assault on the single-minded quest for high ratings and bigger corporate dividends. As he saw it, the medium that had nurtured the anthology writers had turned into a cesspool of fantasy and mediocrity, where nonthinking audiences can hear anything "you want to hear because TV is a goddamned amusement park." So says Howard Beale (Peter Finch), an aging network anchorman who goes insane on the air one night and has inspired revelations about saving mankind from television by using television.

Network programmer Diana Christensen (Faye Dunaway) is delighted with this insanity because the audience for the news show is increasing steadily. But Max Schumacher (William Holden), a programming executive and the film's voice of reason, is disgusted by this exploitation of his old friend's sickness. Network vice-president Frank Hackett (Robert Duvall) fires Schumacher and wastes no time building the network into the business empire he has always dreamed of, turning the news show into an entertainment program with Beale as its "Mad Prophet of the Airwaves." *Network* is a bold movie that would have been even better if Chayefsky had not indulged himself with so many polemical speeches and had told less and shown more.

Chayefsky's last film, *Altered States* (1980), was based on his novel satirizing the scientific research community and its pretensions. But, during pro-

Peter Finch in Network, *the film for which Chayefsky won his third Academy Award for screenwriting*

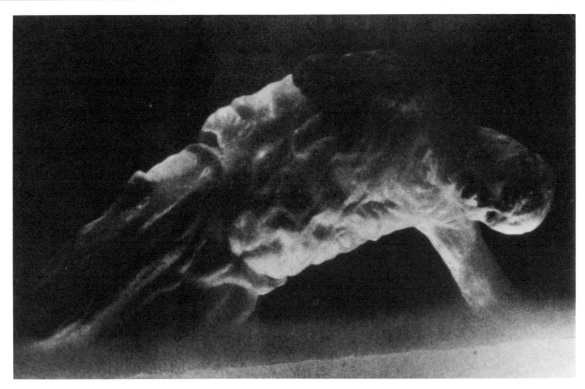

William Hurt as Eddie Jessup during his experimentation with sensory deprivation in Altered States

duction, he had many disagreements with producer and director Ken Russell, who wanted the movie to be more of a symbol-heavy, special-effects laden film than a satire, so Chayefsky withdrew his name from the credits in protest and replaced it with Sidney Aaron. Chayefsky's anger is understandable; *Altered States* is in many ways merely a reworking of old horror movie themes. Eddie Jessup (William Hurt) is experimenting with sensory deprivation, in an effort to discover the secrets of the inner self and human evolution. He imbibes a mixture of Mexican herbal drugs and turns into a murderous ape-man.

There is more to the convoluted plot, including a bewildered wife (Blair Brown), but the film version of *Altered States* manages to dredge up nearly every cliché of the 1960s drug and psychic phenomena culture, missing its intended more mature audience.

Though Chayefsky's output was not prolific, he did have an impact on every entertainment medium he touched. He championed the common man, ripped through the lies and subterfuge of our most pervasive institutions, and dug into his own ethnic background to examine religious and sec-

ular questions. His major strength as a playwright was his ability to create realistic characters and to give them believable and revealing dialogue. Playing with language and turns of phrase for their own sake he wrote some of the best speeches in motion pictures. His was not the edgy urbanity of Rod Serling or the angry social conscience of Reginald Rose—at least not in the early years—but rather the earthy, questioning civility of a man who is sick of illusions and artifice and wants to show human frailty and need in a compassionate if bemused light. His major failings were an overemphasis on the mundane for its own sake, and in his later years an overreliance on speech-making in lieu of characterization and plot.

Ironically, he died just a few weeks before PBS rebroadcast *Marty*, reintroducing the nation to a simpler and more human form of television drama.

References:

John Brady, *The Craft of the Screenwriter* (New York: Touchstone, 1981), pp. 29-83;
John M. Clum, *Paddy Chayefsky* (Boston: Twayne, 1976);

James Vinson, ed. *Contemporary Dramatists* (New
    York: St. Martin's Press, 1973).

Papers:
Paddy Chayefsky's papers are at the Wisconsin
Center for Film and Theatre Research.

Lenore J. Coffee
(1900?-2 July 1984)

Thomas Slater
Northwest Missouri State University

MOTION PICTURES: *The Better Wife* (Garson Stu-
    dios, 1919), story;
The Forbidden Woman (Equity Pictures, 1920), story;
Alias Ladyfingers (Metro, 1921), adaptation; also re-
    leased as *Ladyfingers* (Metro, 1921), scenario;
The Face Between (1922);
The Right That Failed (Metro, 1922), scenario;
Sherlock Brown (Metro, 1922), scenario;
The Age of Desire (First National, 1923), titles;
Daytime Wives (R-C Pictures, 1923), story by Coffee
    and John Goodrich;
Temptation (C.B.C. Film Sales, 1923), story;

Lenore Coffee (courtesy of Culver Pictures)

Thundering Dawn (Universal, 1923), scenario by
    Coffee and Goodrich;
The Six-Fifty (Universal, 1923), scenario by Coffee,
    Harvey Gates, and Doris Schroeder(?);
Wandering Daughters (First National, 1923), titles;
Bread (Metro-Goldwyn, 1924), adaptation;
Fools' Highway (Universal, 1924), scenario by Coffee
    and Gates;
The Rose of Paris (Universal, 1924), adaptation by
    Coffee and Bernard McConville;
East Lynne (Fox, 1925), adaptation by Coffee and
    Emmett Flynn;
Hell's Highroad (Cinema Corp. of America, 1925),
    adaptation by Coffee and Eve Unsell;
For Alimony Only (De Mille Pictures, 1926), story
    and scenario;
The Volga Boatman (De Mille Pictures, 1926), ad-
    aptation;
The Angel of Broadway (De Mille Pictures, 1927),
    screenplay;
Lonesome Ladies (First National, 1927), story;
The Night of Love (Samuel Goldwyn, 1927), adap-
    tation;
Chicago (De Mille Pictures, 1928), scenario;
Desert Nights (M-G-M, 1929), continuity;
The Bishop Murder Case (M-G-M, 1930), adaptation,
    dialogue, and scenario;
Mother's Cry (1930);
Street of Chance (Paramount-Famous Lasky, 1930),
    dialogue;
Possessed (M-G-M, 1931), adaptation, dialogue, and
    continuity;
The Squaw Man (M-G-M, 1931), screenplay by Cof-
    fee and Lucien Hubbard;
Arsene Lupin (M-G-M, 1932), screenplay by Coffee,
    Bayard Veiller, and Carey Wilson;
Night Court (M-G-M, 1932), screenplay by Coffee,
    Mark Hellinger, Veiller, and Charles Beehan;

Torch Singer (Paramount, 1933), screenplay by Coffee and Lynn Sterling;

Evelyn Prentice (M-G-M, 1934), screenplay;

Four Frightened People (Paramount, 1934), screenplay by Coffee and Bartlett Cormack;

Age of Indiscretion (M-G-M, 1935), story;

Vanessa, Her Love Story (M-G-M, 1935), screenplay;

Suzy (M-G-M, 1936), screenplay by Coffee, Dorothy Parker, Alan Campbell, and Horace Jackson;

Four Daughters (Warner Bros., 1938), screenplay by Coffee and Julius Epstein; refilmed as *Young at Heart* (Warner Bros., 1954), screenplay by Coffee and Epstein;

Good Girls Go to Paris (Columbia, 1939), story;

The Way of All Flesh (Paramount, 1939), screenplay;

My Son, My Son (United Artists, 1940), screenplay;

The Great Lie (Warner Bros., 1941), screenplay;

The Gay Sisters (Warner Bros., 1942), screenplay;

Old Acquaintance (Warner Bros., 1943), screenplay by Coffee and John Van Druten;

Marriage Is a Private Affair (M-G-M, 1944), screenplay by Coffee and David Hertz;

Till We Meet Again (Paramount, 1944), screenplay;

Tomorrow Is Forever (RKO, 1946), screenplay;

The Guilt of Janet Ames (Columbia, 1947), screen story;

Beyond the Forest (Warner Bros., 1949), screenplay;

Lightning Strikes Twice (Warner Bros., 1951), screenplay;

Sudden Fear (RKO, 1952), screenplay by Coffee and Robert Smith;

The End of the Affair (Columbia, 1955), screenplay;

Footsteps in the Fog (Columbia, 1955), screenplay by Coffee and Dorothy Reid;

Cash McCall (Warner Bros., 1960), screenplay by Coffee and Marion Hargrove.

BOOKS: *Weep No More* (New York: Castle, 1955);
Storyline: Reflections of a Hollywood Screenwriter (London: Cassell, 1973).

Veteran Hollywood screenwriter Lenore Coffee was born in San Francisco at the turn of the century. As a youngster she became enamoured with the arts, and particularly with the movies, which her parents also loved. She wanted to be an actress and rebelled against her father's urgings to become a writer by tearing to pieces all the poetry she had written. After her parents divorced she returned to writing, beginning her career in the advertising field.

In January of 1919, she answered an item in the back of *The Motion Picture Exhibitors' Herald* which advertised that actress Clara Kimball Young

was in desperate need of a screen story. Having seen Young in several movies and impressed with her beauty, Coffee developed a story for her. In the process, she developed a method that lasted for the rest of her career: she would take a premise or concept that interested her then build a story around it. Many of her pictures can be summarized by their titles alone, such as *For Alimony Only* (1926), *Lonesome Ladies* (1927), *Night Court* (1932), and *The Guilt of Janet Ames* (1947). For Young, she developed a romantic tale in which the actress would meet an unmarried man who had a child.

Coffee titled her story *The Better Wife* (1919) and sent it to Garson Studios. Two weeks later, she received a check for one hundred dollars. In March, she met studio owner Harry Garson, who had been impressed with the fact that Coffee's story had been completely filmable as written. He immediately gave her a one-year contract at fifty dollars a week to come to Hollywood and learn screenwriting. Coffee's career was launched.

She began by providing scenarios, titles, captions, original stories, and other material demanded by Hollywood during its early years. One of her jobs at Garson was re-editing and retitling unreleasable movies, making some of them good enough for distribution. This experience proved to be very valuable, bringing Coffee a great deal of work throughout her career; she was well-known as a "script doctor" and was often called on in desperation to save a project.

The Forbidden Woman (1920) was Coffee's second story; she played a part in the film herself. In 1921 she went to work for playwright and movie producer Bayard Veiller at Metro Studios, choosing his offer of two hundred fifty dollars a week over the two hundred a week promised by Irving Thalberg at Universal. This move was a great benefit to Coffee's career, for working with Veiller allowed her to learn scriptwriting and dialogue years before talking pictures began. Her first task at Metro was to write a series of scripts that Veiller directed, all adventures starring Bert Lytell: *Alias Ladyfingers* (1921), *The Right that Failed* (1922), and *Sherlock Brown* (1922).

Coffee's career was built upon working relationships (not always good) with other producers, besides Garson and Veiller, particularly Cecil B. De Mille, Thalberg, and Louis B. Mayer. Most important of these was her collaboration with De Mille. In 1924 he called her in to help him save a picture called *Hell's Highroad* (1925). He admired her work so much that afterwards he offered her a generous contract. In that year, Coffee also met William J.

Cowen, De Mille's assistant. Coffee later married the future novelist and director, and they had a son and daughter. Later, he asked Coffee if she would like to work directly with him on a script. His idea was to make a movie called *The Volga Boatman* (1926), based on the "Volga Boat Song." Coffee only had to describe one scene that she had in mind to convince De Mille that she was right for the job: a scene showing the corruption of the Bolsheviks once they got into power after the Russian revolution. Coffee described to De Mille how she would present this idea: "When the Bolsheviks are victorious in capturing a palace filled with women in beautiful evening gowns and superb jewels, and the men in court dress with decorations, the Volga boatmen harness these proud people into the ropes which pull the barge while they watch in triumph from the boat." At the conclusion of the movie the boatman leaps down to help the Russian princess pull her rope. In the final scene, he asks that the lives of the prince and princess be spared in exchange for his own. When the picture was finished, De Mille was at first displeased with the results, but *The Volga Boatman* became enormously successful, having long runs all over the country.

Throughout the rest of her career, Coffee maintained a close friendship with De Mille; he was always someone she could turn to whenever she needed help. Her relationships with Irving Thalberg and Louis Mayer at M-G-M were very different; she was hired, fired, and rehired at M-G-M throughout the 1920s and 1930s. At first, Thalberg seemed to admire her, as Coffee herself relates in her memoirs: "I was in one of my interminable waits to see Thalberg when his secretary told me they were having a very heated conference about

William Boyd and Julia Faye in The Volga Boatman, Coffee's *attempt to show how the Bolsheviks had become corrupt after they gained power*

a script which needed work; when the door opened I heard one of the men say, 'Why don't you put Coffee on this? She's free now.' Whereupon Irving replied, 'For Christ's sake, don't give me a writer with any ideas! She'll have them and I'll *listen* to them—and we *just* haven't the time!' Backhanded praise, but it amused me."

Her relations with the two men at M-G-M were not to remain cordial for long. Coffee constructed a detailed outline of a story called "Stepmother" which she offered to the studio for five thousand dollars. Mayer was furious about her asking price and said she would either take half that amount or "get the hell out of the studio." Coffee replied, "Mr. Mayer, I couldn't take twenty-five *thousand* dollars like that." Mayer fired her, threatening that she would never work in pictures again. Coffee packed her belongings and left; she was back five years later. In the interim, she wrote two scripts for De Mille, *For Alimony Only* (1926) and *The Angel of Broadway* (1927).

In 1930 she wrote *The Bishop Murder Case*, her first talking picture. It was adapted from one of S. S. Van Dine's Philo Vance novels, with Basil Rathbone starring as the famous detective. At the time, screenwriters were usually hired only to write a plot, while playwrights were paid to write the dialogue; but Coffee insisted to Thalberg that she should be allowed to write her own dialogue, and he agreed.

She also wrote *Possessed* (1931) on special orders from Thalberg to provide Joan Crawford with a change of pace in her career; Crawford played a small-town factory worker who travels to New York City and becomes the mistress of a politician (Clark Gable). The movie was a success, but for some reason Coffee was never treated well at M-G-M; she had returned in order to write for the best actors and actresses in the business, but was paid half what she had been receiving from De Mille and was shunted aside into a small, dingy office.

The only happiness she found during this period was in working with Veiller again. Together, they wrote *Night Court* (1932), a tough New York hoodlum story, and a new version of the French play *Arsene Lupin* (1932), starring Lionel and John Barrymore as a detective and a jewel thief. Coffee finally left the studio when she inadvertently discovered that Thalberg had been denying all loan-out requests for her even though she was not under contract to the studio.

It is difficult to understand why Coffee had any trouble with studio heads since her talents as script doctor must have saved or earned them

Clark Gable and Joan Crawford in Possessed, *a film that by 1930s standards was considered a frank treatment of illicit sex*

hundreds of thousands of dollars. Her work on *The Night of Love* (1927) is a perfect example of her skill. She was several months pregnant when Samuel Goldwyn called one day pleading for help on the picture. Set in medieval Spain, the film opened with a scene in which Ronald Colman dramatically kidnaps a just-married bride. But nobody could think of a motive for his doing so, and the picture was stuck. Coffee thought for a while and then remembered a ritual in which a Spanish feudal duke had the right to and choice of any bride on his estate on her wedding night. She then wrote the rest of the script in less than three weeks.

After leaving M-G-M, Coffee worked on two scripts for Paramount. She rewrote scenes for *Torch Singer* (1933), adding some good material for Claudette Colbert. De Mille produced and directed *Four*

Frightened People (1934), about a group of people (Colbert, Mary Boland, Herbert Marshall, and Leo Carillo) stranded in the jungle.

In 1934 Coffee returned to M-G-M for the last time, writing four screenplays for the studio. One picture, *Suzy* (1936), saved M-G-M from a possible lawsuit. As part of their block booking policy, the studio had sold a movie starring Jean Harlow and Cary Grant; but Grant had never signed a contract agreeing to such a picture. He was refusing to play his part in *Suzy* as a French pilot during World War I, because he thought it was completely wrong for him. Coffee convinced him that the part would be a perfect springboard to becoming an international star, and he accepted the part. Coffee's other scripts for M-G-M were *Evelyn Prentice* (1934) about the neglected wife (Myrna Loy) of a

Lionel and John Barrymore in Arsene Lupin, *the first film that the two brothers made together*

successful attorney (William Powell), who begins an affair, is blackmailed, and suspected of her lover's murder; *Vanessa, Her Love Story* (1935) about a woman (Helen Hayes) in love with a scoundrel (Robert Montgomery); and *Age of Indiscretion* (1935).

Leaving M-G-M, Coffee wrote one picture apiece at Columbia, United Artists, and Paramount. In *Good Girls Go to Paris* (1939), a waitress (Joan Blondell) pretends to be in love with a wealthy man (Alan Curtis) so he will send her to Paris. A poor man (Brian Aherne) makes a fortune then pampers his own son (Scotty Beckett) in *My Son, My Son* (1940), based on the novel by Howard Spring. *The Way of All Flesh* (1939) was a remake of a 1927 melodrama about an immigrant (Akim Tamiroff) who is swindled when he arrives in the United States.

Coffee became a writer at Warner Bros. in 1941, and although she wrote only a few screenplays there, the "women's pictures" she wrote for that studio are the films with which she is most frequently identified. Bette Davis starred in two:

The Great Lie (1941) and *Old Acquaintance* (1943). In *The Great Lie*, she plays a woman in love with a married man (George Brent) who weds him after his marriage is annulled; he is killed in a plane crash, and she must cope with his pregnant first wife (Mary Astor, who won an Academy Award). *Old Acquaintance* follows two novelists (Davis, Miriam Hopkins) through a twenty-year friendship. Coffee and John Van Druten adapted their script from Van Druten's Broadway play. Her third film was *The Gay Sisters* (1942) about a woman (Barbara Stanwyck) who marries a man (George Brent) for his inheritance. Coffee left Warner's in 1943, but returned in 1949 to write two films. *Beyond the Forest* (1949) is the story of a woman (Davis) who is married to a small-town doctor (Joseph Cotten) and is bored with her life. She drifts into an affair. King Vidor directed both that film and *Lightning Strikes Twice* (1951) in which a man (Richard Todd) just released from prison returns home to find the real killer of his wife.

Despite her unpleasant experiences at M-G-M, Coffee did one rewrite job for them in the 1940s,

Joan Crawford in Sudden Fear, *one of Coffee's few mystery films*

working on the script for *Marriage Is a Private Affair* (1944) about a socialite newlywed (Lana Turner) who rebels against the restraints of marriage. Her other films of the mid-1940s include *Till We Meet Again* (1944), about a nun (Barbara Britton) who helps an American pilot (Ray Milland) caught behind enemy lines. Frank Borzage directed. In *Tomorrow Is Forever* (1946), a man (Orson Welles) who is disfigured during the war lets his wife (Claudette Colbert) believe he is dead, then returns home some time later to find his wife has remarried and he has a grown son (Richard Long). A war widow (Rosalind Russell) feels responsible for her husband's death in *The Guilt of Janet Ames* (1947).

As the 1950s began, Coffee saw fewer screenplays produced, but her services were still highly regarded. *Sudden Fear* (1952) was one of her infre-

quent attempts to write a mystery drama. A recently married woman (Joan Crawford) realizes her husband (Jack Palance) is planning to kill her. *The End of the Affair* (1955), adapted from a novel by Graham Greene, is about a British woman (Deborah Kerr) falling in love with an American (Van Johnson) during World War II. That led to another rewrite job, *Footsteps in the Fog* (1955). Columbia Pictures, who was financing it, had liked her work on *The End of the Affair* and asked for her help on the second film. Coffee had a long meeting with Stewart Granger about the script, after which he agreed to star only if she did the writing. She finished the screenplay—a period murder mystery—in London in five weeks, writing scenes in the order in which the sets were being built. Her final screenplay was *Cash McCall* (1960) which she adapted from Cameron Hawley's best-selling novel about a ruthless businessman (James Garner). She retired from screenwriting that year. Her memoirs *Storyline: Reflections of a Hollywood Screenwriter* were published in 1973. Lenore Coffee died in 1984.

If one word could be used to describe Lenore Coffee's career it would be "dependable." She never wrote a great screenplay, but that was never her exact goal. Coffee measured a picture's success by how well it did at the box office rather than by personal standards of artistic achievement. She prided herself on fulfilling her contracts and having good working relationships with studio heads and producers. Her writing was based on a very simple formula. "Two . . . things which I learned fairly early on—things which a writer, particularly of film scripts, must never forget. The first, that you must never leave out one essential ingredient; it is like baking a cake. No matter how delicate and costly the ingredients may be, if you have left out an essential one, you will not have a cake—you will have a disaster. But if you use cheap and inferior ingredients, but use them all, you will have a cake. Not a good one, but indisputably, a cake. The other thing I learned is that a second-rate idea can be better than a first-rate one, if it permits you to 'ring all the changes.'" Coffee might never have been able to gather the very best ingredients, but she knew very well how to use what was available.

Reference:
Sharon Smith, *Women Who Make Movies* (New York: Hopkinson and Blake, 1975).

Betty Comden
(3 May 1919-   )

Adolph Green
(2 December 1918-   )

Nick Roddick

MOTION PICTURES: *Good News* (M-G-M, 1947), screenplay;

The Barkleys of Broadway (M-G-M, 1949), screen story and screenplay;

On the Town (M-G-M, 1949), screenplay and lyrics, adapted from their musical play;

Take Me Out to the Ball Game (M-G-M, 1949), lyrics;

Singin' in the Rain (M-G-M, 1952), screen story and screenplay;

The Band Wagon (M-G-M, 1953), screen story and screenplay;

It's Always Fair Weather (M-G-M, 1955), screen story, screenplay, and lyrics;

Auntie Mame (Warner Bros., 1958), screenplay;

Bells Are Ringing (M-G-M, 1960), screenplay and lyrics, adapted from their musical play;

What a Way to Go! (20th Century-Fox, 1964), screenplay.

PLAY PRODUCTIONS: *On the Town*, New York, Adelphi Theatre, 28 December 1944, book and lyrics;

Billion Dollar Baby, New York, Alvin Theatre, 21 December 1945, book and lyrics;

Bonanza Bound, Philadelphia, Shubert Theatre, 1947, book and lyrics;

Two on the Aisle, New York, Mark Hellinger Theatre, 19 July 1951, sketches and lyrics;

Wonderful Town, New York, Winter Garden Theatre, 25 February 1953, lyrics;

Peter Pan, New York, Winter Garden Theatre, 20 October 1954, additional lyrics;

Bells Are Ringing, New York, Shubert Theatre, 29 November 1956;

Say, Darling, New York, ANTA Theatre, 3 April 1958, lyrics;

A Party, New York, Cherry Lane Theatre, 10 November 1958; expanded as *A Party with Betty Comden and Adolph Green*, New York, Garden Theatre, 23 December 1958; new version produced, New York, Morosco Theatre, February 1977, sketches and lyrics;

Do Re Mi, New York, St. James Theatre, 26 December 1960, lyrics;

Betty Comden

Subways Are for Sleeping, New York, St. James The-
    atre, 27 December 1961, book and lyrics;
Fade Out—Fade In, New York, Mark Hellinger The-
    atre, 26 May 1964, book and lyrics;
Hallelujah, Baby, New York, Martin Beck Theatre,
    26 April 1967, lyrics;
Applause, New York, Palace Theatre, 20 March
    1970, lyrics;
Lorelei, New York, Palace Theatre, 27 January
    1974, lyrics;
On the Twentieth Century, New York, St. James The-
    atre, 19 February 1978, book and lyrics.

TELEVISION: *I'm Getting Married, Stage 67* (ABC,
    March 1967), script and lyrics;
*A Party with Betty Comden and Adolph Green, Mobil
    Summer Showcase* (July 1980), script and lyrics.

BOOKS: *Bells Are Ringing,* book and lyrics by Com-
    den and Green (New York: Random House,
    1957);
Fade Out—Fade In, book and lyrics by Comden and
    Green (New York: Random House, 1965);
Good Morning, Good Night (New York: Holt, Rine-
    hart & Winston, 1967);
Applause (New York: Random House, 1971);

Singin' in the Rain (New York: Viking Press, 1972).

Betty Comden and Adolph Green have always
been officially billed as a team, and there is not a
single credit in their professional lives which they
do not share. Native New Yorkers born within six
months of one another, they have celebrated their
hometown in musicals from *On the Town* (1944) to
Subways Are for Sleeping (1961). Indeed, their real
milieu is less Hollywood than Broadway, where,
collaborating with several composers, they have
provided books and/or lyrics for such full-scale
Broadway musicals as: *On the Town* (1944), *Billion
Dollar Baby* (1945), *Wonderful Town* (1953), *Peter Pan*
(1954), *Bells Are Ringing* (1956), *Say, Darling* (1958),
Do Re Mi (1960), *Subways Are for Sleeping* (1961),
Hallelujah, Baby (1967), *Applause* (1970), and *On the
Twentieth Century* (1978). They have also been re-
sponsible for three Broadway revues: *Two on the
Aisle* (1951), *A Party with Betty Comden and Adolph
Green* (1958), and *Fade Out—Fade In* (1964).

During their Hollywood career they worked
on a number of well-known musicals, including two
adaptations of their own stage musicals, and two
adaptations of the works of others. They are responsible for writing some of the best-loved and
best-known films in the musical comedy genre: *On
the Town* (1949), *Singin' in the Rain* (1952), and *The
Band Wagon* (1953). Like Jule Styne (with whom
they frequently collaborated) and Gene Kelly (who
made his directorial debut on one of their films),
Comden and Green belong to the second generation of American musical comedy creators. Growing up under the influence of Irving Berlin, Al
Dubin, Harry Warren, and Ira and George Gershwin, they began to make their contributions when
the movie musical had more or less outgrown its
origins in the vaudeville show and the chorus line
(though *Two on the Aisle* was very much in that older
tradition). They have been less active since the decline of the musical comedy genre in the 1960s.

Comden and Green belong to the golden age
of the M-G-M musical. Most of their movies were
for that studio, and they, along with Gene Kelly
and Vincente Minnelli, were to a large measure
responsible for what came to be known as the Arthur Freed unit, so-named for its supervising father
figure and producer. Freed contributed the outstanding production values that have always been
associated with M-G-M, Minnelli, skilled direction
of musical numbers, and Kelly, his own particular
brand of athletic dancing. Yet, Comden and Green
were responsible for the wit and drive of the screenplays that held the Freed unit's musicals together.

*Alvin Hammer, Betty Comden, Judy Holliday, and Adolph Green performing their cabaret act
in the 1944 film* Greenwich Village

Their screenwriting has never seemed to be just something between songs.

Actress, lyricist, dramatist, and screenwriter Betty Comden, born Elizabeth Cohen, in Brooklyn, New York, was the daughter of Leo Cohen and Rebecca Sadvoransky Cohen. Her mother was a schoolteacher and her father a lawyer. She was educated at the Brooklyn Ethical Culture School and Erasmus Hall High School before graduating from New York University with a bachelor of science degree. On 4 January 1942 she married Stephen Kyle, a successful designer and antique dealer, and they had one daughter, Susanna, and one son, Alan. Kyle died on 10 October 1979.

Adolph Green, lyricist, entertainer, and dramatist, was born in the Bronx to Daniel and Helen Green. He was educated at DeWitt Clinton High School and spent one day at a community college in New York before, as he put it, "becoming a full time bum." He is married to actress Phyllis Newman.

The first Comden and Green teaming was a nightclub act called The Revuers which opened in New York at Max Gordon's Village Vanguard nightclub in 1938. (The act was later featured in the 1944 film *Greenwich Village*.) The cast was made up entirely of young unknowns; in addition to Comden and Green (who wrote the script and performed), the act included Alvin Hammer, John Frank, and Judy Holliday. A fairly regular accompanist was the young Leonard Bernstein. At the Village Vanguard the act was such a phenomenal success that it was transferred to Radio City Music Hall. Presumably seeking a more sophisticated crowd, they moved the act to the Rainbow Room, where it failed. But, by that time the entertainment industry had noticed Comden and Green, and they were invited to Hollywood to work on a movie; it was never filmed. Comden returned to New York almost immediately, but Green stayed on for a while. When he returned to New York, he was greeted by a group of cheering admirers organized by Comden and bearing a sign that said "The Adolph Green Fan Club." (The pair later incorporated this event into *The Band Wagon*.)

The hiatus in Comden and Green's career was brief. In 1943 Leonard Bernstein decided to put a musical together using the score he had just written for Jerome Robbin's ballet *Fancy Free*. The result was *On the Town*, which opened shortly after Christmas 1944, with book and lyrics by Comden and Green (who also created the roles of Claire and Ozzie). *On the Town* was an enormous Broadway hit, and it launched the pair on the next phase of their Hollywood career.

Their first film was *Good News* (1947), scripted for Freed at M-G-M from a musical by Lawrence Schwab, Lew Brown, Frank Mandel, B. G. De Sylva, and Ray Henderson. (The musical had been filmed before by M-G-M in 1930.) The story, which takes place in the 1920s, presents the romantic triangle of a football hero (Peter Lawford), a gold-digger (Patricia Marshall) who pursues him because she thinks he is a millionaire, and a teacher's assistant (June Allyson) who loves him. Comden and Green contributed one new song, "The French Lesson," which they wrote with Freed's associate producer and arranger, Roger Evans. *Good News* was a kind of test for Comden and Green to see if they could transfer to film the snappy, sophisticated writing of their Broadway musicals.

Eighteen months and a stage musical later, Comden and Green produced their next screenplay for the Freed unit. *The Barkleys of Broadway* (1949), which was nominated for a Writers Guild award, turned out to be the musical that reunited Fred Astaire and Ginger Rogers, although it had started as an Astaire/Judy Garland vehicle. It was Comden and Green's first original screenplay, incorporating a George and Ira Gershwin classic, "They Can't Take That Away From Me," and some new works by veteran songwriter Harry Warren. By any standard, the story of *The Barkleys of Broadway* is slight, involving a successful dancing duo who become temporarily estranged when the man falls for his partner's understudy, and his partner is almost led into a career as a stage actress. In movie history, the film is important as the last one to pair the greatest dancing team in the history of the cinema. It is significant in the career of Comden and Green, because it shows them creating a story in the environment that would become the frame-

work for many of their later screenplays: show business.

The year 1949 is notable as the year Comden and Green's movie career shifted into high gear with the movie version of *On the Town*, a milestone in the history of the Hollywood musical. The story of three sailors (Gene Kelly, Frank Sinatra, and Jules Munshin) on leave in New York City, it is the first of a trio of films to be directed jointly by Stanley Donen and Gene Kelly, and it represents a stylistic breakthrough in terms of choreography and pacing, much as the stage original did. The music of the film owes little to the original—only four of the Bernstein numbers were retained; the rest of the music was provided by Roger Edens. (Edens won an Oscar which he shared with the film's musical director Lennie Hayton.) The freshness of *On the Town* is due to the teams of Kelly/Donen and Comden/Green. It still seems a very modern musical, with its innovative use of New York locations. But *On the Town*, a Writers Guild award winner, is equally a screenplay achievement. The openly comic satirical numbers register strongly, particularly the "Miss Turnstiles" sequences.

Comden and Green use the selection for a subway "Queen for a Day" (and Kelly's subsequent infatuation with Miss Turnstiles) to ridicule the constant search in Hollywood for new faces and the publicity that goes with it. Though working with six characters, they manage to give the three sailors and their girlfriends (Betty Garrett, Ann Miller, and Vera-Ellen) complete backgrounds, and to differentiate one from another so that they never appear simply to be parts of a convenient formula.

When the next Comden and Green/Kelly and Donen collaboration, *Singin' in the Rain*, was released three years later in 1952, it was overshadowed by the critical reception of its predecessor. In the years that followed, the later film would largely eclipse *On the Town* in popular memory and would come to equal it in critical acclaim. *Singin' in the Rain* has many of the qualities evident in *On the Town*: a sense of freedom from the restrictions of the sound stage (though it was shot almost entirely on sound stages), energy in the choreography and editing, and exuberance among the principal performers (Kelly, Donald O'Connor, and Debbie Reynolds). It is the story of silent-movie star Don Lockwood (Kelly) whose romantic screen partnership with brainless vamp Lina Lamont (Jean Hagen) is threatened by the advent of the talkies. Thanks to the encouragement of his former vaudeville sidekick Cosmo Brown (O'Connor), and the

Gene Kelly in Singin' in the Rain. *This song-and-dance routine is one of the best-known sequences in the history of Hollywood musicals.*

love of aspiring actress Kathy Selden (Reynolds), who turns out to have a wonderful singing voice, Lockwood manages to part with Lina and salvage a disastrous film by turning it into a musical.

The screenplay for *Singin' in the Rain* is undoubtedly superior to that for *On the Town*. Comden and Green set the film during a transitional period in Hollywood history when the development of talking pictures was bringing about great changes in filmmaking. Comden and Green talked to veteran Hollywood employees to gather stories of the problems studios faced when converting to sound, and they used this material to spoof many musical film traditions. The movie opens with a parody of a Hollywood premiere: Kelly, resplen-

dent in white overcoat, tells a gossip columnist a romanticized version of his early career, while the audience sees, accompanied by his voice-over, his tawdry beginnings. Even the traditional meeting scene is handled with wit: Don, escaping from a horde of fans, climbs onto a streetcar and drops into an open automobile driven by Kathy. She finds him conceited and pretends to be a "serious actress," disdainful of his career. Shortly afterwards, at a party celebrating the premiere of Don's latest picture, it is Kathy who bursts out of the surprise cake, prompting Don to remark: "Well, if it isn't Ethel Barrymore." *Singin' in the Rain* won Comden and Green their second Writers Guild award.

Their next screenplay was *The Band Wagon*

Lobby poster for the film in which Comden and Green drew upon their experiences in the New York theater world

(1953), for which Comden and Green received their first Academy Award nomination. The film was inspired by a 1931 Broadway revue, also titled *The Band Wagon,* in which Fred Astaire had appeared. The M-G-M musical is built around songs written by Arthur Schwartz and Howard Dietz for the revue and for four other Broadway plays, plus the song "That's Entertainment," which Schwartz and Dietz wrote specifically for the film. Former Hollywood dancer Tony Hunter (Astaire) comes to New York to try to revive his career. Two writer friends, Lester and Lily Martin (Oscar Levant and Nanette Fabray, playing characters modeled on Green and Comden) have gotten him a starring part in a show, but he quarrels with egotistical director Jeffrey Cordova (Jack Buchanan) and costar Gaby (Cyd Charisse). When the director's attempts to transform the show into an extravagant reworking of the Faust legend fail, Hunter suggests they produce a revue. The show is a success, and he wins over his antagonistic leading lady. Well-directed by Vincente Minnelli, *The Band Wagon* is a triumph not only because it epitomizes the golden rule of musicals—that a conflict should be stated, developed, and finally resolved through music—

but also because it does so with good humor, energy, and wit.

Perhaps inevitably, Comden and Green's next film after *The Band Wagon* seemed an anticlimax. While *It's Always Fair Weather* (1955) is not flawed in all respects, it is below the standards of Comden and Green's three previous films and is probably the weakest of the films directed by Gene Kelly and Stanley Donen. It tells the story of three GIs (Kelly, Michael Kidd, and Dan Dailey) who arrange to meet again ten years after World War II. By then they are all failures, but the men redeem themselves through the interest and affection of a coordinator of a television program (Cyd Charisse). Apart from some extraordinary dance routines, it is the last part of the film, dealing with the television show, that displays the most signs of coming to life. This is because Comden and Green are able to return to a familiar subject: the satirizing of show business. In this case, it is show business's latest offshoot, television, which bears the brunt of the attack, as Comden and Green score on this new target just as well as they had on their previous ones. They were nominated for both an Academy Award and the Writers Guild award for their screenplay.

Michael Kidd, Gene Kelly, and Dan Dailey in It's Always Fair Weather, *the first of their musicals for which Comden and Green wrote all the lyrics*

By the time they wrote *It's Always Fair Weather,* Comden and Green were already referred to as "vets" of the movie musical (less than a decade earlier they had been novices). But by 1955 the golden age of the M-G-M musical was nearly over, and while the previous decade had seen six Comden and Green screenplays, the next would see only three, two of them nonmusicals, and none of them up to the standard of *Singin' in the Rain* or *The Band Wagon. Auntie Mame* (1958) is a fairly straight adaptation of a Broadway hit, less an independent project than a showcase for Rosalind Russell, who stars as the eccentric and outrageous socialite Mame Dennis. Comden and Green's contribution to the movie seems to have been limited, though they were presumably responsible for toning down some of the racier aspects of the original show and for introducing moments of pathos that punctuate the movie.

With *Bells Are Ringing* (1960), directed by Vincente Minnelli, the duo returned to the format of the musical. The script was an adaptation of one of their own Broadway hits, which had opened four years earlier under the direction of Jerome Rob-

bins. The film centers upon an answering service operator (Judy Holliday) who falls in love with one of her clients (Dean Martin), whom she has never seen. When professional troubles strike him, she tries to console him by posing as a sophisticated psychic. The film won Comden and Green their third Writers Guild award; it was their last film for the Freed unit.

Since then they have written only one screenplay, *What a Way to Go!* (1964), an unsuccessful comedy about a woman (Shirley MacLaine) who is widowed several times by wealthy husbands. Their flair for satire can be seen in some of the film's characters, such as an uncultured millionaire (Robert Mitchum), an avant-garde artist (Paul Newman), and, particularly, an egotistical movie star played by Gene Kelly.

The movie-writing career of Comden and Green peaked in the early 1950s. At its zenith, they were the royal family of Hollywood musicals, bringing to their screenplays the well-developed characters and the wit that made *On the Town, Singin' in the Rain,* and *The Band Wagon,* three of the greatest musicals of all time. They are satirists of the

Rosalind Russell in Auntie Mame

1950s school, avoiding political or social material, or else approaching it at one remove, through a satire of show business. Like most classical satirists, they are conservative—the artistic avant-garde is one of their favorite targets. Theirs is a world of solid values, and it is a little exclusive in the sense that a certain level of sophistication is required to appreciate it. In 1961, Comden declared: "We've got no ax to grind. . . . We're not political satirists, we satirize false values. . . ." "Human foolishness, things that last," added Green.

Comden and Green have repeatedly insisted that they cannot say who had what idea; their teamwork is second nature. Or as Comden puts it: "If I'm ever without Adolph, it will simply be because he has been run over by a truck."

References:

Peter Lyon, "Two Minds that Beat as One," *Holiday* (30 December 1961): 149-152, 155, 174-175;

Paul Kresh, "Betty Comden and Adolph Green: A Profile," *Stereo Review*, 30 (April 1973): 54-63.

Francis Ford Coppola
(7 April 1939-   )

Richard Macksey
Johns Hopkins University

MOTION PICTURES: *Tonight for Sure* (Premier Pictures, 1962), screenplay;

The Magic Voyage of Sinbad (American International, 1962), English version adaptation;

Battle Beyond the Sun (American International, 1963), English version adaptation;

Dementia 13 (American International, 1963), screenplay;

You're a Big Boy Now (Warner Bros.-Seven Arts Productions, 1966), screenplay;

Is Paris Burning? (Paramount, 1966), screenplay by Coppola, Gore Vidal, Jean Aurenche, Pierre Bost, and Claude Brulé;

This Property is Condemned (Paramount, 1966), screenplay by Coppola, Fred Coe, and Edith Sommer, based on the one-act play by Tennessee Williams;

The Rain People (Warner Bros.-Seven Arts, 1969), screenplay;

Patton (20th Century-Fox, 1970), screenplay by Coppola and Edmund H. North;

The Godfather (Paramount, 1972), screenplay by Coppola and Mario Puzo;

The Conversation (Paramount, 1974), screenplay;

The Godfather, Part II (Paramount, 1974), screenplay by Coppola and Puzo;

The Great Gatsby (Paramount, 1974), screenplay adapted by Coppola from the novel by F. Scott Fitzgerald;

Apocalypse Now (United Artists, 1979), screenplay by Coppola and John Milius;

One from the Heart (Columbia, 1982), screenplay by Coppola and Armyan Bernstein;

Rumble Fish (Universal, 1983), screenplay by Coppola and S. E. Hinton;

The Cotton Club (Orion, 1984), screenplay by Coppola and William Kennedy; story by Coppola, Kennedy, and Puzo.

Francis Ford Coppola

Francis Ford Coppola is one of the first and most successful graduates of the California film schools. Like many of his peers, he has been fascinated with movies since childhood and has drawn on the whole of American film culture as inspiration for his work. His technical roots are in the conventions of the American genre film, whose formulae he has managed to transform stunningly, from his earliest exploitation and horror films—like *Tonight for Sure* (1962) and *Dementia 13* (1963)—to his recent musical, *One from the Heart* (1982). Master of the gangster film (*The Godfather*, 1972, and its sequel *The Godfather, Part II* in 1974), the detective film (*The Conversation*, 1974), the war epic (*Patton*, 1970, and *Apocalypse Now*, 1979). Coppola has also tried his hand at the youth picture (*You're a Big Boy Now*, 1966 and *Rumble Fish*, 1983), and the road picture (*The Rain People*, 1969). He has also been fascinated by two deeply troubling themes: the seductions of power (corporate and political), its nature and its price, and the claims of the family in its rituals, its ties, and its moral relation to society.

Coppola was born in Detroit on 7 April 1939, the second child of Carmine and Italia Pennino Coppola. The family, which moved to the New York City area shortly after Francis's birth, had an artistic background. Carmine Coppola is a concert flutist, composer, and conductor. The elder Coppola's career was, by his son's account, often frustrating, but he played first flute under Arturo Toscanini in the NBC symphony and did occasional arrangements for Radio City Music Hall. Italia Coppola, daugher of Italian musician Francesco Pennino, had been, briefly, a screen actress. She made appearances in a few Vittorio de Sica films. Francis's older brother, August, who seems to have been a major early influence, became a teacher of comparative literature, and he has published fiction. His younger sister, born in 1947, is actress Talia Shire.

Coppola grew up in a succession of New York City bedroom communities; he claimed on one occasion that the family had moved thirty times during his childhood and youth. Most of these years were spent in Queens and Long Island. At age nine he was stricken with a paralytic polio; he was confined to bed for almost a year and during this time began experimenting with puppets, films, and tapes. He later observed that "the technical thing for gadgetry and the interest in plays and puppets and theatre and musical-comedy sort of came together in film, which was like a playground for all those things."

As a boy he was an accomplished tuba player and won a music scholarship to the New York Military Academy at Cornwall-on-Hudson, which seems to have been more of a trial than his polio. He finally left the military school after a dispute about the book and lyrics he wrote for a class musical that were rewritten without his approval. He transferred to Great Neck High School for his senior year, and, after his graduation in 1955, entered Hofstra College in Hempstead, Long Island, where he majored in dramatic arts. He has said that even then he was committed to film, but he felt the importance (learned from the precept of master filmmaker Sergei Eisenstein) of first applying himself to all the stage crafts that play a role in production. He was elected president of the campus dramatic society, The Green Wig, and, at the same time, of the musical comedy club, the Kaleidoscopians; he merged the two groups into a new organization, the Spectrum Players, which presented a strenuous

weekly series of productions. He wrote the book and lyrics for a musical comedy, "A Delicate Touch," directed several musicals and *A Streetcar Named Desire,* and tried to found a cinema workshop. He contributed some stories to the college literary magazine, *Word:* "The Garden of the Little Punk Princess," "The Battle of the Lions," "Del Vecchio," and "Candide—or Pessimism," and he also served on the school paper as editor of music and drama.

Graduating with a B.A. degree in theater in 1959, he enrolled in the M.F.A. film program of the University of California at Los Angeles, where he studied under Dorothy Arzner. It was during the years at UCLA that Coppola actually received some production experience, working in the growing market for "nudie" films. Russ Meyer, the producer, writer, and director of soft-core pornographic films, had just grossed over one million dollars with *The Immoral Mr. Teas* (1959); "nudie" films were suddenly a legitimate business and student filmmakers in the Los Angeles area could find ready employment as writers, cameramen, and even directors with producers in search of cheap talent. Coppola first worked on a short about voyeurism titled *The Peeper;* later, he shot some "erotic inserts" to be added to a German film, *Mit Eva fing die Sunde an* (1958, distributed in the United States as *The Playgirls and the Bellboy*). Finally, when the producers refused to allow him to direct his own work, he borrowed a few thousand dollars for his own feature, *Tonight for Sure* (1962).

In early 1962, Coppola completed a ninety-nine page manuscript for a film to be called "Pilma, Pilma." The script won him the $2,000 Samuel Goldwyn Award for 1962 and proved to be his introduction to the industry as a "promising young writer," leading eventually to his contract with Seven Arts. Meanwhile, desperate for any employment in the film industry, Coppola took a job with low-budget producer and director Roger Corman; he considers this to be his first true professional work. His first job for Corman was writing English dialogue for a Russian import film, *Sadko* (retitled *The Magic Voyage of Sinbad,* 1962). This job was a highly imaginative one for Coppola since he knew no Russian and was charged with giving the film exploitable elements that would appeal to an American audience. His work for Corman extended to a variety of activities: dialogue coach on *The Tower of London* (1962), assistant director on *The Premature Burial* (1962), associate producer and (uncredited) director of photography for the second unit of *The Terror* (1963). He also wrote English dialogue for another Russian film, *Nebo zovyot* (retitled *Battle Beyond the Sun*, 1963).

When Corman needed a sound man for *The Young Racers* (1963), to be shot on location in Ireland, Coppola did a little homework on the Perfectone recorder and volunteered for the job. This film proved to be a turning point in his life and career for several reasons: while in Ireland he met and subsequently married Eleanor Neal, a young artist with the crew; and he had the opportunity to direct. Coppola proposed to use the sets from *The Young Racers,* making a horror film with the crew and gear already on location at the Irish castle. Corman agreed to finance the project on the basis of a single scene—night at the castle, a naked woman with five dolls, a pond, and the apparition of a seven-year-old girl, her hair floating in the water. The rest of the script for what was to become *Dementia 13* was roughed out later, supposedly in three days. The initial stake from Corman was $20,000, which Coppola managed to double by selling the British rights to Raymond Stross.

In *Dementia 13,* a family has gathered in their Irish castle to await the reading of a will; during the course of one night, several people are murdered with an ax. While the film looks its budget and has the wooden dialogue and sketchy plotting standard for the genre, it is an intelligent, workmanlike use of standard Corman materials. Many of the scenes are very well composed, and the atmosphere is always sustained. The gothic family, the Hallorans, do, in a sense, anticipate the Corleones of *The Godfather* in their drive for power and their appetite for violent solutions. As a twenty-three-year-old's first commercial film it is certainly not a classic, but it did demonstrate that Coppola had passed his apprenticeship. A decade later he said, "It was the only film I've ever *enjoyed* working on."

Shortly after *Dementia 13* was completed, Seven Arts, a corporation that packaged films, offered Coppola a job adapting Carson McCullers's *Reflections in a Golden Eye.* Although his script was not used (the novel was not filmed until 1967), Seven Arts liked his work well enough to sign him as a contract writer. While under contract, Coppola learned the frustrations of the writer cut off from the productions of films. He says that during the period he worked on eleven scripts, but most were aborted or reworked. He collaborated (without credit) on early drafts of scripts for *Arrivederci Baby* (1966), a black comedy about a wife murderer, and wrote three screenplays that were never filmed. He later discussed the frustrations of this period: "The

screenwriter's position is, in a word, impossible. Ridiculous. He gets a lot of money, but he has absolutely nothing to say about his film. . . ." After reiterating that the writer is the one essential element in getting any movie started, "the first bait," and that the writer cannot be hired with the certainty of results with which a producer hires gaffers and cameramen, Coppola adds: "A screenplay, of course, is not a finished piece of art; it's only the blueprint for a film. This becomes clear when you direct from a script you've written. After spending two months visualizing the female lead as short and fat, you must be willing to dump her when you suddenly find a tall, skinny actress who is better for the part. The footage you have shot is not a finished piece of art, either; it's only the basis for the actual picture you end up with. . . . I have written and I have directed, and although I view them both as part of the same process, writing is for me much the more difficult of the two."

Just *how* difficult Coppola was to discover in his frustrating collaborative role on the screenplay of *Is Paris Burning?* (1966). For this adaptation of the book by Larry Collins and Dominique Lapierre, Paramount enlisted a large group of writers that certainly never worked as a team. When the film was completed, Coppola shared credits with Gore Vidal, Jean Aurenche, Pierre Bost, and Claude Brulé. Another screenplay on which he worked during this period was *This Property Is Condemned* (1966), sharing credits with Fred Coe and Edith Sommer. The film, directed by Sydney Pollack, was "suggested" by the Tennessee Williams one-act play of the same title. Williams's play forms only the frame for a rather conventional melodrama; while most of the first and last five minutes of the film are verbatim from Williams, the rest of the picture involves a shift of focus from Willie (Mary Badham) to her older sister Alva (Natalie Wood). As a result of these changes, the film's conclusion seems forced and poorly motivated.

For a screenwriter in his mid-twenties, Coppola was making very good money—one thousand dollars a week—but he hoped to make enough money to finance a film of his own. He put all of his savings (about twenty thousand dollars) into the stock market and lost it all. In an effort to recoup, he accepted an assignment from 20th Century-Fox to write a screenplay on the military career of George S. Patton. The timing of the project and the choice of the writer seem at first strange: a flamboyant military hero was an unlikely subject to attract audiences during the Vietnam war, and Coppola was too young to have had any personal

George C. Scott in Patton, *the film for which Coppola won his first Academy Award*

knowledge of the mystique that once surrounded Patton and the third army. Several writers had already tried their hand at the project, but the screenplay submitted by Coppola would eventually become the film that won him his first Academy Award. Although totally removed from the experience of World War II, Coppola seems to have responded to the paradoxes that he recognized in the general's character, the histrionic crudities of the public self and the nostalgic chivalry of the closet poet. Coppola has stated that he wanted to reveal the Don Quixote in Patton's extravagance. However, amid all this instability, he also develops the strain of Patton's rationalism, allowing the general to recognize that he has become an anachronism. Nearly five years elapsed between Coppola's writing the screenplay and *Patton*'s release in 1970.

It won Academy Awards for best picture, best director (Franklin J. Schafner), best actor (George C. Scott), and best screenplay, which Coppola shared with Edmund H. North, who made the final revisions.

While under contract to Seven Arts, Coppola had been working on an idea for a "personal" film about a nineteen-year-old who discovers the big city. He realized that Seven Arts had a claim on all his writing and that if the script were good, they would assign it to an experienced director. He yearned to direct it himself. He came across a novel by a young English writer, David Benedictus, that followed a callow nineteen-year-old through his discovery of London. He optioned the novel, wrote a screenplay that combined two characters, and used the novel's title: *You're a Big Boy Now.* He now owned a property and could do business with Seven Arts, who agreed to produce the film with Coppola as director. The final screenplay was about a naive young man (Peter Kastner) who leaves his overprotective family to live in New York City, where he comes into contact with a variety of eccentrics. Coppola's only comedy to date, it is a fast-paced, quirky film that shows influences ranging from Richard Lester to the early French new wave films (particularly in the fantasies of the protagonist). Coppola also submitted the film as the thesis for his M.F.A. degree.

With this experience as a director behind him, Coppola was hired by Warner Bros.—now owned by Seven Arts—to direct a contemporary version of the stage musical *Finian's Rainbow* (1968), with Fred Astaire as star. Although he did not write the screenplay, he did rework it to add to the period feeling, adding lines from old Astaire films. Warner Bros. was pleased enough with the film to offer him the assignment of directing *Mame;* he refused. His work on *Finian's Rainbow*, with the constraints of a studio production, had been a frustrating experience; now he was determined to make a film over which he could have artistic control.

That film was *The Rain People*, based on a short story he had written in 1960. It is about a pregnant housewife, Natalie Ravenna (Shirley Knight), who suddenly leaves her home and husband and starts out on an aimless cross-country trip. The scale of the film is deliberately small, with most of the heroine's perplexity quietly established in the early scenes and through flashbacks. The most impressive achievement is the tension Coppola builds between Natalie and the two males she meets on her trip: "Killer" Kilgannon (James Caan), a brain-damaged football player, and Gordon (Robert Duvall), an unstable state trooper. Unfortunately, the film is marred by its abrupt, melodramatic conclusion: Kilgannon intervenes in a fight between Natalie and Gordon, and is shot and killed by Gordon's daughter.

While shooting *The Rain People*, Coppola conceived the idea of an independent film studio for new talent. Funded with $400,000 from Warner Bros., based in an old San Francisco warehouse, and staffed with some of the youngest and brightest people in the industry, American Zoetrope was designed to put the film industry back in the hands of the artists. The original Zoetrope was loosely organized, to say the least, but the nucleus of the group included, in addition to Coppola himself, George Lucas, Walter Murch, John Milius, Willard Huyck and Gloria Katz, John Korty, Carroll Ballard, Martin Scorsese, Hal Barwood, and Matthew Robbins. Zoetrope's first production was *THX-1138*

Elizabeth Hartman and Peter Kastner in You're a Big Boy Now, *the film Coppola submitted as his M.F.A. thesis*

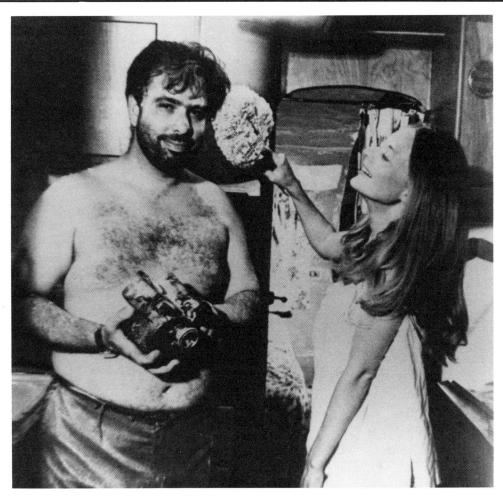

Francis Ford Coppola and Shirley Knight on the set of The Rain People, *based on a short story Coppola wrote in 1960*

produced by Coppola and directed by George Lucas from a script he wrote with Murch. After screening this film, a group of Warner Bros. executives withdrew their sponsorship of Zoetrope, and it ceased to exist as a production company, although it continued as a production facility.

At this juncture, in part to recoup his finances, Coppola took on another screenwriting assignment: an adaptation of F. Scott Fitzgerald's *The Great Gatsby* for Paramount. There were disagreements between Coppola and the film's director, Jack Clayton, from the outset, with Coppola arguing that some of the more elliptical elements in Fitzgerald's novel had to be made explicit. The film was not completed and released until 1974; it was neither a critical nor a financial success, but by that time Coppola's reputation had been firmly established.

A turning point in Coppola's career came with another assignment from Paramount, an offer for

him to adapt and direct Mario Puzo's novel *The Godfather*. Coppola worked effectively with Puzo in bringing shape and visual immediacy to the lengthy novel about a Mafia don. Some aspects of the novel are elided in the adaptation, but the main lines of a plot that brought together Coppola's enduring fascination with the dynamics of family and power are clear and fully articulated. The basic notions of the film are simple but powerfully deployed, with the recurrent family rituals balanced by periodic outbreaks of violence. The conflict between the apparent security of the family and the incipient anarchy of business is sustained. Out of a bestseller, a comfortable dynastic plot, some richly detailed gangster stereotypes, and a good dose of bloodshed, Coppola, aided by a powerful cast and an excellent technical crew, fashioned an enormously popular success, exceeding Paramount's expectations. The Academy of Motion Picture Arts and Sciences certified this success with awards for

Marlon Brando in The Godfather, *adapted from Mario Puzo's best-selling novel*

best film, best actor (Marlon Brando), and best screenplay. Coppola also received the first of his Directors Guild awards. Most important for his career, the acclaim and his share of the profits brought him, at last, the opportunity to make deals and to indulge his dream of personal filmmaking.

The project that Coppola next undertook was one that he had been long nursing. *The Conversation* (1974) was about surveillance expert Harry Caul (Gene Hackman) who, after years in his business, finds himself becoming emotionally involved with two of his subjects, an unfaithful wife (Cindy Williams) and her lover (Frederic Forrest). The idea for the film stemmed from a 1966 conversation Coppola had had with director Irvin Kershner about the diabolic possibilities of "surveillance technology": the ability of sophisticated sound equipment to lift a private conversation out of a crowd. Coppola decided to shift the story from the victims of the surveillance to the man spying on them.

Caul (named in part for Hermann Hesse's

protagonist, Harry Haller, in *Der Steppenwolf*)) has almost no private life; for example, he entertains himself by playing the saxophone alone in his apartment. His birthday goes virtually unnoticed. He has a compulsion for privacy, hides his telephone, avoids business contacts, and denies his landlord entrance to his apartment. Coppola has lent Caul much of himself: his childhood polio, Catholicism, fascination with gadgetry. Harry is eventually destroyed by his guilt and fear and literally dismantles his apartment in a vain attempt to find the bugging device he believes to be hidden in it.

After completing his work on *The Conversation*, Coppola accepted the challenge that followed immediately on the success of *The Godfather*—the gamble of risking his reputation on a sequel. He had already won greater artistic control and a larger working budget, but attempts to repeat earlier successes had proven the undoing of too many careers. If in *The Godfather, Part II* (1974) Coppola

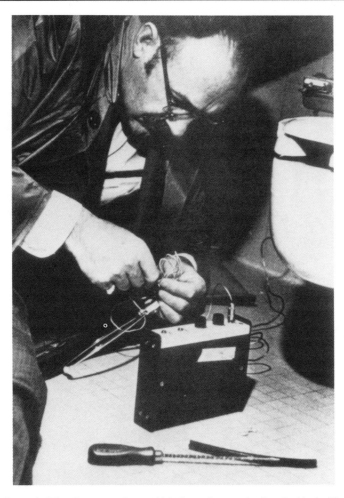

Gene Hackman in The Conversation, *which Coppola conceived as "a kind of horror film"*

failed to achieve quite the popular success of the first film, he still succeeded in making a richer, denser film that powerfully reinterpreted its predecessor.

He collaborated again with the novel's author, Mario Puzo, with Coppola apparently making larger contributions to the story line. The structure that Coppola chose for this lengthy (200-minute) narrative is schematically very simple. After the brief prologue that links Michael Corleone (Al Pacino) to his father's succession, five episodes of flashback trace the career of Vito (Robert De Niro); intercut with Vito's story are the five episodes tracing the career of Michael. The film concludes with a brief but complex epilogue in which Michael poses, perhaps too overtly, the question that colors the entire film: can he lose his family through the pursuit of the power that was supposed to secure it?

The separate stories of Michael and Vito are subtly tied together. We are given not so much a double portrait of the two Corleone dons as a study of Michael's reconstruction of the family history amid his own growing isolation.

Although Coppola has had trouble with the endings of almost all of his films, the epilogue of *The Godfather, Part II* is an extraordinary piece of filmmaking that unites the sequel with its predecessor through the sequence of the final scenes: the execution Michael orders of his brother Fredo; the face of Michael; and then the family dinner table in the old New York home, December 1941. Then Michael sits contemplating his future. His face dissolves again to a brief reprise of Vito's departure from the train station at Corleone after his return to Sicily to settle family accounts with Don Ciccio; the father holds the young Michael at the train window, showing him how to wave goodbye. The last dissolve is back to Michael after Fredo's death, one half of his face masked in shadows. In this sequence Coppola gathers together the themes of both films. As the final, brooding scene suggests, the one inheritance Michael cannot escape is the ethic of the vendetta.

The Godfather, Part II proved to be a worthy successor to *The Godfather*, winning six major Academy Awards, including best picture, best screenplay, best director, and best supporting actor (Robert DeNiro). In November 1977, NBC television broadcast a synoptic version of the two Godfather films as a four-part series entitled *Mario Puzo's The Godfather: The Complete Novel for Television*. The two films were reedited so that events were presented chronologically; seven hours and fourteen minutes of footage were used—including an hour of additional footage, mostly about the young Vito, that was not used in the theatrical prints of the films.

For much of the time immediately following and preceding the release of *The Godfather, Part II* Coppola divided his efforts between screenwriting and work in other areas. He was executive producer of two films directed by friends from his college days: *American Graffiti* (1973), directed by George Lucas, and *The Black Stallion* (1979), directed by Carroll Ballard. He purchased an interest in Cinema 5, a distribution company, bought the Little Fox Theatre in Los Angeles, took an option

on San Francisco radio station KMPX, and became an investor in, and eventually manager of, a weekly magazine titled *City*. In 1972 he directed a revival of Noel Coward's *Private Lives* for the American Conservatory Theatre and staged the American premiere of *The Visit of the Old Lady* by Gottfried von Einem for the San Francisco Opera Company.

Much of this activity had to be abandoned when Coppola began his next film, *Apocalypse Now* (1979). The project, an adaptation of Joseph Conrad's *Heart of Darkness* that would translate the novel to the American experience in Vietnam, began with a treatment by screenwriter John Milius written in 1969. "The most important thing that I wanted to do . . . was to create a film experience that would give its audience a sense of the horror, the madness, the sensuousness, and the moral dilemma of the Vietnam war," Coppola said while filming. After reworking and extending the Milius script during the fall of 1975, Coppola began shooting in the Philippines on 20 March 1976; his schedule called for sixteen weeks on location, and the budget was twelve million dollars. Over a year later, the crew reached its last shooting day; the budget was over thirty million and post-production would take two years longer. A series of problems, including illnesses and typhoons, had delayed shooting, but perhaps the greatest production problem

Robert De Niro in The Godfather, Part II, *one of the few successful film sequels*

Dennis Hopper, Martin Sheen, and Frederic Forrest in Apocalypse Now, *Coppola's Vietnam War version of Joseph Conrad's*
Heart of Darkness

lay in the film's script. As he had done in the past, Coppola began work without a satisfactory ending for his screenplay. He recognized this early enough, and spent long hours closeted with star Marlon Brando experimenting with alternate versions of the script, leaving production at a standstill. "Working on the ending is like trying to climb glass by your fingernails," he confessed.

The film was finally shaped from over two hundred eighty miles of footage, and journalist Michael Herr, author of *Dispatches,* was hired to write the voice-over narration added to the script. The film was finally released in September 1979. Conrad's tale was already a complex story with Marlow (Willard in the film), the company agent, sent to the heart of the Congo to repatriate Kurtz. Coppola's adaptation added another twist, and Willard became the assigned executioner of Kurtz. Much of the film explores the excesses of power gone wild, initially that of the United States in Vietnam,

then, as Willard progresses down the river further from civilization, the power of Kurtz, who has become a virtual god to the natives.

Willard bears a close resemblance to other Coppola protagonists, particularly Harry Caul, in that he is never concerned about the morality of what he is doing—it is just his "mission," his job. (Kurtz calls him "an errand boy sent by grocery clerks to collect a bill.") But Willard changes when he confronts Kurtz, and Coppola begins to explore the similarities between the two. Willard finally kills Kurtz because "everyone wanted it," even Kurtz, but this action causes him to abandon his military life and the amorality that went with it. "I'd never want another (mission)," he realizes, later telling himself, "I wasn't even in their f------ army any more."

Months after the release of *Apocalypse Now,* in early 1980, Coppola purchased the historic Hollywood General Studios, renaming his new plant

Zoetrope Studios. Although some of Coppola's initial projects for Zoetrope fell through, two films went into production in 1980: *The Escape Artist* (1982), directed by Coppola's frequently used cinematographer, Caleb Deschanel, and *Hammett* (1982), the first American film by German director Wim Wenders. Coppola was one of several writers who worked on the screenplay for *Hammett,* based on Joe Gores's novel about mystery novelist Dashiell Hammett, but none of his material was used.

The largest project undertaken by Zoetrope was Coppola's own *One from the Heart* (1982), a contemporary musical filmed entirely on studio sets at a cost of twenty-three million dollars. Coppola directed the film and shared screenplay credit with Armyan Bernstein, who wrote the original screen story. It is about two lovers, Frannie (Terri Garr) and Frank (Frederic Forrest) who become bored with one another, quarrel, separate, take other lovers, then reunite, all in the space of one day. Much of the film is concerned with the dissatisfaction Frannie feels with her life and Frank's inability to understand her. Frank is finally able to win Frannie back when he abandons his dull persona and sings to her at an airport as she prepares to leave with her lover.

Coppola apparently intended *One from the Heart* to be made in the manner of an old-fashioned musical (although the musical numbers are decidedly modern), but he relies entirely on surrealistic sets, elaborate dance numbers, and fantasy sequences, such as when Frank "conducts" an orchestra of wrecked cars that perform by honking their horns, rather then trying to tell a well-developed story. The film was badly received by the critics and never was given national release; it grossed less than one million dollars at the box office, and led to the bankruptcy of Zoetrope.

Two novels by children's novelist S. E. Hinton, *The Outsiders* and *Rumble Fish,* provided the source material for Coppola's next two projects. He received a fan letter from a group of school children telling him that he was their favorite director and Hinton their favorite author, and asking him to film one of Hinton's novels. Coppola acquired the rights to two Hinton books, announcing his intention to make what he termed "art films for teenagers." He directed, but did not write, *The Outsiders* (1983), about the conflicts between upper-and lower-class adolescents in Oklahoma in the 1960s. His screenplay for *Rumble Fish* (1983) was written in collaboration with Hinton. It marked a return to a familiar Coppola theme: the ties of the family. Rusty James (Matt Dillon) is a teenaged boy living with his alcoholic father; the mother had left the family years before. Rusty idolizes his brother Motorcycle Boy (Mickey Rourke), a former gang leader, who has acquired a nearly legendary status among the local youth.

Rumble Fish was another failure for Coppola. Like all of his films since *Apocalypse Now,* it is extremely stylized; in this case, directed in a deliberate attempt to emulate such German expressionists as Robert Wiene and F. W. Murnau. The film is also shot in black and white, probably to suggest the point of view of the color blind Motorcycle Boy; only the rumble fish appear in color. But the main problem of the film is its script; it is nearly plotless, consisting mainly of Rusty James's arguments with his girlfriend, fistfights with other street youth, and visits to a pool hall. The dialogue is extremely trite: "Hey, my brother is cool." "Well, you're better than cool; you're warm." Furthermore, while *The Outsiders* had acceptable box office receipts, *Rumble Fish* did not. The film also received almost unanimously poor reviews, perhaps the worst of Coppola's career. As in the past, Coppola remained undaunted and announced several projects before beginning work on his next film, *The Cotton Club,* about the famous New York jazz club.

The Cotton Club was written by Coppola and novelist William Kennedy from a story by Coppola, Kennedy, and Mario Puzo. The film interweaves two separate stories, that of musician Dixie Dwyer (Richard Gere) and that of dancer Sandman Williams (Gregory Hines). Dwyer saves the life of gangster Dutch Schultz (James Remar), becomes a part of Schultz's entourage, and begins an affair with Schultz's mistress (Diane Lane). Williams, a black man, struggles against racism and falls in love with a woman (Lonette McKee) who passes for white. Both stories reflect some of Coppola's usual concerns—both Dwyer and Williams have problems with their brothers—but it is Williams with whom Coppola most strongly identifies. Ostracized by white society, he is able to force them to accept him because of his great talent; after the movie's release, Coppola stated that he saw parallels between Williams's career and his own.

Francis Ford Coppola's career has tended to blur the traditional distinctions between screenwriter, director, producer, and promoter. As he achieved a position of power in the industry, he was able to explore his conviction that film writing is a continuous process extending from the first concept through to the last stages of editing. He has also worked closely with a creative team who can all make personal contributions to the final "text." As a coordinator of talent he has played many roles, but he still tends to define his own ambitions in terms of writing. "I feel that I'm basically a writer who directs . . . . When people go to see a movie, eighty percent of the effect it has on them was preconceived and precalculated by the writer . . . . So to me, that's the primary act of creation."

Interviews:

Stephen Farber, "Coppola and *The Godfather*," *Sight and Sound*, 41 (Autumn 1972): 217-223;

Brian DePalma, "The Making of *The Conversation*: An Interview with Francis Ford Coppola," *Filmmakers Newsletter*, 7 (May 1974): 30-34;

Marjorie Rosen, "Francis Ford Coppola," *Film Comment*, 10 (July-August 1974): 43-49;

Gabria Belloni and Lorenzo Codelli, "Conversation avec F. F. Coppola," *Positif*, no. 161 (August 1974): 47-54;

W. Murray, "Playboy Interview: Francis Ford Coppola," *Playboy* (July 1975);

Lise Block-Morhange and David Alper, "Entretien avec Francis Ford Coppola," *Cahiers du Cinéma*, no. 304 (October 1979): 7-22;

Fred Robbins, "Interview: Francis Ford Coppola," *Genesis* (April 1980): 41-42, 81;

Francis Coppola and Gay Talese, "The Conversation: Francis Ford Coppola and Gay Talese," *Esquire*, 96 (July 1981): 78-87.

References:

Hal Aigner and Michael Goodwin, "The Bearded Immigrant from Tinsel Town," *City* (July 1974): 12-25;

Randy Baer and Christopher Baffer, "Grooming the Godfather," *Sight and Sound*, 44 (Spring 1975): 83;

Fred Baker, "Francis Ford Coppola on the Director," in *Movie People: At Work in the Business of Film*, edited by Baker and Ross Firestone (New York: Douglas, 1972), pp. 51-69;

Susan Braudy, "Francis Ford Coppola: A Profile," *Atlantic*, 238 (August 1976): 66-73;

Carlos Clarens, "Godfather Sag-a," *Film Comment*, 14 (January-February 1978): 21-23;

Eleanor Coppola, *Notes* (New York: Simon & Schuster, 1979);

Peter Cowie, "Francis Ford Coppola," in *International Film Guide 1976* (London: Tantivy Press, 1975; South Brunswick & New York: A. S. Barnes, 1975), pp. 50-59;

R. D. DeFuria, "*Apocalypse Now:* The Ritual Murder

of Art," *Western Humanities Review*, 34 (Winter 1980); 85-89;

Michael Dempsey, "*Apocalypse Now,*" *Sight and Sound*, 49 (Winter 1979-1980): 5-9;

David Denby, "Stolen Privacy: Coppola's *The Conversation,*" *Sight and Sound*, 43 (Summer 1974): 131-133;

Denby, "The Two Godfathers," *Partisan Review*, 43, no. 1 (1976): 113-118;

Joseph Gellmis, *The Film Director as Superstar* (Garden City: Doubleday, 1970);

Charles Higham, "Director's Guild Winner: Francis Ford Coppola," *Action*, 8 (November 1975): 14-18;

Diane Jacobs, *Hollywood Renaissance* (South Brunswick & New York: A. S. Barnes/London: Tantivy, 1977), pp. 97-121;

Robert K. Johnson, *Francis Ford Coppola* (Boston: G. K. Hall, 1977);

Marsha Kinder, "The Power of Adaptation in *Apocalypse Now,*" *Film Quarterly*, 33 (Winter 1979-1980): 12-20;

Robert Phillip Kolker, *A Cinema of Loneliness* (New York & Oxford: Oxford University Press, 1980);

Axel Madsen, *The New Hollywood: American Movies in the '70s* (New York: Thomas Y. Crowell, 1975);

Joseph McBride, "Coppola Inc.: The Director as Godfather," *American Film* (November 1975): 14-18;

Peter McInerney, "Apocalypse Then: Hollywood Looks Back At Vietnam," *Film Quarterly*, 35 (Winter 1979-1980): 21-32;

James Monaco, *American Film Now* (New York: Oxford University Press, 1979);

Positif, Special issue devoted to Francis Ford Coppola, no. 222 (September 1979);

Michael Pye and Linda Myles, *The Movie Brats: How the Film Generation Took Over Hollywood* (New York: Holt, Rinehart & Winston, 1979);

John Pym, "An Errand Boy's Journey," *Sight and Sound*, 49 (Winter 1979-1980): 9-10;

Lawrence Shaffer, "*The Conversation,*" *Film Quarterly*, 28 (Fall 1974): 54-60;

Garrett Stewart, "Coppola's Conrad: The Repetitions of Complicity," *Critical Inquiry*, 7 (Spring 1981): 455-474;

David Thomson, "The Discreet Charm of *The Godfather,*" *Sight and Sound*, 47 (Spring 1978): 76-80;

Christian Viviani, "L'Opéra des ténèbres," *Positif*, no. 220-221 (July-August 1979): 2-5;

Michael Wood, "Bangs and Whimpers: *Apocalypse*

Now," New York Review of Books, XXVI, 15 (11 October 1979): 17-18;

Joel S. Zuker, *Francis Ford Coppola: A Guide to Ref-* *erences and Resources* (Boston: G. K. Hall, 1984).

Carol Eastman
(Adrien Joyce)
(birth date unknown-   )

Joel Bellman

MOTION PICTURES: *The Shooting* (Walter Reade, 1967), screenplay;

Five Easy Pieces (Columbia, 1970), story by Eastman and Bob Rafelson; screenplay;

Puzzle of a Downfall Child (Universal, 1970), story by Eastman and Jerry Schatzberg; screenplay;

The Fortune (Columbia, 1975), screenplay.

TELEVISION: *Run for Your Life,* two episodes (NBC, 1965-1967).

The career of Carol Eastman—writing as Adrien Joyce—has been characterized primarily by sparsity—sparsity of biographical information, sparsity of output (four films in nine years), and sparseness in the style of her work. The sister of screenwriter Charles Eastman (*Little Fauss and Big Halsy,* 1970), she emerged during the 1970s as an important member of a new generation of filmmakers. In response to the needlessly elaborate, big-budget films of the decade, a smaller European-influenced American film began to appear, championed by filmmakers such as Monte Hellman, Bob Rafelson, and Jack Nicholson. Eastman became part of this group and helped to create a trend of cinema neorealism analogous to the films of the postwar years in Europe.

Eastman's scriptwriting began with two episodes for the television series *Run for Your Life,* which ran from 1965 to 1968, about Paul Bryan (Ben Gazzara), who had a terminal illness and only two years to live; he tried to squeeze a lifetime of experiences into the time he had left, and each episode comprised an adventure on the outskirts of society. This theme of the outsider at odds with society has become a sort of trademark of Eastman's screenwriting.

In 1965 Eastman successfully made the tran-sition to feature films. Her friends Hellman and Nicholson were producing a low-budget Western, *Ride in the Whirlwind* (1965), from their own script. Eastman had a recently completed, similarly themed screenplay; Hellman and Nicholson decided to film the two movies simultaneously. *The Shooting* (1967) is the epitome of the existential Western. In it the three main characters are reduced to their most basic archetypes, and the spare directing style of Monte Hellman was the perfect complement to the unadorned narrative Eastman had fashioned. Willet Gashade (Warren Oates) is searching for the murderer of his friend (Will Hutchins) and for his missing brother Coigne (also played by Oates). He is assisted in the search by a laconic gunfighter named Billy Spear (Jack Nicholson) and a mysterious woman in black (Millie Perkins) who has her own reasons for joining the pursuit. Little is explained of the motivations or origins of any of the characters, and the deliberately ambiguous finale—a climactic shootout involving Gashade's brother—gives the film a weird, dreamlike aura. The two overriding concerns of the film's characters are flight and pursuit; these seem to be the only rationales offered or required.

Produced independently for about $75,000 and distributed by the Walter Reade organization, the film received very limited release and few reviews. Nevertheless, film critics have written well of it retrospectively, and the movie has developed a following over the years.

While Eastman continued to write, Nicholson joined with producer-director Bob Rafelson in another filmmaking venture. They approached Eastman in the late 1960s, and the three of them developed an idea that became her second produced screenplay. The resulting picture starred Nicholson, was directed by Rafelson, and cemented

Jack Nicholson and Millie Perkins in Carol Eastman's existential Western, The Shooting

the reputations of all three: *Five Easy Pieces* (1970), one of the best examples of the disaffected anti-hero cycle of the late 1960s and 1970s. Widely misinterpreted by many critics at the time as an indictment of American society, the film was actually more of a character study of the modern alienated man, a born outcast who has talent but is unable to keep from wasting it (he was an aspiring concert pianist, and the film's title refers to a basic piano lesson book), who cannot sustain a personal relationship (and knows it is largely his own fault), who feels estranged from the world and realizes that this estrangement is due to his lack of focus and direction. The film is a landmark in American cinema, artistically delineating the social and political disorientation that followed in the wake of the intense activism of the middle and late 1960s. Again, the man-on-the-run theme was central to the story, with Rafelson's visual style giving Eastman's script a naturalistic atmosphere. The film earned Academy Award nominations for best picture, best

screenplay, best director, best actor, and best supporting actress (Karen Black).

At that point, while still remaining friends, Eastman parted with Nicholson and Rafelson. Her next project proved a catastrophic mistake, one which may have dealt her career a near-fatal setback. For his feature film directing debut, former fashion photographer Jerry Schatzberg hired Eastman to develop a screenplay based on Schatzberg's story idea about a fashion model suffering a nervous breakdown because of the pressures of her work and inherent emotional instability. *Puzzle of a Downfall Child* (1970) was released a few months after *Five Easy Pieces;* critical reaction was unfavorable, and few critics remembered Eastman's earlier triumph. The problems with the film stemmed partly from a weak premise; a character study of the beauty whose pretty face masks pain was a cliché. Between Eastman's efforts to stretch the idea into a full-length story and Schatzberg's inexperienced directing, the film simply did not work. It

Jack Nicholson as the disaffected protagonist of Eastman's Academy Award-winning Five Easy Pieces

was a disaster for Eastman, Schatzberg, and star Faye Dunaway.

Although Dunaway and Schatzberg recovered, Eastman's momentum virtually stopped. A year later, she talked vaguely in interviews of directing her first feature, to star Jack Nicholson and Jeanne Moreau, but these plans never materialized. Eastman had once been thought to be a major new screenwriting talent, but her early promise seemed destined to go unfulfilled.

After four and a half years, one more Eastman script was produced. In many ways, *The Fortune* (1975) is her most daring screenplay; while it is unconventional in some respects, like her other films, it was released at a time less hospitable to unorthodoxy. The premise is the blackest of black humor: two disreputable schemers, a would-be lothario (Warren Beatty) and a small-time embezzler (Jack Nicholson), plot to murder an heiress (Stockard Channing) for her fortune. The film is written and directed like the most innocent farce. And unlike Eastman's other films, which, though somewhat experimental still reflected the moods of their times, *The Fortune* was released to a public that was not receptive to humor resulting from failed murder attempts. Furthermore, the stars were cast against type, the female lead (Stockard Channing) was an unknown, and the director, Mike Nichols, seemed more at home with realistic social satire. Ignoring almost every rule for success, *The Fortune* was perhaps inevitably a commercial disaster. Still, it elicited praise from some viewers who found the

humor charming and even hilarious in a sinister way. Moreover, underneath the humor there were buried more serious themes.

Freddie, the Channing character, is little more than an object of scorn for the men, but she is so naive that the two men become the objects of real scorn. (One of the causal factors in the trio's badly conceived marriage scheme is the Mann Act, which forbids transporting a woman across state lines for immoral purposes; comment is thus indirectly made on the status of women in the 1920s, when the film takes place, as well as on the sort of morality laws that are absurdly outdated, yet still enforced.) A bittersweet conclusion—in which Freddie elects to stay with the men she now refuses to believe were trying to kill her—leaves a slightly discomfiting feeling with the audience, because the film does not offer the standard comedy resolution. The film demands a tolerance from its audience, and Hollywood comedies traditionally do not make such demands.

Though she still used her pen name, Adrien Joyce, in the credits, Eastman described *The Fortune* as the start of a new trend in her own work, that of using her real name in the credits. But no other screenplays have followed. She has suffered some of the same setbacks as a handful of other promising screenwriters: good notices for initial work, followed by business complications and questionable artistic decisions, then bad luck, loss of confidence, and finally, undeserved neglect.

References:
Norman Dickens, *Jack Nicholson: The Search for a
Superstar* (New York: Signet, 1975);

Danny Peary, *Cult Movies* (New York: Dell, 1981):
318-320.

Lonne Elder III
(26 December 1931-   )

Joseph Millichap
Western Kentucky University

See also the Elder entries in *DLB 7, Twentieth-Century American Dramatists; DLB 38, Afro-American Writers After 1955: Dramatists and Prose Writers.*

MOTION PICTURES: *Melinda* (1972), screenplay;
Sounder (20th Century-Fox, 1972), screenplay;
Part 2, Sounder (Gamma III, 1976), screenplay;
Bustin' Loose (Universal Pictures, 1981), adaptation.

PLAY PRODUCTIONS: *Ceremonies in Dark Old
Men*, Staten Island, New York, Wagner College, July 1965; New York, Saint Marks Playhouse; revised and transferred 28 April 1969
to New York, Pocket Theatre, 4 February
1969;
Charades on East Fourth Street, Montreal, Expo '67,
1967.

BOOK: *Ceremonies in Dark Old Men* (New York:
Farrar, Straus & Giroux, 1969).

TELEVISION: *Camera Three* (CBS, 1963), scripts;
The Terrible Veil (NBC, 1963), script;
N.Y.P.D. (ABC, 1967-1968), scripts;
McCloud (NBC, 1970-1971), scripts;
Ceremonies in Dark Old Men (ABC, 1975), teleplay;
A Woman Called Moses (NBC, 1978), teleplay.

OTHER: *Charades on East Fourth Street*, in *Black
Drama Anthology*, edited by Woodie King, Jr.
and Ron Milner (New York: New American
Library, 1971).

PERIODICAL PUBLICATIONS: "Comment:
Rambled Thoughts," *Black Creation*, 4 (Summer 1973): 48;
"Lorraine Hansberry: Social Consciousness and

*Lonne Elder III (courtesy of the Billy Rose Theatre Collection,
The New York Public Library at Lincoln Center, Astor, Lenox
and Tilden Foundations)*

The Will," *Freedomways*, 19 (Fourth Quarter
1979): 213-218.

Calvin Lockhart in Melinda. *Elder adapted Raymond Cis-theri's screen story, making the central characters black.*

Lonne Elder III is a talented and creative actor, playwright, and screenwriter whose career has evolved from acting and writing for the stage to acting and writing for the screen. Elder has remained committed to a program of raising audience consciousness of racial tensions through his analysis of the black identity in modern America. In particular, his vision has stressed the personal dedication necessary for Afro-Americans to overcome the handicaps imposed by generations of white prejudice and black fear. He has also used his writing to help change the portrayal of blacks in films and on television.

Elder was born in Americus, Georgia, but his family moved to New Jersey when he was an infant. He has two brothers and twin sisters. After losing both his father, Lonne Elder II, and his mother, Quincy Elder, in 1943, he was brought up by his aunt and his uncle (who was a numbers runner); his childhood experiences have provided the basis for his plays. After high school, Elder briefly attended New Jersey State University before being drafted in 1952 into the U.S. Army. Following his discharge from the army, he enrolled at New Jersey State Teachers College (now Trenton State Teachers College). He worked at odd jobs, for example, as a dock worker and waiter, while beginning his career as a writer. Joining the Harlem Writers Guild, Elder met such important writers as Lorraine Hansberry and Douglas Turner Ward, and it was Ward who urged Elder to become a play-

wright. He made his Broadway acting debut in Hansberry's *A Raisin in the Sun* (produced in 1959), and he also played Clem in Ward's *Day of Absence* (produced in 1965).

After getting a job as staff writer on the CBS series *Camera Three* in 1963, Elder began to concentrate on his play writing; his earliest works were produced by black theater groups. An early version of *Ceremonies In Dark Old Men* was produced in 1965; it earned Elder a John Hay Whitney Fellowship to study drama and filmmaking at Yale University from 1965 to 1967. The New York City Mobilization for Youth commissioned him to write *Charades on East Fourth Street* (produced in 1967), about a gang of black youths holding a kangaroo court trial of a white policeman. It was first performed at Expo '67 in Montreal, Canada.

A series of other grants followed Elder's studies at Yale, including the John Golden Fellowship, the Joseph E. Levine Fellowship in Filmmaking, and the ABC Television Writing Fellowship. The latter led to a position as staff writer on the television series *N.Y.P.D.* in 1967-1968; this realistic program about the New York City Police Department was one of the few dramatic series then being made in New York, allowing Elder to work on the show and still remain near the theater district. His job on *N.Y.P.D.* not only gave Elder financial stability but also allowed him to sharpen his dramatic skills and provided an opportunity to write for one of the first black characters seen in a regular series, Detective Jeff Ward (Robert Hooks).

The revised version of *Cermonies in Dark Old Men* was performed in 1969. This play, about a black family's disintegration because of an inability to find purpose in white America, brought Elder his first critical acclaim. It received several awards, including the Los Angeles Drama Critics Award and the Outer Circle and Drama Desk awards, and was second in the Pulitzer Prize voting. The play was also produced on ABC television in 1975.

After working again as a staff writer, this time on the *McCloud* series (1970 to 1971), Elder made his screenwriting debut with *Melinda* (1972). This mystery film was adapted from a screen story by Raymond Cistheri; Elder changed the story, making the central characters black. Disc jockey Frankie J. Parker (Calvin Lockhart) is falsely accused of murdering his girlfriend Melinda (Vonetta McGee). To clear himself, Parker searches for the real killer. Elder also made his only screen appearance in the film, portraying police lieutenant Daniels. *Melinda* is a blending of Elder's commercial efforts for television and his more serious efforts

Paul Winfield and Kevin Hooks as father and son in Sounder, *Elder's examination of a Depression-era black family*

at probing the effects of deprivation and prejudice on black personality. He says he wrote the film quickly to take advantage of the market for exploitation movies like *Shaft* (1971) and *Superfly* (1972) that were aimed at black audiences.

Also in 1972, Elder's most important work, *Sounder,* was filmed. Working in collaboration with producer Robert Radnitz, who specializes in family films, and director Martin Ritt, whose films had shown a knack for dealing with the South, Elder created a moving film which received much critical acclaim and provided an artistic counterpoint to the exploitation film trend. The screenplay was adapted from William H. Armstrong's Newberry-Prize-winning novel, which described the impoverished yet dignified lives of a family of black share-croppers in rural Louisiana during the Depression. The story centers on the maturation of young David (Kevin Hooks) during the year his father (Paul Winfield) has to spend on the chain gang for stealing food to feed his hungry family. David searches out his father on the distant prison farm in a sort of initiation journey which leads him to Miss Johnson, a committed black teacher who promises a way out of poverty and ignorance. Sounder is David's hound dog, a symbol for the family's tough yet warm persistence in their struggle to survive the injustice of the white society, represented by the local sheriff (James Best). *Sounder* was one of the most critically successful films of 1972 earning an Academy Award nomination for best picture.

In 1976 Radnitz and Elder reteamed to make *Part 2, Sounder,* a continuation of the original story. A less effective director and cast kept the film from having the success of the original work. The story of building a school for David (Darryl Young) clearly reveals Elder's continuing interest in self-help and self-realization for blacks.

Several years passed before Elder received another screen credit, *Bustin' Loose* (1981). It was a project conceived by comedian Richard Pryor, who starred, coproduced, and wrote the screen story; Elder is credited as adapting Pryor's story. The film is about an ex-convict (Pryor) who becomes bus driver for a group of handicapped children. He overcomes his initial dislike of the children and gives them new self-esteem.

Most of Lonne Elder's work has been for television. Much of this writing is, like *Melinda,* merely good entertainment. But his plays and his screenplay for *Sounder* reveal Elder to be a committed, intelligent writer whose work is shaped by a responsible vision of the black experience as an important part of modern American life.

Interviews:

Richard F. Sheperd, "Lonne Elder Talks of Theatre in Black and White," *New York Times,* 8 February 1969, I: 22;

Liz Gant, "An Interview With Lonne Elder," *Black World,* 22 (April 1973): 38-48;

Rochelle Reed, "Lonne Elder III on *Sounder,*" *Dialog on Film,* 2 (May 1973): 2-12;

Dan Sullivan, "What's a Nice Black Playwright Doing in a Place Like This?," *New York Times,* 5 January 1975, II: 23.

References:

Lance Jeffers, "Bullins, Baraka, and Elder: The Dawn of Grandeur in Black Drama," *CLA Journal,* 16 (September 1972): 32-48;

Michael Mattox, "The Day Black Movie Stars Got Militant," *Black Creation,* 4 (Winter 1973): 40-42.

Papers:

Transcripts of Elder's one-act plays are at the Hatch-Billops Archives in New York.

William Faulkner

(25 September 1897-6 July 1962)

Bruce Kawin
University of Colorado

See also the Faulkner entries in *DLB 9, American Novelists, 1910-1945; DLB 11, American Humorists, 1800-1950;* and *Documentary Series,* Volume Two.

MOTION PICTURES: *Today We Live* (M-G-M, 1933), story and dialogue;

The Road to Glory (20th Century-Fox, 1936), screenplay by Faulkner and Joel Sayre;

Slave Ship (20th Century-Fox, 1937), story and additional dialogue;

To Have and Have Not (Warner Bros., 1944), screenplay by Faulkner and Jules Furthman;

The Big Sleep (Warner Bros., 1946), screenplay by Faulkner, Furthman, and Leigh Brackett;

Land of the Pharaohs (Warner Bros., 1955), story and screenplay by Faulkner, Harry Kurnitz, and Harold Jack Bloom.

PLAY PRODUCTIONS: *Marionettes,* University, Miss., University of Mississippi, 4 March 1920;

Requiem for a Nun, London, Royal Court Theatre, 26 November 1957; New York, John Golden Theatre, 30 January 1959.

BOOKS: *The Marble Faun* (Boston: Four Seas, 1924);

Soldiers' Pay (New York: Boni & Liveright, 1926; London: Chatto & Windus, 1930);

Mosquitoes (New York: Boni & Liveright, 1927; London: Chatto & Windus, 1964);

William Faulkner, circa 1936 (courtesy of Louis Daniel Brodsky)

Sartoris (New York: Harcourt, Brace, 1929; London: Chatto & Windus, 1932); original, uncut version, *Flags in the Dust,* edited by Douglas Day (New York: Random House, 1973);

The Sound and the Fury (New York: Cape & Smith, 1929; London: Chatto & Windus, 1931);

As I Lay Dying (New York: Cape & Smith, 1930; London: Chatto & Windus, 1935);

Sanctuary (New York: Cape & Smith, 1931; London: Chatto & Windus, 1931); unrevised version, *Sanctuary: The Original Text,* edited by Noel Polk (New York: Random House, 1981);

These 13 (New York: Cape & Smith, 1931; London: Chatto & Windus, 1933);

Light in August (New York: Smith & Haas, 1932; London: Chatto & Windus, 1933);

A Green Bough (New York: Smith & Haas, 1933);

Doctor Martino and Other Stories (New York: Smith & Haas, 1934; London: Chatto & Windus, 1934);

Pylon (New York: Smith & Haas, 1935; London: Chatto & Windus, 1935);

Absalom, Absalom! (New York: Random House, 1936; London: Chatto & Windus, 1937);

The Unvanquished (New York: Random House, 1938; London: Chatto & Windus, 1938);

The Wild Palms (New York: Random House, 1939; London: Chatto & Windus, 1939);

The Hamlet (New York: Random House, 1940; London: Chatto & Windus, 1940);

Go Down, Moses and Other Stories (New York: Random House, 1942; London: Chatto & Windus, 1942);

The Portable Faulkner, edited by Malcolm Cowley (New York: Viking, 1946);

Intruder in the Dust (New York: Random House, 1948; London: Chatto & Windus, 1949);

Knight's Gambit (New York: Random House, 1949; London: Chatto & Windus, 1951);

Collected Stories of William Faulkner (New York: Random House, 1950; London: Chatto & Windus, 1951);

Requiem for a Nun (New York: Random House, 1951; London: Chatto & Windus, 1953);

A Fable (New York: Random House, 1954; London: Chatto & Windus, 1955);

Big Woods (New York: Random House, 1955);

The Town (New York: Random House, 1957; London: Chatto & Windus, 1958);

New Orleans Sketches, edited by Carvel Collins (New Brunswick: Rutgers University Press, 1958; London: Sidgwick & Jackson, 1959);

The Mansion (New York: Random House, 1959; London: Chatto & Windus, 1961);

The Reivers (New York: Random House, 1962; London: Chatto & Windus, 1962);

Early Prose and Poetry, edited by Collins (Boston: Little, Brown, 1962; London: Cape, 1963);

Essays, Speeches & Public Letters, edited by James B. Meriwether (New York: Random House, 1966; London: Chatto & Windus, 1967);

The Wishing Tree (New York: Random House, 1967; London: Chatto & Windus, 1967);

The Big Sleep, by Faulkner, Jules Furthman, and Leigh Brackett (New York: Irvington, 1971);

To Have and Have Not, by Faulkner and Furthman (Madison: University of Wisconsin Press, 1980);

The Road to Glory, by Faulkner and Joel Sayre (Carbondale & Edwardsville: Southern Illinois University Press, 1981);

Faulkner: A Comprehensive Guide to the Brodsky Collection. Volume III: The DeGaulle Story, edited by Lewis Daniel Brodsky and Robert W. Hamblin (Jackson: University Press of Mississippi, 1984).

TELEVISION: *The Graduation Dress* (CBS, 1960), teleplay by Faulkner and Joan Williams.

William Faulkner, one of the great American novelists of the twentieth century, was also a screenwriter. The first of four brothers, he was born in New Albany, Mississippi, the son of Murry Cuthbert and Maud Butler Falkner. They were a prominent Mississippi family with interests in banking and the railroad. Faulkner's father became secretary and then business manager of the University of Mississippi in Oxford after a somewhat checkered vocational career that included working for the family railroad and running a livery stable. William Faulkner spent most of his life in the town of Oxford, Mississippi, where he went to high school through the eleventh grade. In 1918 his childhood sweetheart, Estelle Oldham, became engaged to an established lawyer after Faulkner refused to elope with her. He tried to join the U.S. Army Signal Corps, but was rejected. He enlisted in the Canadian RAF, but World War I ended before he finished his training. At about this time he added the "u" to his family name.

In 1919 he published his first poem and entered the University of Mississippi as a special student; his withdrawal the next year marked the end of his formal education. After a brief stint working at the Fifth Avenue Doubleday Bookstore in New York City, Faulkner returned to Mississippi and went to work as a postmaster, a job that does not seem to have interfered with his writing. In 1924 at the expense of his friend Phil Stone, *The Marble Faun*, a poetry collection, was published by Four Seas Company. His first novel, *Soldiers' Pay*, was published in 1926. Faulkner traveled for a while in Europe, then lived for about a year in New Orleans. *Mosquitoes* (1927) was written in this time, and by 1927 he had finished his first major work, "Flags in the Dust," (the first revision of *Sartoris*, 1929).

While at work on *The Sound and the Fury* (1929) he married his former sweetheart shortly after her divorce in 1929. She had two children from her first marriage. In 1931 the Faulkners first child died a few days after birth. In 1933 their daughter, Jill, was born. From his marriage came an almost lifelong preoccupation with the need for money. The Faulkners' home life was made more stressful by their mutual and excessive dependence on alcohol, and these two factors had a great deal to do with Faulkner's need and sometime desire to get away to Hollywood and make money.

On a visit to New York in 1931 Faulkner met Tallulah Bankhead and discussed the possibility of reworking *Sanctuary* into a screenplay for her. Although this screenplay was never realized as a film, the conversation gave Faulkner the impetus to consider writing for Hollywood. His agent landed him a contract with M-G-M in 1932. At M-G-M Faulkner wrote several screen stories that were not approved for expansion into screenplays: "Manservant" (from the story "Love"), "The College Widow" (perhaps the Bankhead vehicle), "Absolution" (from one of his unpublished short stories), and "Flying the Mail," all in 1932.

M-G-M was about to allow Faulkner's contract to lapse when Howard Hawks asked the studio to assign Faulkner to him to work on an adaptation of Faulkner's *Saturday Evening Post* story "Turn About." After Faulkner had written this screenplay, Irving Thalberg insisted that it be rewritten to include a major role for Joan Crawford; this second draft allowed Faulkner to expand his original story and include many of the dominant themes and childhood scenes from *The Sound and the Fury*. Most of these scenes were not used in the final film due to the inability of child actors to master British accents. In the revised version, Claude and Ronnie (Robert Young and Franchot Tone), British sailors, and Bogard (Gary Cooper), an American flyer, are all emotionally involved with Ronnie's sister Ann (Crawford). Ann and Bogard are married after Claude and Ronnie die in a suicidal mission. Apart from the addition of Ann, Faulkner's treatment is much like his original story. Revised drastically by two other screenwriters, this story became the basis for *Today We Live* (1933), Faulkner's first screen credit. After a brief hiatus, Faulkner returned to M-G-M to write "War Birds," an extension and reworking of his stories "Ad Astra," "All the Dead Pilots," and his novel "Flags in the Dust." "War Birds" was not produced, and in 1933 his contract expired and was not renewed; Faulkner left M-G-M for good. His last works for them were the unproduced "Mythical Latin-American Kingdom Story," written in August 1933, and a partial script for Tod Browning's *Lazy River* (1934).

Faulkner worked with Hawks a great deal during his time in Hollywood; Hawks had discovered Faulkner's talent as a "script doctor" and frequently called upon him to rework screenplays of other writers. Faulkner wrote *Sutter's Gold* for Hawks at Universal, although the 1936 production did not use his script. The following year he began work on another project for Hawks—this time at 20th Century-Fox—called *The Road to Glory* (1936). *The Road to Glory* is the story of two French officers, Denet (Fredric March) and LaRoche (Warner Baxter), in love with the same nurse, Monique (June Lang); the setting is "1916, Somewhere in France,"

Franchot Tone, Joan Crawford, and Robert Young in Today We Live. *In adapting his short story "Turn About" for the screen Faulkner added a major female role for Crawford.*

and the central device is that of repetition that both creates and erases history—a regiment whose members change, but whose identity is constant. Hawks's preoccupation with blindness, death, repetition, and the "two men and a girl" structure complements Faulkner's sense of history, love, glory, and sardonic humor in an uncanny and fortunate collaboration.

Faulkner continued to work at 20th Century-Fox until 1937, often in collaboration with Nunnally Johnson and under the supervision of Darryl F. Zanuck. He wrote some unproduced scenes for *Banjo on My Knee* (1936), much of *Slave Ship* (1937) and *Submarine Patrol* (1938), a few scenes for *Four Men and a Prayer* (1938), *Dance Hall* (1941), and a full-length, unproduced screenplay for *Drums Along the Mohawk* (1939). He also moonlighted at RKO on *Gunga Din* (1939) in 1936. It was during

this period that he began a thirty-year love affair with Hawks's script supervisor, Meta Doherty Wilde.

In 1942, desperate for money, Faulkner signed a long-term contract with Warner Bros. He did some very good work during this period when teamed with such directors as Hawks and Jean Renoir who respected and understood him. He interrupted work on an anti-Vichy screenplay, "The DeGaulle Story" (unproduced), to write two scenes for Hawks's film *Air Force* (1943). Then, with Dudley Murphy, he wrote an experimental, and ultimately unsuccessful, adaptation of his 1936 novel, *Absalom, Absalom!*, called "Revolt in the Earth" that was unproduced. In 1942 he wrote another unproduced treatment called "The Life and Death of a Bomber," which concerned the conflict between patriotism and greed in an American factory. He

Scenes from The Road to Glory: *(top center) Lionel Barrymore and Fredric March; (bottom) Warner Baxter and March leading the troops*

did some work on *Background to Danger* (1943), *Northern Pursuit* (1943), and *Deep Valley* (1947), but his contributions appeared in early drafts and have little or nothing to do with the finished products. He put a great deal of work into an unproduced treatment titled "Country Lawyer," a multigenerational *Romeo and Juliet* set in the South, which has been called his best script after *War Birds.* He worked with Hawks on "Battle Cry," drawing on many of the concerns of his story "Go Down, Moses," but this film was abandoned during a budget dispute with Warner Bros. His last significant work in 1948 was *Who?,* a treatment about the possibility of the Unknown Soldier's having been Christ; this was the germ of his novel *A Fable,* on which he continued to work until 1954.

The year 1944 was a high point of Faulkner's screenwriting career. Faulkner was called upon by

Hawks to salvage Jules Furthman's screenplay for *To Have and Have Not* (1944), which had been banned from production on the grounds that it might offend the Cuban government. Furthman had substantially altered the plot of Hemingway's novel, in accordance with Hawks's and Hemingway's original (1939) plans to tell not the novel's story of Harry Morgan's decline but their own new story of how Morgan and his wife Marie might have met. In Furthman's script, set in Havana, Morgan has to decide whether to hire out his boat to a group of student revolutionaries who want to overthrow the Cuban dictator, Machado; he ends up helping the police. His love-interest is split between "Slim," Marie's nickname, and a rich old flame named Helen; he ends up with Slim. Faulkner changed the story to one of anti-Vichy resistance on Martinique, shunting Helen into a subplot as the wife of a

Walter Sande, Humphrey Bogart, and Lauren Bacall in To Have and Have Not. *Though the film has the same title as Ernest Hemingway's 1937 novel, Faulkner's revision of Jules Furthman's screenplay bears little resemblance to the original source.*

French agitator and leaving Marie much as Furth-man and Hawks created her (it was Hawks, for instance, who wrote the "you know how to whistle" scene). Without entirely abandoning Hawks's concept of Morgan, the political loner and salty lover, Faulkner managed to write a comic melodrama with serious anti-Fascist implications (and almost no resemblance to the original novel, except in the opening deep-sea fishing and café scenes). He thus saved the studio from taking a total loss on an expensive project, and for once his intelligent versatility was appreciated by someone besides Hawks.

Faulkner then did some minor work on *God is My Co-Pilot* (1945), *The Damned Don't Cry* (1950), and *The Adventures of Don Juan* (1949), which he followed with an unproduced treatment called "Fog Over London" (a revision of John Huston's *The Amazing Dr. Clitterhouse*, 1938, but with serious Jekyll/Hyde overtones). He wrote some of his worst material for *Escape in the Desert* (1945), then went outside the studio to help Jean Renoir with the dialogue for *The Southerner* (1945). It is the story of the family of Sam Tucker (Zachary Scott), a tenant farmer who is nearly destroyed by a combination of bad weather and a hostile neighbor, Henry Devers (J. Carroll Naish), but who refuses to give up hope. Although Renoir has screen credit for writing the script, Faulkner later told Malcolm Cowley that he considered *The Southerner* the best of his own Hollywood works and felt it ironic that he should have received no credit for it; it was also the testimony of Zachary Scott, the film's star, that Faulkner had written the script; none of these men mentions Nunnally Johnson, who helped Renoir write at least the first draft.

Faulkner's work with Renoir was, as his work with Hawks had been, a virtually seamless collaboration, especially on the philosophic level. Those parts of *The Southerner* that most directly echo Renoir's other pictures—the contrast between city and country values, the Tucker family's struggle to endure rather than despair, the comic touches, the quality of interpersonal support, and the complex presentation of nature—can also be described as Faulknerian.

Late in 1944, Faulkner and Leigh Brackett adapted Raymond Chandler's *The Big Sleep* for Hawks. Faulkner and Brackett never worked together but instead adapted alternate chapters of the novel; later revisions by Jules Furthman removed much of Faulkner's work from the finished film. Faulkner also wrote a draft of James Cain's novel *Mildred Pierce,* then ended his career at Warner's by collaborating on several unproduced treat-ments: "Barn Burning" (from his own short story), "Continuous Performance," and "One Way to Catch a Horse." He wrote an entire screenplay for *Stallion Road* (1946), though the film was shot from another script. "Dreadful Hollow," an unproduced vampire film written for Hawks and in its own way one of the most compelling incarnations of Faulkner's themes of generation and doom, appears to date from this period.

The publication of *The Portable Faulkner* in 1946 brought Faulkner's name and achievements back into the public eye (he was remembered only as the author of *Sanctuary*) and his 1948 novel, *Intruder in the Dust,* was bought by M-G-M. Faulkner worked on Ben Maddow's script for *Intruder in the Dust* and also helped scout locations around Oxford, where the film was made. He won the 1949 Nobel Prize for Literature, and the screenwriting he did after this date was for friendship and not for money: an unproduced screenplay of *The Left Hand of God* for Hawks in 1951, and *Land of the Pharaohs* in 1955. In *Land of the Pharaohs*, the pharaoh (Jack Hawkins) plans an elaborate tomb that will hold him, his gold, his servants, and his priests after his death. As the pharaoh oversees the building of the tomb, his wife (Joan Collins) schemes to gain control of his kingdom and his wealth. It was Faulkner's last screen work.

One of the most interesting things about Faulkner's two writing careers is that he wrote cinematic fiction and novelistic screenplays: montage and involution dominate his fiction, but his scripts are linear and straightforward. This is probably the result of the influence of Hawks, whom Faulkner admired as a good storyteller and who taught him the business of screenwriting. Faulkner's influence on film is considerable, but that is the result of his novels, in particular *The Sound and the Fury* (1929) and *The Wild Palms* (1939), which have been studied and are often alluded to or even mirrored in the works of such writer-directors as Agnes Varda, Alain Resnais, Marguerite Duras, Alain Robbe-Grillet, and notably, Jean-Luc Godard. Czech filmmaker Jan Nemec and Krzysztof Zanussi of Poland recently credited Faulkner as a decisive influence on them and their whole filmmaking generation.

The impact of Faulkner's fiction on cinema should not be taken to mean, however, that Faulkner's screenplays are negligible. In the first place, they often bear close thematic relations with his fiction and help to explain and enlarge it. In the second place, some of the screenplays are compelling and well-written in their own right; unfortunately, most of these have remained unproduced

Lauren Bacall and Humphrey Bogart in the film version of Raymond Chandler's The Big Sleep

(or, as in the case of *Today We Live*, were substantially revised before production). The very best of these are "War Birds" and "Dreadful Hollow." Among the produced works, that most closely approaching Faulkner's script is *To Have and Have Not*. The best films to which he made major but now partially buried contributions are *Today We Live*, *The Road to Glory*, and *The Big Sleep*. The most interesting treatments are "The College Widow" (1932), "Absolution" (1932), "Flying the Mail" (1932), "Country Lawyer" (1943), and "Fog Over London" (1944). It is to be hoped that someday these scripts will be published, so that the full range of Faulkner's imagination and achievement might be understood and appreciated.

Letters:

The Faulkner-Cowley File: Letters and Memories, 1944-1962, edited by Malcolm Cowley (New York: Viking, 1966);

Selected Letters of William Faulkner, edited by Joseph L. Blotner (New York: Random House, 1976);

Faulkner: A Comprehensive Guide to the Brodsky Collection, Volume II: The Letters, edited by Louis Daniel Brodsky and Robert W. Hamblin (Jackson: University Press of Mississippi, 1984).

Interviews:

Faulkner at Nagano, edited by Robert A. Jelliffe (Tokyo: Kenkyusha, 1956);

Faulkner in the University: Class Conferences at the University of Virginia, 1957-58, edited by Frederick L. Gwynn and Joseph L. Blotner (Charlottesville: University of Virginia Press, 1959);

Faulkner at West Point, edited by Joseph L. Fant III and Robert Ashley (New York: Random House, 1964);

Lion in the Garden: Interviews with William Faulkner, 1926-1962, edited by James B. Meriwether and Michael Millgate (New York: Random House, 1968).

Bibliographies:

James B. Meriwether, *The Literary Career of William Faulkner: A Bibliographical Study* (Princeton: Princeton University Library, 1961; Colum-

Jack Hawkins and Joan Collins in Land of the Pharaohs, *Faulkner's last film*

bia: University of South Carolina Press, 1971);

Linton R. Massey, *William Faulkner: "Man Working," 1919-1962, A Catalogue of the William Faulkner Collections at the University of Virginia* (Charlottesville: Bibliographical Society, University of Virginia, 1968);

John E. Bassett, *William Faulkner: An Annotated Checklist of Criticism* (New York: David Lewis, 1972);

Carl Petersen, *Each in Its Ordered Place: A Faulkner Collector's Notebook* (Ann Arbor, Mich.: Ardis Press, 1975);

Thomas L. McHaney, *William Faulkner: A Reference Guide* (Boston: G. K. Hall, 1975);

Louis Daniel Brodsky, *Faulkner: A Comprehensive Guide to the Brodsky Collection. Volume I: The Bibliography* (Jackson: University Press of Mississippi, 1982).

Biographies:

Robert Coughlan, *The Private World of William Faulkner* (New York: Harper, 1954);

John Faulkner, *My Brother Bill: An Affectionate Reminiscence* (New York: Trident, 1963);

James W. Webb and A. Wigfall Green, eds., *William Faulkner of Oxford* (Baton Rouge: Louisiana State University Press, 1965);

Murry C. Faulkner, *The Falkners of Mississippi: A Memoir* (Baton Rouge: Louisiana State University Press, 1967);

Joseph L. Blotner, *Faulkner: A Biography*, 2 volumes (New York: Random House, 1974);

Meta Carpenter Wilde and Orin Borsten, *A Loving Gentleman* (New York: Simon & Schuster, 1976);

David Minter, *William Faulkner: His Life and Work* (Baltimore: Johns Hopkins University Press, 1980).

Papers:

The major collections of Faulkner papers and manuscripts are located at the University of Virginia, the University of Texas at Austin, Yale University Library, and the New York Public Library.

Jules Feiffer

(26 January 1929-   )

H. Wayne Schuth
University of New Orleans

See also the Feiffer entry in *DLB 7, Twentieth-Century American Dramatists.*

MOTION PICTURES: *Carnal Knowledge* (Avco Embassy, 1971), screenplay;
Little Murders (20th Century-Fox, 1971), screenplay;
Popeye (Paramount/Walt Disney Productions, 1980), screenplay.

PLAY PRODUCTIONS: *The Explainers,* Chicago, Playwright's Cabaret Theatre, 9 May 1961;
Crawling Arnold, Cambridge, Mass., Poets' Theatre, 1961; Spoleto, Italy, Festival of Two Worlds, 28 June 1961;
The World of Jules Feiffer, New Jersey, Hunterdon Hills Playhouse, 1962;
Little Murders, New York, Broadhurst Theatre, 25 April 1967;
The Unexpurgated Memoirs of Bernard Mergendeiler, Los Angeles, Mark Taper Forum, 9 October 1967;
Feiffer's People, Edinburgh, International Festival of Music and Drama, August 1968;
God Bless, New Haven, School of Drama, 10 October 1968;
Dick and Jane, in *Oh! Calcutta!,* New York, Eden Theatre, 17 June 1969;
The White House Murder Case, New York, Circle in the Square, 18 February 1970;
Munro, Brooklyn, N.Y., Prospect Park, 15 August 1971;
Watergate Classics, by Feiffer and others, New Haven, Yale School of Drama, 16 November 1973;
Knock Knock, New York Circle Repertory Theatre, 18 January 1976;
Hold Me!, New York American Place Theatre, 23 January 1977;
Grownups, Cambridge, Mass., Loeb Drama Center, June 1981.

BOOKS: *Sick, Sick, Sick* (New York: McGraw-Hill, 1958; London: Collins, 1959);

Passionella and Other Stories (New York: McGraw-Hill, 1959; London: Collins, 1960);
The Explainers (New York: McGraw-Hill, 1960; London: Collins, 1961);
Boy, Girl, Boy, Girl (New York: Random House, 1961; London: Collins, 1962);
Crawling Arnold (New York: Dramatists Play Service, 1963);
Feiffer's Album (New York: Random House, 1963);
Hold Me! (New York: Random House, 1963);
Harry: the Rat with Women (New York: McGraw-Hill, 1963; London: Collins, 1963);
The Unexpurgated Memoirs of Bernard Mergendeiler (New York: Random House, 1965; London: Collins, 1966);
Feiffer on Civil Rights (New York: Anti-Defamation League of B'nai B'rith, 1966);
The Penguin Feiffer (Baltimore: Penguin, 1966; Harmondsworth: Penguin, 1966);
Feiffer's Marriage Manual (New York: Random House, 1967);
Little Murders (New York: Random House, 1968; London: Cape, 1970);
Feiffer's People: Sketches and Observations (New York: Dramatists Play Service, 1969);
The White House Murder Case and Dick and Jane (New York: Grove Press, 1970);
Pictures at a Prosecution: Drawings and Text from the Chicago Conspiracy Trial (New York: Grove Press, 1971);
Carnal Knowledge (New York: Farrar, Straus & Giroux, 1971; London: Cape, 1971);
Feiffer on Nixon: The Cartoon Presidency (New York: Random House, 1974);
VD Blues, by Feiffer and Israel Horovitz (New York: Avon, 1974);
Knock Knock (New York: Hill & Wang, 1976);
Akroyd (New York: Simon & Schuster, 1977; London: Hutchinson, 1978);
Hold Me! (New York: Dramatists Play Service, 1977);
Tantrum (New York: Knopf, 1979);
Jules Feiffer's America: From Eisenhower to Reagan, edited by Steve Heller (New York: Knopf,

Jules Feiffer (courtesy of the Billy Rose Theatre Collection, The New York Public Library at Lincoln Center, Astor, Lenox and Tilden Foundations)

1982; Harmondsworth: Penguin, 1983);
Marriage Is an Invasion of Privacy and Other Dangerous Views (New York: Andrews McMeel Parker, 1984).

TELEVISION: *Silverlips* (PBS, 1972);
Happy Endings, by Feiffer, Herb Gardner, Peter Stone, and Neil Simon (ABC, 10 August 1975).

OTHER: Robert Mines, *My Mind Went All to Pieces,* illustrated by Feiffer (New York: Dial, 1959);
Norton Juster, *The Phantom Tollbooth,* illustrated by Feiffer (New York: Random House, 1961);
The Great Comic Book Heroes, edited by Feiffer (New York: Dial, 1965; London: Allen Lane, 1967);
Rick Marshall, ed., *The Complete E. C. Segar Popeye,* introduction by Feiffer (Stamford, Conn.: Fantagraphics, 1984).

Satirist Jules Feiffer strips away the illusions and delusions of his characters as he examines the human condition in his screenplays, cartoons, plays, and novels. The seeming simplicity of his work often disguises profound meanings, and though his work deals primarily with contemporary concerns, the issues he addresses are of lasting artistic value.

Jules Ralph Feiffer was born in the Bronx, New York. His father, David Feiffer, held a variety of jobs from dental technician to salesman, and his mother, Rhoda Davis Feiffer, was a fashion designer. Feiffer attended James Monroe High School and then the Arts Students League in 1946 and Pratt Institute in Brooklyn from 1947 to 1951. On 17 September 1961 he married Judith Sheftel, a production executive with Warner Bros.; they have a daughter, Kate. They separated in 1971.

As a child Feiffer drew his own comics, modeled on those of his favorite comic book artists, and peddled them to children in his neighborhood. He became an assistant to cartoonist and comic book artist Will Eisner from 1946 to 1951 and ghostwriter for Eisner's comic book *The Spirit* from 1949 to 1951. (Years later, in the late 1970s, Feiffer was commissioned to write a screenplay for a *Spirit* movie; the script remains unproduced.) He also drew the syndicated cartoon *Clifford* from 1949 to 1951. (Feiffer has written about his experiences with the comics in *The Great Comic Book Heroes,* 1965.) It is significant that he started with comics, because they are similar to storyboards—groups of pictures drawn from scripts, used as an aid to the director in shooting—which are vital in the process of motion picture scripting. Comics also developed at about the same time as film, and *The Spirit* is one of the comic books most heavily influenced by motion pictures. Feiffer learned about writing for the movies from his work in comics, selecting a sparse visual style instead of a complex one, so that what his characters say is extremely important.

From 1951 to 1953, Feiffer worked in a cartoon animation unit of the U.S. Army Signal Corps; afterward, from 1953 to 1956, he held various art jobs, including making slide films, writing cartoons for Terrytoons, and designing booklets for an art firm. He launched his strip *Feiffer* in the then-new *Village Voice* in 1956; it continues to appear weekly.

Even when he is working in other media, Feiffer's simple style is often cinematic. His political play *The White House Murder Case* (1970) reads very much like a film script. The same is true of his book of drawings and text of the Chicago Seven conspiracy trial, *Pictures at a Prosecution* (1971), a documentary-like work of which Feiffer once wrote, "I have raided and rearranged sections of the transcript, lifted out of context, trifled with chronology, and put together what I hope amounts to a cinéma vérité version of the conspiracy trial."

It was, in fact, one of Feiffer's works of fiction that led to his first screenwriting success. In 1960 he adapted a story from his book *Passionella and Other Stories* (1959) to the animated cartoon *Munro*. Munro is a four-year-old boy who is drafted into the U.S. Army and cannot make anyone believe he is only a child. He tries to fit into army life, but without much success, and finally he starts to cry. When a general tells him that only little boys cry, not soldiers, the truth becomes clear. Munro is sent home and praised by the President for trying to help his country at his young age. A bit rebellious before army life, Munro is now very well-behaved when his parents remind him about the army.

This short film is an excellent illustration of Feiffer's style. The animation is simple, with characters and backgrounds only suggested. The plot depends more on the words than on the visuals. Feiffer satirizes the army establishment and characters who see only what they want to see. Characters reacting to their own preconceptions and beliefs regardless of reality can be found in much of Feiffer's work, including *Little Murders* (1971), *Carnal Knowledge* (1971), and *The Feiffer Film* (a short animation of some of his syndicated cartoons, released in 1965).

Just as Feiffer's short fiction led to *Munro*, so did his work as a playwright lead to his first full-length screenplay. In 1967, Feiffer's play *Little Murders* opened in New York, where drama critics lauded the play and named Feiffer "most promising playwright" of the 1966-1967 season. This production of *Little Murders* was not popular with the public, however, and closed within a week. In spite of this poor showing in New York, it was taken for a successful run in London, and then reopened in 1969 for a long off-Broadway stint. The play won an Obie Award and an Outer Circle Award in 1969, and was voted the best play of the year by London critics. Twentieth Century-Fox decided to film the play with a script by Feiffer and direction by Alan Arkin, who had directed the off-Broadway production.

Little Murders is about the Newquist family, New York City residents who live in a world of muggers, assassins, obscene phone calls, blackouts, and polluted air. Nevertheless, daughter Patsy (Marcia Rodd), an "all-American girl," believes that no matter what terrible things happen to her, "life can be beautiful." She meets Alfred Chamberlain (Elliott Gould), a passive man who is regularly beaten by muggers. Patsy tries to convince him to become more assertive, and when he does, they

marry. Patsy is killed by a random shot fired into their apartment by an assassin terrorizing the city, and Alfred feels frustration, then rage. The film concludes with Alfred and the family shooting happily from the window of their apartment at the impersonal society around them.

Little Murders deals with several of the themes found in Feiffer's other work: people seeing only what they wish to see, gratuitous violence, selfishness, lack of communication. As a play, *Little Murders* is very effective: its characters stay in one room and the dialogue is humorous and meaningful. Most of the violence takes place off-stage. The film version is less effective. Feiffer added scenes on the subway (where the blood-spattered Alfred is ignored), at the Concord Hotel, in the park, and on the street. These added scenes open up the play for film, but make the violence too graphic. The audience is not distanced from the events on screen, and cannot laugh comfortably. The visuals overwhelm Feiffer's words, and the satire is lost.

Filmed the same year as *Little Murders*, *Carnal Knowledge* was written by Feiffer and produced and directed by Mike Nichols. Nichols purposely filmed the screenplay in a manner complementary to Feiffer's terse writing style: only a few colors are used, and a character's head is often seen in full close-up, while the background is out of focus or nearly empty. Much must be filled in by the viewer; the screenplay tells little about the two main characters except how they react to each other and how they feel about women.

Carnal Knowledge traces the friendship of Jonathan (Jack Nicholson) and Sandy (Art Garfunkel) from their college years at Amherst in the mid-1940s to their adulthood in Manhattan in the early 1970s. They meet a variety of women, and even marry, but their relationships are largely unsatisfying and do not last. Near the beginning of the film, Sandy says, "I feel the same way about getting laid as I feel about going to college. I'm being pressured into it." When asked about this line, Feiffer told a *Playboy* interviewer, "It's a result of the society that the Jonathans and Sandys were born into, the mythology they were reared in from birth, which geared them to think about themselves as men and about their relationship with women. They were trained to think about women as conveniences, receptacles, appendages . . . it had to do with rivalry and envy, with competition with the other fellows, more than it had to do with women."

Jonathan, who is primarily interested in sex, and Sandy, who is primarily interested in love, do not react to people but to images. They see women,

Jack Nicholson and Ann-Margret in Carnal Knowledge. *According to Feiffer the film "had to do with rivalry and envy, with competition with the other fellows, more than it had to do with women."*

not as three-dimensional people, but as two-dimensional objects. Thus, Sandy and Jonathan remain lost in their fantasies and preconceptions. The final irony of the title is that "carnal knowledge" is just that and nothing more: a knowledge of other people as mindless bodies to be manipulated.

Three years after its release, *Carnal Knowledge* became the subject of controversy due to a Supreme Court ruling that community standards could determine what was legally obscene. A theater owner in Albany, Georgia, was arrested after showing the movie; the Georgia Supreme Court upheld his conviction, but it was later overturned by the United States Supreme Court.

After *Little Murders* and *Carnal Knowledge*, Feiffer turned his attention to other media. In 1979, he returned to screenwriting with the script for a feature film version of *Popeye* (1980). It certainly seemed appropriate for Feiffer, a cartoonist, to be asked to write the script for *Popeye*, a famous newspaper cartoon and later series of animated cartoons. Feiffer cherishes the work of E. C. Segar, who created the comic strip, and he insisted that his screenplay emulate Segar's Popeye, not the animated Popeye of Max and Dave Fleischer's cartoons. After much research through the original strips, Feiffer decided to focus the script on Popeye's (Robin Williams) romance with Olive Oyl (Shelley Duvall) in the seacoast town of Sweethaven and on Popeye's search for his long-lost "Pap" (Ray Walston).

Hal Ashby signed to direct the film but was replaced by Robert Altman, who has a style that is at odds with Feiffer's. Feiffer has a sparse, visual, cartoonish style; Altman loves to fill the frame with detail and have many people talking at once. Feiffer places importance on individual speeches; Alt-

Shelley Duvall in Popeye, *which Feiffer called fifty percent the work of director Robert Altman and "fifty percent me"*

man encourages improvisation on the set. Altman was, according to Feiffer, also more interested in the minor characters than in the principal ones. Disagreements between the two were common; Feiffer has said, "My sense of it is that every important fight I lost." At one time during shooting Feiffer remarked, "the movie Altman is making is fifty percent me and fifty percent him . . . but the fifty percent is to no extent a violation of the Segar world I was trying to construct here and possibly—there is no way I can tell this—is *more* in keeping with it."

The final result of this collaboration does not work. The film is too busy, too confused. Unlike *Carnal Knowledge,* where the audience must infer much of the details, *Popeye* provides the audience with everything. The Popeye character is set against

oppressive forces (uncaring and selfish neighbors, unfriendly townfolk, a mean tax collector) as are many of Feiffer's characters in his other works, but the character becomes lost amid the details and finally becomes part of the background himself.

Richard Corliss, in *Talking Pictures,* summarizes Feiffer's work well when he writes, "Those who say Feiffer's vision is simplistic because he is a cartoonist are wrong; it is simplistic because he is a moralist."

References:

Richard J. Anobile, *Popeye, the Movie Novel* (New York: Avon, 1980);

Richard Corliss, *Talking Pictures: Screenwriters in the American Cinema* (Woodstock, N.Y.: Overlook Press, 1974): 366-370;

Larry Dubois, "An Interview with Jules Feiffer," *Playboy* (September 1971): 82-84;

Robert Geller, "Little Murders," in *Talking Cinemately re Films* (New York: 20th Century-Fox, 1971);

Stanley Kauffmann, "Carnal Knowledge," *New Republic* (21 August 1971): 22-35;

Herb A. Lightman, "On Location with 'Carnal Knowledge,'" *American Cinematographer*, 1(January 1971): 37;

H. Wayne Schuth, *Mike Nichols* (Boston: Twayne, 1978), pp. 85-108;

"The Stormy Saga of Popeye," *American Film*, 6 (December 1980): 3, 36, 73-74.

W. C. Fields

(29 January 1880-25 December 1946)

Joseph Adamson
and
Christopher T. Lee

MOTION PICTURES: *The Dentist* (Sennett, 1932), screenplay;

The Fatal Glass of Beer (Sennett, 1933), screenplay;

The Pharmacist (Sennett, 1933), screenplay;

The Barber Shop (Sennett, 1933), screenplay;

The Old-Fashioned Way (Paramount, 1934), screen story by Fields as Charles Bogle;

It's a Gift (Paramount, 1934), screen story as Bogle;

Man on the Flying Trapeze (Paramount, 1935), screen story by Fields as Bogle, and Sam Hardy;

You Can't Cheat an Honest Man (Universal, 1939), story as Bogle;

My Little Chickadee (Universal, 1940), story and screenplay by Fields and Mae West;

The Bank Dick (Universal, 1940), screen story and screenplay by Fields as Mahatma Kane Jeeves;

Never Give a Sucker an Even Break (Universal, 1941), screen story by Fields as Otis Criblecoblis.

BOOKS: *Fields for President*, by Fields with Charles D. Rice, Jr. (New York: Dodd, Mead, 1940);

Drat! Being the Encapsulated View of Life by W. C. Fields in His Own Words, edited by Richard J. Anobile (New York: New American Library, 1968);

I Never Met a Kid I Liked, edited by Paul Mason (Hollywood: Stanyon, 1970);

Never Trust a Man Who Doesn't Drink, edited by Mason (Hollywood: Stanyon, 1971);

Fields' Day: The Best of W. C. Fields (Kansas City, Mo.: Hallmark Cards, 1972);

W. C. Fields

The Bank Dick (New York: Simon & Schuster, 1972);

W. C. Fields by Himself, edited by Ronald J. Fields (Englewood Cliffs, N.J.: Prentice-Hall, 1973).

OTHER: *Never Give a Sucker an Even Break,* in *Never Give a Sucker an Even Break and Tillie and Gus* (New York: Simon & Schuster, 1973).

W. C. Fields was the stage name for William Claude Dukenfield, a brilliant and highly original comedian. A former vaudeville star, Fields was never comfortable working in the motion picture studio system and began writing his own scripts and story outlines almost out of self-defense. Having entertained himself by reading Mark Twain, William Shakespeare, and particularly Charles Dickens, Fields crammed his scripts with Dickensian humor, outrage, and caricatures bearing such names as Cuthbert J. Twillie, Cleopatra Pepperday, Marmaduke Gump, Ouliotta Hemogloben, and Hookallockah Meshobbab. Even the pseudonyms he adopted for his work—Charles Bogle, Otis Criblecoblis, and Mahatma Kane Jeeves—had the same flavor. Improvisation was commonplace in his movies, and the major contribution of Fields as writer was to anticipate the structure that would work best for Fields as performer; he advised one studio, "I write my scripts short and they develop on the set, which I have found is a far better premise both economically and practically. When they are over-written it makes the picture more costly, and when you begin deleting scenes entirely or cutting them, it ruins the story and the smoothness."

Fields was born in Philadelphia, the son of James Dukenfield, a cockney immigrant, and Kate Felton Dukenfield. Dukenfield earned a meager living by peddling fruits and vegetables. Fields's early fondness for "euphonious appellations" was apparent when he was a youth working on his father's vegetable cart; he was not above hawking produce that bore names that appealed to him (rutabagas, calabashes, pomegranates) whether or not they were actually available to the customers. Later he peddled newspapers but generally shunned calling out the headlines in favor of the obituaries or obscure filler stories that involved names like Bronislaw Gimp. Many of these names later appeared in his movies, and Fields said, "Every name I used is an actual name I've seen somewhere."

When he was nine years old, Fields saw his first vaudeville show. Part of the show was a juggling act, and Fields became determined to learn to juggle. The elder Dukenfield disapproved, primarily because Fields used his father's produce for juggling practice and ruined it in the process. Despite his father's objections, Fields continued practicing, and by the time he was sixteen, he was

Baby LeRoy and W. C. Fields. Fields made a number of films with the child actor, whom he heartily disliked.

proficient enough to appear on stage as "W. C. Fields, the Tramp Juggler."

Fields's devotion to his trade was intense. His early performances, including his famous pool table routine, were mostly in pantomime, and it was not until 1915, at age thirty-five, that he abandoned pantomime in his act and began using his comic delivery effectively. As he told an interviewer in 1926: "I always had made up my own acts; built them out of my knowledge and observation of real life. I'd had wonderful opportunities to study people: and every time I went out on the stage I tried to show the audience some bit of true human nature." Graduating from vaudeville to Florenz Ziegfeld's *Follies,* George White's *Scandals,* and Earl Carroll's *Vanities,* he continued performing brief skits in large shows until 1923, when he landed the lead role of Eustace McGargle in *Poppy,* a Dorothy Donnelly play. The grandiose McGargle, a petty con man, provided Fields with the first meaty and engaging character of his career; variations of this character would occur in much of his later work.

After the success of *Poppy,* Fields offered a

film studio a deal in which he would write, direct, and star in a two-reel comedy for free if the studio would agree to sign him to a contract in the event of the film's success. This deal was turned down, as were many other proposals; Fields was not widely considered a viable film personality, in spite of his stage success and his skill at pantomime. (He did make two brief film appearances in the silent shorts *Pool Sharks* and *His Lordship's Dilemma,* both 1915.) Were it not for the efforts of film producer William LeBaron, Fields might never have had a movie career. LeBaron gave him his first role in a full-length film, *Janice Meredith* (1924). Then D. W. Griffith featured him in the film version of *Poppy,* retitled *Sally of the Sawdust* (1925). When LeBaron became an associate producer at Paramount, he brought Fields to that studio, after which Fields had starring roles in several silent films that were written and directed by others.

Fields was sensitive about the style of comedy that was appropriate to his established image, and he was exceedingly critical of the attempts of Hol-lywood jokesmiths to adapt to what he called "my character." As a result, he often added his old routines to new stories whether or not they seemed appropriate to anybody else, and contributed without credit jokes and concepts to every film in which he appeared. (One writer exclaimed, "No matter what I write, he puts in a pool table.") On the frustrations of working in the studio system, Fields declared, "The writer, director, supervisor, and the assassin of humor, known as the cutter, must have faith in me and believe in me and not hate me or at least be friendly toward me. (I'll settle for neutrality.) All of the aforementioned may be master craftsmen, when they get a toe-hold on accepted formulas, but when they are dealing with me, they must accept me as I am and not gang up on me."

In 1930 LeBaron spent a brief period as vice-president in charge of production at RKO studios. There he arranged for Fields to appear in his first sound film, a short titled *The Golf Specialist* (1930). Fields wrote the screenplay but received no credit. Throughout 1932 and 1933 Fields had both lead-

Harry Watson and W. C. Fields in The Barber Shop, *one of four short films Fields wrote for Mack Sennett Studios in 1932-1933*

W. C. Fields as Mr. Micawber and Freddie Bartholomew as David Copperfield in the 1935 film version of Dickens's novel. Micawber was his favorite role.

ing and supporting roles in Paramount films. He also made a series of four comedy shorts with Mack Sennett. *The Dentist* (1932) includes a dentist's chair routine Fields had done for Ziegfeld. *The Fatal Glass of Beer* (1933) is based on a skit called "Stolen Bonds," while *The Pharmacist* (1933) revives "Drug Store." The final short was *The Barber Shop* (1933).

LeBaron returned to Paramount in 1933, and Fields was now allowed to write his own scripts and screen stories, which he based on comedy skits he had performed on stage and written either alone or in collaboration with J. P. McEvoy. The first of these was released in 1934 as *The Old-Fashioned Way.* Fields wrote his screen story under the name "Charles Bogle," a character name from his previous film, *You're Telling Me* (1933). Fields played

the leader of a traveling acting troupe which performed the Victorian melodrama "The Drunkard." Elements of Fields's juggling act and his silent film *Two Flaming Youths* (1927) were incorporated into the film.

It's a Gift (1934) also contains scenes from Fields's silent films: in this case, *The Potters* (1927) and *It's the Old Army Game* (1926). Several vaudeville skits were also used. The movie is about a grocery store owner who sells his business and buys some useless land in California hoping to start an orange grove. *It's a Gift* has since become a favorite of Fields fans.

After appearing in *David Copperfield* (1935) and *Mississippi* (1935), Fields wrote his third movie, *Man on the Flying Trapeze* (1935). It is one of several movies in which Fields played a miserable, hen-pecked husband. His character in this movie is Ambrose Wolfinger, a memory expert who is easily distracted by trivialities. Fields then appeared in the sound version of *Poppy* in 1936 and in *The Big Broadcast of 1938* (1938) before leaving Paramount.

Universal then hired Fields away from Paramount, paying him $125,000 per film appearance and $25,000 per script. He appeared in five films for the studio and had a hand in writing all but one, *Follow the Boys* (1944). The Charles Bogle pseudonym was used for the last time in *You Can't Cheat an Honest Man* (1939). Fields played Larson E. Whipsnade, the conniving owner of a nearly bankrupt circus. His daughter (Constance Moore) plans to save the circus by marrying into a wealthy family. Ventriloquist Edgar Bergen, along with his dummy Charlie McCarthy, costarred, and much of the film's humor stemmed from conflicts between Fields and McCarthy. Fields was not pleased with the picture; although he had written a detailed screen story, producer Lester Cowan turned the project over to several other writers without showing them Fields's treatment.

Fields also wrote several treatments for *My Little Chickadee* (1940), which Cowan also produced.

When he was not pleased with any of the completed scripts shown him, Fields cabled his costar, Mae West, and told her, "We will probably have to get together in the end and write the tome ourselves." The two of them proceeded to do so, writing their own scenes and maintaining their own styles so clearly that it is no problem to distinguish his work from hers. Fields said, "During my entire experience in the entertainment world, I have never had anyone catch my character as Miss West has. In fact, she is the only author that has ever known what I was trying to do." Flower Belle Lee (West) is run out of a small western town and meets con man Cuthbert J. Twillie (Fields) on the train. They "marry" in what Twillie does not realize is a mock ceremony. They then travel to Greasewood City, where Twillie becomes sheriff.

The Bank Dick (1940) is the only feature film for which Fields received sole writing credit, and that was under the pseudonym Mahatma Kane Jeeves (the name is a variation of a line from a vaudeville sketch: "My hat and cane, Jeeves"). Even then, the script was subject to much censoring and rewriting although it was Fields's first draft that was finally used. The film is a simple story about a shiftless small-town resident (Fields) who is a guard

W. C. Fields, Eddie Anderson, and Grady Sutton in You Can't Cheat an Honest Man, *the last film Fields wrote under the pseudonym Charles Bogle*

Mae West and W. C. Fields in My Little Chickadee. *West and Fields wrote their own scenes, producing a script that reveals two distinct styles.*

at the local bank, but who spends much of his time at a nearby café. When Universal protested that the ending of the movie was weak, Fields rejected their demands for something more physical and exciting. He conceded that it would be possible to use something in the Mack Sennett style of slapstick, and the result was a grand chase scene, staged by Ralph Ceder, that pleased audiences and critics. It remains one of the best of its kind ever filmed.

Never Give a Sucker an Even Break (1941) is an episodic comedy. The main character is Fields himself, and the action comprises a bizarre series of events supposedly contained in a script he prepared for a producer at Esoteric Studios. The device enables Fields to get back at studio executives and writers who had tampered with his work over the preceding ten years. Most of the anti-Hollywood invective is removed from the final version,

but when the Hays Office objected to a scene taking place in a saloon, Fields relocated the action to an ice cream parlor and stated directly to the camera: "This was supposed to be set in a barroom, but the censor cut it out." The film ended with a chase that was even more elaborate than its predecessor.

W. C. Fields's films are probably some of the least glamorous, least charming pictures to come out of the escapist moviemaking of the 1930s. "Bill had only one story," said Eddie Sutherland, one of his directors. "It wasn't a story at all, really—there was just an ugly old man, an ugly old woman, and a brat of a child." Actually, Fields had two stories: *The Old-Fashioned Way, You Can't Cheat an Honest Man,* and *My Little Chickadee* were variations on the McGargle curmudgeon, while the henpecked husband (which Fields swore would get "surefire laughs") appeared in *The Pharmacist, The Barber*

Shop, It's a Gift, Man on the Flying Trapeze, and *The Bank Dick.* In his curmudgeon tales Fields made impropriety charming, and in the henpecked husband stories he made respectability dull; in both he found humor in the petty tragedies of everyday life. His films portrayed people as frauds and charlatans, bumblers and fools, and if there were any distinctions to be drawn between characters, it was simply a distinction between lovable and unlovable frauds. His unhappy marriage to Harriet Hughes (they wed in 1900 and had one son, W. C. Fields, Jr.) left him with a bitter view of family life, and his pictures became bloodthirsty satires of the kind of morality espoused by the rest of Hollywood. His cynical views kept Fields from appealing to a mass audience, but he was able from the beginning of his career to generate a loyal following and has kept a following to this day.

Ill-health and problems associated with alcoholism curtailed Fields's career in the 1940s, and *Never Give a Sucker an Even Break* marked both his

last script and his final starring role. He performed his pool table routine in *Follow the Boys,* then played supporting roles in *Song of the Open Road* (1944) and *Tales of Manhattan* (1942), from which his scenes were cut before the film's release. Fields's last film appearance was in a sketch in the movie *Sensations of 1945.* W. C. Fields died on Christmas day, 1946.

References:

Louise Brooks, "The Other Face of W. C. Fields," *Sight and Sound,* 40 (Spring 1971): 92-96;

Heywood Broun, "W. C. Fields and the Cosmos," *Nation,* 132 (7 January 1931): 24-25;

Teet Carle, "The Man Who Was Fascinated by Names," *Hollywood Studio* (February 1972);

H. Cary, "The Loneliest Man in Movies," *Collier's,* 76 (28 November 1925): 26;

Donald Deschner, *The Films of W. C. Fields* (New York: Citadel Press, 1966);

William K. Everson, *The Art of W. C. Fields* (Indi-

Pierre Watkins, W. C. Fields, and Fay Adler in The Bank Dick, *which Fields wrote under the pseudonym Mahatma Kane Jeeves, a variation on a line from an old vaudeville sketch: "My hat and cane, Jeeves"*

Leon Errol and W. C. Fields in Never Give a Sucker an Even Break, *Fields's humorous, and sometimes vituperative, depiction of the business of filmmaking*

anapolis: Bobbs-Merrill, 1967);

Corey Ford, *The Time of Laughter* (Boston: Little, Brown, 1967);

Alva Johnston, "Profiles Legitimate Nonchalance," *New Yorker,* 10 (2 February): 23-26; (9 February): 25-28;

Johnston, "Who Knows What is Funny?," *Saturday Evening Post* (6 August 1938): 10-11, 43-46;

Dee Lowrance, "Bogeyman's Bluff," *Washington Post: Weekly Star,* 26 October 1941;

Leonard Maltin, *The Great Movie Comedians: From Charlie Chaplin to Woody Allen* (New York: Crown, 1978);

Wallace Markfield, "The Dark Geography of W. C. Fields," *New York Times Magazine,* 24 April 1966, pp. 32-33, 110-120;

Carlotta Monti with Cy Rice, *W. C. Fields and Me* (Englewood Cliffs, N.J.: Prentice-Hall, 1971);

J. B. Priestley, "W. C. Fields," *New Statesman and Nation* (4 January 1947); reprinted in *Atlantic Monthly,* 179 (March 1947): 43-51;

David Robinson, "Dukenfield Meets McGargle," *Sight and Sound* (Summer 1967);

Robert Lewis Taylor, *W. C. Fields: His Follies and Fortunes* (Garden City: Doubleday, 1949).

William Goldman

(12 August 1931-   )

Botham Stone

MOTION PICTURES: *Masquerade* (United Artists, 1965), screenplay by Goldman and Michael Relph;

Harper (Warner Bros., 1966), screenplay;

Butch Cassidy and the Sundance Kid (20th Century-Fox, 1969), screenplay;

The Hot Rock (20th Century-Fox, 1972), screenplay;

The Stepford Wives (Fadsior/Palomar, 1974), screenplay;

The Great Waldo Pepper (Universal, 1975), screenplay;

All the President's Men (Warner Bros., 1976), screenplay;

Marathon Man (Paramount, 1976), screenplay from his novel;

A Bridge Too Far (United Artists, 1977), screenplay;

Magic (Joseph E. Levine, 1978), screenplay from his novel.

PLAY PRODUCTIONS: *Blood, Sweat and Stanley Poole*, New York, Morosco Theatre, 5 October 1961, by Goldman and James Goldman;

A Family Affair, New York, Billy Rose Theatre, 27 January 1962, by Goldman, James Goldman, and John Kander.

BOOKS: *The Temple of Gold* (New York: Knopf, 1957; London: Transworld, 1961);

Your Turn to Curtsy, My Turn to Bow (Garden City: Doubleday, 1958; London: Transworld, 1966);

Soldier in the Rain (New York: Atheneum, 1960; London: Eyre & Spottiswoode, 1960);

Blood, Sweat, and Stanley Poole, by Goldman and James Goldman (New York: Dramatists Play Service, 1962);

Boys and Girls Together (New York: Atheneum, 1964; London: Joseph, 1965);

No Way to Treat a Lady (New York: Harcourt, Brace & World, 1964; London: Hodder Fawcett, 1968);

The Thing of It Is . . . (New York: Harcourt, Brace & World, 1967; London: Joseph, 1967);

The Season: A Candid Look at Broadway (New York: Harcourt, Brace & World, 1969);

Butch Cassidy and the Sundance Kid (London: Corgi, 1969; New York: Bantam, 1971);

Father's Day (New York: Harcourt Brace Jovanovich, 1970; London: Joseph, 1971);

The Princess Bride (New York: Harcourt Brace Jovanovich, 1973; London: Macmillan, 1975);

Marathon Man (New York: Delacorte Press, 1974; London: Macmillan, 1975);

Wigger (New York: Harcourt Brace Jovanovich, 1974);

The Great Waldo Pepper (New York: Dell, 1975);

Magic (New York: Delacorte Press, 1976; London: Macmillan, 1976);

William Goldman's Story of A Bridge Too Far (New York: Dell, 1977);

Tinsel (New York: Delacorte Press, 1979; London: Macmillan, 1979);

William Goldman (photograph by Ilene Jones)

Control (New York: Delacorte, 1982; London: Hodder & Stoughton, 1982);

Adventures in the Screen Trade (New York: Warner, 1983; London: Macdonald, 1984);

The Color of Light (New York: Warner, 1984; London: Granada, 1984);

Heat (New York: Warner, 1985).

TELEVISION: *Mr. Horn* (CBS, 1979), teleplay.

PERIODICAL PUBLICATIONS: "The Ice Cream Eat," *Transatlantic Review*, 2 (Winter 1959-1960): 108-117;

"Da Vinci," *New World Writing 17* (1960);

"Till the Right Girls Come Along," *Transatlantic Review*, 8 (Winter 1961): 50-61.

"I've only been a writer," William Goldman once told a biographer. "My first novel was taken the summer I finished graduate school, so I've never known anything else." His career has spanned three decades and has included several dozen screenplays, novels, plays, and works of criticism. By the end of the 1970s Goldman had established himself as one of the most highly paid writers in America. Many of his works deal with themes stemming from the stresses of male adolescence. Several of his works, most notably his original screenplay *Butch Cassidy and the Sundance Kid* (1969), have become a part of the popular mythology of our time, and as his popularity has increased, it has brought with it increased critical attention, further cementing his reputation as one of film's most dependable screenwriters.

Goldman was born in Chicago, the son of Marion Weil and businessman Maurice Clarence Goldman. Although a native midwesterner, Goldman has spent most of his life in the eastern United States. He received his B.A. at Ohio's Oberlin College in 1952 and M.A. at Columbia University in 1956. His first novel, *The Temple of Gold* (1957), takes its title and central metaphor from *Gunga Din* (1939), a classic film of the "buddy ethic" and one of Goldman's favorite movies. The book established his reputation and the basic theme that would dominate most of his work for the next twenty-five years: the nature of male friendship. Goldman married Ilene Jones on 15 April 1961, and they have a daughter, Jenny Rebecca.

Goldman's fiction is blunt and direct, and he avoids symbolism and elaborate detail. His narrative voice is rarely intrusive, but he will occasionally step away from his omniscient stance and deliver a few words of his own. In his screenplays he has shown the same spare, slightly cocky style. He constructs scenes efficiently and with a deliberate punch line, as if determining the weight and flow of scenes from the very start of the writing process. He very rarely thinks in visual terms, preferring to work with plot and character action as a way of building his themes.

It was his novel *No Way to Treat a Lady* (1964) that led, indirectly, to Goldman's first screenwriting job. Before the book was published, actor Cliff Robertson saw the short (150 pages) typescript and mistook it for a film treatment. He liked it enough to offer Goldman the opportunity to write a film based on the short story "Flowers for Algernon" by Daniel Keyes; Robertson had already appeared in a television dramatization of the story. Goldman accepted, and while he was working on that script, Robertson asked him to work on the screenplay for another film in which Robertson was appearing, *Masquerade* (1965). Thus *Masquerade* became Goldman's first film credit. (His adaptation of "Flowers for Algernon" was never used; the film was made as *Charly*, 1968, from a screenplay by Stirling Silliphant, who had written the television version.) Apparently Goldman did little to *Masquerade* other than rewrite Britisher Michael Relph's script so that it could accommodate the American Robertson, but the film does show his interest in male camaraderie, depicting the attempts of British Colonel Dexter (Jack Hawkins) and his wartime friend David Frazer (Robertson) to find a missing Middle Eastern prince.

As a British production, *Masquerade* received little attention in the United States; it was *Harper* (1966) that became Goldman's first screen success. Goldman had recommended Ross Macdonald's Lew Archer novels to producer Elliott Kastner, who was looking for a new film project. Kastner liked what he read and, at Goldman's suggestion, optioned the first Archer novel, *The Moving Target*. *Harper* is most noteworthy as an oddity in Goldman's career: Lew Harper (as the character was renamed), unlike Goldman's other heroes, is alone, divorced, and friendless. Directed by Jack Smight, the film was a fairly conventional thriller, but Goldman's material for the star, Paul Newman, signaled the start of an acting/writing collaboration that would perfectly mesh. Three years later Goldman wrote *Butch Cassidy and the Sundance Kid* (1969), in which Newman starred, and since then he has associated himself exclusively with big-budget, major films.

Goldman developed *Butch Cassidy and the Sundance Kid* over an eight-year period, and most

Paul Newman in Harper, *adapted from Ross Macdonald's novel* The Moving Target

of the characteristics that mark his work can be found in this screenplay. His heroes are not held together by blood relation (only *Marathon Man,* 1976, violates this premise) but by an instinctive feeling of closeness that transcends individual backgrounds and differences. His heroes are essentially loners who fall in with each other out of necessity, with friendship coming after. Butch (Newman) and Sundance (Robert Redford) are bound together in their profession and partnership, and yet they know very little about each other's lives. It is only after years of riding together that they learn each other's real names: Robert Leroy Parker and Harry Longbaugh. Etta Place (Katherine Ross), the woman who accompanies them to Bolivia when they are fleeing the posse organized to track and kill them, is acutely aware of how much she is left

out of their very special relationship, and when she leaves them in Bolivia, certain of their approaching deaths, she bitterly tells them, "All these years and we don't know each other at all."

In this film, as in almost all his others, the male camaraderie is most obviously shown in constant wisecracking. Especially in extremis, Goldman's males reassert their control and interconnection by transporting the relaxed, he-man atmosphere of a barroom or poker game to wherever they are. Even when pursued inexorably by the posse, Butch and Sundance respond to their predicament with scene after scene of sardonic, irreverent jokes that serve to conceal their fear as well as make them secure in their friendship when faced with mutual enemies. The men are dreamers, living out a boy's romantic ideal of nonviolent, good-natured banditry, and they never cease dreaming even in the face of certain death. Fleeing the posse, Butch and Sundance continually repeat a simple statement that Goldman turns into a comic refrain: "Who *are* those guys?" Their enemies are hazily seen and only partially knowable; they exist as a subject for repartee. Goldman keeps the dialogue terse and humorously downbeat:

BUTCH: "I think we lost 'em. Do you think we lost 'em?"
SUNDANCE: "No."
BUTCH: "Neither do I."

Coming in the wake of *Bonnie and Clyde* (1967), *Butch Cassidy and the Sundance Kid* might have seemed a naive, impossible treatment of criminal behavior, which no doubt accounted for a great

deal of its charm and was a factor in the film's critical and popular success. (The original script was grimmer in tone, but revisions made the film more humorous.) The film was one of the best received in the 1960s. Goldman won his first Academy Award for the screenplay, which continues to be one of the most influential works in Hollywood, still defining a standard for entertainment movies. It was also a breakthrough film, not just for Goldman but for screenwriters in general; Goldman received $400,000 for his script, the first time a screenwriter had ever received so high a payment.

The Hot Rock (1972), which Goldman wrote for the screen from Donald Westlake's comic novel, continues the kind of comic adventure begun with *Butch Cassidy and the Sundance Kid*. The film is about a gang of thieves who try to steal a rare jewel from a museum; the criminals are jovial, somewhat inept

Robert Redford and Paul Newman in Butch Cassidy and the Sundance Kid. *Goldman won his first Academy Award for the screenplay.*

workers who enjoy being with each other as much as they like committing clever thefts. As long as Goldman's characters refrain from real violence, he is able to keep the film humorous and not lose the audience's sympathy. He depicts criminal life as an all-male paradise where the crooks can be as boyish, crude, and enthusiastic as they like. Goldman clearly realizes the need to keep his scripts light in tone and largely removed from brutal realities. Just as he revised the script to *Butch Cassidy and the Sundance Kid* to emphasize the humor, so did he change the ending to *The Hot Rock*. Originally, the criminals, disillusioned and weary, were to dispose of the jewel by selling it for fifty dollars at a swap meet. In the finished screenplay, ringleader Dortmunder (Robert Redford) pulls off one more seemingly impossible heist, and the gang recovers the jewel after a series of double crosses.

A series of failures followed *The Hot Rock*. Goldman was hired to write the screenplay for *Papillon* (1973), but he left the project early on and his screenplay was not used; he says he is responsible for one line in the film. *The Stepford Wives* (1974) was a rarity for Goldman in that it centered on the friendship between two *women*, which is what attracted Goldman to the project. But the screenplay was rewritten by the film's director, Bryan Forbes, and the film, based on Ira Levin's novel about a town where women are gradually replaced by robots, depicts the ultimate dehumanization of females. Goldman asked the producers to take his name off the film but they refused; he refers to the movie now as "an unpleasant experience."

The Great Waldo Pepper (1975) reunited Goldman with George Roy Hill and Robert Redford, the director and costar of *Butch Cassidy and the Sundance Kid*. All three men were at the peaks of their careers—Hill and Redford had just completed *The Sting* (1973)—and decided to collaborate on a small, personal film. But the screenplay, about two barnstorming pilot friends (Redford, Bo Svenson) had to be rewritten several times before a version was produced that pleased Goldman, Hill, and Redford; audiences had trouble accepting the completed film's mixture of comedy and drama.

Much more rewarding for Goldman was his next project, *All the President's Men* (1976), for which he won his second Academy Award. It is based on the best-selling book by Bob Woodward and Carl Bernstein, the two reporters who helped break the Watergate story at the *Washington Post*. Typically, Goldman is interested in the relationship of the two men and balances their personal story with the details of how they "followed the money." There is

actually an explicit author's note on Goldman's final script that suggests the screenplay can be viewed as the story of how two very different individuals grew to like each other. The two reporters, as written into semifiction by Goldman, show a variety of oppositions in their personalities and backgrounds: one is Protestant, the other Jewish; one an introvert, the other an extrovert; one Republican, the other a Democrat, and so forth. It is these differences they need to overcome in order to get the story. *All the President's Men* was a great critical and popular success; besides Goldman's Academy Award for best screenplay, the film received nominations for best picture, and Alan Pakula was nominated for best director.

A Bridge Too Far (1977), based on Cornelius Ryan's book, gave Goldman another chance at adapting a work of nonfiction for the screen, but the results were far less impressive than *All the President's Men*. After reading Ryan's book, about an Allied mission to take the Rhine bridge in Holland, Goldman decided to make two changes when writing the screenplay: he felt that Ryan had told his story entirely from the point of view of the officers, and he wanted to incorporate the point of view of the enlisted men; and since none of the persons described in the book had died in the mission and, according to Goldman, "you can't have a war film in which everybody lives," he created many secondary, fictional characters. Other changes were made, less for aesthetic reasons than due to the needs of a commercial screenplay. Because the producer wanted an all-star cast, Goldman had to create a dozen star parts; then, in order to give the film more appeal to American audiences, he tried to balance the action between American and British characters. The film was lengthy and, perhaps inevitably, severely fragmented. One of the few segments that stood out was also the one that was the most typical of Goldman—a sergeant (James Caan) forces a doctor (Arthur Hill) at gunpoint to examine his wounded captain. Although *A Bridge Too Far* was a success in other countries, particularly England, it did not fare well critically or popularly in the United States. Goldman feels that audiences did not want to see a film in which American troops failed at their mission.

Goldman has often suggested in his work that friendship is the only comfort in an absurd universe in which individual lives are ultimately meaningless, but for commercial reasons this darker slant to the material is usually missing from the final product on the screen. Two of Goldman's scripts do deal effectively with this darker theme,

Dustin Hoffman and Robert Redford in All the President's Men. *Goldman viewed the film as the story of two different individuals growing to like each other.*

however: *Marathon Man* (1976) and *Magic* (1978). Significantly, both films were adapted by Goldman from his own novels: in his fiction he has been more willing to examine the disillusionment that comes with long periods of friendship, while his screenplays usually hold up the "buddy ethic" as an innocent, pure ideal.

In *Marathon Man,* graduate student Thomas "Babe" Levy (Dustin Hoffman) becomes involved with international espionage and murder after his brother "Doc" (Roy Scheider) is killed by his own organization. Ex-Nazi Christian Szell (Laurence Olivier) wrongly thinks Babe has information about a cache of diamonds stolen from Jews headed for Nazi death camps, and tortures Babe with the help of one of Doc's former associates, Janeway (William

Devane). A labyrinth of double crosses follows. After the docile and introverted Babe sees Doc die, he is forced to overcome what he considers his liberal-minded weakness, his victim mentality, and become a killer like his brother. In the final film version, Babe confronts Szell, who had the diamonds, in a water processing plant near a reservoir. He forces Szell to swallow some diamonds in imitation of the Jews who did the same in Germany, but cannot bring himself to kill Szell. Szell dies after falling on his own knife, and the diamonds are washed away. Goldman's novel and first draft of the screenplay show a more dramatic transformation in Babe: he repeatedly and sadistically shoots Szell and throws the diamonds into the reservoir. He has learned to kill but is left alone and bitter.

Goldman disclaims the ending of the completed motion picture.

In *Magic*, the two buddies who die together are a part of the same schizophrenic mind, that of the ventriloquist Corky (Anthony Hopkins) whose lifelong fear of failure and rejection finally leads him to a nervous breakdown and split personality. He uses his dummy Fats to serve as the voice of his manly, extrovert self, but Fats soon becomes the dominant personality. Corky flees to his home town and seeks out Peggy Ann Snow (Ann-Margret), with whom he was infatuated in high school. Fats "forces" Corky to kill anyone who might discover "their" secret, becomes jealous of Peggy, and wants Corky to kill her as well. The continuous stress causes Corky to commit suicide, and he and Fats "die" together. Corky, in a final confrontation with Fats, realizes that he did not need a dummy, magic, or tricks to make people like him. "It was never me . . . always us," Corky says, but Fats tells him, "Us was you . . . it was you all the time." As in other Goldman works, the revelation comes too late. Corky's inability to trust himself makes his tragedy inevitable. He dies with his alter ego and only friend—himself.

The main problem of *Magic* was the difficulty of getting an audience to identify with Corky and not immediately dismiss him as a psychopath. The director, Richard Attenborough, and Goldman worked out a series of silent flashbacks that would not disturb the narrative flow but would depict the beginnings of Corky's career, when he was trained by his mentor Merlin, Jr. "We needed to show their affection for each other, so the audience wouldn't think 'He's a crazy nut and I don't care about him.' He is, after all, a loony killer," says Goldman. Although he succeeded in creating characters and situations of depth on paper, the translation of Goldman's script to the screen was only moderately successful, and critical response to the script was almost entirely negative. By playing down the blood and gore, Attenborough lost the horror aspects of the script and focused almost entirely on the love story, which was too weak to stand on its own. *Magic* is one of Goldman's best scripts, but one of his most disappointing movies.

After *Magic*, Goldman began work on a screenplay about western scout Tom Horn; after it was completed, producers found it too lengthy to become a theatrical release, and the script was filmed as a four-hour film for television in 1979. Goldman has had no more screenplays produced to date, but he has written a few unproduced scripts and has occupied himself with his novels. His memoirs of the film business, *Adventures in the Screen Trade*, appeared in 1983 to critical acclaim.

William Goldman is an instinctive writer who works very quickly and with little revision. His extremely popular screenplays and books have a quality of humanity that sets them apart from formula best-sellers and other, more calculated "blockbuster" films. If his subjects appear trivial and adolescent on occasion, there is no small amount of skill involved in their creation. And yet Goldman is normally unenthusiastic about his work, no matter how flamboyant or comic it might appear on the screen. "I'm not all that crazy about the act of writing, which is probably why I write quickly," he has said. "The sooner I'm done, the sooner I can go to the movies."

References:

John Brady, *The Craft of the Screenwriter* (New York: Touchstone, 1982), pp. 84-176;

Brendan Gill, Review of *Masquerade, New Yorker* (22 May 1965): 41, 168;

Pauline Kael, *Reeling* (Boston: Little, Brown, 1972).

Walter Hill

(10 January 1942-   )

Randall Clark

MOTION PICTURES: *Hickey and Boggs* (United Artists, 1972), screenplay;

The Getaway (Solas/First Artists, 1972), screenplay;

The Thief Who Came to Dinner (Warner Bros., 1973), screenplay;

The Mackintosh Man (Warner Bros., 1973), screenplay;

The Drowning Pool (Warner Bros., 1975), screenplay by Hill, Lorenzo Semple, Jr., and Tracy Keenan Wynn;

Hard Times (Columbia, 1975), screenplay by Hill, Bryan Gindorff, and Bruce Henstell;

The Driver (20th Century-Fox, 1978), screenplay;

The Warriors (Paramount, 1979), screenplay by Hill and David Shaber;

Southern Comfort (20th Century-Fox, 1981), screenplay by Hill, David Giler, and Michael Kane;

48 Hrs. (Paramount, 1982), screenplay by Hill, Larry Gross, Steven de Souza, and Roger Spottiswoode;

Streets of Fire (Universal, 1984), screenplay by Hill and Gross.

TELEVISION: *Dog and Cat* (ABC, 1977), series idea; pilot teleplay by Hill, Owen Morgan, Henry Rosenbaum, and Haywood Gould.

Walter Hill is the author, and later director, of moody, extremely stylized, almost existential action films. His protagonists are silent loners with strong moral codes; other characters are usually little more than stereotypes, and his plots are deceptively simple. Hill sees all his screenwriting as mere reworkings of the film themes that intrigued him as a youth: "I'm always making Westerns. But Hollywood has decided that people don't like Westerns anymore, so I have to make these other movies and pretend they're not Westerns." His films are not just rooted in Westerns, but in American film noir and Japanese samurai films, and even as he reworks established themes, he creates his own unique and original work.

Hill was born in Long Beach, California, and educated at the University of the Americas in Mexico City and at Michigan State University. After graduating, he worked odd jobs, including construction work, while writing magazine articles and short stories. He wrote two educational films to be used in high schools, only one of which was produced. Finally, in 1966 he entered the assistant directors training program of the Directors Guild of America. He served as second assistant director on two films, *Take the Money and Run* (1969) and *The Thomas Crown Affair* (1969). He also wrote his first screenplay "The Streetfighter." It has never been produced.

In the late 1960s Hill was one of many new, young talents signed to work at Warner Bros., where he wrote the screenplay for *Hickey and Boggs* (1972). It was sold to United Artists and substantially rewritten. Hickey (Robert Culp, who also directed) and Boggs (Bill Cosby) are two private

Walter Hill

152

Steve McQueen in The Getaway, *which Hill has called a story of "purification"*

investigators whose missing persons case becomes a search for stolen money wanted by organized crime and two different militant groups. Hill is not pleased with the final film; he feels that the characters were changed from his original concept, and the plot was so altered that it no longer made sense.

The Getaway (1972) is the only one of Hill's scripts he did not direct himself that he is pleased with as a film. He adapted the screenplay from a novel by Jim Thompson; Sam Peckinpah, whom Hill admires and cites as an influence, directed. After his wife Carol (Ali MacGraw) bribes and seduces a parole board member (Ben Johnson), longtime con man Doc McCoy (Steve McQueen) is released from prison on the condition that he organize a bank robbery for that same board member.

After the robbery, one of the criminals, Rudy (Al Lettieri), tries to double-cross McCoy, but McCoy shoots him and flees with all the money. He and Carol must now travel from Texas to Mexico, pursued by Rudy, the police, and the parole board member. What follows is little more than a series of set pieces showing Doc and Carol on their trip; he purchases a shotgun to destroy a police car; she loses their bag of money to a con man in a railroad station; they are forced to hide in a garbage truck. The depiction of characters in trouble and seeking safety is a formula that Hill follows in many of his later films, most notably in *The Warriors* (1979), but also in *Southern Comfort* (1981) and *Streets of Fire* (1984). These films, along with *48 Hrs.* (1982), also share *The Getaway*'s compressed time schedule;

none takes place over a period of more than two days, and *The Warriors'* events occur in a matter of hours.

Hill has called *The Getaway* a story of "purification"; he feels that the McCoys' perseverance and bravery redeem their characters. In contrast, he offers another couple, criminal Rudy and his hostage Fran (Sally Struthers), who begins to enjoy being a part of Rudy's crimes. Hill's characters are never clearly motivated and are usually defined only by their actions. Soldier of fortune Tom Cody's statement in *Streets of Fire*, "I do what I'm good at and I get money for it," could describe nearly any of Hill's protagonists, including private detectives Hickey and Boggs, thief McCoy, the burglar (Ryan O'Neal) in *The Thief Who Came to Dinner* (1973), the boxer in *Hard Times* (1975), *The Driver* (1978) of getaway cars (O'Neal), the police officer (Nick Nolte) in *48 Hrs.*, the soldier (Amy Madigan) in *Streets of Fire*. His screenplays show how these characters react when they are placed in life-threatening situations.

Following *The Getaway*, Hill wrote three scripts for Warner Bros., but he was not pleased with any of the resulting films. *The Thief Who Came to Dinner* is about a computer expert who ingratiates himself into Houston's upper class then robs his acquaintances. In *The Mackintosh Man* (1973), a secret agent (Paul Newman) under cover allows himself to be branded a traitor, then is in real jeopardy when the one person who knows the truth is killed. Hill's script was rewritten by at least four other writers, including the film's director, John Huston; Hill says he is responsible for nine-tenths of the first half and none of the second half of the completed film. The greatest disappointment came with Hill's adaptation of Ross Macdonald's detective novel *The Drowning Pool* in 1975. His screenplay was rewritten twice, first by Lorenzo Semple, Jr., then by Tracy Keenan Wynn; of his original script, which was faithful to the novel, only two scenes remained in the film.

For some time Hill had hoped to become a director as a means of protecting his screenplays. He finally received that opportunity with *Hard Times* (1975), a boxing drama set during the Depression. Producer Lawrence Gordon had a screenplay he was not pleased with and approached Hill about doing a rewrite; Hill wrote a script from Gordon's synopsis (he never read the original screenplay by Bryan Gindorff and Bruce Henstell) based largely on material from his own unproduced "The Streetfighter," which had a boxing protagonist. Chaney (Charles Bronson) is a bare knuckle fighter living off the money won in bets by his manager Speed (James Coburn). In New Orleans, he causes gangsters to lose so much money that they set up a fight between Chaney and a rugged opponent (Nick Dimitri) who is sure to kill him. Chaney goes ahead with the fight, and wins.

Hill has referred to his earlier screenplays as "jobs to which I brought some professional skills. I don't really see them as Avenues of personal expression." By directing *Hard Times*—and thus ensuring that his script would be filmed as written—Hill had taken a step away from the impersonal screenplays at the beginning of his career. His next movie, *The Driver*, remains his most personal project, the only film for which he is both director and sole credited screenwriter. The Driver (Ryan O'Neal)—none of the film's characters has any names—is the best getaway car driver in Los Angeles. The Cop (Bruce Dern), his nemesis, is a man obsessed with catching "the cowboy who's never been caught," so obsessed that he frees other criminals after they promise to set up the Driver on his next job. The Driver learns that the Cop is after him but he goes through with his next job anyway; he is not interested in getting his share of the loot, but merely wants to beat the Cop by successfully pulling off the crime. With this film, Hill developed what he calls the "exaggerated realism" of his pictures; they remain gritty though they are extremely stylized: darkly lit sets with occasional bits of vivid color.

Hard Times brought Hill little attention; *The Driver* received a few, mostly negative, reviews. *The Warriors* placed Hill in the middle of a controversy about film violence. The Warriors are a New York City street gang sent to take part in a meeting of all gangs called by Cyrus (Roger Hill), the leader of New York's biggest gang, the Riffs. Cyrus has called a truce to prove that if all the gangs banded together they could run the city; as he speaks, Cyrus is murdered by Luther (David Patrick Kelly), an insane member of the Rogues who blames the killing on the Warriors. The truce now over, the Warriors have to make a trip back to Coney Island without being captured by the police or the rival gangs (just as the McCoys had to avoid police and rival criminals in *The Getaway*.)

The Warriors was based on a 1965 novel by Sol Yurick, but Hill intended his screenplay to be more of an updated version of Xenophon's play *Anabasis*, about a group of Greek warriors caught in enemy territory after the death of their leader. (In the film the Warriors' leader is captured, and presumably killed, after Cyrus's murder.) To underscore the

Joanne Woodward and Paul Newman in the film version of Ross Macdonald's The Drowning Pool

point, Hill provided a kind of Greek chorus in the form of a disc jockey (Lynne Thigpen) who comments on the film's actions. The movie was never intended to appear realistic; Hill conceived of it as a "comic book" story and directed it to give the film a surreal, nightmarish quality. But it was still too realistic for some critics, who found the violence in the film appalling; three people were killed in theaters showing the film and *The Warriors* was held responsible. At least one state tried to ban the movie, and Paramount studios yanked almost all its advertising. Still, the movie was a financial success; *48 Hrs.* is Hill's only other popular success.

After *The Warriors*, Hill produced *Alien* (1979) and directed *The Long Riders* (1980). He worked on the screenplays for both but received credit for neither. *Alien* is Hill's only science fiction credit (though Paul Schrader says he worked on *Close Encounters of the Third Kind*, 1977), in which the seven-

member crew (Tom Skerritt, Sigourney Weaver, Yaphet Kotto, Veronica Cartwright, John Hurt, Ian Holm, Harry Dean Stanton) of a spaceship are killed, one by one, by an alien creature. Hill and David Giler, his coproducer, rewrote a screenplay by Dan O'Bannon and assigned themselves screen credit, but after an arbitration hearing by the Screen Writers Guild, O'Bannon received sole credit. *The Long Riders* is the story of Jesse James (James Keach) and his gang, covering the last few years of James's life. Hill directed from a screenplay by James and Stacy Keach, Stephen Philip Smith, and Bill Bryden, making only minor script changes before filming.

Hill and Giler next teamed to produce and write *Southern Comfort* (1981) which Hill directed. He had conceived of the picture years before, after meeting some Cajuns during the filming of *Hard Times* and becoming interested in Cajun society. In

Michael Beck (left foreground) and David Patrick Kelly (far right) in The Warriors, *in which Hill imposed elements of Xenophon's* Anabasis *upon the plot of a 1965 novel by Sol Yurick*

1973 a National Guard unit is on maneuvers in Louisiana. As a prank, one man (Lewis Smith) shoots blanks at some Cajuns they see, but the Cajuns think they are being attacked and shoot back, killing the unit's commander (Peter Coyote) and leaving the other men frightened and unable to find their way out of the swamp. The film's premise is similar to that of *The Warriors,* but the remainder of the film is not: while the Warriors are able to work together as a team and make their way home, the Guardsmen quarrel, separate, and are killed off one by one by the Cajuns, the swamp, and each other. The film is both a suspenseful story of men fleeing danger and a study of those men as they break under pressure. Only two of the guardsmen survive by the movie's end.

In many ways, *48 Hrs.* is the prototypical Hill film; in others, it is an oddity among his work. It contains many of his usual trademarks: a seamy urban setting, violent action, a protagonist who is a loner, and a compressed time scheme. But his protagonists (Nick Nolte, Eddie Murphy) are the pursuers, not the pursued; they are not in any real physical danger until the film's climax. There is also much more humor than is usual. After he breaks out of prison, psychopath Ganz (James Remar) murders a police officer (Jonathan Banks) and steals the gun of another officer, Jack Cates (Nolte).

Cates wants to capture Ganz so desperately that he frees Ganz's former partner, Reggie Hammond (Murphy), from prison for forty-eight hours after Hammond agrees to help him. The movie is little more than an extended chase sequence, with Cates and Hammond pursuing Ganz and his associate (Sonny Landham) all over San Francisco. It is also a character study of Cates and Hammond, with the two men developing a growing respect for one another. The screenplay, written with Larry Gross, Roger Spottiswoode, and Steven de Souza, was produced under pressure, since there was a rush to complete the film in just a few months so that it could be released at Christmas; and much ad-libbing went on on the set, so much that Hill said that Nolte and Murphy deserved screen credit. *48 Hrs.* was one of the biggest hits of 1982, and remains Hill's most popular film.

Streets of Fire, like *The Warriors,* was described by Hill as "comic book in concept." It was subtitled "a rock and roll fable" and set in "another time, another place." During a rock concert, singer Ellen Aim (Diane Lane) is kidnapped by gang leader Raven (Willem Dafoe); her manager, Billy Fish (Rick Moranis) hires Aim's ex-lover Tom Cody (Michael Pare) and soldier of fortune McCoy to sneak into the gang's hideout and bring Ellen back. They escape with Aim, but Raven confronts Cody, learns his name, and tracks him home for a climactic street fight. Though it is thinly plotted *Streets of Fire* is an exceptional piece due to Hill's visual sense and the film's underlying theme: its characters have no future and no place to go. The movie begins with Aim singing "We're going nowhere fast"; Fish describes himself, Aim, Cody and McCoy as "nobody going noplace"; after defeating Raven, Cody drives away with McCoy, leaving his hometown though he has no destination in mind. Ellen Aim is plagued with self-doubts; "I'm just a singer," she tells an overzealous fan. But by the film's end, she is back on stage; like all of Hill's characters, she is what she does. Hill followed *Streets of Fire* with two separate projects: an adaptation of Ross Macdonald's forthcoming novel *Blue City*, which he wrote but did not direct, and a remake of *Brewster's Million*, which he directed only.

Throughout his career, Walter Hill's screenplays have been remarkably consistent in theme. Like John Ford and Howard Hawks, two filmmakers he admires, he is less concerned with specific issues than he is with more abstract concerns such as heroism and courage. By his own admission, his screenplays are intended to evoke in his audience the memory of things they might have forgotten. This does not mean Hill is not a creative screenwriter; unlike many of his contemporaries, he is not just remaking the films he loved as a child. Walter Hill is helping to redefine old film genres, and for that he is a filmmaker worthy of respect.

Interviews:

Bob Martin, "Walter Hill," *Starlog* (July 1979): 92-95;

Alain Silver and Elizabeth Ward, "Scriptwriter and Director," *Movie* (Winter 1978/1979): 29-42.

References:

Audie Bock, "Walter Hill's Street Blues," *Moviegoer* (November 1982): 6-7;

Michael Goodwin, "The Hit Master," *Esquire*, 96 (November 1981): 116-122;

Samir Hachem, "Nick Nolte Plays Cops and Robbers for 48 Hrs.," *Prevue* (January 1983): 42-51;

Rick Lyman, "Hill Making Westerns No Matter the Setting," *The Atlanta Constitution* (15 June 1984): 3P;

Michael Sragow, "Don't Jesse James Me!," *Sight and Sound*, 51 (Summer 1982): 194-198;

Sragow, "Ghost Writers in the Cinema," *Film Comment*, 19 (March-April 1983): 9-18.

Ernest Lehman
(1920-)

Nick Roddick

MOTION PICTURES: *The Inside Story* (Republic, 1948), story by Lehman and Gerza Herczeg;

Executive Suite (M-G-M, 1954), screenplay;

Sabrina (Paramount, 1954), screenplay by Lehman, Billy Wilder, and Samuel Taylor;

The King and I (20th Century-Fox, 1956), screenplay;

Somebody Up There Likes Me (M-G-M, 1956), screenplay;

Sweet Smell of Success (United Artists, 1957), story by Lehman, screenplay by Lehman and Clifford Odets, adapted from *Tell Me About it Tomorrow* by Lehman;

North by Northwest (M-G-M, 1959), screen story and screenplay;

From the Terrace (20th Century-Fox, 1960), screenplay;

West Side Story (Mirisch Pictures-Seven Arts Productions/United Artists, 1961), screenplay;

The Prize (M-G-M, 1963), screenplay;

The Sound of Music (20th Century-Fox, 1965), screenplay;

Who's Afraid of Virginia Woolf? (Warner Bros., 1966), screenplay;

Hello, Dolly! (20th Century-Fox, 1969), screenplay;

Portnoy's Complaint (Warner Bros., 1972), screenplay;

Family Plot (Universal, 1976), screenplay;

Black Sunday (Paramount, 1977), screenplay by Lehman, Kenneth Ross, and Ivan Moffat.

Ernest Lehman

BOOKS: *The Comedian and Other Stories* (New York: New American Library, 1957);

Sweet Smell of Success and Other Stories (New York: New American Library, 1957);

North by Northwest (New York: Viking Press, 1972);

The French Atlantic Affair (New York: Atheneum, 1977);

Final Performance (New York: McGraw-Hill, 1983).

TELEVISION: "The Comedian," *Playhouse 90* (CBS, 1957).

Ernest Lehman's scripts defy categorization. They include dramas: *Executive Suite* (1954), *Sweet Smell of Success* (1957), *Who's Afraid of Virginia Woolf?* (1966); musicals: *The King and I* (1956), *West Side Story* (1961), *The Sound of Music* (1965), *Hello, Dolly!* (1969); and thrillers: *North by Northwest* (1959), *Family Plot,* (1976), and *Black Sunday* (1977). His versatility made him one of the most successful screenwriters of the 1960s and 1970s, and as his reputation and earning power grew, so did his involvement in other aspects of the film business. Lehman added the role of producer to his credits with *Who's Afraid of Virginia Woolf.* From there, he went on, through his own Chenault Productions, to both produce and write *Hello, Dolly!* and to produce, write, and direct *Portnoy's Complaint* (1972).

Lehman was born in New York City, but his family moved to Woodmere, Long Island, when he was five years old. His education began at Woodmere Academy, a private school, but when the Depression came he was transferred to Lawrence High School. Lehman entered the College of the City of New York as a science major to study chemical engineering but became interested in literature, changed courses, and graduated with what he calls a "hybrid degree" of bachelor of science in English.

He worked briefly as a copy editor on a Wall Street financial magazine and lost the job when the magazine folded; Lehman tried free-lance writing and immediately sold a profile of bandleader Ted Lewis (coauthored by David Brown) to *Collier's.* He decided he did not like the insecurity of free-lance work and took a job writing copy for a publicity agency specializing in the entertainment business— a background which he was to use in his story (and subsequent screenplay) "Sweet Smell of Success." He continued to write stories and magazine pieces, one of which, "The Inside Story," was filmed in 1948.

After Lehman's short story "The Comedian" appeared in *Collier's* in 1953, Paramount optioned it and brought Lehman to Hollywood and placed him under contract as a screenwriter. But his first screenplay was written for M-G-M, not Paramount. Plans to film "The Comedian" fell through, and Lehman spent an unproductive year at Paramount. Then a former associate from New York who had become an assistant producer at M-G-M introduced Lehman to John Houseman, who needed someone to adapt Cameron Hawley's novel *Executive Suite* for the screen. The film depicts the behind-the-scenes machinations at a major corporation after the chairman of the board has died and several executives compete to succeed him. They include Loren Phineas Shaw (Fredric March), a financier more concerned with profit than quality; Julia O. Treadway (Barbara Stanwyck), daughter of the company's founder working in league with Shaw; and McDonald Walling (William Holden), an idealistic young furniture designer. Walling is named the new chairman, thanks to an impassioned speech to the board stressing the need for positive leadership. Under Robert Wise's direction (they subsequently worked on three other films, a quarter of Lehman's output), Lehman's screenplay creates a convincing business setting, turning the novel into a series of carefully orchestrated scenes which place each character in focus.

Executive Suite established Lehman as a promising talent, and at the request of Billy Wilder he returned to Paramount to work on *Sabrina* (1954). Based on the stage success by Samuel Taylor (who shares screenplay credit with Lehman and Wilder), the film has at least one major resemblance to *Executive Suite:* a slight but crucial business background. Sabrina Fairchild (Audrey Hepburn) is a chauffeur's daughter who falls in love with the playboy son (William Holden) of her father's employer. She is ignored, goes to a Paris cooking school, acquires sophistication, and returns to have the playboy fall in love with her, only to realize that his business-obsessed older brother (Humphrey Bogart) is a better man. *Sabrina* is largely Wilder's film; the main connection between the movie and later Lehman screenplays is the acerbic humor set in a context slightly apart from that of everyday people. Lehman received his first Academy Award nomination for *Sabrina.*

Lehman's next two screenplays, *The King and I* and *Somebody Up There Likes Me* (1956), exemplify the wide range of his writing talent. *The King and I* was based on Margaret Landon's book *Anna and the King of Siam* and the Broadway musical by Richard Rodgers and Oscar Hammerstein II. The story of a determined English governess (Deborah Kerr) who sets about "civilizing" her employer, the King of Siam (Yul Brynner, who won an Oscar), the film is a fairly straight adaptation of the stage success, with more emphasis on the songs than on the dance numbers. It was an enormous commercial success and was nominated for several Academy Awards, including best picture and best screenplay.

The King and I: *Yul Brynner as the King of Siam in the role with which he became identified*

North by Northwest: *Cary Grant and Eva Marie Saint on Mount Rushmore in one of the best-known chase scenes in movie history*

Somebody Up There Likes Me was based on the autobiography of boxer Rocky Graziano. The film follows its hero (Paul Newman) from the East Side, through reform school, the army, the army prison (where he was sent for going AWOL), discovery by promoter Irving Cohen (Everett Sloane), suspension for refusing to reveal who tried to make him take a dive, and finally success and the middleweight championship. The film is dominated by violence that transcends any sentimentality, particularly under the brisk direction of Robert Wise.

With *Sweet Smell of Success,* Lehman returned to familiar ground, the world of the Broadway columnist. Megalomaniac columnist J. J. Hunsecker (Burt Lancaster) coerces struggling publicity agent Sidney Falco (Tony Curtis) into ruining the repu-

tation of Steve Dallas (Martin Milner), who is in love with Hunsecker's sister (Susan Harrison). Falco thinks this will put him in Hunsecker's favor, but Hunsecker betrays him. Lehman had wanted to direct this film himself, but United Artists apparently vetoed the idea, selecting instead British director Alexander Mackendrick. Lehman became ill under the strain of arguments about the direction and was sent to Tahiti by his doctors for a complete rest. When rewrites became necessary, Clifford Odets was called in. Lehman seems to have no hard feelings about this, but there seems little doubt that the final movie shows mostly Odets's influence, especially in its bitterness about the entertainment industry and its penchant for melodramatic confrontations.

Lehman's next project moved off in yet another direction, that of witty thriller. Nominated for best screenplay by the Academy of Motion Picture Arts and Sciences and The Writers Guild, *North by Northwest* is probably his finest work, a model of screenplay construction as well as a fine piece of dramatic writing. The film's success is all the more impressive when one considers that the starting point was just a couple of ideas: a chase vaguely northwest from New York to Alaska, taking in Mount Rushmore, and a United Nations delegate being murdered in broad daylight in the UN building. Both ideas survive in the final screenplay, but are enormously modified. Even by the time shooting started only three quarters of the screenplay was complete and neither Lehman nor director Alfred Hitchcock was sure what the end would be.

North by Northwest combines two favorite Hitchcock themes: mistaken identity and a protracted chase that, in this case, takes up three quarters of the movie. New York advertising executive Roger O. Thornhill (Cary Grant) is abducted by two men convinced he is someone called Kaplan. He escapes and begins his pursuit of the mysterious Kaplan while the criminals pursue him across the country. Hitchcock is renowned for the extent to which he involved himself in the preparatory stages—especially the scripting—of all his films. And given such characteristic Hitchcock devices as the presence of a dangerous blonde, the chase, the mistaken identity, and the general tongue-in-cheek nature of the film, Lehman's precise contributions are hard to determine. The screenplay is, however, constructed with a kind of bitter wit typical of Lehman, as in Thornhill's remark that, "My wives divorced me . . . I think they said I led too dull a life," as he tries to escape a gunman on Mount Rushmore.

His adaptation of John O'Hara's novel *From the Terrace* (1960) took Lehman back to the emotional turmoils of a successful business career.

Julie Andrews, Christopher Plummer, and Peggy Wood in The Sound of Music, *which won an Academy Award for the best picture of 1965*

Richard Burton and Elizabeth Taylor in the film version of Edward Albee's play Who's Afraid of Virginia Woolf?

Alfred Eaton (Paul Newman) rises to success by rescuing the grandson of a Wall Street banker from a frozen lake. Eaton neglects his wife (Joanne Woodward), who has an affair with a psychiatrist (Patrick O'Neal). Eaton takes up with the daughter of a Pennsylvanian businessman, rediscovers love, and leaves his wife, his job, and New York in search of a happier future. Lehman reduced O'Hara's lifetime study of his character to a mere fifteen-year period and gave the story a happy ending. The results were not entirely successful, and it is one of Lehman's least rewarding movies.

West Side Story was both one of Lehman's best screenplays and one of his most successful, earning him his third Academy Award nomination. The play, an updated version of *Romeo and Juliet* set among the street gangs of New York's upper West Side, had been a great stage success, but there was no reason why such a success should necessarily have resulted in a screen hit, especially since the audiences for stage and screen were, by 1961, firmly separated. Lehman's work on *West Side Story* is a great deal more than a simple adaptation. He

both restructured it (rearranging the order of the songs and some of the scenes) and gave a stronger social emphasis to the story's theme. Foremost among the changes was a fairly unequivocal statement that the real villains were racism and poverty. This shift in emphasis received a certain amount of criticism at the time of the movie's release, and there is certainly a tendency in the film to sanitize the Jets, who seem at times to be just another likable bunch of teenagers, complete with comic members and snappy dialogue. But the change nonetheless gives bite to the movie, balancing the tendency for it to become an overly sentimental love story with a downbeat setting.

Mark Robson and Paul Newman, the producer-director and star of *From the Terrace*, reunited with Lehman for *The Prize* (1963). Based on Irving Wallace's novel, the film is about a gathering of Nobel Prize candidates in Stockholm. Lehman's screenplay changed the serious novel into a fast-paced tongue-in-cheek thriller much like *North by Northwest*. Neither audiences nor critics had expected the film to be a humorous thriller and some

Ernest Lehman on the set of Hello, Dolly!

viewers were confused by Lehman's whimsical treatment of the subject. *The Prize* was a financial success, but received mixed reviews.

Like *The King and I, The Sound of Music* was adapted from a hit stage musical by Rodgers and Hammerstein. The film is unabashedly sentimental, telling the story of Maria (Julie Andrews), a postulant preparing to be a nun, who is sent as governess to an unruly family of seven children belonging to the widowed Baron von Trapp (Christopher Plummer), an Austrian aristocrat. Maria wins over the children, then the Baron, while teaching the children to sing, and joins them in their flight from the Nazis. Lehman's script fleshes out the stage musical, showing a great deal of assurance in its handling of the sentimental themes. *The Sound of Music* is not an entirely successful movie, but it is better than its critical reception—or its subsequent reputation—may suggest, for although the film won an Oscar for best picture of 1964, its reception by the critics was lukewarm.

Again, Lehman followed one film with another that was totally different, in this case moving from *The Sound of Music* to *Who's Afraid of Virginia Woolf.* This adaptation of Edward Albee's play was extremely successful, winning a total of five Acad-

emy Awards and earning Lehman another Oscar nomination. The story deals with a climactic, drink-sodden night in the home of college professor George and his wife Martha (Richard Burton and Elizabeth Taylor) to which young colleagues Nick and Honey (George Segal and Sandy Dennis) have been invited after a campus reception. What follows is an evening of bickering, taunts, sexual humiliations, and games played around the imaginary existence of the child Martha and George have never had. The play's acts are designated "Fun and Games," "Walpurgisnacht," and "Exorcism"—an accurate description of the theme of the play as the tensions build, explode, and finally dissipate, indicating the strength of the relationship between George and Martha.

Lehman's script fleshes out the play, though the final screenplay contains very little original work; Lehman says that most of the additions he made in his six drafts were removed at the insistence of director Mike Nichols (whom Lehman, as producer of the film, had hired). Much of the credit for the movie's enormous success, both critical and commercial, must go to Albee's original play, but Lehman deserves some praise, both as writer and producer, for undertaking what at the time was a bold and risky project, a landmark film in its outspoken treatment of sex and its uninhibited language.

Hello, Dolly! was the first film produced by Lehman's own Chenault Productions. With Lehman as screenwriter and producer, Barbra Streisand as star, and Gene Kelly directing his first major musical in over a decade, the film seemed destined to be a success, but it turned out to be a disappointment for everyone involved. As with his other musical screenplays, Lehman attempted to provide the musical numbers with a firmer dramatic framework—in this case, to reintroduce more of the source, Thornton Wilder's *The Matchmaker*, than was possible in the stage version. But *The Matchmaker* revolves around a contrast between small town and big city values, ending up very much in favor of the former, while the musical relies on a lavish recreation of the splendor of turn-of-the-century New York society, and thus glorifies the city. The result is that the Yonkers background is never really established, nor placed into proper conflict with the mammoth New York reconstructions. In subsequent discussions of the film, Lehman has admitted *Hello, Dolly!* was a mistake: "I think the script was kind of weak, but for the life of me I don't know how to make anything really solid out of *The Matchmaker.*"

Bruce Dern and Marthe Keller in Black Sunday, *Lehman's most recent film*

Lehman's next project, *Portnoy's Complaint* (1972) was nearly an outright disaster. Based on Philip Roth's best-selling novel, and produced, written, and directed by Lehman, *Portnoy's Complaint* deals with the sexual hang-ups and fantasies of thirty-three-year-old mother-obsessed Alexander Portnoy (Richard Benjamin). Lehman's semi-serious treatment of his material undermines much of the humor, with only a few scenes rescuing the film from total failure. *Portnoy's Complaint* did undeniable damage to Lehman's career. His next project, a comedy-thriller about a revolutionary plot to blow up Acapulco, which was to have been his first produced original screenplay since *North by Northwest*, was abandoned. He has neither produced nor directed any other movie, and it was not until four years later that his next film was released. Lehman remains philosophical about these developments. "I've been lucky with a lot of pictures that I didn't produce," he told an interviewer in 1976. "Let's face it, most of the best pictures that you see in a list of my credits are pictures that I did not produce."

Family Plot was Alfred Hitchcock's last film.

The story, an immensely complex tale of kidnapping, murder, concealed identity, fake spiritualism, and man's fascination with diamonds, was taken from Victor Canning's novel *The Rainbird Pattern*. To an even greater extent than is normal with Hitchcock, the story is merely a pretext for an elegant development of familiar themes: a deft exercise in keeping the audience simultaneously bemused and on the edge of their seats. Many of the scenes are formal visual exercises rather than integral parts of the story, as in the daring kidnapping of a bishop in the middle of a service in a San Francisco cathedral. *Family Plot* is one of Hitchcock's minor films.

Lehman's next picture, *Black Sunday*, adapted from a novel by Thomas Harris and written in collaboration with Kenneth Rose and Ivan Moffat, is his last to date. It is a political thriller involving an attempt by the Palestinian Black September movement to bomb the Super Bowl game from the Goodyear blimp. The action sequences of the movie—an Israeli commando raid on Black September headquarters, the final struggle between the blimp pilot (Bruce Dern) and the Israeli major

(Robert Shaw)—are directed by John Frankenheimer with his usual flair for suspense. The sequences in between show little of Lehman's wit or flair for narrative construction. The film is well-intentioned but muddled.

Since 1976 Lehman has written no further screenplays and, unlike other screenwriters, he has tended to stay away from television. He has, however, written a novel, *The French Atlantic Affair* (1977), that was produced as a television mini-series in 1979. Since April 1978 he has had a regular column in *American Film,* and in the late 1970s he became a fixture on the college circuit, teaching at Sherman Oaks Experimental College in California and going to Dartmouth College as part of the Academy Visiting Artists Program.

Ernest Lehman's indisputable claim as a major screenwriter rests on a string of critical and commercial successes between 1956 and 1966. His four movies since *Who's Afraid of Virginia Woolf?* have had their good qualities, but none has achieved either the commercial or the artistic success of *North by Northwest, West Side Story* or *The Sound of Music,* and certainly none has achieved both. A champion of the well-crafted, what-happens-next screenplay, he has been somewhat adrift in the formal and narrative experiments of the 1970s and 1980s.

References:
Richard Boeth, "Screenwriters of the 70s," *Cosmopolitan* (July 1975): 168-171, 182;

Richard Corliss, *Talking Pictures: Screenwriters in the American Cinema, 1927-73* (Woodstock: Overlook Press, 1974), pp. 188-195;

Ernest Lehman: An American Film Institute Seminar on his Work (Glen Rock, N.J.: Microfilming Corporation of America, 1977);

Axel Madsen, "Who's Afraid of Alfred Hitchcock?" *Sight and Sound,* 37 (Winter 1967-1968): 26-27;

James Powers, "Dialogue on Film: Ernest Lehman," *American Film,* 2 (October 1976): 33-48;

John Russell Taylor, *Hitch: The Life and Work of Alfred Hitchcock* (London: Faber & Faber, 1978); retitled *Hitch: The Life and Times of Alfred Hitchcock* (New York: Pantheon, 1978).

Papers:
Lehman's manuscripts and correspondence are housed at the University of Texas in Austin.

Isobel Lennart
(18 May 1915-25 January 1971)

Thomas Slater
Northwest Missouri State University

MOTION PICTURES: *The Affairs of Martha* (M-G-M, 1942), screen story and screenplay by Lennart and Lee Gold;

Lost Angel (M-G-M, 1944), screen story and screenplay;

Anchors Aweigh (M-G-M, 1945), screenplay;

Holiday in Mexico (M-G-M, 1946), screenplay;

It Happened in Brooklyn (M-G-M, 1947), screenplay;

The Kissing Bandit (M-G-M, 1949), screen story and screenplay by Lennart and John Briard Harding;

Holiday Affair (RKO, 1949), screenplay;

East Side, West Side (M-G-M, 1950), screenplay;

A Life of Her Own (M-G-M, 1950), screenplay;

"Rosika, the Rose," in *It's a Big Country* (M-G-M, 1952), screenplay;

Skirts Ahoy (M-G-M, 1952), screen story and screenplay;

My Wife's Best Friend (20th Century-Fox, 1952), screenplay;

Latin Lovers (M-G-M, 1953), screen story and screenplay;

The Girl Next Door (20th Century-Fox, 1953), screenplay;

Love Me or Leave Me (M-G-M, 1955), screenplay by Lennart and Daniel Fuchs;

Meet Me in Las Vegas (M-G-M, 1956), screen story and screenplay;

This Could Be the Night (M-G-M, 1957), screenplay;

Isobel Lennart

Merry Andrew (M-G-M, 1958), screenplay by Lennart and I. A. L. Diamond;

The Inn of the Sixth Happiness (20th Century-Fox, 1958), screenplay;

Please Don't Eat the Daisies (M-G-M, 1960), screenplay;

The Sundowners (Warner Bros., 1960), screenplay;

Period of Adjustment (M-G-M, 1962), screenplay;

Two for the Seesaw (United Artists, 1962), screenplay;

Fitzwilly (United Artists, 1967), screenplay;

Funny Girl (Columbia, 1968), screenplay adapted by Lennart from her play.

PLAY PRODUCTION: *Funny Girl*, New York, Winter Garden, 24 March 1961.

Isobel Lennart's career was devoted primarily to writing musicals and light comedy. Though the light touch she aimed for sometimes seemed merely superficial, she was often successful and helped to create several very entertaining movies. Her best pictures are those in which a spirited, robust character is portrayed by an appropriate performer: Gene Kelly in *Anchors Aweigh* (1945), Barbra Streisand in *Funny Girl* (1968).

Lennart was born in Brooklyn, New York, but came to California while in her early twenties, seeking a career in motion pictures. In 1939 she joined the Communist Party; she quit after the signing of the Hitler-Stalin pact but rejoined in 1941 after Germany invaded Russia. She quit again in 1945 and seven years later voluntarily testified about her former activities to a Congressional committee. The knowledge of her involvement with the Party does not seem to have harmed her career, probably because almost all of her films espouse traditional values.

The frothy optimism of Lennart's screenplays may be attributable to the change in her political beliefs; her earliest scripts show a marked sympathy for the working class. In her first picture, *The Affairs of Martha* (1942), a servant embarrasses her employers by writing a revealing book about them. (The film was directed by Jules Dassin, a Communist party member who was later blacklisted.) Lennart's second credit for M-G-M, *Lost Angel* (1944), is about a child prodigy (Margaret O'Brien) who is reared in a scientific institution, runs away, and meets some "common man" characters, including a newspaper reporter (James Craig) and a tough-talking man (Keenan Wynn) who is really soft-hearted. Unfortunately, the girl's character is not well-developed and remains artificial; Lennart was mainly interested in presenting her idealized working-class adults.

Lennart never did abandon her focus on middle- or working-class characters, but beginning with *Anchors Aweigh* her stories took on a different nature. In that film, two sailors (Gene Kelly and Frank Sinatra) on leave try to arrange an audition for an aspiring singer (Kathryn Grayson). Most of Lennart's subsequent scripts involve characters who achieve their goals or fantasies through hard work and struggle, or sometimes just through good fortune. The emphasis is on an optimistic sense of possibilities rather than on characters who merely become satisfied with their lot. Those characters who are satisfied and complacent generally demonstrate the values of family and hard work.

The Lennart scripts that carry a positive message are mainly her musicals, most of which were produced under the aegis of the Joe Pasternak unit at M-G-M. *It Happened in Brooklyn* (1947) and *The Kissing Bandit* (1949) reunited Frank Sinatra and Kathryn Grayson from *Anchors Aweigh*. Lennart drew on her Brooklyn upbringing for *It Happened in Brooklyn* about four young people (Sinatra, Grayson, Peter Lawford, and Gloria Grahame) pursuing show business careers. *The Kissing Bandit* was written in collaboration with John Briard Harding; it is one of the few films on which Lennart worked with a collaborator. In this picture, the son (Frank Sinatra) of an infamous kissing bandit in the Old West decides to follow in his father's footsteps. Neither picture repeated the success of *Anchors Aweigh,* and Lennart's best musical of this period was *Holiday in Mexico* (1946), about the efforts of the teenage daughter (Jane Powell) of the American Ambassador (Walter Pidgeon) to run a motherless home. The movie had both good humor and good music, and the Mexican setting helped Lennart create a lighthearted mood.

Holiday Affair (1949) was Lennart's first attempt at romantic comedy, a genre well-suited for her wish-fulfillment formula. A struggling young widow (Janet Leigh) with a reliable but somewhat

dull fiancé (Wendell Corey) suddenly finds herself being courted by a charming man (Robert Mitchum) she has known only a few days. As usual, Lennart keeps the tone light: no one worries seriously about the characters' problems (although both the main characters are unemployed at one point) and everything ends happily.

Three consecutive scripts followed which examined the problem of infidelity. Lennart adapted *East Side, West Side* (1950) from a best-selling novel by Marcia Davenport. Mervyn LeRoy directed this story of an upper-class New York couple (Barbara Stanwyck and James Mason) whose marriage is destroyed by the husband's affair. *A Life of Her Own* (1950), directed by George Cukor, is about a Kansas woman (Lana Turner) who comes to New York

Margaret O'Brien and Keenan Wynn in Lost Angel, *Lennart's first musical*

Gene Kelly dancing with cartoon characters Tom and Jerry in Anchors Aweigh. *This animation/live-action sequence required two months of filming.*

and becomes a successful model. A Montana miner (Ray Milland) makes her his mistress, but she leaves him when she learns he has a crippled wife who needs him. She gives up both riches and the man she loves. Much lighter in tone was *My Wife's Best Friend* (1952), about a married couple (Anne Baxter and MacDonald Carey) who confess their extramarital affairs when they think the plane they are traveling on is going to crash.

Lennart contributed material to *It's a Big Country* (1952), an episodic film dramatizing the values of American society; seven screenwriters, seven directors, and an all-star cast participated in the project. Lennart's episode is about a Hungarian immigrant (S. Z. Sakall) who is biased against Greeks until his daughter (Janet Leigh) marries a Greek man (Gene Kelly).

Four more musicals followed. *Skirts Ahoy* (1952) is about three WAVEs (Esther Williams, Joan Evans, and Vivian Blaine) on leave, but Lennart's screenplay allows them to achieve their particular goals too easily, and the film lacks dramatic tension. In *Latin Lovers* (1953), a wealthy woman (Lana Turner), fearing men are only interested in her for her money and unhappy with her fiancé (John Lund), flees to Latin America where she is unknown and meets a man (Ricardo Montalban) who genuinely loves her. In *The Girl Next Door* (1953), a cartoonist (Dan Dailey) falls in love with his new neighbor, a singer (June Haver). Similarly, a rancher (Dailey) and a ballerina (Cyd Charisse) meet and fall in love in *Meet Me in Las Vegas* (1956). This is possibly the best film of the four; Lennart's screenplay was humorous and made good use of the Las Vegas setting.

Lennart wrote two other pictures that contained many musical numbers but are not actually musicals. *Love Me or Leave Me* (1955) was based on the true story of the marriage of singer Ruth Etting (Doris Day) to ex-Chicago mobster Martin Snyder (James Cagney). Although Lennart and co-author Daniel Fuchs soften the characters somewhat—Etting sings at the opening of Snyder's night club for old time's sake at the film's end—the picture still achieves a high level of tension.

Merry Andrew (1958), Lennart's other movie with music, was cowritten with I. A. L. Diamond. An English schoolteacher (Danny Kaye) becomes involved with a small traveling circus and falls in love with an aerialist (Pier Angeli). The situation allows the movie's creators to put Kaye in precarious situations (in a lion's cage, on a trapeze) that produce a very entertaining picture.

Love Me or Leave Me and *Merry Andrew* address a consistent theme in Lennart's screenplays. The big city is a place where success is based on questionable terms and marriages have a difficult time surviving. It is an unethical environment in which

dreams and true love are shattered. This description applies mainly to older cities such as New York and Chicago, while Las Vegas is presented as a fantasy playground where good times and happiness abound. Similarly, all other environments outside of the metropolitan areas are places where dreams can still come true. *Funny Girl* is the ultimate model of this theme, for it is based on the premise that even a plain-looking woman can, with enough determination, rise out of the trap of the urban environment.

In *Two for the Seesaw* (1962), Lennart's view of New York again holds true. A successful lawyer (Robert Mitchum) begins a relationship with an eccentric New York woman (Shirley MacLaine), giving her the money for her own dance studio. When he feels that she is paying too much attention to another man, though, he slaps her around and returns to his former wife in Omaha. Bosley Crowther observed, "Thus the picture concludes, not ironically and believably, as did the play, but in a dull wash of phony behavior and sentimen-

Wendell Corey, Janet Leigh, Gordon Gebert, Henry Morgan, Robert Mitchum, Larry J. Blake, and Charles Sullivan in Holiday Affair, *Lennart's first romantic comedy*

James Cagney and Doris Day in Love Me or Leave Me, *based on the marriage of former mobster Martin Snyder and singer Ruth Etting*

tality." Not only was New York again presented as an impossible place for an honest love affair, but William Gibson's play was purposely altered to make it appear that way.

Again, by contrast, *The Inn of the Sixth Happiness* (1958) and *The Sundowners* (1960) were stories about common people who struggle and survive in the rugged rural country of a foreign land. Based on fact, *The Inn of the Sixth Happiness* was about an English housemaid (Ingrid Bergman) who bravely leads a group of Chinese children on a dangerous journey through the mountains in order to escape Japanese invaders. *The Sundowners,* for which Lennart received an Academy Award nomination, studied a poor but happy family of migrant workers struggling to survive in the Australian back

country. Lennart seemed to feel that when people are given enough space to move around in, they are happy and able to rise to new levels of strength and courage even if they are poor.

She seemed to believe that in the city no amount of money can secure happiness, and relationships have a difficult time surviving. *Please Don't Eat the Daisies* (1960) and *Period of Adjustment* (1962) were two movies about marital and family difficulties set in urban locations. *Please Don't Eat the Daisies* was adapted from the book and play by Jean Kerr. MacKay (David Niven), a college drama professor turned drama critic, his wife Kate (Doris Day), and his four sons move from New York to a house in the country. MacKay's commuting to New York, Kate's boredom, and MacKay's friendship with a sexy actress (Janis Paige) cause problems in the MacKays' marriage, though they are worked out by the film's end.

Period of Adjustment, adapted from Tennessee Williams's play, was directed by George Roy Hill, who also directed the stage production. Two married couples—one newlyweds (Jane Fonda and Jim Hutton), the other married for several years (Anthony Franciosa and Lois Nettleton)—go through a "period of adjustment" during which they learn to cope with their marital problems. Critical reception was favorable, and Lennart was praised for her job of transferring Williams's play to the screen.

Lennart is most famous for the last screenplay she produced: *Funny Girl* (1968). Since she also wrote the original play, Lennart's work on *Funny Girl* truly represents the peak of her creative talents and the culmination of the major themes in her movies. The film possesses an ample amount of humor and the kind of "success story" plot that helps a good musical attain an air of fantasy. In this case, the true story of Fanny Brice (portrayed by Barbra Streisand, who won an Academy Award for her performance) helps the humor and adds a degree of believability.

On 25 January 1971 Isobel Lennart suffered severe injuries from a car accident in Hemet, California. She died a short time later in a hospital. Lennart was survived by her husband, actor John Harding, her son, and her daughter.

Sonya Levien

(25 December 1888-19 March 1960)

Edith Hurwitz

MOTION PICTURES: *Who Will Marry Me?* (1919), story;

Cheated Love (Universal, 1921), additional story; scenario by Levien, Doris Schroeder, and Lucien Hubbard;

First Love (Realart Pictures, 1921), story;

Pink Gods (Famous Players-Lasky, 1922), adaptation by Levien and J. E. Nash;

The Top of New York (Realart Pictures, 1922), story;

The Exciters (Famous Players-Lasky, 1923), scenario by Levien and John Colton;

The Snow Bride (Famous Players-Lasky, 1923), story by Levien and Julie Herne; scenario;

Salome of the Tenements (Famous Players-Lasky, 1925), scenario;

Christine of the Big Tops (Banner, 1926), story and scenario;

The Love Toy (Warner Bros., 1926), scenario by Levien as Sonya Hovey;

Why Girls Go Back Home (Warner Bros., 1926), scenario by Levien as Sonya Hovey;

A Harp in Hock (De Mille Pictures, 1927), screenplay;

The Princess from Hoboken (Tiffany Productions, 1927), story and scenario;

The Power of the Press (Columbia, 1928), adaptation and continuity by Levien and Frederick A. Thompson;

A Ship Comes In (De Mille Pictures, 1928), scenario;

Behind That Curtain (Fox, 1929), scenario;

Frozen Justice (Fox, 1929), scenario;

Lucky Star (Fox, 1929), scenario;

They Had To See Paris (Fox, 1929), scenario;

Trial Marriage (Columbia, 1929), story and scenario;

The Younger Generation (Columbia, 1929), scenario;

Lightnin' (Fox, 1930), screenplay, adaptation, and dialogue by Levien and S. N. Behrman;

Liliom (Fox, 1930), continuity;

Song O' My Heart (Fox, 1930), continuity;

So This Is London (Fox, 1930), scenario;

The Brat (Fox, 1931), screenplay by Levien, Behrman, and Maude Fulton;

Daddy Long Legs (Fox, 1931), screenplay by Levien and Behrman;

Sonya Levien (courtesy of the Henry E. Huntington Library and Art Gallery)

Delicious (Fox, 1931), screenplay by Levien and Guy Bolton;

Surrender (Fox, 1931), screenplay by Levien and Behrman;

After Tomorrow (Fox, 1932), screenplay;

Rebecca of Sunnybrook Farm (Fox, 1932), screenplay by Levien and Behrman;

She Wanted A Millionaire (Fox, 1932), original story and continuity;

Tess of the Storm Country (Fox, 1932), screenplay by Levien, Behrman, and Rupert Hughes;

As Husbands Go (Fox, 1933), screenplay by Levien and Behrman;

Berkeley Square (Fox, 1933), screenplay by Levien and John Balderston;

Cavalcade (Fox, 1933), continuity by Levien and Reginald Berkeley;

Mr. Skitch (Fox, 1933), adaptation by Levien and Ralph Spence;

State Fair (Fox, 1933), screenplay by Levien and Paul Green;

Warrior's Husband (Fox, 1933), adaptation by Levien;

Change of Heart (Fox, 1934), screenplay by Levien, James Gleason, and Samuel Hoffenstein;

The White Parade (Fox, 1934), screenplay by Levien and Ernest Pascal;

Here's To Romance (Fox, 1935), story by Levien and Pascal;

Navy Wife (Fox, 1935), screenplay;

The Country Doctor (20th Century-Fox, 1936), screenplay;

Reunion (20th Century-Fox, 1936), screenplay by Levien, Sam Hellman, and Gladys Lehman, with contributions by Walter Ferris;

In Old Chicago (20th Century-Fox, 1937), screenplay by Levien and Trotti;

Kidnapped (20th Century-Fox, 1938), screenplay by Levien, Eleanor Harris, Pascal, and Edwin Harvey Blum;

The Cowboy and the Lady (Goldwyn-United Artists, 1938), screenplay by Levien and Behrman;

Four Men and a Prayer (20th Century-Fox, 1938), screenplay by Levien, Ferris, and Richard Sherman;

Drums Along the Mohawk (20th Century-Fox, 1939), screenplay by Levien and Trotti;

The Hunchback of Notre Dame (RKO, 1939), screenplay;

Ziegfeld Girl (M-G-M, 1941), screenplay by Levien and Marguerite Roberts;

The Amazing Mrs. Holliday (Universal, 1943), screen story;

Rhapsody In Blue (Warner Bros., 1945), screen story;

The Valley of Decision (M-G-M, 1945), screenplay by Levien and John Meehan;

The Green Years (M-G-M, 1946), screenplay by Levien and Robert Ardrey;

Cass Timberlane (M-G-M, 1947), adaptation by Levien and Donald Ogden Stewart;

Three Daring Daughters (M-G-M, 1948), screen story and screenplay by Levien, Meehan, Frederick Kohner, and Albert Mannheimer;

The Great Caruso (M-G-M, 1951), screen story and screenplay by Levien and William Ludwig;

Quo Vadis (M-G-M, 1951), screenplay by Levien, Behrman, and John Lee Mahin;

The Merry Widow (M-G-M, 1952), screenplay by Levien and Ludwig;

Antonio Moreno and Bebe Daniels in The Exciters, *the story of an heiress who falls in love with a gangster but discovers, to her disappointment, that he is a federal agent*

The Student Prince (M-G-M, 1954), screenplay by Levien and Ludwig;

Hit the Deck (M-G-M, 1955), screen story and screenplay by Levien and Ludwig;

Interrupted Melody (M-G-M, 1955), screenplay by Levien and Ludwig;

Oklahoma! (Rodgers & Hammerstein/Magna, 1955), screenplay by Levien and Ludwig;

Bhowani Junction (M-G-M, 1956), screenplay by Levien and Ivan Moffat;

Jeanne Eagels (George Sidney Productions/Columbia, 1957), screenplay by Levien, Daniel Fuchs, and John Fante;

Pepe (George Sidney Posa Films International/Columbia, 1960), screen story by Levien and Leonard Spigelgass.

One of the most prolific screenwriters in the motion picture industry, Sonya Levien was born in Russia near Moscow; her family immigrated to the United States when she was a child. She graduated from New York University with a law degree but practiced law for only six months before deciding she would prefer a writing career. Levien wrote short stories and took a job as secretary to a magazine publisher. An active participant in the woman suffrage movement, she worked for one year as editor of the movement's official publication, *Woman's Journal*. She then joined the staff of *Metropolitan* magazine, eventually becoming an assistant editor. Levien married Carl Hovey, the magazine's editor, on 11 October 1917. They had two children.

Levien's short stories attracted the attention of Jesse Lasky, head of Famous Players studio, and he invited her to Hollywood in 1921. Her first scenario, *Cheated Love* (1921), was adapted by Levien from one of her short stories. Lasky offered her a contract with a starting salary of $24,000 per year, but Levien declined because she did not wish to leave her husband and son in New York. Not long afterward, Hovey accepted a job as story editor for

Cecil B. De Mille at Paramount, and Levien returned to California.

Levien is credited with seventy screenplays; her accomplishment is even more impressive because, unlike most of her contemporaries, she frequently worked without a collaborator. She was the sole screenwriter for thirty-two films. Of the remainder, ten were written with playwright S. N. Behrman and five with William Ludwig. Her early scripts frequently drew on her Jewish heritage or New York City background. *Salome of the Tenements* (1925), for example, which was adapted from a novel by Anzia Yezierska, is about a young Jewish immigrant woman (Jetta Goudal) who is courted by a gentile social worker, causing problems with her family. *The Younger Generation* (1929) is about a Jewish man (Jean Hersholt) who is critical of his children's striving for upward mobility because it

Louise Dresser and Will Rogers in the 1933 version of State Fair. *The film was nominated for an Academy Award as best picture but it lost to another of Levien's films,* Cavalcade.

means leaving the Jewish community. Frank Capra directed the movie; the preceding year, he and Levien had worked on *The Power of the Press* (1928), the story of a ruthless newspaper reporter.

Fox Films Corporation signed Levien to a long-term contract in 1929; she remained at the studio until 1941. She immediately received an important assignment, writing a film starring Fox's popular team of Janet Gaynor and Charles Farrell. *Lucky Star* (1929) is about a young farm woman (Gaynor) in love with a local man (Farrell) who was crippled during World War I; she remains loyal to him and he is eventually cured. Levien particularly enjoyed working with Frank Borzage, who directed *Lucky Star,* and she wrote the screenplays for his next three pictures. *They Had To See Paris* (1929) was the first talking picture for Will Rogers, who plays an Oklahoman who visits Paris. *Liliom* (1930) was Levien's first collaboration with Behrman, who wrote the screenplay and dialogue while she wrote the continuity; their screenplay was adapted from a play by Ferenc Molnár. Liliom (Charles Farrell) is a carnival barker who kills himself after he is arrested for stealing the carnival's payroll. In heaven, he is told he can return to Earth after ten years in purgatory. Levien's final film with Borzage was *Song O' My Heart* (1930).

They Had To See Paris had by now been released and had become such a financial success that Fox placed Will Rogers under contract and assigned Levien to write a follow-up film, *So This Is London* (1930). She and Behrman then wrote a third Rogers film, *Lightnin'* (1930), from a play by Frank Bacon and Winchell Smith. Henry King directed.

Levien and Behrman continued to adapt literary properties to the screen. *The Brat* (1931) was adapted from a play by Maude Fulton, who also collaborated on the script. John Ford directed this movie about an author (Allan Dinehart) who meets an orphaned child (Sally O'Neil) and teaches her proper social behavior. *Daddy Long Legs* (1931), based on Jean Webster's novel, stars Janet Gaynor as a young woman whose school tuition is secretly paid by a playboy (Warner Baxter). *Surrender* (1931) was based on Pierre Benoit's novel *Axelle* (1928). The niece (Leila Hyams) of a World War I German prison camp commander (C. Aubrey Smith) falls in love with one of her uncle's prisoners (Warner Baxter). *Tess of the Storm Country* (1932) was written with Behrman and Rupert Hughes, and is based on Hughes's dramatization of Grace Miller White's novel. This was the third film Levien wrote for Gaynor and Farrell, who star respectively

as Tess, a troubled young woman in a small town, and Frederick Crawford, the young man who loves Tess despite his father's disapproval. Levien and Behrman ended the year by adapting *Rebecca of Sunnybrook Farm* (1932) from the novel by Kate Douglas Wiggins.

In 1933 Levien earned three of her most important screen credits. With John Balderston, she adapted *Berkeley Square* from Balderston's play, based on Henry James's unfinished, posthumously published novel *The Sense of the Past* (1917). Peter Standish (Leslie Howard), a young American, is able to trade places with an ancestor in eighteenth-century London. He then falls in love with Helen Pettigrew, though he knows he is fated to marry her sister. *State Fair* (1933), based on a novel by Phil Stong, allowed Levien to write for both Will Rogers and Janet Gaynor; it also reunited her with *Lightnin'* director Henry King. The film has a fairly simple plot, depicting the adventures of a midwestern farm family at the fair, but it is a good example of Levien's continuing interest in family unity and in American culture. The film also earned her her first Academy Award nomination for screenwriting. The film itself received an Academy Award nomination for best picture of the year, but lost to another of Levien's movies, *Cavalcade* (1933). Based on Noel Coward's play, *Cavalcade* depicts over thirty years in the life of one British family at the turn of the century as they cope with such important events as the Boer War, the death of Queen Victoria, the sinking of the Titanic, and World War I. Levien's other films in 1933 include *As Husbands Go*, which she and Behrman adapted from Rachel Crothers's play about two American couples in Paris, and another vehicle for Will Rogers, *Mr. Skitch*.

Despite the prestigious credits she had earned the preceding year, Levien returned to lightweight material in 1934. *Change of Heart* was the final film for Gaynor and Farrell. After graduating from college four young people (Gaynor, Farrell, Ginger Rogers, and James Dunn) seek employment in New York City. Levien wrote *The White Parade*, a study of a nursing school, in collaboration with Ernest Pascal, with whom she also collaborated on her next film, *Here's To Romance* (1935), a vehicle for Nino Martini, a tenor with the New York Metropolitan Opera. He portrays an opera singer who becomes involved with a married woman (Genevieve Tobin).

Fox Studios' merger with 20th Century in 1935 had no effect on Levien's career; she continued to work for the studio for another five years. She had great success with *The Country Doctor*

Charles Laughton in The Hunchback of Notre Dame, *one of the most successful films of the late 1930s*

(1936), which was inspired by an important news event of the time: the birth of the Dionne sisters, the first set of quintuplets to survive. Levien wrote an outline for her screenplay and then traveled with director Henry King and the film's cast and crew to the children's home town, Callancer, Ontario. Her observations in Callancer gave her a greater appreciation of what had taken place, and she produced a script that was an entertaining mixture of fact and fiction. The film's realistic portrayal of this milestone in medical history made it extremely popular with audiences, though the sequel, *Reunion,* which Levien wrote that same year, did not fare as well.

Levien and King teamed again for *In Old Chicago* (1937). Working from Niven Busch's story, Levien and collaborator Lamar Trotti created a re-

alistic account of the O'Leary family, tracing the feud between the two O'Leary brothers (Don Ameche and Tyrone Power) that culminated in the great fire of 1871. The film was a critical success as well as a popular one—it received an Academy Award nomination for best picture, and Alice Brady won a best supporting actress Oscar for her performance as Mrs. O'Leary.

The Cowboy and the Lady (1938) is noteworthy in Levien's career as one of the only movies of this period that was not filmed by 20th Century-Fox (Samuel Goldwyn produced it) and her last collaboration with Behrman for thirteen years. An heiress (Merle Oberon) runs away from home and gets a job as a maid; she falls in love with an unsophisticated rodeo rider (Gary Cooper).

John Ford directed Levien's next two screen-

Hedy Lamarr, Tony Martin, and Lana Turner in front of the sixty-foot-high, gold and silver staircase created for the finale of Ziegfeld Girl

plays. *Four Men and a Prayer* (1938) is a well-paced mystery about four brothers trying to solve their father's murder. An even greater success was the historical drama *Drums Along the Mohawk* (1939). Adapted from the novel by Walter Edmunds, the film is a story of life on the New York frontier during the Revolutionary War, centering on a young married couple (Henry Fonda and Claudette Colbert) who are trying to establish a farm. Levien collaborated on her screenplay with Trotti, who like Levien had an interest in the early American period.

Critics praised *Drums Along the Mohawk* for its faithful adaptation of the novel; they were less kind to two other Levien adaptations during this period. Both *Kidnapped* (1938) and *The Hunchback of Notre Dame* (1939) were criticized for taking too many liberties with the source novels, though *The Hunchback of Notre Dame* did win praise for its many eerie scenes.

Levien joined M-G-M in 1941. Her first assignment there was to write a musical. It was a genre with which she had little experience, but she would write musicals during most of the 1950s. *Ziegfeld Girl* (1941) relates the lives of three showgirls (Judy Garland, Lana Turner, and Hedy

Eleanor Parker won an Academy Award nomination for her starring role in Interrupted Melody, *the story of opera singer Marjorie Lawrence, who was stricken with polio at the height of her career*

Lamarr). The premise was hardly new to musicals, but Levien gave it a twist: instead of competing ruthlessly with one another for the same job and the same man, a common plot of backstage stories in the 1930s, these women help one another through some unhappy experiences.

Rhapsody In Blue (1945), the biography of George Gershwin, followed. Levien was lent to Warner Bros. for this film and wrote the screen story only. Her influence can be seen mainly in the character of Gershwin's old-fashioned Jewish father (Morris Carnovsky). Her next three scripts dealt with one of Levien's favorite themes, conflicts within the family. *The Valley of Decision* (1945), based on a novel by Marcia Davenport, unlike many of Levien's other scripts depicts how an upper-class family handles the problems that arise when the oldest son (Gregory Peck) marries the family maid (Greer Garson). *The Green Years* (1946) is the story of a young Scottish boy (Dean Stockwell) with stern parents who only receives affection from his grandfather (Charles Coburn). In *Three Daring Daughters* (1948) a divorced career woman (Jeanette Mac-

Donald) considers remarrying, but her daughters do not approve. Levien ended the decade with her adaptation of Sinclair Lewis's novel *Cass Timberlane* in 1947. Townspeople disapprove when a judge (Spencer Tracy) marries a much younger woman (Lana Turner).

Levien began the 1950s with *The Great Caruso* (1951), the first of many musicals she was to write during that decade. Working from Dorothy Caruso's biography of her husband, Enrico, Levien and William Ludwig carefully selected portions of Caruso's life, emphasizing his American years and his triumphs as the Metropolitan Opera's greatest tenor.

Quo Vadis (1951) reunited Levien with Behrman; it was their final work together. Based on a novel by Henryk Sienkiewicz, the film depicts early Christians during the time of Nero. Highly praised by critics, the film received eight Academy Award nominations, including best screenplay, but won no awards—the first time a film received so many nominations and won nothing. It did receive a citation from the National Board of Review, and Levien, Behrman, and collaborator John Lee Mahin shared a Christopher Medal, given annually for "an outstanding creative work of enduring spiritual significance."

Working again with Ludwig, Levien next adapted two operettas to the screen, *The Merry Widow* (1952) by Franz Lehar and *The Student Prince* (1954) by Sigmund Romberg. They then undertook a second musical biography, *Interrupted Melody* (1955), the story of Marjorie Lawrence, an Australian opera singer who was stricken with polio. The depression Lawrence fell into when she contracted the disease and her battle with polio made for powerful screen drama, with Levien and Ludwig basing their script on Lawrence's autobiography and on hours of conversation they had with the singer. The film earned Levien her only Academy Award.

Two mediocre films followed. *Hit the Deck* (1955), the story of a group of sailors on leave, is a more traditional musical than Levien's film biographies. *Bhowani Junction* (1956) is the story of a British officer (Stewart Granger) in Pakistan who falls in love with a native (Ava Gardner). Levien's last important screen credit, however, was *Oklahoma!* (1955). Rodgers and Hammerstein had waited over ten years before bringing their hit musical to the screen; they produced the film themselves and selected Levien and Ludwig to write the screenplay. The film was a great critical and popular success.

Levien received only two more screen credits

Shirley Jones and Gordon MacRae in Oklahoma!, *based on the stage musical by Richard Rodgers and Oscar Hammerstein, who selected Levien and William Ludwig to write the screenplay*

after *Oklahoma*. After she developed cancer in the mid-1950s, and after her husband's death in 1956, she limited her film work. *Jeanne Eagels* (1957), her biography of the 1920s actress, received a poor reception from critics and audiences. Her last film was *Pepe* (1960), a vehicle for the Mexican comedian Cantinflas. Sonya Levien died on 19 March 1960.

References:

S. N. Behrman, *People in a Diary* (Boston: Little, Brown, 1972);

Mel Gussow, *Don't Say Yes Until I Finish Talking: A Biography of Darryl F. Zanuck* (Garden City: Doubleday, 1971);

"Screenwriters Symposium," *Film Comment*, 6 (Winter 1970-1971): 94-95;

Andrew Sinclair, *John Ford* (New York: J. Wade/ Dial Press, 1979);

Anthony Slide, "Jetta Goudal," in *The Idols of Silence* (South Brunswick: A. S. Barnes, 1976).

Papers:

Levien's papers are collected at the Huntington Library, San Marino, California.

Charles MacArthur

(5 November 1895-21 April 1956)

Leslie Clark

See also the MacArthur entries in *DLB 7, Twentieth-Century American Dramatists* and *DLB 25, American Newspaper Journalists, 1901-1925.*

MOTION PICTURES: *Way for a Sailor* (M-G-M, 1930), additional dialogue by MacArthur and Al Boasberg;

Paid (M-G-M, 1930), dialogue; adaptation by MacArthur and Lucien Hubbard;

The Girl Said No (M-G-M, 1930), dialogue;

Billy the Kid (M-G-M, 1930), additional dialogue by MacArthur;

The Sin of Madelon Claudet (M-G-M, 1931), dialogue and continuity;

The Unholy Garden (United Artists, 1931), story and screenplay by MacArthur and Ben Hecht;

New Adventures of Get Rich Quick Wallingford (M-G-M, 1931), adaptation;

Rasputin and the Empress (M-G-M, 1932), story and screenplay;

Crime without Passion (Paramount, 1934), story and screenplay by MacArthur and Hecht;

20th Century (Columbia, 1934), screenplay by MacArthur and Hecht;

Barbary Coast (United Artists, 1935), story and screenplay by MacArthur and Hecht;

Once in a Blue Moon (Paramount, 1935), story and screenplay by MacArthur and Hecht;

The Scoundrel (Paramount, 1935), story and screenplay by MacArthur and Hecht;

Soak the Rich (Paramount, 1936), story and screenplay by MacArthur and Hecht;

Gunga Din (RKO, 1939), story by MacArthur and Hecht;

Wuthering Heights (United Artists, 1939), screenplay by MacArthur and Hecht;

I Take This Woman (M-G-M, 1940), story;

The Senator Was Indiscreet (Universal, 1947), screenplay.

PLAY PRODUCTIONS: *Lulu Belle,* by MacArthur and Edward Sheldon, New York, Belasco Theatre, 9 February 1926;

Salvation, by MacArthur and Sidney Howard, New York, Empire Theatre, 31 January 1928;

The Front Page, by MacArthur and Hecht, New York, Times Square Theatre, 14 August 1928;

Twentieth Century, by MacArthur and Hecht, New York, Broadhurst Theatre, 29 December 1932;

Jumbo, by MacArthur and Hecht, New York, Hippodrome, 16 November 1935;

Ladies and Gentlemen, by MacArthur and Hecht, New York, Martin Beck Theatre, 17 October 1939;

Fun to Be Free. Patriotic Pageant, by MacArthur and Hecht, New York, Madison Square Garden, 1941;

Johnny on the Spot, New York, Plymouth Theatre, 8 January 1942;

Swan Song, by MacArthur and Hecht, New York, Booth Theatre, 15 May 1946;

Stag at Bay, by MacArthur and Nunnally Johnson,

Charles MacArthur and Ben Hecht

Tallahassee, School of Theatre, Florida State University, 6 February 1974.

BOOKS: *A Bug's-Eye View of the War* (Oak Park, Ill.: Pioneer Publishing, 1919);

The Front Page, by MacArthur and Hecht (New York: Covici Friede, 1928; London: Richards and Toumlin, 1929);

War Bugs (Garden City: Doubleday, Doran, 1929; London: Hutchinson, 1929);

Ladies and Gentlemen, by MacArthur and Hecht (New York: French, 1941; London: French, 1941);

Fun to Be Free. Patriotic Pageant, by MacArthur and Hecht (New York: Dramatists Play Service, 1941);

The Stage Works of Charles MacArthur, edited by Arthur Dorlag and John Irvine (Tallahassee: Florida State University Foundation, 1974).

Charles Gordon MacArthur was born in Scranton, Pennsylvania. One of seven children, he was the son of a self-proclaimed evangelical minister, William T. MacArthur, and of Georgiana Welstead MacArthur, one of nineteen offspring of a British former officer in the East India army. MacArthur was educated at Wilson Memorial Academy, a Nyack, New York, school for missionaries. Unhappy living with his stern father, MacArthur left home at age seventeen and went to Chicago, where he spent a summer working on a small newspaper that had been founded by his older sister. He also worked as a reporter for the *Chicago City Press* before serving as a trooper in the First Illinois Cavalry on the Mexican border in 1916. During World War I, MacArthur served in France as a private with the 149th Field Artillery, Rainbow Division. He returned to Chicago and in 1919 went to work for the *Chicago Herald Examiner*, where he remained until 1921. He married *Herald Examiner* reporter Carol Frick in 1920. The following year MacArthur took a job at the *Chicago Tribune*, where he remained until 1924. He then separated from Frick and moved to New York City, where he contributed to the *New York American*, the *New Yorker*, and William Randolph Hearst's *International Magazine*. He also began writing for the theater.

MacArthur's first play, *Lulu Belle* (1926), was written in collaboration with Edward Sheldon, a distant relative, and produced at the Belasco Theatre in New York. After *Lulu Belle*, MacArthur coauthored *Salvation* with Sidney Howard. It opened in New York to poor reviews and closed

following thirty-one performances. MacArthur's next collaborations were with Ben Hecht, whom he knew as a fellow journalist in Chicago. They wrote several plays together, including *The Front Page* (produced in 1928), *Twentieth Century* (produced in 1932), *Jumbo* (produced in 1935), *Ladies and Gentlemen* (produced in 1939), and *Swan Song* (produced in 1946). MacArthur's reputation as a dramatist is founded mainly upon *The Front Page*, a rambunctious, wisecracking depiction of newspaper life that has become one of the best-known works of the American stage.

Frick and MacArthur were divorced in 1926. Two years later MacArthur married actress Helen Hayes. Their daughter, Mary, died of poliomyelitis at age nineteen in 1949; their adopted son, James, has become a successful television actor. Soon after his marriage to Hayes, MacArthur went to Hollywood with Hecht. His earliest work was as a dialogue writer for such early talking pictures as *Billy the Kid* (1930), *The Girl Said No* (1930), and *Way for a Sailor* (1930). With Lucien Hubbard, MacArthur adapted and wrote dialogue for the film version of Bayard Veiller's play *Within the Law*. Retitled *Paid* (1930), the movie is about an innocent woman (Joan Crawford) who, when sent to prison, decides to get revenge on the men responsible for her conviction.

MacArthur wrote his first complete screenplay in 1931, *The Sin of Madelon Claudet*, adapted from Edward Knoblock's play *The Lullaby*. MacArthur had written the movie as a starring vehicle for Helen Hayes, and she won an Academy Award for her performance as a woman who makes countless sacrifices so that her illegitimate son can go to medical school. Because the screenplay emphasizes forgiveness and charity in the face of adversity, it was criticized for its sentimentality and for the unrelenting, somewhat improbable misfortunes that befall Madelon. But Hayes's performance, and the resultant publicity after her Oscar, helped to make the movie a popular success. It remains MacArthur's best-known solo screenplay.

The Unholy Garden (1931) was the first of nine films MacArthur wrote in collaboration with Hecht. It is a romantic spoof regarded more for its clever repartee than for its plot, pitting a suave criminal (Ronald Colman) against the daughter (Fay Wray) of a European baron. MacArthur earned an Academy Award nomination for his next film, *Rasputin and the Empress* (1932), a tale of court intrigue in Czarist Russia. The movie brought together John, Lionel, and Ethel Barrymore for the only time on the screen and was a hit with both critics and au-

Ralph Forbes, Carole Lombard, and John Barrymore in 20th Century, *which MacArthur and Hecht adapted from their 1932 stage play*

diences. MacArthur also worked on the script for *New Adventures of Get Rich Quick Wallingford* (1931), in which three con men decide to help out a young woman (Leila Hyams) after one of their schemes inadvertently costs her her job.

MacArthur and Hecht went to New York to run their own production company in 1934. Paramount gave them the old sound stage facilities in Astoria, Long Island, complete autonomy, and financing for four feature films. They were responsible for all the direction and production, areas in which neither had any experience, but, since Hecht believed that the script was eighty percent of a motion picture, they put most of their energies into writing.

The two men were well-suited as writing partners, so much so that for a six-year period (from 1934 to 1939) all of MacArthur's scripts were written in collaboration with Hecht. Although tem-

peramentally dissimilar, their newspaper backgrounds, their close friendship, and their mutual love of witty ripostes created a partnership that made them a very successful screenwriting team. MacArthur was fastidious and disciplined in his writing, serving as a brake to Hecht's penchant for baroque lines and fanciful plots. He also abhorred pomposity, and his scripts with Hecht often display a cheerful enjoyment of satirizing self-importance and chicanery.

Crime without Passion (1934) was the first of the movies made in Astoria. It is about a dishonest lawyer (Claude Rains) who is driven to murder. It was a great critical success and was followed in 1935 by *Once in a Blue Moon.* A bizarre adventure about Russian aristocrats disguised as circus clowns to escape the revolution, it was a box-office failure. It was also the only one of the Astoria projects that MacArthur did not direct with Hecht.

Although their work in New York occupied most of their time, MacArthur and Hecht continued to provide screenplays for Hollywood pictures. *20th Century* (1934), an adaptation of their own play, was released between *Crime without Passion* and *Once in a Blue Moon*. It is about a Broadway producer (John Barrymore) who is desperate for a new hit. When his leading lady (Carole Lombard) leaves him and heads by train for California, he sneaks onto the train and tries to bring her back. *Barbary Coast* (1935) is a period romance about a Southern woman (Miriam Hopkins) entangled with a gang leader in San Francisco's underworld. Howard Hawks directed both films.

The next Astoria production, *The Scoundrel* (1935), won an Academy Award for best original story. Based on *All He Ever Loved*, a play written by Hecht and his wife, Rose Kaylor, the movie is a biting depiction of the New York literary scene, with Noel Coward playing an immoral publisher whose spirit must wander the Earth until someone cries for him. The last of their four independent films was *Soak the Rich* (1936), a madcap university satire in which the students create a tax system that penalizes the wealthy.

With the Astoria studio shut down, MacArthur and Hecht returned to Hollywood, where they wrote their two final, and most famous, collaborations: *Gunga Din* and *Wuthering Heights* (both 1939). *Gunga Din* was inspired by Rudyard Kipling's poem. The movie is about three British soldiers in India, Cutter (Cary Grant), MacChesney (Victor McLaglen), and Ballantine (Douglas Fairbanks, Jr.), and their water boy, Gunga Din (Sam Jaffe), who battle Indian natives. When Cutter is captured, MacChesney and Ballantine pit themselves against hundreds of Punjabis to rescue him. Under George Stevens's direction, the movie became a classic adventure story, one of the most important and influential in the genre.

Wuthering Heights (1939) was another literary adaptation, and, as they did with *Gunga Din*, MacArthur and Hecht took considerable liberties with their source, adapting only half the novel and making the character of Heathcliffe (Laurence Olivier) more sympathetic. But since the two script-

Sam Jaffe, Cary Grant, Victor McLaglen, and Douglas Fairbanks, Jr., in Gunga Din, *inspired by Rudyard Kipling's poem*

Merle Oberon, Laurence Olivier, and David Niven in the 1939 film version of Wuthering Heights, *one of MacArthur and Hecht's best-known collaborations*

writers shared a lively appreciation for Charlotte Brontë's romantic imagination and flair for tragic passion, they provided a moving rendition of the novel's dramatic themes. Samuel Goldwyn gave the film a lavish production, and William Wyler directed. MacArthur and Hecht were nominated for Academy Awards for their script, and the film was nominated for best picture. It won the New York Film Critics Award for picture of the year.

MacArthur then wrote the screen story for *I Take This Woman* (1940) from his own short story "A New York Cinderella." A doctor (Spencer Tracy) prevents the suicide of a socialite (Hedy Lamarr), marries her, and gives up his slum clinic to go into private practice. The movie was plagued with several problems during shooting, directors Frank Borzage and Josef von Sternberg were replaced by William S. Van Dyke, and filming had to be stopped three times. The completed picture was an uneven and unsuccessful effort.

During World War II MacArthur served as assistant to the Chief of the Chemical Warfare Service in Washington, D.C. He did not write his next motion picture until 1947. *The Senator Was Indiscreet*, directed by playwright George S. Kaufman, is a farce about a long-winded presidential hopeful; the satire was praised by critics. After this film, however, MacArthur withdrew from the movie industry. He spent most of his later years in his home in Nyack, New York, and died in 1956.

Though he wrote some noteworthy dramatic films, Charles MacArthur's most memorable achievements are in comedy. His best works combined eccentric characters with a strongly realistic setting: a newsroom, a lawyer's chambers, chic society, the theater. He was a writer possessing immense charm, wit, and perception about the psychology of human foibles.

Biographies:
Ben Hecht, *Charlie: The Improbable Life and Times of Charles MacArthur* (New York: Harper, 1957);

Jhan Robbins, *Front Page Marriage* (New York: Putnam's, 1982).

References:

Geoff Brown, "Better Than Metro Isn't Good Enough!: Hecht and MacArthur's Own Mov-

ies," *Sight and Sound*, 44 (Summer 1975): 153-155, 196;

Ben Hecht, *A Child of the Century* (New York: Simon & Schuster, 1954).

Jeanie Macpherson
(1884-26 August 1946)

Alexa Foreman

SELECTED MOTION PICTURES: *The Unafraid* (Jesse L. Lasky Feature Play Company, 1915), scenario;

The Captive (Jesse L. Lasky Feature Play Company, 1915), scenario by Macpherson and Cecil B. De Mille;

Chimmie Fadden Out West (Jesse L. Lasky Feature Play Company, 1915), scenario by Macpherson and De Mille;

The Golden Chance (Jesse L. Lasky Feature Play Company, 1916), scenario by Macpherson and De Mille;

The Trail of the Lonesome Pine (Jesse L. Lasky Feature Play Company, 1916), scenario;

The Heart of Nora Flynn (Jesse L. Lasky Feature Play Company, 1916), scenario;

The Dream Girl (Jesse L. Lasky Feature Play Company, 1916), scenario;

Joan the Woman (Cardinal, 1916), scenario;

A Romance of the Redwoods (Artcraft Pictures, 1917), story by Macpherson and De Mille;

The Little American (Artcraft Pictures, 1917), story;

The Woman God Forgot (Artcraft Pictures, 1917), story;

The Devil Stone (Artcraft Pictures, 1917), adaptation;

The Whispering Chorus (Famous Players-Lasky, 1918), scenario;

Old Wives for New (Famous Players-Lasky, 1918), scenario;

Don't Change Your Husband (Famous Players-Lasky-Paramount, 1918), story;

Jeanie Macpherson

For Better, For Worse (Famous Players-Lasky-Paramount, 1919), scenario;

Male and Female (Famous Players-Lasky, 1919), scenario by Macpherson, Elsie Janis, and Gladys Unger;

Something to Think About (Famous Players-Lasky-Paramount, 1920), story;

Forbidden Fruit (Famous Players-Lasky, 1921), story;

The Affairs of Anatol (Famous Players-Lasky, 1921), scenario;

Saturday Night (Famous Players-Lasky, 1921), story and scenario;

Manslaughter (Famous Players-Lasky, 1922), adaptation and scenario;

Adam's Rib (Famous Players-Lasky, 1923), story and scenario;

The Ten Commandments (Famous Players-Lasky, 1923), story and scenario;

Triumph (Famous Players-Lasky, 1924), adaptation;

The Golden Bed (Famous Players-Lasky, 1925), screenplay;

The Road to Yesterday (De Mille Pictures, 1925), adaptation by Macpherson and Beulah Marie Dix;

The King of Kings (De Mille Pictures/Pathé, 1927), story and screenplay;

The Godless Girl (C. B. De Mille Productions, 1929), story, continuity, and dialogue;

Dynamite (M-G-M, 1929), screenplay; dialogue by Macpherson, John Howard Lawson, and Unger;

Madam Satan (M-G-M, 1930), screenplay;

Fra Diavolo/The Devil's Brother (Hal Roach Studios, 1933), adaptation;

The Buccaneer (Paramount, 1938), adaptation.

Jeanie Macpherson was thirty-two years old when she met Cecil B. De Mille, the director with whom she would be most closely identified. Though it was through De Mille that she would become known as a screenwriter, Macpherson had already enjoyed a remarkable career in other areas of motion pictures, including acting and directing.

Born in 1884 in Boston, Massachusetts, to a wealthy family, Macpherson was a petite, fiery girl of Spanish, Scottish, and French descent. As a teenager, she was sent to Mademoiselle DeJacques's school in Paris but was forced to leave when her family lost their money. Returning to the United States, she began to look for a job.

Macpherson was drawn to the stage and began her theatrical career in the chorus of the Chicago Opera House. For the next few years, while taking singing lessons, she took whatever theater-

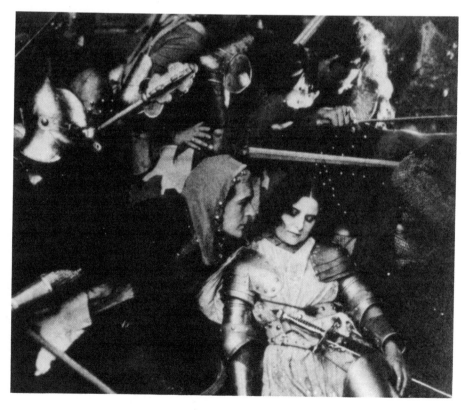

Wallace Reid and Geraldine Farrar in Joan the Woman, *Macpherson's first historical film*

related jobs she could find. Slowly, she was able to work her way up; she acted in the road companies of *Cleopatra* and *Strongheart* and ultimately landed the role of Tita, a Spanish girl, in the Broadway musical *Havana* (1914). The part was a featured one, and the play ran successfully for a year.

Fascinated by motion pictures and ready for a new challenge, Macpherson plunged into a screen career. She convinced D. W. Griffith to hire her for his acting company at Biograph in New York. There she remained for two years, acting in pictures such as *A Corner in Wheat* (1909), *Winning Back His Love* (1910), and *Heart Beats of Long Ago* (1911). Although she enjoyed the work Griffith demanded of his actors, Macpherson left Biograph to go to the Edison Company in 1911, where she worked with director Oscar Apfel. Apfel left for Hollywood soon after to codirect and coproduce *The Squaw Man* (1913) with a young filmmaker named Cecil B. De Mille.

Realizing the opportunities for a screen actress were better in California, where many film companies were migrating from the East, Macpherson accepted a position with Universal Studios in Hollywood. Though employed as an actress, she soon became interested in screenwriting.

One of her first writing endeavors was a motion picture entitled *The Tarantula*, a film in which she had starred. The original negative had been destroyed by accident, and the director, Edwin August, had left for New York. Without a print or director, the studio asked neophyte screenwriter Macpherson not only to recreate the leading role in the film but to direct the feature from her memory of the original. She accepted the challenge and remade the picture. Delighted with the final print, Universal offered Macpherson her own production company, Powers, for which she had the freedom to act, write screenplays, and to direct. During this early period in filmmaking it was not unusual for

Theodore Roberts, Raymond Hatton, Edmund Burns, Gloria Swanson, Mildred Reardon, and Lila Lee in Male and Female, *an updated version of James M. Barrie's play* The Admirable Crichton

Theodore Roberts as Moses in The Ten Commandments

Universal to offer women under contract directing assignments.

Almost a year later, Macpherson moved to Criterion Features, another arm of Universal, where she worked with actor Wilfred Lucas. She became ill from overwork during this period. Shortly after her recuperation, however, she met De Mille, and he asked her to leave Universal and work with him at Jesse L. Lasky Feature Play Company. There were rumors of a romance, though De Mille was married; but, whether or not the two were involved, there was certainly a mutual professional attraction. Drawn to her spirit and courage, he taught her discipline in her writing. She admired his direct style and demand for perfection in his projects. She worked long hours writing and rewriting scripts to meet his standards.

Above all, Macpherson and De Mille held a common belief which would be the basis for every screenplay on which they collaborated: they despised weakness in men and women. Weak men were taken advantage of and degraded, and weak women were shallow, gold digging, and destructive creatures who went from one rich man to the next. Their belief that men and women could change if they learned from experience and corrected their flaws is demonstrated in their early 1920s social dramas. Macpherson and De Mille celebrated the hero and the heroine—biblical, historical, or fictional—and praised their courage and perseverance. Their twenty-seven-year working relationship would rest on these principles.

Macpherson appeared in De Mille's *Rose of the Rancho* (1914), *The Girl of the Golden West* (1914), *The Captive* (1915), which she also wrote, and *Carmen* (1915) before turning exclusively to screenwriting. Perhaps this decision was made because she realized she had to specialize in one area or

The crucifixion scene in The King of Kings

risk becoming exhausted again. She may have come to the conclusion that her dark looks limited her to playing Mediterranean women *(Havana, Rose of the Rancho),* or gypsies *(Carmen),* or a combination of the two *(Spanish Gypsy, 1911).*

When Macpherson began her association with De Mille, he was featuring operatic star Geraldine Farrar in a series of motion pictures highlighting the singer's passionate public image: *Maria Rosa* (1915), *Carmen, Temptation* (1915), and *Joan the Woman* (1916). This last, based on the life of Joan of Arc, was Macpherson's first attempt at recreating a historical episode, and she was particularly good at this type of writing. While De Mille created the huge frame around the French girl's life with his grandiose settings and hundreds of extras, Macpherson fashioned a human drama with which the audience could identify. Thus, while Joan of Arc may be part of a spectacular event, she is revealed as a frightened young girl driven by her spiritual beliefs. The picture's title was Macpherson's idea, as was the view of Joan as a human being rather than an indestructible saint. As Macpherson ad-

mitted to a reporter in 1920, "You must build up your hero so that every young man in the audience pictures himself as that hero. You must build up your heroine so that every young girl will feel herself the heroine, wish herself the heroine—or understand the heroine's feelings. Unless you can do this, you are not in sympathy with your public."

De Mille next made two films written by Macpherson for America's "Sweetheart," Mary Pickford, then a Lasky contract player. The first, *A Romance of the Redwoods* (1917), featured the actress as an orphan sent to live with her uncle during the 1849 gold rush. The second, *The Little American* (1917), was a propaganda film about a young woman involved with a German and an American at the same time. The film featured the sinking of the *Lusitania* and demonstrated that Hollywood had begun fighting World War I in its own way.

After working once more with Geraldine Farrar on *The Woman God Forgot* (1917), about Montezuma's daughter, and *The Devil Stone* (1917), from an original story coauthored by De Mille's mother, De Mille and Macpherson began moving away from escapism and historical projects and toward contemporary drama. The director chose *The Whispering Chorus* (1918) and *For Better, For Worse* (1919) as their vehicles. The former film concerned a man who disfigures a corpse and plants his identification on it; he is executed later for murdering himself. The title of the film refers to his hallucinations of faces which whisper his thoughts in a chorus. Macpherson's screenplay vividly depicted the sleazy side of the fugitive's world and the horror of his execution. *For Better, For Worse* told the story of a doctor who refuses to enlist in the army because he feels that he is needed in a hospital at home. Macpherson portrayed the doctor as an individual as courageous as any fighting soldier who must face those in his own town who believe him a coward.

The end of World War I ushered in the era of the "Roaring Twenties." The liberal moral climate gave rise to the flapper, the sexually aware young woman who rejected conventional mores. Some of the best films De Mille and Macpherson created were responses to the change of America's mood and fashions: *Old Wives for New* (1918), *Don't Change Your Husband* (1918), *Male and Female* (1919), *The Affairs of Anatol* (1921), *Manslaughter* (1922), and *Adam's Rib* (1923). *Male and Female*, featuring Gloria Swanson, was an update of the James M. Barrie play *The Admirable Crichton;* it introduced a new element into Macpherson's screenplays: the blending together of past and present stories. Macpherson carried her talent for recreating historical events a step further by weaving episodes from history into modern dramas to demonstrate moral lessons. The lessons warned audiences about the excesses of the 1920s and what the future would hold if the warnings went unheeded.

One of the excesses of the 1920s, in the opinion of Macpherson and De Mille, was sexual freedom, and they were masters at portraying this and other "sins" on the screen. They used the technique of flashbacks, which were sometimes lessons themselves, as in the case of the prologue to *The Ten Commandments* (1923), which concerned Moses and the story of the Commandments (the original *Ten Commandments* had a modern-day plot). In this case, the modern story showed the excesses of the human race. *Male and Female* contained a flashback to Babylon, *Manslaughter*, to ancient Rome, *Adam's Rib*, to prehistoric times, *Triumph* (1924), to Romeo and Juliet, and *The Road to Yesterday* (1925) contained a visit to seventeenth-century England. Besides offering audiences an admonishment for their money, Macpherson and De Mille felt that America liked watching their stars in a contemporary story plus the added attraction of seeing them in the period costumes that each flashback demanded.

Macpherson had little time for a personal life outside work. She spent what spare moments she had pursuing her hobby, flying. She became an experienced pilot, and magazine interviews with the screenwriter featured pictures of Macpherson wearing her aviatrix clothing. Most of her time was spent writing and rewriting screenplays and researching future projects, a task she took seriously. For *Manslaughter* (1922), for example, at her own suggestion, she entered a Detroit penitentiary posing as a prisoner. For three days, she observed the inner workings of the prison, which housed both first-time offenders and hardened criminals. *Manslaughter's* screenplay concerned a flapper whose imprisonment for accidentally killing a policeman changed her reckless ways.

In 1926 De Mille began work on the first of his well-known biblical epics: *The King of Kings* (1927). Based on the life of Jesus Christ, the film featured H. B. Warner in the title role. Macpherson's character studies portrayed Mary Magdalene as a woman who was not evil but misguided and Jesus as a man who was virile and strong. These representations offended some critics, but the film was a great success. Following *The King of Kings*, Macpherson and De Mille brought to the screen *The Godless Girl* (1929), their first film with sound sequences. The picture concerned the eventual redemption of atheists. For the next two features, *Dynamite* (1929) and *Madam Satan* (1930), Macpherson returned to the subject of marriage and the problems involved in making a successful one. While De Mille charged ahead with *The Sign of the Cross* (1932) and *Cleopatra* (1934), Macpherson ventured into new territory. She wrote the screenplay for the comedy *Fra Diavolo* (1933), starring Laurel and Hardy and based on the 1830 operetta by Daniel Auber.

Macpherson's last research and writing projects for De Mille were done mostly without credit and were concerned primarily with heroes—both real and fictional: King Richard The Lionhearted in *The Crusades* (1935), Wild Bill Hickok in *The Plainsman* (1937), Jean Lafitte in *The Buccaneer* (1938), the men who started the transcontinental railroad in *Union Pacific* (1939), the Canadian Mounties in *North West Mounted Police* (1940), and Dr. Corydon E. Wassell in *The Story of Dr. Wassell* (1944). In 1939 she coauthored and narrated the De Mille film *Land of Liberty*, a historical look at America for the New York World's Fair.

Macpherson had begun research on *Unconquered* (1947), a historical drama, when she became ill with cancer and had to stop work. She died soon after in August 1946. Her screenplays had gone full circle from the early escapist and historical films to the realistic and social dramas, and back to the escapist and historical pictures again. "I shall always be grateful for Mr. De Mille's assistance," Macpherson told a reporter in 1921. "He is a hard taskmaster and he demands that a thing shall be perfect. . . . It was hard, but it taught me that anything worth doing at all was worth doing perfectly."

Interviews:

Alice Martin, "From Wop Parts To Bossing The Jobs," *Photoplay* (October 1916);

Doris Delvigne, "Mind The Little Things," *Motion Picture Magazine* (July 1920);

Barbara Beach, "The Literary Dynamo," *Motion Picture Magazine* (July 1921);

Anthony Slide, "Forgotten Early Women Directors," *Films In Review*, 25 (3 March 1974).

References:

Kevin Brownlow and John Kobal, *Hollywood: The Pioneers* (London: Collins, 1979);

Brownlow, *The Parade's Gone By* (New York: Knopf, 1968);

Ivan Butler, *Religion In The Cinema* (New York: A. S. Barnes, 1969);

Cecil B. De Mille, *The Autobiography*, edited by Donald Hayne (Englewood Cliffs, N.J.: Prentice-Hall, 1959);

William K. Everson, *The Films of Laurel and Hardy* (Secaucus: Citadel Press, 1967);

Charles Higham, *Cecil B. De Mille* (New York: Scribners, 1973);

Al Kilgore and John McCabe, *Laurel and Hardy* (New York: Dutton, 1975);

Richard Koszarski, *Hollywood Directors 1914-1940* (London: Oxford University Press, 1976);

Mike Munn, *The Stories Behind the Scenes of the Great Film Epics* (London: Illustrated Publications, 1982);

David Robinson, *Hollywood in the Twenties* (New York: A. S. Barnes, 1968);

Anthony Slide, *Early Women Directors* (New York: A. S. Barnes, 1974);

John Stewart, *Filmarama: The Formidable Years, 1893-1919*, volume 1 (Metuchen: Scarecrow Press, 1975).

Ben Maddow
(David Wolff)
(1909-)

John Hagan

SELECTED MOTION PICTURES: *Harbor Scenes* (Ralph Steiner Productions, 1935), narration;
The World Today (Nykino, 1936), commentary;
Heart of Spain (Frontier Films, 1937), narration by Maddow and Herbert Kline;
China Strikes Back (Frontier Films, 1937), commentary by Maddow, Irving Lerner (as Peter Ellis), Jay Leyda (as Eugene Hill), and Sidney Meyers (as Robert Stebbins);
People of the Cumberland (Frontier Films, 1937), commentary by Maddow and Erskine Caldwell;
Return to Life (Frontier Films, 1938), narration;
The History and Romance of Transportation (Frontier Films, 1939), commentary by Maddow, Meyers, and Lionel Berman;
United Action (Frontier Films, 1940), commentary by Maddow and Lionel Berman;
White Flood (Frontier Films, 1940), commentary by Maddow, Berman, and Sidney Meyers;
Tall Tales (Brandon Films, 1940), commentary;
Valley Town (University and Documentary Film Distributions, 1940), commentary by Maddow, Willard Van Dyke, and Spencer Pollard;
A Place to Live (Documentary Film Productions, 1941), commentary;
Here Is Tomorrow (Documentary Film Productions, 1941), commentary;
Native Land (Frontier Films, 1942), commentary by Maddow, Leo Hurwitz, and Paul Strand;
The Bridge (Documentary Film Productions, 1944), screenplay;
Northwest, U.S.A. (Office of War Information, 1944), commentary by Maddow, Van Dyke, Meyers, and Philip Dunne;
Framed (Columbia, 1947), screenplay;
The Photographer (Affiliated Film Producers, 1948), commentary by Maddow and Irving Jacoby;
Kiss the Blood Off My Hands (United Artists, 1948), adaptation by Maddow and Walter Bernstein;
The Man from Colorado (Columbia, 1948), screenplay by Maddow and Robert D. Andrews;

Intruder in the Dust (M-G-M, 1949), screenplay by Maddow based on the novel by William Faulkner;
The Asphalt Jungle (M-G-M, 1950), screenplay by Maddow and John Huston;
The Steps of Age (1951), screenplay by Maddow and Helen Levitt;
Shadow in the Sky (M-G-M, 1952), screenplay;
The Stairs (National Mental Health Association, 1953), screenplay;
The Unforgiven (United Artists, 1960), screenplay;
The Savage Eye (Macmillan Films, 1960), screenplay by Maddow, Joseph Strick, and Meyers;
Two Loves (M-G-M, 1961), screenplay;
The Balcony (Kino International, 1963), screenplay by Maddow based on the play by Jean Genet;
An Affair of the Skin (Zenith International, 1964), screen story and screenplay;
The Way West (United Artists, 1967), screenplay by Maddow and Mitch Lindeman;
The Chairman (20th Century-Fox, 1969), screenplay;
The Secret of Santa Vittoria (United Artists, 1969), screenplay by Maddow and William Rose;
Storm of Strangers (MacMillan Films, 1970), screenplay;
The Mephisto Waltz (Quinn Martin, 1971), screenplay.

PLAY PRODUCTIONS: *In a Cold Hotel* and *The Ram's Horn*, New York, Theatre de Lys, December 1963;
Soft Targets, by Maddow and "The Company," New York, La Mama Experimental Theatre Club, March 1981.

BOOKS: *44 Gravel Street* (Boston: Little, Brown, 1952);
The Great Right Horn of the Ram: A Play (New York: French, 1967);
Edward Weston: Fifty Years: The Definitive Volume of His Photographic Work (Millerton, N.Y.: Aperture, 1973); revised and retitled, *Edward*

Weston: His Life and Photographs (Millerton, N.Y.: Aperture, 1979);

Faces: A Narrative History of the Portrait in Photography from 1820 to the Present (New York: New York Graphic Society, 1977);

A Sunday Between Wars; The Course of American Life from 1865 to 1917 (New York: Norton, 1979);

The Asphalt Jungle: A Screenplay, by Maddow and John Huston (Carbondale & Edwardsville: Southern Illinois University Press, 1980);

The Photography of Max Yavno (Berkeley: University of California Press, 1981);

Aperture, No. 92, by Maddow and Marketa Luska-covas (New York: Aperture, 1983).

TELEVISION: "Man on a String" (CBS, 1972), teleplay.

OTHER: "Two Poems" ("Jeu Du Géomètre" and "Surfaces of a Restaurant"), in *American Caravan IV,* edited by Alfred Kreymborg, Lewis Mumford, and Paul Rosenfeld (New York: Macaulay, 1931), pp. 450-451;

"The Front in Darkness" and "Remembering Hart Crane," as David Wolff, in *Proletarian Literature in the United States,* edited by Granville Hicks, et al. (New York: International Publishers, 1935), pp. 200-202;

"Gauntlet of Flowers," *New World Writing 17,* edited by Stewart Richardson and Corlies M. Smith (New York: Lippincott, 1960), pp. 118-150;

"In a Cold Hotel," in *New Theatre in America* (New York: Dell, 1965);

"A Summer Night," as Wolff, in *New Masses: An Anthology of the Rebel Thirties,* edited by Joseph North (New York: International Publishers, 1969), pp. 61-62;

"The Writer's Function in Documentary Film," in *Proceedings of the Writers' Congress, Los Angeles, 1943* (New York: University of California Press, 1944), pp. 98-103;

"Nude In A Social Landscape," in *Nude: Photographs 1850-1980,* edited by Constance Sullivan (New York: Harper & Row, 1980), pp. 181 + ;

Response to questionnaire in *The Hollywood Screenwriters,* edited by Richard Corliss (New York: Discus Books, 1972), pp. 273-275.

PERIODICAL PUBLICATIONS:
FICTION:
"The Life and Death Of," *Front,* 1 (April 1931): 268-276;

"Red Decision," *Symposium,* 3 (October 1932): 443-453;

"The Communist Party of Germany," *Dynamo,* 1 (Summer 1934): 1-6;

"Acts of God," as David Wolff, *Partisan Review,* 2 (April-May 1935): 69-71;

"Green in the Halls," as Wolff, *Dynamo,* 2 (May-June 1935): 16-18;

"Mr. Gold and the Sailor Boy," *Common Ground,* 6, no. 4 (1946): 78-82;

"The Lilacs," *Mademoiselle* (April 1947): 177, 298-302;

"To Hell the Rabbis," *Kenyon Review,* 23 (Summer 1961): 448-459;

"Christmas in Another Skin," *Hudson Review,* 25 (Winter 1962-1963): 534-543;

"On the Square," *Hudson Review,* 16 (Autumn 1963): 369-374;

"Sad Seduction of the Teddy Bear," *Hudson Review,* 16 (Autumn 1963): 362-369;

"Stamp Out Illiteracy, But Slowly," *Genesis West,* 3 (Winter 1965): 79-82;

"The Wind Machine," *Harper's,* 233 (August 1966): 55-60;

"You, Johann Sebastian Bach," *Hudson Review,* 20 (Autumn 1967): 389-416;

"The Circumcision of James Buttonwood," *Playboy,* 15 (December 1968): 187, 301-302, 304-308, 310.

POETRY:
"Sonats," *Blues,* 9 (Fall 1930): 44-45;

"Obsequy," *Poetry,* 38 (May 1931): 79;

"The Trumpeter," as Wolff, *New Masses,* 18 (25 February 1936): 14;

"On Signing Up," as Wolff, *Poetry,* 48, 2 (May 1936): 71;

"The Sign," as Wolff, *New Masses,* 23 (4 May 1937): 20;

"The Defenses," *TAC,* 1 (July 1938): 12;

"The City," as Wolff, *Poetry,* 55, 4 (January 1940): 169-175;

"While We Slept," as Wolff, *Poetry,* 56, 6 (September 1940): 316-317;

"Elegy Upon a Certificate of Birth," *Poetry,* 85 (January 1955): 194-195;

"Psalm of Twelve Fridays," *Poetry,* 105, 6 (March 1965): 355-357.

NONFICTION:
"Wall Street Hollywood," by Maddow and Gertrude Armstrong, *New Masses,* 12 (14 August 1934): 29-30;

"Comrade and Master," as Wolff, *Dynamo,* 21 (May-June 1935): 29-32;

"Harry Alan Potamkin," as Wolff, *New Theatre,* 3 (February 1936): 28, 33;

"Hopes for Poetry," as Wolff, *New Masses,* 20 (4 August 1936): 28;

"Film Into Poem," as Wolff, *New Theatre,* 3 (November 1936): 23, 36;

"Two Poets," as Wolff, *New Masses,* 23 (27 April 1937): 23;

"Fact Into Film: *Confessions of a Nazi Spy,*" as Wolff, *Films,* 1 (November 1939): 81-85;

"Film Intensity: *Shors,*" as Wolff, *Films,* 1 (Spring 1940): 55-61;

"Eisenstein and the Historical Film," *Hollywood Quarterly,* 1 (October 1945): 26-30;

"Hurrell," *American Photographer,* 6 (April 1981): 40-49.

Ben Maddow has gained a reputation as an independent and outspoken artist despite the fact that much of his work as a screenwriter of documentaries and commercial films over the past fifty years has been done pseudonymously, or without credit, or has suffered dilution on commercial projects over which he had little control. Until 1942 Maddow used the name David Wolff for his documentary pictures. Blacklisted in Hollywood from about 1952 to 1960, Maddow apparently continued to write scripts, although it is difficult to ascertain the extent of his contributions to them because he was not given credit. Maddow seems reticent to clarify the matter; in fact, of the many film scripts he has written, he would prefer to be credited only with seven that have established his reputation: *Native Land* (1942), *Intruder in the Dust* (1949), *The Asphalt Jungle* (1950), *The Stairs* (1953), *The Savage Eye* (1960), *The Balcony* (1963), and *Storm of Strangers* (1970).

Maddow's reticence extends to providing precise information on his background, although it is known that he was born in Passaic, New Jersey, and attended Columbia University in New York. Following his graduation in 1930 he was employed as a hospital orderly and then as a social worker. He also began to have his poetry published in literary journals. In 1935 Maddow responded to a magazine advertisement placed by filmmaker Ralph Steiner, who was seeking a poet to write narration for a film that he had shot, *Harbor Scenes.* Maddow was delighted with this job; he felt that his poetry came to life when associated with the images on screen. Through Steiner, Maddow met several well-known photographers, including Paul Strand and Willard Van Dyke, and thus he developed the aesthetic interest that would play a large part in much of his later work. In recent years he has writ-

ten several books about the work of individual photographers.

In the mid-1930s Maddow, Steiner, and other leftist artists formed Nykino, an informal organization that attempted to make films promoting social awareness and the interests of the working class. Nykino was succeeded in 1937 by Frontier Films, which Maddow joined under the pseudonym David Wolff as a writer of narration and commentary. (Pseudonyms were used by many artists during this period since their government-subsidized jobs prevented them from taking additional employment under their own names.) The members of Frontier Films had been impressed by *The March of Time,* a series of films dealing with national and international current events which combined documentary footage and staged scenes; Frontier Films wished to move beyond *The March of Time* and deal with social problems in a more radical and complex political and stylistic fashion. They created the short-lived *The World Today.* Maddow in particular had been impressed with the *March of Time* format; he felt it might be a means through which to achieve a new form of cinema, the "cine-poem," in which a continuous voice would serve "as a sort of ground-bass to the images on screen." He worked on the commentaries of most, if not all, of the seven pictures made by Frontier Films between 1937 and 1942, among them *Heart of Spain* (1937), *People of the Cumberland* (1937), *Return to Life* (1938), *United Action* (1940), and *Native Land* (1942). The last was their final and most famous effort; it was based on a Senate committee investigation into the illegal attempts of large businesses to curb the growing power of trade unions. Maddow's commentary traces the struggle for liberty throughout America's history and creates a parallel between the growth of democracy and the nation's physical and industrial expansion.

When Frontier Films disbanded, Maddow traveled to South America, on his first voyage abroad, to work with Van Dyke on *The Bridge* (1944), a short documentary about the problems faced by South America when its trade relations with Europe and the United States were shattered by the outbreak of World War II. The film suggests that South America rely upon its own resources by using air transportation to break down the trade barriers between its constituent countries. As in *Native Land,* the future of the worker is linked to the development of technology.

After returning to the U.S., Maddow was drafted and served as a sergeant in the Army Air Corps' Hollywood Motion Picture Unit. During this

Claude Jarman, Jr., unidentified actor, and Juano Hernandez in Maddow's film version of William Faulkner's Intruder in the Dust, *an examination of racial antagonism*

time, he wrote the treatment for a film called *Death and Mathematics: A Film on the Meaning of Science* which was to have been made by the Army's Overseas Motion Picture Bureau. The script, about a science teacher who returns home from the war and finds himself scheduled to teach a course in nuclear physics, was never filmed, ostensibly because its discussion of security issues would have created a risk in wartime. Maddow's screenplay was eventually published, though, and this early work both reflects the concerns raised in his previous writing and anticipates the complex, eclectic style of many of the later films over which he maintained control. Close-ups, commentary, photographs, animation, stock footage, and staged scenes were all to be used in an attempt to fuse the "personal" film with the educational documentary.

After completing his stint in the army, Maddow began working on screenplays for Hollywood films; his political concerns may be detected in many of his scripts. In *Framed* (1947) an unemployed mining engineer (Glenn Ford) becomes involved in a robbery and murder scheme with a former model (Janis Carter) who attributes her criminal acts to the fact that she once had to parade in other women's furs. *The Man from Colorado* (1948) concerns a sadistic Civil War colonel (Glenn Ford) turned Federal judge who becomes involved in a territorial dispute with the soldiers who were previously under his command. *Kiss the Blood Off My Hands* (1948), adapted by Maddow and Walter Bernstein from a novel by Gerald Butler, deals with an ex-soldier (Burt Lancaster) who becomes brutally violent after spending time in a Nazi concentration camp.

Maddow's adaptation of William Faulkner's *Intruder in the Dust* (1949) was his first major achievement as a Hollywood screenwriter. The complexities of Faulkner's plot, and the eccentricities of his narrative form led Maddow to "dismember the whole thing and put it back in some kind of order." Besides simplifying plot details and the temporal structure, he eliminated those speeches in the novel in which lawyer Gavin Stevens (Porter Hall) argues that the black man's freedom must be achieved through an alliance of southern blacks and whites rather than through outside Federal interference. Maddow considered these speeches to be absurd; he says that the lines at the end of the script which depict Beauchamp as the conscience of the South were added at the insistence of the film's producer, Dore Schary.

After seeing *Intruder in the Dust*, John Huston asked Maddow to work with him on the screenplay of *The Asphalt Jungle* (1950), which Huston was directing and which was based on W. R. Burnett's novel about a group of men from various backgrounds and social levels, who converge to plan a jewel heist in a large midwestern city. The film's philosophy is summed up in an exchange between one of the characters, a prominent lawyer (Louis Calhern), and his wife (Dorothy Tree), who knows of her husband's acquaintance with thieves but is ignorant of his criminal actions. To her comment,

"When I think about all the awful people you come into contact with . . . I get scared," he replies: "There's nothing so different about them. After all, crime is only a left-handed form of human endeavor." *The Asphalt Jungle*'s sympathetic study of the criminal mind and its detailed description of how a heist is planned have won it a critical reputation that has increased in the years since its release. Maddow and Huston were nominated for an Academy Award for their screenplay.

Following *The Asphalt Jungle*, Maddow wrote a novel, *44 Gravel Street* (1952), as well as the screenplay for *Shadow in the Sky* (1952), about the difficulties faced by a World War II veteran following his release from a mental hospital. He made two documentaries also dealing with social issues: *The Steps of Age* (1951), on the problems of aging, and *The Stairs* (1953), for the National Health Association.

A victim of the Hollywood blacklist, Maddow spent much of the 1950s working without credit on scripts with writer Philip Yordan. The most

Sam Jaffee, Sterling Hayden, James Whitmore (standing), and Antonio Caruso in The Asphalt Jungle, *Maddow's seminal study of the criminal mind*

noteworthy of these were *Johnny Guitar* (1954), a political allegory set in the Old West, and *Men in War* (1957), which examined the mental strain of war on a platoon of soldiers in Korea. Other films Maddow worked on with Yordan include *The Naked Jungle* (1954), *The Last Frontier* (1955), and *God's Little Acre* (1958). There is uncertainty as to the extent of Maddow's contributions to these scripts; some film scholars have suggested that Yordan merely supervised Maddow's work, but this has never been confirmed. Maddow is also said to have written an early draft for *Wild River* (1960), about the Tennessee Valley Authority.

During the 1960s Maddow wrote pseudonymously for several television programs, including *Naked City* and *Kraft Suspense Theatre*. He finally was given a chance to work again under his own name by John Huston, who hired him to write *The Unforgiven* (1960); again, it has been suggested that Maddow worked uncredited on several Huston films. Adapted from Alan LeMay's novel, *The Unforgiven* is about the love affair between a white man (Burt Lancaster) and his adopted Indian sister (Audrey Hepburn). The film was not particularly well received, with even Huston admitting that "it got a little bombastic and overdramatized."

Maddow had planned to make a film for Joseph Strick about the eighteenth-century painter and engraver William Hogarth, applying Hogarth's satirical attitudes toward London society to contemporary Los Angeles. For about three years, Maddow, Strick, and Sidney Meyers worked on several scripts for this independent project, compiling material in their spare time without any definite idea of how the material would be organized. Eventually Hogarth was dropped as a subject, though he obviously remained an influence, and the resulting film, *The Savage Eye* (1960), became what Maddow has called "essentially an anthropological film about Los Angeles, about lower-middle class life."

The Savage Eye consists of an offscreen dialogue between a bitter, recently divorced woman and a man who is apparently her conscience. As the two offscreen voices converse poetically about love and loneliness, a series of disparate images is seen, including graphic sequences of a plastic surgery operation and a roller derby. The correspondence between what is heard on the soundtrack and what is seen on the screen is sometimes direct, sometimes tenuous, and the imagery is so vivid that the film's language often seems overly ripe and superficially psychoanalytic.

Certain themes recur throughout Maddow's

work. Some of the predominant themes of earlier scripts—fear of love, the mental scars of war, cultural differences—appear again in his screenplay for *Two Loves* (1961), derived from Sylvia Ashton-Warner's novel *Spinster* about a sexually inhibited American woman teaching in a primitive section of New Zealand. After resisting the advances of a fellow teacher, an Englishman who has been shaken emotionally by his wartime experiences, she is shocked to learn that he is the father of the child of a pregnant native girl. Moreover, both the girl and her tribe eagerly await the birth. Like the woman in *The Savage Eye* and the one in Maddow's subsequent film *An Affair of the Skin*, the woman teacher in *Two Loves* eventually becomes less emotionally constrained.

The Savage Eye brought to the screen a type of realism rare in fictional films of that period, but Maddow and Strick's next independent venture, a movie of Jean Genet's *The Balcony* (1963), was even more explicit in its depiction of sexual inhibition and the need for emotional fulfillment. Although Genet's play is set in a bordello in which several rooms have been designed to accommodate the various fantasies of the clientele, the film's bordello is a converted movie soundstage. This provided the filmmakers with a more appropriate setting for a "house of illusions" and allowed them to suggest certain similarities between the operation of a movie studio and that of a brothel.

Maddow recognized that essentially the play was about power rather than sex, and he emphasized this in his screenplay. The film takes a more didactic and pragmatic, less lyrical, approach to its subject than does the play. It is more concerned with the social aspects of the bordello as a microcosm than with its metaphysical implications. In an effort to be more realistic and less obscure, Maddow omitted certain of the play's scenes, simplified the stylized dialogue, and tried to clarify some of Genet's concepts. The film is more bluntly satiric than the play in its treatment of bureaucracy, and it avoids some of the play's religious imagery and explicit language, although it is still shocking.

An Affair of the Skin (1964), written and directed by Maddow, was a continuation of the type of independently produced, adult film that he had envisioned with *The Savage Eye* and *The Balcony*. "The audience is ready for the realism of grown-up, contemporary sex, the way people live today, not in England or France or Italy, but here in our own country," he stated. "What has been lacking is a story that is both truthful and exploitable in commercial terms." *An Affair of the Skin*—the story of

Barbara Parkins in Maddow's last credited screenplay, The
Mephisto Waltz

two couples, a four-sided love affair as seen
through the eyes of a black woman photographer—
proved to be a commercial failure and received a
poor critical reception. Both in its wordiness and
in its harsh view of relationships between intelligent, middle-class men and women, the film seems
more akin to the theater of the 1960s than to the
mainstream cinema of that period. The production
of the film had been rushed due to financial reasons; ten years later, having accumulated enough
money to reedit the film, Maddow released it (again
unsuccessfully) as *Love as Disorder.* An offscreen
narration by the photographer was added in order
to make it clear that she was someone watching
from a distance.

With only one exception, Maddow's screen
work to date has been for commercial, Hollywood
films, not the experimental cinema he prefers.
Adapted from A. B. Guthrie's novel, *The Way West*
(1967) is an epic Western centering on the power
struggle between a wagon train leader (Kirk Douglas) and a westbound traveler (Richard Widmark).
The film was not a success, with most critics agree-

ing that the screenplay failed to develop adequately
its many characters and subplots. In *The Chairman*
(1969) celebrated scientist John Hathaway (Gregory Peck) is sent on a spy mission to Red China;
he is unaware of the explosive device implanted in
his skull which can be detonated to kill the chairman of the Chinese government. The most noteworthy thing about the film is Maddow's
characterization of overly zealous general Shelby,
who resembles the men warped by war in other
Maddow films.

Maddow's next commercial works were both
adapted from popular novels and each, in its own
way, deals with an unusual transference of power.
Stanley Kramer directed *The Secret of Santa Vittoria*
(1969), from Robert Crichton's satiric tale of a peasant (Anthony Quinn) who becomes mayor of an
Italian village during the wartime confusion following the death of Mussolini. Though something
of a buffoon, he outwits the Fascists, thus preserv-
ing both democracy and the village's wine supply.
The Mephisto Waltz (1971) centers around a failed
concert pianist (Alan Alda) who, by means of a
supernatural bargain, inherits the talent of a dying
master musician (Curt Jurgens). Sandwiched between these two pictures was *Storm of Strangers*
(1970), an independent production that Maddow
had wanted to do for many years as a tribute to his
immigrant parents. The film depicts the problems
of turn-of-the-century immigrants living in New
York's Lower East Side slums.

Although Maddow has had no screen credits
since 1971, he has continued to write screenplays.
He also continues to be identified, perhaps erroneously, as an uncredited contributor to films, most
recently *Midway* (1976). In the late 1970s and early
1980s, he published two nonfiction books: *A Sunday
Between Wars* (1979), a study of American life between 1865 and 1917, and *The Photography of Max
Yavno* (1981).

Although Ben Maddow's contributions to the
cinema are difficult to enumerate because so much
of his work was done while he was blacklisted, it is
evident he has repeatedly served with distinction
the cause of forthright, issue-oriented American
cinema.

Interviews:
Jay Leyda, ed., Interview with Maddow in *Voices of
    Film Experience: 1894 to the Present* (New York:
    Macmillan, 1977), pp. 291-292;
John Hagan, Interview with Maddow (WNYC, 22
    December 1978).

References:

"*An Affair of the Skin*," *Film Comment*, 1 (1963): 28-29;

William Alexander, *Film on the Left: American Documentary Film from 1931 to 1942* (Princeton: Princeton University Press, 1981);

Russell Campbell, *Cinema Strikes Back: Radical Filmmaking in the United States, 1930-1942* (Ann Arbor: UMI Research Press, 1982);

Regina K. Fadiman, *Faulkner's "Intruder in the Dust": Novel into Film* (Knoxville: University of Tennessee Press, 1978);

Ken Ferguson, "Interview with J. Lee Thompson," *Photoplay* (September 1969);

Verna Fields, "Dialogue on Film," *American Film*, 1 (June 1976): 33-48;

Leo Hurwitz, "*Native Land*: An Interview with Leo Hurwitz," *Cineaste*, 6 (1974): 3-7;

Jack Edmund Nolan, "Films on TV," *Films in Review*, 20 (April 1969): 242-243;

Gerald Pratley, *The Cinema of John Huston* (New York: A. S. Barnes, 1977);

Albert Turner, "*The Unforgiven*," *Films in Review*, 6 (May 1960): 287-288;

Linn Unkefer, "Lookout from Genet's 'Balcony,' " *New York Times*, 12 November 1962, p. 277;

Gerald Weales, "Voices: *A Sunday Between Wars*," *Nation*, 229 (28 July 1979): 88-90.

John Lee Mahin

(1902-17 April 1984)

Kevin Mace

MOTION PICTURES: *Beast of the City* (M-G-M, 1932), dialogue and continuity;

Red Dust (M-G-M, 1932), screenplay;

Scarface (United Artists, 1932), dialogue and continuity by Mahin, Seton I. Miller and W. R. Burnett;

The Wet Parade (M-G-M, 1932), screenplay;

Bombshell (M-G-M, 1933), screenplay by Mahin and Jules Furthman;

Eskimo (M-G-M, 1933), adaptation;

The Prizefighter and the Lady (M-G-M, 1933), screenplay by Mahin and John Meehan;

Hell Below (M-G-M, 1933), dialogue by Mahin and Meehan;

Chained (M-G-M, 1934), screenplay;

Laughing Boy (M-G-M, 1934), screenplay;

Treasure Island (M-G-M, 1934), screenplay;

Naughty Marietta (M-G-M, 1935), screenplay by Mahin, Francis Goodrich, and Albert Hackett;

The Devil is a Sissy (M-G-M, 1936), screenplay by Mahin and Richard Schayer;

Love on the Run (M-G-M, 1936), screenplay by Mahin, Manuel Seff, and Gladys Hurlbut;

Small Town Girl (M-G-M, 1936), screenplay by Mahin, Goodrich, Hackett, and Edith Fitzgerald;

Wife vs. Secretary (M-G-M, 1936), screenplay by Mahin, Norman Krasna, and Alice Duer Miller;

Captains Courageous (M-G-M, 1937), screenplay by Mahin, Marc Connelly, and Dale Van Every, based on the novel by Rudyard Kipling;

The Last Gangster (M-G-M, 1937), screenplay;

Too Hot to Handle (M-G-M, 1938), screenplay by Mahin and Laurence Stallings;

Boom Town (M-G-M, 1940), screenplay;

Dr. Jekyll and Mr. Hyde (M-G-M, 1941), screenplay, based on the novel by Robert Louis Stevenson;

Johnny Eager (M-G-M, 1942), screenplay by Mahin and James Edward Grant;

Tortilla Flat (M-G-M, 1942), screenplay by Mahin and Benjamin Glazer, based on the novel by John Steinbeck;

The Adventures of Tartu (M-G-M, 1943), screenplay by Mahin and Howard Emmett Rogers;

Down to the Sea in Ships (20th Century-Fox, 1949), screenplay by Mahin and Sy Bartlett;

Love That Brute (20th Century-Fox, 1950), screen story and screenplay by Mahin, Darrell Ware, and Karl Tunberg;

Quo Vadis (M-G-M, 1951), screenplay by Mahin,

John Lee Mahin

S. N. Behrman, and Sonya Levien;
Show Boat (M-G-M, 1951), screenplay;
My Son, John (Paramount, 1952), adaptation;
Mogambo (M-G-M, 1953), screenplay;
Elephant Walk (Paramount, 1954), screenplay;
Lucy Gallant (Paramount, 1955), screenplay by Mahin and Winston Miller;
The Bad Seed (Warner Bros., 1956), screenplay;
Heaven Knows, Mr. Allison (20th Century-Fox, 1957), screenplay by Mahin and John Huston;
No Time for Sergeants (Warner Bros., 1958), screenplay;
The Horse Soldiers (United Artists, 1959), screenplay by Mahin and Martin Rackin;
North to Alaska (20th Century-Fox, 1960), screenplay by Mahin, Rackin, and Claude Binyon;
The Spiral Road (Universal, 1962), screenplay by Mahin and Neil Patterson;
Moment to Moment (Universal, 1966), screenplay by Mahin and Alec Coppel.

One of Hollywood's most prolific and versatile screenwriters, John Lee Mahin spent nearly thirty-five years working with some of the best and most colorful writers and directors Hollywood has ever known. Spending most of his career at M-G-M, Mahin became the favorite screenwriter of such

popular stars as Clark Gable, Jean Harlow, and Spencer Tracy and such legendary directors as John Ford, Victor Fleming, and Howard Hawks. While working at M-G-M in the thirties and early forties, Mahin garnered a solid reputation for writing rousing adventure stories—*Red Dust* (1932), *Boom Town* (1940)—and some of the raciest and most sophisticated sexual comedies—*Bombshell* (1933), *Wife vs. Secretary* (1936)—of that period.

Born in Evanston, Illinois, Mahin acquired an interest in writing from his father who was a pioneer in newspaper advertising. While attending Harvard, Mahin worked as a movie editor for the Boston *American*; he later worked as a reporter for various New York newspapers. When he became tired of news reporting, he took up acting at the Provincetown Playhouse, which was run by Robert Edmund Jones and Kenneth McGowan. His acting career ended in the early 1930s, and Mahin returned to writing. He became head copywriter at the Kenyon and Ekhart advertising agency in New York.

While working at the agency and living in Haverstraw, New York, Mahin became good friends with Ben Hecht, who along with his partner Charles MacArthur was working on a film for Samuel Goldwyn called *Unholy Garden* (1931), a romantic adventure film about a sophisticated thief (Ronald Colman). Mahin went out to Hollywood with Hecht and was paid two hundred dollars a week for working on the film; he received no credit but was guaranteed a permanent job as screenwriter by Hecht. The following year Mahin landed his most important screenwriting assignment: *Scarface* (1932). It was the first time he worked for Howard Hawks, who became his close friend for over forty-five years, until Hawks's death in 1977.

Scarface documented the rise and fall of Tony Camonte (Paul Muni), a cruel mobster patterned after Al Capone. Mahin became associated with the film when Hecht, who had already written a treatment and sixty pages of script, abandoned the project. Before leaving for New York, Hecht recommended Mahin to Hawks, who quickly hired Mahin to write dialogue for the final script. Mahin collaborated with Seton I Miller on the screenplay (W. R. Burnett, with whom they shared credit, had already worked on the screenplay before Mahin and Miller entered the project) then remained on the film set rewriting scenes with Hawks, often without Miller's assistance. While Mahin's dialogue for *Scarface* has been praised for its authenticity, Mahin always felt that Hecht and Hawks were responsible for the film's success; according to Mahin,

Osgood Perkins, Karen Morley, and Paul Muni in Scarface. *Mahin was chiefly responsible for the dialogue, which has been praised for its authenticity.*

Hecht devised the film's two most famous elements: the incestuous relationship between Camonte and his sister (Ann Dvorak) and the coin-flipping character played by George Raft.

The growing popularity of gangster pictures alarmed some studio heads, who reacted by making films glorifying crime fighters rather than criminals. Irving Thalberg hired Mahin to write *Beast of the City* (1932), a study of a ruthless police officer (Walter Huston) determined to eliminate the criminal gangs of his city. Mahin's script was an unacknowledged adaptation of W. R. Burnett's Western novel *Saint Johnson*, which was then being filmed as *Law and Order* (1932); Burnett was credited with the original story of *Beast of the City*, and Mahin preserved much of the Western structure, with the police as vigilantes and the criminals an outlaw gang that controlled the town. M-G-M was very unhappy with the completed film; *Beast of the City* was held out of release for over a year and then it was poorly distributed.

The failure of *Beast of the City* had no effect on Mahin's career; he worked on three more scripts that year. For Hawks he worked without credit on *Tiger Shark* (1932), about a tuna fisherman (Edward G. Robinson) who marries the impoverished daughter (Zita Johann) of his late partner; she later falls in love with another man (Richard Arlen). *The Wet Parade* (1932) was about the evils of alcohol and the work of Prohibition agents. It was with *The Wet Parade* that Mahin began his long and successful association with director Victor Fleming, for whom he would write two of his most successful and characteristic films: *Red Dust* (1932) and *Bombshell* (1933).

Red Dust is an adventure story featuring a romantic triangle. Dennis Carson (Clark Gable) is a rubber plantation manager who befriends and is attracted to Vantine (Jean Harlow), a prostitute running from the police. When engineer Gary Willis (Gene Raymond) and his wife arrive at the plantation, Carson begins an affair with Barbara Willis

(Mary Astor) then drives her back to her husband by stating he is in love with Vantine. According to Mahin, John Gilbert was the original choice to play Carson, but Mahin convinced M-G-M to hire Gable and the chemistry between Gable and Harlow made the picture an unexpected success.

If *Red Dust* proved what Mahin could do with an action adventure story, *Bombshell* (1933) revealed his talent for lively repartee. Coauthored with Jules Furthman, *Bombshell* tells the story of a beautiful but lonely movie star (Jean Harlow) who is constantly at odds with her conniving publicity agent (Lee Tracy). The movie became both a critical and popular success and is considered one of the sharpest satires of 1930s Hollywood.

After *Bombshell*, Mahin began work on his most atypical project—adapting two nonfiction studies by Peter Freuchen, *Der Eskimo* and *Der Flucht in Weisse Land* for the movie *Eskimo* (1933), a study of life in the arctic. He returned to more familiar material with *The Prizefighter and the Lady*

(1933). It should have been a perfect project for Mahin, who was working from Francis Marion's screen story about a mismatched couple who fall in love. Clark Gable and Myrna Loy were to star, and Howard Hawks was signed to direct. But Gable was unavailable, and Hawks withdrew to be replaced by W. S. Van Dyke II. Boxing champion Max Baer was cast in the lead, and Mahin had to write a screenplay about a gangland moll who is romanced by a prizefighter, instead of the sailor Gable was to play. Gable did star in *Chained* (1934), a romantic melodrama directed by Clarence Brown and the fourth film to team Gable with Joan Crawford. She plays Diane Loverling, a secretary in love with her married employer (Otto Kruger); Gable is the wealthy rancher who tries to marry her. Lavishly produced by M-G-M, *Chained* was a great success with moviegoers but dismissed by critics as an improbable soap opera. During this same period, Mahin wrote *Hell Below* (1933), a submarine drama centering on the conflict between Lieutenant Com-

Otto Kruger, Joan Crawford, and Clark Gable in Chained, *the fourth film to costar Crawford and Gable*

Jeanette MacDonald and Nelson Eddy in Naughty Marietta, *the first film they made together*

mander Toler (Walter Huston) and Lieutenant Knowlton (Robert Montgomery), the navy officer who loves Toler's daughter (Madge Evans). It is an uneven mixture of drama, romance, and comedy (in one scene, a crew member played by Jimmy Durante boxes with a kangaroo) and an undistinguished film, most noteworthy as an example of Mahin's continuing interest in the society of males. A more prestigious assignment came with *Treasure Island* (1934). This expensive production of Robert Louis Stevenson's novel reunited Mahin with Victor Fleming and was one of the best films in both their careers.

Beginning in 1934, with *Laughing Boy*, Mahin wrote four pictures directed by W. S. Van Dyke. By far, the most successful of these films was *Naughty Marietta* (1935), the first of Mahin's pictures to be nominated for an Academy Award for best picture and the first movie to costar Jeanette MacDonald and Nelson Eddy. Mahin, Francis Goodrich, and Albert Hackett adapted the movie from an operetta by Victor Herbert and Rita Johnson Young, updating the material to give it more modern appeal. *The Devil Is a Sissy* (1936) was a melodrama about children living in the slums of London. *Love on the Run* (1936), a Gable-Crawford vehicle, was a deliberate attempt to create another *It Happened One Night* (1934). Crawford played an American heiress running from her fiancé and Gable was a reporter who helped her. Mahin also made uncredited contributions to another Gable picture, *China Seas* (1935).

It was during the 1930s that Mahin became heavily involved in Hollywood politics. He was an early supporter of the Screen Writers Guild until he decided Guild leaders were too liberal. Feeling that the Communist Party played an important part in the Guild's affairs, Mahin and others like him left the Guild to establish Screen Playwrights, Inc., a more conservative organization consisting mainly of older, established writers like Mahin and Herman Mankiewicz. A bitter power struggle existed between the two factions until the 1940s.

Despite his problems with the Guild, Mahin's career continued to flourish. M-G-M constantly assigned him to write pictures for the studio's biggest stars, particularly Gable. Between 1936 and 1940 Mahin worked on five of Gable's movies. For Janet Gaynor and Robert Taylor he wrote *Small Town Girl* (1936), about a woman who marries a man while he is intoxicated then tries to convince him he really loves her. Another Gable-Harlow teaming followed with *Wife vs. Secretary* (1936), which Mahin, Norman Krasna, and Alice Duer Miller adapted from a novel by Faith Baldwin. A couple's marriage is in trouble when the wife (Myrna Loy) believes rumors about her husband (Gable) and his secretary (Harlow).

Mahin received his first Academy Award nomination for *Captains Courageous* (1937). Victor Fleming directed this adaptation of Rudyard Kipling's novel. The film is not entirely faithful to the novel about a wealthy youth (Freddie Bartholomew) who falls off an ocean liner and is rescued by a fishing boat: the character of Manuel (Spencer Tracy), the seaman who rescues the boy, is built up at the expense of that of Disko Troop (Lionel Barrymore), the ship's captain. But the film was still a critical and financial success; in addition to its best screenplay nomination, it received an Academy Award nomination for best picture and Tracy won the award for best actor.

After writing a crime movie, *The Last Gangster* (1937), and making uncredited contributions to *A Star Is Born* (1937), Mahin worked on four consecutive pictures starring Clark Gable. With Laurence Stallings he wrote *Too Hot to Handle* (1938), a story of newsreel photographers overseas. At the request of Victor Fleming, Mahin did uncredited rewrites on *Test Pilot* (1938), and when Fleming was assigned to replace George Cukor as director of *Gone With the Wind* (1939), Mahin was assigned to the movie

Jean Harlow, Clark Gable, and Hobart Cavanaugh in Wife vs. Secretary, *adapted from a novel by Faith Baldwin*

Spencer Tracy and Freddie Bartholomew in Captains Courageous, *for which Mahin received his first Academy Award nomination*

as well, becoming one of many to work on the film without credit. He was sole screenwriter of *Boom Town* (1940). "Big" John (Gable) and "Square" John (Spencer Tracy) are partners in an oil drilling concern and in love with the same woman (Claudette Colbert). Over a period of years their fortunes rise and fall as they quarrel, separate, and reunite.

Mahin collaborated on *Johnny Eager* (1942), with James Edward Grant, who wrote the original story for *Boom Town*. A gangster (Robert Taylor) is loved by the district attorney's daughter (Lana Turner). As the study of a criminal, the film is very different from *Scarface* and lacks the brutality of *Beast of the City*; Johnny Eager is not as ruthless as the protagonists of the earlier films and by the film's end, even commits an act of self-sacrifice, allowing the police to kill him.

Fleming directed Mahin's next two screenplays, both of them adaptations of novels, *Dr. Jekyll and Mr. Hyde* (1941) and *Tortilla Flat* (1942). Spencer Tracy starred in both films.

Dr. Jekyll and Mr. Hyde was the more successful of the two, with many critics feeling that it compared favorably with the highly acclaimed version filmed in 1931. Mahin also worked without credit on another Tracy film that year, *Woman of the Year* (1942).

In 1945 Mahin returned to the Screen Writers Guild, but he also left M-G-M, ending a fifteen-year period as one of the studio's best paid and most highly regarded writers. His last credit at M-G-M had come in 1943 with *The Adventures of Tartu*, about a British spy (Robert Donat) fighting Nazis in occupied Czechoslovakia. His last uncredited work for M-G-M was again done for Fleming and Gable: he polished scenes in *Adventure* (1945), Gable's first picture after the war. (During the war, while serving as an intelligence officer, Mahin had written a script for Gable about pilots in battle; it became the training film "Combat America.")

Mahin moved to 20th Century-Fox in 1949. His first film there was *Down to the Sea in Ships* (1949), a story reminiscent of *Captains Courageous* in its depiction of a spoiled young boy (Dean Stockwell) who matures when he signs up as a deckhand on his grandfather's whaling vessel. His only other credit at the studio was for *Love That Brute* (1950), about a soft-hearted gangster (Paul Douglas). It was a remake of an earlier film, *Tall, Dark, and Handsome* (1941).

In the early 1950s Mahin returned briefly to M-G-M. He collaborated with Sonya Levien and S. N. Behrman on *Quo Vadis* (1951), a historic epic set during Nero's rule and studying the persecution of early Christians. He next wrote one of his few musical scripts, *Show Boat* (1951), taken from Edna Ferber's novel about life on a Mississippi riverboat. Both films were among M-G-M's greatest successes of the year. Mahin's final project for M-G-M was a remake of *Red Dust*, now titled *Mogambo* (1953). Mahin provided a new screenplay for director John Ford, but Gable still starred (his character was now a big game hunter and guide in Africa) and the plot was still the same. The action was more spectacular and believable, but with Ava Gardner in the Harlow role and Grace Kelly replacing Astor, the chemistry is missing and the film is not as good as its predecessor.

From 1952 to 1955 Mahin worked at Paramount where he wrote three pictures, none of them successful at the box office. Leo McCarey directed *My Son, John* (1952), about a mother (Helen Hayes) who fears her son (Robert Walker) has become a communist. *Elephant Walk* (1954) was an adventure

Ingrid Bergman, Spencer Tracy, and Lana Turner in a publicity photograph for the 1941 version of Dr. Jekyll and Mr. Hyde

Patty McCormack and Henry Jones in The Bad Seed, *one of Mahin's successful adaptations for Warner Bros.*

film set on a Ceylon tea plantation. With Winston Miller, Mahin wrote *Lucy Gallant* (1955), about a woman's (Jane Wyman) rise to wealth in a western town.

Mahin had greater success with assignments from Warner Bros. to adapt two stage plays: *The Bad Seed* (1956) and *No Time for Sergeants* (1958). The former, from Maxwell Anderson's play and William March's novel, is about an evil young girl (Patty McCormack) and suggests that such evil can be inherited. *No Time for Sergeants,* which was based on Ira Levin's hit play, had Andy Griffith and Myron McCormick repeating their roles as a hayseed buck private (Griffith) and a tough sergeant (McCormick) who are constantly at odds.

It was not until 1957 that Mahin worked on the favorite of his films, *Heaven Knows, Mr. Allison.* John Huston directed and coauthored the script. A poignant romance, *Heaven Knows, Mr. Allison* tells the story of a nun (Deborah Kerr) who is stranded during World War II on a Japanese-held island with a gruff marine (Robert Mitchum). Mahin's

script skillfully mixes comedy, pathos, action, and suspense. The film became a box office success for 20th Century-Fox and earned Mahin his second Oscar nomination.

While Mahin was working for Warner Bros., he met Martin Rackin, who worked with Mahin on an adaptation of Pearl Buck's *Letter from Peking.* Although the Buck project was never completed, Mahin and Rackin joined forces to produce and adapt Harold Sinclair's novel *The Horse Soldiers.* John Ford directed and John Wayne and William Holden starred. A violent civil war tale, *The Horse Soldiers* (1959) tells of a Yankee cavalry unit's drive through the South; the hard commander (Wayne) is pitted against a doctor (Holden), a pacifist who opposes his brutal tactics. Considered one of Ford's least successful pictures, *The Horse Soldiers* failed, according to Mahin, because Ford lost interest in the film after his close friend, stuntman Fred Kennedy, was killed during the course of shooting. Ford ended shooting almost immediately with much of the script left unfilmed.

After *The Horse Soldiers,* Mahin and Rackin wrote and produced *North to Alaska* (1960), a boisterous adventure comedy in the vein of *Boom Town.* Two mining partners (John Wayne, Stewart Granger) find gold in Alaska. They become wealthy but quarrel after a misunderstanding over a woman. Mahin and Rackin next collaborated on three television pilots in the early 1960s, but when none of the pilots sold, the partnership was dissolved.

Mahin went to work at Universal studio, where he wrote his last two screenplays: *The Spiral Road* (1962), about a doctor (Rock Hudson) treating lepers in Africa, and *Moment to Moment* (1966), a murder mystery set in France. Mahin retired from screenwriting in 1966, although he occasionally wrote a script for television. He also worked on an adaptation of A. B. Guthrie's novel, *Arfive,* about a high school principal in a western town, but that script has not been filmed. John Lee Mahin died of emphysema in April 1984.

Interview:

Todd McCarthy and James McBride, "Bombshell Days in the Golden Age," *Film Comment,* 16 (March/April 1980).

References:

Carlos Clarens, *Crime Movies: From Griffith to the Godfather and Beyond* (New York: W. W. Norton, 1980), pp. 73-78, 83-100;

Rene Jordan, *Clark Gable* (New York: Pyramid Books, 1973);

Nancy Schwartz, *The Hollywood Writers Wars* (New York: Knopf, 1982).

Daniel Mainwaring
(Geoffrey Homes)
(22 July 1902-31 January 1977)

William Boddy
New York University

MOTION PICTURES: *Secrets of the Underground* (Republic, 1943), screen story as Geoffrey Homes; screenplay by Mainwaring as Homes, and Robert Tasker;

Dangerous Passage (Paramount, 1945), screen story and screenplay as Homes;

Scared Stiff (Paramount, 1945), screen story and screenplay by Mainwaring as Homes, and Maxwell Shane;

Tokyo Rose (Paramount, 1946), screenplay by Mainwaring as Homes, and Shane;

Hot Cargo (Paramount, 1946), screen story and screenplay as Homes;

They Made Me a Killer (Paramount, 1946), screenplay by Mainwaring as Homes, Winston Miller, and Kae Salkow;

Swamp Fox (Paramount, 1946), screenplay;

Big Town (Paramount, 1947), screen story and screenplay by Mainwaring as Homes;

Out of the Past (RKO, 1947), screenplay by Mainwaring as Homes, based on his novel *Build My Gallows High;*

Roughshod (RKO, 1949), screenplay by Mainwaring as Homes, and Hugo Butler;

The Big Steal (RKO, 1949), screenplay by Mainwaring as Homes, and Gerald Drayson Adams;

The Eagle and the Hawk (Paramount, 1950), screenplay by Mainwaring as Homes, and Lewis R. Foster;

The Last Outpost (Paramount, 1950), screenplay by Mainwaring as Homes, George W. Yates, and Winston Miller;

The Lawless (Paramount, 1950), screen story and screenplay as Homes, from his short story "The Voice of Stephen Wilder";

Roadblock (RKO, 1951), screen story by Mainwaring as Homes, and Richard Landau;

The Tall Target (M-G-M, 1951), screen story by Mainwaring as Homes, and Yates;

This Woman is Dangerous (Warner Bros., 1952), screenplay by Mainwaring as Homes, and Yates;

Bugles in the Afternoon (Warner Bros., 1952), screen-

Daniel Mainwaring (photograph ©1946 Ernest A. Bachrach)

play by Mainwaring as Homes, and Harry Brown;

Powder River (20th Century-Fox, 1953), screenplay by Mainwaring as Homes;

Those Redheads from Seattle (Paramount, 1953), screen story and screenplay by Mainwaring as Homes, Foster, and Yates;

Alaska Seas (Paramount, 1954), screenplay by Mainwaring as Homes, and Walter Doniger;

Black Horse Canyon (Universal, 1954), screenplay as Homes;

Southwest Passage (United Artists, 1954), screenplay by Mainwaring as Homes, and Harry Essex;

The Desperado (Allied Artists, 1954), screenplay as Homes;

The Annapolis Story (Allied Artists, 1955), screenplay by Mainwaring as Homes, and Daniel Ullman;

A Bullet for Joey (United Artists, 1955), screenplay by Mainwaring as Homes, and A. I. Bezzerides;

The Phenix City Story (Allied Artists, 1955), screenplay by Mainwaring and Crane Wilbur;

Invasion of the Body Snatchers (Allied Artists, 1956), screenplay;

Thunderstorm (Allied Artists, 1956), screenplay;

Baby Face Nelson (United Artists, 1957), screenplay;

Cole Younger, Gunfighter (Allied Artists, 1957), screenplay;

Space Master X-7 (20th Century-Fox, 1958), screen story and screenplay by Mainwaring and Yates;

The Gun Runners (United Artists, 1958), screenplay by Mainwaring and Paul Monash;

Walk Like a Dragon (Paramount, 1960), screen story and screenplay by Mainwaring and James Clavell;

Atlantis, the Lost Continent (M-G-M, 1961), screenplay;

The Minotaur (United Artists, 1961), screen story and screenplay by Mainwaring, Sandro Continenza, and Gian Paolo Callegari;

Revolt of the Slaves (United Artists, 1961), English dialogue;

East of Kilimanjaro (Independent Productions, 1962), screen story by Mainwaring and Richard Gladstone;

Convict Stage (20th Century-Fox, 1966), screenplay;

The Woman Who Wouldn't Die (Warner Bros., 1966), screenplay.

BOOKS: *One Against the Earth* (New York: R. Long & R. R. Smith, 1933);

The Man Who Murdered Himself, as Homes (New York: Morrow, 1936);

The Doctor Died at Dusk, as Homes (New York: Morrow, 1936);

The Man Who Didn't Exist, as Homes (New York: Morrow, 1937);

The Man Who Murdered Goliath, as Homes (New York: Morrow, 1938);

Then There Were Three, as Homes (New York: Morrow, 1938);

No Hands on the Clock, as Homes (New York: Morrow, 1939);

Finders Keepers, as Homes (New York: Morrow, 1940);

Forty Whacks, as Homes (New York: Morrow, 1941);

Street of the Crying Women, as Homes (New York: Morrow, 1942);

Hill of the Terrified Monk, as Homes (New York: Morrow, 1943);

Six Silver Handles, as Homes (New York: Morrow, 1944);

Build My Gallows High, as Homes (New York: Morrow, 1946).

TELEVISION: *Rustler's Gun* (Syndicated, 1957), teleplay;

The Californians (NBC, 1958), teleplay;

The Thin Man (NBC, 1958), teleplay;

Adventures in Paradise (ABC, 1960), two-episode
     teleplay;
The Legend of Jesse James (ABC, 1965), teleplay;
A Man Called Shenandoah (ABC, 1966), teleplay;
"The Night of the Deadly Blossom," *The Wild, Wild
     West* (CBS, 1967), teleplay;
Mannix (CBS, 1967), teleplay;
Cimmaron Strip (CBS, 1967), teleplay.

Daniel Geoffrey Homes Mainwaring, a prolific novelist and screenwriter, spent most of his long career in Hollywood working on "B" films and independent productions. Although he helped to write more than forty scripts in twenty-five years, Mainwaring's major work spanned a ten-year period, beginning with *Out of the Past* (1947), and including *The Lawless* (1950), *The Phenix City Story* (1955), and *Invasion of the Body Snatchers* (1956). He wrote several Westerns and two science fiction scripts but seemed most comfortable in the crime genre, reflecting his background as a crime reporter and mystery writer.

Mainwaring was born in Oakland, California, and grew up on a family farm in the Sierra Nevadas. After graduating from Fresno State Teachers College and teaching briefly, Mainwaring worked as a journalist for several New York dailies before returning to California as a crime reporter for the *Los Angeles Examiner*.

One Against the Earth, Mainwaring's first novel, was published in 1933. A caustic portrayal of a violent America which culminated in the lynching of the hero, the book was not a popular success. Depression America wanted to be entertained, Mainwaring decided, and he turned to the flourishing market for detective fiction, writing under his middle names, Geoffrey Homes. (He also used this name for his screenwriting credits until 1955.) Mainwaring found success in crime fiction and wrote twelve detective novels between 1936 and 1946.

In 1934 Mainwaring began working in Hollywood as a publicist for Warner Bros. He later wrote publicity for Columbia, RKO, and Paramount studios. He said this publicity work gave him a broader familiarity with film production than he would have garnered simply as a screenwriter. In this job, he was introduced to many writers, actors, and directors with whom he later worked. While a publicist, Mainwaring also wrote occasional articles for magazines and newspapers, including profiles of behind-the-scenes workers in Hollywood. His cynical attitude toward the motion picture industry can be seen in an article he wrote for the *Richmond*

News Leader in 1938, in which he observed: "The studios look like factories and by the looks of some of the pictures, that's what they are. Why, with all the talent in the world, are 95% of the pictures dull?" Mainwaring worked as a publicist until 1943.

Two of Mainwaring's mystery novels, *No Hands on the Clock* (1939) and *Forty Whacks* (1941), had been sold to motion picture studios during the war, and this led to Republic studios asking Mainwaring to work on a low budget film, *Secrets of the Underground* (1943). His screenwriting career did not fully develop, however, until he was signed to a 1945 six-picture contract with independent producers William Pine and William Thomas. Thus Mainwaring began writing for the screen when he was forty-one years old, with long experience in journalism, publicity, and fiction writing behind him. The professional background is reflected in many ways in the scripts Mainwaring wrote. He claimed journalism taught him how to write quickly, and such efficiency was surely an asset within the constraints of the low budget film; the six scripts he wrote for Pine and Thomas were all written in a single year. With few exceptions, production budgets and deadlines remained tight throughout his career. He wrote *Baby Face Nelson* (1957) in two weeks, and many of his scripts faced similarly constricted shooting schedules. *Baby Face Nelson*, *Invasion of the Body Snatchers*, and *The Lawless* were also shot under stringent time limits.

Mainwaring's training in crime reporting in newspapers, where, as he described it, "the formula was founded in the exploitation of violence," suited the action melodramas of Pine and Thomas. Though Mainwaring was pleased with only one of his early scripts—*Big Town* (1947)—most of the films were well-received by the trade press. Many of his early scripts highlight journalistic protagonists and address the battle against economic corruption, foreshadowing many of his later works. The reporter-detectives in *Scared Stiff* (1945) and *Tokyo Rose* (1946) and the sensationalistic newspaper editor in *Big Town* point to a familiar journalistic milieu. *Hot Cargo* (1946) combines a vengeance plot with a fight against economic autocracy in a tale of two returning soldiers who clean up the western timber industry, thus fulfilling a pledge to a dying friend.

At the end of his one-year contract with Pine and Thomas, Mainwaring was eager for a change and left Hollywood to concentrate on his final novel, *Build My Gallows High* (1946). Mainwaring's early detective novels had combined the hero and plot of the traditional mystery with social commentary. *Build My Gallows High*, however, moves away from the classic detective novel's concern with plot and motivation and moves toward the complex narrative structure, physical action, and tone of hard-boiled detective fiction.

RKO production head William Dozier bought *Build My Gallows High* and gave Mainwaring a studio contract in 1946. Mainwaring was assigned the adaptation of the novel to the screen, and after drafts by James M. Cain and Frank Fenton, Mainwaring's own script was filmed under the new title *Out of the Past* (1947). The film gave Mainwaring his first chance to work with an "A" budget and first-rate director, Jacques Tourneur.

In *Out of the Past* a former private detective, Jeff Markham (Robert Mitchum), runs a garage under an assumed name in a quiet California town. Calling himself Jeff Bailey, he lives a peaceful life with his sweetheart (Virginia Huston) until his former life catches up with him and he is framed for an old murder by gangster Whit Sterling (Kirk Douglas) and his moll Kathie Moffat (Jane Greer). Bailey, who had loved Kathie earlier, is caught up

in a complex series of events that culminate in his death.

Out of the Past is an important and prototypical film noir, with its convoluted narrative structure, somber tone, and femme fatale. A screen of lies, deals, and double deals disguises the real motives of the characters. The elaborate flashbacks with Bailey's sardonic voice-over pull the spectator into the hero's own confusion and obsession. The tone of failure and cynicism is clearest in the acid dialogue, perhaps the best Mainwaring wrote for the screen. "Is there a way to win?," Kathie asks Bailey in a Mexican gambling house. "No, but there's a way to lose more slowly," is his reply. "I don't want to die," Kathie pleads to Bailey as she prepares to change sides once again. "Neither do I, baby," he says, "but if I have to, I'm going to die last." In the bitter world of *Out of the Past* losing more slowly and dying last are the best one can hope for, and Bailey regains a degree of moral credibility at the end of the film only in the self-destructive act of entering the police ambush.

Mainwaring wrote two other significant

Jane Greer and Robert Mitchum in Out of the Past, *Mainwaring's film version of his 1946 novel*

scripts while at RKO: *Roughshod* (1949) and *The Big Steal* (1949). Directed by Mark Robson, *Roughshod* is a Western about a rancher who is convinced that three cattle rustlers are out to kill him. *The Big Steal*, the first of several collaborations with director Don Siegel, is about an American serviceman (Robert Mitchum) chasing some stolen money across Mexico; he is pursued by his crooked superior (William Bendix) and the police. The movie is little more than an extended chase, but the thin plot is sustained by the excitement of the multiple chase and the clever dialogue.

His support of the Screen Writers Guild cut short Mainwaring's RKO career. He had long been active in the guild, serving as the guild's RKO Studio chairman. When Howard Hughes acquired RKO in 1948 and undertook a purge of politically "unreliable" employees, he assigned Mainwaring the politically conservative *I Married a Communist*, a project Hughes used as a kind of studio loyalty oath. When Mainwaring refused to work on the film, Hughes dismissed him. He further punished Mainwaring by denying him screen credit for his final RKO movie, *The Hitch-Hiker* (1953); Mainwaring had written the screen story for this highly regarded motion picture about a psychopath (William Talman) who terrorizes the two men (Edmond O'Brien and Frank Lovejoy) who offer him a ride.

After he was fired by RKO, Mainwaring developed a project with another RKO exile, Joseph Losey. *The Lawless* (1950) was made for independent producers Pine and Thomas. Mainwaring had an unusually large role in the production of the movie, proposing the subject to the producers, suggesting Losey as director, and adapting his own unpublished short story for the screenplay. During production, Mainwaring scouted locations with Losey and acted as a sort of liaison between the director and the producers. He later said that he had learned more from working with Losey than from any other director.

In *The Lawless*, newspaper editor Larry Wilder (MacDonald Carey), returning from Europe to edit a local newspaper in the small California town of Santa Clara, defends a young Chicano fruit picker (Lalo Rios) accused of assaulting a policeman and attacking a white woman (Gail Patrick). Spurred on by sensationalist big city reporters and the local television station, the townspeople hunt down the fugitive and try to lynch him after his arrest; later, they attack innocent Chicanos in the street and destroy the newspaper offices. Like several other Mainwaring scripts, *The Lawless* is the story of the hero's moving from moral complacency into action;

Wilder must also battle the social pressures of his own community, which turns on him after he defends the accused Chicano in his paper. The movie also points to Mainwaring's liberal-reformist politics, a liberalism he attributed in part to his experiences as a journalist, and partly to his youth spent in agricultural communities among migrant workers. The small town setting of *The Lawless* is similar to the one in which Mainwaring became aware of social injustice, he once said, and like settings recur throughout his fiction and screenplays.

The movie's social criticism was unexpected from producers Pine and Thomas, who specialized in "B" movies; in fact, they demanded a script rewrite and delayed production for six weeks, although Mainwaring steadfastly refused to make any changes. The producers finally decided they had invested too much money in the film to abandon it, and the movie was completed using the original screenplay. Even so, Mainwaring was unhappy with the movie's ending, in which a businessman apologizes for the town's violence and puts the newspaper back in business. Mainwaring insisted that pressures from Pine and Thomas and the short production schedule prevented a more satisfactory ending.

After *The Lawless*, Mainwaring worked on *Roadblock* (1951), a minor film noir, and *The Last Outpost* (1950), a Civil War adventure, before working with director Anthony Mann on another Civil War era project, *The Tall Target* (1951). Mainwaring shared screen story credit with veteran screenwriter George W. Yates, and Joseph Losey also made contributions to the screenplay. The movie is about a New York City policeman (Dick Powell) who stumbles across a conspiracy to assassinate Abraham Lincoln as he rides the train to his inauguration. The policeman is forced to solve the case himself when his superiors do not believe him. What follows is a mixture of classic detective plot and a political subplot involving a secret organization similar to the Ku Klux Klan. While *The Tall Target* is more effective as a period piece and detective melodrama than it is a political thriller, the amount of political argument in the movie is striking, and its mixture of genres is interesting.

A series of relatively undistinguished films, mostly Westerns, written for a variety of studios, followed *The Tall Target*. Mainwaring then went to work for Allied Artists. His first screenplay at the studio was *The Desperado* (1954); three years later the script was reworked by Mainwaring as *Cole Younger, Gunfighter* (1957). Based on a novel by Clifton Adams, the movie depicts the attempts of

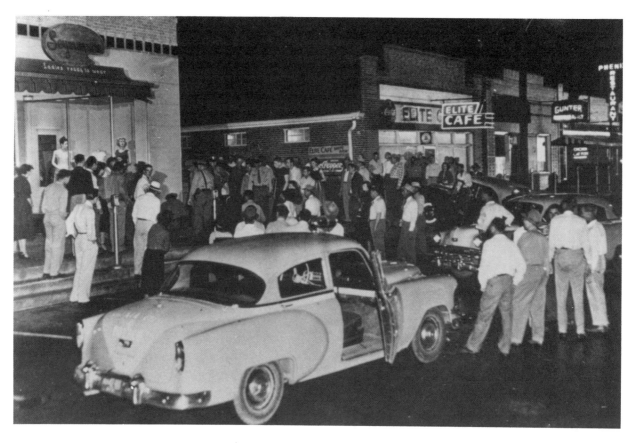

Crowd scene in The Phenix City Story, *a film praised for its documentary realism*

young Kit Caswell (James Lydon) to battle the crooked lawmen who killed his father and who control a small Texas town. The conflict in *The Desperado* prefigures Mainwaring's better-known 1955 script, *The Phenix City Story:* the protagonist's campaign for social justice, answered by violence and murder, becomes a pursuit of private vengeance. In *The Phenix City Story, The Desperado,* and *Cole Younger, Gunfighter,* the hero's vengeance is provoked by the murder of his father. The desire for revenge pushes the protagonist to the margins of a corrupt society, although not totally outside the law. The hero is reintegrated into society at the film's conclusion, not simply through the individual actions of the hero but through reformed social machinery: honest elections in *The Desperado* and *Cole Younger, Gunfighter,* and the occupation of the National Guard in *The Phenix City Story.* The reformism of many of Mainwaring's vengeance plots blunts the anarchistic tendencies of his heroes; it is precisely the possibility of institutional reform which restrains the heroes' private vengeance.

Mainwaring coauthored *The Phenix City Story* with Crane Wilbur (who did the research in Phenix

City) for director Phil Karlson at Allied Artists. Earlier, Mainwaring had spent a few days on the project with Don Siegel before Siegel left the film due to a salary dispute. With this film, Mainwaring dropped the Geoffrey Homes pseudonym and began using his first and last names.

The Phenix City Story dramatized then-recent events in the infamous Alabama vice town across the river from Fort Benning in Georgia, where a national syndicate controlled a hundred-million-dollars-a-year gambling and prostitution racket. A campaign by reform-minded citizens to turn out the mob-controlled town officials provoked the mob's violent retaliation, culminating in the murder of the State Attorney General-elect, Albert Patterson. Forced into action by the national scandal, Alabama's governor called in the National Guard and Patterson's son John was elected Attorney General. Within six months, over 700 local indictments were issued.

After a sequence of newsreel interviews with townspeople describing the events in Phenix City, Mainwaring's narrative begins, showing the gradual deepening of the Pattersons' involvement with

Panic-stricken townspeople in Invasion of the Body Snatchers, *a psychological study of paranoia in the guise of science-fiction melodrama*

the problem. John Patterson (Richard Kiley) agrees to join the fight against the gangster's political machine; Albert (John McIntyre), who has learned to ignore the criminal activity, is slowly drawn from his complacency and agrees to run for Attorney General. Over the course of the film the reformers' battle is at first implicitly linked with young Patterson's legal prosecutions of fascist war criminals in Europe; after his father's murder, however, vengeance overtakes John Patterson's desire for simple social justice. The tension between a desire for vengeance and fidelity to legal justice splits the protagonist in *The Phenix City Story* more sharply than did similar conflicts in earlier Mainwaring plots.

Between *The Desperado* and *The Phenix City Story*, Mainwaring had coscripted two undistinguished and uncharacteristically jingoistic screen-

plays, *The Annapolis Story* (1955) and *A Bullet for Joey* (1955). Don Siegel directed the former, about two brothers (John Derek and Kevin McCarthy), Navy cadets in love with the same woman (Diana Lynn). *A Bullet for Joey*, which was cowritten with A. I. Bezzerides, pits Royal Canadian Mounted Police inspector (Edward G. Robinson) against a gangster (George Raft) during the cold war; the gangster eventually succumbs to the inspector's patriotic appeals and helps free a Canadian scientist kidnapped by a "foreign power."

The emotional descent of the protagonist into hysteria, hinted at in *The Phenix City Story*, is placed at the center of Mainwaring's next film, *Invasion of the Body Snatchers* (1956). Dr. Miles Bennett (Kevin McCarthy), returning from a medical convention to his small California town, slowly realizes that his neighbors are being replaced in their sleep by humanoids, who emerge from alien pods, identical to their human models except for a complete lack of emotion. Bennett allies with his girlfriend Becky (Dana Wynter) and friends Jack and Theodora Balacek (King Donovan and Carolyn Jones), but one by one the others become humanoids.

In adapting Jack Finney's short novel *The Body Snatchers* for the screen, Mainwaring avoided both Finney's scientific speculations on the origins and motives of the aliens and the distracting spectacular machinery of the conventional science fiction film. *Invasion of the Body Snatchers* is as much a psychological study of paranoia as the recounting of the confrontation of two worlds. The ordinary small-town setting and the lack of manifest differences between pod people and humans motivate Miles's paranoid reaction: appearances are not to be trusted. This dark perspective is epitomized by the view from his office window over Main Street on a Saturday morning "just like any other morning": none of the townspeople is human. Miles moves from reason and reassurance at the beginning of the script to a frenzied hysteria, echoing the emotional progression of John Patterson in *The Phenix City Story.*

Finney ends his novel with Jack Balacek and the FBI rescuing Miles, but Mainwaring's original script leaves Miles alone on the highway, appealing to an indifferent world. Allied Artists threatened to replace Mainwaring and director Don Siegel if a new ending were not substituted, so Mainwaring created a framing device: Miles tells the story in flashback to the authorities and evidence is found to back up his story; again, the protagonist is saved by the prevailing social order. (In the 1970s, *Invasion of the Body Snatchers* was rereleased with the original ending restored.)

With the shift from the explicit threats of such films as *The Lawless* and *The Phenix City Story* to the vague terrors of *Invasion of the Body Snatchers* came a consequent shift from explicit political commentary to looser allegory. *Invasion of the Body Snatchers* has been interpreted as an anti-Communist and as an anti-anti-Communist parable, but the reading proposed by Siegel is probably closest to Mainwaring's design: the film's criticism of McCarthyism is intentional though understated in favor of a dramatization of more general 1950s anxieties over conformism. The common features of *Invasion of the Body Snatchers* and Mainwaring's other scripts support such a sociological interpretation. The film is remarkable not only as effective science fiction melodrama, but in the degree to which it reworks the themes and conflicts of Mainwaring's work in other genres.

Thunderstorm (1956), Mainwaring's next script, was directed by John Guillerman at Allied Artists. The film is set in the small fishing village of San Lorenzo, controlled by a fleet owner and a local merchant. Diego (Carlos Thompson), a poor fisherman, attempts to organize a fishing cooperative in the village. The movie recalls the earlier *Alaska Seas* (1954) which Mainwaring coauthored with Walter Doniger; both films pit a fledgling cooperative against a powerful businessman who tries to frame the hero for murder. But while the dramatic skeleton of *Thunderstorm* reworks conflicts familiar from other Mainwaring action melodramas, opposing forces move without much novelty or conviction, making the film less interesting than earlier incarnations of similar dramatic material.

In the late 1950s Mainwaring wrote his two final screenplays for Don Siegel, *The Gun Runners* (1958) and *Baby Face Nelson* (1957). The former was an adaptation by Mainwaring and Paul Monash of Ernest Hemingway's *To Have and Have Not;* neither Siegel nor Mainwaring was pleased with the picture. More interesting is *Baby Face Nelson*, the details for which were drawn from newspaper files on the gangster. The film is a prototype of the 1960s gangster biography genre, with Nelson depicted as an infantile psychopath. Just out of prison, Nelson (Mickey Rooney), tries to reconstruct John Dillinger's gang. The story follows Nelson's increasing loss of self-control as his gang disintegrates in betrayals and murder. The film ends in Nelson's death at the hands of his girlfriend.

Walk Like a Dragon (1960), Mainwaring's last major script, recalls his earlier work in its fusion of melodrama and didacticism. The story, set in the 1870s, concerns a frontiersman (Jack Lord) who buys a young Chinese prostitute (Nobu McCarthy) out of slavery in San Francisco, brings her back to his small California town, and falls in love with her. He must then battle a Chinese-American rival (James Shigeta) and the racial intolerance of his own community.

In the early 1960s Mainwaring worked on three routine spectacle films for European producers, mainly writing English dialogue and receiving full screenplay credit only on the final film, *Atlantis, the Lost Continent* (1961). Even on this project, Mainwaring complained that producer-director George Pal "rewrote every line of dialogue and let me take the blame." Moreover, it is clear that Mainwaring's talents as a writer—a certain verisimilitude of landscape and speech, tightly plotted narratives and social commentary—are basically unsuited to the spectacle film.

Mainwaring worked on two more screenplays, both in familiar genres: *Convict Stage* (1966), a Western, and *The Woman Who Wouldn't Die* (1966), a mystery. Most of the writing in the 1960s was for television; from 1957 to 1967 he wrote ten episodes for various crime and Western series. Daniel Mainwaring died of cancer in Los Angeles in 1977.

Mainwaring's achievement as a screenwriter

rests not merely in his classic genre scripts which reflect his skill in narrative structure, character, and dialogue but also in his ability to adapt and mix elements of different genres. While such stylistic consistency may be unexpected within the constraints of the low-budget film, more remarkable is Mainwaring's persistent social criticism. He succeeded in integrating reformist politics into action melodrama in a postwar Hollywood which was itself often politically intimidated and complacent.

Joseph L. Mankiewicz
(11 February 1909-)

Randall Clark

MOTION PICTURES: *The Dummy* (Paramount Famous Lasky, 1929), titles;

Close Harmony (Paramount Famous Lasky, 1929), titles;

The Man I Love (Paramount Famous Lasky, 1929), titles;

The Studio Murder Mystery (Paramount Famous Lasky, 1929), titles;

Thunderbolt (Paramount Famous Lasky, 1929), titles;

River of Romance (Paramount Famous Lasky, 1929), titles;

The Mysterious Dr. Fu Manchu (Paramount Famous Lasky, 1929), titles;

The Saturday Night Kid (Paramount Famous Lasky, 1929), titles;

Fast Company (Paramount Famous Lasky, 1929), dialogue;

The Virginian (Paramount Famous Lasky, 1929), titles;

Slightly Scarlet (Paramount Famous Lasky, 1930), screenplay and dialogue by Mankiewicz and Howard Estabrook;

The Social Lion (Paramount-Publix, 1930), adaptation and dialogue;

Only Saps Work (Paramount-Publix, 1930), dialogue;

The Gang Buster (Paramount-Publix, 1931), dialogue;

Joseph L. Mankiewicz

Finn and Hattie (Paramount-Publix, 1931), dialogue;

June Moon (Paramount-Publix, 1931), scenario by Mankiewicz and Keene Thompson; dialogue by Mankiewicz, Thompson, and Vincent Lawrence;

Skippy (Paramount-Publix, 1931), scenario by Mankiewicz and Norman Z. McLeod; dialogue by Mankiewicz, McLeod, and Don Marquis;

Newly Rich/Forbidden Adventure (Paramount-Publix, 1931), scenario by Mankiewicz, McLeod, and Edward Paramore, Jr.; dialogue by Mankiewicz and McLeod;

Sooky (Paramount-Publix, 1931), scenario and dialogue by Mankiewicz, McLeod, and Sam Mintz;

This Reckless Age (Paramount-Publix, 1932), scenario and dialogue;

Sky Bride (Paramount-Publix, 1932), scenario and dialogue by Mankiewicz, Agnes Brand Leahy, and Grover Jones;

Million Dollar Legs (Paramount-Publix, 1932), story by Mankiewicz; scenario and dialogue by Mankiewicz and Henry Myers;

If I Had a Million (Paramount-Publix, 1932), screenplay by Mankiewicz and others;

Diplomaniacs (RKO, 1933), story by Mankiewicz; screenplay by Mankiewicz and Myers;

Emergency Call (RKO, 1933), screenplay by Mankiewicz and John B. Clymer;

Too Much Harmony (Paramount, 1933), scenario;

Alice in Wonderland (Paramount, 1933), screenplay by Mankiewicz and William Cameron Menzies;

Manhattan Melodrama (M-G-M, 1934), screenplay by Mankiewicz and Oliver H. P. Garrett;

Our Daily Bread (United Artists, 1934), dialogue;

Forsaking All Others (M-G-M, 1934), screenplay;

I Live My Life (M-G-M, 1935), screenplay;

The Keys of the Kingdom (20th Century-Fox, 1944), screenplay by Mankiewicz and Nunnally Johnson;

Dragonwyck (20th Century-Fox, 1946), screenplay;

Somewhere in the Night (20th Century-Fox, 1946), screenplay by Mankiewicz and Howard Dimsdale;

A Letter to Three Wives (20th Century-Fox, 1949), screenplay;

No Way Out (20th Century-Fox, 1950), screen story and screenplay by Mankiewicz and Lesser Samuels;

All About Eve (20th Century-Fox, 1950), screenplay;

People Will Talk (20th Century-Fox, 1951), screenplay;

Julius Caesar (M-G-M, 1953), screenplay;

The Barefoot Contessa (United Artists, 1954), screenplay;

Guys and Dolls (M-G-M, 1955), screenplay;

The Quiet American (United Artists, 1958), screenplay;

Cleopatra (20th Century-Fox, 1963), screenplay by Mankiewicz, Sidney Buchman, and Ranald MacDougal;

The Honey Pot (United Artists, 1967), screenplay.

BOOKS: *All About Eve: A Screenplay* (New York: Random House, 1951);

More About All About Eve: A Colloquy, by Mankiewicz and Gary Carey (New York: Random House, 1972).

One of the first and most important screenwriters of talking films, Joseph Mankiewicz was born in Wilkes-Barre, Pennsylvania, the son of Johanna Blumenau and Frank Mankiewicz, German immigrants who had met in New York City. When Mankiewicz was a child, his family—including his brother Herman, with whom Joseph would share a lifelong rivalry—moved to New York where his father had a job teaching high school. Mankiewicz was an unusually bright student; he graduated from high school at fifteen and entered Columbia University that year, receiving a bachelor of arts degree when he was nineteen years old.

After graduating from Columbia, Mankiewicz got a job with the *Chicago Tribune* as a foreign correspondent in Berlin. In Germany he first found employment in the film industry, translating titles from German to English for Universum Film Aktien, the largest film distributor in the country. He was never able to live within his means in Europe and finally had to turn to his brother Herman for help. Herman Mankiewicz, at the time one of the highest-paid writers at Paramount, arranged for Joseph to take a junior writer's job at sixty dollars a week.

Mankiewicz's first job in Hollywood was as title writer for silent films (or sound films released with silent versions); he wrote nine sets of titles in 1929. He then became a dialogue writer, working mostly on pictures starring Jack Oakie, including *Fast Company* (1929), *The Social Lion* (1930), *Only Saps Work* (1930), *The Gang Buster* (1931), and *June Moon* (1931). His first screenplay was *Slightly Scarlet* (1930), the story of a gang of jewel thieves after a necklace worth half a million dollars. *Skippy* (1931), Mankiewicz's second screenplay, earned him an Academy Award nomination; the picture was also nominated for the best film of the year award.

Jackie Cooper and Robert Coogan in Skippy, *adapted by Mankiewicz and Norman McLeod from a popular comic strip*

Based on a comic strip by Percy Crosby, it is the story of a health inspector's son (Jackie Cooper) and the friends he makes in the slums. Mankiewicz collaborated with Norman McLeod on the screenplay, and they also collaborated on his next two scripts, *Newly Rich* (1931) and *Sooky* (1931). *Newly Rich,* also known as *Forbidden Adventure,* was adapted from Sinclair Lewis's "Let's Play King," about a child actress (Mitzi Green) who meets a child king (Bruce Line).

This Reckless Age (1932) is the second film version of the play *The Goose Hangs High* by Lewis Beach. A mining company manager (Richard Bennett) is so happy his estranged children are coming to visit that he lets an unscrupulous employee keep the company's records; when the employee frames the manager for embezzlement, the children (Frances Dee and Buddy Rogers) come to their father's defense. Another 1932 film Mankiewicz wrote was *Sky Bride* (1932), in which one pilot accidentally causes the death of another.

Million Dollar Legs (1932), an important screen credit for Mankiewicz, created a small controversy;

Herman Mankiewicz produced the picture and claimed to have written much of it without credit. When the film, a comedy about a mythical country that enters the Olympics, became a great success the long-running rivalry between the two brothers came to a head, with each wanting credit for the film. The attention gained from this film resulted in Joseph Mankiewicz receiving more prestigious assignments, including an adaptation of *Alice in Wonderland* (1933) filmed with an all-star cast.

Mankiewicz was one of nineteen writers who worked on *If I Had a Million* (1932), an episodic film about several people who are given one million dollars by an eccentric millionaire (Richard Bennett). Mankiewicz wrote two segments, "The Three Marines," featuring Gary Cooper, and perhaps the best-known segment, "Rollo and the Roadhogs" with W. C. Fields as a man who gets revenge on reckless drivers. He also contributed to the other segments. Mankiewicz's last screenplay for Paramount was *Too Much Harmony* (1933), about a singer (Bing Crosby) torn between two women (Judith Allen and Lillyan Tashman).

After leaving Paramount, Mankiewicz wrote two films for RKO. *Diplomaniacs,* (1933) starred the comedy team of Bert Wheeler and Robert Woolsey as two bumblers who represent an Indian tribe at the Geneva Convention. In *Emergency Call* (1933) a doctor and an ambulance driver team up to battle criminals faking automobile accidents for insurance payments. He then wrote dialogue for *Our Daily Bread* (1934), a highly regarded drama about farmers during the Depression. King Vidor directed.

In 1934 Mankiewicz married Elizabeth Young; they were divorced in 1937. In 1939 he married Rosa Strader, who died in 1958; and in 1962 he married Rosemary Matthews. He has four children: Eric, Christopher, Thomas, and Alexander.

Mankiewicz wrote three scripts for M-G-M in 1934, all of them directed by W. S. Van Dyke II. *Manhattan Melodrama* (1934), on which he shared credit with Oliver H. P. Garrett, is about two slum boys, one (Clark Gable) who becomes a gangster and the other (William Powell) who becomes a district attorney. In *Forsaking All Others* (1934), Dill Todd (Robert Montgomery) leaves his fiancée Mary Clay (Joan Crawford) in order to marry his mistress (Frances Drake); Mary is consoled by Jeff Williams (Clark Gable) who has loved her since childhood. Mary takes Dill back, but they separate again, and she realizes she truly loves Jeff. *I Live My Life* (1935) is the story of an unhappy romance

W. C. Fields and Hugh Herbert in Million Dollar Legs. *A long-standing rivalry between two brothers came to a head when Herman and Joseph Mankiewicz each claimed sole credit for writing this successful film.*

between a shallow woman (Joan Crawford) and an archaeologist (Brian Aherne) devoted to his work.

Mankiewicz became a producer for M-G-M in 1935 and took the same position at 20th Century-Fox in 1943. Consequently, he began writing fewer scripts; only one was produced during the decade that followed, although he is known to have worked without credit on one of his productions, *Fury* (1940), the story of an innocent man who is lynched. His one screenplay of this period was *The Keys of the Kingdom* (1944) which he and Nunnally Johnson adapted from a novel by A. J. Cronin. It is the study of an elderly priest (Gregory Peck) near the end of his career; at first his superiors consider him an unremarkable member of the clergy, but as they study his record they begin to realize that he has made great accomplishments for the church. This was to become a theme in Mankiewicz's work: the character who is not what he seems to be. Mankiewicz enjoyed examining the way his protagonists were viewed by their peers.

This same notion recurs in Mankiewicz's next

film, *Dragonwyck* (1946), which he adapted from one of Anya Seton's gothic novels. Young Miranda (Gene Tierney) comes to Dragonwyck, the estate of Nicholas Van Ryn, to serve as the governess of his daughter (Connie Marshall). After the death of Van Ryn's first wife (Vivienne Osborne), Miranda marries him, only to discover he is an insane killer. *Dragonwyck* provided Mankiewicz with his first opportunity to direct a film: he took over for ailing Ernst Lubitsch. From this time until his retirement in 1972, he directed all his own screenplays, as well as scripts by other writers, including films such as *The Late George Apley* (1947), *The Ghost and Mrs. Muir* (1947), *Escape* (1948), *House of Strangers* (1949), *Five Fingers* (1952), *Suddenly Last Summer* (1959), *There Was a Crooked Man* (1970), and *Sleuth* (1972). He is known to have worked without credit on the script of *House of Strangers* (about a businessman who manipulates his family) and *Five Fingers* (about a Briton who spies for the Germans during World War II).

Somewhere in the Night (1946), his only attempt

Joan Crawford and Clark Gable in Forsaking All Others, *one of the three films Mankiewicz wrote for M-G-M in 1934*

to write in the film-noir genre that was so popular in post-World War II, is an oddity among Mankiewicz's works. Amnesiac George Taylor (John Hodiak) has only one thing that can help him uncover his true identity: a letter signed "Larry Cravat." His attempts to find Cravat lead to a beating at the hands of gangsters and the knowledge that Cravat is wanted for murder and for the theft of two million dollars. Finally, Taylor learns that he is Cravat, but he is innocent of these charges; the real culprit is his former business partner (Richard Conte).

With *A Letter to Three Wives* (1949), Mankiewicz earned his first two Academy Awards, one for his screenplay and one for his direction. Three women (Linda Darnell, Jeanne Crain, and Ann Southern) receive letters from a woman who claims

she has run away with the husband of one; the film then becomes three separate stories, as each wife reflects on her marriage and wonders whether it is her husband who left. This film introduced a Mankiewicz trademark: the story told by several different narrators, expressing divergent points of view.

Mankiewicz followed the success of *A Letter to Three Wives* with another artistic triumph, his most famous film, *All About Eve* (1950). His script was based on Mary Orr's short story "The Wisdom of Eve" and her subsequent radio play, which were in turn based on a true story told Orr by an actress friend. Told in flashback, the film traces the success of unscrupulous actress Eve Harrington (Anne Baxter) who comes to New York and attaches herself to Broadway star Margo Channing (Bette Davis). Eve becomes Margo's understudy, replaces

Linda Darnell, Ann Southern, and Jeanne Crain in A Letter to Three Wives. *Mankiewicz won his first two Academy Awards—
best screenplay and best director—for this film.*

her in a play, pursues her lover (Gary Merrill), and becomes a success with the assistance of critic Addison de Witt (George Sanders, who won an Oscar). De Witt provides cynical commentary on the theater throughout the movie, and it is largely through him that *All About Eve* becomes one of the most biting portrayals of show business ever filmed. It is the cornerstone of Mankiewicz's reputation as a witty, literate screenwriter (though it is also one of the films most frequently cited by his detractors, who find his screenplays too wordy and his direction too static). For the second consecutive year, he won best screenplay and best director Academy Awards, an unprecedented accomplishment.

No Way Out (1950) was a far more serious drama, a study of racial tensions in the 1950s. After his brother dies under the care of a black doctor (Sidney Poitier), a bigot (Richard Widmark) has his friends stir up racial problems. *People Will Talk,*

written in 1951 by Mankiewicz, was adapted from a play by Don Praetorius and Curt Goetz. A doctor (Cary Grant) marries a pregnant, unwed patient (Jeanne Crain) in this comedy-drama. *Julius Caesar* (1953) was Mankiewicz's ambitious production of the Shakespearean play. The film was a critical success and earned an Academy Award nomination for best picture of the year.

With *The Barefoot Contessa* (1954), Mankiewicz returned to the material he had used in *All About Eve,* this time examining the rise of a Hollywood movie actress. Harry Dawes (Humphrey Bogart), a has-been director, and Kirk Edwards (Warren Stevens), his producer, cast beautiful, unknown Maria Vargas (Ava Gardner) in their new picture. The story then follows Maria from her first Hollywood success to her murder at the hands of an impotent husband (Rossano Brazzi) to whom she had been unfaithful. *The Barefoot Contessa* is similar

Anne Baxter, Bette Davis, Marilyn Monroe, and George Sanders in All About Eve, *Mankiewicz's best-known film*

to *All About Eve* in many ways: both films are told in flashback, so that the central character's fate is known to the audience; both are concerned with the way in which the protagonist is perceived by others; both films are bitter depictions of show business marked by the cynical commentary of a supporting player (in *The Barefoot Contessa* the cynic is press agent Oscar Muldoon [Edmond O'Brien]). That both George Sanders as Addison de Witt and O'Brien as Muldoon won Academy Awards for their work can be attributed, at least in part, to Mankiewicz's ability to create strong supporting characters and provide them with sharp dialogue.

The Barefoot Contessa was Mankiewicz's last genuine success as a screenwriter. His next film, *Guys and Dolls* (1955) was a musical based on Abe Burrows and Jo Swerling's play, itself based on Damon Runyon's short stories about a group of New York gamblers, one of whom (Marlon Brando) romances a Salvation Army officer (Jean Simmons) to win a bet. Critics disagreed as to whether the

film was a successful adaptation of the play, but were nearly unanimous in their disapproval of the casting of Marlon Brando in the lead role. *The Quiet American* (1958) is based on Graham Greene's novel about an American (Audie Murphy) in Saigon during the early days of the Vietnam War. It is certainly Mankiewicz's most obscure film of this period.

It was *Cleopatra* (1963) that damaged and nearly ruined Mankiewicz's career. The film was intended to be a big-budget history of the Egyptian queen, directed by Rouben Mamoulian and starring Elizabeth Taylor and Richard Burton. The screenplay went through many revisions—Mankiewicz ended up sharing screen credit with Sidney Buchman and Ranald MacDougal—and when Mamoulian withdrew from the film, Mankiewicz took over as director. As he usually did, he emphasized the film's dialogue at the expense of its visuals, but no one was willing to accept this in a historical epic; Mankiewicz's films had always been criticized for being excessively wordy and theatrical, but none were criticized more than *Cleopatra*. Even after its release in a shortened form—the original ran well over four hours—the film continued to be primarily a source of gossip regarding Burton and Taylor's love affair and subsequent marriage.

The Honey Pot (1967), Mankiewicz's last film as screenwriter, has a rather complicated history: it is based on the play *Mr. Fox of Venice* by Frederick Knotti, which is itself based on a novel, *The Evil of the Day* by Thomas Sterling, which was inspired by Ben Johnson's play *Volpone*. In order to test the loyalties of his three mistresses (Capucine, Edie Adams, and Susan Hayward) a millionaire (Rex Harrison) pretends to be dying, only to inspire one of the women to plot his murder. The film had the sort of witty, sophisticated script that Mankiewicz was famous for, but the movie was only moderately successful, critically and financially. After that, Mankiewicz directed two more films, *There Was a Crooked Man* and *Sleuth*, then retired.

Since his retirement, Mankiewicz's reputation has decreased somewhat. The very things that earned him praise in the past—the literate, witty qualities of his screenplays—have become the things that are most frequently criticized in his films. But it cannot be denied that Mankiewicz wrote some of the most intelligent films of the 1950s, and that his best work has aged well.

Biography:

Kenneth L. Geist, *Pictures Will Talk: The Life and Films of Joseph Mankiewicz* (New York: Scribners, 1978).

References:

Jack Brodsky and Nathan Weiss, *The Cleopatra Papers: A Private Correspondence* (New York: Simon & Schuster, 1963);

Frank Nugent, "All About Joe," *Collier's*, 127 (24 March 1951): 24-25, 68-70;

John Springer, "The Films of Joseph Mankiewicz," *Films in Review* (March 1971).

Abby Mann
(1 December 1927-)

Dale Winogura

MOTION PICTURES: *Judgment at Nuremburg* (United Artists, 1961), story and screenplay, adapted from his teleplay;

A Child is Waiting (United Artists, 1963), screen story and screenplay, adapted from his television story;

The Condemned of Altona (20th Century-Fox, 1963), screenplay;

Ship of Fools (Columbia, 1965), screenplay;

The Detective (20th Century-Fox, 1968), screenplay;

Report to the Commissioner (United Artists, 1975), screenplay by Mann and Ernest Tidyman;

War and Love (Cannon, 1985), screenplay.

BOOKS: *A Child Is Waiting* (New York: Popular Library, 1963);

Medical Story (New York: Signet, 1975);

Tuesdays and Thursdays (Garden City: Doubleday, 1978).

SELECTED TELEVISION: "A Child is Waiting," *Studio One* (CBS, 1957), teleplay;

"Judgment at Nuremberg," *Playhouse 90* (CBS, 1959), teleplay;

The Marcus-Nelson Murders (CBS, 1973), teleplay;

Kojak (CBS, 1973-1978), creator;

Medical Story (NBC, 1975), creator and producer; author of pilot;

King (NBC, 1978), teleplay;

Skag (NBC, 1980), producer and creator;

The Atlanta Child Murders (CBS, 1985), teleplay.

Abby Mann is one of the foremost writers of prestigious social problem movies. In his handful of screenplays Mann has addressed such problems as fascism, police corruption, and mental retardation. His films are often powerful, thought-provoking experiences.

Born Abraham Goodman, in Philadelphia,

Born Abraham Goodman, in Philadelphia, Mann was educated at public schools before attending Temple University in Pennsylvania and New York University. He became involved with the theater while at college, writing five plays for student productions: "Freud Has a Word for It," "The Happiest Days," "Exodus," "Sweet Lorraine," and "Just Around the Corner." When World War II erupted Mann joined the army.

In the 1950s Mann began writing for television, working on such dramatic anthology series as *Playhouse 90*, *Studio One*, and *Alcoa Goodyear Theatre*. It was one of his television scripts that brought him his first screenwriting assignment; in 1961, Stanley Kramer hired him to expand "Judgment at Nuremberg" to feature film length. Mann turned his fifty-minute teleplay into a three-hour movie about the trial of Nazi war criminals. Though the primary conflict is between flamboyant prosecutor Tad Lawson (Richard Widmark) and the defense attorney Hans Rolfe (Maximilian Schell), there is also much emphasis on the peripheral roles: Judge Dan Haywood (Spencer Tracy); witnesses Irene Hoffman (Judy Garland), who is the friend of a murdered Jew, and Rudolph Petersen (Montgomery Clift), who is the victim of medical experiments; and the defendants, particularly Ernst Janning (Burt Lancaster), the most conscience-stricken of the war criminals. Mann succeeds to an extraordinary extent in giving all his characters definition and impact. The movie is consistently engrossing and surprising; Mann drew upon actual trial transcripts to produce strong courtroom drama. As with all of Mann's screenplays, *Judgment at Nuremberg* relies heavily on the spoken word, but his dialogue is concise and revealing, rarely self-conscious and never calling attention to the mechanics of the script. He earned his first Academy Award for the

Maximilian Schell in Judgment at Nuremburg, *which earned Mann an Academy Award for his screenplay*

film, which was also nominated as best picture.

Another exceptional screenplay came the following year: *A Child is Waiting* (1963), again adapted from Mann's own television script. Kramer produced the film and John Cassavetes directed. It is set in a school for retarded children, with Dr. Clark (Burt Lancaster), the head of the school, trying to find adequate funds for the center while he instructs a new therapist, Jean Hansen (Judy Garland). Hansen takes a special interest in one child, a mildly retarded boy whose parents seem to care little for him. This interest leads to a conflict between Hansen and Clark, who insists it is wrong to become personally involved with any of the children. *A Child is Waiting*, overlooked upon its release, gained critical attention in later years. It is Mann's most modest, yet poignant screenplay.

There were many impressive credits associated with *The Condemned of Altona* (1963). The movie was based on Jean-Paul Sartre's play *Les Sequestres d'Altoona*, which was first produced in Paris in 1959; an English version was produced in New York City in 1966. Vittorio De Sica directed, and Fredric March and Maximilian Schell headed a strong cast. But the completed film was a static version of Sartre's story about a dying German magnate (March) and his two sons, one a war criminal (Schell), the other a playboy (Robert Wagner). Little more than a filmed stage play, the movie was of limited interest to critics and to viewers.

Mann recovered on his next project, however, reteaming with Kramer to film Katherine Anne Porter's *Ship of Fools* in 1965. By cutting, condensing, and changing the text, adding some characters and situations not in the book, Mann created a vivid and captivating motion picture. Just prior to World War II, a German liner is carrying a multitude of passengers from Vera Cruz to Bremerhaven. On

Oskar Werner, Simone Signoret, and Stanley Kramer on the set of Ship of Fools, *for which Mann received an Academy Award nomination*

Telly Savalas and Abby Mann

the top decks reside the elite, including wealthy and struggling Americans, arrogant Germans, and tolerant and intolerant Jews, all heading for probable disaster. Below, there are hundreds of poor, starving Spanish peasant laborers being sent home through a humanitarian action. The central characters are Schumann (Oskar Werner), the ship's doctor, and La Condessa (Simone Signoret), the woman responsible for the workers' deportation. Their old-fashioned values are contrasted with the shallow, purposeless nature and motivations of most of the other characters. The spokesman for balance and understanding is the dwarf Karl Glocken (Michael Dunn), who is sharply aware of everything; he opens and closes the film with cynical, but meaningful, observations. At the movie's end, he directly addresses the audience: "Oh, I can just hear you saying, 'What has all this to do with us?' Nothing!" Mann's screenplay makes the ship and passengers more than just representative of the kind of corruption, stupidity, ignorance, and hatred that fed the rise of Hitler and war; they are a timeless study of prejudice and emotional conflict. *Ship of Fools* earned Mann an Academy Award nomination.

Busy with television and other projects, Mann did not write another screenplay until 1968. *The Detective*, adapted from Roderick Thorp's novel and directed by Gordon Douglas, is one of his most underrated efforts. Police detective Joe Leland (Frank Sinatra) is investigating two deaths—Teddy Leikman, a homosexual who was brutally slain, and McIver, officially a suicide, though his wife (Jacqueline Bissett) insists he was murdered. Leland finds that Leikman and McIver were lovers; McIver killed Leikman, then himself, and Leikman's wealthy father covered up everything. Disgusted by police complicity in the cover-up, Leland resigns from the force and vows to fight police corruption. Action and social comment are interwoven neatly in *The Detective*. It is a minor work, but not an unimportant one.

Before writing his next screenplay, Mann became involved with a variety of television productions, the most noteworthy of which were *The Marcus-Nelson Murders* (1973) and *Medical Story* (1975). *The Marcus-Nelson Murders* is a fictional depiction of two murders in 1963 that eventually resulted in the Supreme Court's Miranda decision. In this telefilm, a police lieutenant (Telly Savalas) tries to prevent a black youth (Gene Woodbury) from being wrongly convicted for the murders. The movie earned Mann an Emmy award and was the basis for the long-running *Kojak* series. *Medical Story* was the account of an intern's struggle to convince his superiors that a highly respected surgeon (Jose Ferrer) is performing unnecessary surgery. Mann based his script on his wife's experiences when she was hospitalized; he produced the subsequent television series in 1975.

Adapted from James Mills's novel, *Report to the Commissioner* (1975) is another police film, one that is even more uncompromising and brutal than *The Detective* and *The Marcus-Nelson Murders*. During the raid on the headquarters of a known drug dealer, rookie police officer Bo Lockley (Michael Moriarty) shoots and kills the man's mistress (Susan Blakely), then learns she was an undercover policewoman. The department immediately hushes up everything, but Lockley feels that the matter is unresolved and continues to investigate. His efforts result in his imprisonment and eventual suicide. Mann's hard-hitting, realistic screenplay was written in collaboration with Ernest Tidyman; Milton Katselas directed.

Since 1975 Mann has devoted his efforts to television. He wrote and directed the biographical miniseries *King*, about Martin Luther King, Jr., in 1978. He received Emmy nominations as writer and director. In 1979 he developed the television series *Skag* about a fifty-six-year-old steelworker trying to cope with health, financial, and personal problems. The series was praised by critics, but unpopular with viewers and ran only briefly.

In 1984 Mann announced his return to motion pictures, beginning work on a project about German children who survived the Holocaust. The resulting film was *War and Love* (1985), based on producer Jack Eisner's experiences as a Polish youth, fighting the Nazis in a Warsaw ghetto and romancing a pretty young girl. Easily Mann's least dramatic work, it was harmed by excessive sentimentality.

Abby Mann's screenplays prove that message cinema can convey genuine dramatic excitement. Though some critics charge that Mann's films depend too much on talk and characterization to be pure cinema, Mann creates dialogue and drama that translate meaningfully to film.

Frances Marion
(18 November 1886-12 May 1973)

Joyce Olin

SELECTED MOTION PICTURES: *Camille* (World, 1915), scenario;

The Foundling (Mary Pickford/Famous Players, 1915; reshot and reedited, 1916), scenario;

The Yellow Passport (Shubert-World, 1916), adaptation by Marion and Edwin August;

Then I'll Come Back to You (World-Frohman, 1916), scenario;

The Social Highwayman (Peerless-World, 1916), scenario;

The Feast of Life (Paragon-World, 1916), scenario;

Tangled Fates (Peerless-World, 1916), scenario;

La Vie de Bohème (Paragon-World, 1916), scenario;

The Crucial Test (Paragon-World, 1916), scenario;

A Woman's Way (Peerless-World, 1916), scenario;

The Summer Girl (Peerless-World, 1916), scenario;

Friday, the 13th (Peerless-World, 1916), scenario;

The Revolt (Peerless-World, 1916), scenario;

The Hidden Scar (Peerless-World, 1916), scenario;

The Gilded Cage (Peerless-World, 1916), scenario;

Bought and Paid For (Peerless-World, 1916), scenario;

All Man (Peerless-World, 1916), scenario;

The Rise of Susan (Peerless-World, 1916), scenario;

On Dangerous Ground (Peerless-World, 1916), scenario;

A Woman Alone (Peerless-World, 1917), scenario;

Tillie Wakes Up (Peerless-World, 1917), scenario;

The Hungry Heart (Peerless-World, 1917), scenario;

A Square Deal (Peerless-World, 1917), scenario;

Frances Marion

A Girl's Folly (Paragon-World, 1917), scenario;

The Web of Desire (Peerless-World, 1917), scenario;

A Poor Little Rich Girl (Paramount-Artcraft, 1917), scenario;

As Man Made Her (Peerless-World, 1917), scenario;

The Social Leper (Peerless-World, 1917), scenario;

Forget-Me-Not (Brady-Peerless-World, 1917), scenario;

Darkest Russia (Brady-World, 1917), scenario;

The Crimson Dove (World, 1917), scenario;

The Stolen Paradise (World, 1917), story and scenario;

The Divorce Game (Brady-Peerless-World, 1917), scenario;

The Beloved Adventuress (World, 1917), story and scenario;

The Amazons (Famous Players, 1917), scenario;

Rebecca of Sunnybrook Farm (Paramount-Artcraft, 1917), adaptation;

A Little Princess (Paramount-Artcraft, 1917), adaptation;

Stella Maris (Paramount-Artcraft, 1918), scenario;

Amarilly of Clothes-Line Alley (Famous Players-Lasky, 1918), scenario;

M'liss (Famous Players-Lasky, 1918), scenario;

How Could You, Jean? (Famous Players-Lasky, 1918), adaptation;

The City of Dim Faces (Famous Players-Lasky-Paramount, 1918), story;

Johanna Enlists (Pickford, 1918), scenario;

He Comes Up Smiling (Famous Players-Lasky, 1918), scenario;

The Temple of Dusk (Haworth/Exhibitors-Mutual, 1918), scenario;

The Goat (Paramount-Artcraft, 1918), story and scenario;

Captain Kidd, Jr. (Paramount-Artcraft, 1918), adaptation;

The Misleading Widow (Paramount-Artcraft, 1919), scenario;

Anne of Green Gables (Realart, 1919), scenario;

A Regular Girl (Selznick-Select, 1919), story by Marion and Edmund Goulding;

The Cinema Murder (Paramount-Cosmopolitan, 1919), scenario;

Pollyanna (United Artists, 1920), scenario;

Humoresque (Cosmopolitan, 1920), scenario;

The Flapper (Selznick, 1920), story;

The Restless Sex (Cosmopolitan, 1920), scenario;

The World and His Wife (Paramount-Cosmopolitan, 1920), scenario;

The Love Light (United Artists, 1921), scenario;

Straight Is the Way (Cosmopolitan, 1921), scenario;

Just Around the Corner (Cosmopolitan, 1922), adaptation;

Back Pay (Cosmopolitan, 1922), scenario;

The Primitive Lover (Schenck-First National, 1922), scenario;

Sonny (Inspiration, 1922), adaptation;

East Is West (Schenck-First National, 1922), adaptation and scenario;

The Eternal Flame (Norma Talmadge Film, 1922), adaptation;

The Toll of the Sea (Technicolor, 1922), story;

Minnie (Neilan, 1922), titles;

The Voice from the Minaret (Schenck-First National, 1923), adaptation;

The Famous Mrs. Fair (Mayer, 1923), scenario;

The Nth Commandment (Cosmopolitan, 1923), scenario;

Within the Law (Schenck-First National, 1923), adaptation;

The Love Piker (Cosmopolitan, 1923), scenario;

Potash and Perlmutter (Goldwyn, 1923), scenario;

The French Doll (Tiffany, 1923), adaptation;

The Song of Love (Schenck-First National, 1923), adaptation;

Through the Dark (Cosmopolitan, 1924), scenario;

Abraham Lincoln (Rockett-Lincoln, 1924), scenario;

Marion wrote two versions of Camille. *The 1915 silent film (left) starred Clara Kimball Young, while the 1937 talkie (right) featured Greta Garbo, shown here with Robert Taylor and Jessie Ralph.*

Secrets (Schenck-First National, 1924), adaptation;

Cytherea (Madison, 1924), adaptation;

Tarnish (Goldwyn, 1924), scenario;

In Hollywood with Potash and Perlmutter (Goldwyn, 1924), adaptation;

Sundown (First National, 1924), scenario by Marion and Kenneth B. Clarke;

The Flaming Forties (Producers Distributing Corp., 1924), scenario;

A Thief in Paradise (Goldwyn-First National, 1925), adaptation;

The Lady (Schenck-First National, 1925), screenplay;

His Supreme Moment (Goldwyn, 1925), adaptation;

Zander the Great (Cosmopolitan, 1925), adaptation;

Lightnin' (Fox, 1925), scenario;

Graustark (Schenck-First National, 1925), adaptation;

The Dark Angel (Goldwyn, 1925), scenario;

Lazybones (Fox, 1925), scenario;

Thank You (Fox, 1925), scenario;

Simon, the Jester (Metropolitan, 1925), adaptation;

Stella Dallas (Goldwyn, 1925), scenario;

The First Year (Fox, 1926), scenario;

Partners Again (Goldwyn, 1926), adaptation;

Paris at Midnight (Metropolitan, 1926), adaptation;

The Son of the Sheik (Feature, 1926), adaptation by Marion and Fred de Gresac;

The Scarlet Letter (M-G-M, 1926), adaptation, scenario, and titles;

The Winning of Barbara Worth (Goldwyn, 1926), adaptation;

The Red Mill (Cosmopolitan, 1927), adaptation and scenario;

The Callahans and the Murphys (M-G-M, 1927), scenario;

Madame Pompadour (Paramount, 1927), scenario;

Love (M-G-M, 1927), continuity;

Bringing Up Father (M-G-M, 1928), continuity;

The Cossacks (M-G-M, 1928), adaptation and continuity;

Excess Baggage (M-G-M, 1928), continuity;

The Wind (M-G-M, 1928), scenario;

The Awakening (Goldwyn, 1928), story;

The Masks of the Devil (M-G-M, 1928), continuity;

Their Own Desire (M-G-M, 1929), screenplay;

Anna Christie (M-G-M, 1930), adaptation;

The Rogue Song (M-G-M, 1930), screenplay by Marion and John Colton;

The Big House (Cosmopolitan, 1930), story, scenario, and dialogue;

Let Us Be Gay (M-G-M, 1930), continuity and dialogue;

Good News (M-G-M, 1930), screenplay;

Min and Bill (M-G-M, 1930), scenario and dialogue by Marion and Marion Jackson;

The Secret Six (M-G-M, 1931), story and screenplay;

The Champ (M-G-M, 1931); refilmed as *The Clown* (M-G-M, 1953); refilmed as *The Champ* (MGM, 1979), story;

Emma (M-G-M, 1932), story;

Blondie of the Follies (M-G-M, 1932), story;

Cynara (Goldwyn, 1932), adaptation by Marion;

Secrets (United Artists, 1933), adaptation and screenplay;

Peg O' My Heart (M-G-M, 1933), adaptation;

Dinner at Eight (M-G-M, 1933), screenplay by Marion and Herman J. Mankiewicz;

The Prizefighter and the Lady (M-G-M, 1933), story;

Going Hollywood (M-G-M, 1933), story;

Riffraff (M-G-M, 1935), story; screenplay by Marion, H. W. Hanemann, and Anita Loos;

Camille (M-G-M, 1937), screenplay by Marion, Zoë Akins, and James Hilton;

Love from a Stranger (United Artists, 1937), screenplay;

Knight without Armour (London Films-United Artists, 1937), adaptation;

Green Hell (Universal, 1940), story and screenplay.

BOOKS: *Minnie Flynn* (New York: Boni & Liveright, 1925);

The Secret Six (New York: Grossett & Dunlap, 1931);

Mary Pickford and Josephine Crowell in Rebecca of Sunnybrook Farm, *Marion's first assignment under her exclusive contract with Paramount*

Marion's husband Fred Thomson and Mary Pickford in
The Love Light

Valley People (New York: Raynal & Hitchcock,
1935);

Molly, Bless Her (New York: Harper, 1937);

How to Write and Sell Film Stories (New York: Covici,
Friede, 1937);

Westward the Dream (Garden City: Doubleday,
1948);

The Powder Keg (Boston: Little, Brown, 1953);

Off With Their Heads: A Serio-Comic Tale of Hollywood
(New York: Macmillan, 1972).

One of the few women to rise high in the
ranks of screenwriters, Frances Marion was an important silent film writer who weathered the transition to sound movies and reestablished herself as
a major screenwriter. Marion had worked on a
number of films before she wrote *The Foundling*
(1916), but this script for Mary Pickford is generally
considered to mark the beginning of one of the
most prolific careers in Hollywood. While most
filmographies give Marion credit for fewer than
150 films, estimates of the number of films attributable to her go as high as 300, including works
written under various pseudonyms.

Named for her distant paternal relative, Francis Marion, the Revolutionary War's "Swamp Fox,"
Frances Marion Owens was born and brought up
in San Francisco. She was the middle child of pianist Minnie Hall (who had studied with a student
of Liszt) and the entrepreneurial Len Douglas Owens, whose father had immigrated to Council Bluffs

from South Carolina when the Iowa territory had
been opened to settlers.

Expelled from Hamilton Grammar School for
drawing satiric cartoons of her teachers, Marion
was placed in a private preparatory school, St. Margaret's Hall. Although she had an older brother
and younger sister, she apparently led a solitary,
but imaginatively rich, childhood; she attended sé-
ances with a great aunt and spent time on the waterfront, with her retired sea captain uncle and his
cronies, listening to sea tales and tall stories. She
spent her summers studying at the Mark Hopkins
Art School. After her father's business security collapsed with the 1906 San Francisco earthquake and
fire, Marion attended the University of California
at Berkeley, instead of Bryn Mawr, as her family
had planned. She also studied for a time at the
Sorbonne.

At sixteen Marion eloped with nineteen-year-
old art instructor Wesley De Lappé. She dropped
out of Berkeley, and they lived "very *La Bohème*,"
until their divorce almost two years later. She took
a job cub reporting for the *San Francisco Examiner,*
but was fired for being "too soft" on "hot leads."
During this period, she did meet actress Marie
Dressler, who would later be a valuable contact.

Her next job was designing advertisements
for Western Pacific Railway and Baker's Chocolate,
which led to a modeling job with photographer
Arnold Genthe. At twenty Marion married Robert
Pike, an older man without Marion's taste for the
bohemian. She painted under the name Marion
Pike during her short-lived second marriage.

Frances Marion came to Hollywood in 1913
as a commercial artist contracted by Oliver Morosco
to draw theatrical posters of the players in his Los
Angeles stock company. The film industry was just
beginning to assert itself as a serious medium, and
Marion's new circle of acquaintances—including
Adela Rogers St. John, Erich von Stroheim, Frank
Borzage, and Sessue Hayakawa—urged her to become involved. Rogers St. John arranged an interview for Marion with Lois Weber, one of the first
women directors in Hollywood. Weber signed Marion to a contract with Hobart Bosworth, an independent producer.

Although Marion's salary was a meager fifteen dollars a week (in contrast to the $1,700 weekly
salary she was drawing during her most successful
period in the 1930s), she acted as leading lady opposite Monte Blue in *The Wild Girl from the Hills*
(1915), learned to interpret scenarios, edited, and
wrote publicity, continuities, and titles. Six months
later she wrote her first scenario, *The Foundling.*

Adolph Zukor paid her for the scenario under the conditions that she also write the continuity and titles and do the editing. Much of the film, however, was destroyed in a storeroom fire at Famous Players, before the premiere (it was reshot and released in 1916). Marion wrote to all the New York studio heads for a job. William A. Brady at World Films was interested, but when Marion tried to convince him that she could write, she had nothing concrete to show him. What she could offer was a demonstration of her tenacity and ingenuity. She suggested to Brady that she would work without pay for two weeks; if he was pleased by her work, she would stay on at $250 a week. Her first project was to take an unmarketable film starring Brady's daughter Alice, rewrite the story using most of the available footage, and salvage the company's thirteen-thousand-dollar investment. She was hired by Brady at the end of the two weeks and in the next

several years wrote fifty to sixty films for World Films. Her first fully credited film was *Camille* (1915), an adaptation of the novel by Alexandre Dumas *fils*, and it starred Clara Kimball Young. (Over twenty years later, Marion wrote a more successful and famous version, with Greta Garbo in the lead.) Her other films for World included *A Woman's Way* (1916), *The Gilded Cage* (1916), and *The Summer Girl* (1916).

In 1917 Marion reestablished her professional relationship with Pickford, writing *A Poor Little Rich Girl* for Pickford's Artcraft Company. In the next several years she wrote some of Pickford's favorite starring roles, including *Rebecca of Sunnybrook Farm* (1917), *A Little Princess* (1917), *Stella Maris* (1918), *Amarilly of Clothes-Line Alley* (1918), *M'liss* (1918), and *Pollyanna* (1920).

In 1919, like much of the rest of Hollywood, Marion became involved with the war effort, work-

Rudolph Valentino and Vilma Banky in The Son of the Sheik. *Valentino died before the film was released.*

Lars Hansen and Lillian Gish in The Wind. *M-G-M forced Marion to write a happy ending to this story of a woman driven to murder.*

ing with Wesley Ruggles and Harry Thorpe on a film about women's war activities for the Committee on Public Information. She was interested in making a picture that would show how women, through the Red Cross, Salvation Army, and other organizations, "stuck to the doughboy from the time he landed on French soil until the armistice was signed." The regard for her film-writing skills led to the army's allowing her to become the first American woman in Germany to ride in trucks taking supplies to American prisoners who had been released along the Rhine. During this time, she met Fred Thomson, an army chaplain whom she married and helped launch as a cowboy star. She and Thomson had two sons, Fred, Jr., and Richard.

After the war, Marion renewed her writing and her first directorial effort was *The Love Light* (1921) which starred Pickford and Thomson. Thomson also starred in her second film, *Just Around the Corner* (1921). Her third directing project was her adaptation of *The Song of Love* (1923), which was codirected with Chester Franklin.

Marion's autobiography, *Off With Their Heads* (1972), credits her with the scenarios for sixty-four films during the 1920s, including *The Flapper* (1920), *Sonny* (1922), *The Eternal Flame* (1922, adapted from Honoré de Balzac's *La Duchess de Congeais*), *Abraham Lincoln* (1924), *Graustark* (1925), *Paris at Midnight* (1926, adapted from Balzac's *Pere Goriot*), *Madame Pompadour* (1927), and *Bringing Up Father* (1928, from the comic strip and screen story by George McManus). She wrote eight silent films for Norma Talmadge and six for Ronald Colman. Notable among the latter was *The Dark Angel* (1925), the first of the celebrated teaming of Colman with Vilma Banky. Based upon the play by H. B. Trevelyan, it tells of Alan Trent (Colman), a soldier blinded in World War I, who allows himself to be believed dead by the woman (Banky) he loves. On the day she is to marry his wartime comrade she learns Trent is still alive and rushes to see him; he hides his blindness and sends her away, but they are later reunited.

The Dark Angel was a box office hit and elevated Colman to the front rank of male stars. Its producer told Marion he intended to make a great woman's picture starring Colman. The film was *Stella Dallas* (1925), an adaptation of the novel by Olive Higgins Prouty. *Stella Dallas* later became synonymous with soap opera, but the 1925 version is a sensitive and moving film, thanks to outstanding performances, Henry King's direction, and Marion's scenario. Stella (Belle Bennett) is a lower-class woman who marries a cultured gentleman (Ronald Colman); they prove incompatible and divorce. Feeling she is unable to raise their daughter Laurel (Lois Moran) properly, Stella eventually sends her to live with her father and his aristocratic second wife. Laurel becomes a refined lady and enters into a marriage in a famous scene in which Stella, stand-

ing outside in the rain, watches the ceremony through the window of the mansion. The film was well received critically, and when it was remade in 1938 most of the structure of Marion's original scenario was reused.

Marion wrote another memorable film for Colman, Banky, and director Henry King in 1926. *The Winning of Barbara Worth*, based on a novel by Harold Bell Wright, is about the harnessing of the Colorado River to irrigate the Imperial Valley of California. Orphan Barbara (Banky) is adopted by rancher Jefferson Worth, one of the backers of a plan to bring water into the valley. When Willard Holmes (Ronald Colman) comes to town as an engineer on the dam, he and Worth argue as to whether the project is safe. Holmes also becomes

Inmates take over the prison in The Big House. *Though the film was successful, it was criticized for its sympathetic portrayal of the prisoners.*

Jackie Cooper and Wallace Beery in The Champ, *which earned Academy Awards for both Beery and Marion*

involved in a romantic triangle with Barbara and local man Abe Lee (Gary Cooper).

In the same year Marion wrote the sequel to *The Sheik,* titled *The Son of the Sheik* (1926). It is a romantic film that focuses on revenge over a misunderstanding and dissolves into a windswept swashbuckling western love story in Arabian costumes. The aggressive son of Sheik Ahmed (Rudolph Valentino plays both the father and son roles) falls in love with the daughter (Banky) of a French swindler, and he is later captured and tortured. Believing the woman betrayed him, he takes revenge, but later learns that she did, in fact, love him; he makes amends by bringing her to live in elegant desert splendor in his father's kingdom. When she is abducted by the villains, both the Sheik and his son go to the rescue in a climax replete with spectacular chases and swordplay. Despite its having followed the formula of *The Sheik, The Son*

of the Sheik was an improvement on the earlier picture and has been Valentino's most popular film and the one most frequently revived.

Marion next turned to an adaptation of Hawthorne's *The Scarlet Letter* (1926). When Lillian Gish proposed filming it, Louis B. Mayer told her it was taboo, and she ran into a storm of protest from women's clubs, which denounced the project as immoral and unworthy of its star. Gish then personally campaigned and reassured the women that the film would not offend their sensibilities. Actually, Marion's scenario is more sexually suggestive than Hawthorne's austere novel, for she begins with a dramatization of the events leading up to the seduction. She shows Hester Prynne's first meeting with the Reverend Arthur Dimmesdale after she has been accused of blasphemy and witchcraft for whistling at her pet bird on the Sabbath. Later, Dimmesdale comes upon Prynne as she washes her undergarments in the river. He walks away, but returns to kiss her fiercely.

After Prynne has an illegitimate baby, the film becomes a fairly faithful transcription of Hawthorne's novel and an example of the simple, direct storytelling that Marion favored throughout her career. She did make one other significant change, however, adding for comic relief a clownish character who scoffs at Puritan prudishness and eventually has her nemesis, Mistress Hibbins, punished in the ducking stool. Purists might protest at the liberties taken with Hawthorne's classic, but in cinematic terms the film is impressive. It marked the American directing debut of Sweden's Victor Seastrom, who also directed Gish in Marion's *The Wind* (1928).

The Wind tells of a sensitive young eastern woman (Gish) who, when left alone and helpless, goes west to live with a coarse and unsympathetic family. There, she is forced into marriage with a

crude ranch hand and into a sexual relationship that is frightening and repellent. Her hopeless situation, echoed and exacerbated by the relentless wind, dust, and endless desert sky, eventually drive her to panic, terror, madness, and murder. A compelling psychological and environmental study, it was quite unorthodox and avant-garde for its time.

After Hawthorne, Marion turned to the Russian classics, writing the scenario for *Love* (1927), the first of two versions of *Anna Karenina* starring Greta Garbo. This version, directed by Edmund Goulding, was played in modern dress and has a happy ending. When Karenin divorces Anna, she is free to marry her lover, Count Vronsky (John Gilbert). The next year, Marion wrote a film adaptation of Leo Tolstoy's *The Cossacks* (1928), also for Gilbert.

Many performers and screenwriters had difficulty in making the transition from silent films to sound but among the most successful writers to

Grant Mitchell, George Baxter, Louise Closser Hale, Jean Harlow, Wallace Beery, Edmund Lowe, Karen Morley, and Billie Burke in Dinner at Eight, *one of Marion's last films*

effect this transition were Marion and Anita Loos. Marion and Garbo made their sound debuts together with *Anna Christie* (1930), which drew a great deal of attention because critics and audiences alike were anxious to see if a talking Garbo would succeed. An adaptation of Eugene O'Neill's play, *Anna Christie* is a somewhat outmoded moral fable about a young woman who was left with abusive relatives as a child and has become embittered by having to support herself as a prostitute. She is reunited with her father, a coal barge operator, and she falls in love with a young sailor (Charles Bickford), neither of whom knows anything about her past.

In 1928 Fred Thomson died of pneumonia, and two years later Marion married director George Hill. They divorced in 1931, but during their brief marriage they collaborated on three successful pictures, *The Big House, The Secret Six,* and *Min and Bill. The Big House* (1930), centered around an attempted jailbreak, contains powerful and disquieting scenes showing the prisoners' discomfort. Criticized mildly for celebrating the inmates as martyrs, it was one of the first films that portrayed the details of life in a maximum security prison. The film won Marion her first Oscar. *The Secret Six* (1931) is one of Marion's rare forays into the gang-

ster film genre that was so popular in the 1930s. It follows the career of Scorpio (Wallace Beery), a small-time butcher who becomes the leader of the criminal underworld in a major (but fictional) city. *Min and Bill* (1930), from a novel by Lorna Moon, is the story of a pair of waterfront toughs who try to prevent Min's daughter from being taken from her and placed in a "proper" home. Its sentimentality was redeemed by the salty dialogue and performances of its stars, Wallace Beery and Marie Dressler, who won an Academy Award.

With *The Big House, Secret Six,* and *Min and Bill,* Marion had proven she was capable of writing good material for Wallace Beery, one of M-G-M's biggest stars. In 1931 she provided Beery with the role for which he won his Academy Award. *The Champ,* a modest, sentimental vehicle, tells the story of Purcell (Beery), a once-successful boxer who is trying to overcome his drinking habit and stage a comeback for the sake of his son Dink (Jackie Cooper). When Purcell finally gets a match, he struggles in the ring, successfully defends his honor before his son by knocking out his opponent, but collapses from a heart attack. Beery's performance as the champ not only won him an Oscar but established him in the type of role he was to play for much of his career.

Dinner at Eight (1933), one of Marion's best-remembered films, was adapted by Marion and Herman Mankiewicz from the play by George S. Kaufman and Edna Ferber. The film featured an all-star cast—John and Lionel Barrymore, Beery, Dressler, Jean Harlow, Lee Tracy, and Billie Burke—whose separate stories are linked by the fact that they are all invited to a posh society dinner. The most poignant episode in *Dinner at Eight* featured John Barrymore as a once great and now unemployable actor, too fond of drink and women, a part that for Barrymore was practically autobiographical. George Cukor directed.

Cukor also directed the remake of *Camille* (1937), which Marion, together with Zoë Akins and James Hilton, adapted from the novel and play by Alexandre Dumas *fils.* In it Garbo gave one of her finest performances, and she was nominated for an Academy Award as best actress.

In 1940 Marion wrote her last screenplay, *Green Hell,* an original story of adventure in the South American jungles that starred Douglas Fairbanks, Jr. Though she was only fifty-four, she wrote no more films. Her novel *Molly, Bless Her* (1937) was filmed in 1945 as *Molly and Me,* and *The Clown* (1953) was based upon the same story that Marion used in writing her film *The Champ.* An-

Frances Marion

other version of *The Champ* was released in 1979.

Though she retired young, Frances Marion had a distinguished career for twenty-five years, during which she wrote practically every kind of film with reliable professionalism—musicals (*The Rogue Song, Good News,* 1930); Westerns (*The Winning of Barbara Worth, The Flaming Forties,* 1924); adventure stories (*Son of the Sheik, Green Hell*); comedies (*Peg O' My Heart,* 1933); adaptations of classics, and straight drama of almost every variety. Her scripts were directed by such notable figures as Henry King, King Vidor, Frank Borzage, Frank Lloyd, Fred Niblo, John Ford, Edmund Goulding,

George Cukor, Clarence Brown, Raoul Walsh, and James Whale. Between 1915 and 1940 she wrote a great many films that are classics of the era; and, along with Anita Loos (with whom she occasionally collaborated) and Isobel Lennart, she stands as one of the most notable women in American screenwriting.

Reference:

DeWitt Bodeen, "Frances Marion," in *More From Hollywood* (South Brunswick & New York: A. S. Barnes/London: Tantivy Press, 1977), pp. 89-128.

Richard Matheson
(20 February 1926-)

Roberta Sharp

See also the Matheson entry in *DLB 8, Twentieth-Century Science Fiction Writers.*

MOTION PICTURES: *The Incredible Shrinking Man* (Universal, 1957), screenplay from his novel *The Shrinking Man;*
The Beat Generation (M-G-M, 1959), screenplay by Matheson and Lewis Meltzer;
The House of Usher (American International, 1960), screenplay;
Master of the World (American International, 1961), screenplay;
The Pit and the Pendulum (American International, 1961), screenplay;
Tales of Terror (American International, 1962), screenplay;
Burn, Witch, Burn (American International, 1962), screenplay by Matheson and Charles Beaumont;
The Raven (American International, 1963), screenplay;
The Comedy of Terrors (American International, 1964), screenplay;
The Last Man on Earth (American International, 1964), screenplay by Matheson as Logan Swanson, and William Leicester;
Die! Die! My Darling (Columbia, 1965), screenplay;
The Young Warriors (Universal, 1967), screenplay from his novel *The Beardless Warriors;*
The Devil's Bride, also released as *The Devil Rides Out* (20th Century-Fox, 1968), screenplay;
De Sade (American International, 1969), story and screenplay;
The Legend of Hell House (20th Century-Fox, 1973), screenplay from his novel *Hell House;*
Somewhere in Time (Universal, 1980), screenplay from his novel *Bid Time Return;*
Twilight Zone—The Movie (Warner Bros., 1983)— "Kick the Can," screenplay by Matheson, George Clayton Johnson, and Mellisa Mathison (as Josh Rogan); "It's a *Good* Life," screenplay by Matheson; "Nightmare at 30,000 Feet," story and screenplay by Matheson;
Jaws 3D (Universal, 1983), screenplay by Matheson and Carl Gottlieb.

BOOKS: *Fury on Sunday* (New York: Lion Books, 1953);
Someone Is Bleeding (New York: Lion Books, 1953);
I Am Legend (New York: Fawcett, 1954; London: Corgi, 1956);
Born of Man and Woman: Tales of Science Fiction and Fantasy (Philadelphia: Chamberlain Press, 1954; London: Reinhardt, 1956); abridged as *Third From the Sun* (New York: Bantam, 1955; London: Corgi, 1961);

Richard Matheson

The Shrinking Man (New York: Fawcett, 1956; London: Muller, 1958);

The Shores of Space (New York: Bantam, 1957; London: Transworld, 1958);

A Stir of Echoes (Philadelphia: Lippincott, 1958; London: Cassell, 1958);

Ride the Nightmare (New York: Ballantine, 1959; London: World, 1961);

The Beardless Warriors (Boston & Toronto: Little, Brown, 1960; London: Heinemann, 1961);

Shock! (New York: Dell, 1961; London: Corgi, 1962);

Shock II (New York: Dell, 1964; London: Corgi, 1965);

Shock III (New York: Dell, 1966; London: Corgi, 1967);

Hell House (New York: Viking, 1971; London: Corgi, 1973);

Bid Time Return (New York: Viking, 1975; London: Sphere, 1977);

What Dreams May Come (New York: Putnam's, 1978; London: M. Joseph, 1979).

SELECTED TELEVISION: "The Last Flight" (1960), "A World of His Own" (1960), "Nick of Time" (1960), "The Invaders" (1961), "Once Upon a Time" (1961), "Little Girl Lost" (1962), "Young Man's Fancy" (1962), "Mute" (1962), "Death Ship" (1962), "Steel" (1962), "Night Call" (1964), "Spur of the Moment" (1964), *The Twilight Zone* (CBS), teleplays;

"The Return of Andrew Bentley," *Thriller* (NBC, 1962), teleplay;

"The Enemy Within," *Star Trek* (NBC, 1966), teleplay;

Duel, *ABC Movie of the Week* (ABC, 13 November 1971), teleplay from his short story;

The Night Stalker, *ABC Movie of the Week* (ABC, 11 January 1972), teleplay;

Ghost Story (NBC, 1972), teleplay;

The Night Strangler (ABC, 1973), teleplay;

The Morning After (ABC, 1974), teleplay;

Dying Room Only, *ABC Movie of the Week* (ABC, 18 September 1974), teleplay from his short story;

Scream of the Wolf, *ABC Movie of the Week* (ABC, 16 January 1974), teleplay;

Dracula (CBS, 8 February 1974), teleplay;

The Stranger Within (ABC, 1974), teleplay based on his short story;

"Amelia," *Trilogy of Terror* (ABC, 1975), teleplay based on his short story;

Dead of Night (NBC, 1977), teleplay;

The Strange Possession of Mrs. Oliver (NBC, 1977), teleplay;

The Martian Chronicles (NBC, 1980), teleplay.

OTHER: "Afterword," *Magic Man and Other Science-Fantasy Stories* (New York: Fawcett Crest Books, 1965).

Richard Matheson, screenwriter and novelist, a contemporary master of the suspense story, was born in Allendale, New Jersey, and grew up in Brooklyn, New York. After serving in the Army in France and Germany during WWII, he studied journalism at the University of Missouri at Columbia, where he earned his bachelor of journalism degree in 1949. While in Columbia, Matheson wrote fiction for a campus magazine and music reviews for the *Columbia Missourian*. He began his professional writing career, while working at night as a linotype machine operator, with the sale of his story "Born of Man and Woman" to *The Magazine of Fantasy and Science Fiction*. Since then he has published more than eighty-five stories in magazines,

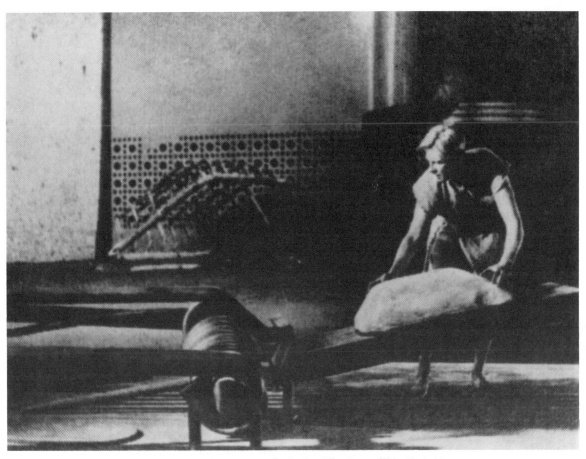

Grant Williams in Matheson's award-winning The Incredible Shrinking Man

six story collections, and ten novels, and he has written extensively for both movies and television. Matheson lives in Woodland Hills, California, with his wife Ruth. Their four children are grown, and his son, Richard Christian Matheson, is a writer of short stories and teleplays.

Based on his own novel *The Shrinking Man* (1956), Matheson's first screenplay, *The Incredible Shrinking Man,* was filmed by Universal in 1957. Directed by Jack Arnold, the film earned the Hugo Award for the best motion picture of 1958. Usually categorized as science fiction, the tale develops the plight of a man (Grant Williams) whose body shrinks an inch a week after his accidental exposure to radioactivity. As he diminishes, the world becomes an increasingly terrifying place. When he reaches only six inches in height, his own cat becomes a menace, and eventually he must defend himself against a spider. As Williams becomes too small to be seen, his voice can still be heard delivering the metaphysical report: "So close—the infinitesimal and the infinite. But suddenly I knew they were really the two ends of the same concept.

The unbelievably small and the unbelievably vast eventually meet—like the closing of a gigantic circle." The last philosophical line, though somewhat equivocal in the context of the movie, bespeaks Matheson's interest in the questions of man's place in the universe and man's fate after death: "All this vast majesty of creation—it had to mean something too! Yes, smaller than the smallest, I meant something too. To God there is no zero. I still exist!"

On the basis of Matheson's early work, he has often been classified, somewhat erroneously, as a science fiction writer; most of his work is more accurately described as fantasy. His novel *I Am Legend* (1954), in which he attempts to explain vampirism in medical and psychological terms, probably comes closer than any of his other works to being science fiction. In it, the main character, Robert Neville, discovers that the epidemic which, so far as he knows, has left him the last surviving human being on earth, was caused by an identifiable bacillus, carried by the wind but dependent on a human host. Two films were based on this novel, but, since he had sold the rights to his book in 1957, he had no control over the scripts. The first movie version, *The Last Man on Earth* (1964), was filmed in Italy in 1963 and starred Vincent Price. Matheson disliked the film so much that he used his pseudonym, Logan Swanson, in the screen credits. *The Omega Man* (1971) was also based on *I Am Legend*, but Matheson did not write the script for it. Interestingly, Matheson did not think Price right for the part of Neville in *The Last Man on Earth*, but apparently he did think him right for the protagonist roles in the scripts he wrote for four films at least loosely based on tales by Edgar Allan Poe.

These films, directed by Roger Corman for American International, include *The House of Usher* (1960), *The Pit and the Pendulum* (1961), *Tales of Terror* (1962), and *The Raven* (1963). Of these, *The House of Usher* is the most true to the action of Poe's tale, despite the violation of its gloomy atmosphere

by the technicolor production. The belief of Poe's Roderick Usher in the sentience of all things provides a basis for the animation of the house in the film. Even so, the movie version does not preserve the original's limitation to the narrator's point of view nor the relationship between Roderick and Madeline as twins. Instead, Usher (Price) appears old enough to be the father of the lady Madeline, who becomes the object of the narrator's suit in the film. Roderick's objections create conflict with Winthrop (Mark Damon) and provide padding necessary for Poe's slender plot to become a feature-length film. The original's "all insoluble" mystery, especially the puzzle of Madeline's escape, not only from the sealed coffin but also from behind the secured iron door of the vault, diminishes with the fairly obvious film treatment. The film concludes with the insane Madeline strangling Rod-

Mark Damon, Myrna Fahey, and Vincent Price in The House of Usher, *the first of Matheson's Edgar Allan Poe adaptations*

erick as the house burns. While this conflagration is not part of the original, both stories end with the houses sinking into the tarn.

Despite these distortions, Matheson attempted to recreate the tale, the only one of Poe's stories he worked with that he felt adapted well to film. The early reviews of *The House of Usher* were generally favorable, but the film was credited with being a far more accurate representation of Poe than it is. The film's financial success and its favorable reviews led to more assignments for loose adaptations of Poe's work. The other Corman-Matheson-Price movies bear even less plot resemblance to their prototypes than did *The House of Usher.*

Matheson's *The Pit and the Pendulum* superimposes an elaborate story on Poe's tale. Set in the period of the Inquisition, the film casts Price as Nicholas, whose wife, Elizabeth (Barbara Steele), has supposedly died of fright in the dungeon—the same place where his mother had been buried alive because of her infidelity. Fearing that he has buried Elizabeth alive, Nicholas visits the burial vault, sees Elizabeth escape from her coffin, learns that she and his best friend—her lover—are plotting against him, and loses his mind. Nicholas then forces the lover into the pit and inters Elizabeth alive.

Matheson next adapted four Poe tales into a film trilogy titled *Tales of Terror.* All three star Vincent Price. The story "Morella," which has hints of Poe's "Ligeia," probably comes closest to capturing Poe's spirit; in it, Morella's spirit leaves her corpse and possesses the body of her daughter Lenora. In what is almost a parody of Poe, "The Black Cat" incorporates "The Cask of Amontillado" into the original tale. Montressor (Peter Lorre) is a besotted drunk who entombs his wife and her lover (Price) behind the cellar wall. The third segment, "The Facts in the Case of M. Valdemar," also deviated from Poe's original. In the story, Valdemar is mesmerized while dying and, therefore, supposedly suspended between life and death, only to become a mass of liquid putrescence when the spell is broken. But in the film, Valdemar (Price) rises up to envelop the mesmerist (Basil Rathbone), who dies of fright as a result of being surrounded by the oozing liquid.

The Raven was the final film of the series which Matheson wrote for Price and Corman, who made three other Poe films with other writers. By this time, Matheson admits that he was "sick and tired of writing Poe." The film's sarcastic tone is set in the opening scene when Poe asks the raven the whereabouts of the lost Lenore only to hear it reply (in the voice of Peter Lorre), "How the hell should I know?" As a spoof of horror films, the movie has numerous parallels with Poe's tales. Written and played for laughs, *The Raven* ends with a hilarious duel of magic between rival wizards (Price and Boris Karloff).

Soon after *The Raven* was made, Matheson wrote an original filmscript called *The Comedy of Terrors* (1964) starring Price, Lorre, Karloff, and Rathbone. (Matheson was also listed as coproducer, but says he has no idea why he was given this credit.) In this film Price plays a sardonic undertaker whose economies include surreptitiously dumping bodies into the grave in order to recycle the coffin. The director of the film, Jacques Tourneur, described it as "a beautiful script. It was a parody on Shakespeare, a comedy on horror films . . . and it is a finished film that was not understood very well. . . .Our film was deliberately aimed at mature thinking people who appreciate satire, who appreciate cynical humour."

During the 1960s Matheson was not exclusively occupied with Poe and satire of Poe. In 1961 he wrote the script for a tale of a balloon journey, *Master of the World,* which starred Price and which was based on two novels by Jules Verne. In the same year he collaborated with Charles Beaumont on a British-made film titled *Night of the Eagle,* released in the United States as *Burn, Witch, Burn* (1962). The film was about a schoolteacher and his wife who are threatened by black magic and witchcraft. In 1965 Matheson adapted Dennis Wheatley's novel *The Devil Rides Out;* his screenplay was not filmed until 1968 and the film was released in America as *The Devil's Bride.* Terrence Fisher directed and Christopher Lee starred in this story about contemporary satan worship. Meanwhile, Matheson also wrote the screenplay for *Die! Die! My Darling* (1965), about a religious fanatic (Tallulah Bankhead) who mourns the death of her son and keeps his fiancée (Stefanie Powers) a prisoner. During this productive decade, Matheson adapted his own novel *The Beardless Warriors* for *The Young Warriors* (1967), a war film about inexperienced troops in combat. Matheson ended the sixties with his script for the biographical film *De Sade* (1969).

In 1973 Matheson wrote *The Legend of Hell House,* based on his own novel *Hell House.* This tale of a haunted house borrows its atmosphere and setting, complete with tarn and miasma, from Poe's "The Fall of the House of Usher." Unlike most ghost stories, *The Legend of Hell House* tries to account scientifically for the manifestations of the haunting as remnants of psychic energy left in the house. Physicist Dr. Barrett (Clive Revill) plans to destroy this energy scientifically by demagnetizing the house with an electromagnetic radiation machine of his own invention. Even this machine fails to break the evil power of the surviving ego; the only one of the four visitors who has a chance of thwarting it is medium Benjamin Franklin Fischer (Roddy McDowall). The tale is truly a horror story, one which reflects Matheson's growing interest in occult and extrasensory phenomena.

For several years following *The Legend of Hell House*, Matheson devoted himself to writing fiction and teleplays and doing extensive research of psychic phenomena. In 1979 he began work on an adaptation of another of his novels, *Bid Time Return*, which was released as *Somewhere in Time* (1980). The film is a fantasy about a playwright (Christopher Reeve) who becomes obsessed with a

deceased actress (Jane Seymour) and finds a way to travel into the past and meet her. The film was neither a critical nor a popular success; most critics felt the film's old-fashioned romantic atmosphere was inappropriate for the 1980s.

The summer of 1983 saw two big-budgeted films made from Matheson's screenplays: *Twilight Zone—The Movie* and *Jaws 3D*. *Twilight Zone* was inspired by the old television series, for which Matheson had been a regular writer. The film consisted of four segments, one original by John Landis and three by Matheson—"Kick the Can," "It's a *Good* Life," and "Nightmare at 30,000 Feet"— which were based on episodes of the television series, the episodes themselves based on short stories by, respectively, George Clayton Johnson, Jerome Bixby, and Matheson. "Kick the Can," directed by Steven Spielberg, was about the residents of a retirement home who find they can become young

Publicity photograph of Vincent Price, Peter Lorre, and Boris Karloff on the set of The Raven

Roddy McDowall, Gayle Hunnicutt, and Clive Revill in The Legend of Hell House. *Though the film is based on Matheson's own novel, its atmosphere is reminiscent of Poe's "The Fall of the House of Usher."*

again by playing children's games. In "It's a *Good Life*," a boy's psychic powers keep his family terrorized. In "Nightmare at 30,000 Feet," a passenger (John Lithgow) on an airliner sees a mysterious creature perched on the plane's wing.

Saying that "the prospect of trying to make something fresh out of a theme that's really been overdone by now is what appealed to me," Matheson agreed to work on the second sequel to *Jaws* (1975), *Jaws 3D*. (He had turned down an earlier offer to rewrite the original.) The setting of the third film was changed from New England to a Florida amusement park on the sea, and there were two sharks instead of one. *Jaws 3D* was a financial success, though not a blockbuster like its predecessors; it received unanimously poor reviews.

Since 1959 Matheson has primarily devoted himself to writing for television; at first he often collaborated with Charles Beaumont, with whom

he worked on early scripts for *The Twilight Zone*. He later wrote sixteen scripts for *The Twilight Zone* by himself. He has contributed scripts for such top series as *The Chrysler Playhouse*, *Thriller*, *The Alfred Hitchcock Theatre*, *Star Trek*, *Have Gun—Will Travel*, *Wanted, Dead or Alive*, and *Night Gallery*. He has also written some highly acclaimed movies for television. Among these was *Duel* (1971), an adaptation of his own *Playboy* novelette about a man driving along a desert road who finds himself drawn into a battle with a truck driver. Directed by Steven Spielberg, it was nominated by the Writers Guild of America as one of the five best television movies of 1971. *The Night Stalker* (1972), Matheson's adaptation of "The Kolchak Papers" by Jeff Rice, won him the 1973 Writer's Guild Award for the year's best film adaptation. This story of a vampire in contemporary Las Vegas was, according to Nielsen ratings, the most widely viewed television film ever when first aired; Matheson wrote an original sequel, *The Night Strangler,* in 1973 and the two films inspired a television series. Matheson's other television work includes *Dracula* (1974); *The Morning After* (1974), an acclaimed drama about an alcoholic; and a miniseries based on Ray Bradbury's *The Martian Chronicles* (1980).

Unlike many screenwriters, Richard Matheson has always been able to move freely from one medium to another. But whether he is writing films, novels, or for television, his primary purpose seems to be to keep audiences at the edges of their seats.

References:

Rhea Anger, "Notes," *Toronto Film Society Newsletter,* 12 February 1962, pp. 7-8; 9 December 1974, pp. 9-13;

John Brosnan, *Future Tense: The Cinema of Science Fiction* (New York: St. Martin's, 1979);

Brosnan, *The Horror People* (New York: St. Martin's, 1970), pp. 132-153, 196;

Carlos Clarens, *An Illustrated History of the Horror Film* (New York: Putnam's, 1967);

Drake Douglas, *Horror!* (New York: Macmillan, 1966);

Joseph Gelmis, *The Film Director as Superstar* (Garden City: Doubleday, 1970);

Stephen H. Goldman, "I Am Legend," in *Survey of Science Fiction Literature,* volume 2, edited by Frank N. MaGill (Englewood Cliffs, N.J.: Salem Press, 1979), pp. 986-990;

William Johnson, ed., *Focus on the Science Fiction Film* (Englewood Cliffs, N. J.: Prentice-Hall, 1972);

David Pirie, "Roger Corman's Descent into the Maelstrom," in *The Millenic Vision,* edited by David Weill and Paul Willeman (Edinburgh Film Festival, 1970), p. 48;

R. Reginald, *Contemporary Science Fiction Authors* (New York: Arno Press, 1975), p. 177;

Jess Rovin, *From Jules Verne to Star Trek* (New York: Drake Publishers, 1977), pp. 60, 84;

Barry Ulanov, "Science Fiction and Fantasy," in *The Two Worlds of American Art: The Private and the Popular* (New York: Macmillan, 1965), pp. 298-308;

Geoffrey Wagner, *The Novel and the Cinema* (Rutherford: Fairleigh Dickinson University Press, 1975).

June Mathis
(1892-27 July 1927)

Thomas Slater
Northwest Missouri State University

MOTION PICTURES: *To Hell with the Kaiser* (Screen Classics/Metro, 1918), scenario;

An Eye for an Eye (Metro, 1918), screenplay; adaptation by Mathis and Albert Capellani;

Out of the Fog (Metro, 1919), scenario by Mathis and Capellani;

The Red Lantern (Metro, 1919), adaptation;

The Brat (Metro, 1919), scenario;

Old Lady 31 (Metro, 1920), scenario;

Hearts Are Trumps (Metro, 1920), screenplay;

Polly with a Past (Metro, 1920), scenario by Mathis and Arthur Zellner;

The Four Horsemen of the Apocalypse (Metro, 1921), adaptation;

The Conquering Power (Metro, 1921), adaptation;

A Trip to Paradise (Metro, 1921), scenario;

Camille (Metro, 1921), scenario and adaptation;

The Idle Rich (Metro, 1921), adaptation;

Turn to the Right (Metro, 1922), scenario by Mathis and Mary O'Hara;

Kisses (Metro, 1922), adaptation and scenario;

Hate (Metro, 1922), adaptation;

Blood and Sand (Famous Players-Lasky, 1922), scenario;

The Young Rajah (Famous Players-Lasky, 1922), adaptation and scenario;

Three Wise Fools (Goldwyn, 1923), screenplay;

The Spanish Dancer (Famous Players-Lasky, 1923), adaptation by Mathis and Beulah Marie Dix;

June Mathis

In the Palace of the King (Goldwyn, 1923), adaptation;

Greed (M-G-M, 1923), titles;

Sally (First National, 1925), scenario;

The Desert Flower (First National, 1925), scenario;

Classified (Corinne Griffith, 1925), screenplay;

We Moderns (John McCormick, 1925), scenario;

Ben-Hur (M-G-M, 1925), adaptation;

Irene (First National, 1926), continuity;

The Greater Glory (First National, 1926), scenario;

The Masked Woman (First National, 1927), scenario;

The Magic Flame (Goldwyn, 1927), continuity.

The screen credits of June Mathis, one of the major figures of the silent film, include some of the best-known films ever made: *The Four Horsemen of the Apocalypse* (1921), *Blood and Sand* (1922), and *Ben-Hur* (1925). She was also personally responsible for bringing Rudolph Valentino to prominence in *The Four Horsemen of the Apocalypse*. A determined woman, Mathis became at one point in the early 1920s one of the most powerful behind-the-scenes figures in Hollywood.

June Mathis was born in Leadville, Colorado, into a theatrical family. During her youth, she worked for several years as an actress in California

in order to support herself and her mother after the death of her father. She worked in vaudeville and acted in several plays, some with the well-known stage actor Julian Eltinge. She was plagued by ill health for much of her short life. The poor quality of the movies in those days encouraged Mathis's belief that she could contribute to their improvement by entering the business as a writer. But, having no experience in the craft and little education for the job, she began by saving enough money to give herself two years of time to learn. She and her mother then moved to New York. During the day she studied, and at night she went to the movies.

Her big break came when she entered a script-writing competition. She did not win, but her handling of her material brought job offers, and in 1918 she joined Metro studios. Mathis later credited her success to a strong concentration on plot and theme. She once advised budding scenario writers, "No story that did not possess a theme has ever really lived. . . . Occasionally one may make money and perhaps be popular for a time, but in the end it dies."

Much of Mathis's work as a screenwriter was the adaptation of the works of other authors to film. She once said she was always disappointed when a director altered a novel or play beyond recognition: "To me it was almost like taking the cover of a book and producing any old story that would fit in it. I thought that even the picturized versions of plays were so altered that the big climaxes were entirely forgotten. I wanted so much to see in the pictures what I had read or what I had seen on the stage— that is, as near to it as possible." Claiming to take her themes straight from the original works, she said, "Personally I feel that when I am adapting a book or a play I am only a servant of the author." She said that at the beginning of her career she often had to sacrifice her own desires, but "gradually I began to get my own way so far as the story was concerned, and I think I can claim that directors found that adherence to a good, smooth scenario was easier for them than trying to do it some other way."

Despite Mathis's ideals about the screenwriter's profession, she did not immediately do much to improve the quality of the movies. The first production that she was involved with was *To Hell with the Kaiser* (1918), which the *New York Times* called "a travesty of the war and of America's serious purpose in it." Mathis's devotion to plot was not very evident in this work; the filmmakers attempted to fit in every possible situation that they assumed

Mathis's first screen credit was for the propagandistic To Hell with the Kaiser, *which featured Lawrence Grant*

their audience would like to see, including having the Kaiser captured and eventually killed by an American girl.

The early years of Mathis's career were marked by her association with the accomplished stage and screen actress Alla Nazimova; however, many of the films they did together seem to suffer from too much sentimentality. The movies *An Eye for an Eye* (1918), *The Red Lantern* (1919), and *Out of the Fog* (1919) follow similar romantic plots about a young girl who violates social customs by marrying someone of another race. Rejected by the bigotry in her husband's society, she is also unable to fit back in with her own people and dies tragically alone at the end. What little praise these movies received was more for Nazimova's acting than for the conventional and melodramatic stories. In another movie, *The Brat* (1919), Nazimova plays a poor girl who is brought into the home of a wealthy family by a novelist who wishes to study her. While there, she is able to put some love into the calloused family's hearts. A *Times* commentary praised the

actors for their portrayals of the stock characters but noted, "more than a few persons will undoubtedly regret that those responsible for it spread the melodrama and sentimentality on so thick."

In 1920 Mathis's screenplays for *Old Lady 31* and *Polly with a Past* were produced, both of which were still praised more for the performances than for the story, possibly because both pictures were based on successful Broadway plays and both starred the leading stage performers recreating their roles. *Old Lady 31* is based on a play by Rachel Crothers; Emma Dunn plays the spirited resident of a retirement home. *Polly with a Past* was taken from a play by George Middleton and Guy Bolton; Ina Claire stars as a woman with a shady background.

In February of 1921 Metro released one of the most commercially successful silent movies ever made, thanks largely to the efforts of June Mathis. *The Four Horsemen of the Apocalypse* grossed $4,500,000 in the United States alone. Mathis was responsible for many elements of its success, and the movie brought her recognition and important executive power in Hollywood. Vicente Blasco Ibáñez's novel of two brothers fighting on opposite sides during World War I had been considered by every motion picture studio but was believed to be impossible to film when Mathis began arguing for its production. Finally, Metro agreed to produce it, but Mathis went further in her demands, insisting that her scenario be shot exactly as written and that the practically unknown Rudolph Valentino be given a leading role. Mathis had never met Valentino and had only seen him in one movie, *Eyes of Youth* (1919), but was convinced he was right for the part. Besides writing the script and being responsible for Valentino's casting, Mathis also edited the film.

The Four Horsemen of the Apocalypse marked the beginning of a fruitful relationship between Mathis and director Rex Ingram. In fact, Ingram's work

on the picture was more highly praised than Mathis's. Although Mathis was praised for following "the main trend and thought" of Ibáñez's novel, some critics found the story overlong and the characters ill-defined. The movie also reflects Mathis's taste for the romantic and melodramatic; the love affair between central characters Julio (Valentino) and Marguerite (Alice Terry) is idealized, and Julio's death is more melodramatic than it was in the novel. She also injected a subplot involving spiritualism (one of Mathis's own concerns), and her presentation of the Germans was influenced by the bigoted notions of the war days. But she was able to transfer successfully to the screen the crucial antiwar theme of the novel, for which she must be given due credit.

After the release of *The Four Horsemen of the Apocalypse*, Mathis began struggling with the enormous problems of creating another epic picture,

Nazimova and Warner Oland in Mathis's drama of the Boxer Rebellion, The Red Lantern

Rudolph Valentino and Alice Terry in The Four Horsemen of the Apocalypse, *Mathis's successful antiwar story*

Ben-Hur (1925). She had become one of the powerful people in Hollywood, and she was given complete control over the project. Attempting to follow
her success with Valentino in *The Four Horsemen of
the Apocalypse*, she cast the obscure George Walsh
(brother of director Raoul) as the lead and rejected
Ingram's offers to direct in favor of George Brabin.
Her decision to film the picture in Italy was disastrous. Labor problems there forced the movie over
schedule and over budget. Mathis was replaced by
Bess Meredyth and Carey Wilson, Walsh by Ramon
Novarro, and Brabin by Fred Niblo. When *Ben-
Hur* premiered in New York little, if any, of Mathis's script remained in the completed film. *Ben-Hur*
lost nearly one million dollars for M-G-M, but it
was critically acclaimed and has remained an item
of prestige.

Mathis, Ingram, and Valentino were reunited
in *The Conquering Power* (1921), with Valentino star-

ring as a young man who temporarily abandons his
morals for money. The picture was criticized for
being too wordy, but Mathis received unusually
high praise for her writing from the *New York Times:*
"its characters are true. They do things and have
done to them things that are hardly plausible, but
if you accept the artificial world in which they move,
you will see them moving as true types of humanity,
exaggerated somewhat for emphasis, but always
fundamentally genuine." Mathis and Ingram then
collaborated on *Turn to the Right* (1922); the film
was based on familiar material—an innocent man
in prison—and Mathis and cowriter Mary O'Hara
used stock characters. Ingram's direction, however,
keeps the film interesting.

Though she wrote three other scripts for Valentino, Mathis never seemed quite able to provide
him with suitable material. In *Blood and Sand* (1922)
he plays a bullfighter in love with one woman (Lila

Lee) but attracted to another (Nita Naldi). The movie never fulfills the promise of romance and adventure suggested by its premise; instead, Valentino is made to display almost Puritan stoicism in the face of temptation. *The Young Rajah* (1922) is an Indian prince who goes to live in New England after his father is deposed; he attends Harvard, falls in love, and develops psychic powers. *Camille* (1921) is an adaptation of Alexander Dumas's novel, with Nazimova as the dying heroine and Valentino as her lover. Mathis's scripts support traditional morality; adventure is the result of breaking social rules for which the protagonist is generally punished in the end. This undercuts both the potential excitement in her scenarios and Valentino's performances. *The Spanish Dancer* (1923) was also written for Valentino, but he did not appear in it. The script was altered to become the story of a gypsy woman in Spain so that it would be suitable for Pola Negri.

King Vidor directed *Three Wise Fools* (1923). One of her best films, it is a charming fantasy in which three elderly men (William Crane, Alec Francis, and Claude Gillingwater) take care of a young girl (Eleanor Boardman); Mathis adapted her script from a play by John Golden.

Mathis earned a degree of notoriety for her rewriting and final editing of *Greed* (1923), an action that some film commentators have criticized for having obscured the true genius of Erich von Stroheim and destroying what was potentially the greatest silent film ever made. Von Stroheim once said, "I consider I have made only one real picture in my life and nobody ever saw that. The poor, mangled, mutilated remains were shown as *Greed*." Yet the movie still stands as a classic even in its final form. Mathis has been cast in the unfortunate historical role of the upholder of corporate mentality against the expression of individual genius. But some film scholars have defended her work on the picture. Von Stroheim had filmed Frank Norris's novel *McTeague* in great detail; Mathis cut the movie from eighteen reels to ten. Perhaps in all the furor over the final version of the film, not enough attention has been paid to what Mathis accomplished. *Greed* remains a powerful film; she made it an accessible one.

Through the remainder of the 1920s Mathis wrote a series of movies for Colleen Moore, one of the biggest stars at First National studios. *Sally* (1925) was based on a successful Florenz Ziegfeld musical about a young woman who impersonates a famous Russian dancer. In *The Desert Flower,* (1925) Moore is a poor girl victimized by a cruel stepfather. *Classified* (1925), based on a short story by Edna Ferber, depicts the romantic adventures of a young woman working in the classified advertisements section of a newspaper. A rebellious flapper worries her parents in *We Moderns* (1925). *Irene*

Ramon Novarro and Francis X. Bushman in Ben-Hur, *considered state-of-the-art cinema in 1925*

(1926) is a poor Irish girl who becomes a successful model.

The Magic Flame (1927), Mathis's final movie, is one of her best pictures, thanks in part to a strong cast led by Ronald Colman and good direction by Henry King. The story is familiar Mathis material: the leader of an obscure country becomes involved with a foreigner. Colman plays a dual role as a king and his look-alike, a clown.

On 27 July 1927 thirty-five-year-old June Mathis was attending a performance of *The Squall* at New York's Forty-Eighth Street Theatre with her mother. During the final act, the play was brought to a halt by Mathis's screams from the balcony: "Oh mother, I'm dying, I'm dying." She threw her arms around her mother and sobbed convulsively.

Mathis was carried outside and placed on the ground where a doctor pronounced her dead. Her death ended a career of service to the ideal of quality motion pictures.

References:

Kevin Brownlow, *The Parade's Gone By* (New York: Knopf, 1968);

Joe Franklin, *Classics of the Silent Screen: A Pictorial Treasury* (New York: Bramhall House, 1959);

"Scenario Writers Must Find Theme," *New York Times*, 15 April 1923, VII:3;

Sharon Smith, *Women Who Make Movies* (New York: Hopkinson & Blake, 1975);

Kaye Sullivan, *Films For, By and About Women* (Metuchen, N.J.: Scarecrow Press, 1980).

Elaine May
(21 April 1932-   )

Linda Malm

MOTION PICTURES: *Such Good Friends* (Paramount, 1971), screenplay as Esther Dale;

A New Leaf (Paramount, 1971), screenplay;

The Heartbreak Kid (20th Century-Fox, 1972), screenplay by May and Neil Simon;

Mikey and Nicky (Paramount, 1976), screenplay;

Heaven Can Wait (Paramount, 1978), screenplay by May and Warren Beatty.

PLAY PRODUCTIONS: *An Evening with Mike Nichols and Elaine May*, New York, John Golden Theatre, October 1960;

Not Enough Rope, in *3 by 3*, New York, Maidmon Playhouse, March 1962;

A Matter of Position, Philadelphia, Walnut Street Theatre, 29 September 1962;

Name of a Soup, New York, HB Studio Workshop, 8 June 1963;

Adaptation, in *Adaptation and Next*, New York, Greenwich Mews Theatre, February 1969.

Screenwriter, actress, comedienne, dramatist, and film director, Elaine May has enriched her five major screenplays with a mix of these talents.

May was born Elaine Berlin in Philadelphia, Pennsylvania, the daughter of Yiddish actor Jack Berlin. In 1949, still in her teens, she married Marvin May. The marriage was dissolved. (Her daughter Jeannie uses the Berlin name.)

Elaine May's professional talents surfaced early. Before graduating from high school she already had many stage and radio appearances to her credit. She studied the Stanislavsky method of acting with Maria Ouspenskaya. She became a performer in Chicago, where she appeared in repertory at the Playwrights Theater, in an improvisational group at the Compass Players, and in *Miss Julie* at the University of Chicago. In Chicago she met Mike Nichols, and by 1957 Nichols and May were doing improvisational skits together at supper clubs. They made television appearances and released a comedy improvisational record for Mercury before performing in their highly successful 1960 New York City theater production, *An Evening with Mike Nichols and Elaine May.* The ad lib comedy was a mix of gentle satire and dry, good-natured humor, often full of surprises, much like the best in May's screenplays.

Elaine May

In 1962 May married lyricist Sheldon Harneck; they divorced the next year. Also in 1962 director Fred Coe asked May to write a *Playhouse 90* script that was expanded into the full-length play *A Matter of Position*. The show opened and closed quickly after May refused to provide the revisions the producers felt necessary. Her statement to the press provides insight into this play and into her future screenplays: "Cuts and revisions were made up to the point where they would change the nature of the play. A play is more than a formula made up of words and jokes and scenes. Somewhere it must have something to do with the realities of human behavior." This would not be the last time May put her convictions ahead of a production.

In 1964 May was hired to adapt for the screen *The Loved One*, based on Evelyn Waugh's satire of Forest Lawn cemetery in Hollywood and the American conventions surrounding the burial. May's writing was reworked by Terry Southern and Christopher Isherwood, and she received no screen credit when the film was released in 1965.

In 1964 May appeared in two Columbia feature films. In *Enter Laughing*, she is Angela, an actress who successfully uses her pseudoglamour to hold a young would-be pharmacist in her seedy little theater group. In the romantic farce *Luv*, May

portrays the disgruntled intellectual wife Ellen caught in a triangle with Jack Lemmon and Peter Falk. In both films, critics said that she played herself, coping with situations brought about by falling in love.

In 1969 May received a Drama Desk Award as a promising playwright for her one-act comedy play *Adaptation* which she directed in a double bill with Terence McNally's *Next*. She received an Outer Circle Award for writing *Adaptation* and directing the two plays in 1969. *Adaptation* became an off-Broadway hit.

Such Good Friends (1971) was May's first screenplay. The film listed the screenplay as being written by Esther Dale, but the *New York Times* reported unconfirmed rumors that the script was by May. In fact, she had become upset with the production and had withdrawn her name. Vincent Canby said that "her voice could be heard in the dialogue," and the plot could certainly be her invention. Adapted from Lois Gould's novel, *Such Good Friends* concerns a magazine editor and writer (Laurence Luckinbill) who enters the hospital for minor surgery. Through a variety of medical errors his condition worsens and he eventually dies. During this period his wife (Dyan Cannon) learns about his many affairs from his concerned women friends. Love and desperation, handled with a

May as the wealthy botanist Henrietta in A New Leaf

Charles Grodin and Jeannie Berlin as the newlywed couple in The Heartbreak Kid

touching lack of bitterness, have become thematic trademarks of May.

May's first screenplay credit under her own name was a nearly total individual effort. She was sole author and director, and she acted a lead in the film. *A New Leaf* (1971), adapted from a short story by Jack Ritchie, is a tightly constructed comedy with characters that remain well-defined throughout the wacky twists of plot. A wealthy but extravagant bachelor (Walter Matthau) has exhausted his fortune and has no means of making money other than by marrying a rich woman. He chooses botanist Henrietta (May), who is naive, dull, and sloppy, but also very well-off. He plans to marry, then murder her, but instead winds up rescuing her when she nearly drowns on a botanical expedition. He has truly turned over a new leaf, and there is a happy ending for these two eccentrics.

Although *A New Leaf* was an artistic and financial success, May was far from satisfied with the finished film. She unsuccessfully sought an injunction against Paramount for using her name on the film because she did not approve of the release cut. May publicly disowned the film.

May's next produced screenplay was *The Heartbreak Kid* (1972), based upon the story by Bruce J. Friedman. It was directed by May and written in collaboration with Neil Simon, although some sources list only Simon as the writer. Here the occasional cruelties of a Simon comedy seem to be tempered by May. Like *A New Leaf*, *The Heartbreak Kid* is about a man pursuing a woman for his own ulterior motives, but in this film the character does not reform and he remains unlikable. Still, May's strong sense of character dominates and makes the film succeed.

Egocentric sports equipment salesman Lenny

Warren Beatty in Heaven Can Wait

(Charles Grodin) marries the undelicious, average Lila (Jeannie Berlin), then meets and falls in love with beautiful, upper-class Kelly (Cybil Shepherd), while on his honeymoon. He promptly annuls his marriage and follows Kelly home. At first he seems doomed to fail, but he eventually succeeds in his quest to obtain Kelly. Lenny and Kelly are linked by their mutual shallowness; they deserve each other.

After two successful romantic comedies, Elaine May wrote and directed a melodrama. Taken from a real-life incident, *Mikey and Nicky* (1976) is a story of two childhood friends who are members of the same criminal mob. Nicky (John Cassavetes) is no longer useful to the gang, and Mikey (Peter Falk) is the hit man on the contract for his old friend's life. Ironically, Nicky has sought his help. The film is mostly a character study, as the two men spend twelve hours wandering from

a fleabag hotel to the bars and streets of the city. Originally conceived as a play, *Mikey and Nicky* retains some of the spatial confinement of a stage production. It was years in the making—May wrote the screenplay in 1973—and legal problems hampered the film's distribution, which guaranteed it little publicity and a resultant limited distribution.

Elaine May returned to romantic comedy with *Heaven Can Wait* (1978), a remake of the film *Here Comes Mr. Jordan* (1941), based on the play by Harry Segall. May's exact contributions to the final film are difficult to trace. She was announced as the film's coauthor, along with Warren Beatty, who also produced, codirected, and starred in the film. A working copy of the script very close to the final version, however, lists Beatty and codirector Buck Henry as authors. It is likely May did the first draft and revisions were done by the producer/directors. In *Heaven Can Wait*, the spirit of athlete Joe Pendleton (Beatty) is taken prematurely from his body by an anxious heavenly messenger. Because Pendleton's body has been cremated, he is placed instead in the body of the recently murdered millionaire Leo Farnsworth. As Pendleton attempts to realize his dreams of playing in the Superbowl, he must deal with Farnsworth's disloyal wife (Dyan Cannon) and his secretary (Charles Grodin) who plotted the murder. He also falls in love with Betty Logan (Julie Christie), a schoolteacher who has come from England to prevent Farnsworth from building a plant in her home town. *Heaven Can Wait* was one of the most successful films of 1978; its Academy Award nominations included best picture, best screenplay, and best director.

May followed *Heaven Can Wait* with uncredited rewrite work on *Reds* (1981) and *Tootsie* (1982). *Reds* is the biography of John Reed, an American journalist who became involved with the Russian revolution and the American Communist Party. Warren Beatty, who produced, directed, coauthored, and starred in the picture, called May in to work on scenes featuring the romance between Reed (Beatty) and fellow journalist/activist Louise Bryant (Diane Keaton). *Tootsie* is about an unemployed actor (Dustin Hoffman) who is forced to disguise himself as a woman in order to find work. The screenplay went through many drafts and rewrites, with May brought in to give the project a feminine slant. She refused any screen credit, despite having made some significant contributions to the script.

Film is a collaborative medium, and when the screenwriter does not also direct, it is often difficult to reconstruct exact individual contributions. However, in all Elaine May scripts, there is an unfailing cohesiveness of characters and an improvisational naturalness in the dialogue. Her comic style is eclectic and her vision satirical. She sees the problems and behaviors of contemporary society sharply, and yet she remains kind and optimistic. She presents a world where sham is exposed and innocence prevails; a crazy equality of personalities and sexual roles exists, a certain justice dominates.

References:

"Elaine May Charges Par Perjury: Ryan 'Disheartened by Her Ways,'" *Variety,* 5 November 1975, II: 22;

Joyce Haber, "Elaine Comments on Rumor," *Los Angeles Times,* 17 January 1973;

Haber, "Elaine May Has a Thing on Not Talking to the Press," *Los Angeles Times,* 7 July 1968;

Michael Rivlin, "Elaine May Too Tough for Hollywood?," *Millimeter,* 3 (October 1975): 16-18, 46;

Michael Scogon, "Ghostwriters in the Cinema," *Film Comment,* 19 (March-April 1983): 9-18;

Richard F. Shephard, "Elaine May: Q&A About Her Play," *New York Times,* 23 September 1962, II:1.

Papers:

The University of California, Los Angeles, has manuscripts of *The Heartbreak Kid* and *Heaven Can Wait.* The University of Southern California has manuscripts for *Such Good Friends* and *A New Leaf.*

Paul Mazursky

(25 April 1930-   )

James Moore

MOTION PICTURES: *I Love You, Alice B. Toklas!* (Warner Bros., 1968), screenplay by Mazursky and Larry Tucker;

Bob & Carol & Ted & Alice (Columbia, 1969), screenplay by Mazursky and Tucker;

Alex in Wonderland (M-G-M, 1970), screenplay by Mazursky and Tucker;

Blume in Love (Warner Bros., 1973), screenplay;

Harry and Tonto (Warner Bros., 1974), screenplay by Mazursky and Josh Greenfeld;

Next Stop, Greenwich Village (20th Century-Fox, 1976), screenplay;

An Unmarried Woman (20th Century-Fox, 1978), screenplay;

Willie and Phil (20th Century-Fox, 1980), screenplay;

The Tempest (Columbia, 1981), screenplay by Mazursky and Leon Capetanos;

Moscow on the Hudson (Columbia, 1984), screenplay by Mazursky and Capetanos.

Paul Mazursky is a filmmaker who maintains a rare control over his work. He has directed all but one of his screenplays and has never directed anyone else's work. Generally he produces his films, and even appears as an actor in some of them. The success of his second film, *Bob & Carol & Ted & Alice* (1969) gave him an artistic freedom infrequently obtained in American motion pictures. Despite that freedom, Mazursky has said that even if he had to give up every other aspect of filmmaking, he would continue to write screenplays.

Irwin Mazursky ("I changed it because Paul would look better on a marquee," he told an old friend in 1971) was born in Brownsville, a Jewish community in Brooklyn. His father was a laborer who was on WPA for several years; his grandfather, a Russian immigrant, ran a candy store and gave Mazursky a love of literature. He graduated from Brooklyn College in 1950. Most of his family and childhood friends have served as models for his films' characters, particularly his mother, who was fictionalized in *Next Stop, Greenwich Village* (1976). His wife Betsy, whom he married in 1951, is the model for most of the women in his films. He had starred in Brooklyn College productions during his senior year and began to get acting jobs in early live New York television programs. He also directed an off-Broadway revue, *Kaleidoscope,* which opened on 13 June 1957. To support himself during this period, he worked in a health food store in Greenwich Village where he met and became

Paul Mazursky

friends with John Cassavetes, who later starred in *The Tempest* (1981).

Mazursky's acting break came in 1953 when he was cast in Stanley Kubrick's first film, *Fear and Desire*. He played in *The Blackboard Jungle* (1955) as well, but he spent most of his time in New York, acting and directing for the stage. He appeared in William Saroyan's *Hello Out There*, and had starring roles in productions of *Death of a Salesman* and *Major Barbara*, but usually, he says, "I was getting juvenile delinquent parts because I looked like a juvenile delinquent."

In the later 1950s Mazursky began to develop his comic gifts as a nightclub performer at the Bon Soir, Gate of Horn, Down in the Depths, and San Francisco's Hungry i. He met Larry Tucker, another comedian and writer, and after producing and directing the off-Broadway *He Who Gets Slapped*, Mazursky joined Tucker in California as part of the regional Second City troupe. From there, Mazursky and Tucker went to television, and in the early and middle 1960s they wrote for the

inventive *Danny Kaye Show* and created and wrote for *The Monkees* (1966 to 1968), a satiric series about a rock band.

While in California, Mazursky acted in the UCLA repertory company and took classes in film editing at the University of Southern California. He and Tucker made a short film spoof of *Last Year at Marienbad* (1962) titled "Last Year at Malibu." Their first full-length script, "H-Bomb Beach Party," was sold, but never filmed; it led to their first motion picture, the only one of Mazursky's scripts he did not direct.

I Love You, Alice B. Toklas! (1968) prefigures a good deal of Mazursky's later themes and concerns. The film is about Harold (Peter Sellers), a Beverly Hills lawyer bored with his job; Mazursky has said that he was really writing about his own attempts to escape from television gag-writing. Harold leaves his bland fiancée Joyce (Joyce van Patten) for hippie Nancy (Leigh Taylor-Young), but he is too responsible to live happily in a commune, and he returns to Beverly Hills in time for

Elliott Gould, Natalie Wood, Robert Culp, and Dyan Cannon in Bob & Carol & Ted & Alice, *inspired by Mazursky's experiences at a group-encounter session*

his long-planned marriage to Joyce. In the type of open-ended conclusion that has become Mazursky's hallmark, Harold runs away from the wedding, not knowing where he is headed, but he has a smile on his face. He is free, if only momentarily.

Bob & Carol & Ted & Alice (1969) sprang from a group-encounter session that Mazursky attended. Written in five days, it remains Mazursky's tightest, most economical film, one in which the plot—never his forte—stems naturally from character. After a visit to a psychiatric institute, Bob (Robert Culp) and Carol (Natalie Wood) decide to have an open marriage. They try to convince their more conservative friends Ted (Elliott Gould) and Alice (Dyan Cannon) to do likewise; Ted and Alice are at first reluctant, but finally agree to an orgy with Carol and Bob. Nothing happens, and the film concludes with the four friends walking away laughing.

Although there are various cuts and camera-angle switches, there are really only sixteen scenes

in *Bob & Carol & Ted & Alice.* The longer, fully developed scenes give the film an air of seriousness; Mazursky is carefully treating characters who, for all their babble, may have something worthwhile to say. In another writer's hands, the dialogue could be cuttingly satiric, but Mazursky lets audiences laugh a little *for* his characters, a little at themselves.

Alex in Wonderland (1970), the most critically condemned and least commercially successful of his films, followed. Director Alex (Donald Sutherland) has just had one stunning success and cannot decide what his next project should be; he finally ends up directing the graduation ceremony at his children's grammar school. The film is thinly plotted, consisting largely of Alex's fantasy sequences. Critics accused Mazursky of imitating director Federico Fellini (who appears briefly in the film). The failure of *Alex in Wonderland* did serious damage to Mazursky's career: it ended his working relationship with Larry Tucker, and nearly two years elapsed before he was able to sell another screenplay.

After spending several months trying to interest a studio in his screenplay for *Harry and Tonto* (1974) and receiving fourteen rejections, Mazursky left the United States to live in Europe. Arguments he had there with his wife inspired him to write *Blume in Love* (1973), about a man who is devastated when his wife leaves him. Told in flashback, the film begins with Stephen Blume (George Segal) telling the audience: "I'm in love with Nina, that's my tragedy. To be in love with your ex-wife is a tragedy." Nina (Susan Anspach) left Blume when she found him in bed with his secretary; for a while, he spends time with divorced friend Arlene (Marsha Mason), but when Nina begins dating rock musician Elmo (Kris Kristofferson) Blume becomes determined to win her back. Blume visits Nina, vows to change, becomes enraged, and rapes her,

then sends a relentless stream of letters. Finally Nina tells him to go to Venice, where they honeymooned. Blume has been there three weeks when the film opens. He wins Nina back, but it is on her own terms: "I love you," she says, "but I won't marry you." The success of *Blume in Love* made up for the failure of *Alex in Wonderland;* many critics consider it to be Mazursky's best film.

Mazursky's next logical step in developing his theory of modern love would be *An Unmarried Woman* (1978), but he had two sidesteps first: *Harry and Tonto* and *Next Stop, Greenwich Village.* The former, written in collaboration with old Greenwich Village friend Josh Greenfeld, was finally filmed following the success of *Blume in Love.* Elderly Harry (Art Carney) decides to leave New York after his apartment is torn down and his best friend, Rivetowsky, dies. He starts out to live with his children, but winds up, with his cat Tonto, on a cross-

Art Carney in Harry and Tonto, *the story of an old man's cross-country journey with his cat*

Lenny Baker and Shelley Winters in Next Stop, Greenwich Village

country odyssey, a nearly surrealistic journey filled with wonder and revelation. The general critical evaluation was that Mazursky was depicting the inexhaustible possibilities of life which lie around you if you can only see them. Harry learns something from all the characters he meets on his trip: his children, his grandson, a pregnant hitchhiker, an aging cowboy, a prostitute, a 106-year-old Indian. Tonto dies, but Harry finds a place at Muscle Beach, where he can carry on philosophical discussions like those with Rivetowsky. At the end, his lady friend wants him to move in with her, but Harry says, "I'm not ready for marriage yet." The script that draws least from Mazursky's own experiences, *Harry and Tonto* is the film that is most accessible to moviegoers. The film earned Mazursky his second Academy Award nomination for best screenplay, and Art Carney was voted best actor.

Next Stop, Greenwich Village is Mazursky's only period film and his most clearly autobiographical. It is set in Greenwich Village in the 1950s, a setting Mazursky obviously feels great attachment to—then and there, he says, "the idea of doing something good was not a foolish, dirty notion." But he also realized that the young people of the period hid behind empty poses, and *Next Stop, Greenwich Village* contains such characters as Robert (Christopher Walken), the icy poet; Bernstein (Antonio Fargas), the gay aristocrat; Anita (Lois Smith), who makes frequent suicide attempts; and Connie (Dori Brenner), everyone's best friend. Mazursky himself is dramatized as struggling actor Larry Lapinsky (Lenny Baker). In typical Mazursky fashion, although the characters act out their fates, the future remains unpredictable. Mazursky's most personal film since *Alex in Wonderland, Next Stop, Greenwich Village* was not much more successful.

The film that brought Mazursky to popular

attention as a writer-director was *An Unmarried Woman*. It was not a significantly better film than its predecessors, but it was most readily recognized by the public as a serious comment on social change. The film grew from conversations Mazursky had with recently divorced women friends, as well as from his wife's frustrations at trying to return to work for the first time in years. Erica (Jill Clayburgh) is jolted from the complacency of married life when her husband (Michael Murphy) tells her he has been having an affair. Suddenly "unmarried," she must confront altered relationships with her job, her daughter, and men in general. Some critics complained that it was too convenient for Erica to find a happy relationship with an artist (Alan Bates). But Mazursky had Erica leave the artist, and he concluded the film with her trudging along a cluttered street, smiling, and unsure of where she is going. *An Unmarried Woman* earned Mazursky his third Academy Award nomination for best screenplay and his first for best director;

the film was nominated for best picture and Jill Clayburgh for best actress.

Borrowing lightly from the François Truffaut film *Jules and Jim* (1961), *Willie and Phil* (1980) is the story of two friends who fall in love with the same woman. Willie (Michael Ontkean) is a Jewish teacher; Phil (Ray Sharkey) is an Italian photographer; both love Jeanette (Margot Kidder), a Kentuckian out to make her fortune in New York. The film covers a period of years during which Jeanette marries Willie, has a child, becomes Phil's lover, then leaves both Willie and Phil for another man. After fighting it out on a Malibu beach, Phil and Willie make up and go to see *Jules and Jim*. A variation on the monogamous-love-is-best theme that has recurred throughout Mazursky's work, *Wille and Phil* was both comic and serious at once. As one of the stars, Michael Ontkean, remarked, "Paul has a light touch that cuts very deep."

Mazursky's next project was one that had intrigued him for nearly a decade; *The Tempest* (1981)

John Cassavetes in a scene from The Tempest, *Mazursky's modern version of Shakespeare's play*

is a modern version of the Shakespeare play. Philip (John Cassevetes) is a successful architect who has grown bored with his work. He leaves his wife Antonia (Gena Rowlands) and goes to live for a year on an unpopulated island, taking along his daughter (Molly Ringwald) and a woman (Susan Sarandon) he has met only recently. Once on the island, Philip grows more eccentric and overbearing; still, he is willing to be reconciled with Antonia when she and a ship full of their friends come looking for him. *The Tempest* is Mazursky's most ambitious movie, done in a deliberate free-form style that permits musical interludes, fantasy sequences, and flashbacks interspersed with the narrative. But the film was not a success; at 140 minutes it was overlong, and despite the stylistic differences, many critics felt Mazursky was covering familiar ground.

Apparently he agreed, because his next film was an even greater departure from his normal style. *Moscow on the Hudson* (1984), about a Russian (Robin Williams) who defects to the United States, was an attempt to do a populist comedy in the manner of Frank Capra. Vladimir is a musician with the Russian circus who suddenly decides to defect while on a shopping trip in Bloomingdale's. Once he is settled in America, Vladimir finds not just the differences between the two countries (he becomes hysterical when confronted with an entire aisle of coffee in a grocery store) but the similarities as well (the ghetto family that offers him a place to live shares a cramped apartment just as his own family did in Moscow). The film also shows that in Vladimir's world, everyone is an alien, from his attorney (Alejandro Rey), a Cuban refugee, to his best friend (Cleavant Derricks), a black man who moved

to New York from Alabama, to his lover (Maria Conchita Alonso), an Italian immigrant. The film concludes with Vladimir, who has finally found a job as a musician, writing a letter to his family and hoping they might someday be able to join him.

A meticulous craftsman who values hard work and consistency, Paul Mazursky has created a remarkably coherent body of work. Critics may assail his excesses, and he may have failed more than once, but to Mazursky these are the risks a filmmaker must take. "You can fail anyway, doing what you *don't* want to do," he said in the early 1970s, "so if I fail, at least it's with something I believe in."

References:

Josh Greenfeld, "Paul Mazursky in Wonderland," *Life*, 69 (4 September 1970): 51-56;

Leticia Kent, "Mazursky: It's OK Not to Be Married," *New York Times*, 5 March 1978, II. 1, 13;

Joan Lurie, "Writer-director Mazursky: the Best of Both Worlds," *Los Angeles Times*, 30 December 1977, IV, 20;

James Monaco, *American Film Now* (New York: New American Library, 1979);

Monaco, "Paul Mazursky and Willie and Phil," *American Film* (July-August 1980);

Clarke Taylor, "The Flip Side of Mazursky," *Los Angeles Times*, 8 July 1979, 27;

David Thomson, *A Biographical Dictionary of Film* (New York: Morrow, 1976), 401, 402.

Papers:
Original screenplays by Mazursky are on file at the American Film Institute, Beverly Hills, California.

John Milius

(11 April 1944-   )

Richard Braverman

MOTION PICTURES: *The Devil's 8* (American International, 1969), screenplay by Milius, James Gordon White, and Willard Huyck;
Evel Knievel (Fanfare, 1971), screenplay by Milius and Alan Caillou;
Jeremiah Johnson (Warner Bros., 1972), screenplay by Milius and Edward Anhalt;
The Life and Times of Judge Roy Bean (First Artists-National General, 1972), story and screenplay;
Dillinger (American International, 1973), story and screenplay;
Magnum Force (Warner Bros., 1973), story; screenplay by Milius and Michael Cimino;
The Wind and the Lion (M-G-M, 1975), story and screenplay;
Big Wednesday (Warner Bros., 1978), screenplay by Milius and Dennis Aaberg;

Apocalypse Now (United Artists, 1979), screenplay by Milius and Francis Ford Coppola;
1941 (Warner Bros., 1979), screen story by Milius, Robert Zemeckis, and Bob Gale;
Conan, the Barbarian (Universal, 1981), screenplay by Milius and Oliver Stone;
Red Dawn (M-G-M, 1984), screenplay by Milius and Kevin Reynolds.

BOOK: *The Life and Times of Judge Roy Bean* (New York: Bantam, 1973).

TELEVISION: *Melvin Purvis, G-Man* (ABC, 1974), story; teleplay by Milius and William F. Nolan.

John Milius pioneered a path from screenwriter to director that many other American filmmakers of the 1970s would eventually follow. His reputation derives not only from the quantity of his writing that has been produced but also from the infusion of his own colorful character into his bold, brutal, and uncompromising work. Milius's screenplays portray changing times, the legends that emerge from the clash of cultures, and the prices people pay for becoming those legends. Beyond the inescapable violence, Milius's work focuses on the spiritual dimensions of great men and the codes of honor and skill by which they live.

The son of William Styx Milius (a shoe manufacturer) and Elizabeth Roe, John Frederick Milius was born in St. Louis, Missouri. His family moved to Los Angeles when he was seven. Raised in a strict Victorian environment, Milius disliked school and found companionship in books, especially by Herman Melville, and movies, primarily by John Ford, that kindled his deep, sentimental love of historical storytelling. Milius received an equally vital education through various boyhood experiences: at the ocean, surfing nearly every day; on the road, riding freight trains; and in a remote cabin in Colorado, living as a mountain man.

While surfing in Hawaii in the early 1960s, Milius repeatedly witnessed violence in the form of street fighting between natives and sailors. This ex-

John Milius

posure to violence left so profound an effect on him that he began investigating its nature. At the same time, Milius discovered the films of Akira Kurosawa, which instigated his study of Japanese art and martial-arts philosophies, where he found a code to deal with violence. Weaponry and war also commanded his interest. Though Milius saw the Vietnam war as "a terrible thing," he also recognized it as "history in the making." He attempted to enlist but was rejected because of a chronic respiratory illness.

Facing an unfulfilling future as a lifeguard, Milius briefly studied at Los Angeles City College, then enrolled in the film department at the University of Southern California in 1965. The film school environment fueled his creative desires, and he began writing. While at USC he established friendships with fellow students George Lucas, Willard Huyck, and Gloria Katz, beginning relationships that would extend into professional careers. With a revolutionary zeal aimed at the cynicism of the "Bel-Air circuit," student films were made by young filmmakers who believed they had no real chance of becoming part of the established film industry. Milius's short film, *Marcello, I'm So Bored* (1966), parodied the European films of that era.

Milius was married in 1967 to Renee Fabri; he has a son, Ethan Jedediah. After his marriage he left USC and soon was offered a production job, along with Willard Huyck, at American International Pictures. Although AIP often provided encouragement to young people, the company fired Milius and Huyck for insubordination. AIP's story editor Larry Gordon apparently saw their potential, and offered them a writing assignment: *The Devil's 8* (1969), an example of the AIP pattern of creating low-budget versions of already proven films, in this case *The Dirty Dozen* (1967). Milius and Huyck finished the screenplay—Milius's first—in ten days. It is the story of a federal agent (Christopher George) who, posing as a convict, engineers the escape of a hardened gang of criminals, and utilizes their force in infiltrating and attacking a corrupt statewide moonshine syndicate. Milius later commented, "They crash cars into each other and shoot at each other and stuff like that. It's just absurd."

After *The Devil's 8*, Milius wrote several unproduced scripts, including "The Texans," "Truck Driver," and "Last Resort." Wanting to write of explorer Jedediah Smith, Milius was instead commissioned by Warner Bros. to adapt Raymond Thorp and Robert Bunker's *Crow Killer*, the saga of a nineteenth-century mountain man. Written in

six weeks in 1968, *Jeremiah Johnson* (1972) traces the metamorphosis of ex-soldier Johnson from his initiation into a trapper's life of solitude to his becoming the liver-eating killer of hundreds of Crow Indians. Milius's screenplay conveys more the sense of an odyssey into the darker depths of the American frontier than does the "ecological Western" the movie would eventually become. The screenplay represents Milius's first serious dramatization of his "greatest fantasy—that of a man becoming a legend in a foreign land."

Warner Bros. originally intended *Jeremiah Johnson* to be directed by Sam Peckinpah and star Lee Marvin, but instead offered it to Robert Redford, who chose Sydney Pollack to direct. Milius's uncompromising point of view was softened. He was fired from the project and rehired several times—subsequently developing his reputation for being unpredictable—as additional rewrites cut the last half of the screenplay, toning down Johnson's dedication to revenge. Finally, Milius shared credit with Edward Anhalt. Although he later said he liked the film, Milius added that Pollack, while a very good director, did not understand the script.

Jeremiah Johnson was a great success at the 1972 Cannes Film Festival and was praised for capturing the life of a mountain dweller. The film has achieved an unusual long-term popularity, grossing over seventy million dollars.

In 1969 Milius wrote a treatment for the Vietnam war adventure *Apocalypse Now* (1979), under the Warner Bros. development program. Using Joseph Conrad's *Heart of Darkness* as basis for the allegory, Milius plotted another legend of a man achieving enormous power in an uncivilized land. Colonel Kurtz (Marlon Brando), a U.S. Army special forces commander, is sent to Cambodia with a contingent of twelve Americans, ostensibly to train the Montagnards and resist enemy infiltration. Instead, he becomes a warlord, fighting only for himself. The American command employs Captain Willard (Martin Sheen) to assassinate Kurtz. The ensuing odyssey follows Willard upriver into the insane, savage depths of war, including his confrontation with the Milius version of the Cyclops— a mad surfing colonel (Robert Duvall).

Millius's script was turned over to Francis Ford Coppola, who had commissioned it. George Lucas was chosen to direct. Initial excitement over the script was dampened by Warner Bros. executive decisions deeming the Vietnam war a taboo subject. Simultaneously, both Coppola and Lucas fell from studio favor, and Warner Bros. decided not to make the picture. They also refused to sell

Paul Newman in The Life and Times of Judge Roy Bean. *Milius wrote the screenplay, but he was paid $300,000 not to direct it.*

the property, and several years passed before Coppola was finally able to film the movie. Coppola reworked Milius's original screen treatment, and by the time the movie was shot the script was greatly altered.

His next picture, *Evel Knievel* (1971), depicts the life of the motorcycle daredevil, tracing his career, his brushes with the law, his kidnapping of his high school sweetheart (Sue Lyon), and his dream of jumping the Grand Canyon. George Hamilton, who played Knievel, asked Milius to rewrite Alan Caillou's first draft, but Milius instead wrote an original script. As was the case with *Jeremiah Johnson,* Milius ended up sharing credit with a writer whose work he had not read. Writing his script in five days "as a lark," Milius infused life and vitality into a character "already full of hot air."

Milius wrote *The Life and Times of Judge Roy Bean* (1972) out of love for the men who built the American West. Roy Bean (Paul Newman) takes the law into his own hands, hoping to form a civilization out of chaos. Like Jeremiah Johnson, he discovers that the resulting changes have destroyed the world he knew. The screenplay represents still another version of the author's favorite fantasy of a man becoming a legend in a strange land. Although originally intended to be a modestly budgeted picture directed by Milius in Spain, the property was acquired by First Artists Productions for Paul Newman. Milius was paid $300,000—double his usual fee—not to direct the film, and the assignment was given to John Huston. According to Milius, the experienced Huston provided a climate—tortuous to the writer, yet highly influential to the would-be director—in which to study directing.

Dirty Harry is the only script to which Milius significantly contributed that does not bear his

Clint Eastwood and Felton Perry in Magnum Force

name. Milius worked on Harry and R. M. Fink's screenplay about a San Francisco homicide detective's pursuit of a maniac rooftop sniper. Despite orders to the contrary, Harry Callahan (Clint Eastwood) hunts the killer (Andrew Robinson) down, risking his life and his badge. The film is a portrait of a man living by his own code and abilities, confronting loneliness and a sense of isolation in an urban wilderness. Detective Callahan, not unlike Judge Roy Bean, Colonel Kurtz, and Jeremiah Johnson, goes beyond the law, becoming the law himself. Influenced by Kurosawa's *Stray Dog* (1949), Milius expanded the Finks' script, adding more violence, a ruthlessness to Harry's character, and the idea of the similarities between cop and killer. Director Don Siegel toned down the script's violence.

Warner Bros. commissioned Milius to write a sequel. In *Magnum Force* (1973), a group of over-zealous police rookies abuse their power by murdering criminals. Although Harry shares some of the rookies' attitudes, he begins to question their methods. Harry becomes an enemy of their style of vigilante justice, and must kill or be killed. Milius was not pleased with *Magnum Force*; his conception of Harry as a bitter, lonely man who liked his work

was lost in the completed film. The subtleties of character in the original screenplay were abandoned in favor of a barrage of violence and car crashes.

Milius finally had an opportunity to direct one of his own screenplays when Larry Gordon, now American International's vice-president in charge of production, hired him to write and direct a screenplay, provided the screenplay adhered to American International's configurations. The resulting film was *Dillinger* (1973). Milius developed the story as a historical folk tale, depicting a gang of criminals and psychotic killers led by Dillinger, who is not actually known to have killed anyone. Much of the film centered on the conflict between Dillinger (Warren Oates) and his nemesis Melvin Purvis (Ben Johnson), the federal agent determined to hunt him down. Purvis was based on a combination of several law enforcement agents, and the character fits the Milius mold of the friendless man, bigger than his contemporaries, who is ultimately left with nothing once his quarry has been killed. In this collision of two larger-than-life characters, Milius infused the script with violence. As a spin-off, Milius wrote *Melvin Purvis, G-Man,* a movie made for television. However, the limita-

John Milius on the set of Dillinger

allies. Together they join forces in a spectacular culminating battle. As director, Milius had to overcome enormous logistical and personnel problems in the sixteen weeks it took to shoot the film in Morocco and Spain, but if "making the movie was like going to war," as Milius has said, it was well worth the effort. In recreating on the screen the marvelous characters and thundering, savage, romantic elements first conceived on paper, *The Wind and the Lion* achieved Milius's first substantial critical success.

In the years following, Milius became involved in rewriting what had become Coppola's *Apocalypse Now,* and contributing to the screenplay of *Jaws* (1975). He also wrote several scripts that were not produced. *Big Wednesday* (1978) marked the initial effort of Milius's own A-Team Productions.

Directed and written by Milius, *Big Wednesday* was originally intended as a novel—"a surfing *How Green Was My Valley.*" The film focuses on the maturing friendship of three young surfers (Jan-Michael Vincent, William Katt, Gary Busey), their

tions of working for television and disappointment in Dan Curtis's direction convinced Milius to refuse all subsequent television involvement, including a proposed second Melvin Purvis film.

Dillinger was successful enough financially to allow Milius to continue directing his own scripts. His next project, *The Wind and the Lion* (1975), had its origins in an *American Heritage* article about El Raisuli, Sultan to the Berbers, that Willard Huyck had shown Milius while they were students at USC. Further investigation unearthed Edith Rosa Forbe's *The Sultan of the Mountain,* in which the author interviews El Raisuli. Influenced by the film *High Wind in Jamaica* (1965), Milius envisioned "an old-time boy's adventure story, very romantic, back-lit, and beautiful to look at." Herbert Jaffe at United Artists liked the idea, and three months later the financed script was completed.

In *The Wind and the Lion,* El Raisuli (Sean Connery) kidnaps a beautiful American woman, Eden Pedicaris (Candice Bergen), and her two children. He sweeps them off to his desert domain, only to outrage President Theodore Roosevelt (Brian Keith) who sends the United States Marines to her rescue. The capture of Raisuli draws together international forces in Morocco; Pedicaris becomes Raisuli's benefactor and the marines become his

Sean Connery and Candice Bergen in The Wind and the Lion, *filmed in Morocco and Spain. Milius later commented that "making the movie was like going to war."*

relationship with the ocean, and the events in their lives from 1963 to 1973. Although not entirely autobiographical, the story, coauthored with longtime surfing partner Dennis Aaberg, is based on Milius's experiences. Prior to filming, Milius explained, "The surf is just an exotic background. This movie is about friendship, the value of friendship, and the passing of a more innocent time into a more complex one." Unfortunately, Milius's "most personal film" would also be his most disappointing; *Big Wednesday* received neither audience nor critical recognition. By substituting reverence for the pragmatism that had colored past achievements, Milius seemed at fault for taking himself too seriously. (He later recut the film for television showings.)

Despite the negative reaction to *Big Wednesday*, A-Team Productions continued, with Milius serving as Executive Producer on Paul Schrader's *Hardcore* (1979). In addition to producing *1941* (1979), a comedy about a California city's hysterical reaction to Pearl Harbor, he also coauthored the film's original story with its director, Stephen Spielberg. Plans to film the story of explorer Jedediah Smith were laid aside in favor of adapting Robert Howard's *Conan, the Barbarian* (1981) to the screen.

Conan (Arnold Schwarzenegger) is a warrior living in a mythical age some twelve thousand years past. It is a time when science does not exist and magic is commonplace. The film is the story of Conan's early years, beginning with his parents' deaths when he is a child. Sold into slavery, he escapes, travels across country, encounters many dangers, and finally battles Thulsa Doom (James Earl Jones), the murderer of his parents and leader of an evil cult. A thinly plotted, highly episodic picture, *Conan, the Barbarian* is perhaps noteworthy for its protagonist. Most of Milius's characters have been in conflict with social custom, but Conan is his first protagonist to operate without any restraint whatsoever; he is a warrior and thief whose primary concern is his own survival.

Though *Conan, the Barbarian* was condemned by most critics, it was a financial success and Milius began planning a sequel. Those plans were never realized (the sequel was made without Milius in 1984), and instead he began work as producer of *Uncommon Valor* (1983), about a group of Vietnam veterans who return to southeast Asia to search for American soldiers who are officially missing in action. The film bears Milius's stamp in many ways: the interest in Vietnam, the heroics of the characters, and the concept of a character placed in a foreign land. The film's plot, when reduced to its simplest terms—man looking for missing relative—is the same as that of the John Ford film *The Searchers* (1956), a Milius favorite, and one that he says influenced him greatly.

Red Dawn (1984) was Milius's next picture as writer and director; he wrote the script with Kevin Reynolds from Reynolds's story. In the near future, the Russian army invades the United States and places most of its citizens in internment camps. In Colorado, one group of teenagers evades capture and fights back against the Soviets. *Red Dawn* earned Milius some of the worst reviews of his career; critics found the picture needlessly violent and implausible, and the characters stereotyped. Milius's by now familiar interest in "macho" heroics was said to be heavy-handed.

Though John Milius has had an impressive career as a screenwriter, his films are not without flaws. These flaws are often not of Milius's doing; some of his screenplays have been revised by other writers or directors, and sometimes he has rewritten the work of others. But his work as a screenwriter, and later as a director, has always been interesting, and shows a rare consistency in theme.

Interviews:

Andrew C. Bobrow, "The Making of Dillinger," *Filmmakers' Newsletter* (November 1973): 20-25;

Richard Thompson, "Stoked," *Film Comment* (July-August 1976): 10-21.

References:

Jon Landau, "Dillinger: Cops, Robbers & Superstardom," *Rolling Stone*, 142 (30 August 1973): 96-99;

Robert Lindsey, "The New Wave of Film Makers," *New York Times Magazine*, 28 May 1978, pp. 11-15, 33-36;

Linda Strawn, "Blood-and-Guts Milius at War," *Los Angeles Times*, 5 August 1973;

Wayne Varga, "Milius Waxes Up Big Wednesday," *Los Angeles Times*, 21 August 1977, p. 7.

Frank Nugent

(27 May 1908-29 December 1965)

Barton Palmer
Georgia State University

MOTION PICTURES: *Fort Apache* (RKO, 1948), screenplay;

Three Godfathers (M-G-M, 1949), screenplay by Nugent and Laurence Stallings;

Tulsa (Eagle-Lion, 1949), screenplay by Nugent and Curtis Kenyon;

She Wore a Yellow Ribbon (RKO, 1949), screenplay by Nugent and Stallings;

Wagonmaster (RKO, 1950), screen story and screenplay by Nugent and Patrick Ford;

Two Flags West (20th Century-Fox, 1950), story by Nugent and Kenyon;

The Quiet Man (Republic, 1952), screenplay;

Angel Face (RKO, 1952), screenplay by Nugent and Oscar Millard;

The Paratrooper (Columbia, 1954), screenplay by Nugent, Richard Maibaum, and Sy Bartlett;

Trouble in the Glen (Republic, 1954), screenplay;

They Rode West (Columbia, 1954), screenplay by Nugent and De Vallon Scott;

Mister Roberts (Warner Bros., 1955), screenplay by Nugent and Joshua Logan;

The Tall Men (20th Century-Fox, 1955), screenplay by Nugent and Sydney Boehm;

The Searchers (Warner Bros., 1956), screenplay;

The Rising of the Moon (Warner Bros., 1957), screenplay;

Gunman's Walk (Columbia, 1958), screenplay;

The Last Hurrah (Columbia, 1958), screenplay;

Two Rode Together (Columbia, 1961), screenplay;

Donovan's Reef (Paramount, 1963), screenplay by Nugent and James Edward Grant;

Incident at Phantom Hill (Universal, 1967), screenplay by Nugent and Ken Pettus.

TELEVISION: *Empire* (NBC, September 1962-September 1963), series developed by Nugent.

OTHER: *New York Times Directory of the Film*, reviews by Nugent (New York: Arno Press/Random House, 1971), pp. 54-70.

PERIODICAL PUBLICATIONS: "Hollywood

Frank Nugent

Waves the Flag," *Nation* (8 April 1939);

"Hollywood Faces Reality," *New York Times Magazine,* 8 March 1942;

"How Long Should a Movie Be?," *New York Times Magazine,* 18 February 1945;

"Going Hollywood," *Good Housekeeping* (July, August, September 1945);

"Assignment in Hollywood," *Good Housekeeping* (October, November, December 1945, January 1946);

"Hollywood Invades Mexico," *New York Times Magazine,* 23 March 1947;

"Cavalcade of Hollywood Heroes," *New York Times
    Magazine*, 4 May 1947;
"Writer or Director, Who Makes the Movie?," *New
    York Times Magazine*, 21 December 1947.
"Hollywood's Favorite Rebel," *Saturday Evening Post*
    (23 July 1949);
"All About Joe," *Colliers* (24 March 1951);
"Golden Holden," *Colliers* (2 June 1951);
"Good Ol' Joel," *Colliers* (15 September 1951);
"Stanwyck," *Colliers*, 12 July 1952;

In a 1947 article for the *New York Times* entitled "Writer or Director, Who Makes the Movie?" Frank Nugent was to prove prophetic about his own career. After surveying the opinions of contemporary directors like Alfred Hitchcock and Cecil B. De Mille, Nugent concluded that, contrary to what they might think, "some of the directors' best friends are writers." The problem is, Nugent went on to state, "they just don't see enough of each other." Nugent's piece appeared at a time when the Screen Writers Guild was mounting an intense campaign to improve recognition and credit for scriptwriters, but Nugent himself never became bitter about the screenwriter's obscured role in the shooting process or the inadequate recognition he received for the finished film. His professional satisfaction must be traced in large measure to Nugent's relationship with John Ford, a director who, unlike many of his peers, recognized that the screenwriter was indeed one of his best friends. And Nugent's filmography, which includes successful films made with Ford, as well as failures or mediocre pictures made with other directors, suggests directors are often screenwriters' best friends as well.

After graduating from Columbia University in 1929, where he majored in journalism, Nugent went immediately to work for the *New York Times*, spending from 1930 to 1940 as a reporter and rewrite man. He was promoted in 1934 to motion picture critic and reporter, a job he held until 1940. While Nugent's reviews reveal a haughtiness about the movies—they fault the medium's escapism, its lightweight themes, and its slim production values—they also display his genuine enthusiasm for film when he addressed such prestigious literary adaptations as *Captains Courageous* (1937), *The Good Earth* (1937), and *Wuthering Heights* (1939). Nugent was not above expressing pure excitement over a swashbuckler like *The Adventures of Robin Hood* (1938).

As a result of Nugent's review of *The Grapes of Wrath* (1940), Darryl F. Zanuck, then head of production at 20th Century-Fox, offered Nugent a job as script doctor. During his tenure at the studio he did no significant screenwriting, working only as a story consultant and rewriting many screenplays without credit. He also continued writing occasional pieces about Hollywood life for the *Times* magazine and periodicals such as *Colliers*. In 1944, seeing no future at 20th Century-Fox, he left to become a free-lance writer.

Nugent met John Ford while the director was in Mexico filming *The Fugitive* (1947). Nugent accompanied the Ford crew on their trip south, writing a piece for the *Times* magazine on Hollywood's "invasion" of Mexico. At that time, Ford was considering making a film about the U.S. Cavalry, that standard subject of Western films whose real story had never been told. As Nugent related, what happened next was a surprise: "I said it sounded great. And then he knocked me right off my seat by asking how I'd like to write it for him. When I stumbled and stammered, he grinned and said he thought it would be fun. He gave me a list of about fifty books to read. . . . Later he sent me down into the Old Apache country to nose around." When writing this screenplay, Nugent said, Ford made him "do something that had never occurred to me before—but something I've practiced ever since: write out complete biographies of every character in the picture. Where born, educated, politics, drinking habits (if any), quirks. You take the character from his childhood and write out all the salient events in his life leading up to the moment the picture finds him—or her."

The film that came of this initial collaboration was *Fort Apache* (1948), which Nugent adapted from a James Warner Bellah story based on the Custer legend. As Nugent pointed out, the story contained little more than an account of the climactic battle itself, which comes near the end of the film. Everything else in the script, including the complex interactions of cavalry officers, enlisted men, and their families, was built up by Nugent, working in close collaboration with Ford. The film was a disappointment at the box office, possibly a result of a rushed production schedule (three weeks). Whatever its final realization, the story itself is intriguing. The Custer figure, martinet Colonel Thursday (Henry Fonda), is balanced against a worldly wise and humane subordinate, Captain Kirby (John Wayne). Thursday, a former Civil War general, is sent west where he arranges a meeting with Cochise, then secretly attacks Cochise and his followers. Following the slaughter of Thursday and his men, York demonstrates his loyalty to military tra-

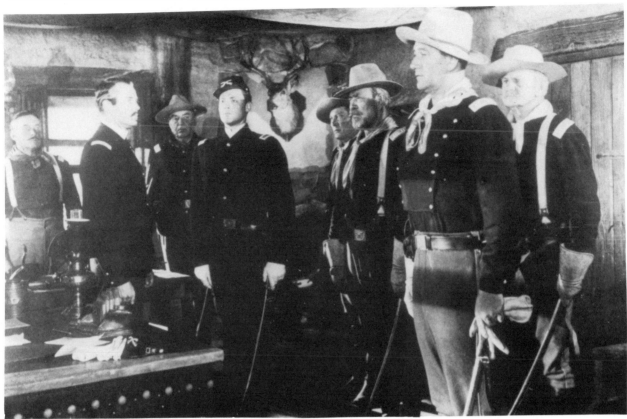

Henry Fonda (second from left), John Agar (fourth from left), and John Wayne (second from right) in Fort Apache, *Nugent's first film, which also began his long and successful career with John Ford*

dition by refusing to acknowledge the defeat as the result of Thursday's error. Then by assuming the role of commander York insures that the cavalry will not have to endure such disaster again. In this way, *Fort Apache* gives some positive meaning to the death of Thursday and his troops.

The following year, Nugent shared his enthusiasm for Ford in an article about the director, "Hollywood's Favorite Rebel," published in the *Saturday Evening Post*. Nugent suggested that working for Ford involved some drastic accommodations for the screenwriter: "Ford has never formally surrendered to the talkies. His writers are under standing orders to keep dialogue to an 'irreducible medium.' Ford usually manages to trim this 'irreducible medium' still more." Since Nugent, especially when working as part of a scriptwriting team, was usually called upon to either write or rewrite dialogue, Ford's bias against dialogue often meant his contribution to the finished picture was correspondingly minor. This was obviously the case with *Three Godfathers* (1949), the fourth and best-known film version of Peter B. Kyne's short story about three men (John Wayne, Harry Carey, Jr., and

Pedro Armendariz) who care for a baby orphaned in the desert.

Nugent followed this picture with his third script, and the first not directed by Ford, the contemporary Western *Tulsa* (1949). After the death of her father, Cherokee Lansing (Susan Hayward) takes charge of his property and becomes determined to bring in an oil well. *Tulsa* was not the critical success that *Fort Apache* and *Three Godfathers* had been, but it did well financially, becoming the most profitable film produced by Eagle-Lion studios.

Nugent got another opportunity to work for Ford when he agreed to rewrite Laurence Stallings's screenplay for *She Wore a Yellow Ribbon* (1949), which was based on Bellah's short story "War Party," the center film in what has come to be referred to as Ford's "cavalry trilogy." (Nugent did not write the third film, *Rio Grande*, 1950.) In *She Wore a Yellow Ribbon*, Captain Nathan Brittles (John Wayne), an about-to-retire cavalry officer, is faced with the threat of war by a tribe of Cheyenne, and he is unable to transfer the wife (Mildred

Natwick) and niece (Joanne Dru) of his commanding officer to a safer place.

It is a much more sentimental film than *Fort Apache*, showing Brittles as he visits the grave of his wife and as he prepares himself for his retirement from the military service that has given his life meaning. Finally the army gives him the position of chief scout for the remainder of his life.

Nugent next collaborated on *Wagonmaster* (1950) with Ford's son Patrick. Wiggs (Ward Bond), an elder in the Mormon church, hires Travis Blue (Ben Johnson) and Sandy Owens (Harry Carey, Jr.) to lead a group of Mormons into Utah. On the way, the wagon train is joined by a group of outlaws who take the Mormons prisoner. Nugent's screenplay is an entertaining Western story that clearly pits good against bad, and it is a depiction of Americans searching for a place to put down roots (a notion in keeping with Ford's view of American history). Nugent ended the decade with *Two Flags West* which was produced in 1950 from a treatment he had written two years before. A group of Confederate prisoners are sent west to aid in the fight against Indians; they are placed under the com-

mand of an officer (Jeff Chandler) who hates both Indians and Confederates. Robert Wise directed.

The Quiet Man (1952) earned Nugent his only Academy Award nomination. Working from a short story by Maurice Walsh, Nugent gives his Irish characters biographical depth. Sean Thornton (John Wayne) and Mary Kate Danaher (Maureen O'Hara) are characters whose pasts interfere with their present attempts to make a life together. Danaher places great value on her dowry; to her, it represents her worth as a wife. When her brother (Victor McLaglen) refuses to give her a dowry, and when Thornton refuses to fight him for it, Danaher feels rejected. Thornton will not fight because he is an ex-boxer who killed a man in the ring and has not overcome his feelings of guilt. John Ford directed, setting the tale in the romanticized Ireland of Walsh's original story. Nugent won the Screen Writers Guild award for best written comedy, and was also presented the *Look* magazine film achievement award.

Angel Face (1952) is another story of a couple trying to accept each other, but there the resemblance to *The Quiet Man* ends; *Angel Face* is Nugent's

Ruth Clifford, Alan Mowbray, and Joanne Dru in Wagonmaster, *one of John Ford's favorites among the films he directed*

Maureen O'Hara and John Wayne in The Quiet Man, *which earned Nugent an Academy Award nomination and awards from the Screen Writers Guild and* Look *magazine*

bleakest screenplay. Ambulance driver Frank Jessup (Robert Mitchum) meets Diane Tremayne (Jean Simmons) when he is called to her home after her stepmother is nearly asphyxiated. He is attracted to Diane even though he realizes she tried to murder her stepmother, but the mentally unstable Diane eventually kills her stepmother, her father, Frank, and herself. Nugent collaborated on the script with Oscar Millard; Otto Preminger directed.

In 1953 Nugent married Jean Lavell. They had one son.

Three minor screenplays followed *Angel Face*. *The Paratrooper* (1954) was adapted by Nugent, Richard Maibaum, and Sy Bartlett from H. St. G. Saungers's book, but it became a routine melodrama despite Nugent's crisp dialogue; it is most

noteworthy as another screenplay with a guilt-ridden protagonist (Alan Ladd). *They Rode West* (1954), directed by Phil Karlson, was Nugent's first Western in four years. A doctor (Robert Francis) insists on treating the Kiowa Indians despite the protests of others. *Trouble in the Glen* (1954) was an attempt to capitalize on the success of *The Quiet Man*, with Nugent adapting another Walsh story. But here Nugent was unable to make much of Walsh's Scottish stereotypes and, saddled with a picturesque but static story, was not able to construct an interesting narrative.

Raoul Walsh directed Nugent's next Western, *The Tall Men* (1955), which was written in collaboration with Sydney Boehm. It is about the competition between two men for the same woman (Jane Russell); one man (Robert Ryan) offers her wealth, while the other man (Clark Gable) has only a simple homestead. Critics disliked the picture (though, again, Nugent's dialogue was praised) but it was one of the financial successes of its year.

Nugent was reunited with Ford on *Mister Roberts* (1955), a faithful filming of the Broadway play based on Thomas Heggen's novel. He won his second Screen Writers Guild award for this picture. More important was Nugent's screenplay for *The Searchers* (1956), also directed by Ford. Nugent reduced Alan LeMay's novel to its narrative essentials, and in the process deepened the one-dimensional characters. Following the massacre of his brother and his brother's family by Indians, Ethan Edwards (John Wayne) devotes himself to finding the one survivor, his niece Debbie (Natalie Wood), but becomes gradually embittered as his search takes years. In Nugent's hands Edwards's bitterness becomes not just a character trait, but an element in the myth of the West. Edwards is defined by his refusals: his refusal to marry the girl he loves; his refusal to accept the confining nature of settled life; his refusal to give up anger and hatred; and his refusal to accept the Indian as human being. In allowing Edwards a single moment of acceptance, which comes when he takes the res-

cued Debbie in his arms and says "Let's go home," the script locates his bitterness in a romantic disappointment with the world.

With only two exceptions—*Gunman's Walk* (1958) and *Incident at Phantom Hill* (1967)—all of Nugent's remaining screenplays were for Ford. *The Rising of the Moon* (1957) is an underrated film, dealing with the 1916 Irish rebellion, which Nugent effectively adapted from three disparate sources. The movie was intended as a fund-raising project for the Irish Abbey Theatre, and Nugent, like everyone else who worked on the film, received minimum scale pay rather than his normal salary. *The Last Hurrah* (1958) was adapted from the novel by Edwin O'Connor. It is the story of Frank Skeffington (Spencer Tracy), the mayor of an unnamed northern city. (Skeffington is loosely based on Boston mayor James Curley.) *Two Rode Together* (1961) was a surprisingly cynical picture for Nugent and Ford. The story of a sheriff (James Stewart) who is hired to rescue white captives of Indians, the movie strongly implies that the captives would be better off with their captors. Nugent, Ford, and John Wayne were reunited in *Donovan's Reef* (1963), but the movie was not a Western and was a critical failure. A prim Boston woman (Elizabeth Allen) comes to visit her father (Jack Warden) who lives on a Pacific island; Wayne plays Donovan, who becomes the woman's romantic interest.

Gunman's Walk and *Incident at Phantom Hill* were both Westerns and were of varying quality. The first, Nugent's second script for director Phil Karlson, was a well-made story of a father (Van Heflin) in conflict with his son (Tab Hunter), a killer. The *Los Angeles Times* selected the film as one of the year's ten best. Nugent's last screenplay was *Incident at Phantom Hill*, about a group of men searching for stolen gold after the end of the Civil War. The movie owes much to both *The Treasure of Sierra Madre* and Anthony Mann's adult Westerns of the 1950s, but it was a critical and commercial failure. It was released after Nugent's death. He died in December 1965, six weeks after undergoing open-heart surgery.

References:

Lindsay Anderson, *About John Ford* (New York: McGraw-Hill, 1981);

J. A. Place, *The Western Films of John Ford* (Secausus, N.J.: Citadel, 1974).

James Cagney and Henry Fonda in Mister Roberts, *for which Nugent won his second Screen Writers Guild award*

Samuel Ornitz

(15 November 1890-11 March 1957)

Gabriel Miller
Rutgers University

See also the Ornitz entry in *DLB 28, Twentieth-Century American-Jewish Fiction Writers.*

MOTION PICTURES: *The Case of Lena Smith* (Paramount Famous Lasky, 1929), story;

Sins of the Children (Cosmopolitan, 1930), adaptation;

Thirteen Women (RKO, 1932), screenplay by Ornitz and Bartlett Cormack;

Hell's Highway (RKO, 1932), screenplay by Ornitz, Robert Tasker, and Rowland Brown;

Secrets of the French Police (RKO, 1932), story; screenplay by Ornitz and Tasker based on Ornitz's "The Lost Empress";

Men of America (RKO, 1932), screenplay by Ornitz and Jack Jungmeyer;

One Man's Journey (RKO, 1933), screenplay;

One Exciting Adventure (Universal, 1934), dialogue;

The Man Who Reclaimed His Head (Universal, 1935), screenplay by Ornitz and Jean Bart;

Three Kids and a Queen (Universal, 1935), screenplay by Ornitz and Barry Trivers;

Fatal Lady (Paramount, 1936), screenplay;

Follow Your Heart (Republic, 1936), screenplay by Ornitz, Nathanael West, and Lester Cole;

A Doctor's Diary (Paramount, 1937), screen story by Ornitz and Joseph Anthony;

The Hit Parade (Republic, 1937), screenplay by Ornitz and Bradford Ropes;

It Could Happen to You (Republic, 1937), screenplay by Ornitz and West;

Portia on Trial (Republic, 1937), screenplay;

Two Wise Maids (Republic, 1937), screenplay;

Army Girl (Republic, 1938), screenplay;

King of the Newsboys (Republic, 1938), screen story by Ornitz and Horace McCoy;

Little Orphan Annie (Paramount, 1938), screenplay by Ornitz and Budd Schulberg; story by Ornitz and Endre Bohem;

A Miracle on Main Street (Columbia, 1940), screen story by Ornitz and Boris Ingster;

Three Faces West (Republic, 1940), screen story and screenplay by Ornitz, F. Hugh Herbert, and Joseph Moncure March;

Little Devils (Monogram, 1944), screenplay;

They Live in Fear (Columbia, 1944), screenplay by Ornitz and Michael Simmons;

Circumstantial Evidence (20th Century-Fox, 1945), adaptation.

BOOKS: *The Sock*, as Don Orno (Brooklyn, N.Y.: Three Pamphleteers, 1918);

Haunch, Paunch and Jowl: An Anonymous Autobiography (New York: Boni & Liveright, 1923; London: Wishart, 1929);

Round the World with Jocko the Great (New York: Macaulay, 1925);

A Yankee Passional (New York: Boni & Liveright, 1927);

Bride of the Sabbath (New York: Rinehart, 1951).

PERIODICAL PUBLICATIONS: "What the 'Gun-Fighter' Thinks About It," anonymous, *Review* (August 1912);

"In New Kentucky," *New Masses* (3 April 1934): 17-28;

"Lester Loven Jumps Both Ways," *Clipper*, 2 (November 1941): 6-15;

"A Jew Confronts the Un-American Committee," *Jewish Life* (December 1947).

Samuel Badisch Ornitz was born in New York City, the son of Polish Jewish immigrants. Raised on New York's Lower East Side, a setting that dominates two of his novels, he became committed to social causes at an early age. As a boy he attended a religious school and participated in programs at the Henry Street Settlement House. After a sporadic college education and a few odd jobs he chose a career in social work. As an employee of the Prison Association, which gave legal support and help to the poor, he had free access to New York's The Tombs prison, where he encountered firsthand the extreme results of social neglect and abuse. He later served the Society for the Prevention of Cruelty to Children as assistant superintendent.

In 1914 Ornitz married Sadie Lesser; they

Samuel Ornitz (courtesy of Culver Pictures)

had two sons. His first novel, *Haunch, Paunch and Jowl,* published anonymously in 1923, became a cause célèbre. A provocative story of political corruption and the excesses of capitalism, it follows the rise of a streetwise boy to his position on the Supreme Court. It was as enthusiastically damned as it was praised, and it remains to this day Ornitz's best-known work. After writing a children's book about the adventures of a monkey (*Round the World with Jocko the Great,* 1925), Ornitz wrote the novel *A Yankee Passional* (1927), a sprawling and extremely impressive work about the rise and fall of a New England mystic who founds a home for wayward boys in New York City; picaresque and panoramic, it is Ornitz's finest work and an unjustly neglected novel.

Ornitz would not write another novel for many years; encouraged by Herman Mankiewicz, he came to Hollywood in 1928 to work for Paramount Studios. His first film, *The Case of Lena Smith* (1929), was based loosely on someone Ornitz had met while working in The Tombs. Esther Ralston

plays Lena Schmidt (whose name changes in the course of the film), a Hungarian peasant who marries a young lieutenant (James Hall); he and his father (Gustav von Seyffertitz) treat her as if she were a servant. Josef von Sternberg directed. Ornitz's next film, *Sins of the Children* (1930), is the story of a working-class man troubled by his grown children. He mortgages his barber shop so his oldest son can marry; later, his daughter begins an affair with a rich man's son and causes a scandal. Finally the youngest son comes to his father's aid with money made from his inventions. Ornitz's devotion to social justice caused him frequently to interrupt his early film career with trips to places where he felt justice needed a hand. He was outspoken about the Scottsboro boys' case and worked to help free them. Later, Ornitz, Theodore Dreiser, John Dos Passos, and others went to investigate labor conditions in Harlan County, Kentucky. This experience inspired Ornitz to write a short play, *In New Kentucky* (1934). When he returned to Hollywood he went to work at RKO studios. Ornitz's commitment to social causes never abated; during the 1930s and 1940s, he was a vocal and active protester against fascism, anti-Semitism, and the travesties of war worldwide. He traveled in the U. S. and abroad, speaking out against injustice wherever he saw it. When he could, he expressed some of his concerns in his scripts.

One of his first films for RKO reflects his social interests: *Hell's Highway* (1932) is about a highway chain gang that rebels against cruel treatment. Rowland Brown and Roland Tasker collaborated on the screenplay. *Secrets of the French Police* (1932) is a realistic and detailed look at the Parisian police force. *One Man's Journey* (1933) studies the problems of a country doctor (Lionel Barrymore).

In 1935 Ornitz moved to Universal studios, where he wrote *The Man Who Reclaimed His Head* (1935). A writer and political activist (Claude Rains) rebels against the publisher (Lionel Atwill) he feels has exploited him. Ornitz and Jean Bart adapted the screenplay from Bart's play. *Three Kids and a Queen* (1935) is about three orphans who are helped by a wealthy woman. Ornitz wrote *Fatal Lady*

(1936), about a mysterious woman who kills seemingly at random. In *A Doctor's Diary* (1937), Dr. Dan Norris (John Trent) keeps a record of the improper behavior he observes in a hospital.

In 1936 Ornitz moved to Republic, a studio that specialized in cranking out inexpensive movies. He wrote six films in three years. *Follow Your Heart* (1936) is about an aspiring singer (Marion Talley) who leaves Kentucky to join her uncle's opera company and falls in love with another member (Michael Bartlett). Nathanael West, with whom Ornitz worked several times, and Lester Cole collaborated with Ornitz on the screenplay. In *The Hit Parade* (1937) radio-show producer Pete Garland (Phil Ragan) seeks a new singer for his show and finds one in ex-convict Ruth Allison (Frances Langford). *Portia on Trial* (1937) is the melodramatic tale of lawyer Portia Merriman (Frieda Inescort) who defends Elizabeth Manners (Heather Angel) for the murder of Earle Kolb (Neil Hamilton), without revealing that she is Kolb's mother. An army captain (Preston Foster) falls in love with his colonel's daughter (Madge Evans) in *Army Girl* (1938). Or-

Lionel Barrymore and Joel McCrea in One Man's Journey, *a critical and popular success*

Alvah Bessie, Albert Maltz, Samuel Ornitz, Herbert Biberman, Ring Lardner, Jr., Lester Cole, and Edward Dmytryk, seven of the Hollywood Ten in Washington, D.C., in 1948 awaiting sentencing by the District Court

nitz's other Republic films were *Two Wise Maids* (1937) and *King of the Newsboys* (1938), about a slum dweller (Lew Ayres) who finds romance despite his poverty.

It Could Happen to You (1937) is a sardonic look at office politics. Office worker MacKinley Winslow (Stu Erwin) finds a dead body after an office party; he and his wife (Gloria Stuart) use this information to blackmail Winslow's way to a vice-presidential position. Budd Schulberg and Ornitz coauthored *Little Orphan Annie* for Paramount in 1938. Critics were somewhat dismayed by this film version of Harold Gray's popular comic strip, which centered more on the prizefighter Annie befriends than on Annie herself. *A Miracle on Main Street* (1940) is about a singer (Margo) who plans to adopt a baby, only to be stopped by her criminal husband (Walter Abel).

Ornitz returned to Republic studios to write *Three Faces West* (1940), about a dust bowl community helping an Austrian doctor (Charles Coburn) escape from the Nazis. Ornitz's last screenplay, *Circumstantial Evidence* (1945), was written for 20th Century-Fox. It is the story of an innocent man accused of murder.

When the House Un-American Activities Committee began investigating the possible influence of the Communist party in Hollywood, Ornitz, an outspoken supporter of the party, was one of the first ten witnesses—known as the Hollywood Ten—called to testify. Although he had not written a screenplay for some time, his outrage at the threat of political repression in the film industry compelled him to take a stand. Like all the other witnesses, Ornitz refused to confirm or deny his status as a party member, or as a member of the Screenwriters Guild. Instead, he prepared a statement defending his right to silence and accusing the committee of racism and anti-Semitism, but he was not allowed to read it. He was found guilty of contempt of Congress and sentenced to one year in prison in Springfield, Missouri. He was also blacklisted in Hollywood, unable to get any more film work.

Unlike most of the other screenwriters who were put on the blacklist, Ornitz never took any

sub-rosa screenwriting assignments. While in prison, he learned he was dying of cancer and decided to devote his time to writing novels. His final work, *Bride of the Sabbath* (1951), is a historical novel recording the way in which the first two generations of Jewish people in America grappled with their identity. Ornitz died of a cerebral hemorrhage in 1957.

John Paxton

(21 March 1911-5 January 1985)

Ellen Feldman

MOTION PICTURES: *My Pal, Wolf* (RKO, 1944), screenplay by Paxton, Lillie Hayward, and Leonard Praskins;

Murder, My Sweet (RKO, 1945), screenplay;

Cornered (RKO, 1946), screenplay;

Crack-Up (RKO, 1946), screen story and screenplay by Paxton, Ben Bengal, and Ray Spencer;

Crossfire (RKO, 1947), screenplay;

So Well Remembered (RKO, 1948), screenplay;

Rope of Sand (Paramount, 1949), additional dialogue;

Of Men and Music (20th Century-Fox, 1951), screen story and screenplay by Paxton, Liam O'Brien, Harry Kurnitz, and David Epstein;

Fourteen Hours (20th Century-Fox, 1951), screenplay;

The Wild One (Columbia, 1954), screenplay;

The Cobweb (M-G-M, 1955), screenplay;

A Prize of Gold (Columbia, 1955), screenplay by Paxton and Robert H. Buckner;

How to Murder a Rich Uncle (Columbia, 1957), screenplay by Paxton and Robert H. Buckner;

Pickup Alley (Columbia, 1957), screenplay;

On the Beach (United Artists, 1960), screenplay;

Kotch (Cinerama, 1971), screenplay.

TELEVISION: *The Great Man's Whiskers* (ABC, 1973), teleplay.

John Paxton's work is distinguished by the mating of socially significant themes with potent drama. His choice of themes reflects his interest in probing contemporary problems; anti-Semitism,

fascism, juvenile delinquency, suicide, and nuclear war were among the topics he addressed in his screenplays. Critics have praised his lack of didacticism and his ability to create suspenseful drama.

Paxton was born in Kansas City, Missouri, as he described years later at a Friends of UCLA Library screening of his film *Kotch* (1971), "under towering elms and maples, long gone, on Victor Street.... Happy boyhood in the Midwest, great deal of it riding free on trains alone or with my father, who managed dining cars, railroad hotels; also on farms in Kansas and Colorado...." Paxton attended Kansas City's Central High School where he joined the literary society, which forced him into writing under the threat of a fine.

At the University of Missouri Paxton studied journalism—it "had the reputation of being easy"—rather than the acting he was interested in, because he was a stutterer. He was sent for voice re-education to overcome this problem. He graduated with what he called "a spurious degree in journalism" in 1934. In 1935 a relative who was Katharine Cornell's press agent got him a job working on a playwriting contest sponsored by the Theatre Guild in New York. Paxton's next job (from 1937 to 1938) was as associate editor of *Stage* magazine, where he was encouraged to do whatever he wanted. There, in what he called the dungeon, he met Adrian Scott, who was later to give Paxton the career opportunity of adapting Raymond Chandler's *Farewell, My Lovely* for film. After *Stage* folded, he worked as a free-lance author (1939-

John Paxton

1941), and then as publicist for the New York Theater Guild (1941).

Paxton came to Hollywood in 1942 and soon became a scriptwriter at RKO. At one point, he was looking for a place to live in the country. Bill Goodley, his dentist, who jointly owned a thousand chickens with Sam Goldwyn's ailing publicist, Johnny Miles, suggested Paxton move into Miles's farmhouse and take over the care of the chickens while Miles went east for an operation. Paxton moved in with the Goodleys and continued to care for the chickens, even after Miles died and his widow, Sarah Jane, returned home. Paxton and Sarah Jane Miles were married in December 1948.

Paxton's first film for RKO, *My Pal, Wolf* (1944), had been written with two other screenwriters, Lillie Hayward and Leonard Praskins. It was received by critics as an unexciting melodrama of a girl's escapades with an army dog. This unpromising first assignment was followed by a more important project, possibly the most important of Paxton's career. Brought in by producer Adrian Scott, he was teamed up with director Edward

Dmytryk in the endeavor of making a film of Chandler's novel *Farewell, My Lovely*. Paxton, Dmytryk, and Scott were well-suited to one another, and they remained a team after completing *Murder, My Sweet* (as the film was titled) in 1945, making three more films: *Cornered* (1946), *Crossfire* (1947), and *So Well Remembered* (1948).

Murder, My Sweet concerns the gradual deepening of private investigator Philip Marlowe's (Dick Powell) entrapment by the underworld characters he is hired to investigate. The story centers on the simultaneous investigation of two linked cases: one to find the former girlfriend of the barely rational, easily provoked Moose Malloy (Mike Mazurki), the other to find a missing jade necklace, an object at the center of a blackmail scheme planned by the dispassionate Jules Amthor (Otto Druger). Marlowe can operate as a reasoning detective, but too frequently his passions and confusions hamper his investigation. Although Chandler's works had been filmed before, this was the first time the Marlowe character had appeared in a picture. As portrayed in *Murder, My Sweet,* he is more vulnerable than the version in a later, better-known adaptation of another Chandler novel, *The Big Sleep* (1946). The film emphasizes Marlowe's point of view by retaining the first-person narration of the novel. His moral detachment from the scenes he witnesses is conveyed by the ironic comments delivered in voice-over narration. Scott had hoped to cast Humphrey Bogart, or at least John Garfield, for the Marlowe role. When Dick Powell was cast, Paxton was astonished that the former band singer was playing Marlowe for laughs and "creating a flip detective." But Chandler wrote that he was pleased with the choice of Powell.

Murder, My Sweet was one of the earliest and most influential works of the film noir genre, which flourished throughout the 1940s primarily as a result of the social change and unrest brought about by the war. All of Paxton's remaining screenplays for RKO were film noir, and all of them dealt with the lingering effects of World War II. *Cornered* reunited most of the creative team behind *Murder, My Sweet,* including Paxton, Scott, Dmytryk, Powell, and cinematographer Harry J. Wild. Powell played Canadian pilot Laurence Gerard, a recently freed prisoner of war seeking revenge on Marcel Jarnac (Luther Adler), the Vichy officer responsible for the death of Gerard's wife. He trails Jarnac to Argentina, where he finds a secret anti-Fascist group in operation. Gerard refuses to join the group, and tracks and kills Jarnac on his own. Made during the final days of the war—it was completed just two

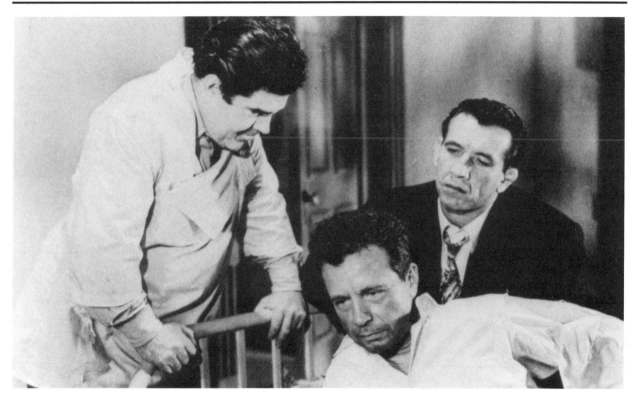

Dick Powell (center) and Mike Mazurki (right) in Murder, My Sweet, *the first film to feature Raymond Chandler's private investigator Philip Marlowe*

days after the Japanese surrendered—*Cornered* is not just a well-crafted mystery, but a study of the disruptive effect the war had on people's lives; nearly every character in the film lives an uncertain and aimless existence. Gerard lives only to avenge his wife's murder and frequently lapses into a trance as a result of his stay in a P.O.W. camp. The German expatriates live in luxury in Argentina, but they are also the targets of the anti-Fascist group, so their luxury cannot last.

Crack-Up (1946) was the only film of this period Paxton worked on without Scott or Dmytryk. It was a rare collaborative effort, written with Ben Bengal and Ray Spencer and based on a short story by Fredric Brown. George Steele (Pat O'Brien) is a tour guide and lecturer on art at the New York Metropolitan Museum. Years before, he had helped identify some Nazi art forgeries. His erratic behavior one evening causes him to be accused of drunkenness, but he has actually been drugged by an art forger who is afraid Steele will discover his plot to replace the museum's paintings with his counterfeits. Steele is discredited and eventually framed for murder but is able to find the mastermind behind the scheme.

Two of the motifs of *Murder, My Sweet,* the

examination of moral corruption and the use of first-person narration, were used again in *Crossfire.* The initial scene of the film depicts a murder; the remainder of the film concerns the search for the murderer, one among a group of soldiers. The crime appears motiveless until it is gradually determined that the victim, a civilian, was killed because he was a Jew. (In the novel on which the film is based, *The Brick Foxhole* by Richard Brooks, the victim is a homosexual, but the filmmakers changed this in order to present the then-more-relevant topic of anti-Semitism.)

The time immediately preceding the murder is depicted in flashbacks, but they are subjective flashbacks, representing the points of view of two characters, including the murderer (Robert Ryan). This technique allows audiences to see the murderer as a deceitful bigot, but it also renders the film somewhat static and denies it the subtlety normally found in Paxton's work. *Crossfire* is also one of the few Paxton films in which a character seems to be directly lecturing the audience—there is an interruption of the action toward the film's climax in which the detective (Robert Young) investigating the murder delivers a moralistic tale about the nature of anti-Semitism. But despite these flaws, *Cross-*

Robert Ryan as the rabid anti-Semite and Sam Levene as the murder victim in the controversial Crossfire, *based on Richard Brooks's novel* The Brick Foxhole

fire is still an effective film. It was particularly well-regarded upon its release, when the importance of its message seemed to outweigh any shortcomings the film might have. It earned Paxton an Academy Award nomination, but the 1947 Oscar went to *Miracle on 34th Street.*

After completing *Crossfire,* Paxton wrote *So Well Remembered* (1948), about a newspaper editor (John Mills) who crusades for better living conditions in a British factory town. Paxton then left RKO, and worked for several studios. After providing additional dialogue for Paramount's *Rope of Sand* (1949), a desert adventure film, Paxton worked briefly at 20th Century-Fox, where he wrote one of his more highly regarded films, *Fourteen Hours* (1951). Directed by Henry Hathaway, the film is based on a true story about a young man's attempt to commit suicide by jumping from a hotel

window. Paxton took this material and created a drama centering on the alienation of contemporary urban life. He focused attention on the interaction between the individual and the depersonalized, destructive mob in the street below. The script received a Writers Guild nomination and the film was named one of the year's ten best by the *New York Times.*

Another socially conscious filmmaker, Stanley Kramer, hired Paxton to write the now classic *The Wild One* (1954), about two small towns invaded by a motorcycle gang. Paxton built a plot in which contemporary social issues are played out among a small group of people. The film has the structure of a parable: a motorcycle gang, representing the lawlessness and impulsiveness of a group uncontrolled by society's institutions, invades two communities (each with its own level of social

Marlon Brando as the motorcycle-gang leader in
The Wild One

responsibility) and tests their moral strength. The first community's stability is demonstrated by the internalization of the law by the citizenry and by the law enforcement of the police. This society casts the gang out. The second town's response is a mixture of fear and attraction, reflecting its moral malaise. The citizens react in turn by welcoming the gang's business, weakly trying to placate it, or by resorting to mob violence. The different nature of the two towns' law enforcers represents an opposition present in many of Paxton's films: between the well-meaning, but ineffectual humanist, and the savvy tactician who is finally the more effective humanist.

The gang itself has largely been formed in opposition to the stifling restrictions of society. The liberation is not satisfying nor is it portrayed as a viable alternative to society, partly because its leader, Johnny (Marlon Brando), still harbors a residual longing for society's acceptance. He may be an outsider, but he gives expression to and provides release for conditions—such as boredom, malaise, and frustration—experienced by the societally constricted. Unfortunately, Johnny is romanticized, and the town leaders are too bland to arouse the audience's sense of approval. Still, this movie re-

mains one of the best attempts to examine the alienation of youth in the 1950s.

Paxton's *The Cobweb* (1955) was a study of the problems of the patients in a mental clinic, and an examination of the interaction between the patients and staff. Directed by Vincente Minnelli, the film is interesting but overlong. Paxton next wrote three crime films for a British company, Warwick Productions. The story of an attempt to steal a large shipment of gold in Berlin, *A Prize of Gold* (1955) was written in collaboration with Robert Buckner and directed by Mark Robson. Paxton produced, as well as wrote, *How to Murder a Rich Uncle* (1957), a comedy about a wealthy man (Charles Coburn) whose family tries to kill him. *Pickup Alley* (1957) is about a federal agent (Victor Mature) battling drug smugglers.

The powerful *On the Beach* (1960) signaled Paxton's return to the gripping drama and contemporary social issues that mark the best of his work. Stanley Kramer produced and directed this film, which centers on the reactions of the last survivors of a nuclear holocaust who have only a few months to live. It is indicative of Paxton's work in that the central focus is upon the characters' sense of impending doom rather than upon the dramatization of the war itself. In fact, the protagonists in the war are never mentioned. Rather than a partisan approach, Paxton prefers to make a general statement about people's will to survive.

In 1971 Paxton wrote his last film, *Kotch*, about a seventy-two-year-old man (Walter Matthau) with a zest for life. When his family decides to place him in a nursing home, Kotch flees and eventually takes up with another social misfit, an unmarried pregnant teenager (Deborah Winters). Like *Murder, My Sweet* and *Crossfire*, *Kotch* relies extensively on flashbacks; some of the film's best moments come from Kotch's reflections on his life with his now-deceased wife (Ellen Geer). Paxton won a Writers Guild Award for the film.

During the course of Paxton's career in Hollywood he and his wife had been building their home, "Hill House," in Laurel Canyon. Almost finished with their work there, the Paxtons were taking a holiday during the 1984 Christmas season, when Sarah Jane, returning from a walk, found John slumped in a chair (he had suffered from angina and chronic obstructive pulmonary disease). "I'm dying," he said. "I've run out of breath. I called the paramedics. It's been a good life. Thank you."

John Paxton worked within the limits of the studio system, becoming part of a team and staying

Gregory Peck and Fred Astaire in On the Beach, *an examination of the psychological effects of nuclear war*

within the familiar genres of the times. Yet his films bear his signature in both tone and theme. His scripts develop narratives which depict, in microcosm, a social dilemma of large dimensions. A small group of people is isolated in each film, and a network of interrelationships is carefully developed. Paxton creates strong and vivid characters. They are, however, emotionally and ideologically narrowly defined. By proscribing the characters' dimensions, he can give them appropriate positions in the microcosm. The exciting drama and full-bodied expressiveness of the characters prevent one from thinking of them as abstractions.

Writing of himself, in the third person singular, he once gave an overview of his career that reveals the pleasure he took from his career and the good humor he brought to life:

> To California in the Forties, started screenwriting by accident, been at it sporadically ever since. . . . Wide variety of films, some considered trail-blazers or socially significant, but really much happier with comedy. . . . Slightly singed by Senators Thomas and McCarthy, but never suffered or put in

jail, as were his close friends . . . MURDER, MY SWEET, a Raymond Chandler adaptation, influenced a flood of private-eye nonsense that followed in movies and TV. . . . CROSSFIRE, an early message picture (Anti-Semitism) in melodramatic clothing probably influenced the grim, terse style of such shows as *Dragnet* . . . THE WILD ONE made Marlon Brando the idol of the Hell's Angels generation, spurred the sale of leather jackets and was the embarrassed parent of such motorcycle cliches as "Go-Go, Man" and "Varoom, Varoom" . . . FOURTEEN HOURS, a semi-journalistic cliffhanger, eventually became highly regarded by addicts of the late and late-late shows . . . ON THE BEACH imagined a world with hardly anybody left but Ava Gardner and Gregory Peck. . . . HOW TO MURDER A RICH UNCLE was fun and games, a cheerful black comedy that perhaps came too soon and disillusioned him about producing his own material . . . dismayed by one called THE COBWEB, believes it probably set psychiatry back a good twenty years. . . . Is happier with KOTCH than any of these, or any of the ones lying around on shelves somewhere, unmade . . .

The current use of the term "film-maker" makes him irrational. . . . Once a dedicated woodsman and trout fisherman, but no longer. The ground got too hard for sleeping and the trout started looking at him in an unpleasant way.

References:

"Symposium on Screenwriters," *Film Comment*, 6 (Winter 1970-1971);

John D. Weaver, "John Paxton: Mr. Fix-It to the End," *Los Angeles Times*, 10 March 1985 ;

Weaver, "John Weaver on John Paxton," *UCLA Librarian*, 31 (July-August 1978).

S. J. Perelman
(1 February 1904-17 October 1979)

Christopher Adcock

See also the Perelman entry in *DLB 11, American Humorists, 1800-1950.*

MOTION PICTURES: *Monkey Business* (Paramount, 1931), screenplay by Perelman, Will B. Johnstone, and Arthur Sheekman;

Horse Feathers (Paramount, 1932), screenplay by Perelman, Bert Kalmar, and Harry Ruby;

Sitting Pretty (Paramount, 1933), screenplay by Perelman, Jack McGowan, and Lou Breslow;

Paris Interlude (M-G-M, 1934), screenplay by Perelman and Laura Perelman, from their play *All Good Americans;*

Florida Special (Paramount, 1936), screenplay by Perelman, Laura Perelman, David Boehm, and Marguerite Roberts;

Ambush (Paramount, 1939), screenplay by Perelman and Laura Perelman;

Boy Trouble (Paramount, 1939), screenplay by Perelman and Laura Perelman;

The Golden Fleecing (M-G-M, 1940), screenplay by Perelman, Laura Perelman, and Marion Parsonnet;

Around the World in 80 Days (United Artists, 1956), screenplay by Perelman, James Poe, and John Farrow.

PLAY PRODUCTIONS: *The Third Little Show,* sketches by Perelman, New York, Music Box Theatre, 1 June 1931;

Walk a Little Faster, sketches by Perelman and Robert MacGunigle, New York, St. James Theatre, 7 December 1932;

All Good Americans, by Perelman and Laura Perelman, New York, Henry Miller's Theatre, 5 December 1933;

Two Weeks with Pay, sketches by Perelman, tour, 1940;

The Night Before Christmas, by Perelman and Laura Perelman, New York, Morosco Theatre, 10 April 1941;

One Touch of Venus, by Perelman and Ogden Nash, New York, Imperial Theatre, 7 October 1943;

Sweet Bye and Bye, by Perelman and Al Hirschfeld, New Haven, Conn., Shubert Theatre, 10 October 1946;

The Beauty Part, by Perelman and Nash, New York, Music Box Theatre, 26 December 1962.

BOOKS: *Dawn Ginsbergh's Revenge* (New York: Liveright, 1929);

Parlor, Bedlam and Bath, by Perelman and Quentin J. Reynolds (New York: Liveright, 1930);

Strictly from Hunger (New York: Random House, 1937);

Look Who's Talking! (New York: Random House, 1940);

The Night Before Christmas, by Perelman and Laura Perelman (New York: French, 1942);

The Dream Department (New York: Random House, 1943);

One Touch of Venus, by Perelman and Ogden Nash (Boston: Little, Brown, 1944);

S. J. and Laura Perelman in Hollywood

The Best of S. J. Perelman (New York: Random House, 1944; London: Heinemann, 1945); republished as *Crazy Like a Fox* (New York: Modern Library, 1947);

Keep it Crisp (New York: Random House, 1946; London: Heinemann, 1947);

Acres and Pains (New York: Reynal & Hitchcock, 1947; London: Heinemann, 1948);

Westward Ha! or Around the World in Eighty Clichés (New York: Simon & Schuster, 1948; London: Reinhardt & Evans, 1949);

Listen to the Mocking Bird (New York: Simon & Schuster, 1949; London: Reinhardt & Evans, 1951);

The Swiss Family Perelman (New York: Simon & Schuster, 1950; London: Reinhardt & Evans, 1951);

A Child's Garden of Curses (London: Heinemann, 1951)—includes *Crazy Like a Fox, Keep it Crisp,* and *Acres and Pains;*

The Ill-Tempered Clavichord (New York: Simon & Schuster, 1952; London: Max Reinhardt, 1953);

Hold That Christmas Tiger! (Berkeley: Hart, 1954);

Perelman's Home Companion: A Collector's Item (the Collector Being S. J. Perelman) of 36 Otherwise Unavailable Pieces by Himself (New York: Simon & Schuster, 1955);

The Road to Miltown; or, Under the Spreading Atrophy (New York: Simon & Schuster, 1957); republished as *Bite on the Bullet; or, Under the Spreading Atrophy* (London: Heinemann, 1957);

The Most of S. J. Perelman (New York: Simon & Schuster, 1958; London: Heinemann, 1959);

The Rising Gorge (New York: Simon & Schuster, 1961; London: Heinemann, 1962);

The Beauty Part, by Perelman and Nash (New York: Simon & Schuster, 1963);

Chicken Inspector No. 23 (New York: Simon & Schuster, 1966; London: Hodder & Stoughton, 1967);

Baby, It's Cold Inside (New York: Simon & Schuster, 1970; London: Weidenfeld & Nicolson, 1970);

Vinegar Puss (New York: Simon & Schuster, 1975; London: Weidenfeld & Nicolson, 1976);

Eastward Ha! (New York: Simon & Schuster, 1977; London: Eyre Methuen, 1978);

The Last Laugh (New York: Simon & Schuster, 1981).

TELEVISION: *Omnibus* (NBC, 1957-1959), scripts;
"The Changing Ways of Love," *Seven Lively Arts* (CBS, 3 November 1957);
Elizabeth Taylor's London (CBS, 6 October 1963).

Sidney Joseph Perelman was born in Brooklyn, New York, to immigrant Joseph and Sophia Perelman. When Perelman was still a child his family moved to Providence, Rhode Island, where his father worked as a machinist, a dry goods merchant, and a would-be poultry farmer. Young Perelman, whose ambition was to become a cartoonist, practiced his drawing on cardboard from his father's dry goods store and spent many hours reading popular novels and going to movies; these books and motion pictures later helped influence his satiric style and his choice of subject matter.

From 1921 to 1925 Perelman attended Brown University as a premedical student. One of his classmates was Nathanael West, who's sister Perelman married. While in school, he began contributing cartoons to the campus humor magazine *Brown Jug;* he later became its editor. After graduation he became a regular contributor to the humor weekly *Judge,* and it was for this magazine that he first began writing humorous essays. But his satiric style did not develop until he went to work for *College Humor* in 1930. Influenced by such writers as Donald Ogden Stewart, Ring Lardner, and Robert Benchley, Perelman's work was a mixture of parody, puns, and non sequitur; his gift for wordplay, evident in his books, plays, and scripts, helped shape twentieth-century American humor.

In 1929 Perelman married Laura West, who collaborated with him on his screenplays *Paris Interlude* (1934), *Florida Special* (1936), *Boy Trouble* (1939), *Ambush* (1939), and *The Golden Fleecing* (1940), and on his plays *All Good Americans* (1933) and *The Night Before Christmas* (1941). The Perelmans had two children, Adam and Abby Laura.

Perelman's first book, *Dawn Ginsbergh's Revenge,* was published in 1929, and it was this book that led to Perelman's filmwriting career. Groucho Marx had been asked to provide a blurb for the book's dust jacket; two years later, when the Marx Brothers were searching for a project for radio, Groucho remembered Perelman and hired him to write a script. Working with Will B. Johnstone, Perelman devised a story of four stowaways on a luxury liner. The Marxes read the treatment and decided to use it for their next movie rather than for a radio show; Perelman and Johnstone were brought to California and put on Paramount Studio's payroll. Their screenplay went through several drafts (with another writer, Arthur Sheekman, eventually brought in) before the Marxes were pleased; the movie, *Monkey Business,* was finally released in 1931.

Like most of the Marx Brothers' movies, *Monkey Business* is virtually without plot—for the first half of the film, the brothers stow away on a ship and wreak havoc on the unsuspecting crew and travelers, and in the second part they go ashore and somehow become involved with gangsters. But plotting is clearly not important here; humor is, and the Marxes proved to be ideal performers of Perelman's material. He could introduce characters and situations at will, with no regard for logic, and Groucho Marx in particular was well suited for Perelman's wordplay.

Monkey Business, the Marx Brothers' third

Harpo, Zeppo, Chico, and Groucho Marx in Monkey Business, *Perelman's first film for the Marx Brothers*

Groucho Marx (center) in Horse Feathers. *Though Perelman's humor was well-suited to the Marx Brothers' technique, he was not fond of them.*

film, was well received by critics and audiences, and Perelman, who had mixed feelings about Hollywood and the Marx Brothers, worked on another picture for them, *Horse Feathers* (1932), the next year. Groucho played the head of Huxley University; desperate for a winning football team he attempts to recruit some new players and winds up with Chico and Harpo. Some gangsters who have wagered on the final game of the season take the new players prisoner, but they escape and win a zany game. Directed by Norman McLeod, the screenplay was a product of the work of Perelman, Bert Kalmar, and Harry Ruby.

Never happy in Hollywood—he once called it "a dreary industrial town controlled by hoodlums of enormous wealth,"—Perelman wrote only one more screenplay before leaving Paramount, *Sitting Pretty* (1933). The movie is a Hollywood satire that allowed Perelman to display some of the low regard

he had for the film community. Two aspiring songwriters (Jack Haley and Jack Oakie) hitchhike to Hollywood hoping for movie careers. They meet a series of eccentric characters, including a producer (Lew Cody), an agent (Gregory Ratoff), and a vampish actress (Thelma Todd).

After returning to New York, Perelman began writing for the stage. He began with two collections of sketches, *The Third Little Show* (produced in 1931) and *Walk a Little Faster* (produced in 1932) which he wrote with Robert MacGunigle. He wrote his first full play, *All Good Americans,* in 1933. The story of Americans living in Paris was a mild success, and when M-G-M optioned it for filming, Perelman and Laura Perelman wrote the screenplay. He returned to work for Paramount in 1935 and remained there until 1940; all of his films during this period were written with Laura Perelman. Their first screenplay was for *Paris Interlude,* which

Cantinflas, David Niven, Marlene Dietrich, and Frank Sinatra in Around the World in Eighty Days, *which Perelman referred to as "Around the Bend in Eighty Days"*

they adapted from their play *All Good Americans.* Next came *Florida Special,* a vehicle for Jack Oakie that was conceived as a comic *Grand Hotel* in a railroad setting. On a Florida-bound train, salesman Bangs Carter (Oakie) meddles in the affairs of most of his fellow passengers, including a group of thieves trying to get the jewels of greedy Simeon Stafford (Claude Gillingwater).

Partly because Perelman had other commitments, including regular contributions to *The New Yorker,* and partly because some film projects fell through, it was three more years before another of Perelman's scripts was filmed. In *Boy Trouble,* a childless couple, the Fitches (Charlie Ruggles and Mary Boland) take two orphan boys (Billy Lee and Donald O'Connor) into their home. At first Mr. Fitch is unable to accept the boys, but finally the four become a family. *Boy Trouble* is a sentimental film, unusually so for Perelman, but was highly popular nonetheless.

Ambush was Perelman's final script for Paramount. A group of bank robbers escape after taking a secretary (Gladys Swarthout) hostage. They hijack a truck, and she falls in love with the driver. After completing this film, the Perelmans wrote a screenplay more typical of their style for M-G-M: *The Golden Fleecing,* a witty comedy. Insurance salesman Henry Twinkle (Lew Ayres) sells a policy to gangster Gus Fender (Lloyd Nolan), then must secretly protect Nolan from encountering the violent end he is almost sure to meet.

Perelman contributed to only two more films before leaving Hollywood again. He worked on the screen story for *Larceny, Inc.* (1942), which was based on his play *The Night Before Christmas.* It was a well-received comedy about a trio of ex-convicts (Edward G. Robinson, Broderick Crawford, and Edward Brophy) whose luggage store is a front for their crimes. With his wife, Perelman worked on an M-G-M musical, *Greenwich Village* (1944), in which a serious musician is forced to write songs for a Broadway revue. Perelman called the movie "loathsome" and declined any screen credit.

For over a decade, Perelman stayed away from Hollywood, devoting his time to essays and plays. He was finally lured back in 1956 when producer Mike Todd hired him to rework James Poe's adaptation of *Around the World in 80 Days.* The story of Phileas Fogg and his bet that he could make the trip around the world provided much opportunity for Perelman to develop a variety of comic vignettes, and David Niven's urbane portrayal of Fogg allowed Perelman's wit to shine through. The script is intelligent and amusing, though most of the success of the picture may be attributed to the nearly four dozen famous performers who took cameo roles in the film. In any case, collaborators Poe, Perelman, and John Farrow received an Academy Award for their work, and the film was voted best picture.

Around the World in 80 Days was Perelman's final screenplay. He had found working on the film to be an extremely unpleasant experience (as he revealed in "Around the Bend in Eighty Days," a series of six articles he wrote in the early 1970s) and firmly decided to have no more to do with

Hollywood. He spent the remainder of his life working on essays and articles, publishing eight more collections before his death. When Laura Perelman died in 1970, Perelman immigrated to England, but returned to the United States a few years later. In 1978 he was presented with a special National Book Award for his contribution to American letters. S. J. Perelman died in October 1979.

Interviews:

William Cole and George Plimpton, "S. J. Perelman," *Paris Review,* 30 (Fall 1963): 147;

William Zinsser, "That Perelman of Great Price is 65," *New York Times Magazine,* 26 January 1969, pp. 24-27, 72, 74, 76.

Bibliography:

Steven H. Gale, "Sidney Joseph Perelman: Twenty Years of American Humor," *Bulletin of Bibliography,* 29 (January-March 1972): 10-12.

Reference:

J. A. Ward, "The Hollywood Metaphor: The Marx Brothers, S. J. Perelman, Nathanael West," *Southern Review,* 12 (Summer 1976): 659-672.

Eleanor Perry
(Eleanor Bayer)
(1915-14 March 1981)

Thomas Slater
Northwest Missouri State University

MOTION PICTURES: *David and Lisa* (Continental, 1962);
Ladybug, Ladybug (United Artists, 1963), screenplay;
The Swimmer (Columbia, 1968), screenplay;
Trilogy (Allied Artists, 1969), screenplay by Perry and Truman Capote;
Last Summer (Frank Perry-Alsid, 1969), screenplay;
Diary of a Mad Housewife (Universal, 1970), screenplay;
The Lady in the Car with Glasses and a Gun (Columbia, 1970), screenplay by Perry and Richard Harris;

Eleanor Perry

The Deadly Trap (National General Pictures, 1972), screenplay by Perry and Sidney Buchman;
The Man Who Loved Cat Dancing (M-G-M, 1973), screenplay.

PLAY PRODUCTION: *Third Best Sport*, as Eleanor Bayer, with L. G. Bayer, New York, Theatre Guild, 1958.

BOOKS: *Paper Chase*, by Perry and Leo G. Bayer, as Oliver Weld Bayer (New York: Doubleday, Doran, 1943);
No Little Enemy, as Oliver Weld Bayer (New York: Doubleday, Doran, 1944);
An Eye for an Eye, as Oliver Weld Bayer (New York: Doubleday, Doran, 1945);
Brutal Question, as Oliver Weld Bayer (New York: Doubleday, 1947);
Dirty Hands Across the Sea, as Eleanor Bayer, with L. G. Bayer (Cleveland: Collins-World, 1952);
The Swimmer (New York: Pyramid, 1968);
Trilogy: An Experiment in Multimedia, by Perry, Truman Capote, and Frank Perry (New York: Macmillan, 1969);
Blue Pages (Philadelphia: Lippincott, 1979).

TELEVISION: *A Christmas Memory* (1966);
The House Without a Christmas Tree (ABC, 1973), teleplay.

PERIODICAL PUBLICATION: "We're All Human," *New York Times*, 17 December 1972, II:19.

Eleanor Perry's screenwriting career covers only an eleven-year period, but it is still a remarkable one, including such films as *David and Lisa* (1962), for which she was nominated for an Academy Award, *Last Summer* (1969), and *Diary of a Mad Housewife* (1970), all made under the direction of her husband Frank Perry. The screenplays of Eleanor Perry generally concentrated on an individual's search for identity, and in that sense they were reflective of her life: her career was full of struggle against the Hollywood establishment and against male domination in the motion picture business. Perry's fight for more power for women in the industry led her into producing in the 1970s, though only one of her proposed projects, *The Man Who Loved Cat Dancing* (1973), ever reached the screen, and that was a film over which she had little control.

Perry was born Eleanor Rosenfeld in Cleveland, Ohio, the daughter of a pharmaceutical company executive. She received a master's degree in psychiatric social work from Western Reserve University. Her education provided a good background for the subjects of her screenplays. After graduation, she married Leo G. Bayer, a lawyer. They had two children, Bill and Ann, both of whom went on to have writing careers. While in Cleveland, Perry became a prominent figure within the local literary and theater circles.

She wrote plays and mystery novels with her husband under the joint pseudonym Oliver Weld Bayer; she also wrote by herself, under the name Eleanor Bayer. She went to New York in 1958 for the production of their play *Third Best Sport* by the Theatre Guild. There she met producer Frank Perry, sixteen years her junior; she never returned to her life in Cleveland.

In 1961 Perry's daughter brought the book *David and Lisa* home with her from college and showed it to her mother. The short novel, by Dr. Theodore Isaac Rubin, was little more than two fictionalized case histories with dialogue about two teenagers in a suburban mental institution who develop a mutually curative love. After reading the book, the Perrys agreed it would make a good movie; despite having no experience with screenplays, they took on the project themselves. Eleanor Perry wrote a script that expanded the book, and Frank Perry directed. But no Hollywood studio would finance the project. The Perrys raised money the same way they would for a play, selling shares for $312.50 apiece. They paid $2,000 to an Armenian church group for the use of an abandoned mansion and shot the movie in twenty-five days, screening rushes on two pieces of paper tacked up on their hotel room wall at night. The actors, Keir Dullea and Janet Margolin, were similarly inexperienced but turned in fine performances and were eventually named best actor and actress at the San Francisco International Film Festival. *David and Lisa* gained other honors as well, winning best film by a new director at the Venice Film Festival and being named best movie of 1962 by *Time* mag-

Carrie Snodgress and Richard Benjamin in Diary of a Mad Housewife, *the last film Eleanor and Frank Perry made together*

azine. Frank Perry was also nominated for an Academy Award for best director.

The success of *David and Lisa* marked the beginning of a decade-long fight with the movie industry for the Perrys. (Eleanor Perry characterized her entire career in 1970 when she remarked, "I hate the establishment.") In their next two movies, the Perrys continued to struggle both artistically and with Hollywood. In both cases, they were unsuccessful.

Based on fact, *Ladybug, Ladybug* (1963) is about a group of rural schoolchildren who are suddenly caught in the situation of not knowing whether a civil defense alarm is indicating an actual attack or merely a test. The dramatic possibilities of the incident proved too slight for a feature film; at the conclusion, one youngster is refused admittance to a bomb shelter by two others, but by then it has already been revealed that the alarm is merely a test. The situation provides the only tension and dramatic irony of the movie, which was not enough to redeem it.

In 1968 the Perrys collaborated on *The Swimmer*, based on a John Cheever story. Eleanor Perry had to expand a short work into a feature-length film. She and her husband might have done a good job on the project, but that will never be known; less than half of what Frank Perry filmed ended up in the final version. Three other directors, including Sydney Pollack, worked on the movie after Frank Perry had finished with it. Still, the Perrys were demonstrating their affinity for small, personal stories. *The Swimmer* is a tale of an aging suburbanite (Burt Lancaster) who is forced to face certain ugly truths about himself. *New York Times* critic Vincent Canby remarked, "Although literal in style, the film has the shape of an open-ended hallucination. It is a grim, disturbing and sometimes funny view of a very small, very special segment of upper-middle-class American life. As a box-office proposition it obviously is an uncertain quantity and one that few major producers might have undertaken without Lancaster's name."

In their final three movies together, the Perrys maintained their intimate exposition approach, but they were also able to incorporate sufficient amounts of dramatic tension and thus achieve greater success. *Last Summer* (1969) was based on Evan Hunter's novel of the same title. The story is about three adolescents, Sandy (Barbara Hershey), Peter (Bruce Davison), and Dan (Richard Thomas), who have a very close and apparently rewarding relationship. But underneath their pleasant friendship and personalities are uncertainties, sexual longings, and desires for power that eventually emerge. Rhoda (Cathy Burns), a somewhat shy and awkward girl, enters the group. At the end, she is raped by Peter and Dan with Sandy's help. Canby indicated that in this movie, for the first time, Eleanor's script was of greater quality than Frank's direction: "Mrs. Perry's screenplay, like the novel, is tough and laconic and exclusively centered on the young people, an isolation that spares us most of the familiar, easy explanations about How They Got That Way. With the parents little more than illusive, dim, off-screen voices *Last Summer* can unfold as a simple, summary horror story." *Last Summer* was shocking to some, but it emphasized the theme of an individual's responsibility for his or her own actions.

The next Perry project was *Trilogy* (1969), a collection of three short films based on Truman Capote stories; the film was originally made for television. Perry collaborated with Capote on the scripts, one of which, "A Christmas Memory," won Perry her first Emmy award. Dialogue predominates over action in the stories, each an examination of human loneliness. The Perrys finally seemed to have hit the mark they had always been

aiming at. Howard Thompson remarked that *Trilogy* "quietly says and conveys more about the human heart and spirit than most of today's free-wheeling blastaways on the screen. Delicately, it towers."

The Perrys' final movie together was also their best. *Diary of a Mad Housewife* (1970) continued their focus on East-Coast, upper-middle-class people at some point of emotional crisis. Perry's screenplay exposed the social mannerisms of the self-consciously hip people whom she knew very well, demonstrating how a shallow personality can become a trap. The familiar settings of Manhattan apartments were also exploited to examine people dealing with enclosed spaces. Tina (Carrie Snodgress) is the housewife—mad at her husband Jonathan (Richard Benjamin) and being driven mad by him as well. Her husband, her obnoxious daughters, the family dog, and New York City itself all seem to be trying to drive her crazy. She attempts to escape by having an affair, but the man (Frank Langella) is a woman hater who adds to her torment. At the end, Jonathan is finally forced to face Tina's situation, but whether the marriage will survive has been left in doubt.

At the time of its release, *Diary of a Mad House-*

Sarah Miles and Burt Reynolds in The Man Who Loved Cat Dancing. *Perry was outraged when a rape scene was added to the film.*

wife was viewed by some critics as a feminist film, exposing the entrapment of the typical American housewife. The movie could also be seen as fitting in with the established formula of the responsible wife having to tolerate an incompetent husband; the movie was more comedy than drama. The conclusion left the wife with no means of escape, but three years later, Eleanor Perry claimed she would write the ending differently if she were writing it then: "I would carry it one step further, to show Tina liberating herself, but not through a man. She'd get a job, or go back to school, or whatever women do to liberate themselves."

Diary of a Mad Housewife may not have been a feminist picture, but it did mark the beginning of Perry's liberated thinking. At this time, Frank Perry obtained a divorce. Following her divorce, Perry became a vehement spokesperson for the women's movement, arguing that women needed to obtain positions of power in the movie industry; she led a feminist protest at the 1972 Cannes Film Festival. (Eight years after her divorce, Perry published a novel, *Blue Pages*, 1979, about a woman screenwriter who is exploited by her director husband.)

For her first projects on her own, Perry wrote the screenplays for two psychological thrillers: *The Lady in the Car with Glasses and a Gun* (1970) and *The Deadly Trap* (1972). In the first of these films, a secretary (Samantha Eggar) is invited to spend the weekend with her employer (Oliver Reed) and his wife (Stephane Audran) who are planning to frame her for a crime they committed and drive her insane. Perry adapted her screenplay from a highly regarded novel by French author Sebastien Japrisot, but was unable to transfer Japrisot's moody, existential prose to film, and the movie never completely works.

The Deadly Trap is possibly the worst movie of Perry's career. A former industrial spy (Frank Langella) refuses to cooperate with his early associates, who retaliate by terrorizing his neurotic wife (Faye Dunaway). Perry was only one of several writers who worked on the script (in the end she shared screen credit with Sidney Buchman), and though she was working with familiar material here—upper-middle-class ethics, neurotic housewives—she was never able to make the script anything more than a muddled thriller. Direction by the respected

French filmmaker René Clement did little to help.

In 1973 Perry coproduced *The Man Who Loved Cat Dancing* with Martin Poll. But her working relationship with Poll was poor, and at least five writers altered her script. She was appalled to see her protagonist (Sarah Miles) turned into a weak, ineffective sex object. Perry denounced a rape scene that was added to the film: "I thought she would defend herself; she would not be raped. But the director and my coproducer thought otherwise. The rape scene is in the film. One of the men told me, 'Well rape turns some men on.'" The film, about a frontier wife who becomes involved with an outlaw gang, was neither a critical nor box office success.

The Man Who Loved Cat Dancing was Perry's last screenplay. That same year she wrote one script for television, *The House Without a Christmas Tree*, about an embittered, widowed man (Jason Robards) who refuses to allow his daughter to buy a Christmas tree for their home. Perry won her second Emmy for her teleplay. She then abandoned scriptwriting and turned her time to producing, but none of her announced projects—"Clout," "Memoirs of an Ex-Prom Queen," "Hatter Fox"— ever made it to the screen.

Eleanor Perry died of cancer in 1981. She perhaps never realized her full potential, but she did write at least four memorable movies in a career spanning little more than a decade.

References:

"The Hard Way," *Time* (25 January 1963): 59, 61;

Aljean Harmetz, "Rape—an Ugly Movie Trend," *New York Times*, 30 September 1973, II:1;

Judy Klemesrud, "The Woman Who Hated 'Cat Dancing,'" *New York Times*, 29 July 1973, II:1;

Sue Nirenberg, "Collaboration Also Sets the Scene at Home," *House Beautiful*, 112 (August 1970): 72, 128-129;

Sharon Smith, *Women Who Make Movies* (New York: Hopkinson & Blake, 1975);

Kaye Sullivan, *Films For, By, and About Women* (Metuchen, N.J.: Scarecrow Press, 1980);

A. H. Weiler, "News of the Screen," *New York Times*, 4 November 1973;

Weiler, "Pity the Poor Prom Queen," *New York Times*, 1 October 1972, II:1.

James Poe

(4 October 1921-24 January 1980)

Malvin Wald

MOTION PICTURES: *Close-Up* (Eagle Lion, 1948), story;

Without Honor (United Artists, 1949), screen story and screenplay;

Scandal Sheet (Columbia, 1952), screenplay by Poe, Ted Sherderman, and Eugene Ling;

Paula (Columbia, 1952), screenplay by Poe and William Sackheim;

A Slight Case of Larceny (M-G-M, 1953), story;

The Big Knife (United Artists, 1955), adaptation;

Around the World in 80 Days (United Artists, 1956), screenplay by Poe, John Farrow, and S. J. Perelman;

Attack! (United Artists, 1956), screenplay;

Hot Spell (Paramount, 1958), screenplay;

Cat on a Hot Tin Roof (M-G-M, 1958), screenplay by Poe and Richard Brooks;

Last Train from Gun Hill (Paramount, 1959), screenplay by Poe and Edward Lewis;

Summer and Smoke (Paramount, 1961), screenplay by Poe and Meade Roberts;

Sanctuary (20th Century-Fox, 1961), screenplay;

Lilies of the Field (United Artists, 1963), screenplay;

Toys in the Attic (United Artists, 1963), screenplay;

The Bedford Incident (Columbia, 1965), screenplay;

Riot (Paramount, 1969), screenplay;

They Shoot Horses, Don't They? (Warner Bros., 1969), screenplay by Poe and Robert E. Thompson.

BOOK: *They Shoot Horses, Don't They?*, Poe's screenplay (credited to Robert E. Thompson) and Horace McCoy's novel (New York: Avon, 1970).

TELEVISION: *The Gathering* (ABC, 1977), teleplay;

Enola Gay: The Men, the Mission, the Atomic Bomb (NBC, 1980), teleplay by Poe and Millard Kaufman.

Unlike many formula writers who throughout their screenwriting employment merely echo their studio's master plan, James Poe was fortunate in being able to make his own voice known. Through his deliberate apprenticeship—first studying screenplays to learn technique, then working on documentaries before attempting screenplays—Poe made himself the screenwriter he wanted to be. He acquired a reputation as one of the most literate screenwriters in Hollywood, and he was frequently called on to adapt literary works for the screen.

Poe was born in Dobbs Ferry, New York. After studying at St. John's College in Annapolis, Maryland, he began his writing career in 1941 as a member of the *March of Time*, a monthly magazine-format screen series headed by Louis de Rochemont, a pioneer in the field of the semi-documentary. The *March of Time*, initiated by Time, Inc. and drawing upon its resources, was made up of theatrical shorts, using actors to re-enact news events. Exciting and informative, these short subjects became a valuable training ground for Poe.

During World War II, Poe served as a blimp pilot on submarine patrol duty with the United States Navy. After the war he wrote a series of short films for the United States Army. One of these, about a soldier adjusting to civilian life, met with strong Congressional disapproval and all prints were destroyed. But the narrator of the film, actor James Cagney, took an interest in the screenwriting skills Poe exhibited and suggested he take his talents to Hollywood. Poe took the advice.

Poe wanted to familiarize himself with the format and structure of the screenplay before attempting to do any writing for motion pictures, and in Hollywood he had ready access to the material he wanted to study. He read as many published scripts as he could find, supporting himself during this period of research by writing free-lance radio scripts. Several of his stories were purchased by CBS for their adventure series *Escape*. His writing skills, unpolished at this point, nevertheless contained vivid imagery, a quality essential to radio drama. Poe also managed to secure a position writing documentary films for the State Department and the Veterans Administration.

Soon after these years of study and apprenticeship, Poe began to earn his first screen credits beginning with his story for *Close-Up* (1948). Poe's

Jack Palance in Attack!, *a film notable for documentary realism and lack of war-movie clichés*

experiences with the *March of Time* unit are reflected in this film about a newsreel cameraman searching for missing film footage of an escaped Nazi leader. *Without Honor* (1949), Poe's first dramatic screenplay, was produced the following year. It is an overly talky film about a young woman (Laraine Day) who thinks she has killed her married lover (Franchot Tone) and is blackmailed by her brother-in-law (Dane Clark).

Scandal Sheet (1952) was Poe's first noteworthy movie, and it contained what was to become a trademark of a James Poe script: a collection of vividly drawn, sometimes eccentric characters. Based on a novel by Samuel Fuller, *Scandal Sheet* is about an unscrupulous newspaper editor (Broderick Crawford) who kills his wife, then realizes his two best reporters are close to solving the crime. Directed by Phil Karlson, the movie is a tightly made "B" picture, and Poe's screenplay ably brings to the

screen the colorful characters of Fuller's novel.

Following *Scandal Sheet*, Poe collaborated on the screenplay for *Paula* (1952) about a woman (Loretta Young) who deafens a child in an auto accident and helps him learn to cope with his handicap. He then provided the screen story for *A Slight Case of Larceny* (1953), about two gas station owners (Mickey Rooney and Eddie Bracken) who steal gasoline from an oil company. Although most of Poe's work to that point had not been major films, his next three screenplays—*The Big Knife* (1955), *Around the World in 80 Days* (1956), and *Attack!* (1956)—brought him critical notice and established him as a screenwriter and as a talented adaptor.

Based on a play by Clifford Odets, *The Big Knife* is a cynical study of Hollywood, centering on embittered actor Charlie Castle (Jack Palance), an alcoholic with a failing career and a broken marriage. The film is really more Odets's creation than

Poe's, particularly in its depiction of an amoral society in which blackmail and even murder can be casually committed to advance a career. But Poe and director Robert Aldrich added the light touch of black humor to the movie; Odets's already grotesque characters were made even more outrageous, almost ludicrous.

Aldrich had produced, as well as directed, *The Big Knife*, and he was pleased enough with Poe's work to hire him for his next production, *Attack!* Again, Poe was adapting a play, *Fragile Fox*—by Norman Brooks—but this time he was able to make more contributions to the screenplay, giving a documentary flavor to this re-enactment of the Battle of the Bulge. In a script that avoids wartime clichés, a small company of men have been left to hold a town during the battle; the men have no confidence in their cowardly Captain Cooney (Eddie Albert) and dissension results.

There was some controversy surrounding the screen credits of *Around the World in 80 Days*. Michael Todd, the film's producer, hired Poe to write a screenplay based on the Jules Verne novel. Poe provided him with a charming romantic comedy about Phileas Fogg (David Niven), his valet Pasepartout (Cantinflas), and the nearly fifty unusual characters they encounter in their travels. Todd used Poe's script to obtain financial backing for the film, then had the screenplay rewritten by S. J. Perelman and John Farrow. When the film was released, Poe was not credited as screenwriter. Acting on his behalf, the Writers Guild of America successfully sued Todd, and Poe was given first credit on the screenplay. The film went on to win an Academy Award for best picture, and Poe won an Oscar for best screenplay.

As a result of the success of *Around the World in 80 Days*, Poe began to receive more prestigious screenwriting assignments, and he soon discovered another field of specialty: adapting works by Southern writers. In his youth, Poe had lived in several Southern states, and he felt that writing movies set in the South would allow him to make good use of his flair for unusual characterizations. "The public seems willing to forgive gross eccentricity in the South," he explained. "Your characters can be outrageous without being considered insane." *Hot Spell* (1958) was an adaptation of Lonnie Coleman's play about a domineering mother (Shirley Booth) trying to hold together her neurotic family in the wake of the father's (Anthony Quinn) infidelity. More successful was his adaptation of Tennessee Wiliams's *Cat on a Hot Tin Roof* (1958). Poe received both Academy Award and Writers Guild nomina-

tions for his work with Richard Brooks, who co-authored the screenplay and directed the film.

In 1959 Poe worked on *Last Train from Gun Hill*, a Western about a lawman (Kirk Douglas) on the trail of the man who raped and murdered his wife. The murderer (Earl Holliman) turns out to be the son of the lawman's best friend (Anthony Quinn), a powerful figure in a nearby town, and when the sheriff tries to arrest him, virtually the entire town unites to prevent him from boarding a train with his prisoner. The movie was well made and suspenseful, with direction by John Sturges, but was somewhat overshadowed by *3:10 to Yuma*, a similar film that had been released the previous year.

Two more literary adaptations followed *Last Train from Gun Hill: Summer and Smoke* (1961), from the Tennessee Williams' play, and *Sanctuary* (1961), based on the novel by William Faulkner. In *Summer and Smoke*, doctor John Buchanan (Laurence Harvey) is loved by repressed Alma Winemiller (Geraldine Page), but he rejects her for the sluttish Rosa (Rita Moreno). As directed by Peter Glenville, who had mounted the original stage production, the film was one of the better adaptations of a Williams play from stage to screen, although it did seem somewhat static and hampered by its theatrical origins.

Sanctuary suffered from censorship problems, and almost did not make it to the screen. The movie was adapted from one of Faulkner's most shocking novels, about an impotent homicidal maniac who rapes a girl with a corn cob. An earlier film version, *The Story of Temple Drake* (1932) had bowdlerized the plot almost beyond recognition, and even by 1961, when Poe undertook a new adaptation, there was no way Faulkner's plot would have been approved intact. Partly to get around the censors and partly to combine *Sanctuary* with its sequel, *Requiem for a Nun*, Poe combined the impotent killer Popeye with Big Red, Temple's lover in a Memphis brothel, and with Big Red's brother. The composite character, named Candy Man (Yves Montand), ruined the credibility of an otherwise serious attempt to render Faulkner on the screen. The results were so disastrous that director Tony Richardson tried to disassociate himself from the film.

In 1963 Poe became involved in a modest project which seemed unlikely ever to reach the screen. He adapted a story by William E. Barrett into a sentimental screenplay in which Sidney Poitier agreed to star. The United Artists executives to whom the project was presented were reluctant to finance the film, claiming that it lacked wide box-

Sidney Poitier and Lilia Skala in Lilies of the Field, *for which Poe received an Academy Award nomination and a Writers Guild award.*

office appeal. One official protested, "What boy will take his girlfriend to a drive-in on Saturday night to see a movie about a black carpenter building a chapel for some German nuns?"

The project was able to find some supporters at United Artists, though, and *Lilies of the Field* (1963) was finally put into production. Poe observed that "Everything I learned in twenty years of writing went into that screenplay. The picture was shot in ten days and cost less than $250,000. We were absolutely stunned with the way *Lilies* was accepted." Critics commended it enthusiastically, and Poe was nominated for an Academy Award for his screenplay. He won the Writers Guild Award for the best written American comedy of 1963, and Sidney Poitier won an Oscar for his performance. Perhaps the most satisfied party was the United States State Department; officials there regarded

the movie as a delightful tale of interracial harmony during a time of great racial strife in America, and as such, the film became an important instrument of counterpropaganda abroad, especially when it was entered in foreign film festivals.

Toys in the Attic (1963), Poe's next film, was adapted from the play by Lillian Hellman; it was Poe's last play adaptation. Julian Berniers (Dean Martin) brings home his youthful bride Lily Prine (Yvette Mimieux); once there, Lily learns she has to contend with Julian's overbearing and possessive sisters (Geraldine Page and Wendy Hiller).

The political allegory *The Bedford Incident* (1965) was filmed because producer James B. Harris was determined to make a film about the dangers of nuclear weapons. He decided to film Mark Rascovich's novel about a NATO destroyer trying to track a Soviet submarine, and he hired Poe,

Jane Fonda and Michael Sarrazin in They Shoot Horses, Don't They?, *Poe's last film*

whom he had long admired, to write the screenplay. Typically, Poe's script focused on the conflicts between the many characters on board the ship, particularly the rigid commander (Richard Widmark) and the civilian journalist (Sidney Poitier). When the destroyer finds a submarine off the coast of Greenland, the commander forces a confrontation, and both ship and submarine are destroyed.

During the late 1960s Poe was active in the Screen Writers Guild. In 1969 he had two films produced. *Riot* was a violent prison drama, distinguished only by Poe's usual assortment of character types. His much greater accomplishment was *They Shoot Horses, Don't They?*

Poe was originally signed to direct as well as adapt the film version of Horace McCoy's novel about a dance marathon during the Depression. Poe created new characters for the film and wrote one role expressly for his second wife, actress Bar-

bara Steele. However, when he finished the screenplay he was replaced by Sydney Pollack as director. Robert E. Thompson was brought in to rewrite the script and subsequently shared the screenwriting credit. Poe later said the film remained ninety-nine percent his work. The film received considerable critical acclaim, and earned Academy Award nominations for best picture, best screenplay, best director, best actress (Jane Fonda), and best supporting actress (Susannah York, in the role Steele was to have played). Gig Young was chosen best supporting actor for his performance as the dissipated emcee of the contest.

They Shoot Horses, Don't They? was Poe's last produced screenplay. He was largely inactive during the 1970s, but in 1977 wrote a script for television, *The Gathering,* about a fatally ill business executive (Ed Asner) who arranges a Christmas reunion with the family he deserted a few years before. *The Gathering* received an Emmy award for best dramatic special, and Poe was nominated for an Emmy for his teleplay. In 1980 he wrote for television *Enola Gay: The Men, the Mission, the Atomic Bomb*. It was the last dramatic writing he was to do; Poe died of a heart attack in January 1980.

Samson Raphaelson

(30 March 1896-16 July 1983)

Barry Sabath

MOTION PICTURES: *The Smiling Lieutenant* (Paramount, 1931), scenario and dialogue by Raphaelson and Ernest Vajda;

The Magnificent Lie (Paramount, 1931), screenplay by Raphaelson and Vincent Lawrence;

One Hour With You (Paramount, 1932), screenplay;

The Man I Killed, retitled *Broken Lullaby* (Paramount-Publix, 1932), screenplay by Raphaelson and Vajda;

Trouble in Paradise (Paramount, 1932), screenplay;

The Merry Widow (M-G-M, 1934), screenplay by Raphaelson and Vajda;

Caravan (Fox, 1934), screenplay;

Servant's Entrance (Fox, 1934), screenplay;

Ladies Love Danger (20th Century-Fox, 1935), story;

Dressed to Thrill (20th Century-Fox, 1935), screenplay;

The Last of Mrs. Cheyney (M-G-M, 1937), screenplay by Raphaelson, Leon Gordon, and Monckton Hoffe;

Angel (Paramount, 1937), screenplay;

The Shop Around the Corner (M-G-M, 1940), screenplay;

Suspicion (RKO, 1941), screenplay by Raphaelson, Joan Harrison, and Alma Reville;

Heaven Can Wait (20th Century-Fox, 1943), screenplay;

The Harvey Girls (M-G-M, 1946), screenplay by Raphaelson, Harry Crane, Nathaniel Curtis, James O'Hanlan, and Edmund Beloin;

Green Dolphin Street (M-G-M, 1947), screenplay;

That Lady in Ermine (20th Century-Fox, 1948), screen story and screenplay;

Main Street to Broadway (Lester Cowan Productions, 1953), screenplay.

PLAY PRODUCTIONS: *The Jazz Singer*, New

Samson Raphaelson

York, Fulton Theatre, 14 September 1925;

Young Love, New York, Theatre Masque, 30 October 1928;

The Magnificent Heel, Stanford, Conn., 1929;

The Wooden Slipper, New York, Ritz Theatre, 3 January 1934;

Accent on Youth, New York, Plymouth Theatre, 25 December 1934;

White Man, New York, National Theatre, 17 October 1936;

Skylark, New York, Morosco Theatre, 11 October 1939;

Jason, New York, Hudson Theatre, 2 January 1942;

The Perfect Marriage, New York, Ethel Barrymore Theatre, 26 October 1944;

Hilda Crane, New York, Coronet Theatre, 1 November 1950.

BOOKS: *The Jazz Singer* (New York: Brentano's, 1925);

Young Love (New York: Brentano's, 1928);

The Wooden Slipper (Evanston, Ill. & New York: Row, Peterson, 1934);

Accent on Youth and *White Man* (New York, Los Angeles & London: Samuel French, 1935);

Skylark [novel] (New York & London: Knopf, 1939); originally serialized and published in *Saturday Evening Post* as "Streamlined Heart";

Skylark [play] (New York: Random House, 1939).

OTHER: Arch Oboler and Stephen Longstreet, eds., *Free World Theatre,* contributions by Raphaelson (New York: Random House, 1944);

Martha Foley, ed., *Best American Short Stories,* contributions by Raphaelson (Boston: Houghton Mifflin, 1952);

"Lost on 44th Street," *Editor's Choice, 26 Modern Short Stories from Good Housekeeping,* edited by Herbert Mayes (New York: Random House, 1956), pp. 306-320.

Samson Raphaelson was born in the Jewish community of New York City's Lower East Side. When he was five his father, cap manufacturer Ralph Raphaelson, received a business offer that required relocating in Denver. The senior Raphaelson's parents agreed to give him the necessary money for the venture on the condition that he and his wife, Anna Marks Raphaelson, leave behind Samson for them to raise. The young Samson was separated from his parents until about the age of thirteen, when, tired of his old-fashioned upbringing, he decided to live with his parents and brothers and sisters who were by then residing in Chicago. After graduating from a Chicago high school and working for a year in a mail-order house, Raphaelson began to write short stories. He decided to learn his craft by taking a bachelor's degree, and entered the Lewis Institute in Chicago, later transferring to the University of Illinois. He took creative writing classes, edited a literary magazine, and organized a banquet and revue given by the journalism fraternity to honor and "roast" faculty members.

After graduation in 1917 Raphaelson briefly worked for a Chicago advertising firm. He traveled to New York that fall and sold his first short story to *Hearst's* magazine. Encouraged by the sale, he decided to marry, and in January 1918 he returned to Chicago and wed his college sweetheart, Raina, a young intellectual and revolutionary. Raphaelson then began reading manuscripts for and working as assistant to the publisher of a group of popular magazines. During this period he found time to write his own short stories.

In the fall of 1920 Raphaelson became a teaching assistant in rhetoric at the University of Illinois. When he was still in his twenties he left Illinois, returned to New York, and worked as a police reporter for the *New York Times* before finding employment in the advertising business. He continued to write short stories; "The Day of Atonement," inspired by an Al Jolson revue he saw while in college, was published in January 1922. At the insistence of his secretary, Raphaelson expanded the story into a play. *The Jazz Singer* was finally produced in 1925; at age twenty-nine, Raphaelson had a hit play running on Broadway. *The Jazz Singer* would become the first American "talkie" in 1927. His second play, *Young Love* (1928), updated the Romeo and Juliet story to the flapper era.

Like many prominent newspaper writers and playwrights, Raphaelson had been approached to write for film after the advent of sound motion pictures in Hollywood. He refused early offers, confident in his Broadway success and feeling that movie writing was degrading. (He was also dismayed by the screen version of *The Jazz Singer* and completely disassociated himself from that historic film.) Financial problems caused him to change his mind in 1929. His third play, *The Magnificent Heel* (1929), had failed; the stock market had crashed, wiping out most of his savings; he had remarried in 1927, and his second wife, Deborah Wegman was pregnant. Raphaelson became a contract writer at RKO, where he earned $750 a week.

The job at RKO was not a fruitful one. Raphaelson remained at the studio for only six months, and his one screenplay written there—an adaptation of A. A. Milne's *The Dover Road*—went unproduced. Raphaelson left the studio in the spring of 1930. He had become good friends with director William Wyler and his brother Robert, who were related to Universal executive Carl Laemmle. The Wylers had been assigned to film the 1927 Broadway comedy hit *The Command to Love,* and they convinced Laemmle to hire Raphaelson to write the screenplay. He wrote a complete script, entitled *Boudoir Diplomat* (1930), but Laemmle became nervous about trusting the property to such an inexperienced writer and had Benjamin Glazer rewrite the script. Raphaelson received no screen credit for his work, but the movie's plot—a handsome attaché is ordered by his ambassador to woo the wife of a politician in order to gain her husband's consent to a treaty—introduced Raphaelson to the sort of sophisticated comedy he would later write for Ernst Lubitsch.

In September of 1930 Raphaelson was put under contract at Paramount and almost immediately introduced to Lubitsch. Lubitsch was about to begin work on the script of *The Man I Killed* (1932), his first sound drama, and he felt that the author of *The Jazz Singer* would be able to help achieve the strong degree of pathos which the script called for. When Lubitsch was put in control of Paramount's Astoria studios in New York, he took Raphaelson and screenwriter Ernest Vajda with him. Instead of putting *The Man I Killed* into production, Lu-

Jeanette MacDonald and Maurice Chevalier in
The Merry Widow

bitsch decided to prepare *The Smiling Lieutenant* (1931), a "mythical kingdom" musical vehicle for Maurice Chevalier. Army lieutenant Niki (Chevalier) smiles across the street to his girlfriend Franzi (Claudette Colbert) just as Princess Anna (Miriam Hopkins) passes by in a parade. She thinks that Niki has winked at her, and he is ordered to marry her. The marriage remains unconsummated until Franzi meets the drab princess and teaches her to become more attractive.

Paramount renewed Raphaelson's contract at the end of six months and assigned him to work on *The Magnificent Lie* (1931), adapted from Leonard Merrick's short story, "Laurels and the Lady." A temporarily blinded soldier falls in love with a famous actress; as a joke, a cabaret singer impersonates the actress. Despite its somewhat grim plot, the film was intended as a comedy; critics chided the filmmakers for the picture's overall poor taste and its lack of humor.

Lubitsch returned to Hollywood in the spring of 1931, and he and Raphaelson prepared the final script of *The Man I Killed*, retitled *Broken Lullaby* (without the participation of Vajda, who had been involved in the earlier draft written in New York). The film was Lubitsch's only sound drama, an unusually sentimental tale of a young Frenchman (Phillips Holmes) in World War I. He kills a German soldier in the last days of the war, then feels compelled to visit the German's hometown and family. He gradually assumes the place of the dead man, becoming accepted by his family and engaged to his fiancée (Nancy Carroll).

Raphaelson and Lubitsch next decided to remake one of Lubitsch's silent pictures, *The Marriage Circle* (1924). In *One Hour With You* (1932), Mitzi Olivier (Genevieve Tobin), bored with her marriage, tries to seduce André Bertier (Maurice Chevalier), the husband of her best friend, Colette (Jeanette MacDonald). When Colette Bertier finds out what is going on, she tells her husband that his business partner has tried to seduce her. The film received mixed reviews and was a box-office failure, but it did little damage to either Raphaelson's or Lubitsch's career.

When Raphaelson and Lubitsch began work on *One Hour With You*, they also conceived of *Love Me Tonight* (1932), about a tailor (Maurice Chevalier) who falls in love with a princess (Jeanette MacDonald). Lubitsch became busy directing *One Hour With You*, and Rouben Mamoulian was assigned to direct *Love Me Tonight*. He and Raphaelson could not get along, and Raphaelson left the movie after writing only a first draft; his script was rewritten and none of his material seems to have been used.

The argument with Mamoulian did further harm to Raphaelson's already poor working relationship with his superiors at Paramount. He had long been unhappy with his low salary and in 1932 decided to leave the studio. He agreed to stay only after Lubitsch promised to intercede on Raphaelson's behalf and speak to studio executives about the terms of his contract. Lubitsch never did this, however, and an air of hostility pervaded their next picture, *Trouble in Paradise* (1932), with Raphaelson vowing "I'll never have anything to do with this man again, as long as I live."

Working under these strained conditions, Raphaelson wrote the script about thieves Gaston (Herbert Marshall) and Lily (Miriam Hopkins) who meet in Italy, pick each other's pockets, and fall in love. They travel to France and steal the purse of heiress Mariette (Kay Francis). Gaston returns the purse for a reward, and eventually he and Lily get jobs in Mariette's perfume factory. They begin stealing from her and are discovered, but she permits them to flee the country. *Trouble in Paradise* was well received upon its initial release, and its critical reputation has continued to grow.

Raphaelson left Paramount in 1933. He accepted an assignment from a British film studio early that year, but the picture was never produced. He then turned down Lubitsch's invitation to adapt Noel Coward's *Design for Living* for the screen, not just because he was angry with Lubitsch, but because he felt he could not improve upon Coward's work. He chose instead to work on his own play, *The Wooden Slipper*. It opened in early 1934 under Raphaelson's direction, but closed after five performances. Much of Raphaelson's own money had been invested in the play, and after its failure he was forced to accept Lubitsch's invitation to work on *The Merry Widow* (1934).

Unlike other Raphaelson-Lubitsch collaborations, the structure of *The Merry Widow* had already been planned before Raphaelson began work on the project, and Ernest Vajda had already begun writing the screenplay. Thus Raphaelson viewed the assignment only as a chore to earn some much-needed money: "I didn't have any colossal interest in *The Merry Widow*. We were doing the same thing we'd done in *Trouble in Paradise* . . . and frankly I was a little bored with it." When wealthy widow Sonia (Jeanette MacDonald) leaves the mythical nation of Marshovia, the King (George Barbier) fears the nation will become bankrupt and orders Captain Danilo (Maurice Chevalier) to woo her and

bring her back. Danilo meets Sonia, falls in love, quarrels with her, and returns home alone. He is tried for treason for failing to complete his mission, but Sonia comes to his defense, and the King locks them in the same cell, where he feels certain they will become lovers.

While working on *The Merry Widow*, Raphaelson was also writing the script for another film, *Caravan* (1934). Produced at Fox, the film was intended to be a spectacular musical, budgeted at over $1,000,000. Raphaelson was brought in to rewrite a screenplay by Robert Liebman, and to his astonishment, he was asked by director Erik Charell to deliberately write a mediocre script. Charell was interested in spectacle and used a slight, sometimes trite, screenplay as an excuse to hold the massive musical numbers. The story is set in the rural vineyards of Hungary where a band of gypsies has been brought in to provide music to insure a rich harvest; political circumstances force a countess (Loretta Young) to marry one of the gypsies (Charles Boyer). Much of the dialogue is made up of obvious song cues, and the songs, in turn, grow into elaborate production numbers.

Caravan might have been an artistic failure, but it did trigger Raphaelson's move to a higher salary. He received $2,500 a week for the picture, and turned down an offer from Irving Thalberg to work at M-G-M in favor of Fox's higher pay. He spent May and June of 1934 writing *Servants' Entrance* (1934), which was directed by Frank Lloyd. A wealthy woman (Janet Gaynor) is forced to take a job as a domestic, then falls in love with another servant (Lew Ayres). *The Wooden Slipper* had a similar plot.

In 1934 Raphaelson took a leave of absence from Fox and returned to the east coast to complete his play *Accent on Youth*, about a middle-aged playwright who falls in love with a younger woman after he completes a play about a middle-aged man in love with a younger woman. It was a great success, and became one of Raphaelson's best-known plays. He was offered the chance to adapt the play for the screen in 1935, but declined. Instead he resumed his Fox contract, but he was only a part of an assembly line of writers and his work achieved little distinction. He received screenplay credit for *Ladies Love Danger* (1935), but Robert Ellis and Helen Logan were also credited for "adaptation" and Ilya Zorn for story; Raphaelson's contributions seem to have been minimal. The movie was a detective melodrama and certainly not Raphaelson's forte, except for the fact that the amateur sleuth was a playwright. Despite some good reviews, the film opened on the lower half of a double bill in most cities. The same fate befell *Dressed to Thrill* (1935), which Raphaelson adapted from Alfred Savoir's play *La Couturière de Luneville.* He also rewrote the dialogue for *The Gay Deception,* a comedy about a prince disguising himself as a servant to win the affections of a woman, but his involvement was uncredited.

After spending several months working on ideas and drafts of new plays, Raphaelson started a new M-G-M contract in January 1936. This resulted in only one screen credit: the remake of *The Last of Mrs. Cheyney* (1937). Based on Frederick Lonsdale's play, the movie was a British drawing-room comedy populated by suave criminals. Raphaelson's script went through an extensive rewrite by Leon Gordon, then was further reworked by Monckton Hoffe.

Raphaelson went back to work at Paramount, but when an early project there fell through he returned to New York for the production of his new play *White Man* (1936), a drama about misce-

genation. While the play was in preparation, Lubitsch went east to work with Raphaelson on *Angel* (1937). Lady Maria Barker (Marlene Dietrich) meets Anthony Halton (Melvyn Douglas), spends one night with him, then returns to her husband (Herbert Marshall). Halton shows up at her home, claiming to be a wartime friend of Barker. With her husband ignoring her because of his duties as a diplomat, Maria agrees to meet Halton in Paris but Barker rushes there in an attempt to save his marriage.

Upon completion of *Angel,* Raphaelson was signed by Mervyn LeRoy to write a treatment of *The Great Garrick* (1937) for Warner Bros. Raphaelson left the project without writing a screenplay, then undertook a film at Columbia at the request of Harry Cohn. But the film was never realized and Raphaelson received no further offers for over a year. He was at work on another play, *Skylark* (1939), when Lubitsch asked him to write *The Shop Around the Corner* (1940) for M-G-M. Set in Budapest, the movie focuses on two employees of a

Margaret Sullavan, Frank Morgan, and James Stewart in The Shop Around the Corner

Advertisement for one of Raphaelson's best-known films

leather goods shop, Klara Novak (Margaret Sullavan) and Alfred Kralik (James Stewart), who feud at work, but unknowingly correspond through the mail. The film is gentler in tone than other Raphaelson-Lubitsch pictures and was a critical and popular favorite when released.

Raphaelson's next screenplay became, along with the Lubitsch pictures, one of his best-known: *Suspicion* (1941). Alfred Hitchcock had been interested in filming Francis Iles's novel *Before the Fact* (1932) but had had problems finding a suitable screenplay. Raphaelson was hired in 1940 and produced a reasonably faithful version of the novel, about a shy heiress (Joan Fontaine) who discovers that the handsome man (Cary Grant) she has married is a swindler and thief and comes to believe that he is going to murder her. Raphaelson changed only the novel's ending, making the woman's suspicion groundless. His screenplay was

changed somewhat by Joan Harrison, Hitchcock's assistant, and Alma Reville, Hitchcock's wife. Raphaelson was not consulted about these changes and did not know about them until he viewed the film for the first time, decades later. *Suspicion* was one of the great film successes of 1941; it earned an Academy Award nomination for best picture and Joan Fontaine was voted best actress.

After successfully launching his play *Jason* (1942) on Broadway, Raphaelson went to work for RKO. As with his earlier stint at the studio, none of his work was produced. He went back to work with Lubitsch again, adapting *Heaven Can Wait* (1943) from Laszlo Bus-Fekete's play, *Birthday*. Henry Van Cleve (Don Ameche) dies, goes to Hell, and tells his life's story to Satan (Laird Cregar), discussing the significant events that coincided with his birthdays: getting drunk at fifteen, marrying at twenty-six, separating and reconciling at thirty-six, dying at seventy. Satan tells Henry he is not welcome in Hell and suggests that he try Heaven.

Raphaelson has said that beginning with *Angel* he became more deeply involved in the structure of the Lubitsch films. One can easily sense in *The Shop Around the Corner* and *Heaven Can Wait* a shift from Lubitsch's earlier work. The stories are more refined; the emotional qualities of the characters are more developed and the humor is more mellow. Of course, as in every other aspect of the collaborative process, the maturity of these two later films cannot be solely traced to Raphaelson. As Lubitsch settled into middle age, he became more aware that the milieu of his "continental comedies" was rapidly disappearing.

After a project at Warner Bros. fell through, Raphaelson signed a two-year contract at M-G-M with the understanding that he could spend six months at a time away from the studio writing plays. His first assignment was *Without Love* (1945),

a comedy about two people (Spencer Tracy and Katherine Hepburn) who marry for convenience and then fall in love. Donald Ogden Stewart rewrote Raphaelson's screenplay and Raphaelson received no screen credit though some of his material was used. He took a leave of absence to work on his play *The Perfect Marriage* (1944); when he returned to M-G-M, he received no full screenwriting assignments. Rather, as a member of the writing assembly line, he made minor contributions to ten films, including *In the Good Old Summertime* (a 1949 musical remake of *The Shop Around the Corner*), *Till the Clouds Roll By* (1946), and *Our Vines Have Tender Grapes* (1945). He contributed additional dialogue, a prologue, and an epilogue for the musical revue film *Ziegfeld Follies* (1946). The only one of the ten films he received screen credit for was *The Harvey Girls* (1946). Seven writers had already written unsatisfactory screenplays for this musical about waitresses in a restaurant chain in the Old West.

Don Ameche and Gene Tierney in Heaven Can Wait *(courtesy of Culver Pictures)*

Raphaelson took all the screenplays and combined them into one workable script, adding his own material. This version was further rewritten by George Wells.

The final M-G-M assignment was a special studio project. In 1944 Louis B. Mayer initiated an annual cash award to a selected work of fiction, which the studio then acquired for filming. The initial winner was Elizabeth Goudge's *Green Dolphin Street*, a historical romance, set in New Zealand and the Channel Islands, about two sisters who fall in love with the same man. Raphaelson wrote the screenplay in his home in New York, then mailed his work in sections to producer Carey Wilson, who rewrote the material without Raphaelson's knowledge. Although Raphaelson received sole screen credit, the finished film of 1947 bore little resemblance to the original script. Still it was a commercially successful movie and allowed Raphaelson to negotiate a new contract with the studio: he was to be employed for a minimum of three work periods, his salary would escalate from $2,750 to $3,000 a week, he could work in the East and be loaned out to another studio at any time.

Despite the lucrative and flexible terms of his contract, Raphaelson completed little work at M-G-M. He had not begun any films when he was loaned out to 20th Century-Fox so that he could work with Lubitsch on *That Lady in Ermine* (1948). Lubitsch died of a heart attack while shooting and was replaced by Otto Preminger. On the day Queen Angelina (Betty Grable) of Bergamo is to marry, her principality is invaded by Hungarian troops. Their leader, Colonel Karoly (Douglas Fairbanks, Jr.) becomes obsessed with a painting of Angelina's ancestor Francesca wearing only an ermine coat. He promises to free Angelina's husband (Cesar Romero) if Angelina will come to him in an ermine coat, just as Francesca did to an earlier invader. Angelina refuses but the painting of Francesca comes to life and appears before Karoly. Angelina has her marriage annulled, and marries Karoly.

It was not until 1949 that Raphaelson started work on an M-G-M film, and though he worked on two projects, neither of his scripts was used and his contract was suspended in August 1951. Part of the reason that he had not written more for M-G-M was that he was continuing to work on short stories—including a series for *Good Housekeeping*—and plays. His last Broadway play, *Hilda Crane*, was produced in 1950. Shortly after its opening, Raphaelson became interested in photography and virtually retired from writing to study that field. A

series of his photographs was published in 1961 in *Popular Photography*.

Raphaelson's final produced screenplay was *Main Street to Broadway* (1953), a film undertaken to benefit the Council of the Living Theatre, an organization formed to encourage legitimate-theater attendance. Robert E. Sherwood, the Council's first president, wrote a story about the problems surrounding a young playwright's first play, and Raphaelson adapted the story into a screenplay. The resulting film, directed by Tay Garnett, was little more than a series of cameo performances by Broadway luminaries, including Tallulah Bankhead, Shirley Booth, Ethel and Lionel Barrymore, Rex Harrison, Lili Palmer, Helen Hayes, Mary Martin, Richard Rodgers, and Oscar Hammerstein II.

In the 1970s Raphaelson contributed his knowledge and experience to the development of the fledgling Israeli film industry. He also immersed himself in the growing field of film theory and history, serving as an adjunct professor of cinema at Columbia University from 1976 until his death. In 1977 he was honored by the Writers Guild with the presentation of the Laurel Award in recognition of lifetime achievement for screenwriting. Raphaelson died in 1983 at age eighty-seven.

Throughout his long career, Samson Raphaelson always believed that if lasting fame were to come to him it would be through his plays. His screenplays, even his best work for Lubitsch, were regarded by him as only a means of supporting himself. The irony of his career never escaped him. "To think," he said in 1974, "that I should be remembered for the bloody movies! It's simply absurd!"

References:

Hugh Fordin, *The World of Entertainment* (Garden City: Doubleday, 1975);

Denis Giles, "The Ghost of Thalberg: M-G-M 1946-1951," *Velvet Light Trap* (Spring 1948): 9;

Tom Milne, *Rouben Mamoulian* (Bloomington: Indiana University Press, 1970);

Nancy Schwartz, "Lubitsch's Widow: The Meaning of a Waltz," *Film Comment* (March-April 1975): 13-17.

Papers:

A collection of Raphaelson's papers, screenplays, and plays is held at the University of Illinois at Champaign-Urbana.

Walter Reisch
(23 May 1903-28 March 1983)

Evan William Cameron
Washington State University

MOTION PICTURES: *Los vom Mann* (Helios Films, 1925), scenario;

Frauen aus der Wiener Vorstadt (Hanus Films, 1925), scenario;

Die Pratermizzi (Sascha Film, 1926), scenario;

Hotel Erzherzogin Victoria (Asta Films, 1926), scenario;

Ein Walzer von Strauss (Helios Films, 1926), scenario;

Trommelfeuer der Liebe (Sascha Film, 1927), scenario by Reisch and Carl Hartl;

Die Schutzenliesl (AAFA Film, 1927), scenario;

Der Bettelstudent (AAFA Film, 1927), scenario;

Das Heiratsnest (AAFA Film, 1927), scenario;

Ein Mädel aus dem Volke (AAFA Film, 1927), scenario;

Donauwalzer (AAFA Film, 1927), scenario;

Einquartierung (AAFA Film, 1927), scenario;

Die elf Teufel (National Studio, 1927), screenplay;

Der lustige Witwer (Superfilm A. G., 1927), screenplay;

Der Fluch (Superfilm A. G., 1927), screenplay;

Der Faschingsprinz (AAFA Film, 1928), scenario;

Der Held aller Mädchenträume (Superfilm A. G., 1928), screenplay;

Die Dollar-Prinzessin und ihre Freier (Herrmann Millakovsky, 1928), screenplay;

Fräulein Fähnrich (Demo-Film, 1928), screenplay;

Dich hab' ich geliebt (AAFA Film, 1929), screenplay;

La nuit est à nous (Tobis-Patent, 1929), screenplay by Reisch and Walter Suppers;

Brand in der Oper (Tobis-Patent, 1930), screenplay by Reisch and Suppers;

Das Flötenkonzert von SansSouci (UFA, 1930), screenplay;

Die Frau, die Jeder Liebt (Tobis-Patent, 1930), screenplay by Reisch and Suppers;

Hokuspokus (UFA, 1930), screenplay;

Das Lied ist aus (Superfilm, 1930), screenplay;

Ein Tango fur Dich (Superfilm, 1930), screenplay;

Wie werde ich reich und glücklich (Tobis-Patent, 1930), screenplay;

Zwei Herzen im 3/4 Takt (Superfilm, 1930), screenplay by Reisch and F. Schultz;

Das Dirnen-Lied (Tobis-Patent, 1931), screenplay;

Die lustigen Weiber von Wien (Superfilm, 1931), screenplay;

Der Raub der Mona Lisa (Superfilm, 1931), screenplay;

Ein Blonder Traum (UFA, 1932), screenplay by Reisch and Billy Wilder;

Die Gräfin von Monte Christo (UFA, 1932), screenplay; remade as *The Countess of Monte Cristo* (Universal, 1952), story;

Der Prinz von Arkadien (Tobis-Patent, 1932), screenplay;

Ich und die Kaiserin (UFA, 1933), screenplay by Reisch, Robert Leibman, and Felix Selter;

Im Geheimdienst (UFA, 1933), screenplay;

Leise flehen meine Lieder (Sascha Film, 1933), screenplay;

Saison in Kairo (UFA, 1933), screenplay;

F. P. 1 Antwortet Nicht (UFA, 1932), adaptation; released in an English language edition as *F. P. 1* (Fox-Gaumont-British-UFA, 1933), screenplay by Reisch and Curt Siodmak;

Der Herr auf Bestellung (Superfilm, 1934), screenplay;

Maskerade (Sascha Film, 1934), screenplay; remade as *Escapade* (M-G-M, 1935), story;

Episode (Sascha Film, 1935), screenplay; remade as *My Love Came Back* (Warner Bros., 1940);

Silhouettes (Sascha Film, 1936);

Men are Not Gods (United Artists, 1937), screen story and screenplay;

The Great Waltz (M-G-M, 1938), screenplay by Reisch and Samuel Hoffenstein;

Gateway (20th Century-Fox, 1938), story;

Ninotchka (M-G-M, 1939), screenplay by Reisch, Billy Wilder, and Charles Brackett;

Comrade X (M-G-M, 1940), story;

That Hamilton Woman (United Artists, 1941), screen story and screenplay by Reisch and R. C. Sherriff;

That Uncertain Feeling (United Artists, 1941), adaptation;

Seven Sweethearts (M-G-M, 1942), screenplay and screen story by Reisch and Leo Townsend;

Walter Reisch

Somewhere I'll Find You (M-G-M, 1942), adaptation;
The Heavenly Body (M-G-M, 1943), screenplay by Reisch and Michael Arlen;
Gaslight (M-G-M, 1944), screenplay by Reisch, John Van Druten, and John Balderston;
Song of Scheherazade (Universal, 1946), screen story and screenplay;
The Fan (20th Century-Fox, 1949), screenplay by Reisch, Dorothy Parker, and Ross Evans;
The Model and the Marriage Broker (20th Century-Fox, 1951), screen story and screenplay by Reisch, Brackett, and Richard Breen;
The Mating Season (Paramount, 1951), screenplay by Reisch, Brackett, and Breen;
Niagara (20th Century-Fox, 1953), screen story and screenplay by Reisch, Brackett, and Breen;
Titanic (20th Century-Fox, 1953), screen story and screenplay by Reisch, Brackett, and Breen;
Die Muecke (Fama Film, 1954), screenplay;
The Girl in the Red Velvet Swing (20th Century-Fox, 1955), screenplay by Reisch and Brackett;
Der Cornet (Fama Film, 1955), screenplay;

Teenage Rebel (20th Century-Fox, 1956), screenplay by Reisch and Brackett;
Stopover Tokyo (20th Century-Fox, 1957), screenplay by Reisch and Breen;
The Remarkable Mr. Pennypacker (20th Century-Fox, 1959), screenplay;
Journey to the Center of the Earth (20th Century-Fox, 1959), screenplay by Reisch and Brackett.

Walter Reisch exerted a distinguished and civilizing influence on the cinema of Vienna, Berlin, Paris, London, and Hollywood for more than half a century. He was a man of culture and erudition and his screenplays are marked by his sensitivity, sentiment, and sophistication.

Reisch was born in Vienna to A. T. Reisch, a bookseller, and Gisela Kreisler Reisch, an author of romantic poetry. Through his father's bookstore, Reisch had easy access to the best of classic and modern literature, a rare advantage in Vienna where books were prohibitively expensive. From 1913 to 1922 he attended the Reform-Real Gymnasium in Vienna. Students on state scholarship, like Reisch, were often drafted as extras for the performances of the state theaters or for locally filmed motion pictures. Reisch worked frequently for Sascha Film, one of Vienna's most successful studios. Also working for Sascha Film were two Hungarian directors, Michael Curtiz and Alexander Korda, neither of whom spoke fluent German or French, the languages in which the titles for their silent films were written. Because of his language facility, Reisch was promoted from extra to author of title cards for the two directors, and eventually to assistant director and editor of Korda's pictures.

When the great inflation hit Vienna in 1921 the Austrian film industry collapsed. Reisch briefly wrote poetry and aphorisms for satiric magazines but in 1923 decided to go to Berlin where the motion picture industry still flourished. He became camera assistant to Stefan Lorant; then, in Geneva, was assistant cameraman for "International News-

reels" at the Société des Nations.

By 1925 the Austrian film industry had recovered. Reisch returned to Vienna and wrote screenplays on Viennese themes for several film studios. The most noteworthy of these early films is *Ein Walzer von Strauss (A Waltz by Strauss*, 1926), the first of many films Reisch was to write about music and the ballet.

Reisch was working steadily as assistant director and occasional screenwriter by 1927; still, he realized that Berlin, not Vienna, was the center of German-language film production. In September 1927 Reisch married Ina Schulthess, a Viennese dancer, and the couple left for Berlin. (The marriage was to end in divorce in 1930.) Reisch, under contract to AAFA Film, wrote a series of silent film scripts that established his reputation as an original writer capable of working with extraordinary speed within popular genres, particularly those genres close to the dramatic temper of the Viennese musical theater.

Miliza Korjus in The Great Waltz, *one of Reisch's early films for M-G-M*

When synchronous sound equipment for films was introduced into Berlin late in 1927, the equipment could accurately reproduce music, but not dialogue. Suddenly there was a demand for screenplays incorporating music. During the next seven years, Reisch's reputation grew as he wrote original sound screenplays to order for various companies, eventually securing a position at UFA, one of Germany's largest studios. He also wrote six Viennese musicals for Superfilm, all starring Willy Forst and receiving worldwide distribution. One of these, *Der Raub der Mona Lisa (The Theft of the Mona Lisa*, 1931), remains among the finest of his works.

By 1933 Reisch was among the most successful screenwriters in Europe, but when the Nazis came to power in Germany, Reisch fled Berlin for Vienna. There he wrote *Leise flehen meine Lieder (The Unfinished Symphony*, 1933), a well-received film biography of Franz Schubert. He also wrote two scripts for actress Paula Wessely, *Maskerade* (1934) and *Episode* (1935); he directed the latter. Both films became world famous, and *Episode* won the award for best screenplay of 1935 at the Biennale in Venice. It is the story of young people struggling through college and art school. An older man attempts to aid a talented female student; this gesture disrupts many lives and nearly ends his marriage of many years. After Reisch came to Hollywood, both these pictures were remade: *Maskerade* became *Escapade* (1935) and *Episode* became *My Love Came Back* (1940). Reisch received screen credit for both remakes.

Episode was the last picture with Reisch's name that was distributed in Germany; *Silhouettes* (1936), which he wrote and directed, received worldwide release, but was banned in Germany. Starring Lisl Handl, a dancer with the Vienna State Opera whom Reisch later married, the film was one of the first pictures concerned with the classical ballet.

For the next ten years, Reisch wrote under contract to M-G-M. His familiarity with classical music earned him a prestigious first assignment: *The Great Waltz* (1938). The picture was a largely fictionalized biography of Johann Strauss (played by Fernand Gravet). Reisch and collaborator Samuel Hoffenstein devised a script which featured prominently most of Strauss's best-known works, as they centered on the married Strauss's infatuation with singer Carla Donner (Miliza Korjus).

An Academy Award nomination came with *Ninotchka* (1939), which Reisch wrote with Billy Wilder and Charles Brackett. (Reisch and Brackett later collaborated on a series of films in the 1950s.) Ernst Lubitsch directed this romantic comedy about a communist official (Greta Garbo) sent to Paris to sell state-owned jewels, who falls in love with a Russian aristocrat (Melvyn Douglas). Reisch was respected for both his ability to write sophisticated comedy and his skill at creating roles for women, and *Ninotchka* allowed him to put both those abilities to good use: the movie contained some political satire that was quite daring for its period and provided Garbo with a change of image. The following year, Reisch wrote the screen story for *Comrade X* (1940), a variation on the same theme. It earned him his second Academy Award nomination.

A series of somewhat lesser films followed these three early successes. Frank Borzage directed *Seven Sweethearts* (1942), a comedy about a man (S. Z. Sakall) who denies his daughters permission to wed until the oldest is married. In *Somewhere I'll Find You* (1942), two brothers (Clark Gable and Robert Sterling) fall in love with the same woman (Lana Turner) during the war. An astrologer (William Powell) neglects his wife (Hedy Lamarr), then suspects her of infidelity in *The Heavenly Body* (1943).

Paula Anton (Ingrid Bergman), the heroine in *Gaslight* (1944), stands with Ninotchka as Reisch's best-known female characterization. Paula and her husband, Gregory (Charles Boyer), move into her aunt's house where Gregory believes jewels to be hidden. He tries to drive his wife insane to gain control of the property. Reisch, John Balderston, and John Van Druten adapted their script from a play by Patrick Hamilton. They earned an Academy Award nomination for their work, and Ingrid Bergman was voted best actress. *Gaslight* marked the end of Reisch's contract with M-G-M.

Even while he had worked for M-G-M, Reisch wrote occasional scripts for other studios. One of his earliest film projects was written for 20th Century-Fox: *Gateway* (1938), the story of immigrants arriving at Ellis Island. For Alexander Korda, he wrote *That Hamilton Woman* in 1941, a film version of the romance between Lady Hamilton (Vivien Leigh) and Admiral Nelson (Laurence Olivier). That same year Reisch wrote *That Uncertain Feeling* for United Artists. Ernst Lubitsch directed this story of a married couple (Merle Oberon and Melvyn Douglas) bored with their lives.

Song of Scheherazade (1946), written for Universal after Reisch's M-G-M contract expired, was the only American film he wrote and directed. The film is another study of a famous composer, centering on the woman (Yvonne deCarlo) who inspired Rimsky-Korsakov (Brian Donlevy). Reisch then went to work for 20th Century-Fox, where he remained throughout the 1950s. His first picture there was *The Fan* (1949), a film version of Oscar Wilde's *Lady Windermere's Fan*. It was only moderately successful.

With *The Model and the Marriage Broker* (1951), Reisch was reteamed with Charles Brackett, with whom he had collaborated on *Ninotchka*. A marriage broker (Thelma Ritter) brings together a busy doctor (Scott Brady) and a lonely model (Jeanne Crain). Richard Breen also worked on the script, and from this point forward all but one of Reisch's American screenplays were to be written with Brackett, Breen, or both. Their next collaboration, *The Mating Season* (1951), is another romantic comedy, but more serious in tone: a working-class woman (Ritter) becomes an embarrassment to her son (John Lund) who has married into a wealthy family.

Reisch moved from comedy to drama with *Niagara* (1953). A woman (Marilyn Monroe) honeymooning with her husband (Joseph Cotten) is secretly plotting his murder. The plot backfires, and the husband murders her coconspirator and lover (Richard Allan). This picture was followed by *Titanic* (1953), a study of the sinking of the ship, done in a semidocumentary style and examining the lives of many passengers. The film earned Reisch his only Academy Award.

Titanic was Reisch's last success for many years. On vacation from 20th Century-Fox, he returned to Germany where he wrote and directed two pictures: *Die Muecke* (1954) and *Der Cornet* (1955). When he returned to Hollywood, he began work on *The Girl in the Red Velvet Swing* (1955), a fictionalized version of the murder of Stanford White (Ray Milland), who was shot during a quarrel over a woman (Joan Collins). *Teenage Rebel* (1956) examines the relationship between a divorced woman (Ginger Rogers) and her teenaged daughter (Betty Lou Keim). *Stopover Tokyo* (1957) is a muddled spy thriller, adapted from John P. Marquand's novel. *The Remarkable Mr. Pennypacker* (1959), based on a play by Liam O'Brien, was Reisch's first solo American screenplay after *Song of Scheherazade*. The film is about an egotistical man (Clifton Webb) whose vanity drives him to marry twice and raise two families.

Greta Garbo and Melvyn Douglas in Ninotchka, *a sophisticated comedy now recognized as a classic*

Ingrid Bergman, Charles Boyer, and Barbara Everest in Gaslight, *Reisch's last film for M-G-M*

With *Journey to the Center of the Earth* (1959), his last American film, Reisch had another critical and financial success. This adaptation of Jules Verne's famous novel was not entirely faithful to its source, but is a well-made, enjoyable adventure movie.

In the 1960s the studio system in Hollywood and Europe collapsed under pressure of competition with television. With full-time employment unavailable, Reisch worked as a free-lance writer and script doctor in Hollywood and Europe. In the later years of his life, he was in great demand as a lecturer on film at major universities and film festivals and in 1973 was awarded The Great Gold Medal of Vienna for his artistic achievements. Walter Reisch died of cancer in 1983. At the time of his death, he was working on a screenplay for the noted German director Volker Schloendorff.

Throughout his career, Walter Reisch remained the consummate craftsman, sure of his art, cautious of its boundaries, and incapable of pretense. He is one of the unheralded screenwriters, prolific yet unrecognized, who created many memorable moments in film.

Arthur Ripley

(1895-13 February 1961)

Joyce Rheuban

SELECTED MOTION PICTURES: *Life's Darn Funny* (Metro, 1921), scenario by Ripley and Mary O'Hara;

A Lady of Quality (Universal, 1924), adaptation by Ripley and Marian Ainslee;

The Strong Man (Harry Langdon/First National, 1926), story;

Long Pants (Langdon/First National, 1927), story;

His First Flame (Mack Sennett Productions, 1927), scenario by Ripley and Frank Capra;

Three's a Crowd (Langdon/First National, 1927), story;

The Chaser (Langdon/First National, 1928), story;

Heart Trouble (Langdon/First National, 1928), story;

Barnum Was Right (Universal, 1929), adaptation by Ripley and Ewart Adamson;

Hide-Out (Universal, 1930), story and scenario by Ripley and Lambert Hillyer;

Captain of the Guard (Universal, 1930), adaptation;

Hypnotized (World-Wide, 1932), story by Ripley and Mack Sennet;

Waterfront (Warner Bros., 1939), screenplay by Ripley and Lee Katz;

Voice in the Wind (United Artists, 1944), screen story.

Harry Langdon (right) in Long Pants

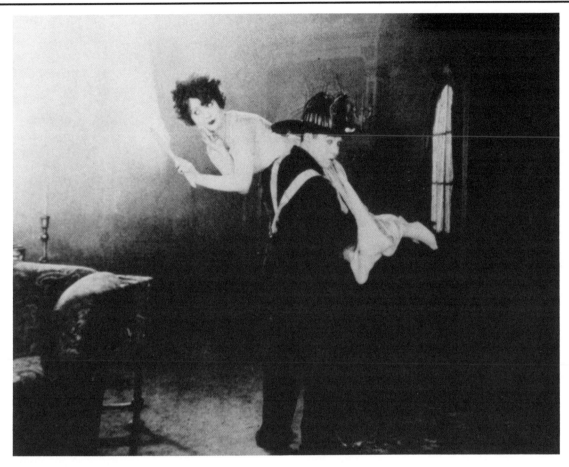

Natalie Kingston and Harry Langdon in His First Flame

Arthur Ripley, whose screenwriting style combined the unlikely elements of gag writing and literary erudition, was born in the Bronx, New York. At fifteen he began his film career, cleaning negatives for the Kalem company. In 1912 he became a film cutter at Vitagraph and later went to California to work as a film editor, first for the Metro Company, then for Universal and Fox.

By 1924 he was established as a writer at Mack Sennett's Keystone Studio and there collaborated with other writers on gags and stories for many two- and three-reel comedies. He worked mostly with Frank Capra on projects for comedian Harry Langdon, and was soon writing feature-length comedies for Langdon; he also directed short films starring Robert Benchley, W. C. Fields, Langdon, and Edgar Kennedy. Capra and Ripley had differing views of Langdon: Capra saw him as an innocent protected by God; Ripley saw him as man and child in the same body, and he exploited the Langdon character's poorly developed sexual identity. His scripts are full of sexual innuendoes and

scatological humor. Thematic motifs include mother as prostitute and vice versa, the linking of sex and violence, and the linking of love and death.

An intellectual gagman, well-read in classical and contemporary literature, Ripley often suggested themes and motifs from literature and applied aesthetic theories to two-reel comedy construction. It is this quality in Ripley's work that kept him from becoming successful by Hollywood standards—critically, financially, and popularly. *His New Mamma* (1924), for example, is a two-reel comedy version of Eugene O'Neill's tragedy *Desire Under the Elms* (1924), complete with Oedipal overtones. The themes of Ripley's films were often judged by critics as too esoteric for the general audience; other critics deemed both his comedies and his dramas too morbid, since they frequently employ brutal violence or spectacular violence and nightmarish atmospheres. Furthermore, his narrative techniques were often confusing: improbable plot twists, flashbacks, flashforwards, memory, dream, and fantasy sequences. His scripts drew on

Ronald Colman and Constance Talmadge in Heart Trouble

his experience as a film editor and director; he exercised the freedom inherent in the film medium to manipulate time, space, and causal relationships. Ripley also capitalized on a trademark of Langdon's character (Harry is often drunk, dazed, drugged, or in a limbo somewhere between falling asleep and waking) by using dreams and fantasies as subject matter and as structural devices in the Langdon stories.

Long Pants (1927) utilizes thematic and stylistic elements typical in Ripley's work on the Langdon comedies and demonstrates the dark humor that links his comedies with later dramatic films written or directed by him. Langdon portrays a sexually-repressed adult who hides in his attic to indulge in romantic fantasies; he also dreams of murdering his fiancée, an act that would free him to join the woman who embodies his fantasies. But when he tries to act out the murder, the fantasy becomes a nightmare of frustration: he cannot get the pistol out of his pants, and when he does, he is incapable of firing it. When he finally finds his dream girl again, she is an ex-convict who is currently smuggling heroin; she involves him in a criminal spree that culminates in murder. Langdon's belated and physically violent initiation into manhood is traumatic and is symbolized by a gunshot wound he receives. With some relief he retreats to the protective custody of his domineering mother and her chosen successor, his unwanted fiancée. Ripley's other scripts for Langdon—*The Strong Man* (1926), *Three's a Crowd* (1927), and *The Chaser* (1928)—employ similar themes.

Ripley's feature films of the early 1930s are minor works. *Hide-Out* (1930) is about a gangster (James Murray) who, on the run from the police, hides at a college and becomes a football hero. In *Hypnotized* (1932), which Ripley coauthored with Sennett, an evil professor (Ernest Torrance) hypnotizes several people as part of a plot to find a five-hundred-thousand-dollar sweepstakes prize.

After the Langdon films, the first script of any interest is *Waterfront* (1939), a story of revenge in which a young waterfront tough (Dennis Morgan) seeks the killer of his brother and nearly murders his own bride by mistake. *Prisoner of Japan* (1942), which Ripley directed, is the story of a drunken, pacifist American astronomer who finds love, death, and spiritual redemption on a remote Pacific island as he and his lover die, sacrificing themselves for the American war effort.

Voice in the Wind (1944) is a tragic story of star-crossed lovers (Francis Lederer and Sigrid Gurie) who are victims of Nazi tyranny. Volny, a Czech

John Boles and Laura La Plante in Captain of the Guard

pianist, and his wife Marie are separated when she is smuggled out of the country, and he is arrested by the occupying Nazis. Eventually they both arrive in Guadeloupe, neither character aware of the presence of the other. He is an amnesiac playing piano in a bar; she is in a coma in a sickroom across the street. His performing rouses her from her coma, but she dies before reaching him and he discovers the body without knowing who it is. The picture has a complicated narrative structure that does not present events in a linear form; it is told partly in flashbacks, the only scenes in which the two main characters speak. Incidents are recalled by two of the secondary characters, or through Volny's point of view in a kind of interior monologue. Most of the film's crucial actions take place off-camera. In *Voice in the Wind* Ripley creates a milieu in which the external environment reflects the characters' states of mind, a technique used in varying degrees in his other films.

Voice in the Wind received some critical acclaim, but other critics found it arty and confusing. Ripley never had another screenplay produced, though he did option Thomas Wolfe's novel *Look Homeward, Angel* and prepared a script. For the rest of his career he functioned as a director of stage, television, and, infrequently, of film. *The Chase* (1946), which Philip Yordan adapted from Cornell Woolrich's novel *The Black Path of Fear,* shows many of Ripley's continuing motifs. Impoverished Chuck Scott (Robert Cummings) becomes the chauffeur of disreputable businessman Eddie Roman (Steve Cochran). Roman's wife Lorna (Michelle Morgan) asks Scott's help in escaping from her husband, and what follows is an extended dream sequence in which Scott dreams he is blamed for Lorna's murder. At the film's end, some parts of his dream seem to be coming true.

The Chase was Ripley's last screen credit for over a decade (though he is said to have directed without credit scenes in *Siren of Atlantis,* 1948). He retired from the film industry in 1954 to become head of the motion-picture division at the University of California at Los Angeles, a position he held until his death in 1961. He returned to filmmaking briefly in 1958, directing *Thunder Road,* an effective film noir dealing with Georgia moonshiners battling both federal authorities and organized crime.

Arthur Ripley's best films as writer and director have always had a limited popular appeal; since his death his films have attracted a cult following. *Voice in the Wind,* although not one of the masterpieces of cinematic art, derives much impact from its rather daring departures from safe Hollywood formulas and customs. As the author of this very personal statement, Ripley merits recognition and respect. In a 1944 interview he said, "The nicest thing you could say about me is that you met somebody in this town who still has good intentions, someone who will try to bring poetry and imagination back to the screen."

Casey Robinson
(17 October 1903-6 December 1979)

Christopher Adcock

MOTION PICTURES: *The Private Life of Helen of Troy* (First National, 1927), titles by Robinson, Ralph Spence, and Gerald Duffy;

Bare Knees (Gotham, 1928), titles;

Mad Hour (First National, 1928), titles;

Turn Back the Hours (Gotham, 1928), titles;

The Chorus Kid (Gotham, 1928), titles;

The Hawk's Nest (First National, 1928), titles;

United States Smith (Gotham, 1928), titles;

Out of the Ruins (First National, 1928), titles;

Waterfront (First National, 1928), titles by Robinson and Gene Towne;

Do Your Duty (First National, 1928), titles by Robinson and Towne;

The Companionate Marriage (C. M./First National, 1928), titles;

The Head of the Family (Gotham, 1928), titles;

Times Square (Gotham, 1929), titles;

The Squealer (Columbia, 1930), continuity;

The Last Parade (Columbia, 1931), story;

Masquerade (Warner Bros., 1931), screenplay;

Is My Face Red? (RKO, 1932), screenplay by Robinson and Ben Markson;

Strictly Personal (Paramount, 1933), additional dialogue;

Lucky Devils (RKO, 1933), story by Robinson and Bob Rose;

Song of the Eagle (Paramount, 1933), screenplay by Robinson and Willard Mack;

I Love That Man (Paramount, 1933), screenplay by Robinson, Towne, and Graham Baker;

Golden Harvest (Paramount, 1933), screenplay;

Eight Girls in a Boat (Paramount, 1934), screenplay;

She Made Her Bed (Paramount, 1934), screenplay by Robinson and Frank R. Adams;

Here Comes the Groom (Paramount, 1934), screenplay by Robinson and Leonard Praskins;

McFadden's Flats (Paramount, 1935), adaptation;

Stella Parish (First National-Vitaphone, 1935); retitled, *I Found Stella Parish* (Warner Bros., 1935), screenplay;

Captain Blood (Warner Bros., 1935), screenplay;

I Married A Doctor (Warner Bros., 1936), screenplay;

Hearts Divided (Warner Bros., 1936), screenplay by Robinson and Laird Doyle;

Give Me Your Heart (Warner Bros., 1936), screenplay;

Stolen Holiday (Warner Bros., 1936), screenplay;

Call It a Day (Warner Bros., 1937), screenplay;

It's Love I'm After (Warner Bros., 1937), screenplay;

Tovarich (Warner Bros., 1937), screenplay;

Four's a Crowd (Warner Bros., 1938), screenplay by Robinson and Sig Herzig;

Dark Victory (Warner Bros., 1939), screenplay;

Yes, My Darling Daughter (Warner Bros., 1939), screenplay;

The Old Maid (Warner Bros., 1939), screenplay;

All This and Heaven Too (Warner Bros., 1940), screenplay;

Million Dollar Baby (Warner Bros., 1941), screenplay by Robinson, Richard Macaulay, and Jerry Wald;

Kings Row (Warner Bros., 1941), screenplay;

One Foot in Heaven (Warner Bros., 1941), screenplay;

Now, Voyager (Warner Bros., 1942), screenplay;

This Is the Army (Warner Bros., 1943), screenplay by Robinson and Claude Binyon;

The Racket Man (Columbia, 1943), screen story;

Passage to Marseille (Warner Bros., 1944), screenplay by Robinson and Jack Moffitt;

Days of Glory (RKO, 1944), screenplay;

The Corn Is Green (Warner Bros., 1945), screenplay by Robinson and Frank Cavett;

Saratoga Trunk (Warner Bros., 1946), screenplay;

The Macomber Affair (United Artists, 1946), screenplay by Robinson and Seymour Bennett;

Desire Me (M-G-M, 1947), adaptation;

Father Was a Fullback (20th Century-Fox, 1949), screenplay by Robinson, Aleen Leslie, Mary Loos, and Richard Sale;

Under My Skin (20th Century-Fox, 1950), screenplay;

Two Flags West (20th Century-Fox, 1950), screenplay;

Diplomatic Courier (20th Century-Fox, 1952), screenplay by Robinson and Liam O'Brien;

Snows of Kilimanjaro (20th Century-Fox, 1952),
screenplay;

The Egyptian (20th Century-Fox, 1954), screenplay
by Robinson and Philip Dunne;

A Bullet Is Waiting (Columbia, 1954), story by Robinson and Thames Williamson;

While the City Sleeps (RKO, 1956), screenplay;

This Earth Is Mine (Universal, 1959), screenplay;

Son of Captain Blood (Paramount, 1964), screen
story and screenplay.

BOOK: *Now, Voyager* (Madison: University of Wisconsin Press, 1984).

Casey Robinson was a versatile screenwriter,
able to change genres and style at will. He was an
ideal choice for adapting literary works to the
screen, retaining the essential flavor of the originals
while creating good dramatic scenes. Robinson
seemed able to work and write in any genre: comedy, melodrama, adventure, mystery, Western.

Ricardo Cortez and Maria Corda in The Private Life of
Helen of Troy, *the film for which Robinson received his first
screen credit*

Robinson was born Kenneth C. Robinson in
Logan, Utah. He attended Cornell University before working as a newspaper reporter on the *New
York World*. His original intention had been to study
law, but he switched to English in college. In addition to his newspaper work, Robinson taught
English in high school in Brigham City, Utah. In
1927 he visited a friend in Hollywood who was
writing subtitles for *The Patent Leather Kid* and was
offered a job as an assistant for $100 a week, which
was more than he was paid as a teacher. Robinson
took the job. During 1927 and 1928, Robinson
helped write titles for thirteen films. His first was
The Private Life of Helen of Troy (1927), a humorous
depiction of historical characters, which was directed by Alexander Korda.

Robinson made a gradual transition from silent to sound pictures. His last silent film, *Times
Square* (1929), was released with some dialogue. He
wrote continuity only for *The Squealer* (1930), about
a criminal who turns himself in to aid his son. Robinson wrote the screen story for *The Last Parade*
(1931), a gangster movie, then wrote his first
screenplay for *Masquerade* (1931), a twenty-minute
short that he also directed. His first feature-length
script was for *Is My Face Red?* (1932), which he
adapted with Ben Markson from Markson and Allen Rivkins's play, in which a gossip columnist (Ricardo Cortez) is shot by an unknown enemy. Other
significant works of this period include *Lucky Devils*
(1933), about movie stuntmen; *She Made Her Bed*
(1934), a melodrama adapted from James Cain's
story "The Baby in the Ice Box"; and *I Love That
Man* (1933), coauthored with Gene Towne and
Graham Baker, about a con man who attempts to
reform.

In 1935 Harry Joe Brown, who had directed
The Squealer and *I Love That Man*, was made a producer at Warner Bros., and he hired Robinson as
a screenwriter. Their first collaboration was *I Found
Stella Parish* (1935), about an actress (Kay Francis)
who must flee England after being blackmailed,
leaving behind her career and her child. She finally
becomes a burlesque star in America. The film was
an example of the so-called "women's picture" in
which Robinson would excel later in his career.

His first big success, however, was in quite a
different genre—the swashbuckler. Warner Bros.
was encouraged by the success of period adventure
films at that time and decided to remake *Captain
Blood*, which had been filmed in 1924. The new
version starred Errol Flynn, and it made him a star.
The screenplay was a faithful adaption of Raphael
Sabatini's novel. Doctor Peter Blood is discovered

treating a wounded rebel and is convicted of treason, sent to Jamaica to be sold into slavery, and there treats the governor's gout and wins special privileges. Eventually he escapes and becomes a pirate. The character had all the traits that Flynn would epitomize in his later roles as the reckless, roguish hero. The critical reviews were generally excellent, and equally important was the favorable reception accorded the film by the public. *Captain Blood* (1935) revived the swashbuckler genre even as it discovered in Flynn the perfect hero for that type. It also made Flynn and his costar Olivia de Havilland a screen couple; they made eight pictures together, one of which, *Four's a Crowd* (1938), was written by Robinson. Though the many imitators that have followed have diluted the effectiveness of the swashbuckling genre, *Captain Blood* remains an exciting film.

In spite of this success, Robinson's next few assignments were routine. *I Married A Doctor* (1936)

was a poor adaptation of Sinclair Lewis's *Main Street*, and critical reception was not favorable toward what had become a soap opera rather than a satire. Frank Borzage directed *Hearts Divided* (1936), a satire about the romance between an American woman (Marion Davies) and the brother (Dick Powell) of Napoleon. *Give Me Your Heart* (1936) and *Stolen Holiday* (1936) were both vehicles for Kay Francis. In *Give Me Your Heart*, she played an unwed mother who turns the baby over to his father (George Brent), an English lord. *Stolen Holiday* is a fictionalized account of Sacha Stavisky, a swindler in 1930s Paris; Francis played the model who trys to reform him.

Robinson wrote six movies for Bette Davis. Mostly, these were melodramas filled with adultery, sexual innuendo, and Freudian secrets. His first script for Davis, though, was a light romantic comedy: *It's Love I'm After* (1937), directed by Archie Mayo. Joyce Arden (Davis) and Basil Underwood

Errol Flynn and Basil Rathbone in the swashbuckling Captain Blood, *which established Flynn as the rogue hero*

(Leslie Howard) are a star acting team who fight constantly offstage though they really love each other. A young actress (Olivia de Havilland) causes the triangle: Underwood must convince her to go back to her fiancé (Patric Knowles) before he can marry Arden. In the same year, Robinson wrote a similar, less successful romantic comedy, *Call It a Day* (1937), also directed by Mayo. The film was about the members of a British family who fall in and out of love in one afternoon.

Taken from Robert E. Sherwood's play, *Tovarich* (1937) was another successful literary adaptation by Robinson. Two Russian nobles (Charles Boyer and Claudette Colbert) hold the Czar's fortune and refuse to touch a penny for their own needs. They pose as a butler and a maid in order to hide out from Russian agents seeking the fortune. This film was followed by *Four's a Crowd* (1938), the least rewarding teaming of Flynn and de Havilland. A public relations man (Flynn) romances a young woman (de Havilland) in the hope of winning a contract from her father (Walter Connolly); his fiancée (Rosalind Russell) and her boyfriend (Patric Knowles) also become romantically involved before things are straightened out in the end.

Dark Victory (1939) has been remade twice and copied many times, but none of these versions has the power of Robinson's original screenplay. Judy Traherne (Bette Davis), an heiress embittered by a terminal illness, is redeemed through the love of Dr. Frederick Steele (George Brent), who marries her and devotes himself to searching for a cure. The final moments of the film are memorable: Judy, realizing she is about to die as blindness overcomes her, refuses to allow her husband to see her plight as she says goodbye to him and sends him off to a medical convention. The film rises above its melodramatic plot due to the fine performances (including Humphrey Bogart as the earthy stableman), Robinson's dialogue, and Edmund Goulding's direction.

Robinson, Davis, Goulding, and Brent were reunited in *The Old Maid* (1939). Robinson's script was based on Zoë Akin's play, which was itself a dramatization of Edith Wharton's novel. Charlotte Lovell (Davis) has an illegitimate daughter who is reared by her cousin (Miriam Hopkins); the girl never knows that Charlotte is her real mother. Davis also starred in *All This and Heaven Too* (1940), which Robinson adapted from Rachel Fields's novel of the same title. Set in nineteenth-century France, the film is about a governess (Davis) who is thought to be having an affair with the Duke De Praslin

(Charles Boyer), the father of her charges.

One of Robinson's more interesting literary adaptations is *Kings Row* (1941), from a popular novel by Henry Bellamann. The film is set in a small town at the turn of the century, and Robinson retains an air of suspense as he presents his many characters and subplots, keeping each distinct and identifiable. The film is structurally flawed, because the disparate subplots are strung together rather weakly. As melodrama, however, it works wonderfully, containing many powerful scenes and engrossing characters. The weakest scenes are those that try to address the then-topical interest in psychoanalysis. One character (Robert Cummings), the small-town boy who has studied psychoanalysis in Vienna, mouths the Freudian simplicities that mar the movement of the film. Still, Robinson's script skillfully underplays the sexual foibles of his characters, and Sam Wood's direction gives the film a refreshing vitality.

Like *Kings Row*, *One Foot in Heaven* (1941) is set at the turn of the century, but that is where similarities end. The picture follows its leading characters, minister William Spence (Fredric March) and his wife Hope (Martha Scott), through twenty-five years in their life, examining how changing times affect them and their family (and by extension, the rest of the country). Robinson followed this piece with uncredited work on two of the most successful films of the early 1940s: *Pride of the Yankees* (1942) and *Casablanca* (1943). Robinson's work on *Casablanca* was extensive; he helped to define and strengthen the romantic relationship between the two main characters, and it was at his suggestion that the Ilsa Lund character became a European, rather than the American woman of the original play.

Now, Voyager (1942) contains one of the best-remembered moments in screen history: Jerry Durrence (Paul Henreid) lights two cigarettes at once, then hands one to Charlotte Vale (Bette Davis). Vale is an emotionally disturbed middle-aged woman who meets Durrence on a cruise; she falls in love with him, then learns he is married. Robinson handles material such as insanity and adultery with taste and style; for all the unseemly behavior inherent in the plot, the film is quite inoffensive, a triumph of screenwriting for that era (though some critics feel it has caused the film to become rather badly dated). Indeed, it is possible to view *Now, Voyager* with a feeling that the sinners have been cleansed even in the act of sinning.

Robinson ended the years at Warner Bros.— the most productive period of his career—with *Pas-*

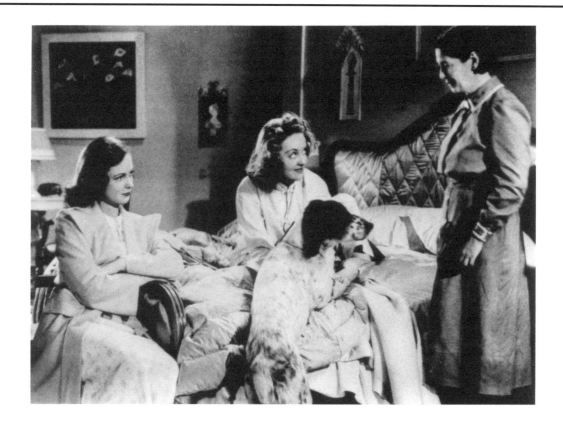

Scenes from two of Robinson's films for Bette Davis. (Top) Geraldine Fitzgerald, Davis, and Virginia Brissac in Dark Victory.
(Bottom) Paul Henreid and Davis in Now, Voyager.

Helmut Dantine, George Tobias, Humphrey Bogart, Billy Roy, and Philip Dorn in Passage to Marseille

sage to Marseille (1944), *The Corn Is Green* (1945), and *Saratoga Trunk* (1946). In *Passage to Marseille*, French journalist Matrac (Humphrey Bogart), framed by enemies after he opposes the Munich pact between England and Germany, is sent to Devil's Island, from which he escapes with four other convicts. They are picked up by a French freighter, and they prevent a mutiny by fascist sympathizers who want to turn the ship over to the Vichy government. *The Corn Is Green* was Robinson's last script for Bette Davis; it was adapted from Emlyn Williams's play and directed by Irving Rapper, who had also directed *Now, Voyager*. Davis is a schoolteacher in a Welsh mining town, determined that one of her students (John Dall) will be educated at Oxford. *Saratoga Trunk* was written by Robinson in 1943, but not released until 1946. It is an overlong adaptation of Edna Ferber's novel, about the romance between a Texas cowboy (Gary Cooper), trying to get control of a spur line, and a Creole (Ingrid Bergman), who wants to marry a rich man.

After leaving Warner Bros., Robinson an-nounced that he would start his own production company and release pictures through International Studios. Nothing came of this plan, and for several years Robinson worked free-lance at RKO, Columbia, M-G-M, and United Artists. His sole screenplay credits of this period are as follows: *The Macomber Affair* (1946), which he adapted from Hemingway's "The Short, Happy Life of Francis Macomber" (he also coproduced); and *Days of Glory* (1944), about Russians battling Nazis during World War II; and the screen story only for *The Racket Man* (1943), about a reformed gangster (Tom Neal) who becomes an undercover operative. Robinson worked without credit on the scripts for *Adventure* (1946), Clark Gable's first postwar film, and *The Mating of Millie* (1948), a romantic comedy which he also produced. He was credited with adaptation only for *Desire Me* (1947), taken from the novel, *Carl and Anna*, by Leonhard Frank. This production was remarkably troubled; four writers and two directors had to be hired before filming was completed. The movie, about a soldier (Richard Hart)

Thomas Mitchell, Vincent Price, and George Sanders in While the City Sleeps, *a crime thriller*

who becomes obsessed with the wife (Greer Garson) of a friend (Robert Mitchum), was a box office disaster.

In 1949 Robinson went to work for 20th Century-Fox, where he remained until 1954. His first film there was *Father Was a Fullback* (1949), about a high school football coach (Fred MacMurray) who has problems at work and at home. He produced his next three screenplays, *Under My Skin* (1950), *Two Flags West* (1950), and *Diplomatic Courier* (1952). *Under My Skin* was another Hemingway adaptation, taken from the story "My Old Man"; a jockey (John Garfield) who has begun taking bribes reforms for the sake of his son (Orley Lindgren). *Two Flags West* was Robinson's first attempt at writing a Western, and though it was based on a story by Frank Nugent, one of the best screenwriters in the Western genre, it was not a success. Robert Wise, also new to Westerns, directed. *Diplomatic Courier* was one of the first postwar spy films, and one of the best of the fifties. Henry Hathaway directed this story of an international spy (Tyrone Power) trying to avenge the death of a close friend.

Snows of Kilimanjaro (1952) was Robinson's third Hemingway adaptation. A novelist (Gregory Peck) tries to come to terms with himself as he prepares to die. Henry King directed. His last screenplay at 20th Century-Fox was for *The Egyptian* (1954), which was directed by Michael Curtiz, an old Warner Bros. associate. Robinson's original script contained many of the elements of his Warner Bros. successes, including an action-packed plot. But his screenplay was rewritten by Philip Dunne, and the resulting film is somewhat uneven.

After leaving 20th Century-Fox, Robinson produced and wrote his only other Western screenplay, *A Bullet Is Waiting* (1954), for Columbia studios. While they are stranded in the wilderness, a sheriff (Stephen McNally) begins to believe his prisoner's claim that he is innocent. John Farrow directed. *While the City Sleeps* (1956) was a crime thriller directed by Fritz Lang. As a psychopathic killer terrorizes a city, a newspaper publisher (Vincent Price) promises an editorial position to the first of his employees who catches the man. *This Earth*

Is Mine (1959) was an overlong study of vineyard owners in the 1930s.

In 1960, at the time he was married to ballerina Tamara Toumanova, Robinson oversaw production of *The Copenhagen Ballet*, a documentary film. He then wrote one final screenplay, the sequel to his first success, *Captain Blood. Son of Captain Blood* (1964), released nearly thirty years after the original, starred Sean Flynn, son of Errol, but it was unable to duplicate the earlier film's success. In the 1970s, Robinson retired from screenwriting and immigrated to Australia, the home of his third wife. There he served for many years as an advisor

to the growing Australian film industry. Casey Robinson died in 1979.

References:

Rudy Behlmer, *America's Favorite Movies: Behind the Scenes* (New York: Ungar, 1982), pp. 160-171;

Joel Greenberg and Allen Eyles, "Writing for the Movies," *Focus on Film*, 32 (April 1979);

Molly Johnson, "Casey Now at Bat Down Under," *Los Angeles Times*, 20 July 1975;

Profile of Casey Robinson, *Writer's Guild Newsletter* (November 1970).

Waldo Salt
(18 October 1914-   )

Stephen Lesser

SELECTED MOTION PICTURES: *The Shopworn Angel* (M-G-M, 1938), screenplay;

Wild Man of Borneo (M-G-M, 1941), screenplay by Salt and John Mcclain;

Tonight We Raid Calais (20th Century-Fox, 1943), screenplay;

Mr. Winkle Goes to War (Columbia, 1944), screen story and screenplay by Salt, George Corey, and Louis Solomon;

A Likely Story (RKO, 1947), additional dialogue;

Rachel and the Stranger (RKO, 1948), screenplay;

The Flame and the Arrow (Warner Bros., 1950), screen story and screenplay;

M (Columbia, 1951), additional dialogue;

Taras Bulba (United Artists, 1962), screenplay by Salt and Karl Tunberg;

Wild and Wonderful (Universal, 1963), screenplay by Salt, Larry Markes, and Michael Morris;

Flight from Ashiya (United Artists, 1964), screenplay by Salt and Elliott Arnold;

Midnight Cowboy (United Artists, 1969), screenplay;

The Gang That Couldn't Shoot Straight (M-G-M, 1971), screenplay;

Serpico (Paramount, 1973), screenplay by Salt and Norman Wexler;

Day of the Locust (Paramount, 1975), screenplay;

Coming Home (United Artists, 1978), screenplay by Salt and Robert C. Jones.

The film career of Waldo Salt may be broken into three periods. During the first period he was a professional, competent but unexceptional writer. In 1951 he testified before the House Un-American Activities Committee and was consequently blacklisted for approximately eleven years. During this time Salt was not able to work in motion pictures and turned his efforts to other media. Following his re-emergence as a recognized screenwriter in 1962, he wrote a few mediocre films but moved to a new plateau by the end of the 1960s, producing compelling, memorable screenplays.

Salt was born in Chicago, Illinois. Educated at a private school in Victoria, British Columbia, he also attended the San Raphael Military Academy in California, then Stanford University, graduating in 1934. Salt has been married three times; his daughter Jennifer is an actress.

After teaching one year at Menlo Junior College, Salt was hired as a junior writer at M-G-M. He began as an uncredited contributor of dialogue to such movies as *Double Wedding* (1937) and *The Adventures of Huckleberry Finn* (1938); he wrote his first screenplay, *The Shopworn Angel*, in 1938. A cynical Broadway actress (Margaret Sullavan) marries a naive soldier (James Stewart) about to go to battle, then realizes she loves another man (Walter

William Holden and Loretta Young in Rachel and the Stranger, *the last film Salt wrote for RKO before he was blacklisted in 1951*

Pidgeon). Salt won praise for this first screenplay credit, with critics commenting on his well-developed characters and believable dialogue. His next assignment was *Wild Man of Borneo* (1941), adapted from Herman Mankiewicz and Marc Connelly's play about a con man (Frank Morgan) who reforms for the sake of his daughter (Mary Howard).

At the beginning of World War II, Salt left M-G-M to become a civilian consultant to the Office of War Information, where he wrote films for the army. He also advised on a government film about the 1945 San Francisco Conference that established the United Nations. The only commercial movies he worked on during this period were two very different films about the war: *Tonight We Raid Calais* (1943) and *Mr. Winkle Goes to War* (1944). In *Tonight We Raid Calais* a British agent (John Sutton) is sent into occupied France to locate a factory set for an RAF bombing raid. In *Mr. Winkle Goes to War* a mild-mannered man (Edward G. Robinson) in his forties is drafted and becomes a hero.

Salt returned to full-time screenwriting after the war, providing additional dialogue for the comedy *A Likely Story* (1947). His next solo screenplay credit came with *Rachel and the Stranger* (1948), an offbeat frontier romance. Based on short stories by Howard Fast, the story takes place in a backwoods section of the Northwest Territory in the early days of the country. A frontier widower (William Hol-

den) marries again to provide his young son with a caretaker. He treats his wife (Loretta Young) as a servant, rebuffing her attempts at affection until a visiting stranger (Robert Mitchum) begins to show an interest in her. *Rachel and the Stranger* earned Salt a nomination for a Writers Guild award. Salt seemed on the verge of emerging from the obscurity of the contract writer who has little control over his assignments. But his career was disrupted in 1947 when he received a subpoena to testify before the House Un-American Activities Committee. He went to New York but was not called to testify. When he returned to Hollywood, he was informed that his contract with RKO would not be renewed.

Unable to find work at any studio, Salt went to work for independent producer Harold Hecht, writing *The Flame and the Arrow* (1950). The movie is a tongue-in-cheek adventure set in medieval Italy, with a peasant (Burt Lancaster) leading the populace against the cruel rulers. Though the film was perceived as little more than light entertainment, there is some slight political comment in its "poor people versus rich oppressors" theme. Still, Salt was not pleased with the completed film; he later said it was "really supposed to be about a medieval Yippy—an Abby Hoffman . . . I really wanted to do a Marx brothers swashbuckler. Jack Warner didn't like the idea." Joseph Losey then hired Salt to write dialogue for the remake of *M* in 1951; it was his last assignment before being blacklisted. That same year Salt was finally called before the House Committee. He refused to answer questions about affiliation with the Communist party or to identify other party members.

"As a matter of confidence towards those who helped me during that period" Salt refuses to identify any films he worked on without credit while blacklisted, though he will admit to polishing the script of *The Crimson Pirate* (1952), the follow-up film to *The Flame and the Arrow.* He also says that M-G-M bought his script for *Ivanhoe* (1952), but "it was deliberately rewritten to get rid of my credit." Under pseudonyms, Salt worked in New York as a television writer and story editor. He also completed a folk opera, *Sandhog,* with singer Earl Robinson that opened in an Off-Broadway production at the Phoenix Theatre.

Harold Hecht finally brought Salt off the blacklist in 1962, hiring him to write *Taras Bulba* (1962), *Wild and Wonderful* (1963), and *Flight from Ashiya* (1964). *Taras Bulba,* based on the novel by Nicolai Gogol, is a historical drama depicting a rul-

ing family in nineteenth-century Ukraine. *Flight from Ashiya* is about an escape from an Iron Curtain country. *Wild and Wonderful* is a comedy—a genre Salt seems ill-suited for—about a poodle that becomes a movie star. None of these movies shows Salt working at the peak of his form; it was not until *Midnight Cowboy* (1969) that Salt established himself as a master screenwriter.

Salt was signed to write *Midnight Cowboy* after his agent, George Litto, brought him together with director John Schlesinger. The screenplay was adapted from the novel by James Leo Herlihy. Salt has said that in transferring the material to the screen "the main thing was to keep it, to translate it," but his screenplay did more than just "keep it"; it fleshed out the characters of Joe Buck (Jon Voight), a Texas hustler lost in New York, and Rizzo (Dustin Hoffman), the seedy street character who befriends him. It was a sensitive, well-crafted script that made good use of Salt's chief writing talent: the ability to depict strong characters and allow the viewer to identify with them. *Midnight Cowboy* was one of the landmark films of the 1960s:

Dustin Hoffman and Jon Voight in Midnight Cowboy, *which established Salt's reputation as a major screenwriter*

Tony Roberts and Al Pacino in Serpico, *based on Peter Maas's book about police corruption in New York City*

from the police force. Salt had begun working on the movie in 1972, with John Avildsen to direct; when Avildsen was replaced by Sidney Lumet, Salt departed as well, and Norman Wexler reworked his screenplay somewhat. The shooting script seems to have been mostly Salt's, however; he and Wexler received an Academy Award nomination for their work.

Shortly after the release of *Midnight Cowboy*, Paramount studios had approached John Schlesinger with the idea of filming Nathaneal West's novel *The Day of the Locust*. Schlesinger and Salt worked on the project for several years before coming up with a suitable script and cast. When the film was released in 1975, it became the center of a controversy: some critics praised it as a faithful adaptation of West's grim Hollywood novel, with others calling it heavy-handed and overlong, lacking a narrative focus. There is some validity to both views. The film is faithful to the material in the novel, and finds the visual equivalents to communicate the emptiness of the characters' lives and the sense of doom hanging over the community. But it lacks West's apocalyptic vision, which gave the story its meaning and coherence. Salt's talents lie on a smaller scale, writing in a more realistic world, a talent he shows in his next film, *Coming Home* (1978).

Coming Home went through a complicated path from conception to final production. Screenwriter Nancy Dowd developed the original story, with Salt brought in to revise her work. He spent fourteen months researching the lives of paraplegic Vietnam veterans then became ill before completing the shooting script; Robert Jones completed the screenplay. Director John Schlesinger was replaced by Hal Ashby, who had his cast improvise much of the material while filming.

Possibly because it avoids political issues and concentrates on the effect the war had on human lives, *Coming Home* was the first Vietnam film to find a large audience. It presents a romantic triangle of paraplegic Luke Martin (Jon Voight); Sally Hyde (Jane Fonda), who works at Martin's veteran's hospital; and Sally's husband Bob (Bruce Dern), a captain in Vietnam. As in *Serpico*, the screenplay shows one person responding to social changes, with Sally becoming more independent after meeting Luke. The movie recreates the social tensions of the 1960s; but its ending hurts the movie. Salt had intended for Bob Hyde to go berserk, become a sniper, and get run over on a freeway. Ashby replaced this climax with Bob drowning himself, while Luke gives an antiwar speech and

its frank depiction of seamy city life loosened the restrictions on what could be shown in the cinema. Some critics found fault with the film, particularly in its grotesque characters and frequent flashbacks to Buck's childhood, but on the whole it was very highly regarded. It won an Academy Award for best picture; Salt won another for his screenplay; and Schlesinger was chosen best director.

From the career high point of *Midnight Cowboy*, Salt next moved to a low—*The Gang That Couldn't Shoot Straight* (1971). It is a comic story of criminal gangs feuding in New York City, adapted from Jimmy Breslin's novel. The humor is forced and the characters stereotyped; the movie received the worst reviews of any in Salt's career.

Salt was able to demonstrate his skill in characterization more to his advantage in *Serpico* (1973). Based on the book by Peter Maas, it tells the story of an honest cop (Al Pacino) whose tenacity and courage led to the formation of the Knapp Commission to investigate police corruption in New York. The film is told in flashbacks, following the near-fatal shooting of Serpico, possibly by another police officer. As he lies hospitalized, the audience sees Serpico's growth from naive rookie to a disillusioned man of the street; he eventually resigns

Sally shops for groceries. Despite this problem, the film was well received by critics. Salt, Fonda, and Voight all won Academy Awards and the film received other nominations for best picture, best director, and best supporting actor (Dern).

At best, Waldo Salt's screenplays seek to make sense of society by depicting characters who are either alienated or seeking new values in a changing world. He focuses on what he sees as common human characteristics, the resilient qualities of courage and compassion. Despite elements of cinematic exaggeration and sentimentality, Salt's screenplays remain rooted in his characterizations of normal persons trying to cope with social problems.

References:

John Cogley, *Report on Blacklisting* (Fund for the Republic, 1956);

Hearings before the House Un-American Activities Committee, eighty-second Congress, First Session, "Communist Infiltration of Hollywood," testimony on 13 April 1951, pp. 259-274.

Papers:

The Theatre Arts Library in the UCLA Research Library, Los Angeles, houses the manuscripts for *Coming Home, Serpico,* and *The Shopworn Angel.*

John Thomas Sayles

(28 September 1950-   )

Terry L. Andrews
Chadwick School

MOTION PICTURES: *Piranha* (New World Pictures, 1978), screenplay;

The Lady in Red (New World Pictures, 1979), screenplay;

Battle Beyond the Stars (New World Pictures, 1980), screen story by Sayles and Anne Dyer; screenplay;

The Return of the Secaucus Seven (Salsipuedes, 1980), screenplay;

The Howling (Avco-Embassy, 1981), screenplay by Sayles and Terence H. Winkless;

Alligator (BLC, 1981), screen story by Sayles and Frank Ray Perilli; screenplay;

The Challenge (CBS, 1982), screenplay by Sayles and Richard Maxwell;

Lianna (Windwood, 1983), screenplay;

Baby, It's You (Double Play, 1983), screenplay;

The Brother from Another Planet (Cinecom International, 1984), screenplay.

PLAY PRODUCTION: *New Hope for the Dead* and *Turnbuckle,* New York, 1981.

BOOKS: *The Pride of the Bimbos* (Boston: Little, Brown, 1975);

Union Dues (Boston: Little, Brown, 1977);

The Anarchists' Convention (Boston: Little, Brown, 1979).

TELEVISION: *A Perfect Match* (CBS, 1980), teleplay.

PERIODICAL PUBLICATIONS: "At the Republican Convention," *New Republic,* 183 (2 August 1980): 20-25;

"I Never Think of Posterity," *New York Times Book Review,* 6 September 1981, pp. 3, 21-22;

Review of William Golding's *Adventures in the Screen Trade, Film Comment,* 19 (May-June 1983): 72-73.

In the years since 1978, John Sayles has fashioned one of the most vital and versatile careers in contemporary American film. With a rare combination of commercial adaptability and clear-eyed independence, Sayles has achieved a remarkable dual success both within and outside the Hollywood system. On the one hand, by writing screenplays for such filmmakers as Roger Corman, Sayles has established himself as an agile craftsman of plot and dialogue in the conventional Hollywood genres: horror, science fiction, gangster, and martial-arts films. On the other hand, he has used his screenplay earnings and growing "bankability" to finance more personal features on subjects which Hollywood considers too risky for the kind of direct, open treatment which Sayles prefers. Yet despite the obvious differences between the Hollywood genre films he scripts and the personal films he both writes and directs (and often acts in and edits), there is an impressive unity in Sayles's work, a unity which shines forth in his published writings as well. Ultimately, John Sayles is an extraordinary comic humanist—an entertainer and satirist, but above all a believer in people, whose humor affirms the value and the resilience of his all-too-human characters.

The prevailing stance of Sayles's work—a committed inner seriousness expressed through a relaxed outer humor—may be traced to his origins. The son of two educators, Sayles was born and raised an Irish-German Catholic in Schenectady, New York, and these roots may partially account for the interest in cultural diversity and the strong social conscience which is always evident in his work. But the serious social commitment at the core of Sayles's writing is well masked by a working-class nonchalance and humor which shun pretense and intellectualism. He claims that in his youth he never thought of being a writer as a vocation or an identity; it was just that writing was always easy and fun for him. To amuse himself, Sayles wrote stories based on popular television shows like *The Untouchables,* but he took sports much more seriously than writing or studies, and with a strong six-foot-four-inch frame, he earned letters in four sports at Mount Pleasant High School in Schenectady.

Despite his professed lack of interest in scholarship, Sayles enrolled in Williams College, where he claims to have spent more time playing pool and intramural athletics than studying. Nonetheless, he majored in psychology (partly due to an interest in reading case studies), kept his grades up through his prolific output in creative-writing courses, and studied foreign film in classes taught by Charles Thomas Samuels. Sayles acted in several college drama productions, and made friends with several people who would later collaborate on his film projects, including Maggie Renzi, his long-time companion, who has worked as a producer, an actress, or both on three of his four independent films.

After graduating from Williams in 1972, Sayles drifted through various jobs and locales while writing in his spare time. He worked as an orderly in an Albany nursing home, a day laborer shoveling clay in Atlanta, and a meat packer in a sausage factory in Boston. In the summers he would return to New England, where he acted in a summer stock theater in North Conway, New Hampshire. After two years of receiving rejection slips from magazines, Sayles sold the story "I-80 Nebraska, m.490-m.205" to the *Atlantic Monthly* in May 1975. A tall tale of a crazed truck driver told largely in citizen's band slang, "I-80 Nebraska" won an O. Henry Short Story Award, and Sayles's career as a writer was launched.

In the years since "I-80 Nebraska," Sayles has published two novels, many short stories, and several nonfiction articles—all notable for their interest in American dialects, quirky characters, and social issues. His first novel, *The Pride of the Bimbos* (1975), tells the story of a bedraggled five-man softball team which barnstorms the South playing exhibition games in women's clothing. His second novel, *Union Dues* (1977), follows two protagonists from West Virginia to Boston: young Hobie McNatt, who runs away to find his brother but instead gets involved in violent New Left politics, and Hobie's father Hunter, a coal miner who leaves his struggling union to search for Hobie. This wide-ranging, dispassionate political novel was the only work of fiction to be nominated for both the National Book Award and the National Book Critics' Circle Award in 1977.

Sayles's collection of short stories written from 1975 to 1979, *The Anarchists' Convention* (1979), contains a broad range of humorous but affecting stories about misfits and workers. One of the stories, "Breed," earned Sayles a second O. Henry Award in 1977. His other writings besides his scripts include two one-act plays—*New Hope for the Dead* and *Turnbuckle*—which Sayles directed in a 1981 Off-Broadway production which was panned by critics.

Sayles was eager to turn his success as an author of fiction into opportunities to work in the movies. In 1978 his literary agent for *Union Dues* put him in touch with a Hollywood agency, and Sayles wasted no time: he sent in a sample screenplay based on the 1919 Chicago Black Sox bribery scandal, and he moved to Santa Barbara to be closer to movie industry activity. Like many of Sayles's later film projects, the Black Sox screenplay never reached the screen. But Roger Corman, the surviving dean of Hollywood's B-movie producers, soon gave Sayles a rewrite job on *Piranha* (directed

As soon as Sayles heard the title Piranha, *he "knew the film would make money," but first he had to rewrite the script to explain how the man-eating fish were released into a North American river and "once everyone knew the fish were in the water, why didn't they just stay out of there?"*

by Joe Dante, 1978), Corman's attempt to cash in on the lingering popularity of *Jaws* (1975).

With its exhilarating combination of self-conscious mockery, social commentary, and intriguing character development, Sayles's screenplay for *Piranha* (1978) sets the terms and the standard for his successful career in genre movies. The picture is filled with in-jokes that ironically counterpoint the horror to come: an allusion to *Citizen Kane*, brief glimpses of piranha in a video game, a girl reading *Moby-Dick* on a crowded beach. But there is a more serious side to *Piranha* as well. The essence of Sayles's rewrite assignment was to provide credible premises for the plot: how do ravenous piranha come to inhabit a North American river, and why don't people hear about them and simply stay out of the water? To answer these questions, Sayles provides social underpinnings which are remarkably well developed for a low-budget horror film. During the Vietnam War the army had set up a secret research project, Operation Razorteeth, to

develop a super species of piranha to destroy the river systems of the North Vietnamese. When the piranha are accidentally released into the American river, Paul and Maggie must struggle not only against them but against a corrupt conspiracy of the military, scientists, and a resort owner, all of whom want to cover up the escape of the fish.

Piranha was a box-office hit, but Sayles's second film for Corman, *The Lady in Red* (also released as *Guns, Sin, and Bathtub Gin*, 1979), went virtually unnoticed by critics and died after a very short run. Its commercial failure is unfortunate, for it began with Sayles's most ambitious and carefully researched screenplay, and the film deserves more attention than it has received. Sayles has expressed disappointment in the way his screenplay was treated, saying that massive cuts reduced the film to a sometimes incomprehensible bloodbath. But whatever Sayles's opinion of the film, *The Lady in Red* holds up as a satisfying genre movie with a strong social conscience.

A caustic, fatalistic study of American social conditions in the 1930s, *The Lady in Red* is a gangster film told from a woman's (and feminist) point of view. The movie approaches the famed shooting of Dillinger outside the Biograph theater in Chicago through the imagined history of Polly Franklin (Pamela Sue Martin), the woman who supposedly set him up for the police. Bad luck, bad judgment, and hostile social conditions reduce Polly from a bank robbery hostage, to a naive victim of seduction, to a sexually harassed garment worker, to a dime-a-dance girl, to a convict, to a prostitute, and eventually to a bank robber. Sayles's screenplay also deftly traces the collusion between gangsters, prison guards, police, press, and politicians—an exploitative network which puts relentless and eventually murderous pressure on the underdogs. *The Lady in Red* is not all bleak fatalism, however. What is most memorable and moving about the film are the moments of tenderness and support, and eventually the strong alliances, that Sayles shows the downtrodden characters sharing with each other.

Sayles's third and last film for Corman's New World Pictures was a second hit, and was (like *Piranha*) designed to follow on the coattails of a previous blockbuster. *Battle Beyond the Stars* (1980) copied the *Star Wars* format of outer space adventure with copious special effects and alien characters, but the Corman idea which Sayles developed to his own intriguing ends was to use the plot of *The Magnificent Seven* (1960). The picaresque structure of the young hero Shad (Richard Thomas) recruiting mercenaries to defeat the evil forces of Sador (John Saxon) allows Sayles to include a wide range of entertaining characters, all allusions to other works. From Greek mythology comes Dr. Hephaestus (Sam Jaffe); from the German, the Valkyrie warrior St. Exmin (Sybil Danning); from the film *Dark Star* (1974) comes a female talking spaceship, Nell. The movie also has an underlying serious theme which Sayles describes as "death, different life forms' attitudes toward death." Though he claims the death theme is not meant to be solemn or profound, it does add a surprising resonance to some of the characters, particularly

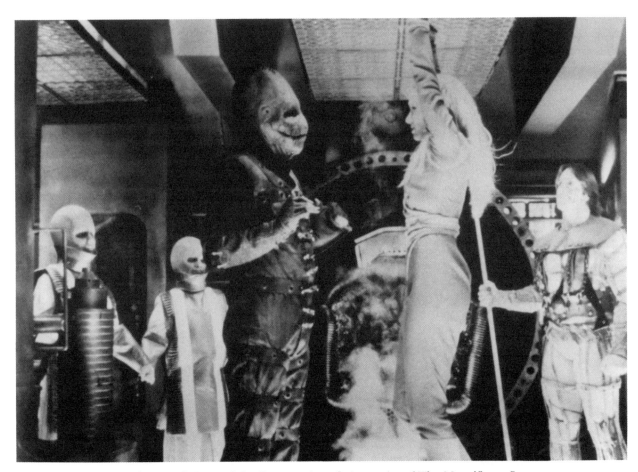

Scene from Battle Beyond the Stars, *a science-fiction version of* The Magnificent Seven

St. Exmin and aging mercenary Gelt (Robert Vaughn).

As with his previous scripts, Sayles enjoyed writing these genre movies, but he was frustrated with the cuts and changes which appeared in the finished product. Thus he decided to make a low-budget display film to convince the Hollywood studios that he would make good use of their money to direct his own material. This display piece, *The Return of the Secaucus Seven* (1980), is still the most critically acclaimed and financially successful (in relation to its costs) of the four films Sayles has written and directed. Shot on a budget of $40,000 (with an additional $20,000 needed later for editing and lab costs), *The Return of the Secaucus Seven* was based on a screenplay that won both the Los Angeles Film Critics Award and an Academy Award nomination. In addition, the movie was cited as one of the ten best films of the year by *Time*, the *Boston Globe*, and the *Los Angeles Times*, and it continues to take in profits on the revival theater circuit, grossing over two million dollars to date.

Sayles's creation of *The Return of the Secaucus Seven* is a case study in the low-budget filmmaking principles of tailoring one's project to one's resources and of turning limitations into expressive strengths. With only $40,000 saved from his own screenplay and fiction earnings, Sayles knew that he could not afford guild actors, and with little knowledge of the technical side of filmmaking, Sayles knew the film would have to be based on dialogue rather than camera movement. To keep the film from seeming too static, he decided to use a structure like *Nashville* (1975), cutting from one conversation to another. When he thought about the actors from Williams and New Hampshire summer stock he would be using, Sayles realized they were all turning thirty, so he made that the film's theme. Finally, he decided to set the film in North Conway, New Hampshire, which he knew from his work in summer stock, and where he could vary the action between scenes shot indoors and out, daytime and nighttime.

Less intentional perhaps than these conscious decisions is the way in which Sayles's spare style complements the action on the screen. The central characters are seven former political activists (based on people Sayles knew in Boston in the mid-1970s) who return to a New Hampshire resort town each fall for a weekend reunion. To broaden the film's frame of social reference, Sayles shows these seven interacting not only with each other, but also with Chip (Gordon Clapp), a more conventional liberal Democrat who is the new boyfriend of one of them,

and with Ron (David Stathairn) and Howie (played by Sayles himself), locals who are old high school friends of another of the seven. On the one hand, Sayles's style in his dialogue and juxtaposition of scenes is often razor-sharp, as he accentuates the ironies of these characters' struggles with the passage into adulthood: struggles involving vocation, relationships, marriage, parenthood, and continued political commitment. On the other hand, Sayles's visual style within each scene has a relaxed, improvisational quality which sometimes borders on the awkwardness of a home movie, and this casualness enhances the reunion intimacy of these characters meeting or rediscovering each other.

The shooting of *The Return of the Secaucus Seven* was completed in 1978, but Sayles needed an extra $20,000 for rental of an editing machine (which he taught himself to use as he was editing the film) and for postproduction costs to enlarge the film from 16 to 35 mm. To raise these funds, he wrote three scripts: a melodrama for a made-for-television movie (*A Perfect Match*, 1980) and two more horror films (*The Howling*, 1981 and *Alligator*, 1981).

In *A Perfect Match*, directed by Mel Damski, Sayles uses the genre of "the women's film," a type popular from the 1930s to the 1950s until it was largely replaced by television soap operas. Coleen Dewhurst stars as a woman who is stricken by a bone-marrow illness and seeks the daughter (Linda Kelsey) she gave up for adoption years before. Despite its sentimental content, Sayles was pleased with the film and sorry that it debuted on television at the same time that *Jaws* and *The End* (1978) were being shown, and thus did not attract much of the viewing audience.

The Howling marks Sayles's second collaboration with director Joe Dante, and like *Piranha*, their previous film together, it made remarkable use of its low budget (this time $1 million) and was successful at the box office. But *The Howling* drew more critical attention than *Piranha:* most of the reviews were positive, and some recognized the sophistication of its visual and narrative style.

The Howling intensifies the three elements present in all of Sayles's horror films—genre conventions, self-conscious humor, and social commentary—in a way which some critics found disconcerting, but which ultimately make it Sayles's most interesting work in the genre. When compared with Frankenstein or Dracula, the myth of man turning into wolf has had relatively few screen incarnations, but *The Howling* revives the genre with compelling force. Sayles and Dante tap into

Lobby poster for one of Sayles's 1983 films (courtesy of Dale Campbell, The Nickelodeon, Columbia, S.C.)

audience dread of urban violence by staging the first werewolf attack in a downtown pornography store, and later scenes in a more traditional country setting create steadily increasing terror as it becomes clear that an entire community is comprised of werewolves.

Even as *The Howling* is making the werewolf menace horrifyingly real, the film is just as busy mocking the genre it is so effectively reviving. In-jokes, allusive names, and cameo appearances (including Sayles himself as a morgue attendant) are so frequent and emphasized that some reviewers complained that these elements dissipate the horror and suspense. And as before, Sayles offers social commentary in the movie that seems partly playful, partly serious. In a lighthearted satire on trendy psychological movements, the plot traces the werewolf threat to an Esalenlike community on the California coast, where the clientele are encouraged to liberate their instinctual selves, but

then become werewolves. More disturbing is the theme, common to many of Sayles's works, that the media are untrustworthy, more concerned with sensationalism or expediency than with the truth. At the beginning of *The Howling* television station manager Fred Francis (Kevin McCarthy) is anxious to boost his ratings by having his reporter (Dee Wallace) meet a psychotic killer, but at the film's end, Francis tries to prevent her from revealing her own transformation into a werewolf.

A third commercial success for Sayles in the horror genre was *Alligator*, a remake of *Piranha* in an urban environment. Rather than piranha loose in a backcountry river, the menace this time is a thirty-foot alligator loose in the sewer system of a midwestern city, but the culprits responsible for the terror are, again, irresponsible scientists and politicians. Baby alligator Ramon is flushed into the city sewer, where it grows to monstrous proportions by feeding on a scientific research company's illegal

Advertisement for the modern-day tale of werewolves by Sayles and Terence Winkless

refuse: hormone-treated animal carcasses. Unfortunately, company president Slade (Dean Jagger) is so powerful that he controls the city's mayor; as in *Piranha*, the hero and heroine—a police officer (Robert Forster) and a herpetologist (Robin Riker)—must struggle not only against the animal menace but also against a political conspiracy which wants to cover up the origins of the problem. As in the case of earlier films, Sayles was somewhat disappointed with the way his screenplay for *Alligator* was filmed and edited. He had intended to show how Ramon "eats [his] way through the whole socio-economic system," from ghetto to the mayor's exclusive neighborhood, but the social commentary was mostly obscured by frenzied action sequences.

In a marathon three-day rewrite session, Sayles worked on one other genre script which did reach the screen—*The Challenge* (directed by John Frankenheimer, 1982)—but it is by far the weakest of the films he has written. The story of washed-up American boxer Rick Murphy (Scott Glenn) who comes to join forces with Japanese martial arts master Yoshida (Toshiro Mifune), *The Challenge* is hindered by a highly improbable plot and hackneyed dialogue. But in typical Sayles fashion, the final action scenes do contain some outrageous humor and social commentary. Using the traditional weapons of an earlier Japan, Rick and Yoshida manage to fight their way into the mammoth fortress of a modern Japanese corporation. But in a final frenetic battle, Rick uses anything that comes to hand—office furniture, a stapler, a typewriter cable—to defeat Yoshida's evil brother and recover a treasured family sword.

Finally, in 1983, Sayles's efforts to gain more control over the filming of his screenplays came to fruition with the release of two independently produced features, *Lianna* and *Baby, It's You*, both written and directed (and the first one edited) by Sayles.

Sayles had written the screenplay for *Lianna* before *The Return of the Secaucus Seven*, but he judged it too controversial and too expensive to try to finance until he had established himself. Following the success of *Secaucus*, Sayles hoped to raise at least $800,000 for *Lianna* so the film could be made in 35mm, but he found the studios wanted too many changes in his story of a woman who leaves her husband and children to commit herself to a lesbian relationship. So with a $300,000 budget, Sayles made *Lianna* in 16mm in Hoboken, New Jersey, and had the film enlarged to 35mm. Some reviewers criticized *Lianna* for being cinematically awkward or insufficiently dramatized, but most praised the film for its offbeat candor, witty dia-

logue, and warmly humorous characterizations. In the cities where *Lianna* played, audiences were receptive, and the film grossed a respectable $800,000.

According to a reviewer for *Ms.*, *Lianna* is "the best-ever gay-theme film," and it may be Sayles's best film as well, for it deals not only with the romantic, subjective side of his heroine's lesbian awakening but with its social consequences as well. Further, Sayles set out to make a movie not only about coming out as a lesbian but also about the issues that arise when any woman without a career leaves her family: what happens to the children, and how does a woman who has never been on her own face the problems of housing, employment, and loneliness? To these complex issues, well portrayed by Linda Griffiths as Lianna, Sayles also adds an insightful satire of academia: Lianna's husband Dick (Jon DeVries) is a philandering junior faculty member who is struggling for tenure, her lover Ruth (Jane Hallaren) is an established professor who insists on keeping their romance a discreet secret, and Sayles himself plays Jerry, a licentious film production teacher who tries to capitalize on Lianna's loneliness. But the real triumph of the film is that, for all its social seriousness, *Lianna* is an entertaining comedy. By dramatizing Lianna's sexual awakening and quest for autonomy in relation to a detailed network of articulate people, Sayles continually delights the viewer with the variety of feelings at play, and of perspectives which can be entertained, in a narrative which might easily have lapsed into ponderous "problem" drama.

Baby, It's You, which Sayles developed from a story by coproducer Amy Robinson, was his most expensive independent production. Because the story deals with a comically mismatched couple in a high school romance, the producers were able to raise $2.9 million for a youth-oriented film with a rock and roll soundtrack. For once, Sayles was able to hire a more skilled editor than himself, and a top-notch cinematographer: Michael Ballhaus, who shot most of R. W. Fassbinder's films. Paramount gave the film major studio distribution and publicity, and the reviews were generally favorable, but, curiously, *Baby, It's You* was only modestly successful at the box office.

The story of *Baby, It's You* appealed to Sayles because, like his own *Union Dues* and *The Return of the Secaucus Seven*, it deals with issues of the 1960s, with class distinctions, and with rites of passage into adulthood. The first half of the film is set in Trenton, New Jersey—an ethnic melting pot much like

Sayles's Schenectady. He was drawn to the idea that a large public high school in the 1960s was "the last bastion of true democracy in our society"—a place where ethnic groups and social classes could still mix, and an overachieving Jewish princess headed for Sarah Lawrence could fall in love with a macho Italian hood who was headed nowhere.

But Sayles was also drawn to the idea of going beyond teenage comedies like *American Graffiti* (1973) to dramatize the struggles of his characters Jill (Rosanna Arquette) and Sheik (Vincent Spano) after high school. With poignant humor, Sayles shows how Sheik's grandiose plan—to emulate his idol Frank Sinatra in Miami Beach—falls predictably flat. But more ironically, Sayles shows how Jill is also disillusioned, for her earnest overachieving style is out of place at a college where marijuana and a new counterculture are making inroads, and her hopes for a glorious college drama career and social life are dashed by arrogant or juvenile males. At the end, Jill and Sheik find welcome refuge in coming back together (for however brief a time), and the film's conclusion shows them dancing at Jill's college prom to the ironic, yet affecting accompaniment of Sinatra's "Strangers in the Night."

Sayles's need to continuously scramble for the funds to make his films was alleviated somewhat in January 1983, when he received a five-year tax-free "genius award" of $35,000 a year from the MacArthur Foundation. He initally wanted to start production on "Matewan"—a "low-budget epic" about the bloody 1920s struggle to unionize West Virginia miners—for this project would have allowed him to put black actors to work in feature roles.

Finding the project too ambitious, however, Sayles turned to another in which black actors and technicians would be equally crucial: a science-fiction comedy in which an extraterrestrial black slave escapes to Harlem. Starting with a budget of $200,000 (which eventually grew to $350,000), Sayles wrote *The Brother from Another Planet* (1984) in a week, filmed it in four (with difficult location work in Harlem), and edited it himself. Reviewers had high praise for the film's social comedy and the charming mute character of the Brother (Joe Morton), but criticized two aspects of the production: Sayles's attempt to stretch the film into an indictment of heroin trafficking, and the confusing developments involving two white aliens (one played by Sayles) who come to recapture the Brother. Despite these flaws, *The Brother from Another Planet* proved to be Sayles's biggest box-office

success since *The Return of the Secaucus Seven*.

It is ironic that Sayles, who struggled so long to free himself from the strictures of genre movies, and who is celebrated most for his ability to write witty dialogue, should turn to science fiction and a mute protagonist for one of his most successful independent films. But Sayles's use of the science fiction genre in *The Brother from Another Planet* does not show him conforming to some imagined need to fit his vision into conventional forms. Rather, it shows him fitting the genre to his vision, shows a pragmatic humanist who is not bound by any fixed notions of what type of film will best allow him to explore his characters in any given situation. In a way, the character of the Brother is a metaphor for John Sayles at his best, for the central irony of the film is that the Brother fits in anywhere, is less "alien" than any of the other characters, because he seems to be so willing to pay attention while other people express themselves.

Interviews:

Al Auster and Leonard Quart, "Counterculture Revisited," *Cineaste*, 11, no. 1 (1980-1981);

"And Then I Just Go Ahead and Write That Dialogue," *Movietone News*, nos. 66, 67 (March 1981);

David Chute, "John Sayles: Designated Writer," *Film Comment*, 17 (May-June 1981);

Tom Schlesinger, "Putting People Together," *Film Quarterly*, 34 (Summer 1981): 1-8;

David Osborn, "John Sayles: From Hoboken to Hollywood—and Back," *American Film* (October 1982): 30-36, 68;

Randy Sue Coburn, "This Generation Isn't Lost; It's Living in Hoboken," *Esquire*, 98 (November 1982): 68-78;

T. Crawley, "Report from a Small Planet," *Monthly Film Bulletin*, 49 (December 1982);

C. Chase, "At the Movies," *New York Times*, 28 January 1983, III: 8;

J. Wells, "John Sayles: Notes on a One-Man Band," *Film Journal* (28 January 1983);

Kenneth M. Chanko, "John Sayles: The Things That I Write and Direct Are Things I'm Not Going to See Unless I Do Them," *Films in Review*, 34 (February 1983): 94-98;

"Interview with John Sayles," *American Cinematographer* (April 1983);

Lindsy Van Gelder, "Director-Screenwriter John Sayles: At Home on Our Turf," *Ms.*, 10 (June 1983).

Paul Schrader
(22 July 1946-   )

Joel Bellman

MOTION PICTURES: *The Yakuza* (Warner Bros., 1975), screenplay by Schrader and Robert Towne;

Taxi Driver (Columbia, 1976), screenplay;

Obsession (Columbia, 1976), story by Schrader and Brian De Palma; screenplay;

Rolling Thunder (American International, 1977), story; screenplay by Schrader and Heywood Gould;

Blue Collar (T.A.T. Communications, 1978), screenplay by Schrader and Leonard Schrader;

Hardcore (Columbia, 1979), screenplay;

Old Boyfriends (Avco Embassy, 1979), screenplay by Schrader and Leonard Schrader;

American Gigolo (Paramount, 1980), screenplay;

Raging Bull (United Artists, 1980), screenplay by Schrader and Mardik Martin;

Mishima (Zoetrope, 1985), screenplay by Schrader and Leonard Schrader.

BOOK: *Transcendental Style in Film: Ozu, Bresson, Dreyer* (Berkeley: University of California Press, 1972).

PERIODICAL PUBLICATIONS: "They're Young . . . They're In Love . . . They Kill People," *Cinema*, 5, no. 2 (1969): 28-30;

"Poetry of Ideas: The Films of Charles Eames," *Film Quarterly*, 23 (Spring 1970): 2-19;

"Notes on Film Noir," *Film Comment*, 8 (Spring 1972): 8-13;

"Robert Bresson, Possibly" (interview), *Film Comment*, 13 (September-October 1977): 26-30;

"Paul Schrader's Guilty Pleasures," *Film Comment*, 15 (January-February 1979): 61-62.

Paul Schrader

Paul Joseph Schrader was born in Grand Rapids, Michigan. Despite his often-demonstrated "confessional" style of writing, Schrader's childhood remains largely a mystery. What emerges from his sketchy comments on the subject is a loving but strict religious upbringing. Schrader's home was Dutch Calvinist, a religion which through a church synodical decree in 1928 declared movies to be a "worldly amusement," along with card playing, dancing, drinking, and smoking. Films and music were completely forbidden, and television was closely regulated.

Schrader remembers pleading to be allowed to see a Disney film. His mother told him, "Your money goes to support an evil industry; therefore, you can't judge the individual movie." He continues, "I remember getting on my knees and crying to see *King Creole*. What broke the church control structure was television, because if you didn't have it in your house, you'd go next door to your friend's house; they couldn't stop it from coming through. Today, they've had to revise and change. Movies are no longer forbidden." Music, too, for Schrader, was considered sinful. "I can remember my mother finding me listening to a Pat Boone song and taking the radio and throwing it against the wall. I remember her anger at losing control, at the insidious effect of the media, destroying and undermining the family structure, which it did."

Schrader's father had been forced to drop out of seminary training during the Depression, and his highest hopes were that his sons Paul and Leonard would enter the ministry. Though Leonard eventually became a teacher and missionary in Japan, Paul's religious training was deflected when, at the age of seventeen, he and two friends slipped downtown to sneak into a showing of *The Absent-Minded Professor.* "I was disappointed," he says now. "After all, movies were forbidden, and this one hardly seemed to qualify. But it was the beginning of a legitimate form of rebellion, and one with an artistic mantle to boot." Schrader's recurring observation on the subject is, "I came to movies as an adult, but I saw them as a child."

Following high school Schrader entered the seminary at Calvin College. He began writing film criticism for his college newspaper and began to evolve his theory of a "transcendental style" of filmmaking as exemplified by Yasujiro Ozu, Robert Bresson, and Carl Dreyer. Schrader felt all three of these directors sought, through a very formalized film structure, to express something of the "transcendent," an all-powerful divine presence in man's life.

During his term at Calvin College, Schrader journeyed to New York one summer to take film courses at Columbia University and made the first of several lucky contacts. While at the West End Bar one night—Schrader had, by this time, slipped rather comfortably into the secular life—he struck up a conversation with another student, who happened to be Paul Warshow, son of the critic Robert Warshow. The subject of their discussion was Pauline Kael's book *I Lost It At the Movies.* Warshow suggested that they drop in to visit Kael; she had just come to New York, was writing for *McCall's,* and lived on West End Avenue. Schrader wound up talking to her all night and sleeping on the couch. The next morning Kael offered to get Schrader into the University of California Film School. He accepted her offer later after graduating from Calvin.

Once in California, Schrader plunged in head first. A professor at UCLA got him his first commercial writing job as a critic for the *Los Angeles Free Press.* Schrader's experience in so-called urban underground still influences his work. Also in 1968, around the time he entered UCLA, Schrader found time to enter two magazine writing competitions, for the *Atlantic* and *Story: The Magazine of Discovery.* He placed first in both.

Schrader graduated from UCLA in 1970 with an M.A. in film. His master's thesis, *Some Criticisms,* expanded ideas he had begun to develop in an earlier (1969) essay for the magazine *Cinema* called "They're Young . . . They're In Love . . . They Kill People." In this essay Schrader embarked on an exploration of the motivations behind the then-current outbreak of cinematic violence. He drew parallels between the late 1960s folk heroes and the gangster heroes of the 1930s and 1940s. The crucial difference, Schrader felt, was the almost mindless, psychopathic energy the 1960s figures had, compared to the grim, environmental factors that motivated the traditional gangster figures. The psychopathology of the criminal—and more importantly, the noncriminal who was pushed over the edge by internal or external forces—later became the focus of Schrader's screenplays *Taxi Driver* (1976) and *Rolling Thunder* (1977).

By his last year at UCLA Schrader had established himself at *Cinema* as a reviewer and no longer needed to write for the *Free Press.* After graduation he continued at *Cinema* and assumed the position of editor, which he held until 1973. While writing for *Cinema,* he also began to free-lance for other publications; in 1970 he briefly wrote for *Coast* magazine, a glossy publication reflecting the prototypical California life-style, and *Film Quarterly,* where he placed an article on the films of Charles Eames, the architect-designer-filmmaker.

By 1971, however, despite the fact that he was editing *Cinema* (and transforming it from a slick picture magazine to a serious film journal), Schrader was itching to try screenwriting, and he signed on as a fellow at the American Film Institute. While this job soured him on Hollywood filmmaking—"I could see that the money was being wasted and the wrong decisions were being made," he says—Schrader was able to make some more useful contacts. He embarked on his first project, a script titled "Pipeliner," concerning a dying man who goes home to northern Michigan for sympathy and ends up ruining the lives of everyone around him. "Pipeliner" apparently was conceived as a strictly commercial proposition; the goal, according to Schrader, was to write a script that could be produced for under $100,000. The script got to an agent, but after being kicked around for a year, with no financing, it was permanently shelved.

Just prior to "Pipeliner," Schrader had finished writing his book—"A real monkey-off-my-back book, something I felt I had to write," he says—which was published in 1972 as *Transcendental Style in Film: Ozu, Bresson, Dreyer.* In it Schrader

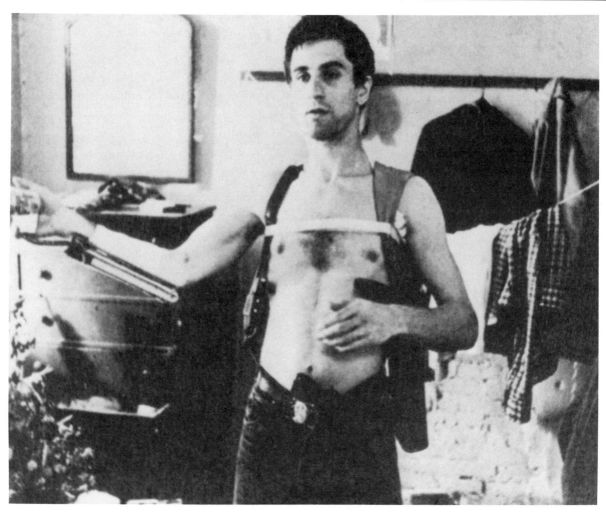

Robert De Niro prepares himself for urban warfare in Schrader's Taxi Driver

argues persuasively his case that the ascetic, almost impenetrable styles of those three directors were actually examples of a stylized evocation—through ritualized filmmaking techniques—of the "Wholly Other," the transcendent presence in man's life. Through a sequential presentation of the four stages—the mundane, purposeless Everyday; the injection of a spiritual/spiritless Disparity; the catalyzing Decisive Action, which proves the existence of the Transcendent; and Stasis, the Everyday, but transformed by the new spiritual consciousness— Schrader felt a discerning viewer could glimpse this transcendent presence and come to accept it on a deeper level than, say, a simple depiction of a saint or Christ-figure could accomplish. Through this presentation the characters, and the viewer, could come to an emerging spiritual realization. Schrader had high hopes for the book, which the University of California Press agreed to publish. The book

attracted little attention, however, dealing Schrader the first in a series of major setbacks.

With the book failing and "Pipeliner" unsold and unproduced, Schrader was hit with another severe blow. His marriage ended, and he fell into a state of depression. Schrader finally developed an ulcer and had to be hospitalized. The stay in the hospital got Schrader his health back and furnished him with some crucial ideas that developed into what is surely his artistic high point, his screenplay for *Taxi Driver* (1976). Finally, all the personal problems, intellectual theories, and struggling emotional expression fused into a fully integrated whole. Two chance occurrences in the hospital ignited the spark: in March 1972, Alabama governor and presidential aspirant George Wallace was shot by a strange, psychopathic young man named Arthur Bremer; and, while lying in the hospital bed, Schrader heard over and over again on the radio a pop song by Harry Chapin called "Taxi."

The first-person story of the song's taxi driver narrator, combined with Schrader's own depression, suggested the perfect metaphor for urban despair and loneliness: a faceless, anonymous figure, who does nothing but drive people from one place to another, unable to relate to anyone on a meaningful level, unknown and unknowing, but all the while seething inside with an ever intensifying, mindless rage, primed to explode at any moment.

Schrader painstakingly structured the story to mirror his personal view of the transcendent through the story of Travis Bickle (Robert De Niro), a young Vietnam veteran suffering from insomnia, depression, and a general inability to relate to the world. Travis takes a job driving a cab at night, and as he sees more and more of life's degradation, he moves from the numbness of the "Everyday" to a building crisis of the spirit. Meeting two women, an upper-class and beautiful campaign

worker (Cybil Shepherd) and a twelve-year-old prostitute (Jodie Foster), Travis gradually develops a way to channel the inarticulate rage that he feels; he has become aware of the "Disparity." The "Decisive Action" occurs when Travis, having reached the flash point, sets out on a violent purification of all the filth and corruption in which he has been submerged. After he commits murder, due to an ironic plot twist, Travis is acclaimed a hero for his actions and finds himself driving a cab once again. *Taxi Driver* was finished in about fifteen days. Schrader deposited it with his agent and left Los Angeles.

It was while traveling around the country in 1973 that he received a letter from his brother in Japan with the nugget of an idea for a third screenplay. Schrader's brother Leonard had been seeing a lot of Japanese gangster, or *yakuza*, films. He suggested that it might be interesting to place a foreigner in a position that forced him to take part in

Robert Mitchum pits himself against a Japanese crime organization in The Yakuza

the very Japanese world of the *yakuza:* the sword-play, the ritual, the codes of honor and obligation that are somewhat alien to Western culture. Schrader spoke to his agent, who promptly offered them the chance to come back to Los Angeles and write it up as a script. The two brothers hammered out a story line, and while Paul worked on the screenplay, Leonard drafted a novel. *The Yakuza* instantly established Paul Schrader as a hot new writer in Hollywood when it was sold to Warner Bros. for $300,000.

While it was his third script, *The Yakuza* was actually Schrader's first sale. Thus it was especially galling when Warner Bros., having decided that the script was still not right after Schrader had already rewritten it twice, hired Robert Towne to do yet another rewrite. Towne kept Schrader's basic scenario, but added dialogue; the result was a somewhat compromised version of the "blood, duty, and obligation" script that Schrader was striving for. Further problems arose when the studio hired Sydney Pollack to direct. Schrader's original conception called for a tough, violent, action picture, using the angle of East-West cultural disparity to sharpen the dramatic conflict, and spice up the plot. But Pollack visualized the story differently, making instead what Schrader describes as a "rich, romantic, transcultural film." The completed film failed to satisfy on either count. Reviews were mostly harsh or indifferent; as his first film failed, Schrader entered another depression.

Fortunately, Schrader's fortunes soon improved. While *The Yakuza* was dying a slow death, things seemed to be coming together on *Taxi Driver.* Schrader had been able to interest producers Michael and Julia Phillips in the script in 1973, and, after screening a rough cut of *Mean Streets,* Schrader and the Phillipses settled on director Martin Scorcese and actors Robert De Niro and Harvey Keitel for *Taxi Driver.* Everyone entered into the project with the same goal in mind; there was general agreement on tone, look, and the motivating forces for the characters. Financial arrangements took a bit of time, but in the same spirit of cooperation, those involved agreed to considerably lower salaries than they could have gotten elsewhere. Total production costs were around $1.9 million.

When *Taxi Driver* was released in February 1976 critical reaction was swift and positive. It rapidly became the most talked-about film of the year and won Academy Award nominations for best picture, actor (De Niro), and supporting actress (Jodie Foster) as well as garnering several foreign awards.

But the film also had its share of detractors, who found the film overly cynical and unbelievable. As Schrader ruefully pointed out, "The film is too damn controversial, too hot. You don't make a picture like this expecting it to get nominated. This is not your 'win friends and influence people' type of script."

Taxi Driver brought Schrader instant respectability as a screenwriter. Fulfilling a long-standing ambition, he began to teach both at UCLA and at Sherman Oaks Experimental College, a small independently run institution which relies primarily on visiting luminaries to lecture on film and media.

In August 1976 the third Schrader film was released. *Obsession,* originally titled "Deja Vu" and directed by Brian De Palma, was a variation on the Alfred Hitchcock film *Vertigo,* incorporating elements of film noir (corrupt society, a trusting man victimized by his business partner) and Schrader's by now familiar psychological touches. After his wife (Genevieve Bujold) is kidnapped and killed, Michael Courtland (Cliff Robertson) continues to brood over her death and his responsibility for it. Fifteen years later, he meets a woman (Bujold) who looks identical to his dead wife and proceeds to fall in love again, only to find she is his grown daughter, who blames him for the death of her mother. Schrader had intended for the film to have a third section in which the daughter is kidnapped, but budgetary restrictions forced De Palma to cut the movie to two parts; Schrader has never forgiven him for changing his ending.

The script for *Rolling Thunder* (1977) was sold to American International soon after Schrader wrote it in 1973. When producer Lawrence Gordon left American International, he took the screenplay to Columbia, where a deal was made that would have allowed Schrader a chance to direct the film. When that fell through, 20th Century-Fox agreed to finance the project but insisted on another director, John Flynn. The studio also had Heywood Gould rewrite the screenplay after Schrader, who had been determined to retain sole writing credit, had already rewritten it more than ten times. *Rolling Thunder* is about former prisoner of war Charles Rane (William Devane) who returns home to his family from Vietnam. When Rane is victimized by criminals at home, he transfers his killing instinct from combat in Vietnam to fighting his enemies in America. The film was so violent that 20th Century-Fox refused to distribute it and American International took over the distribution. Reviews were overwhelmingly negative, but Schrader, already heavily involved in other projects, hardly noticed.

George C. Scott, Paul Schrader, and Season Hubley on location for Hardcore

In December 1977 *Close Encounters of the Third Kind* was released. Though Steven Spielberg received sole writing credit, the story conception, original script, and title come from Schrader. Spielberg rewrote the script extensively. The original idea was an updated version of the life of Saint Paul, about an air force debunker who spends his time disproving UFO sightings until he sees a genuine spaceship and the government orders him to make contact with the aliens. He realizes that the aliens live at an elevated level of consciousness and he must contact them mentally, not physically. The final version of the film was radically different in every respect, and Schrader gladly disassociated himself from the project.

After speaking to the Writer's Guild one night in 1975, Schrader was approached by a young man named Sydney Glass who sought advice about a script he was working on concerning auto workers. Glass went to Schrader's house to discuss the idea further, and a plot was conceived. Some time later,

Schrader decided Glass would never write the screenplay, so he began working on the project with his brother Leonard. After the project was announced, Glass threatened to sue Schrader; he settled for a payment of $18,000, a percentage of the film's profits, and the screen credit "Suggested by source material from Sydney A. Glass."

Blue Collar became Schrader's first film as a director and proved to be a controversial and complex film about labor. The story examines the problems of three auto workers (Harvey Keitel, Richard Pryor, and Yaphet Kotto) who, dissatisfied with their union representation, decide to rob its safe. Instead of money, they discover records of illegal loans. In their attempt to blackmail the union, they find out they are in over their heads; the system is more powerful than they realized, and an individual stands virtually no chance of changing it. Schrader later said, "I didn't set out to make a left-wing film. While I was working on the script, I realized it had come to a very specific Marxist conclusion."

Hardcore (1979) had been completed and sold to Warner Bros. in 1975, but the failure of *The Yakuza* and the studio's misgivings about the subject matter caused them to abandon the project. Schrader's friend John Milius finally produced the film in 1979 through his A-Team production company. The protagonist is Jake Van Dorn (George C. Scott), a strongly religious Calvinist who comes to California searching for his runaway daughter, now an actress in pornographic films. Oddly enough, given Schrader's own personal ambivalence about violence, pornography, and "worldly pleasures," one of the recurring criticisms of *Hardcore* was that Van Doren seemed completely untainted by the porno underground. The way the film is constructed, no real moral conquest is possible. The conclusion reveals a rigid character whose moral foundations are shown to be a serious impediment in his development and a contributing factor to the breakup of his family. Schrader acknowledged the mistake when he said, "the ending I originally sold in *Hardcore* is the one I wish I had shot. I changed it and the whole thing went out of whack."

Schrader's second full screenplay collaboration with his brother, *Old Boyfriends*, was released in 1979. It is the story of a woman (Talia Shire) who reaches into her past to look up former lovers in an attempt to settle some old scores and come

Richard Gere in the title role of American Gigolo

to terms with her own identity and sexuality. Screenwriter Joan Tewkesbury made her directing debut on the film and also did an uncredited rewrite of the script; "It needed an aggressive, feminine sensibility," Schrader said. The completed motion picture is a somewhat uneasy blend of the kind of compulsive violent and sexual energy that characterizes many Schrader protagonists with the softer, more sympathetic treatment of Tewkesbury.

American Gigolo (1980) was written in 1976, and Schrader described it as "the flip side of *Taxi Driver*. It's very light, where *Taxi Driver* was dark. It's a story of redemption by blood. Finally, I'm making a movie about grace." That description is a bit misleading, as virtually all of Schrader's films concern protagonists who suffer assorted ignominious fates until redeemed either through the catharsis of violence (*The Yakuza, Taxi Driver, Rolling Thunder*) or confession (*Blue Collar, American Gigolo*). Nevertheless, the film is lighter in tone and Schrader's third directorial effort shows a surprising ease and fluidity of camera movement. Gigolo Julian Kaye (Richard Gere) is framed for murder; he spends his time trying to clear himself and beginning a love affair with the wife (Lauren Hutton) of a powerful politician. But the plotting of the film is of secondary importance to its lengthy character study of Kaye, a man with a drive to improve himself and his position in life. Schrader sees him as "a man who's compulsively sexual, but he only knows how to give pleasure, not receive it." The critical reception to *American Gigolo* was polite, but not enthusiastic; the box office reception was more generous.

It is difficult to accurately assess Schrader's contributions to *Raging Bull* (1980), the story of boxer Jake La Motta (Robert De Niro). Schrader was brought in to rewrite and polish Mardik Martin's adaptation of La Motta's 1970 autobiography; this rewrite was then reworked by director Martin Scorcese and De Niro. The story—the rise, fall, and attempted comeback of a former middleweight boxing champion—is very much in keeping with the suppressed redemption modes of previous Schrader work, but it is impossible to separate La Motta's life, Martin's treatment, Scorcese's and De Niro's interpretation of the character, and Schrader's polishing from the final amalgam. Considering the difficulties Scorcese has acknowledged in framing the story properly for film, it is a remarkably seamless piece of work. Scorcese, De Niro, and Schrader all received Academy Award nominations for their work, and the film was nominated for best picture.

Schrader's rewrite of *Raging Bull* had been accomplished after he suffered a creative block while working on "Born in the U.S.A.," a screenplay about two midwestern, blue-collar brothers who became rock musicians. When Schrader found himself still unable to complete the script after working on *Raging Bull,* he decided to take some time off from screenwriting. For six months he taught a screenwriting class at Columbia University, followed by working as director only on *Cat People* (1982), a remake of the 1942 horror film. (He is also said to have made some uncredited contributions to the screenplay.) The experience helped to cure him of his writer's block: "Once I got started with this picture," he said while still shooting *Cat People,* " 'Born in the U.S.A.' suddenly began to materialize . . . I've finally been able to work again as a good writer." With "Born in the U.S.A." completed but unproduced, he began work in 1983 on a long-planned project, a film about Japanese novelist and political leader Yukio Mishima. It was released in 1985.

Paul Schrader, perhaps more than any other screenwriter currently working, has established a personal style and staked out his moral territory. From his earliest scripts, Schrader has known exactly what he has wanted to say, even as he was struggling to find the proper voice with which to say it. He explains: "I did not see movies as a child, which I think is probably the greatest thing that ever happened to me—because I have no adoles-

cent memories of movies. I have no desire to make the movies I saw when I was a child because I never saw movies as a child. So I can approach movies as an adult, and make movies for adults. I don't have to make . . . all the kids' movies my peers are making now."

Interviews:

Mark Patrick Carducci, "Paul Schrader on CE3K," *Cinefantastique,* 7 (Winter 1978): 36;

Gary Crowdus and Dan Georgakas, "*Blue Collar:* An Interview with Paul Schrader," *Cineaste,* 8 (Winter 1978): 34-37, 59;

Carducci, "Interview with Paul Schrader," *Millimeter* (February 1979): 60-72.

References:

"Dialogue: Screenwriters," *Film Comment,* 14 (July-August 1978): 45;

Charles Higham, "When I Do It, It's Not Gote, Says Writer Paul Schrader," *New York Times,* 5 February 1978;

Fiona Lewis, "Paul Schrader: 'It's Time for Me to Do a Masterful Job,' " *Los Angeles Times,* 15 April 1979;

Stephen Rebello, "*Cat People:* Paul Schrader Changes His Spots," *American Film* (April 1982): 38-45;

Richard Thompson, "Screenwriter: *Taxi Driver's* Paul Schrader," *Film Comment,* 12 (March-April 1976): 6-19;

Wayne Warga, "The Anti-Homecoming of Paul Schrader," *Los Angeles Times,* 12 March 1978.

George Seaton

(17 April 1911-29 July 1979)

James Desmarais

MOTION PICTURES: *Student Tour* (M-G-M, 1934), story by Seaton, Arthur Bloch, and Samuel Marx;

The Winning Ticket (M-G-M, 1935), story by Seaton and Robert Pirosh;

A Day at the Races (M-G-M, 1937), screen story by Seaton and Pirosh; screenplay by Seaton, Pirosh, and George Oppenheimer;

The Doctor Takes a Wife (Columbia, 1940), screenplay by Seaton and Ken Englund;

This Thing Called Love (Columbia, 1941), screenplay by Seaton, Englund, and P. J. Wolfson;

That Night in Rio (20th Century-Fox, 1941), screenplay by Seaton, Bess Meredyth, and Hal Long;

Moon Over Miami (20th Century-Fox, 1941), adaptation by Seaton and Lynn Starling;

Charley's Aunt (20th Century-Fox, 1941), screenplay;

Ten Gentlemen from West Point (20th Century-Fox, 1941), additional dialogue;

Bedtime Story (Columbia, 1942), contribution to treatment;

The Magnificent Dope (20th Century-Fox, 1942), screenplay;

The Meanest Man in the World (20th Century-Fox, 1943), screenplay by Seaton and Allan House;

Coney Island (20th Century-Fox, 1943), screen story and screenplay;

The Song of Bernadette (20th Century-Fox, 1943), screenplay;

The Eve of St. Mark (20th Century-Fox, 1944), screenplay;

Billy Rose's Diamond Horseshoe (20th Century-Fox, 1945), screenplay;

Junior Miss (20th Century-Fox, 1945), screenplay;

The Shocking Miss Pilgrim (20th Century-Fox, 1946), screenplay;

Miracle on 34th Street (20th Century-Fox, 1947), screenplay;

Apartment for Peggy (20th Century-Fox, 1948), screenplay;

Chicken Every Sunday (20th Century-Fox, 1948), screenplay by Seaton and Valentine Davies;

For Heaven's Sake (20th Century-Fox, 1949), screenplay;

The Big Lift (20th Century-Fox, 1950), screen story and screenplay;

Anything Can Happen (20th Century-Fox, 1952), screenplay by Seaton and Oppenheimer;

Little Boy Lost (Paramount, 1953), screenplay;

The Country Girl (Paramount, 1954), screenplay;

The Proud and the Profane (Paramount, 1956), screenplay;

The Counterfeit Traitor (Paramount, 1962), screenplay;

36 Hours (M-G-M, 1965), screenplay;

What's So Bad About Feeling Good? (Universal, 1968), screen story and screenplay by Seaton and Pirosh;

Airport (Universal, 1970), screenplay.

George Seaton

BOOK: *But Not Goodbye* (New York & Los Angeles: French, 1944).

PERIODICAL PUBLICATION: "One Track Mind on a Two Way Ticket," *The Screen Writer* (September 1947).

George Seaton is probably best known as a director and producer, but for over thirty-five years he had a highly successful career as a screenwriter. He wrote scripts in almost every genre, nearly always appealing to popular taste; his career was not without critical acclaim, including two Academy Awards, but this acclaim was never the equal of his financial success.

Seaton was born George Stenius, son of Olga Berglund and chef Charles Stenius, in South Bend, Indiana. After the family moved to Detroit, Seaton enrolled in Phillips Exeter Academy in preparation for attending Yale. At Exeter he became interested in theater and wrote several one-act plays; finally deciding he wanted to be an actor, he left Exeter after one year and never attended college. His parents convinced him to try the business world, and Seaton became employed at a brokerage firm in October 1929. The stock market crashed the next day, and Seaton joined a little theater group with

Anne Revere and Jennifer Jones in The Song of Bernadette, *the film that established Seaton's reputation as a screenwriter*

which he remained for two years. The love of theater also gave him his new name: he took Seaton from one of the characters in Philip Barry's *Holiday;* in 1937 he made the change legal.

Eventually Seaton went to New York City, hoping to further his stage career. But acting jobs were scarce, and he turned to writing True Confession style stories for McFadden Publications in order to support himself. Seaton's play about rumrunning was optioned by producer Jed Harris for a movie, but restrictions by the Hays Office prevented its production. Nevertheless, the novelization of the play made Seaton enough money to return to Detroit where he became a radio writer and actor; he played the Lone Ranger for eight months on station WXYZ. Several of his radio plays were brought to the attention of M-G-M's story editor Samuel Marx, who hired Seaton as a junior writer in August 1933. His first assignments were writing screen stories for the lightweight comedies *Student Tour* (1934), about college students on a world cruise, and *The Winning Ticket* (1935), in which a barber (Leo Carillo) can claim $150,000 if he can find his lottery ticket. In 1936 Seaton married Phyllis Laughton, an actress and drama instructor he had met while active in the theater. They had two children.

Irving Thalberg gave Seaton a career break when he assigned him to write a new Marx Brothers movie. A perfectionist, Thalberg demanded eighteen complete rewrites of *A Day at the Races* (1937) from Seaton and cowriter Robert Pirosh before he was satisfied with the script. He worked closely with the writers, suggesting they retain one character from one script or expand an idea from another until they combined all the workable elements into the final screenplay. The result was a witty vehicle for the Marx Brothers in which Groucho plays Dr. Hugo Z. Hackenbush, a veterinarian who masquerades as a physician at a sanitorium owned by Judy Standish (Maureen O'Sullivan). In an effort to save the hospital from its creditors, the Marx Brothers take a horse owned by Standish's fiancé and enter it in a race. Enormously popular, *A Day at the Races* grossed over four million dollars, more than any other Marx Brothers movie, and its success resulted in Seaton being loaned out to Columbia. His first picture there was *The Doctor Takes a Wife* (1940), a comedy about a writer (Loretta Young) and a doctor (Ray Milland) who pretend to be married. William Perlberg produced the movie and began a twenty-five-year professional relationship with Seaton, during which they collaborated on more than thirty films.

Seaton worked on two more films before leaving Columbia in 1940. He received the unusual credit of "contributor to treatment" for his work on the screen story for *Bedtime Story* (1942), about a playwright trying to convince his actress wife (Loretta Young) to star in his newest production. Adapted from Edwin Burke's play, *This Thing Called Love* (1941) showed the conflict between a married couple (Rosalind Russell and Melvyn Douglas) when the wife insists on remaining chaste for three months after their marriage.

In 1941 Seaton went to work for 20th Century-Fox, where he remained for the rest of the decade. At this time the studio was making a series of colorful musicals with such stars as Betty Grable, Don Ameche, Alice Faye, and Carmen Miranda. Seaton's early work for 20th Century-Fox includes three such musicals: *That Night in Rio* (1941), with Ameche, Faye, and Miranda; *Moon Over Miami* (1941), with Ameche and Grable; and *Coney Island* (1943) with Grable. He also helped transform two plays, Brandon Thomas's *Charley's Aunt* in 1941 and George M. Cohan's *The Meanest Man in the World* in 1943, into vehicles for Jack Benny.

Many of Seaton's screenplays had been adaptations of plays, and it was this apparent skill for bringing other writers' work to the screen that gave him the chance to write his first serious screenplay. *The Song of Bernadette* (1943), based on the novel by Franz Werfel, told of a young French peasant (Jennifer Jones) who claims to have had a vision of the Virgin Mary telling her that the spring waters had curative powers. Her story is doubted but she sticks to it, even when she is faced with possible commitment to an asylum. The movie was 20th Century-Fox's biggest project of the year, lavishly produced and overseen by David O. Selznick; even with its three-hour running time, the film was never boring due to Seaton's script and Henry King's direction. The movie was extremely popular with audiences and critics and earned five Academy Awards, including one for Jennifer Jones as best actress. It was also nominated for best picture, and Seaton received his first nomination for best screenplay.

The Song of Bernadette brought Seaton fame and more prestigious projects. He adapted Maxwell Anderson's play *The Eve of St. Mark* (1941) in 1944; the play, about a small group of soldiers fighting off Japanese troops, had been highly acclaimed, but it was dated somewhat by the time the movie was made and the studio-added happy ending did further damage to its appeal. The movie's director, John Stahl, later told Seaton that the only

way a writer could protect his work in its transition to the screen was to direct his own scripts. With that advice in mind, Seaton began directing in 1945 and continued to direct all his screenplays. He strongly believed that writers should direct their own work but, indicative of his working relationship with Perlberg, also felt that a strong producer was essential for providing an objective opinion.

Despite the success of *The Song of Bernadette* and fairly good reviews for *The Eve of St. Mark*, Seaton returned to lightweight fare. He wrote two more vehicles for Betty Grable, *Billy Rose's Diamond Horseshoe* (1945) and *The Shocking Miss Pilgrim* (1946). In between came *Junior Miss* (1945), from Sally Benson's stories (and a subsequent Broadway play) about a precocious teenaged girl (Peggy Ann Garner). His next picture, though, was to become one of his most popular: *Miracle on 34th Street* (1947). Doris Walker (Maureen O'Hara) hires Kris Kringle (Edmund Gwenn) as a Santa Claus for Macy's; he begins to convince everyone, with the exception of Walker (a bitter divorcée), that he is Santa Claus. Kringle is accused of insanity and brought to trial, but the court rules he truly is Santa Claus when the post office delivers him all of Santa's mail. Seaton wrote his screenplay from a story by Valentine Davies and both won Academy Awards, as did Gwenn. The movie was also nominated for best picture.

Miracle on 34th Street had revealed Seaton's optimistic nature and belief that society is naturally good; the remainder of his screenplays at 20th Century-Fox were equally sentimental and hopeful. He collaborated with Davies on *Chicken Every Sunday* (1948), a turn-of-the-century story about a family man (Dan Dailey) who dreams of striking it rich. *Apartment for Peggy* (1948) shows his belief that the young and old can live and work together—a belief also demonstrated by Seaton's involvement with and encouragement of young filmmakers. Newlywed Peggy (Jeanne Crain) enrolls in college and meets lonely professor Henry Barnes (Edmund Gwenn); because she and her husband (William Holden) need a place to live, Peggy convinces Barnes to let them move into his attic, and he finds renewed interest in life through her exuberance and energy. *The Big Lift* (1950) is about a pilot airlifting refugees, mostly children, out of post-World War II Berlin. In *For Heaven's Sake* (1949) an angel (Clifton Webb) is sent to Earth to convince a couple (Joan Bennett and Robert Cummings) to have a child.

In 1952 Seaton and Perlberg formed Perlberg-Seaton Productions, which produced Seaton's

Edmund Gwenn and Natalie Wood in Miracle on 34th Street. *Seaton won an Academy Award for his screenplay.*

own scripts, and seven other films, including *Rhubarb* (1951), *Somebody Loves Me* (1952), *The Bridges at Toko-Ri* (1955), *The Tin Star* (1957), *But Not for Me* (1959), *The Rat Race* (1960), and *Twilight of Honor* (1963). Perlberg-Seaton released their films through Paramount. Seaton was inactive as a screenwriter for two years, finally returning to writing and directing with *Anything Can Happen* (1952), about a Russian immigrant (Jose Ferrer) in the United States.

Little Boy Lost (1953) signaled a change in Seaton's attitude; most of his subsequent screenplays have been less hopeful, more realistic, and some have been outright bitter. Like *The Big Lift, Little Boy Lost* concerns the fate of children in Europe after the war, but the film is more cynical in tone than its predecessor, having an American (Bing Crosby) manipulated into believing that a war orphan is his own lost son.

The Country Girl (1954) won Seaton an Acad-

emy Award. His script was adapted from a play by Clifford Odets, and the completed film shows more of Odets's influence than Seaton's. It centers on Frank Elgin (Bing Crosby), an alcoholic singer trying for a comeback in a Broadway play; Bernie Dodd (William Holden), his director; and Georgie Elgin (Grace Kelly, who won an Oscar), Frank's bitter but loyal wife. Unlike other Seaton characters, Elgin is not inherently good; rather, he is a spineless, manipulative, deceitful man who blames his alcoholism on the death of his son but in fact turned to drink simply out of weakness. Dodd at first thinks Georgie is responsible for Elgin's problems but comes to realize it is Elgin himself who is at fault. He also falls in love with Georgie and begs her to leave Frank if she ever realizes her dream to see him "on his feet again, so I can get out from under." Although the movie is not without hope, it offers no easy resolutions.

Seaton followed *The Country Girl* with *The*

Grace Kelly, Gene Reynolds, Bing Crosby, and William Holden in Seaton's film version of Clifford Odets's play The Country Girl

Proud and the Profane (1956), about the romance between an arrogant American officer (William Holden) and an Englishwoman (Deborah Kerr) during World War II. By this time he was busy with his production company and did little screenwriting for the next several years. He also began directing others' scripts with the documentary *Williamsburg: The Story of a Patriot* (1956), later making *Teacher's Pet* (1958) and *The Pleasure of His Company* (1961).

It was not until 1962 that Seaton wrote his next motion picture. *The Counterfeit Traitor* was a fact-based spy film in which an American businessman (William Holden), living and working in Switzerland, uses his business contacts in Germany to spy for the Allies. The film was a realistic, nonglamorous view of espionage. Its protagonist acts not out of principle but because he is being blackmailed by British authorities; he in turn pressures his friends into working with him to fight the Nazis. Even the one person (Lilli Palmer) who willingly

aids the Allies is conscience-stricken when she realizes the information she passes on leads to bombing raids and German deaths. Seaton followed this project with another espionage drama, *36 Hours* (1965), about an American agent (James Garner) caught in Germany during the war. It was an uneven effort, inferior to *The Counterfeit Traitor*. It was also the last film for Perlberg-Seaton production.

What's So Bad About Feeling Good? (1968) is noteworthy mainly as a return to Seaton's earlier optimistic themes, presenting the idea that all the world's problems are solvable with the proper change of attitude. An infected toucan, loose in New York City, is spreading a disease that causes people to be happy; many of the victims remain good-natured even after the illness has been treated.

Seaton's last screenplay was *Airport* (1970), his greatest financial success and the first of the series of disaster films made in the 1970s. Based on Arthur Hailey's novel, the film depicts the disastrous events of one evening at a metropolitan airport; there is a stowaway (Helen Hayes), a bomber (Van Heflin) on board the plane, and a severe snowstorm. Seaton interwove a series of subplots involving most of the characters and wrote individual biographies for each of the 104 passengers on the plane. In addition to its great popular success, *Airport* received critical praise for its return to old-fashioned entertainment. It was nominated for an Academy Award as best picture of 1970.

Seaton did no more screenwriting after *Air-*

port. He produced and directed a final film, the Western *Showdown* (1973), then retired in 1973. Following a long bout with cancer, George Seaton died in July 1979.

References:

Vanessa Brown, "How Hunter and Seaton Tackled *Airport* Task," *Los Angeles Times*, 6 April 1969;

Jerome S. Simon, "George Seaton," *Films in Review*, 22 (November 1971): 521-540.

Curt Siodmak
(10 August 1902-   )

Kevin Mace
Oklahoma State University

SELECTED MOTION PICTURES: *Menschen am Sonntag ("People on Sunday")* (documentary) (Filmstudio, Germany, 1929), screenplay by Siodmak and Billy Wilder;

Der Mann, der seinen Mörder sucht ("The Man Who Looked for His Murderer") (UFA, 1931), screenplay by Siodmak, Wilder, and Ludwig Hirschfield;

Le Bal ("The Party") (Germany, 1931), screenplay by Siodmak and S. Fodor;

F. P. 1 (Fox-Gaumont-British UFA, 1933), screenplay by Siodmak and Walter Reisch;

La Crise est finie ("The Crisis is Over") (Nero Film, France, 1934), screenplay by Siodmak and Frederic Kohner, based on a story by Siodmak;

The Tunnel/Transatlantic Tunnel (Gaumont-British, 1935), story and screenplay;

I Give My Heart (B.P., 1936), screenplay by Siodmak, Frank Launder, and Roger Burford;

Non-Stop New York (Gaumont-British, 1937), screenplay by Siodmak, Roland Pertwee, J. O. C. Orton, and Derek Twist;

Her Jungle Love (Paramount, 1938), story by Siodmak and Gerald Geraghty;

The Invisible Man Returns (Universal, 1940), screen story by Siodmak and Joe May; screenplay by Siodmak and Lester Cole;

Black Friday (Independent, 1940), screen story and screenplay by Siodmak and Eric Taylor;

The Ape (Monogram, 1940), screenplay by Siodmak and Richard Carroll;

Pacific Blackout (Paramount, 1941), screen story by Siodmak and Franz Spencer;

The Invisible Woman (Universal, 1941), screen story by Siodmak and May;

Aloma of the South Seas (Paramount, 1941), screen story by Siodmak and Seena Owen;

Invisible Agent (Universal, 1942), screen story and screenplay;

London Black-Out Murders (Republic, 1942), screen story and screenplay;

The Wolf Man (Universal, 1942), screen story and screenplay by Siodmak and Gordon Kahn;

Son of Dracula (Universal, 1943), screen story by Siodmak;

Frankenstein Meets the Wolf Man (Universal, 1943), screen story and screenplay;

I Walked with a Zombie (RKO, 1943), screenplay by Siodmak and Ardel Wray;

The Purple V (Republic, 1943), screenplay by Siodmak and Bertram Millhauser;

The Mantrap (Republic, 1943), screenplay;

False Faces (Republic, 1943), screen story and screenplay;

House of Frankenstein (Universal, 1944), screen story by Siodmak;

The Climax (Universal, 1944), adaptation; screenplay by Siodmak and Lynn Starling;

Shady Lady (Universal, 1945), screen story and

Virginia Bruce in the title role of the comedy film The Invisible Woman. *Although Siodmak did not write the screenplay for* The Invisible Man, *he wrote or coauthored most of its sequels.*

screenplay by Siodmak, Geraghty, and M. M. Musselman;

Frisco Sal (Universal, 1945), screen story and screenplay by Siodmak and Geraghty;

The Return of Monte Cristo (Columbia, 1946), screen story by Siodmak and Arnold Phillips;

The Beast with Five Fingers (Warner Bros., 1947), screenplay;

Berlin Express (RKO, 1948), screen story;

Tarzan's Magic Fountain (RKO, 1949), screen story and screenplay by Siodmak and Harry Chandlee;

Four Days' Leave (Film Classics, 1949), screenplay by Siodmak, Leopold Lindtberg, and Richard Schweitzer;

Bride of the Gorilla (Realart, 1951), screen story and screenplay;

The Magnetic Monster (United Artists, 1953), screen story and screenplay by Siodmak and Ivan Tors;

Riders to the Stars (United Artists, 1954), screen story and screenplay;

Creature with the Atom Brain (Columbia, 1955), screen story and screenplay;

Earth vs. Flying Saucers (Columbia, 1956), story;

Curucu, Beast of the Amazon (Universal, 1956), screen story and screenplay;

Love Slaves of the Amazon (Universal, 1957), screen story and screenplay;

Sherlock Holmes und das Halsband des Todes (Constantin, 1962), screenplay; English version, *Sherlock Holmes and the Deadly Necklace* (CCC Films, 1968), screenplay;

The Devil's Messenger (Herts Lion, 1962), screenplay;

Ski Fever (Allied Artists, 1969), screenplay by Siodmak and Robert L. Joseph.

BOOKS: *Schuss in Tonfilmatelier* (Berlin: Scherl, 1930);

F. P. 1 antwortet nicht (Berlin: Scherl, 1931); re-

350

published as *F. P. 1 Does Not Reply* (Boston: Little, Brown, 1933); republished as *F. P. 1 Fails to Reply* (London: Collins, 1933);

Stadt hinter Nebeln (Berlin: Verlag der Seit-Romane, 1931);

Bis ans Ende der Welt (Leipzig: Goldmann, 1932);

Die Madonna aus der Markusstrasse (Leipzig: Goldmann, 1932);

Rache im Äther (Leipzig: Goldmann, 1932);

Die Macht im Dunkeln (Zurich: Morgarten, 1937);

Donovan's Brain (New York: Knopf, 1943; London: Chapman & Hall, 1944);

Whomsoever I Shall Kiss (New York: Crown, 1952);

Skyport (New York: Crown, 1959);

For Kings Only (New York: Crown, 1961);

Hauser's Memory (New York: Putnam's, 1968; London: Jenkins, 1969);

The Third Ear (New York: Putnam's, 1971);

City in the Sky (New York: Putnam's, 1974; London: Barrie & Jenkins, 1975).

PERIODICAL PUBLICATIONS: "In Defense of Ghouls," *Screen Writer*, 1 (February 1946);

"Medium-Close Shot in Belair," *Screen Writer*, 3 (November 1947);

"Filming Behind the Iron Curtain," *Action*, 1 (November-December 1966);

"Sci-Fi or Sci-Fact," *Films and Filming*, 15 (November 1968);

"Variations on a Theme," *Magazine of Fantasy and Science Fiction* (June 1972);

"The P Factor," *Magazine of Fantasy and Science Fiction* (September 1976).

Advertisement for a 1941 film that is a radical departure from the horror pictures Siodmak typically wrote

Lon Chaney, Jr., as Lawrence Talbot and Maria Ouspenskaya as the gypsy in The Wolf Man

TELEVISION: *Thirteen Demon Street* (Denmark, 1959), teleplay.

Onetime railroad engineer and factory worker, bilingual novelist, short-story writer, film director, and screenwriter, German-born Curt Siodmak made his mark in American cinema in the low-budget horror and science-fiction film genres. Siodmak has been responsible for terrorizing the adolescent imaginations of five generations of viewers.

Siodmak is best known as a writer of the fantastic, both in his novels and in such well-known motion pictures as *The Wolf Man* (1942), *I Walked with a Zombie* (1943), and *The Beast with Five Fingers* (1947). His films are known for their strange, exotic settings, cursed but sympathetic heroes, and such creatures as werewolves, zombies, and vampires. Siodmak has shown that the horror film can be literate and imaginative without resorting to exploitive thrills or unnecessary gore or violence.

Kurt (as his name was originally spelled) was born in Dresden just after the turn of the century. The son of Leipzig banker Ignatz and Rose Siod-

mak, he is the younger brother of American film director Robert Siodmak, who has worked in the same film genres. He received a doctorate in 1927 from the University of Zurich and did further graduate work at the Technische Hochschule in Dresden and Stuttgart, Germany. Beginning his career as a reporter, he did free-lance writing as well. In 1931 he married Henrietta de Perrot, with whom he had a son, Geoffrey Curt de Perrot. A neophyte screenwriter and sometime motion picture director, Siodmak had six books published in pre-World War II Germany, before he fled to England from the Nazis in 1933. He has had two other German-language novels published since then. Siodmak's reputation as a novelist was established with *F. P. 1 antwortet nicht* (1931), his first novel to be published in America and England. It proposed the idea of building aircraft-landing platforms in the Atlantic to facilitate intercontinental flights. Siodmak's best-known novel, *Donovan's Brain*, was published in 1943. This story of a revived brain of a dead criminal that controls other people has been filmed three times, as *The Lady and the Monster* (1944), *Donovan's Brain* (1953; Siodmak did not work on the screenplay), and *The Brain* (1966). In 1968, Siodmak wrote a sequel to *Donovan's Brain* called *Hauser's Memory;* it was filmed for television in 1970.

While Siodmak's literary career was flourishing in Germany in the late 1920s he decided to attempt screenwriting. His first film work was on a picture his brother was directing, *Menschen am Sonntag/People on Sunday* (1929). It is the story of four strangers traveling together across Germany one afternoon; Siodmak worked on the script with Billy Wilder. With Walter Reisch, Siodmak adapted his novel *F. P. 1 antwortet nicht;* it was a box-office success in Germany and was released in the United States as *Floating Platform One Does Not Reply* in 1932. After writing another film for his brother, *La Crise est finie* (1934), Siodmak went to England.

In London he worked for four years at the motion picture studio of Gaumont-British. His first assignment there was *Transatlantic Tunnel* (1935), a science fiction film in the vein of *Floating Platform*

One Does Not Reply. (For American release, the film was titled simply *The Tunnel.*) Adapted from Bernhard Kellerman's novel *From the Land Beyond Beyond,* the film depicts the building of the first transatlantic tunnel from London to New York. Siodmak's script was actually filmed three times: simultaneous shootings were done in English, German, and French with three different casts. Siodmak's final picture before coming to the U.S. was *Non-Stop New York* (1937), a mystery with a science-fiction setting; a murder is committed on a huge experimental plane flying from London to New York.

Siodmak began his American screenwriting career at Paramount, where he wrote one picture, *Her Jungle Love* (1938), as a vehicle for Dorothy Lamour. She plays a native woman on a South Seas island, helping two stranded pilots (Ray Milland and Lynne Overton) battle the villain (J. Carroll Naish). After this film, Siodmak was hired by Universal, which was enjoying great success with a se-

Bela Lugosi and Lon Chaney, Jr., in their classic make-ups in Frankenstein Meets the Wolf Man

Christine Gordon, Frances Dee, and Darby Jones in the cult favorite I Walked with a Zombie

ries of supernatural films, such as *Frankenstein* (1931) and *The Invisible Man* (1933). Siodmak was assigned to *The Invisible Man Returns* (1940). After he is falsely accused of murdering his brother, Geoffrey Radcliffe (Vincent Price) uses the formula for invisibility to hunt the real killer (Sir Cedric Hardwicke). The film garnered good reviews and became a box-office success. That same year Siodmak worked on *Black Friday* (1940), a strange combination of gangster film and Robert Louis Stevenson's Jekyll and Hyde story: a mad scientist (Boris Karloff) transplants the brain of a dead gangster into an English professor (Stanley Ridges). Siodmak finished the year writing *The Ape* (1940) for Monogram studios. Boris Karloff again plays a crazed scientist in this picture.

In 1941 Siodmak wrote one of the finest horror pictures of his career and of Universal's horror series. *The Wolf Man* (1942) has become one of the

most popular films of the genre, spawning three direct sequels *(Frankenstein Meets the Wolf Man,* 1943; *House of Frankenstein,* 1944; and *House of Dracula,* 1945), as well as many imitators. Lawrence Talbot (Lon Chaney, Jr.) is bitten by a werewolf and becomes a wolf man himself; his subsequent attempts to convince people that he is a wolf man are not believed. The story may seem simple, but Siodmak's screenplay sympathetically depicts Talbot's plight and the film becomes a sad, almost mournful horror picture in which the audience comes to feel and fear for Talbot. The tone of the movie can be summed up with the poem that Siodmak wrote for the film, spoken by an old gypsy (Maria Ouspenskaya) who befriends Talbot:

Even a man who is pure at heart
And says his prayers by night
May become a wolf when the wolfbane blooms

And the autumn moon is bright.

Siodmak established many film traditions with *The Wolf Man*, such as the pentagram as the sign of the werewolf and the silver-tipped cane (often the cane's handle is shaped like a wolf's head) to destroy the werewolf. The film became a critical success and one of Universal's most popular films of the 1940s.

Two more "invisible" movies followed *The Wolf Man: The Invisible Woman* (1941) and *Invisible Agent* (1942). *The Invisible Woman* is a comedy about a scientist (John Barrymore) who turns an attractive young model (Virginia Bruce) invisible; the humor comes from the reactions of people to the invisible woman's activities. Siodmak cowrote the screenplay with Joe May, who had directed *The Invisible Man Returns*. The invisible agent (Jon Hall) is an American during World War II who turns invisible and becomes a spy in Nazi Germany.

Although he was doing much work for Universal during this period, Siodmak also wrote an occasional script for other studios. For Paramount, he wrote another Dorothy Lamour vehicle, *Aloma of the South Seas* (1941). He also wrote two wartime thrillers dealing with crimes committed during the blackouts made necessary by the war: *London Black-Out Murders* (1942) and *Pacific Blackout* (1941).

Continuing in the horror film genre, Siodmak wrote *Frankenstein Meets the Wolf Man* (1943) and *Son of Dracula* (1943) for Universal. Robert Siodmak directed *Son of Dracula*, in which vampire Count Alucard (Lon Chaney, Jr.) arrives in the decadent, mist-enshrouded world of the Deep South where he terrorizes a small community before being destroyed by the sun's rays. Despite a somewhat ludicrous premise, *Son of Dracula* is an enjoyable horror film replete with dark, expressionistic cinematography and a sinister, swirling fog that permeates the entire film. Chaney reprised his role of Lawrence Talbot in *Frankenstein Meets the Wolf Man*, with Talbot searching for Dr. Frankenstein in the hopes that the doctor can cure him. The film was not a hit with critics, but became a box-office success.

In 1943 Siodmak was hired to write a screenplay for Val Lewton, producer of a series of highly regarded, low-budget horror films for RKO studios. Siodmak based his script loosely on a factual account of Haitian zombies written by reporter Inez Wallace. The resulting film, *I Walked with a Zombie* (1943), is one of the most unusual and intelligent horror films ever made. The movie, described by Lewton as "Jane Eyre in the Indies," is about a nurse (Frances Dee) who is brought to a Caribbean island to care for a woman in a zombie-like state; she falls in love with her employer (Tom Conway), but fears he may be responsible for his wife's condition. Directed by Jacques Tourneur, the film is rich in voodoo atmosphere and filled with beautiful, often eerie scenes, such as one in which a native with a skeletal face stalks two women in a canefield. *I Walked with a Zombie* is considered one of the best of the Lewton-RKO horror films, with a powerful and sensual style rare for a horror film made in the early 1940s.

Returning to Universal, Siodmak wrote two of the last movies in the studio's horror cycle. *House of Frankenstein*, like *Frankenstein Meets the Wolf Man*, featured both the Wolf Man and the Frankenstein monster; both have now been made part of a sinister traveling carnival. A low-budget effort, *The Climax* (1944), was produced mainly as a means of utilizing old sets from *The Phantom of the Opera* (1943). Boris Karloff plays a crazed doctor who hypnotizes a young singer (Susanna Foster) as part of a murder plot. Siodmak based his script on a play by Edward Cochran, and George Waggner (of *The Wolf Man*) directed.

The horror series had run its course by now, but Siodmak stayed with Universal for two more pictures. In *Shady Lady* (1945), a gambler (Charles Coburn) helps the police capture other criminals. Siodmak collaborated on the script with Gerald Geraghty and M. M. Musselman, and Geraghty also coauthored the next picture, *Frisco Sal* (1945). It was a musical written especially for Susanna Foster, a former opera singer whom Universal hoped to make into a star. She plays a young New England woman who travels to California to avenge her brother's murder.

Warner Bros. next hired Siodmak to write *The Beast with Five Fingers* (1947), a strange and moody film based on a short story by William F. Harvey. The severed hand of an insane pianist (Victor Francen) kills anyone who attempts to harm his beautiful young ward (Andrea King). Siodmak never makes it clear whether the hand is real or if it is the product of the imagination of the dead pianist's somewhat unbalanced secretary (Peter Lorre). Bizarre touches are scattered throughout the picture: the hand playing Mozart on the piano, the secretary nailing the hand to a desk so that it will not escape, and the final confrontation between the secretary and the hand, which culminates with the hand crawling up his chest and strangling him. The film may have been too strange for audiences' tastes in the 1940s; it failed at the box office and with the critics, but since its rerelease it has developed a following among horror film buffs.

In the years that followed, Siodmak was involved with only a handful of somewhat pedestrian projects. In *The Return of Monte Cristo* (1946), the descendant (Louis Hayward) of the count must fight for his inheritance. *Tarzan's Magic Fountain* (1949) has Tarzan (Lex Barker) defending a jungle fountain of youth against exploitation by English civilization. An American soldier (Cornel Wilde) on leave and a Swiss woman (Josette Day) fall in love in *Four Day's Leave* (1949). By far the best film of this period was *Berlin Express* (1948), for which Siodmak wrote only the screen story. Jacques Tourneur directed this story of a Nazi organization that kidnaps a statesman (Paul Lukas) working to unite postwar Germany.

As Siodmak's career entered the 1950s, he began to direct as well as write his own films; unfortunately, his films of the fifties sometimes lack the complex style and sympathetic characters that graced his films of the 1940s. *Bride of the Gorilla* (1951), Siodmak's first project as a writer-director, was little more than a reworking of *The Wolf Man:* a big-game hunter (Raymond Burr) becomes a victim of an African curse that transforms him into a marauding gorilla. Bereft of logic, suspense, or any attempts on Siodmak's part to extract atmosphere from the jungle sets, the film was a critical and box-office failure.

Shortly after filming *Bride of the Gorilla*, Siodmak was approached by producer Ivan Tors, who was working on a pilot for a possible science-fiction television series. He wanted Siodmak to write a script that could be filmed cheaply—for around one hundred thousand dollars—using footage Tors had acquired from the 1934 German film *Gold*. Siodmak had a screenplay he thought would be appropriate, and he and Tors formed a production company. *The Magnetic Monster* (1953) is a low-key thriller, with two scientists (Richard Carlson and King Donovan) realizing a recently created element is unstable and must absorb energy periodically; as its needs grow, it will drain the entire planet of its resources. Because the low-budget film emphasized the logic and thought of its protagonists rather than special effects, *The Magnetic Monster* was a critical success. Oddly, although the movie had helped to give Siodmak greater credibility as a director, he did not direct another picture until *Curucu, Beast of the Amazon* in 1956.

The success of *The Magnetic Monster* gave Siodmak's career new direction, and he devoted several years to writing science-fiction films, with mixed results. He and Tors had another mild success with *Riders to the Stars* (1954). Three rockets are sent into outer space to retrieve meteors, with scientists hoping to make a friction-resistant spaceship coating from the meteors. *Earth vs. Flying Saucers* (1956) was inspired by *Flying Saucers from Outer Space,* a nonfiction study of UFOs by army major Donald F. Keyhoe. Siodmak used Keyhoe's information as the basis for a fictional account of extraterrestrials on Earth.

On occasion, Siodmak would incorporate ideas from his earlier horror films into his science fiction screenplays. *Creature with the Atom Brain* (1955) was reminiscent of *Black Friday:* a gangster (Richard Denning) commands recently dead beings whose brains have been electrically recharged. Even more derivative of his earlier work was *Curucu, Beast of the Amazon,* in which an evil witch doctor dresses up as a monster to scare away an African safari. Siodmak wrote the film for Universal studios, employing many of the techniques of his earlier horror films.

In the early 1960s Siodmak returned to Germany. He was hired to write what was intended to be a faithful adaptation of Arthur Conan Doyle's Sherlock Holmes novel *The Valley of Fear.* What resulted bore no resemblance to Doyle's work; titled *Sherlock Holmes und das Halsband des Todes* (*Sherlock Holmes and the Deadly Necklace,* 1962), the film pitted Holmes (Christopher Lee) against Professor Moriarty in a search for a rare gem. The film was never released in America.

Traveling to Denmark, Siodmak became the writer of a television series titled *Thirteen Demon Street,* about Satan's efforts to corrupt humans in contemporary society. Three episodes of that series were reedited and released in the United States as the film *The Devil's Messenger* (1962), with a beautiful woman (Karen Kadler) sent to Earth to trigger a nuclear holocaust. Siodmak was also credited as the film's director.

Seven years elapsed before Siodmak received another screen credit. *Ski Fever* (1969) was an atypical project, a youth-oriented romantic comedy about an American ski instructor (Martin Milner) in Austria. It was not a success critically or financially, and remains Siodmak's last film effort to date. He retired shortly thereafter, devoting himself to writing novels.

It is perhaps easy to underestimate Curt Siodmak's contributions to the American motion picture. He has worked almost entirely within the science-fiction and horror genres, has had many failures, and is most immediately associated with a film he did not even write: *Donovan's Brain*. But to view Siodmak's contributions to film as only minor would be to misunderstand completely his career. His horror films of the 1940s—with their emphasis on story and characterization—have done a great deal to make the horror film an important genre with its own style and characteristics. Siodmak has shown that the horror film does not have to rely on shocks to be effective. With such films as *The Wolf Man* and *I Walked with a Zombie*, Siodmak has proven that the most effective thrills are the ones which are quiet and unseen, and which do not fill the screen with unnecessary violence or gore.

References:
James Robert Parish and Michael R. Pitts, "Christopher Lee: A Career Article," *Cinefantastique* (Fall 1973): 11;

Danny Peary, *Cult Movies* (New York: Dell, 1981), pp. 150-153;

Kenneth von Gunden and Stuart H. Stock, *Twenty All-Time Great Science Fiction Films* (New York: Crown, 1982), pp. 69-77.

Laurence Stallings

(25 November 1894-28 February 1968)

John Driscoll
University of Washington

See also the Stallings entry in *DLB 7, Twentieth-Century American Dramatists*.

MOTION PICTURES: *The Big Parade* (M-G-M, 1925), story;
Old Ironsides (Paramount Famous Lasky, 1926), story;
Show People (M-G-M, 1928), treatment by Stallings and Agnes Christine Johnston;
Billy the Kid (M-G-M, 1930), dialogue;
Way for a Sailor (M-G-M, 1930), scenario and dialogue by Stallings and W. L. Rivers;
After Office Hours (M-G-M, 1935), story by Stallings and Dale Van Eveky;
So Red the Rose (Paramount, 1935), screenplay by Stallings, Edwin Justus Mayer, and Maxwell Anderson;
Too Hot to Handle (M-G-M, 1938), screenplay by Stallings, John Lee Mahin, and Len Hammond;
Stand Up and Fight (M-G-M, 1939), additional dialogue;
The Man from Dakota (M-G-M, 1940), screenplay;
Northwest Passage (M-G-M, 1940), screenplay by Stallings and Talbot Jennings;
The Jungle Book (United Artists, 1942), screenplay;

Salome, Where She Danced (Universal, 1945), screenplay;
Christmas Eve (United Artists, 1947), story by Stallings, Arch Oboler, and Richard H. Landau; screenplay; retitled *Sinners' Holiday*;
A Miracle Can Happen (United Artists, 1948), screenplay by Stallings and Lou Breslow; retitled *On Our Merry Way;*
Three Godfathers (M-G-M, 1949), screenplay by Stallings and Frank Nugent;
She Wore a Yellow Ribbon (RKO, 1949), screenplay by Stallings and Nugent;
The Sun Shines Bright (Republic, 1954), screenplay.

PLAY PRODUCTIONS: *What Price Glory?*, by Stallings and Maxwell Anderson, New York, Plymouth Theatre, 5 September 1924;
First Flight, by Stallings and Anderson, New York, Plymouth Theatre, 17 September 1925;
The Buccaneer, by Stallings and Anderson, New York, Plymouth Theatre, 2 October 1925;
Deep River, New York, Imperial Theatre, 4 October 1926;
Rainbow, by Stallings and Oscar Hammerstein II, New York, Gallo Theatre, 21 November 1928;

Laurence Stallings (courtesy of The Billy Rose Theatre Collection, The New York Public Library at Lincoln Center, Astor, Lenox and Tilden Foundations)

A Farewell to Arms, New York, National Theatre, 22 September 1930;

Eldorado, by Stallings and George S. Kaufman, New Haven, 19 October 1931;

Virginia, by Stallings and Owen Davis, New York, Center Theatre, 2 September 1937;

The Streets Are Guarded, New York, Miller's Theatre, 20 November 1944.

BOOKS: *Plumes* (New York: Harcourt, Brace, 1924; London: Cape, 1925;

Three American Plays, by Stallings and Maxwell Anderson (New York: Harcourt, Brace, 1926)—includes *What Price Glory?*, *First Flight*, and *The Buccaneer*;

The Doughboys (New York: Harper & Row, 1963).

OTHER: *The First World War—A Photographic History*, edited by Stallings (New York: Simon & Schuster, 1933; London: Daily Express, 1933).

PERIODICAL PUBLICATIONS: "Celluloid Psychology," *New Republic*, 33 (7 February 1923): 282-284;

"The Whole Art of a Wooden Leg," *Smart Set*, 70 (March 1923): 107-111;

"The Big Parade," *New Republic*, 40 (17 September 1924): 66-69;

"How a 'Great' Play Is Written," *Current Opinion*, 77 (November 1924): 617-618;

"Esprit de Corps," *Scribner's*, 84 (August 1928): 212-215;

"Turn Out the Guard," *Saturday Evening Post*, 201 (13 October 1928): 16-17, 96, 99-100;

"Gentleman in Blue," *Saturday Evening Post*, 204 (20 February 1932): 8-9, 95;

"Return to the Woods," *Collier's*, 89 (5 March 1932): 30-31, 52;

"Lt. Richard Plume Comes Home from the War," *Scholastic*, 25 (10 November 1934): 4-6;

"Bush Brigades and Blackamoors," *American Mercury*, 37 (April 1936): 411-419;

"The War to End War," *American Heritage*, 10 (October 1959): 4-17, 84-85;

"Bloody Belleau Wood," *American Heritage*, 14 (June 1963): 65-77.

Laurence Stallings was a rarity among American screenwriters, one of the few playwrights who went to Hollywood and did significant motion picture work before the era of sound films. Like many other writers who came to the movies with a background in the theater, Stallings never enjoyed working in motion pictures, and his film career was interrupted by several periods of retirement and by military service during World War II. A screenwriter for nearly three decades, he displayed a skill for writing realistic, usually fact-based drama.

Laurence Tucker Stallings was born in Macon, Georgia, the son of Larkin Tucker Stallings, a bank clerk, and Aurora Brooks Stallings, who instilled in her son a love of literature. Growing up in turn-of-the-century Georgia, Stallings was exposed to stories of Southern Civil War heroes, and he developed a fascination with war. He entered Wake Forest University in North Carolina in 1912 and became the editor of the campus literary magazine, *Old Gold and Black*. At the university he met Helen Poteat, the daughter of the college president and the sister of Stallings's classics professor. Stallings and Poteat were married in 1919; they had two daughters.

Larkin and Aurora Stallings had moved to Atlanta in 1911. After graduating in 1915, Stallings joined them there and took a job as reporter for the *Atlanta Journal*. He was commissioned a second lieutenant in the United States Marines in 1917 and the following year was badly wounded while lead-

John Gilbert (in barrel) and Renée Adorée in The Big Parade, *acclaimed as the best war film since D. W. Griffith's 1915 classic*
The Birth of a Nation

ing his platoon against German troops at Belleau Wood: he lost his right kneecap. (His leg was amputated after he reinjured it in a fall in 1922.) Stallings resumed his journalistic career with a reporting job on the *Washington Times*, working simultaneously on a master's degree at Georgetown University.

In 1922 Stallings joined the staff of the *New York World* and advanced rather rapidly through the ranks: copywriting assistant, drama critic, theater reporter, feature writer, and ultimately literary editor of the *World*. While still a drama critic, he became friends with Maxwell Anderson, a colleague at the *World* and an aspiring playwright. Working from Stallings's reminiscences of the war, Anderson wrote the first draft of *What Price Glory?* (1924). Stallings then rewrote the entire second act and converted the dialogue to more realistic military conversation. A chance meeting with producer Arthur Hopkins on the day the typist returned the manuscript resulted in an immediate contract. The play was a resounding success, running on Broad-

way for 299 performances and launching a touring company in 1924. Stallings and Anderson were able to dramatize the unglamorous life of men at war in the unique study of the conflict between two professional soldiers, a Marine captain and his first sergeant, over an innkeeper's daughter. It was the true-to-life nature of the play that made it a hit; Stallings admitted that the characters were composites of people he had known in the war.

Besides bringing fame to its authors, *What Price Glory?* spawned many imitations. After the popularity of the film version (which Stallings and Anderson did not write) in 1926, the title became a virtual stock phrase. The play was also translated into German for the Berlin stage. The robust characterizations of Captain Flagg and Sergeant Quirt gave Stallings a reputation as a dramatist whose best work depicted the relationships among men during battle.

In 1924 Stallings published his only novel, *Plumes*, which traces the history of one American family. In each generation a member of the Plume family had fought in an American war, and Richard Plume becomes disillusioned after World War I. *Plumes* was not well received but sold some twenty thousand copies. During the next year Stallings and Maxwell Anderson saw the production of two more of their plays, *First Flight* (1925) and *The Buccaneer* (1925), which were not successful and the collaboration ended. A third play, *Deep River* (1926), which Stallings wrote alone, also failed.

Turning to motion pictures, Stallings created another war story, *The Big Parade* (1925). Directed by King Vidor and produced by Irving Thalberg, the movie became a huge box-office success and is an enduring classic of the silent cinema. It is the story of a young soldier (John Gilbert), of his conflict between duty and love for a French village woman (Renée Adorée), and of comradeship. His script avoided unrealistic heroics and concentrated instead on three common soldiers: wealthy Jim Apperson (Gilbert); Slim, the bartender (Karl Dane); and riveter Bull (Tom O'Brien). It was suggested that the script was autobiographic—Jim loses a leg, as had Stallings—but Stallings based the story on a wartime acquaintance, not himself. The movie was more a comment on the futility and horror of war than had been the ironic *What Price Glory?*, and it was acclaimed as the best film depiction of war since *The Birth of a Nation* (1915). The success of *The Big Parade* was also responsible for the host of large-scale war films that were made in the late 1920s. Modestly Stallings pointed out years later that he had been fortunate when *The Big Parade* had been filmed. "You know that King Vidor and Irving Thalberg were the two men responsible for the great success of *The Big Parade*. We did not have Academy Awards in those days. The equivalent was the *Photoplay* Gold Medal, and our picture got that."

In 1926 Stallings gave up his post on the *World* and wrote another screenplay, *Old Ironsides* (1926). It was not the equal of *The Big Parade,* but it was a successful, swashbuckling story of the American fight against the Barbary pirates. The historical setting did not draw upon audiences' wartime emotions, as had *The Big Parade,* but Stallings's script apparently struck a different patriotic feeling; viewers were said to have jumped to their feet at the pictures' first showings.

Stallings retired to a farm in North Carolina following his work on *Old Ironsides,* but he grew restless and soon returned to screenwriting. He was reunited with King Vidor on *Show People* (1928), a satiric film that was publicized as *The Front Page* of Hollywood. The film centered on Peggy Pepper (Marian Davies), a young woman who leaves Georgia to become a star in Hollywood. Many big stars of the period, including Charlie Chaplin and Douglas Fairbanks, spoofed themselves in the movie. That same year Stallings had a Broadway success with *Rainbow* (1928), a musical comedy he had written with Oscar Hammerstein II.

Still semiretired, Stallings agreed to accept some assignments from M-G-M in 1930; he worked sporadically for that studio throughout the decade. He began by contributing dialogue to *Billy the Kid* (1930), a well-received film about the outlaw, then collaborated with W. L. Rivers on *Way for a Sailor* (1930). John Gilbert stars as Jack, a young man working on a freighter and in love with shipping clerk Joan (Leila Hyams). She will not marry him unless he takes a job on land, and eventually he lies to her and says he has found such a job.

In 1931 Stallings officially came out of retirement and busied himself with several projects. He began work on a pictorial history of World War I, published several short stories, and became a regular contributor to the *New York Sun*. Stallings returned to playwriting with his dramatization of Ernest Hemingway's *A Farewell to Arms* (1930) which opened to mixed reviews and a very brief run on Broadway in 1930. He also took over as editor of *American Mercury* in 1935. But his most significant work of the period was done for motion pictures. He had a big success with *So Red the Rose* (1935), a historical drama adapted from Stark Young's novel about a young Southerner (Randolph Scott), reluctant to fight in the Civil War, who becomes embittered by his experiences in battle. He also wrote *After Office Hours* (1935), about a newspaper editor (Clark Gable) who agrees to hire a socialite (Constance Bennett) when he thinks she can provide him with a big murder story.

In 1934 Stallings became writer-editor for Fox-Movietone News. It was in connection with this new kind of screenwriting that he began the second great adventure of his life, as head of the Fox-North American Newspaper Alliance Ethiopian Expedition, sailing in August 1935 with an entourage of cameramen, trunks, motorcycles, portable generators, and film processors. Besides his war experience and years as a journalist, Stallings brought a mature enthusiasm to the job. He later covered the civil war in Spain. Helen and Laurence Stallings were divorced in 1936, and in 1937 he married Louise Vance, who worked at Movietone.

Back at M-G-M, Stallings devised an adventure film script, *Too Hot to Handle* (1938), as a vehicle for Clark Gable. Stallings built the screenplay

Myrna Loy and Clark Gable in Too Hot to Handle, *the story of a newsreel cameraman, based on Stallings's experiences as a writer-editor for Fox-Movietone News.*

around the life of a newsreel cameraman. Gable plays cameraman Chris Hunter, who travels the world and cannot settle down with the woman he loves, aviatrix Alma Harding (Myrna Loy).

Stallings's final scripts for M-G-M were all period pieces. He contributed additional dialogue to James M. Cain's screenplay for *Stand Up and Fight* (1939), about a stagecoach employee (Robert Taylor) who feuds with his slave-owning employer (Wallace Beery). *The Man from Dakota* (1940) was adapted from a novel by Mackinlay Kantor about two Union spies (Wallace Beery and John Howard) stuck behind Confederate lines during the Civil War. Talbot Jennings joined Stallings on the difficult task of adapting Kenneth Roberts's novel *Northwest Passage*, which was filmed under the direction of King Vidor. M-G-M had planned to film the entire novel as a two-part epic to compete with *Gone with the Wind* but eventually made only one

movie, omitting the novel's story of the search for the Northwest Passage and featuring the Rangers' massacre of the Abenaki Indians in the French and Indian war. Stallings describes the debilitating effects of war on the men who fight it. Critics complained about the movie's muddled script, unclear motivation, and poorly developed characters.

When the United States entered World War II, Stallings was called back into active service. He was commissioned in the Army Air Corps and served as an adviser and interviewer in Europe, Africa, and the Middle East. Discharged as a lieutenant colonel, he returned to Hollywood in 1943. Stallings's screenplay for *The Jungle Book* (1942) had been filmed by Alexander Korda after Stallings had returned to military duty, providing him with his only screen credit for a five-year period. This lavish production of Rudyard Kipling's stories received mixed reviews.

Advertisement for one of John Ford's best-known Westerns. The script by Stallings and Frank Nugent is notable for its portrayal of male comradeship.

Though he became a permanent resident of Hollywood after the war, Stallings did not go back to full-time screenwriting until 1945. Instead, he devoted his time to a play, *The Streets Are Guarded* (1944), a military drama set in the Pacific during World War II. It had a disappointing run of twenty-four performances. He had another failure with his first postwar screenplay, *Salome, Where She Danced* (1945), a poorly made film about an exotic Viennese dancer (Yvonne De Carlo) who flees Europe during the Franco-Prussian War and goes to a lawless Arizona town.

Working for United Artists in the late 1940s, Stallings wrote two pictures, neither a true success: *Christmas Eve* (1947) and *A Miracle Can Happen* (1948). (The films were retitled *Sinners' Holiday* and *On Our Merry Way*, respectively, after their initial releases.) In *Christmas Eve*, three men (Randolph Scott, George Raft, and George Brent) return to

the home of their foster mother (Ann Harding) just in time to prevent her from being victimized by greedy relatives; it is a slow-moving picture that earned Stallings some of the worst reviews of his career. He had slightly better success with *A Miracle Can Happen*, his fourth script for King Vidor. Stallings and Lou Breslow wrote two segments of this episodic film, which depicts varying responses to a reporter's questions: "How has a child changed your life?" Stallings's first episode centered on two extras (Dorothy Ford and Victor Moore) in a motion picture; his second was a reworking of O. Henry's "The Ransom of Red Chief."

John Ford directed Stallings's final three screenplays, and they are considered to represent the best of his postwar work. *Three Godfathers* (1949) was written with Frank Nugent and was the fourth film version of a story by Peter Kyne. (Ford had directed one earlier version, *Marked Men*, in 1916.)

Three outlaws, Robert Hightower (John Wayne), Pedro Fuerte (Pedro Armendariz), and William Kearney (Harry Carey, Jr.), flee an Arizona town after a bank robbery and find a pregnant woman (Mildred Natwick) abandoned in the desert; after she dies, they care for her baby. The film then becomes almost a religious parable, with the three men following a star to take the baby to the town of New Jerusalem.

Stallings and Nugent also collaborated on *She Wore a Yellow Ribbon* (1949), the second in Ford's renowned trilogy of cavalry pictures. Captain Nathan Brittles (John Wayne), facing retirement, takes on one last mission: to prevent an impending Indian war. Stallings's script presents his finest study of masculine comradeship since *What Price Glory?*

The Sun Shines Bright (1954) was Stallings's final screenplay. Adapted from Irwin Cobb's Judge Priest stories, it is the story of a wise jurist (Charles Winninger) in a small Kentucky town; he wins re-election, helps stop the persecution of a woman born illegitimately, and prevents a lynching. Ford had filmed the same material before as *Judge Priest* (1935), but he vastly preferred this version, and the picture represents some of Stallings's best work.

Stallings declined to write any further screenplays after 1954. For the remainder of his life he devoted his time primarily to writing nonfiction; at least two novels were begun but left uncompleted. His history of World War I, *The Doughboys*, was published in 1963 to good reviews. The following year he was honored by the United States Marine Corps for his contributions to his country. He died in 1968.

References:

Joan T. Brittain, *Laurence Stallings* (Boston: Twayne, 1975);

Hedda Hopper, "A Man of Courage," *Los Angeles Times,* 7 July 1964.

Jo Swerling
(8 April 1897-   )

Thomas Slater
Northwest Missouri State University

MOTION PICTURES: *Melody Lane* (Universal, 1929), source;

Ladies of Leisure (Columbia, 1930), adaptation and dialogue;

Sisters (Columbia, 1930), scenario and dialogue;

Rain or Shine (Columbia, 1930), dialogue and continuity by Swerling and Dorothy Howell;

Hell's Island (Columbia, 1930), adaptation, continuity, and dialogue;

The Last Parade (Columbia, 1931), screenplay;

Dirigible (Columbia, 1931), adaptation and dialogue;

Ten Cents a Dance (Columbia, 1931), story and dialogue;

The Miracle Woman (Columbia, 1931), screenplay and dialogue;

Platinum Blonde (Columbia, 1931), adaptation;

Forbidden (Columbia, 1932), adaptation and dialogue;

Behind the Mask (Columbia, 1932), story, adaptation, and dialogue;

War Correspondent (Columbia, 1932), adaptation;

Washington Merry-Go-Round (Columbia, 1932), screenplay;

Below the Sea (Columbia, 1933), story and screenplay;

Man's Castle (Columbia, 1933), screenplay;

No Greater Glory (Columbia, 1934), screenplay;

The Defense Rests (Columbia, 1934), story and screenplay;

Lady by Choice (Columbia, 1934), screenplay;

The Whole Town's Talking (Columbia, 1935), screenplay by Swerling and Robert Riskin;

Love Me Forever (Columbia, 1935), screenplay by Swerling and Sidney Buchman;

The Music Goes 'Round (Columbia, 1936), screenplay;

Pennies from Heaven (Columbia, 1936), screenplay;

Double Wedding (M-G-M, 1937), screenplay;

I Am the Law (Columbia, 1938), screenplay;

Doctor Rhythm (Paramount, 1938), screenplay by Swerling and Richard Connell;

Made for Each Other (United Artists, 1939), screen story and screenplay;

The Real Glory (United Artists, 1939), screenplay by Swerling and Robert Presnell, Sr.;

The Westerner (United Artists, 1940), screenplay by Swerling and Niven Busch;

Blood and Sand (20th Century-Fox, 1941), screenplay;

New York Town (Paramount, 1941), story;

Confirm or Deny (20th Century-Fox, 1941), screenplay;

The Pride of the Yankees (RKO, 1942), screenplay by Swerling and Herman J. Mankiewicz;

Crash Dive (20th Century-Fox, 1943), screenplay;

A Lady Takes a Chance (RKO, 1943), screen story;

Lifeboat (20th Century-Fox, 1944), screenplay;

Leave Her to Heaven (20th Century-Fox, 1945), screenplay;

Thunder in the East (Paramount, 1953), screenplay;

King of the Roaring '20s (Allied Artists, 1962), screenplay.

PLAY PRODUCTIONS: *One of Us*, New York, Bijou Theatre, 9 September 1918;

One Helluva Night, New York, Sam H. Harris Theatre, 4 June 1924;

The New Yorkers, New York, Edith Totton Theatre, 10 March 1927;

Kibitzer, by Swerling and Edward G. Robinson, New York, Royale Theatre, 18 February 1929;

Guys and Dolls, New York, 46th Street Theatre, 24 November 1950.

BOOKS: *Typo Tales and Verses* (Chicago: Ertman, 1915);

Kibitzer (New York, Los Angeles & London: French, 1929).

TELEVISION: *The Lord Don't Play Favorites, Producers' Showcase* (NBC, 17 September 1956), book by Swerling and Hal Stanley.

Dramatist and screenwriter Jo Swerling was born in Bardichov, Russia. As a child, he and his family barely escaped a pogrom. With his parents, four brothers, and two sisters, Swerling fled Czarist Russia and after a dangerous journey arrived in New York. The Swerlings were poor, and Jo helped support his family by selling newspapers on street corners and by running errands. As a young man he moved to Chicago and found a job with the

Chicago Herald and Examiner. In a twelve-year journalism career, he worked as a reporter, rewrite man, editorial writer, columnist, and author of a comic strip titled "Gallagher and Shean," based on two vaudeville stars. Swerling is married and has two children. His son, Jo Swerling, Jr., is a television writer and producer.

While working as the Chicago correspondent for *Variety*, Swerling wrote a rave review of the Marx Brothers' vaudeville act. The brothers visited Swerling to thank him for the review; this visit led to Swerling's writing a musical comedy for the Marxes, *Street Cinderella*, which quickly folded. Swerling decided to return to New York and devote his writing efforts to the theater. His play *One of Us* premiered in September 1918. He then wrote *Kibitzer* and sought out Edward G. Robinson to star; Robinson agreed to appear in the play and became Swerling's collaborator on the rewrite. *Kibitzer* opened in New York in 1929.

After the success of his plays and after making his first fiction sale—a short story in *The Nation*—Swerling decided to pursue a screenwriting career. He felt certain he could fill the motion picture industry's need for good stories. In 1935 Swerling told screenwriter Frank Nugent: "The writer is the kingpin of the motion-picture business today. . . . The smart studios have decided there's no denying the play's the thing. A popular star can get an audience into a theatre, but it takes a story to keep them there, or bring them back next time. If they disregard that rule the box office white cow becomes the white elephant."

In his screenplays Swerling praises individual ingenuity, common sense, and the goodness of the common man, who is usually right in following his natural inclinations, as opposed to the amoral rich and powerful who abide by a book of rules that leaves no room for humanitarianism. Swerling's characters may sometimes be scoundrels, but they are essentially good people who understand that the world is cockeyed and do not take it too seriously. His typical male hero is a strong, silent type, played by actors like Jack Holt in many of Swerling's Columbia pictures, and by Gary Cooper in *The Westerner* (1940) and *The Pride of the Yankees* (1942). The typical female lead is similarly strong; a woman who is tough and brassy and able to make her way in the world by herself, but who eventually gives up everything for the right man and the promise of domestic bliss. Often the heroines' former lives had been morally questionable. Barbara Stanwyck played these roles in the early Columbia movies; Jean Arthur played them in *The Defense*

Rests (1934), *The Whole Town's Talking* (1935), and *Made for Each Other* (1939).

The Swerling screenplay usually found characters who do wrong revolting against their own bad behavior and being transformed into good and honest people. These upstanding types of individuals were the ones Swerling most admired, and therein lies both the nature of the problem and the measure of accomplishment in his work. For it is often difficult to write a good screenplay when no real sense of conflict is involved in the plot, and most of Swerling's weak writing results from this problem. His characters triumph by hard work, honesty, common sense, and luck, opposing patently good virtues to ones that are so plainly bad that they are easily defeated. Nonetheless, the mark of achievement in Swerling's career is that he made the formula work in many good scripts.

Swerling's first screen credit came with *Melody Lane* (1929), which was based on his unproduced play "The Understander"; Swerling was credited as the source. He went to work at Columbia studios in 1930 and remained there until 1936. His first

assignment at that studio began his long association with director Frank Capra, who shared many of Swerling's ideas about human nature. Capra directed Swerling's first screenplay, *Ladies of Leisure* (1930). A big-city gold digger (Barbara Stanwyck) realizes the tawdry nature of her life when she is asked to pose for a painting to be called "Hope." She sacrifices her comfortable way of life to win the love of her man (Ralph Graves).

Swerling and Capra then worked on another picture together, *Rain or Shine* (1930). The owners of a small circus are threatened with the possibility that their employees will go on strike. Swerling wrote his script in collaboration with Dorothy Howell, with whom he also wrote *Dirigible* (1931). The story of a navy expedition to the South Pole, the picture shows that true heroism is based on human compassion, and success only comes when the dirigible pilot (Jack Holt) and the airplane pilot (Ralph Graves) learn to cooperate. It was the third of Swerling's screenplays to be directed by Capra.

Three more screenplays for Stanwyck followed. In *Ten Cents a Dance* (1931), she played a

Robert Williams, Jean Harlow, Louise Closser Hale, Reginald Owen, and Donald Dillaway in Platinum Blonde

taxi dancer in love with a criminal (Ricardo Cortez). Capra directed *The Miracle Woman* (1931), which Swerling adapted from Robert Riskin and John Meehan's play *Bless You, Sister* (1927). Inspired by Aimee Semple McPherson, the movie is about a sham evangelist (Stanwyck) who eventually finds faith. In *Forbidden* (1932), a woman (Stanwyck) has her illegitimate baby adopted by a wealthy family, then later kills a vindictive city editor who is out to ruin the child's adoptive father by exposing an incident that happened far in his past. Capra directed and collaborated with Swerling on the script.

Platinum Blonde (1931) was Swerling's last work with Capra for many years. A newspaper reporter (Lee Tracy) marries a wealthy woman (Jean Harlow) and struggles uncomfortably with his new fortune. Swerling then worked on *Behind the Mask* (1932), an action melodrama atypical of Swerling's writings. A Secret Service agent (Jack Holt) goes undercover to find the leader of a drug-smuggling ring.

Directed by James Cruze, *Washington Merry-Go-Round* (1932) anticipates the Capra film *Mr. Smith Goes to Washington*. Young and naive Button Gwinnett Brown (Lee Tracy) is elected to the House of Representatives. While in Washington, he falls in love with a callous native (Constance Cummings) of the city and exposes a great deal of graft and corruption, incriminating the man who controls his state.

Swerling's favorite script of these years was *No Greater Glory* (1934), a movie based on a Polish novel called *The Paul Street Boys*. The story had already been filmed under that title in 1929. In the Swerling version, a young boy named Nemecsek is the only private in a local "army" consisting of a group of other young boys. In a bit of political analogy, the enemies of the Paul Street Boys are called "the Reds." They are nothing but a gang of ruffians, but even they show admiration for the courage and grit of the heroes. Nemecsek is extremely loyal to his army and has the one goal in life of becoming an officer in it. At the end, he dies of pneumonia with an officer's cap on his head.

Another favorite of Swerling's was *Man's Castle* (1933), which starred Spencer Tracy and Loretta Young. Tracy plays a hobo who gets by on doing odd jobs now and then but basically hates working. Young falls in love with him after he proves particularly adept at getting them a restaurant meal without paying. They are both very happy living in his Hooverville shack until Young gets pregnant and Tracy decides to help out on a safecracking job in order to support them. Together, these two

movies demonstrate Swerling's love of patriotism and loyalty, his hatred of communism, and his admiration for self-sufficiency and ingenuity.

His other early screenplays are largely average. *Hell's Island* (1930) is set in a prison camp where one man (Ralph Graves) is a guard and his close friend (Jack Holt) has become a prisoner; the guard allows his friend to escape to be with the woman they both love. In *The Last Parade* (1931), a gangster (Holt) tries to find the murderer of his brother. A diver (Ralph Bellamy), a wealthy woman (Fay Wray), and a German army officer (Frederick Vogeding) search for three million dollars worth of gold in *Below the Sea* (1933). *The Defense Rests* (1934) pits an unscrupulous attorney (Holt) against an idealistic one (Jean Arthur). *Lady by Choice* (1934) was a follow-up film to *Lady for a Day* (1933), which Capra had directed. In the Capra film, an impoverished woman (May Robson) is introduced to upper-class society.

Swerling had another success with *The Whole Town's Talking* (1935), which he coauthored with Robert Riskin; John Ford directed. Swerling's typical American character, here portrayed by his friend Edward G. Robinson, faces problems when his look-alike, a convicted murderer, escapes from prison. Robinson's performance of both passive Arthur Jones and evil killer Mannion re-established him as a major star, and Andre Sennwald of the *New York Times* called the movie "the best of the new year's screen comedies."

For the next three years, Swerling concentrated on musicals and comedies. He achieved critical success with *Love Me Forever* (1935), about a washed-up singer (Grace Moore) making a comeback. The script was written with Sidney Buchman, and the picture was directed by Victor Schertzinger. The three of them teamed up again in 1936 (Swerling writing the script from Buchman's story) to make *The Music Goes 'Round* (1936), which used both a well-known popular song and a familiar plot to make a lackluster movie about a vaudeville star who exploits an untalented band. Later that year, Swerling wrote *Pennies from Heaven* (1936), which featured Bing Crosby and Louis Armstrong. In it Crosby plays a wandering singer who inadvertently becomes responsible for a large, destitute family which he helps with the aid of a beautiful social worker (Madge Evans). Frank Nugent found the film to be one of Crosby's best, but Swerling was not able to repeat the success when he, Armstrong, and Crosby were reunited in *Doctor Rhythm* (1938), adapted from the O. Henry story "The Badge of Policeman O' Roon." Crosby played a doctor who

Edward G. Robinson in The Whole Town's Talking, *in which Robinson plays an average American and his double, a convicted murderer who has escaped from prison*

substitutes for his policeman friend (Andy Devine) trying to prevent the niece (Mary Carlisle) of a wealthy woman (Beatrice Lillie) from eloping.

Swerling's final screenplay before leaving Columbia was *I Am the Law* (1938), which he wrote for Robinson, who played a law professor who becomes a criminal prosecutor. Swerling's action-packed script helped make the film a box-office success. He then went to M-G-M, where the studio wanted a screwball comedy for William Powell and Myrna Loy (it was to be their seventh picture together) in the hopes of cashing in on Powell's success in *My Man Godfrey* (1936). In *Double Wedding* (1937), Loy played Margaret Agnew, a domineering woman who runs her sister's life, and Powell is free-spirited painter Charlie Lodge, who helps the sister (Florence Rice) rebel by announcing he intends to marry her; when Margaret and Charlie meet, they first quarrel, then fall in love.

In his last two movies of the 1930s, Swerling scored successes with a domestic tale and an ad-

venture story. Frank Nugent recognized his touch and his formula in *Made for Each Other* (1939), about the struggles of a young married couple (James Stewart and Carole Lombard). "Mr. Swerling hasn't said a new thing, taken a stand pro or con, or shed a bit of light on the murky course of human destiny. He simply has found a pleasant young couple, or let them find each other, and has permitted nature to have its fling. It is an unusual procedure for a script writer. Habitually they toss nature aside and think up the darndest things for their people to do. It's amazing how interesting normal human behavior can be." Such a statement could adequately stand for all of Swerling's career. His other movie of 1939, *The Real Glory*, was a patriotic film showing American soldiers helping to save a small foreign nation from destruction. An army surgeon (Gary Cooper) working in the Philippines in 1906 helps to save the society from some fierce native tribal warriors. Henry Hathaway directed.

Cooper also starred in *The Westerner* (1940),

James Stewart and Carole Lombard in Made for Each Other. *Frank Nugent praised Swerling's screenplay, commenting, "It's amazing how interesting normal behavior can be."*

which Swerling wrote in collaboration with Niven Busch and which William Wyler directed. Cooper is a drifter who gets caught up in a range war, but the film is really about Judge Roy Bean (Walter Brennen, who won an Oscar), his irascible friend. This critical success was followed by a string of weak pictures, beginning with a remake of *Blood and Sand* (1941), about a bullfighter (Tyrone Power) torn between two women (Rita Hayworth and Linda Darnell). Swerling wrote two war stories during the 1940s, but they were little more than romances using the war as a backdrop: *Confirm or Deny* (1941), about a reporter (Don Ameche) in love with a telegraph operator (Joan Bennett), and *Crash Dive* (1943), about two navy men (Tyrone Power and Dana Andrews) in love with the same woman (Anne Baxter).

The Pride of the Yankees (1942) was one of Swerling's best films of this period, earning him his only Academy Award nomination. This biography of Lou Gehrig illustrates the strengths and weaknesses of Swerling's work; Bosley Crowther commented that: "It is, without being pretentious, a real saga of American life—homely, humorous, sentimental and composed in patient detail. But,

by the very nature of its subject, it lacks conflict till well on toward its end. And that is its principal dramatic weakness. . . . Illness and death are the only adversaries faced by Lou."

A Lady Takes A Chance (1943) was the best of Swerling's post-Depression comedies, the story of a city woman (Jean Arthur) who travels west and falls in love with a rodeo star (John Wayne). This was followed by his finest screenplay, *Lifeboat* (1944), which was directed by Alfred Hitchcock. In it Swerling was able to achieve dramatic tension because the conflict of the movie existed naturally in its premise. Nine people, one of them a Nazi (Walter Slezak), are adrift in a lifeboat after a German submarine sinks a passenger liner and is sunk in turn. Some typical Swerling elements are present: cold and calculating authority is opposed by the confused Americans who must figure out how to lead themselves after killing the Nazi. Salvation comes by means of good fortune. But the ending does not promise a bright future, foreshadowing the complex nature of the postwar world.

One gets the impression that Swerling was not comfortable in a world in which his characters could not settle down into a happy, optimistic community. Over the last twenty years of his career, he had only three screenplays made into movies. *Leave Her to Heaven* (1945), adapted from the novel by Ben Ames Williams, was the last full-length script Swerling had produced in the 1940s. Crowther judged that: "Assuming that there are now such women as the one Gene Tierney plays in this film— a thoroughly ornery creature who is so jealous of her author-husband's love that she permits his adored younger brother to drown, kills her own unborn child, and finally destroys herself by trickery when she finds that her husband and her sister are in love—the description of such in this picture is far from skillful or acute. The reason for the lady's disposition is never convincingly revealed, and the whole plot—especially a courtroom climax—is arbitrary, artificial and inane."

Swerling's last success was also his last film for Capra. In 1946 Capra was having problems with the screenplay for *It's a Wonderful Life* (1946), the story of a man (James Stewart) who attempts suicide and is shown by his guardian angel what the world would have been like if he had never been born. Swerling came in to write additional scenes for the film, which was a commercial failure when first released but has since gone on to become a classic motion picture.

During the 1950s and 1960s, Swerling had only one screenplay produced per decade. *Thunder*

Babe Ruth and Gary Cooper in The Pride of the Yankees, *Swerling and Herman J. Mankiewicz's film biography of Lou Gehrig. Because of Cooper's limited baseball skills, the movie contained surprisingly little baseball footage.*

in the East (1953) was about an amoral gunrunner (Alan Ladd) in India who reforms when he meets a blind woman (Deborah Kerr). *King of the Roaring '20s* (1962) was a film biography of 1920s gangster Arnold Rothstein (played by David Janssen). Swerling's greatest achievement during these years came outside of movies: he coauthored the stage success

Guys and Dolls, which opened on Broadway in 1950 and ran for two years.

Jo Swerling retired from filmmaking in 1964. Though it has been over two decades since his last screenplay, he is still one of Hollywood's most highly respected screenwriters.

Daniel Taradash
(29 January 1913-   )

Jay Boyer
Arizona State University

MOTION PICTURES: *Golden Boy* (Columbia, 1939), screenplay by Taradash, Lewis Meltzer, Sarah Y. Mason, and Victor Heerman;

For Love or Money (Universal, 1939), screen story by Taradash, Julien Blaustein, and Bernard Feins; filmed again as *The Noose Hangs High* (Eagle-Lion, 1948);

A Little Bit of Heaven (Universal, 1940), screenplay by Taradash, Gertrude Purcell, and Harold Goldman;

Knock on Any Door (Columbia, 1949), screenplay by Taradash and John Monks, Jr.;

Rancho Notorious (RKO, 1952), screenplay;

Don't Bother to Knock (20th Century-Fox, 1952), screenplay;

From Here to Eternity (Columbia, 1953), screenplay;

Desirée (20th Century-Fox, 1954), screenplay;

Picnic (Columbia, 1955), screenplay;

Storm Center (Columbia, 1956), screen story and screenplay by Taradash and Elick Moll;

Bell, Book and Candle (Columbia, 1958), screenplay;

Morituri (20th Century-Fox, 1965), screenplay;

Hawaii (United Artists, 1966), screenplay by Taradash and Dalton Trumbo;

Castle Keep (Columbia, 1969), screenplay by Taradash and David Rayfiel;

Doctors' Wives (Columbia, 1971), screenplay;

The Other Side of Midnight (20th Century-Fox, 1977), screenplay by Taradash and Herman Raucher.

PLAY PRODUCTIONS: *Red Gloves*, New York, Mansfield Theatre, 1948;

There Was a Little Girl, New York, Cort Theatre, 1960.

TELEVISION: *Bogie* (CBS, 1980), teleplay;

OTHER: "Oscar Turns Fifty," *1979 Britannica Book of the Year* (London: Encyclopaedia Britannica, 1979), pp. 545-546.

Daniel Taradash

PERIODICAL PUBLICATION: "Into Another World," *Films and Filming*, 8 (1959): 9-35.

Daniel Taradash's gifts are adaptation and adaptability. He has over fifteen screenplays to his credit, and all but two were first stories, novels, or plays written by others. There is no one style or sort of film with which he is identified; his work includes a Western, a gangster film, thrillers, a musical, war movies, historical dramas, comedies, and romantic melodramas. Nor is there one era in which he seems inherently more comfortable than another. Taradash works with equal grace and knowledge in any setting: the heartland Kansas of *Picnic* (1955), the Greenwich Village of *Bell, Book and Candle* (1958), the Southwestern Badlands of

Rancho Notorious (1952), or the nineteenth-century island of *Hawaii* (1966).

Since his work is so diverse and since it is, in part, the original creation of others, it is difficult to find a single, consistent, personal theme, although there is a situation which recurs periodically with varying degrees of importance assigned it from film to film, and which appears most explicitly in *Golden Boy* (1939), *From Here to Eternity* (1953), and *Storm Center* (1956). The protagonists in these films have tried to live their lives by reconciling two codes, one private, the other the code of the community in which they live. In the course of these motion pictures the values inherent in one prove to be diametrically opposed to those of the other, and thus the protagonists find themselves forced to choose between the two. They choose the former more times than not, to remain true to themselves, but in either case they are likely to suffer for their choice.

Taradash was born in Louisville, Kentucky. He received his bachelor of arts degree from Har-

vard in 1933 and his bachelor of law from Harvard Law School three years later. (He has never practiced.) Hired by Columbia studios after winning a playwriting contest, Taradash went to Hollywood in 1938 to collaborate with Lewis Meltzer on the screen adaptation of Clifford Odets's Broadway success *Golden Boy*.

Directed by Rouben Mamoulian, *Golden Boy* is the story of Joe Bonaparte (William Holden), a former child prodigy now starting to pursue a career as a concert violinist. But the Great Depression is beginning, and Joe fears a musical career will result in a life of poverty; he chooses instead to seek his fortune as a prizefighter. He finds success in the ring but at great personal cost. His father (Lee J. Cobb), a poor, honest immigrant, takes Joe's boxing and obsession with money and fame as a personal betrayal, a rejection—epitomized by Joe's rejection of the violin—of everything in which he believes and for which he has worked. The spiritual and emotional changes which Joe undergoes complicate his relationship with Lorna Moon (Barbara

William Holden, Don Beddoe, Adolphe Menjou, and Barbara Stanwyck in the film version of Clifford Odets's play Golden Boy

Stanwyck), who is drawn to him by his sensitivity but sees him become as mercenary and brutal as others in the fighting game. The film comes to a climax once Joe gets his chance at the big time; only after he has killed his opponent in the ring does Joe fully comprehend the dimensions of the change he has undergone, and this comprehension results in his return to the music and values with which he has been raised.

In adapting Odets's play, Taradash and Meltzer stripped it of much of its populist/socialist dogma and many of its rhetorical excesses. Odets's play framed Joe's dilemma primarily in terms of a struggle between capital and labor, extending Joe's situation to global proportions through the speeches of Frank, a labor organizer. The screenwriters removed Frank entirely from the film and then proceeded to modify the Lorna character. In the play she was a sentimental figure whose speeches balanced out the brutality of the boxing world, but in the movie she is more hard-bitten and cynical; her instincts are those of self-preservation. The major difference between the stage and screen versions, though, is the terms in which Taradash and Meltzer define Joe's dilemma. It is a personal rather than an ideological conflict: Joe's father calls it "big trouble in his heart." Joe is caught in a tug between the nineteenth-century European values with which he has been raised and those of the modern world. This conflict is developed in the simplest terms through one central metaphor: hands and fists. Joe's hands are capable of producing great music, yet it is only through his fists that he can succeed in twentieth-century America.

After the release of *Golden Boy*, Taradash went to work for Universal, where he collaborated on two minor pictures. *For Love or Money* (1939), cowritten with Julian Blaustein and Bernard Feins, is about two bumbling window washers who lose a large sum of money belonging to bookies. In *A Little Bit of Heaven* (1940), a twelve-year-old girl (Gloria Jean) becomes a successful singer, which leads to problems with her disapproving family. Taradash, Gertrude Purcell, and Harold Goldman wrote their screenplay from a story by Grover Jones.

In May 1941 Taradash entered the army. Drafted as a private, he was trained as an officer and was eventually promoted to captain. He served in the infantry and with the Signal Corps, for which he wrote and produced training and industrial incentive films. He received official commendation from the commanding general of the army ground forces for his scripts for the "Fighting Men" series, in particular "Kill or Be Killed," which was shown to every entering infantryman and was featured in *Life* magazine. Taradash was discharged in November 1944. That same month he married Madeleine Forbes; they have three children.

Although he received screen credit for *The Noose Hangs High* (1948), a remake of *For Love or Money* that starred Abbott and Costello, Taradash's first full screenplay after the war was actually *Knock on Any Door* (1949). Taradash and John Monks, Jr., adapted Willard Motley's novel; Nicholas Ray directed. Like many postwar films, *Knock on Any Door* attempted to examine a social problem. Nick Romano (John Derek), a young man raised in a ghetto, is accused of killing a police officer. Attorney Andrew Norton (Humphrey Bogart), also from the slums, believes Romano is innocent and agrees to defend him. When the district attorney elicits an admission of guilt from Romano, Morton pleads that Romano's background is to blame for his crimes and any slum youth might have acted the same way, but Romano is found guilty and executed.

Never a prolific writer, Taradash went three years before writing his next screenplay, the Western *Rancho Notorious*, which he adapted from Sylvia Richards's screen story. Vern Haskell (Arthur Kennedy) searches for the murderer of his fiancée and tracks the man to a ranch owned by Altar Keine (Marlene Dietrich); Haskell's growing love for Keine conflicts with his desire for vengeance. Although Taradash was working with standard Western materials, his script and Fritz Lang's direction gave the movie an offbeat quality that has kept critical opinion of the film divided since its release. There was more agreement about the merits of *Don't Bother to Knock* (1952), a muddled thriller about a psychotic woman (Marilyn Monroe) who works as a babysitter for a hotel and threatens to kill one of her charges. Though the presence of Monroe has given the film something of a following, critics viewed it as a tedious, unsatisfying thriller. Taradash's screenplay was taken from the novel *Love from Anybody*, by Clifford Hanley.

In his 1953 adaptation of James Jones's novel *From Here to Eternity*, Taradash addresses the same moral dilemmas he posed in *Golden Boy*. Despite its popular appeal, the book was an unlikely film property. It is filled with obscenities, brutality, and illicit sex and is a lengthy, rambling tour de force. Jones was originally hired to do the adaptation himself, and when he failed the assignment was undertaken by Taradash. He produced a 100-page treatment which solved censorship problems, then created a 161-page screenplay which straightened out the

Humphrey Bogart, George Macready (behind Bogart), and John Derek (in dark coat) in Knock on Any Door, *an examination of the social origins of crime*

novel's convolutions and eliminated in the process enough of its complexities to bring it sparely to the screen (121 minutes). Removing many of Jones's characters entirely and reducing others to minor roles, Taradash focused on the lives of three soldiers—Prewitt, Maggio, and Warden—in pre-Pearl Harbor Hawaii.

Private Prewitt (Montgomery Clift) is a stubborn Kentuckian, an expert prizefighter who suffers endless harassment when he refuses to box in the regional tournament. His closest friend is Angelo Maggio (Frank Sinatra), who openly rebels against military authority and its restrictions. Warden (Burt Lancaster) is the company's first sergeant, a career soldier who both detests the army and its leaders and loves and needs the military way of life. Prewitt and Warden are juxtaposed by Taradash, both in terms of their moral code—Prewitt's private values supercede his public, while the opposite is true for Warden—and in terms of the women with whom they fall in love. Warden begins an affair with Karen Holmes (Deborah

Kerr), the seemingly proper wife of the company commander, and Prewitt is in love with Alma (Donna Reed), a prostitute longing for respectability.

From Here to Eternity earned Taradash an Academy Award (it was also voted best picture; Sinatra and Reed were chosen best supporting actor and actress; and Fred Zinneman won best director). It also brought him financial reward: he had agreed to write the screenplay for two and one-half percent of the film's profits. Unfortunately, Taradash's next project was not a success by any standard. *Desirée* (1954), based on a novel by Annemarie Selinko, is the story of the Emperor Napoleon (Marlon Brando) and the seamstress (Jean Simmons) he loved, though both were married to others. The film does address the conflict between private desire and public responsibility, but it never becomes anything more than a romantic melodrama.

Picnic (1955) was considered a better film. Taradash's script was based on the play by William

From Here to Eternity: *(top) Montgomery Clift and Frank Sinatra; (bottom) Burt Lancaster and Deborah Kerr*

Marlon Brando, Jean Simmons, and Merle Oberon in Desirée

Inge; Joshua Logan directed. Drifter Hal Carter (William Holden) comes to the small Kansas hometown of his army friend Alan Benson (Cliff Robertson). He also falls in love with Madge Owens (Kim Novak), Benson's fiancée, and asks her to run away with him. Madge is at first uncertain what to do, but after being encouraged by her younger sister (Susan Strasberg), she agrees to leave town with Carter. *Picnic* is another fine example of Taradash's skills as an adaptor; he provides a faithful version of the play that is neither theatrical nor static.

Storm Center (1956) most blatantly depicts the Taradash theme that what keeps the community together—mediation, subjugation, sublimation—is precisely that which pulls the individual apart. The only Hollywood film of the 1950s that openly confronts McCarthyism, it was awarded the Chevalier de la Barre Award at Cannes in 1957 as the film "which did most for tolerance and understanding." But *Storm Center* is significant to an appreciation of

Taradash's work for other reasons—he wrote the original screenplay (with Elick Moll) and directed the film, his only directorial effort. For a screenwriter who has spent so much of his life adapting the work of others, this is a uniquely personal film.

For the first half of the film, *Storm Center* deals with Alicia Hull (Bette Davis), the prim librarian of a modest American community who is asked by the city council to remove from the library *The Communist Dream*, a book of propaganda. She at first refuses, then gives in to the council's bribe—a new children's wing. But later she refuses, and the city council accuses her of being a Communist. The second half of the film contains little of Alicia Hull; instead Taradash examines the disintegration of the town, particularly one family, as civilized life falls prey to McCarthyism. He sees the process in three phases: a threat to the town's well-being generates suspicion which becomes fear; the fear is replaced by guilt; and the guilt leads to madness which threatens to replace reason entirely.

Betty Field, Cliff Robertson, Verna Felton, Kim Novak, William Holden, Rosalind Russell, Arthur O'Connell, and Susan Strasberg in the film version of William Inge's play Picnic

Despite its important theme, *Storm Center* was not a success. Reviewing the picture for the *New York Times*, Bosley Crowther argued that the story was neither strong enough to carry the theme nor sufficiently interesting to make the movie entertaining. His review is typical of those of *Storm Center* and suggestive about Taradash's work when considered in its entirety.

Taradash is generally as good as the original short story, play, or novel from which he works. The films for which he has been most consistently criticized are those based on properties of dubious merit. *Bell, Book and Candle* (1958) might serve as a case in point. It is a film adapted from John Van Druten's play about a sorceress (Kim Novak) who bewitches a man (James Stewart). The *New York Times* called Van Druten's play "silly and banal" and added, "as Daniel Taradash has reduced it in a screenplay . . . it is not distinguished by any consistent witchery or bounce." Perhaps the most poorly received of any of Taradash's films, *Morituri* (1965) was taken from a novel by W. J. Luedecke.

It is a too-complicated thriller about an Allied agent (Marlon Brando) who sets out to subvert the mission of a Nazi blockade runner (Yul Brynner). The film was rejected by critics and the public alike.

Hawaii (1966) was beset with problems from the beginning. Several screenwriters and directors had already undertaken the filming of James Michener's massive novel about the Hawaiian Islands in the nineteenth century. Finally, George Roy Hill directed the picture from a screenplay by Taradash and Dalton Trumbo. The script carefully pared down the novel, centering on a missionary (Max von Sydow) who lets nothing stand in the way of what he feels is his duty—to bring religion to the islands.

Castle Keep (1969), also adapted from a bestselling novel, fared less well than did *Hawaii*. Taradash and David Rayfield adapted their script, about a group of soldiers trying to hold a castle on the French border during World War II, from a book by William Eastlake. But after preview screenings, the film was severely edited and lost much of

Scene from Storm Center, *an open confrontation
of McCarthyism*

its continuity and subplots; both critics and audiences were confused, and neither liked the movie.

Taradash's final two screenplays were simplistic melodramas that did little to enhance his reputation: *Doctors' Wives* (1971) and *The Other Side of Midnight* (1977). *Doctors' Wives* is a sensationalized study of the medical profession, complete with drug abuse, alcoholism, infidelity, blackmail, and the murder of an unfaithful spouse (Dyan Can-

non). *The Other Side of Midnight*, taken from Sidney Sheldon's novel, follows the romance of three characters during the 1940s: Noelle (Marie France Pisier), a poor Parisian who becomes a successful model, Catherine (Susan Sarandon), a somewhat naive American, and Larry (John Beck), the callous pilot they both love.

Taradash has done little screenwriting since 1965; instead, he has devoted his time to trying to improve the American film industry and the place of the screenwriter in it. He has been the president of the Writers Guild of America's screen branch, a member of some thirty of its committees, and has served as both the vice president (1968 to 1970) and the president (1970 to 1973) of the Academy of Motion Picture Arts and Sciences. One of the most respected men in Hollywood, he has received numerous awards, including the Guild's Valentine Davies award "for bringing dignity and honor to writers everywhere."

Though not a great original talent, Daniel Taradash is a master craftsman. He is a meticulous writer, often taking from six months to a year to complete a script, sometimes sitting before his typewriter for two or three weeks (a "percolating period" he calls it) prior to writing a word. He has an ear for dialogue, a sense of its rhythms, and hence he is able to develop a character successfully through short passages of speech. His plots are generally expertly executed, wasting no time in moving from exposition to conflict to complication to climax and resolution.

References:

Tom Milne, *Rouben Mamoulian* (Bloomington: Indiana University Press, 1969);

Bob Thomas, *King Cohn* (New York: Putnam's, 1968).

Frank Tashlin

(19 February 1913-5 May 1972)

Randall Clark

MOTION PICTURES: *Delightfully Dangerous* (United Artists, 1945), story by Tashlin, Irving Phillips, and Edward Verdier;

Variety Girl (Paramount, 1947), screen story and screenplay by Tashlin, Edmund L. Hartmann, Monte Brice, and Robert Welch;

The Paleface (Paramount, 1948), screen story and screenplay by Tashlin and Hartmann;

The Fuller Brush Man (Columbia, 1948), screenplay by Tashlin and Devery Freeman;

One Touch of Venus (Universal, 1948), screenplay by Tashlin and Harry Kurnitz;

Love Happy (United Artists, 1949), screenplay by Tashlin and Mac Benoff;

Miss Grant Takes Richmond (Columbia, 1949), screenplay by Tashlin, Freeman, and Nat Perrin;

A Woman of Distinction (Columbia, 1950), additional dialogue;

Kill the Umpire (Columbia, 1950), screen story and screenplay;

The Good Humor Man (Columbia, 1950), screenplay;

The Fuller Brush Girl (Columbia, 1950), screen story and screenplay;

The Lemon Drop Kid (Paramount, 1951), screenplay by Tashlin, Hartmann, and Robert O'Brien;

Son of Paleface (Paramount, 1952), screen story and screenplay by Tashlin, Welch, and Joseph Quillan;

Marry Me Again (RKO, 1953), screenplay;

Artists and Models (Paramount, 1955), screenplay by Tashlin, Hal Kanter, and Herbert Baker;

The Scarlet Hour (Paramount, 1955), screen story by Tashlin and Rip Van Ronkel; screenplay by Tashlin, Van Ronkel, and Meredyth Lucas;

The Lieutenant Wore Skirts (20th Century-Fox, 1956), screenplay by Tashlin and Albert Beich;

The Girl Can't Help It (20th Century-Fox, 1957), screenplay by Tashlin and Herbert Baker;

Will Success Spoil Rock Hunter? (20th Century-Fox, 1957), screen story and screenplay;

Rock-a-Bye Baby (Paramount, 1958), screenplay;

The Geisha Boy (Paramount, 1958), screen story and screenplay;

Cinderfella (Paramount, 1960), screen story and screenplay;

Bachelor Flat (20th Century-Fox, 1962), screenplay by Tashlin and Budd Grossman;

Who's Minding the Store? (Paramount, 1963), screenplay by Tashlin and Harry Tugend;

The Disorderly Orderly (Paramount, 1964), screenplay;

Caprice (20th Century-Fox, 1967), screenplay by Tashlin and Jay Jayson;

The Private Navy of Sergeant O'Farrell (United Artists, 1968), screenplay.

Frank Tashlin was one of the foremost comedy writers of the 1950s and 1960s, providing screenplays for such performers as Bob Hope, Dean Martin and Jerry Lewis (and later, Lewis alone), Red Skelton, Lucille Ball, and the Marx Brothers. His films were usually mild comedies about American life. Popular culture—movies, comic books, advertising—fascinated him and provided the inspiration for much of his work. There is a surreal quality to his humor; he came to screenwriting after many years as a cartoonist, bringing with him an exaggerated, visual sense of comedy.

Tashlin was born in Weehawken, New Jersey, but his family moved to Astoria in Queens, New York, when he was a child. His education ended with grammar school; by age thirteen he was making a living delivering newspapers and working for local merchants. His career break came in 1928, when he got a job running errands for Max Fleischer, an animation pioneer. This affiliation led to a series of minor jobs in the cartoon industry, and finally to a position as animator at Van Beuren studios, where he worked on a series of cartoons based on Aesop's fables. (A few years later, Tashlin parodied his employer Amadee Van Beuren with a comic strip titled "Van Boring.") He also began submitting cartoons to various magazines, usually under the name Tish-Tash.

In 1933 Tashlin came to Hollywood where he worked at several animation studios, including Ub Iwerks, M-G-M, and Warner Bros. One particularly noteworthy cartoon that Tashlin wrote and

Sheree North and Frank Tashlin on the set of The Lieutenant Wore Skirts

supervised during this period was "The Fox and the Grapes," about a fox that is trying to snatch a bunch of grapes from a crow but never succeeds. Chuck Jones, an animator who worked with Tashlin at Warner Bros., has acknowledged the cartoon as the inspiration for his long-running "Roadrunner" series.

In addition to his cartoon work, Tashlin was a gagman at Hal Roach studios, writing jokes for the Little Rascals, Thelma Todd, and Charlie Chase. Tashlin learned a great deal from Roach, a comedy writer and producer who emphasized plot over jokes. But the most important influence on his movie scripts was his work in the Warner Bros. animation unit. There he learned the frenetic pacing, frequent scene changes, and broad visual humor, including comic violence and outrageous double takes, that mark his feature films. And in one cartoon, *Porky's Romance* (1937), in which a nervous Porky Pig is introduced as "one of Warner Bros.' 'brightest stars' " and is too nervous to go "onstage," Tashlin discovered another of his trademarks: self-reference in film. His characters, par-

ticularly in his films with Bob Hope, step out of character and directly address the audience; in *The Girl Can't Help It* (1957), Tom Ewell steps into a small-screen, black-and-white film and makes technicians transform it into a Cinemascope, stereo, Technicolor masterpiece; and in *Will Success Spoil Rock Hunter?* (1957), Tony Randall, playing the film's theme music, at one point reduces the size of the picture "so television viewers will feel at home." It is this quality that makes his films stand apart from those of his contemporaries and that earned Tashlin a favorable reputation in France, where he has always been taken more seriously than in the United States; he is considered to be one of the greatest influences of the French "nouvelle vague" cinema.

Tashlin worked at Warner Bros. from 1937 to 1938 and again from 1943 to 1945. He wrote and directed twenty-eight cartoons at the studio, nearly half of which featured Porky Pig. One of these, *The Swooner Crooner* (1944), received an Academy Award nomination for best animated short feature. In between jobs at Warner Bros.,

Bob Hope and Tashlin on the set for Son of Paleface, *a spoof on Westerns*

Tashlin worked at Walt Disney Studios, where he wrote a Mickey Mouse cartoon, *Mickey and the Beanstalk,* was story director for other Mickey Mouse and Donald Duck cartoons, and worked on an early screenplay for *Sleeping Beauty,* though none of his work seems to have been used in the film. A firm union supporter, Tashlin left Disney over a labor disagreement and become an executive producer at Screen Gems Cartoon Studios. He immediately brought many of Disney's animators to Screen Gems in the hopes of making it one of the best animation studios in the country. John Hubley, one of the animators who worked under Tashlin, remembered: "We tried some very experimental things; none of them quite got off the ground but there was a lot of ground broken. We were doing crazy things that were anti the classic Disney approach." This experimentation ended with Tashlin's return to Warner Bros.

During World War II, Tashlin wrote and directed cartoons for the *Army Navy Screen Magazine.* The cartoons featured Private Snafu, a bumbling soldier. There was less censorship here than there had been at Tashlin's earlier jobs, and these car-

toons contain much of the risqué humor that appears in his film scripts.

Delightfully Dangerous (1945) was Tashlin's first feature film. A young woman (Jane Powell) goes to visit her sister (Constance Moore), whom she believes is a successful dancer, only to find she is a burlesque performer; later the two fall in love with the same man (Ralph Bellamy). Because Tashlin wrote only the screen story, not the full screenplay, and because he wrote that story with two others, it is difficult to determine his precise contributions to the film. Still, certain themes that recur in his work may be found here: the character who pretends or aspires to be something she is not, the interest in show business, and the unfulfilled romance.

Following the release of *Delightfully Dangerous,* Tashlin was signed as a joke writer at Paramount; he is known to have written sight gags for Harpo Marx in *A Night in Casablanca* (1946), and his work certainly was used in other pictures. His first screenplay credit (shared with three other writers) was for *Variety Girl* (1947), about two aspiring performers who travel to Hollywood, one of whom (Mary Hatcher) becomes a star. It is noteworthy only as the first time Tashlin wrote material for Bob Hope, who had a cameo role in the film. The next year, Tashlin and Edmund Hartmann, one of his collaborators on *Variety Girl,* wrote an entire screenplay for Hope, *The Paleface* (1948). Calamity Jane (Jane Russell) has been promised a pardon by the governor if she can find the men who are selling guns to the Indians. She is supposed to travel across country undercover, posing as the wife of a secret service man, but when he is found murdered, she marries Painless Peter Potter (Hope), an inept dentist who knows nothing about her plan. The movie also contains a running joke that is typical of the humor Tashlin borrows from cartoons: whenever Potter tries to kiss Jane, she knocks him unconscious with her gun. *The Paleface* was a financial success, but Tashlin was unhappy with the completed film; what he had intended to be a satire of *The Virginian* seemed to him to be little more than a conventional Western with some humor. He became determined to direct his own material, a goal he achieved three years later.

Tashlin was always interested in the working class, almost invariably finding humor in the occupations of his characters. His next two pictures, *The Fuller Brush Man* (1948) and *One Touch of Venus* (1948) both have protagonists who run into trouble while on the job. In *The Fuller Brush Man,* street sweeper Red (Red Skelton) is told by his fiancée

(Janet Blair) that he must make something of himself, so he becomes a door-to-door salesman, but stumbles into a murder while making his rounds. Tashlin and Harry Kurnitz adapted *One Touch of Venus* from a Broadway hit by S. J. Perelman and Ogden Nash. A window dresser (Robert Walker) impulsively kisses a statue of Venus in a department store; his kiss brings her to life (Ava Gardner plays the living Venus), and she falls in love with him.

Love Happy (1949) provided Tashlin with the opportunity to write a screenplay for the Marx Brothers. Unfortunately, the film was one of the brothers' worst. Chico and Harpo play two musicians in an unsuccessful show, while Groucho appears as a private detective in an unrelated subplot. The three Marxes had few scenes together, and the film was a failure. Groucho Marx was used to better advantage in a cameo role in *Will Success Spoil Rock Hunter?* (1957).

Lloyd Bacon, a former comedy actor and director for Mack Sennett, directed Tashlin's next four films (the last screenplays before Tashlin began directing his own work). Two of these pictures were vehicles for Lucille Ball. In *Miss Grant Takes Richmond* (1949), she is a secretary who uncovers a criminal plot connected with the housing shortage in postwar America. *The Fuller Brush Girl* (1950) is very similar to *The Fuller Brush Man*. A saleswoman (Ball) is framed for murder and must find the real criminals; at the film's climax, she chases them into a burlesque house and disguises herself as a performer. *The Good Humor Man* (1950) is also similar to *The Fuller Brush Man* (both pictures were based on short stories by mystery writer Roy Huggins). An ice cream salesman (Jack Carson) witnesses a crime, is captured by criminals, but is saved by a group of children who are fellow members in the Captain Marvel club.

In *Kill the Umpire* (1950), a former baseball player (William Bendix) is pressured by his father-in-law (Ray Collins) to become the one thing he hates most in the world: an umpire. When he is set to umpire a major league game, gangsters ask him to rule in favor of the team on which they have wagered heavily. The film ends in a wild chase scene which is clearly influenced by Tashlin's work on cartoons.

In 1951 Tashlin, Hartmann, and Robert O'Brien adapted Damon Runyon's story "The Lemon Drop Kid" into a vehicle for Bob Hope. The Kid (Hope) is a racetrack tout who uses an old-age home as a front for a gambling den. After the movie had begun filming, Hope was dissatisfied with director Sidney Lanfield and suggested that Tashlin be allowed to take over the film. After that, Tashlin directed all his own scripts with the exception of *The Scarlet Hour* (1955).

Son of Paleface (1952) was Tashlin's next film for Hope. This sequel was closer to the Western spoof that Tashlin had intended *The Paleface* to be, with Roy Rogers joining the cast and satirizing his own screen image. Tashlin then began working as a comedy writer for NBC and, later, CBS television and wrote fewer screenplays. *Marry Me Again* (1953) was about a young woman (Marie Wilson) who inherits one million dollars, which threatens her relationship with her fiancé (Robert Cummings), a gas station attendant too proud to live off her money. Tashlin directed *Susan Slept Here* (1954), and worked on the screenplay without credit. Seventeen-year-old Susan (Debbie Reynolds), fearing she will jeopardize her mother's remarriage, runs away from home and is taken in by a successful writer (Dick Powell). She falls in love with him, despite the difference in their ages, and they marry.

Artists and Models (1955) was a milestone in Tashlin's career. It is, with *The Paleface*, his best-known and most popular work; it is the only time he wrote a film about cartooning; and it introduced him to Jerry Lewis, with whom he maintained a working relationship for a decade, and in whom he found the best performer for his material. The movie satirizes the comic book industry, which was the subject of great controversy when *Artists and Models* was filmed. Rick Todd (Dean Martin) is an aspiring artist who finds great success drawing and writing comic books based on the gruesome nightmares of his roommate Eugene Fullstack (Lewis). Todd falls in love with another artist, Abigail Parker (Dorothy Malone), and Fullstack falls in love with her friend Bessie Sparrowbrush (Shirley MacLaine), who models for his favorite comic book character, The Bat Lady. The collaboration between Tashlin and Lewis, nine films in all, resulted in some of the best work of both men and Lewis's later directorial efforts reveal much of Tashlin's influence.

Directed by Michael Curtiz, *The Scarlet Hour* (1955) is an oddity among Tashlin's work, his sole attempt at melodrama. He coauthored the script with Meredyth Lucas and Alford "Rip" Van Ronkel. A bored housewife (Carol Ohmart) takes a lover (Tom Tryon) then pushes him toward a life of crime. Tashlin was back to more familiar material with *The Lieutenant Wore Skirts* (1956), about a woman (Sheree North) who reenlists in the army

Advertisement for one of Tashlin's most popular films

to be near her husband, whom she mistakenly believes has been drafted. He follows her around the country in an attempt to save their marriage. Tashlin worked without credit on the screenplay for *Hollywood or Bust* (1955), the last movie for the Martin and Lewis team. They play two men who win a car and travel cross-country to Hollywood, where Lewis is determined to meet Anita Ekberg.

Though *The Girl Can't Help It* (1957) and *Will Success Spoil Rock Hunter?* are about rock music and the advertising business, respectively, the films have a common target for their satire: the artificially created celebrity. In *The Girl Can't Help It*, gangster Fats Murdock (Edmond O'Brien), who feels it is beneath him to marry a woman who is not famous, hires press agent Tom Miller (Tom Ewell) to make his fiancée Jerri Jordan (Jayne

Mansfield) into a successful singer. Jordan has agreed to marry Murdock because she feels she owes him a debt, another recurring theme in Tashlin's work. Jordan cannot sing (or so everyone believes; she is really disguising her voice to avoid a career she does not want) and only becomes a success because of her looks. Tashlin fills his screenplay with jokes about her physique and has his characters do exaggerated double takes whenever they see her.

Will Success Spoil Rock Hunter? was adapted from a play by George Axelrod, though Tashlin's script deviated from Axelrod's play. Rockwell Hunter (Tony Randall) is an advertising executive who needs a celebrity endorsement for a new brand of lipstick; actress Rita Marlowe (Mansfield, who had starred in the play) agrees to the endorsement to make her boyfriend jealous of Hunter. When the public believes that Hunter is Rita's lover, he becomes a sex symbol in his own right. While Hunter is the manufactured celebrity in this film, Tashlin spends most of his time spoofing the image of Mansfield (who was herself groomed by 20th Century-Fox as another Marilyn Monroe).

A series of Jerry Lewis films followed this picture. *Rock-a-Bye Baby* (1958) is about an actress (Connie Stevens) who wants to keep her triplets secret from her public and hires a full-time sitter (Lewis). *The Geisha Boy* (1958) has Lewis as an inept magician on a USO tour of Japan. *Cinderfella* (1960) updates a classic fairy tale; Lewis is a mistreated young man, kept from his family fortune by a cruel stepmother (Judith Anderson), until his fairy godfather (Ed Wynn) intervenes, transforming him into a confident character capable of dealing with his problems. Tashlin also directed *It's Only Money* (1963), with Lewis as a television repairman who aspires to become a private investigator.

Although *Bachelor Flat* (1962) was adapted by Tashlin and Budd Grossman from Grossman's play *Lily*, the film's basic premise is similar to that of *Susan Slept Here:* a seventeen-year-old girl (Tuesday Weld) meets her mother's fiancé (Terry-Thomas), who does not know she exists. Rather than ruin her mother's engagement, she pretends to be a runaway juvenile delinquent. In *Who's Minding the Store?* (1963), Lewis is a clumsy department store employee kept apart from his fiancée (Jill St. John) by her cruel mother (Agnes Moorehead). Much better was *The Disorderly Orderly* (1964), about a hospital orderly who develops "neurotic identification empathy" that causes him to experience the symptoms of the patients. The movie is noteworthy for a scene in which Tashlin mixes live action and animation: Lewis, crawling on the floor in a straitjacket, is passed by a cartoon snail.

The Disorderly Orderly was Tashlin's last work with Lewis and his last genuine success. He took three more directing jobs: *The Man from the Diner's*

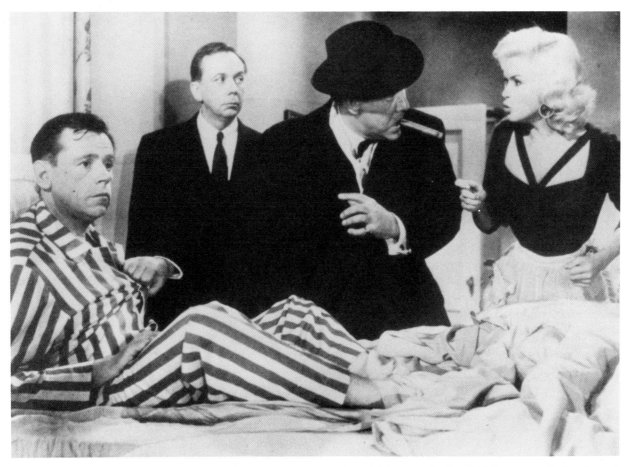

Tom Ewell, Henry Jones, Edmond O'Brien, and Jayne Mansfield in The Girl Can't Help It, *which became a cult favorite and was rereleased in the 1970s*

Club (1963), *The Alphabet Murders* (1966), and *The Glass Bottom Boat* (1966). Doris Day starred in the last, and Tashlin both wrote and directed her next film, *Caprice* (1967), a spy spoof about an industrial spy (Day) trying to solve the murder of her father, an Interpol agent. The film contains many of Tashlin's favorite themes, including a satire of business, Day mocking her screen image, and self-referential remarks about the movie (Day enters a theater that is showing *Caprice*). But much of the material falls flat, and *Caprice* is one of Tashlin's worst pictures. He followed it with one final Bob Hope vehicle, their first collaboration in seventeen years, *The Private Navy of Sergeant O'Farrell* (1968). During World War II, a navy sergeant (Hope) searches desperately for a missing ship carrying a load of beer for his men. The film was a critical and commercial failure; in 1969 nobody wanted to see a traditional service comedy. The time for Tashlin's humor was past. He retired that year and died in 1972 of a heart attack. He was survived by his wife and two children.

The career of Frank Tashlin has always been subject to some controversy; even at the height of his success he was dismissed by many critics as being vulgar. As the years passed, much of his best work was associated less with him than with the films' performers, so that now he has been largely forgotten. But he was a formative influence on filmmakers as dissimilar as Chuck Jones, Jerry Lewis, and Woody Allen. As long as movie comedy is to be studied, so should be the work of Frank Tashlin.

References:

Peter Bogdanovich, "Frank Tashlin—An Interview and an Appreciation," *Film Culture*, no. 26 (Fall 1962): 21-33;

Leonard Maltin, *The Great Movie Comedians: From Charlie Chaplin to Woody Allen* (New York: Crown, 1978), pp. 185-196, 217-226;

Maltin, *Of Mice and Magic: A History of American Animated Cartoons* (New York: McGraw-Hill, 1980).

Robert Towne
(1936-)

Joel Bellman

MOTION PICTURES: *The Last Woman on Earth* (Filmgroup, 1960), screenplay;

The Tomb of Ligeia (American International, 1965), screenplay;

Villa Rides (Paramount, 1968), screenplay by Towne and Sam Peckinpah;

The Last Detail (Columbia, 1973), screenplay;

Chinatown (Paramount, 1974), screenplay;

Shampoo (Columbia, 1975), screenplay by Towne and Warren Beatty;

The Yakuza (Warner Bros., 1975), screenplay by Towne and Paul Schrader;

Personal Best (Warner Bros., 1982), screenplay;

Greystoke: The Legend of Tarzan, Lord of the Apes (Warner Bros., 1984), screenplay by Towne (as P. H. Vazak) and Michael Austin.

TELEVISION: *The Outer Limits,* "The Chameleon" (ABC, 1964);

The Man From U.N.C.L.E., "The Dove Affair" (NBC, 1964);

Breaking Point, "So Many Pretty Girls, So Little Time" (ABC, 1964);

The Lloyd Bridges Show (CBS, 1962-1963), four episodes;

The Richard Boone Show (NBC, 1964).

OTHER: "A Screenwriter on Screenwriting," in *Anatomy of the Movies*, edited by David Pirie (New York: Macmillan, 1981), pp. 150-153.

Robert Towne is the sort of screenwriter who is very important to but largely unrecognized outside of the film industry. He is a script doctor, most of whose work involves rewriting or polishing other writers' scripts; he is credited in less than half the films on which he has worked. This is hardly the way to become famous, but it has earned Towne a

Robert Towne

reputation as one of Hollywood's consummate professionals.

Towne grew up in the San Pedro harbor district, the son of Russian-Rumanian immigrants. He says, "I was born . . . before World War II, so I can remember Los Angeles . . . when it was an entirely different place. It had a beauty which is lost forever." He studied philosophy and literature at Pomona State College before dropping out of school to join the army. After he was discharged and having done "everything from selling real estate to working as a commerical fisherman," he began taking a series of acting classes under drama instructor Jeff Corey. It was these classes that provided Towne with his entrance into the movie industry. Among his classmates were Sally Kellerman, Jack Nicholson, James Coburn, and Roger Corman, who was just beginning his career as producer and director of low-budget movies. Ever on the lookout for inexpensive talent, Corman hired twenty-one-year-old Towne as writer, actor, and general errand boy, for what Towne calls "a dreadful science fiction movie."

The Last Woman on Earth (1960) was Towne's first produced screenplay. The plot was standard science fiction fare of the period: three survivors of a nuclear holocaust, one woman (Betsy Jones-Moreland) and two men, are caught in a love triangle. Towne's script gave the picture more substance than others in the genre, largely due to the conflict he established between the two male survivors: one, a small-time gangster (Anthony Carbone) wants to rebuild civilization while the other,

his attorney, accepts and almost enjoys his life as one of the few people living on Earth. Because Towne had not finished his screenplay when Corman was to begin shooting the movie, and because Corman's budget did not allow him to bring along his screenwriter, he gave Towne a role in the film: Towne, as Edward Wain, plays the gangster's attorney. The movie contained enough exploitable elements to become a financial success, and Towne and Corman continued working together.

Persistent allergies left Towne in ill health throughout the 1960s. He was able to work only sporadically during this time, one reason he began rewriting others' work rather than undertaking the more demanding task of writing an entire screenplay. It was Corman who first asked him to polish a script, hiring him to rework Charles Griffith's screenplay for *The Creature from the Haunted Sea* (1961), about a criminal gang that uses a fake sea monster to frighten people away from their hideout. Two years later, Towne was hired to rewrite *The Long Ride Home*, about a Union officer (Glenn Ford) pursuing escaped Confederate prisoners. The picture was released in 1967 as *A Time for Killing*, with Halstead Welles receiving sole screenplay credit.

Towne began writing for television in 1964, starting with a script titled "The Chameleon" written for *The Outer Limits*. He later wrote scripts for *The Man From U.N.C.L.E.*, *The Lloyd Bridges Show*, and *The Richard Boone Show*. Interestingly, one script from this period, "So Many Pretty Girls, So Little Time," written for *Breaking Point*, anticipates the theme of Towne's later screenplay for *Shampoo* (1975); both concern a compulsive Don Juan who gets his comeuppance.

Corman hired Towne in 1965 to write *The Tomb of Ligeia*, the last film in Corman's series of Edgar Allan Poe adaptations. In Poe's original work, a second wife's dead body is seemingly reanimated by the spirit of her husband's first wife. Realizing that this story was too short to sustain a full-length movie, Towne expanded the plot, elaborating on the themes of necrophilia and mesmerism that he thought Poe had only hinted at, and he borrowed material from other of Poe's works. In the movie, both wives reappear and battle each other; the husband (Vincent Price) tries to kill both, but to no avail; a corpse is exhumed, but then is discovered to be a wax dummy; even the black cat from another story appears. Finally, a fiery holocaust occurs that destroys everyone and everything. Critics responded favorably to Towne's outrageous plot, giving *The Tomb of Ligeia* the best reviews of

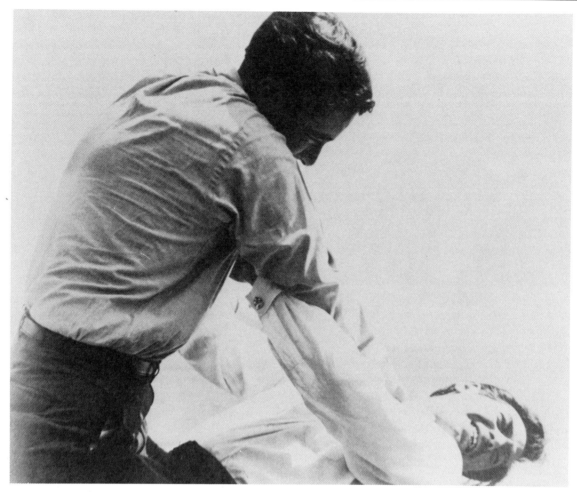

Edward Wain (Robert Towne) and Anthony Carbone as the last males in The Last Woman on Earth, *the film for which Towne earned his first screen credit*

any of the Poe films. Towne later said he worked harder on this movie than on any other.

Warren Beatty had read Towne's rewrite of *The Long Ride Home* and was impressed with it, so when he ran into problems with the screenplay for *Bonnie and Clyde* (1967), Towne was brought in to do a final polish. His major contribution was redefining the relationship between Clyde (Beatty), Bonnie (Faye Dunaway), and their driver C. W. Moss (Michael J. Pollard); in the original screenplay by Robert Benton and David Newman, the characters were involved in a ménage a trois, with Clyde unable to perform sexually unless C. W. was present. This element was removed from the final version. Towne altered the structure of the movie, rearranging the sequence of certain scenes in order to heighten the tension as audiences waited for the inevitable deaths of Bonnie and Clyde. This is one

of the rare times that Towne ever received any official credit for his rewrite work; he is billed in the film as "special consultant."

Towne has said of *Villa Rides* (1968), his next project: "It was one of the most interesting experiences I have ever had working on a film. And it was also one of the least successful. It was a textbook on *How Not to Make a Movie*." The movie was a historically inaccurate account of Mexican revolutionary Pancho Villa (Yul Brynner), his closest associate (Charles Bronson), and an amoral American pilot (Robert Mitchum) who is first their prisoner, later a compatriot. The screenplay was adapted from a novel by William Douglas Lansford; Towne shared scripting credit with Sam Peckinpah, who seems to have had a greater influence on the final film. Television veteran Buzz Kulik directed. Reviews complained that the movie was needlessly violent, though some of the violence was done with a grim humor that escaped most critics.

In 1971, again uncredited, Towne lent his skills to a final draft of *Cisco Pike*, a gritty crime drama about a former pusher (Kris Kristofferson) caught between his parole board and a crooked cop (Gene Hackman). The film had a tough, convincing edge to it, although it was largely overlooked on its initial release. Another uncredited polishing job done that same year resulted in a public acknowledgement from an unlikely source. After accepting the 1972 Oscar for best screen adaptation of *The Godfather*, Francis Ford Coppola praised Towne for his help in rewriting some scenes, including the crucial one in which Vito Corleone passes his empire to his son Michael. "Coppola basically wanted a scene where the two men would say that they loved each other. . . . It sounds simple; but you cannot write a love scene by just having two people say they love each other. . . . eventually I wrote the

scene so that it was ostensibly about the succession of power, about youth taking over and the reluctance of the old to give way. The older man is telling his son to be careful in the future and mentions some of the people who might pose a threat, while the son reassures him with a touch of impatience—'I can handle it.' And you can tell the father's obsessive concern for these details reflects his anxiety that his son is having to adopt a role that the old man never wanted him to have, as well as the father's reluctance to give up his power. Underlying all of this is the feeling that they care for each other."

At the same time Towne was contributing so successfully to *The Godfather*, however, he ran into difficulties with another project, an adaptation of Joseph Wambaugh's novel *The New Centurions* (1970). Towne worked carefully with Wambaugh when preparing his screenplay, but the producers made so many changes in his work that he withdrew

Vincent Price and Elizabeth Shepherd in Tomb of Ligeia. *The screenplay, by Towne, was written for Roger Corman's last Poe film.*

his name from the picture. Stirling Silliphant received final credit.

The Last Detail (1973) finally brought Towne into the limelight. Jack Nicholson, former roommate from his acting-class days, had read Daryl Ponicsan's novel while it was still in galleys, bought it, and had Towne write the screenplay. The movie was not only Towne's first major screen credit, but it also brought him his first Academy Award nomination. Ponicsan's novel was a variation on the "three sailors on the town" theme, with the bitter twist that the two career sailors, Buddusky (Nicholson) and Mulhall (Otis Young) are escorting naive young Meadows (Randy Quaid) to the brig for an eight-year sentence. When Buddusky and Mulhall realize how inexperienced Meadows is, they decide to introduce him to such pleasures as drinking, sex, and fist fights. The offbeat humor present in almost all of Towne's work is used to good advantage in

the film. His penchant for working strange anecdotes into his scripts rises to the fore, and the film essentially becomes a kind of long shaggy-dog story. Towne says he has Buddusky turn Meadows over to the brig, rather than allowing him to escape, so that the audience would identify with the film's theme: people are nice until they have to "risk" their own skin.

Towne's next film was only his second original script, but *Chinatown* (1974) is clearly his masterwork. The themes underlying *Chinatown* are social and ecological. As Towne explains: "I wanted to tell a story about a man who raped the land and his daughter in the name of the future. Men like Cross (the film's villain) believe that as long as they keep building and reproducing, they'll live forever." In 1937 Los Angeles, private eye Jake Gittes (Nicholson) is hired for what seems to be a standard marital infidelity case but is rapidly drawn into a

Otis Young and Jack Nicholson escort Randy Quaid (center) to prison in The Last Detail

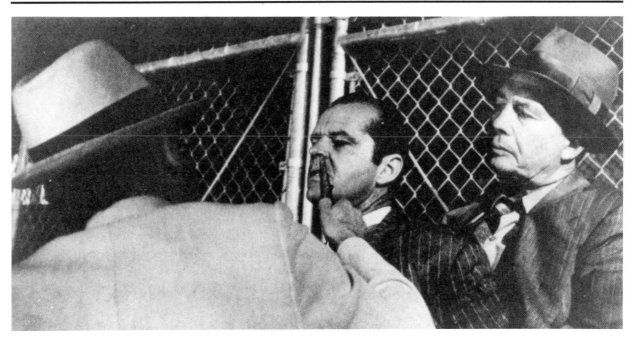

Roman Polanski (with knife), Jack Nicholson, and Roy Jensen in Chinatown

maelstrom of moral and political corruption that affects the entire city. The metaphor of Chinatown is used throughout the story as the recurring example of an unknowable, terrifying place. Something happened to Jake when he was a policeman in Chinatown, but all he will say by way of explanation is, "I tried to prevent someone from getting hurt. I ended up making sure she got hurt." In other words, even an aggressive guy like Gittes can get into a situation over his head and cause more problems than he can solve.

The plot was a synthesis of Towne's personal experiences (including his childhood in the San Pedro harbor district of Los Angeles), political concerns, and affection for the private eye literature of the 1930s. Researching the film, he read both factual histories of California, especially Carey McWilliams's *Southern California: An Island on the Land,* and fiction, particularly the novels of Raymond Chandler and John Fante. (Towne is a great admirer of Fante, and has made attempts to film his novels.)

Commercially and artistically successful as *Chinatown* ultimately was, serious tension developed between Towne and director Roman Polanski over the structure of the plot. Polanski altered Towne's ending—in which Cross's daughter Evelyn (Faye Dunaway) kills her father to protect her daughter—to a more despairing one in which Evelyn is killed by the police. Towne thought a slightly

more hopeful ending was called for; he feels Polanski's version is "so relentlessly cynical it works against itself." Despite his misgivings, Towne won the Academy Award for best screenplay.

While *Chinatown* was still in production, Towne was hired to rewrite *The Yakuza* (1975), which Paul Schrader had written from a story by his brother Leonard. The movie centers on a retired American detective (Robert Mitchum) who owes a friend a favor and travels to Japan searching for the friend's missing daughter. In Japan, the detective becomes involved with the Japanese underworld of the *yakuza*, and must enlist the help of a wartime acquaintance (Takakura Ken), himself a former underworld member. Towne preserved the structure of the script, deleting scenes that he felt would not work and improving the dialogue. Unfortunately, neither Towne nor Schrader adequately developed the characters, and director Sidney Pollack had little feel for the material, particularly the action sequences. *The Yakuza* became an expensive failure.

Warren Beatty had remained friends with Towne since they had worked on *Bonnie and Clyde,* and Beatty eventually became Towne's collaborator on his screenplay for *Shampoo* (1975). Towne had first conceived of the plot in 1970—he would invert the cliché of the gay male hairdresser, making him a heterosexual superman. In so doing, the character George (Beatty) would embody all the social

Julie Christie and Warren Beatty in Shampoo, *which Towne and Beatty wrote together*

contradictions and manic energy of the 1960s; the point was made clearer by setting the story on election day 1968. Against the backdrop of miniskirts, strobe lights, psychedelia, and politics, George's life crashes around him. He is finally left abandoned, and uncertain of his future.

The exact contributions of Towne and Beatty to the script are difficult to determine. Each man worked on separate drafts, sometimes rewriting each other's work, and further rewriting was done once the film started shooting. Towne has said, "The history of that thing is so convoluted and involved and my relationship with Beatty so close it's impossible to disentangle to show who did what." Whoever was responsible, *Shampoo* became one of the most acclaimed motion pictures of the 1970s; it is said to have been on more critics' ten-best lists than any film that year.

The combined success of *The Last Detail*, *Chinatown*, and *Shampoo* made Towne one of the most

sought-after screenwriters in Hollywood. He was reportedly earning $300,000 for an original script, $150,000 for an adaptation, and receiving a percentage of the box office receipts of his films. But following *Shampoo* he began writing less, and he did not receive another screen credit until 1982 with *Personal Best*. He still did occasional script doctoring: he polished William Goldman's script for *Marathon Man* (1976) and advised Warren Beatty on *Reds* (1981), which Beatty produced, directed, and coauthored. Towne also devoted his time to personal concerns, including spending nearly a year in the late 1970s working as a negotiator between San Pedro tuna fishermen and environmentalists. But most of his time was spent on two pet projects: *Personal Best* (1982), about two women pentathletes, and *Greystoke* (1984), an epic version of the life of Tarzan.

Personal Best is Towne's most personal film to date. He says that he has always identified with women: "You are always the one at home sweating over the hot typewriter while the authority figure is on the set telling people what to do." *Personal Best* is also the result of his developing fascination with women athletes he met at the gymnasium where he works out to combat his allergic attacks. "I have an absolutely blatant prejudice for women athletes, for their bodies, the way they move, their temperaments," Towne told a *Newsweek* reporter while *Personal Best* was filming. The movie centers on two pentathletes, Chris Cahill (Mariel Hemingway) and Tory Skinner (Patrice Donnelly), following them from the 1976 Olympic trials to the 1980 trials. Cahill is the less experienced of the two, and much of the film is devoted to her development as an athlete and her emotional growth: she and Tory move from competitors to friends to lovers to competitors again, and Chris eventually begins a romance with another athlete (Kenny More). Towne described the film as a "story about innocence, purity, growing up. My idea is that they're children discovering who they are with their bodies," and the film was to a a degree inspired by his infant daughter Katharine.

Personal Best began filming in 1981 with Towne making his directorial debut. Almost immediately it was beset with production problems; the film ran over budget and at one point the money ran out completely and filming had to be stopped. Towne finally secured further financing, but he had to release Warner Bros. from their agreement to let him direct *Greystoke*, a project he had worked on for eight years. *Personal Best* was finally released in 1982, but given limited distribution; despite good reviews, it was a box office failure.

When *Greystoke: The Legend of Tarzan, Lord of the Apes,* directed by Hugh Hudson, was released in 1984, Towne removed his name from the credits and substituted the pseudonym P. H. Vazak. He had intended the movie to be a faithful adaptation of Edgar Rice Burroughs's Tarzan novels, set almost entirely in Africa, but the script was rewritten by Michael Austin who added scenes showing the problems Tarzan (Christopher Lambert) faces when returning to English society. Still, the movie was a critical success and earned Towne and Austin Academy Award nominations. Towne, in the meantime, had returned to the role of script doctor; he provided some last minute changes in *Swing Shift* (1984), a comedy about women factory workers during World War II.

Robert Towne's talent as a screenwriter lies in the film craftsman's instinct for telling a story in a cinematically effective way. He possesses the gift of being able to construct plausible, yet highly entertaining dialogue, and he can sense a story's narrative rhythms; even some of his less successful efforts are creatively paced. Where other writers worry about getting screen credit for their work, Towne sometimes exerts pressure to have his name removed from the credits. His financial position established, Towne's primary concern is maintaining his integrity as a master screenwriter.

References:

John Brady, *The Craft of the Screenwriter* (New York: Simon & Schuster, 1981), pp. 366-432;

Norman Dickens, *Jack Nicholson: The Search for a Superstar* (New York: NAL, 1975), pp. 124,132-134;

Martin Kasindorf, "Hot Writer," *Newsweek,* 84 (14 October 1974): 114;

Jack Kroll, "Chariots of Desire," *Newsweek* (8 February 1982): 60;

Kenny Moore, "You Oughta Be in Pictures," *Sports Illustrated,* 56 (1 February 1982): 50-62;

Ed Naha, *The Films of Roger Corman* (New York: Arco, 1982);

Michael Sragow, "Ghost Writers Unraveling the Enigma of Movie Authorship," *Film Comment,* 19 (March-April 1983): 9-18.

Lamar Trotti

(18 October 1898-28 August 1952)

Maynard Tereba Smith

MOTION PICTURES: *The Man Who Dared* (Fox, 1933), screenplay by Trotti and Dudley Nichols;

You Can't Buy Everything (M-G-M, 1934), screenplay by Trotti and Nichols;

Hold That Girl (Fox, 1934), screenplay and dialogue by Trotti and Nichols;

Call It Luck (Fox, 1934), screenplay by Trotti and Nichols;

Judge Priest (Fox, 1934), screenplay by Trotti and Nichols;

Bachelor of Arts (Fox, 1934), screenplay;

Life Begins at Forty (20th Century-Fox, 1935), screenplay;

Steamboat Round the Bend (20th Century-Fox, 1935), screenplay by Trotti and Nichols;

This Is the Life (20th Century-Fox, 1935), screenplay by Trotti and Arthur Horman;

Gentle Julia (20th Century-Fox, 1936), screenplay;

The First Baby (20th Century-Fox, 1936), screen story and screenplay;

Country Beyond (20th Century-Fox, 1936), screenplay by Trotti and Adele Comandini;

Pepper (20th Century-Fox, 1936), screenplay;

Ramona (20th Century-Fox, 1936), screenplay;

Can This Be Dixie? (20th Century-Fox, 1936), screen story by Trotti and George Marshall; screenplay;

Career Woman (20th Century-Fox, 1936), screenplay;

This Is My Affair (20th Century-Fox, 1937), screen story and screenplay by Trotti and Allen Rivkin;

Slave Ship (20th Century-Fox, 1937), screenplay by Trotti, Sam Hellman, and Gladys Lehman;

Wife, Doctor and Nurse (20th Century-Fox, 1937), screenplay by Trotti, Kathryn Scola, and Darrell Ware;

In Old Chicago (20th Century-Fox, 1937), screenplay by Trotti and Sonya Levien;

The Baroness and the Butler (20th Century-Fox, 1938), screenplay by Trotti, Scola, and Hellman;

Gateway (20th Century-Fox, 1938), screenplay;

Alexander's Ragtime Band (20th Century-Fox, 1938), screenplay by Trotti and Scola;

Kentucky (20th Century-Fox, 1938), screenplay by Trotti and John Taintor Foote;

The Story of Alexander Graham Bell (20th Century-Fox, 1939), screenplay;

Young Mr. Lincoln (20th Century-Fox, 1939), screen story and screenplay;

Drums Along the Mohawk (20th Century-Fox, 1939), screenplay by Trotti and Levien;

Brigham Young—Frontiersman (20th Century-Fox, 1940), screenplay;

Hudson's Bay (20th Century-Fox, 1940), screen story and screenplay;

Belle Starr (20th Century-Fox, 1941), screenplay;

To the Shores of Tripoli (20th Century-Fox, 1942), screenplay;

Tales of Manhattan (20th Century-Fox, 1942), screen story and screenplay by Trotti, Donald Ogden Stewart, Ben Hecht, Ferenc Molnár, Samuel Hoffenstein, Alan Campbell, L. Vadnai, L. Gorog, Ladislas Fodor, and Henry Blankfort;

Thunder Birds (20th Century-Fox, 1942), screenplay;

The Immortal Sergeant (20th Century-Fox, 1943), screenplay;

The Ox-Bow Incident (20th Century-Fox, 1943), screenplay;

Guadalcanal Diary (20th Century-Fox, 1943), screenplay;

Wilson (20th Century-Fox, 1944), screen story and screenplay;

A Bell for Adano (20th Century-Fox, 1945), screenplay by Trotti and Norman Reilly Raine;

The Razor's Edge (20th Century-Fox, 1946), screenplay;

Mother Wore Tights (20th Century-Fox, 1947), screenplay;

Captain from Castille (20 Century-Fox, 1947), screenplay;

The Walls of Jericho (20th Century-Fox, 1948), screenplay;

When My Baby Smiles at Me (20th Century-Fox, 1948), screenplay;

Yellow Sky (20th Century-Fox, 1949), screenplay;

You're My Everything (20th Century-Fox, 1949), screenplay by Trotti and Will Hays, Jr.;

Cheaper by the Dozen (20th Century-Fox, 1950), screenplay;

My Blue Heaven (20th Century-Fox, 1950), screenplay by Trotti and Claude Binyon;

American Guerrilla in the Philippines (20th Century-Fox, 1950), screenplay;

I'd Climb the Highest Mountain (20th Century-Fox, 1951), screenplay;

As Young as You Feel (20th Century-Fox, 1951), screenplay;

With a Song in My Heart (20th Century-Fox, 1952), screen story and screenplay;

O. Henry's Full House (20th Century-Fox, 1952), screenplay by Trotti, Richard Breen, Walter Bullock, Ivan Goff, and Ben Roberts;

Stars and Stripes Forever (20th Century-Fox, 1952), screenplay;

There's No Business Like Show Business (20th Century-Fox, 1954), screen story.

Lamar Jefferson Trotti was born in Atlanta, Georgia. He graduated from the University of Georgia with a degree in journalism in 1921. From 1922 to 1925 he was city editor of William Randolph Hearst's *Atlanta Georgian*. His first contact with the movie industry was made through Jason Joy, a representative of the Hays Office who was on business in Atlanta in 1924. Joy offered Trotti a job as a publicist in the New York office of what is now known as the Motion Picture Association of America. Trotti spent six years doing public relations work, including editing and publishing a promotional magazine for newly released movies. During his spare time he took short-story courses at Columbia University.

As the film industry migrated to California, Joy was transferred west and Trotti was invited to come along. When Joy became head of the story department at Fox a year later, Trotti followed and settled into a twenty-year tenure as a screenwriter. Although he worked in many genres, Trotti exhibited a distinct affinity for historical Americana. When he was given the freedom to do so, he concerned himself with moralistic tales set in old or rural America, such films as *The Ox-Bow Incident* (1943) and *Young Mr. Lincoln* (1939).

Trotti's earliest screenplays were written in collaboration with Dudley Nichols. *The Man Who Dared* (1933) was based on the life of Anton Cermak, the Chicago mayor who had been killed the year before during an assassination attempt on Franklin Roosevelt. It was the first of many bio-

graphical pictures to be written by Trotti. The second script with Nichols, *You Can't Buy Everything* (1934), deals with events in the life of the eccentric financier Hetty Green, and was the only screenplay Trotti wrote which was not produced by 20th Century-Fox. (It was filmed at M-G-M.) *Hold That Girl* (1934) is a fast-paced mystery with wisecracking detectives and reporters, and *Call It Luck* (1934) is about a London cabdriver (Pat Peterson) who wins £ 25,000, comes to New York City, is robbed, but wins all his money back in a horse race.

In 1934 Trotti and Nichols wrote *Judge Priest*, an adaptation of Irwin Cobb's novel, the first of a series of films starring Will Rogers. John Ford directed this story of an easygoing small-town judge (Rogers) whose sensible but unorthodox methods make him the center of controversy. It was a great success and was the basis for Ford's later work, *The Sun Shines Bright* (1953). *Life Begins at Forty* (1935) was the second film in the series. After an innocent man is framed for bank robbery, the local newspaper publisher (Rogers) tries to clear him. Ford also directed the final Rogers picture, *Steamboat Round the Bend* (1935), with Rogers playing a riverboat captain involved with a swamp woman. Rogers died in 1936, bringing an end to Trotti's collaborations with Nichols.

Trotti next wrote another series of films for one artist, this time for child actress Jane Withers. *Gentle Julia* (1936) was adapted from a novel by Booth Tarkington; Withers plays a girl who saves her aunt (Marsha Hunt) from a bad marriage. In *Pepper* (1936) she prevents a rich woman from marrying a golddigger and keeps a widow and her children from being evicted. The other films written by Trotti for Withers were *This Is the Life* (1935) and *Can This Be Dixie?* (1936).

Tentative plans were made to use Trotti's screenplay for *Ramona* (1936) as the first feature to be photographed in Technicolor's new three-color process, although in 1935 *Becky Sharp* became the first Technicolor film; 20th Century-Fox produced *Ramona* in color, nonetheless. This film version of Helen Hunt Jackson's novel about a Spanish woman (Loretta Young) and an Indian man (Don Ameche) who fall in love and face white prejudice was a great popular success. Henry King directed; this was the first of seven films he made with Trotti.

Two oddities stand out among Trotti's next several screenplays. *Wife, Doctor and Nurse* (1937) is a romantic comedy about a successful doctor (Warner Baxter) who places his work ahead of his marriage, but also remains oblivious to his nurse's advances. *Slave Ship* (1937) is one of the few proj-

Anne Shirley, John McGuire, Eugene Pallette, and Will Rogers in Steamboat Round the Bend, *one of the films Trotti and Dudley Nichols wrote for Rogers*

ects Trotti worked on that was not his original idea; he was brought in on the film after Nunnally Johnson, William Faulkner (who is credited with additional dialogue), Sam Hellman, and Gladys Lehman were unable to provide a workable adaptation of *The Last Slaver*, George S. King's novel about the disastrous voyage of a slave-carrying ship.

Most of Trotti's efforts during this period were devoted to historical pictures. *This Is My Affair* (1937) is the story of President McKinley's risky but ultimately successful scheme to end a wave of bank robberies in the Old West. It centers on an undercover agent (Robert Taylor) who is accused of conspiring with McKinley's assassins. Trotti reunited with King to make *In Old Chicago* (1937), collaborating on the script with Sonya Levien. A dramatization of the great Chicago Fire of 1871, the film centers on Molly O'Leary (Alice Brady, who won an Oscar) and her sons Jack (Don Ameche), an

attorney, and Dion (Tyrone Power), a gambler. *In Old Chicago* was one of Trotti's first films to become both a critical and financial success, and it received an Academy Award nomination for best picture.

Trotti had another success with *Kentucky* (1938), a story of two rival horse-breeding families which he adapted from John Tainter Foote's story "The Look of Eagles."

This project was followed by one of his most ambitious ones, *Alexander's Ragtime Band* (1938). The movie was two years in production and was, at the time, the most expensive musical ever made. Trotti's screenplay established a pattern he would follow in almost all his later musicals; he combined the requisite musical numbers with his love of American history, showing the development of popular music over nearly a quarter of a century, from 1915 to 1938. The movie was a great success,

Advertisement for one of the earliest Technicolor films

earning an Academy Award nomination for best picture.

In 1939 Trotti wrote the three films that provided him with his first real critical acclaim: *The Story of Alexander Graham Bell*, *Young Mr. Lincoln*, and *Drums Along the Mohawk*. The first two were biographical pictures that covered only a segment of their subjects' lives. *The Story of Alexander Graham Bell* begins with Bell (Don Ameche) as a struggling inventor; depicts his marriage to his deaf wife (Loretta Young); then shows Bell and his assistant Watson (Henry Fonda) as their experiments lead to the invention of the telephone. *Young Mr. Lincoln* is about the beginnings of Abraham Lincoln's (Henry Fonda) legal career. John Ford directed the movie, and he and Trotti worked closely together on the screenplay, which earned Trotti his first Academy Award nomination. Ford also directed *Drums Along the Mohawk*, which Trotti and Sonya Levien adapted from Walter D. Edmonds's novel. Set during the American Revolution, the movie shows the problems of settlers of the Mohawk Valley in New York, centering on one married couple (Henry Fonda and Claudette Colbert) dealing with such problems as Indian attack and loss of crops.

Two more biographies followed with less successful results. *Brigham Young—Frontiersman* (1940) is ostensibly about the Mormon leader (Dean Jagger), but the movie downplays Mormon doctrine and concentrates on the epic trek to Utah and a romance between two young lovers (Tyrone Power and Linda Darnell). It was lavishly produced and extensively promoted by Darryl F. Zanuck, but never made back its $2.5 million budget. *Hudson's Bay* (1940) is the story of Pierre Esprit Radisson (Paul Muni), the French-Canadian who in 1667 founded one of the world's largest fur trading businesses. Slowly paced and historically inaccurate, the movie was neither a critical nor a popular success.

Trotti's last prewar film was *Belle Starr* (1941), which he adapted from Burton Rascoe's *Belle Starr: The Bandit Queen*. In this considerably romanticized story, Starr (Gene Tierney) is a Southern aristocrat driven to crime because of injustices suffered at the hands of Union officials. She falls in love with Cole Younger (Randolph Scott), a Confederate hero turned outlaw, and after the war they team up for a series of robberies.

Moviegoers were beginning to exhibit a more somber, patriotic mood in light of the new world war, and for the next two years Trotti turned his attentions to scripts about the American war effort. *To the Shores of Tripoli*, released 1 April 1942, became the first American-made film about the war. Wealthy and undisciplined Chris Winters (John Payne) joins the marines and is gradually reformed by his commanding officer Dixie Smith (Randolph Scott) and by his love for military nurse Mary Carter (Maureen O'Hara). Closely following was *Thunder Birds* (1942), depicting the training of the British, Chinese, and American cadets at Thunderbird Field in Arizona. William Wellman directed, and Trotti also served as producer. *The Immortal Sergeant* (1943) was adapted from a novel by John Brophy and directed by John Stahl. It is an account of the campaign in Libya as seen through the eyes of Corporal Spence (Henry Fonda), a mild-mannered former journalist who gradually becomes a hardened soldier. *Guadalcanal Diary* (1943) was based on a best-selling book by Richard Tregaskis, a nonfiction account of a battle in the Pacific.

During these war years, Trotti was also involved with two other films. He was one of ten scriptwriters on *Tales of Manhattan* (1942), an episodic film about a tailcoat passed from owner to owner. A more important credit came with Trotti's adaptation of Walter Van Tilburg Clark's novel *The Ox-Bow Incident* in 1943. The "incident" was the

1880 lynching of three innocent men (Dana Andrews, Anthony Quinn, and Francis Ford) in Nevada; two men (Henry Fonda and Harry Morgan) try to prevent the lynching but fail. Trotti drew upon firsthand knowledge when writing the script, having witnessed several lynchings while growing up in turn-of-the-century Georgia (a scene in *Young Mr. Lincoln*, in which two brothers are hanged for a crime only one committed, also came from these experiences). *The Ox-Bow Incident* did not receive enthusiastic acclaim from a war-weary public in 1943, but critics ranked it among the best films of the year.

Trotti returned to biographical pictures with *Wilson* (1944), for which he won his only Academy Award. It was an elaborate production of the life of Woodrow Wilson, with a 150-minute running time, 143 speaking parts, and a budget of over three million dollars. The movie was a box office failure, but it became a critical success; in addition to Trotti's best screenplay award, the movie was nominated for an Academy Award for best picture, and Alexander Knox's portrayal of Wilson earned him a nomination as best actor.

Two literary adaptations followed *Wilson*. *A Bell for Adano* (1945) was taken from John Hersey's novel and subsequent stage play about the American troops occupying an Italian village during World War II; it was the fourth screenplay by Trotti to be directed by Henry King. Edmund Goulding directed Trotti's screen version of Somerset Maugham's *The Razor's Edge* in 1946. This story of one man's (Tyrone Power) search for spiritual fulfillment was well received, if not entirely faithful to the novel, with Anne Baxter winning an Oscar for her role as a woman addicted to opium and alcohol.

Beginning in 1947 with *Mother Wore Tights*, Trotti acted as producer of all his own screenplays. That film was one of many musicals he wrote in the late 1940s and early 1950s, and was taken from Miriam Young's true account of a family of vaude-

Advertisement for the 1938 film that at the time was the most expensive musical ever made

Drums Along the Mohawk: *(center) Claudette Colbert, Edna May Oliver, and Henry Fonda*

ville performers. Trotti again teamed with King on *Captain from Castille* (1947), which was taken from the first half of a lengthy historical novel by Samuel Shellabarger. The movie is about a fifteenth-century Spaniard (Tyrone Power) who joins Cortez's expedition to Mexico. John Stahl directed *The Walls of Jericho* (1948), about a small-town lawyer (Cornell Wilde) whose devotion to his work leads to marital troubles.

Between 1948 and 1950 Trotti wrote three musicals starring Dan Dailey: *When My Baby Smiles at Me* (1948), *You're My Everything* (1949), and *My Blue Heaven* (1950). Walter Lang directed the first two pictures, Henry Koster the last. *When My Baby Smiles at Me* was the third film version of George Manter Walters's play *Burlesque* about a vaudeville performer (Dailey) whose career declines while his wife (Betty Grable) becomes a Broadway star. Trotti examines the early days of Hollywood in

You're My Everything, which focuses on a 1920s socialite (Anne Baxter) who becomes an actress. In *My Blue Heaven*, two radio performers (Dailey and Grable) decide they want a family and try to adopt a child.

Five years after the release of *The Ox-Bow Incident* Trotti and William Wellman were reunited on another Western, *Yellow Sky* (1949). In a nearly deserted western town, an aging miner and his daughter (Anne Baxter) fight off a group of men who are after their gold; one of the outlaws softens and joins the miners in their battle. Wellman's direction perfectly matched the austere quality of Trotti's screenplay; the film did not receive the critical acclaim of *The Ox-Bow Incident*, but it is a well-made and entertaining film.

With *Cheaper by the Dozen* (1950) Trotti returned to the turn-of-the-century period about which he did some of his best work. This film was

The Ox-Bow Incident: *Frank Conroy (in cavalry uniform), Marc Lawrence (holding noose), and (without hats) Dana Andrews, Francis Ford, and Anthony Quinn*

an adaptation of Frank and Ernestine Gilbreth's account of their family: twelve children, stern father (Clifton Webb), and understanding mother (Myrna Loy). It was an extremely popular film that inspired a sequel, *Belles on Their Toes*, with a screenplay by Henry and Phoebe Ephron, two years later. Trotti next wrote *American Guerrilla in the Philippines* (1950), about two American sailors (Tyrone Power and Tom Ewell) in World War II who are stranded after MacArthur surrenders Bataan and must make their way to Australia. They organize the island natives and fight the Japanese. The film was not a success: Trotti's patriotism, which had seemed appropriate during the war now was out of place, and audiences were not interested in the years-old story. Fritz Lang directed.

In 1951 Trotti wrote one of his rare contemporary screenplays, *As Young as You Feel*. A loyal employee (Monty Woolley) is fired from his corporation after he reaches their mandatory retirement age; determined to prove he is still a valuable worker, he hatches a plan that saves the business from bankruptcy. Next came *O. Henry's Full House* (1952), an episodic film consisting of five adaptations of O. Henry short stories. Trotti wrote the script for "The Cop and the Anthem" segment; Henry Kester directed.

Trotti's final pictures were combinations: musicals/biographies. *With a Song in My Heart* (1952) is about the life of Jane Froman (Susan Hayward), a popular radio singer of the time. *Stars and Stripes Forever* (1952) was adapted from John Philip Sousa's autobiography *Marching Along*. It was Trotti's last full screenplay; his career was interrupted by the death of his son Lamar, Jr., whom Trotti had hoped would also have a screenwriting career.

Ethel Merman, Dan Dailey, Mitzi Gaynor, Donald O'Connor, and Marilyn Monroe in There's No Business Like Show Business, *the film on which Trotti was working at the time of his death*

Perhaps aggravated by this trauma, Trotti suffered a fatal heart attack in 1952. He had begun work on, but had not completed, *There's No Business Like Show Business* (1954), an account of a fictional family of musical performers. He received screen credit for the film, along with a posthumous Academy Award nomination for best story.

While most of his film ideas were his own, Lamar Trotti is often still considered a formula writer, a dependable screenwriter whose work assured a general, if moderate, box office success. Alexander Knox maintained that Trotti might have made a greater name for himself as a writer and producer if he had not limited himself to one stu-dio. Yet, as his list of films attests, Trotti managed to make himself known as a serious and prolific screenwriter, and in the opinion of William Wellman he was "one of the best." His most notable achievement was his recreation of America's past in a diverse assortment of films.

References:

"John Ford's *Young Mr. Lincoln*," *Cahiers du Cinema*, 13 (1972);

W. Franklin Moshier, *The Alice Faye Movie Book* (Harrisburg, Pa.: Stackpole Books, 1974), pp. 101-104.

Ernest Vajda

(27 May 1887-3 April 1954)

Audrey Kupferberg

SELECTED MOTION PICTURES: *The Crown of Lies* (Famous Players-Lasky, 1926), story;
You Never Know Women (Famous Players-Lasky, 1926), story;
The Cat's Pajamas (Famous Players-Lasky, 1926), story;
Service for Ladies (Paramount Famous Lasky, 1927), story;
Serenade (Paramount Famous Lasky, 1927), author and scenario;
A Night of Mystery (Paramount Famous Lasky, 1928), adaptation and scenario;
His Tiger Lady (Paramount Famous Lasky, 1928), adaptation;
Loves of an Actress (Paramount Famous Lasky, 1928), story;
Manhattan Cowboy (El Dorado Productions, 1928), scenario by Vajda and Sally Winters;
His Private Life (Paramount Famous Lasky, 1928), story by Vajda and Keene Thompson;
Manhattan Cocktail (Paramount Famous Lasky, 1928), story;
Innocents of Paris (Paramount Famous Lasky, 1929), adaptation and dialogue;
The Love Parade (Paramount Famous Lasky, 1929), story;
Marquis Preferred (Paramount Famous Lasky, 1929), story;
Such Men Are Dangerous (Fox, 1930), adaptation and dialogue;
Monte Carlo (Paramount-Publix, 1930), screenplay;
The Smiling Lieutenant (Paramount-Publix, 1931), dialogue and scenario by Vajda and Samson Raphaelson;
Son of India (M-G-M, 1931), continuity and dialogue;
The Guardsman (M-G-M, 1931), dialogue and screenplay by Vajda and Claudine West;
Tonight or Never (Feature Productions/United Artists, 1931), screenplay;
The Man I Killed, retitled *Broken Lullaby* (Paramount-Publix, 1932), screenplay by Vajda and Raphaelson;
Smilin' Through (M-G-M, 1932), screenplay by Vajda and West;
Payment Deferred (M-G-M, 1932), screenplay by Vajda and West;
Reserved for Ladies (Paramount-Publix, 1932), story;
Reunion in Vienna (M-G-M, 1933), screenplay by Vajda and West;
The Barretts of Wimpole Street (M-G-M, 1934), screenplay by Vajda, West, and Donald Ogden Stewart;
The Merry Widow (M-G-M, 1934), screenplay by Vajda and Raphaelson;
A Woman Rebels (RKO, 1936), screenplay by Vajda and Anthony Veiller;
Personal Property (M-G-M, 1937), screenplay by Vajda and Hugh Mills;
The Great Garrick (Warner Bros., 1937), screen story and screenplay;

Ernest Vajda

Marie Antoinette (M-G-M, 1938), screenplay by Vajda, West, and Stewart;

Dramatic School (M-G-M, 1939), screenplay by Vajda and Mary C. McCall;

He Stayed for Breakfast (Columbia, 1940), screenplay by Vajda, P. J. Wolfson, and Michael Fessier;

They Dare Not Love (Columbia, 1941), screenplay by Vajda and Charles Bennett.

PLAY PRODUCTIONS: *Rozmarin Neni (Aunt Rose Marie)* Budapest, Magyar Szinhaz, 1909;

Ludas Matyi, Budapest, Nemzeti Szinhaz, 1911;

Mister Bobby, Budapest, Nemzeti Szinhaz, 1912;

Varatlan Vendeg (The Unexpected Guest), Budapest, Magyat Szinhaz, 1915;

Fata Morgana, Copenhagen, 1918; New York, Garrick Theatre, 3 March 1924;

Szerelem Vasara, Budapest, 1920;

Farsangi Lakadalom, Budapest, 1920;

Confession, Budapest, Gaiety Theatre, 1922;

The Crown Prince, Budapest, 1923; Atlantic City, Apollo Theatre, 26 February 1927;

Harem, Budapest, 1923; New York, Belasco Theatre, 2 December 1924;

Carnival Marriage, Budapest, Royal Opera, 1923;

Váloperes Hölgy (Grounds for Divorce), New York, Empire Theatre, 23 September 1924;

The Littlest Angel, New York, Frazee Theatre, 27 September 1924;

Bottom of the Pile, Pasadena Playhouse, 1951;

Royal Suite, Stockholm, New Theatre, 1954.

BOOK: *The Monkey Man and the Man Monkey* (Budapest, 1916).

Ernest Vajda was an accomplished playwright in Europe before coming to the United States to write for motion pictures in 1925. Though his screenwriting career spanned over twenty-five years, his best work was done in the late 1920s and the 1930s. Vajda was a specialist in sophisticated, romantic comedy. His favorite comic motifs included mistaken identity and the mingling of common folk with royalty or the wealthy.

Vajda was born Erno Vajda, the son of Terez Fischer and Lajos Vajda, in Komaron, Hungary. His father, a lawyer and captain in the Royal Hussars, was able to give Vajda an excellent education. He attended the College of the Benedictine Monks in Papa, Hungary, where he received a degree in electrochemistry in 1904, then received a doctorate in civil law, literature, and philosophy from Peter Pazmany University in Budapest in 1908. After graduation, Vajda devoted himself to a literary ca-

reer. He was secretary to the Thalia Theatre Company; editor of *A Het*, a literary magazine; founder and editor of *Kepes Ujsag*, a news weekly; and editorial writer for the Magyar *Hirlap*.

Aunt Rose Marie, Vajda's first play, was produced in 1909; more plays followed over the next fourteen years. *Fata Morgana*, his best-known work, was first performed in Denmark in 1918; it was produced in New York in 1924, and that same year Vajda was invited to Hollywood. He became a contract writer for Famous Players-Lasky at Paramount studios, supplying the screen stories for several silent films.

His first picture was *The Crown of Lies* (1926), in which a lodging-house employee (Pola Negri) is mistaken for the long lost Queen of Sylvania. The men who "recognize" her then blackmail the current ruler of Sylvania, threatening to restore the queen to her throne. Vadja next supplied the story for *You Never Know Women* (1926), about a Russian circus performer (Florence Vidor) torn between two men—the circus's knife thrower (Clive Brook) and the mysterious Mr. Foster (Lovell Sherman), who is finally revealed to be a criminal.

Service for Ladies (1927) was the breakthrough film for Vajda. It is the story of Albert Leroux (Adolphe Menjou), headwaiter at a posh Parisian hotel restaurant, who falls in love with American heiress Elizabeth Foster (Kathryn Carver) and follows her to a winter resort in the Swiss Alps, passing himself off as a nobleman. The movie was directed by Harry D'Arrast, a French director known for his witty, sophisticated films. It was such a success that the studio immediately reteamed Vajda, D'Arrast, Menjou, and Carver for *Serenade* (1927) and gave Vajda his first opportunity to write an entire script. Composer Franz Rossi (Menjou) ignores his wife (Carver) for the actress (Lina Basquette) appearing in an opera he has written. When his wife learns of the affair, Rossi repents and returns to her.

Vajda never worked again with D'Arrast, but he continued to write films for Menjou, with Carver (who had married Menjou) occasionally costarring. In *A Night of Mystery* (1928), French Army Captain Ferreal (Menjou) uncovers a murderer but cannot turn the man in because the killer threatens to compromise Ferreal's lover (Nora Lane). *His Tiger Lady* (1928) is about a theater worker (Menjou) in love with a succesful actress (Evelyn Brent); in order to impress her, he disguises himself as a character from her play, a wealthy Indian Rajah. Vajda collaborated with Keene Thompson on his screenplay for *His Private Life* (1928). Menjou and Carver both appeared in this film about a man who insists all women are the same, until he becomes obsessed with a beautiful stranger.

Vajda wrote a second film for Pola Negri, *Loves of an Actress* (1928). She plays an actress who uses her influential lovers to build a successful career; then she is blackmailed by one lover after she marries. Dorothy Arzner directed *Manhattan Cocktail* (1928) from Vajda's story. A theatrical producer suspects his wife has taken a lover and frames the man for murder. *Innocents of Paris* (1929) introduced Maurice Chevalier to American audiences; he played a carefree Parisian who saves a boy (Russell Simpson) from drowning, then falls in love with the boy's aunt (Sylvia Beecher).

Director Ernst Lubitsch worked frequently with Vajda in the late 1920s and early 1930s. At that time, Paramount was a haven for Eastern European filmmakers and was generating many romantic comedies of the continental style favored by both Vajda and Lubitsch. Able to speak fluent German and English, Vajda could exchange ideas freely with the Berlin-born Lubitsch and translate them into acceptable scripts for American filmgoers.

Their first collaboration, *The Love Parade* (1929), based on a story by Vajda and Guy Bolton, is considered a classic of the early sound period. While other talking pictures of the late 1920s used dialogue merely as a substitute for titles, *The Love Parade* is filled with sly wit and stylized banter. And while musicals of the transitional sound period were for the most part revues, *The Love Parade* incorporates its musical numbers into the plot. The story revolves around Queen Louise (Jeanette MacDonald) of Sylvania who, much to the chagrin of her cabinet ministers, remains unmarried. Sylvania's French Ambassador Count Alfred (Maurice Chevalier) is recalled in disgrace, having developed notoriety as a lover of great prowess. Intending to reprimand Alfred, the Queen instead falls in love with him. A subplot places Alfred's valet Jacques (Lupino Lane) and Queen Louise's maid Lulu (Lillian Roth) in a similar romantic situation—a comic

Adolphe Menjou and Kathryn Carver in Service for Ladies

Charles Laughton and Norma Shearer in The Barretts of Wimpole Street

device Vajda and Lubitsch were to use in their second film together, *Monte Carlo* (1930).

Before making the second film with Lubitsch, Vajda wrote the story for his final picture for Menjou, *Marquis Preferred* (1929). The penniless Marquis d'Argenville (Menjou) plans to marry a wealthy heiress (Dot Farley) but falls in love with her friend (Nora Lane). Vajda also worked on the script for *Such Men Are Dangerous* (1930). When his newlywed wife leaves him, ugly Ludwig Krane (Warner Baxter) decides to have plastic surgery; then, as the handsome Pierre Veillard, he begins courting his wife (Catherine Dale Owen).

The final three motion pictures Vajda wrote before leaving Paramount were all directed by Lubitsch. *Monte Carlo* tells of an impoverished countess (MacDonald) who escapes marriage to a wealthy but unattractive duke (Claude Allister) only to fall in love with her new hairdresser (Jack Buchanan), actually a wealthy count in disguise. Vajda collab-

orated with Samson Raphaelson on *The Smiling Lieutenant* (1931) and *The Man I Killed* (1932). *The Smiling Lieutenant* is a variation on Vajda's theme of love among the nobility. Franzi (Claudette Colbert), a violinist, and Niki (Chevalier), an officer of the guards, share a love nest in Vienna. One afternoon, as the visiting Princess Anna (Miriam Hopkins) rides by in a parade, Niki smiles past her at Franzi across the street; the Princess thinks the smile was meant for her and considers it a rude flirtation. King Adolf XV (George Barbier) sees Niki as hope for his unwed daughter and declares a royal wedding. Franzi and Niki reunite; but when Franzi meets the princess, she takes pity on her and helps to glamorize the dowdy princess. Niki decides that the marriage will not be as boring as he had imagined.

The Man I Killed (reissued as *Broken Lullaby*) was Lubitsch's only dramatic sound film, an uncompromising pacifist drama. Vajda and Raphael-

Robert Taylor and Jean Harlow in Personal Property

son collaborated on the screenplay. French soldier Paul (Phillips Holmes) kills young German Walter Holderlin (Tom Douglas) in battle. After the war, Paul's sense of guilt drives him to Walter's hometown where he takes a room in the Holderlin home. There he experiences the German hatred for the French, particularly from Walter's father Dr. Holderlin (Lionel Barrymore); only Walter's fiancée Elsa (Nancy Carroll) is sympathetic to him. In time the Holderlins accept Paul, and Dr. Holderlin realizes that his hatred was responsible for Walter's death; he proclaims that he and others his age were too old to fight, but not too old to hate.

In 1931 Vajda moved to M-G-M, where he remained until 1938. He and Claudine West adapted Ferenc Molnar's play *The Guardsman* (1931) for the only sound film to star Alfred Lunt and Lynn Fontanne. An actor (Lunt) becomes jealous and decides to test his wife's (Fontanne) fidelity; he tells her he is leaving town, then comes back disguised as a dashing Russian count. She allows him to woo her but the next day claims that she always knew it was her husband in disguise.

Vajda continued collaborating with West throughout his stay at M-G-M. Their next film together was *Smilin' Through* (1932), a Victorian melodrama about a woman (Norma Shearer) in love with the son (Fredric March) of a murderer. In

Payment Deferred (1932) a man (Charles Laughton) plots to murder his nephew and inherit the nephew's fortune. *Reunion in Vienna* (1933) was adapted from a play by Robert Sherwood; an exiled nobleman (John Barrymore) returns to his native land and rekindles an old romance. Vajda, West, and Donald Ogden Stewart wrote *The Barretts of Wimpole Street* (1934), based on the 1930 play by Rudolph Besier. It is a romanticized version of the life of Elizabeth Barrett (Norma Shearer) and Robert Browning (Fredric March). During this time, Vajda also received story credit for *Reserved for Ladies* (1932), a remake of *Service for Ladies*, but he had little to do with this second version.

Vajda and Raphaelson reunited in 1934 to write *The Merry Widow* for Lubitsch at M-G-M; it was one of the most polished of Vajda's comedies. The King (George Barbier) orders Prince Danilo (Maurice Chevalier) to return to Marshovia the widow Sonia (Jeanette MacDonald) who controls fifty-two percent of the nation's wealth. Danilo and Sonia meet in Paris and fall in love, but neither knows the other's identity. When Sonia learns of Danilo's mission, she threatens to abandon Marshovia forever, and Danilo is sentenced to prison for treason. The King tricks Sonia into visiting Danilo and then locks them into a cell together; subsequently they marry and insure financial well-being for Marshovia.

At M-G-M, Vajda had slackened his pace; by 1936 he was writing only one or two films a year, and West became the writer of the team more in demand. In 1936 he collaborated with Anthony Veiller on the screenplay for *A Woman Rebels;* the film was a highlight in Vajda's later career. Set in nineteenth-century England, the film covers twenty years in the life of Pamela Thistlewaite (Katharine Hepburn), an unwed mother trying to raise her daughter and make a career for herself as a journalist. The movie was a failure when it was first released, but has found new audiences in recent years; the determination of its protagonist to make a life for herself and her child has a strong contemporary appeal.

A Woman Rebels was something of an oddity among Vajda's films; he returned to more traditional material with *Personal Property* (1937). An im-poverished American widow (Jean Harlow) living in England is sent to jail because she cannot pay her debts. She falls in love with the bailiff (Robert Taylor). *The Great Garrick* (1937) was one of Vajda's few solo screenplays; in this film, an acting troupe decides to pull a prank on a pompous actor (Leslie Howard) and pass themselves off as untalented country bumpkins seeking roles in his new play.

Vajda reteamed with West and Donald Ogden Stewart, his collaborators on *The Barretts of Wimpole Street*, to write another historical melodrama, *Marie Antoinette* (1938), a lavishly produced but only moderately successful biography of the French queen. It was Vajda's last collaboration with West, and his penultimate script for M-G-M. His final screenplay at that studio was *Dramatic School* (1939), written with Mary C. McCall, about an acting class of young hopefuls. It was similar in plot and theme to *Stage Door* (1937) and completely overshadowed by the earlier film. A similar fate befell *He Stayed for Break-*

Norma Shearer in the title role of the lavish historical melodrama Marie Antoinette

fast (1940), about a Russian man (Melvyn Douglas) who falls in love with an American woman (Loretta Young). Coming only a year after *Ninotchka*, it was dismissed as a poor copy of the original.

They Dare Not Love (1941) was Vajda's next, and last, screenplay. After Nazi forces invade his country, an Austrian prince (George Brent) flees to America; he falls in love but has to leave his fiancée (Martha Scott) behind when he returns to Austria. The film's poor financial return virtually ended Vajda's career, although he was involved with two more screen projects. He and West made contributions to the screenplay for *The Chocolate Soldier* (1941), a remake of *The Guardsman*. Over a decade later, Vajda's original story was used for

Stars and Stripes Forever (1952), a biography of John Philip Sousa. Ernest Vajda died in Woodland Hills, California, on 3 April 1954.

Vajda's decline in popularity was partly due to the movement in American films away from continental, escapist romance to realism. The suave Hungarian screenwriter was deemed passé by the studios, which saw no market for his sophisticated comedies and imaginary kingdoms. Like so many other screenwriters, Ernest Vajda was the product of an older era, whose films expressed the romantic vision that helped shape American cinema in the 1930s.

Anthony Veiller
(23 June 1903-27 June 1965)

Thomas Slater
Northwest Missouri State University

MOTION PICTURES: *Breach of Promise* (Benjamin Verschleiser, 1932), dialogue;

The Notorious Sophie Lang (Paramount, 1934), screenplay;

Star of Midnight (RKO, 1935), screenplay by Veiller, Howard J. Green, and Edward Kaufman;

Break of Hearts (RKO, 1935), screenplay by Veiller, Sarah Y. Mason, and Victor Heerman;

Jalna (RKO, 1935), screenplay;

Seven Keys to Baldpate (RKO, 1935), screenplay by Veiller and Wallace Smith;

The Lady Consents (RKO, 1936), screenplay by Veiller and P. J. Wolfson;

The Ex-Mrs. Bradford (RKO, 1936), screenplay;

A Woman Rebels (RKO, 1936), screenplay by Veiller and Ernest Vajda;

Winterset (RKO, 1936), screenplay;

The Soldier and the Lady (RKO, 1937), screenplay by Veiller, Mortimer Offner, and Anne Morrison Chapin;

Stage Door (RKO, 1937), screenplay by Veiller and Morrie Ryskind;

Radio City Revels (RKO, 1938), screenplay by Veiller, Offner, Matt Brooks, and Eddie Davis;

Let Us Live (Columbia, 1939), screenplay by Veiller and Allen Rivkin;

Barricade (20th Century-Fox, 1939), screenplay by Veiller and Darrell Ware;

Disputed Passage (Paramount, 1939), screenplay by Veiller and Sheridan Gibney;

Her Cardboard Lover (M-G-M, 1942), screenplay by Veiller, William H. Wright, and Jacques Duval;

Assignment in Brittany (M-G-M, 1943), screenplay by Veiller, Wright, and Howard Emmett Rogers;

The Battle of Russia (U.S. War Documentary, 1943), continuity and commentary;

Tunisian Victory (British War Documentary, 1944), screenplay by Veiller as Major Tony Veiller, J. L. Hodson, Captain Roy Boulting, Captain Alfred Black, and Captain John Huston;

Adventure (M-G-M, 1946), adaptation by Veiller and Wright;

The Stranger (RKO, 1946), screenplay;

The Killers (Universal, 1946), screenplay;

State of the Union (M-G-M, 1948), screenplay by Veiller and Myles Connolly;

Red Planet Mars (United Artists, 1952), screen story and screenplay by Veiller and John L. Balderston;

Moulin Rouge (United Artists, 1953), screenplay by Veiller and John Huston;

That Lady (20th Century-Fox, 1955), screenplay by Veiller and Sy Bartlett;

Safari (Columbia, 1956), screenplay;

Monkey on My Back (United Artists, 1957), screen story and screenplay by Veiller, Paul Dudley, and Wilbur Crane;

Solomon and Sheba (United Artists, 1959), screenplay by Veiller, Dudley, and George Bruce;

Timbuktu (United Artists, 1959), screen story and screenplay by Veiller and Dudley;

The List of Adrian Messenger (Universal, 1963), screenplay;

The Night of the Iguana (M-G-M/Seven Arts, 1964), screenplay by Veiller and Huston.

Reporter, theater manager, publicist, and screenwriter, Anthony Veiller was born in New York City, the son of Bayard Veiller, himself a screenwriter, director, and producer. Veiller came to Hollywood in 1930 to begin the screenwriting career that would last for the rest of his life.

Veiller's first work on a feature film was as a dialogue writer for *Breach of Promise* (1932). This picture was followed by two crime/comedy screenplays. The first was *The Notorious Sophie Lang* (1934), which Veiller's father produced at Paramount. Two competing criminals manage to commit all their crimes under the noses of the police. The picture received good reviews, and Veiller stayed with this type of material for his next film, *Star of Midnight* (1935). This time, however, the comedy was told from the point of view of the law, in this case, a private detective. The film featured William Powell, who played Clay Dalzell, a lawyer-turned-detective who was modeled very closely on the Nick Charles character in the popular *Thin Man* series, with Dalzell forced to clear himself of the murder of his new client.

Veiller returned to this formula once more during the decade with *The Ex-Mrs. Bradford* (1936), again with Powell in the lead role. Jean Arthur costarred as his former wife, helping him find a

Burgess Meredith, Margo, Maurice Moscovitch, Edward Ellis, Alec Craig, and Eduardo Ciannelli in the highly acclaimed Winterset, *Veiller's adaptation of Maxwell Anderson's examination of the Sacco and Vanzetti case*

murderer. The film was well received, and Frank Nugent commented in the *New York Times,* "It makes us wonder how Metro will fare with its sequel, tentatively called 'After the Thin Man,' for the postscript—it would seem—already has been written."

In between *Star of Midnight* and *The Ex-Mrs. Bradford,* Veiller only wrote one film on his own, but he coauthored a string of domestic romances and melodramas: *Break of Hearts* (1935), *Jalna* (1935), *Seven Keys to Baldpate* (1935), and *The Lady Consents* (1936). The film which received the highest critical applause, *Jalna,* is the one which Veiller wrote alone. It is based on the first of a series of novels by Maza de la Roche depicting the White-oaks family of Canada; Veiller's screenplay was praised for its compression of the novel's series of complicated relationships into a single, effective film. John Cromwell directed. *The Lady Consents,* written with P. J. Wolfson, is about a man (Herbert Marshall) who divorces, remarries, then decides he still loves his first wife (Ann Harding). Both *Seven Keys to Baldpate* and *Break of Hearts* were stories that had already been filmed more than twice before. *Seven Keys to Baldpate,* adapted from a novel by Earl Derr Biggers, is about a mystery writer who becomes involved in a murder. *Break of Hearts* is significant for providing the first of several roles that Veiller created for Katharine Hepburn. In this film, she is a married woman coping with an unfaithful husband (Charles Boyer).

Hepburn reteamed with Veiller for *A Woman Rebels* (1936), which he wrote with Ernest Vajda. Set in nineteenth-century England, the film depicts a stubborn, independent woman (Hepburn) who has a child out of wedlock and pursues a career as a journalist. The film did not do well on its initial release, but its reputation has grown over the years.

The 1930s was a prolific period for Veiller; he authored or coauthored thirteen screenplays between 1934 and 1939, most of them for RKO Pictures. Not all of these films were successful, but these were the years in which he was learning his craft; also, he was required to work within the constraints of Hollywood formulas or to adapt well-known works of fiction. Veiller's best films of the decade were those which had notable casts or directors or were based on an above average original work. Both of Veiller's greatest successes of the thirties, *Winterset* (1936) and *Stage Door* (1937), meet these criteria.

Winterset was adapted from a play by Maxwell Anderson, which in turn was inspired by the Sacco-Vanzetti case. In the film, a man (Burgess Mere-

Edward G. Robinson, Loretta Young, and Orson Welles in a promotional still for The Stranger

dith) whose father was executed for a crime he did not commit sets out to find the real criminal. The film earned Veiller good reviews, and he was singled out for praise for the first time in his career. The *New York Times* critic wrote: "Anthony Veiller's screenplay, as directed by Alfred Santell, is a smooth blend of theatre and cinema. It combines the peculiar attributes of each in such a way as to maintain tension in action and plot development without serious damage to Mr. Anderson's majestically cadenced dialogue."

Stage Door provided Veiller with all the elements he needed for a successful picture. The cast included Hepburn, Ginger Rogers, Lucille Ball, Eve Arden, and Adolphe Menjou. The director was Gregory La Cava and the original work was a play by Edna Ferber and George S. Kaufman. Frank Nugent singled out Veiller and coauthor Morrie Ryskind for special praise, saying they "have taken the play's name, its setting and part of its theme and have built a whole new structure which is wittier than its original, more dramatic than the original, more meaningful than the original, more cogent than the original." *Stage Door* proved that when Veiller was presented with good material, he was usually able to enhance it. He earned his first

Academy Award nomination for the picture.

With *Let Us Live* (1939), Veiller returned to the theme of miscarried justice. The film had a factual basis: five years earlier, two Boston cab drivers had been falsely accused of murder and sent to prison. *Let Us Live* centers on one of the men (Henry Fonda) and his supportive fiancée (Maureen O'Sullivan). Veiller wrote the screenplay with Allen Rivkin.

For his other work of the 1930s, Veiller wrote an adventure picture, *The Soldier and the Lady* (1937), with Mortimer Offner and Anne Morrison Chapin. Based on Jules Verne's novel *Michael Strogoff*, the movie, set in Siberia during the Tartar revolt of 1870, was praised for its action sequences. *Radio City Revels* (1938), written by Veiller, Offner, Matt Brooks, and Eddie Davis, is a musical comedy about two songwriters (Milton Berle and Jack Oakie) who steal material from a young writer who sings in his sleep. *Disputed Passage* (1939), directed by Frank Borzage, was a study of scientists at work. Veiller also worked as an uncredited story consultant on *Gunga Din* (1939), helping to condense its too lengthy original screenplay.

At the beginning of the 1940s, Veiller turned to producing for a two-year period. He returned to writing with *Her Cardboard Lover* (1942), which he, William Wright, and Jacques Duval, with John Collier, adapted from Duval's play of the same title. A woman (Norma Shearer) pays a man (Robert Taylor) to pretend to be her lover as part of a scheme to make her fiancé (George Sanders) jealous. *Assignment in Brittany* (1943), written with Wright and Howard Emmett Rogers, is about a French resistance fighter (Jean-Pierre Aumont) who discovers he is a physical double for a German officer. He uses his resemblance to spy behind German lines.

During the war, Veiller worked on documentaries to promote the war effort: *The Battle of Russia* (1943) and *Tunisian Victory* (1944), part of the film series "Why We Fight." He resumed his Hollywood career with a final collaboration with William Wright; they adapted the novel *The Strange Adventure* by Clyde Brion Davis. *Adventure* (1946) was the first postwar Clark Gable picture. He plays a sailor who marries a librarian (Greer Garson), deserts her, then returns. The film did very badly both critically and financially and was one of the biggest disappointments of the 1940s.

The Stranger (1946) was brought to the screen under the direction of Orson Welles, who also played the lead role. (He is also thought to have worked without credit on the script, as John Hus-

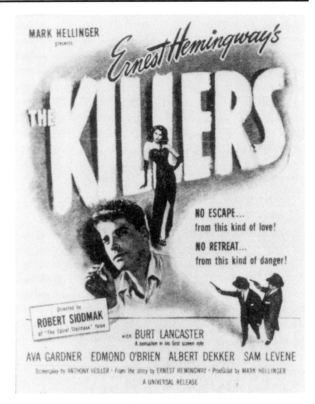

Advertisement for Veiller's 1946 adaptation of Ernest Hemingway's story

ton did.) A Nazi war criminal (Welles), married to an unsuspecting young woman (Loretta Young), now lives incognito in the United States. A Federal inspector (Edward G. Robinson) suspects his true identity. The film received mixed reviews; some found it suspenseful, but Bosley Crowther summed up the opinion of others when he called the picture "a routine and mechanical cat and mouse chase, with the outcome completely apparent."

At this point in his career, Veiller seemed to be having trouble creating characters who were as appealing as the strong women and sophisticated men who peopled his movies in the 1930s. In his next picture, he solved the problem by creating an effective, troubled, male character. *The Killers* (1946) is based on a short story by Ernest Hemingway. The director was Robert Siodmak, and the cast included Burt Lancaster and Ava Gardner. The picture may represent Veiller's most difficult task of adapting an original work—he had to expand Hemingway's story of a man who knows he is to be murdered to explain why the killers were after him. The movie earned Veiller his second and final Academy Award nomination.

Two years later, Veiller saw his final screenplay of the decade produced before he again turned to a period of production work. Frank Capra directed *State of the Union* (1948), which Veiller and Myles Connolly had adapted from a play by Russel Crouse and Howard Lindsay. Industrialist Grant Matthews (Spencer Tracy) is convinced to run for president but soon learns he must compromise his ideals. His estranged wife (Katharine Hepburn) tries to win him back from the manipulative newspaper heiress (Angela Lansbury) who is backing his campaign. The film was a success, and Veiller and Connolly were commended for inserting more commentary on current issues into the script than had been in the play.

Veiller returned to scriptwriting with *Red Planet Mars* (1952), which he produced and coauthored with John Balderston, adapting Balderston's play. It is a heavily moralistic science fiction work, with evil represented by an ex-Nazi scientist (Herbert Berghoff). There is a final plea for a return to religion.

Over the next seven years, Veiller had six screenplays produced. The most notable was the first, *Moulin Rouge* (1953), a biography of Toulouse-Lautrec that was named the year's best picture by the *New York Times*. The movie was Veiller's first project with director John Huston, who coauthored it. They received a Writers Guild nomination for their work.

Veiller's next two scripts were filmed in England and directed by Terence Young. *That Lady* (1955) is a romantic melodrama set in sixteenth-century Spain. Veiller and Sy Bartlett adapted their script from Kate O'Brien's novel and subsequent play. Ana de Mendoza (Olivia de Havilland), the rejected mistress of King Philip II (Paul Scofield), falls in love with the king's minister Antonio Perez (Gilbert Roland), causing the king's jealousy. *Safari* (1956) is about an American expedition to Africa caught in a battle with the Mau Mau tribe.

Monkey on My Back (1957) received some notoriety as the second United Artists movie about

Suzanne Flon, Zsa Zsa Gabor, and José Ferrer in Moulin Rouge, *the story of Toulouse-Lautrec*

drug addiction to be released without a Production Code Seal of Approval, following *The Man with the Golden Arm* (1955). But while *Monkey on My Back* contained a few tense sequences, it was not the success its predecessor had been. Veiller collaborated with Paul Dudley and Wilbur Crane; later he, Dudley, and George Bruce worked together on *Solomon and Sheba* (1959). King Vidor directed this biblical epic which stressed the sexual relationship between the two characters.

In 1963 Veiller once again collaborated with John Huston. *The List of Adrian Messenger* was a mystery film with the added gimmick of disguised guest stars placed throughout. The movie was talky, but enjoyable. Huston and Veiller adapted Tennessee Williams's play *The Night of the Iguana* to film the following year. Unfortunately, the elements for success did not work for Veiller; despite a fine cast and Huston's direction, the film is overlong, wordy, and tedious.

Anthony Veiller died of cancer on 27 June 1965. He was survived by his wife, two children, a stepson, and two grandchildren. Veiller had just completed an adaptation of Budd Schulberg's *The Disenchanted* and was working with Huston on the screenplay of Rudyard Kipling's *The Man Who Would be King*.

Throughout its course, Veiller's career remained an interesting one. Its highs and lows marked the journey of a writer who took on each new popular formula as it arrived—meeting with various levels of success, but finishing with a respectable body of work over a forty-year period. His movies demonstrate traditional loyalty to country and family, but also a healthy disrespect for authority and restrictive social codes.

Reference:

Gerald Pratley, *The Cinema of John Huston* (South Brunswick: A. S. Barnes, 1976).

Mae West
(17 August 1892-22 November 1980)

Eugene L. Huddleston
Michigan State University

MOTION PICTURES: *I'm No Angel* (Paramount, 1933), screen story, screenplay, and dialogue;
Belle of the Nineties (Paramount, 1934), story and screenplay;
Goin' to Town (Paramount, 1935), screenplay and dialogue;
Klondike Annie (Paramount, 1936), screen story and screenplay;
Go West, Young Man (Paramount, 1936), screenplay;
Every Day's a Holiday (Paramount, 1939), screen story and screenplay;
My Little Chickadee (Universal, 1940), story and screenplay by West and W. C. Fields.

PLAY PRODUCTIONS: *Sex*, as Jane Mast, New York, Daly's, 26 April 1926;
The Wicked Age, as Anton Scibilia, New York, Daly's, 4 November 1927;
The Drag, touring company, 1927;

Diamond Lil, New York, Royale Theatre, 9 April 1928;
Pleasure Man, New York, Biltmore Theatre, 1 October 1928;
The Constant Sinner, New York, Royale Theatre, 14 September 1931;
Catherine Was Great, New York, Schubert Theatre, 22 August 1944;
Sextet, Chicago, Edgewater Beach Hotel, 1952.

BOOKS: *Babe Gordon* (New York: Macaulay, 1930); republished as *The Constant Sinner* (New York: Macaulay, 1931);
Diamond Lil (New York: Macaulay, 1932);
Goodness Had Nothing to Do With It; The Autobiography of Mae West (Englewood Cliffs, N.J.: Prentice-Hall, 1959; revised edition, New York: Macfadden-Bartell, 1970);
The Wit and Wisdom of Mae West, edited by Joseph Weintraub (New York: Putnam's, 1967);

Mae West

Mae West on Sex, Health, and ESP (London & New York: W. H. Allen, 1975);
Pleasure Man (New York: Dell, 1975).

Mae West's career as a screenwriter grew out of her background in vaudeville and her desire to fashion a distinctive identity as a sex symbol. By 1919 she was writing many of her vaudeville sketches, and her interest in writing increased as she realized that the sexy persona could be the source of "much good material for drama, satire, and some kind of ironic comment on the war of the sexes." West turned to screenwriting to provide material that would reinforce the image she had created for herself.

Born in Brooklyn, New York, West was the first of three children of John and Matilda West. Her father, a former heavyweight boxer, provided a good living for his family, and West's parents gave her nearly everything she asked for. Still, West and her father were never close; she felt alienated from him because of his stern manner and was put off by his strong-smelling cigars. She was her mother's

favorite child, however, and as soon as she was able to walk, her mother took her to vaudeville shows. At five she was performing in church socials, and at seven she enrolled in dancing school, soon making a debut in a song-and-dance number with a twelve-piece orchestra. In her preteens she had child parts, both with stock companies in New York and on the road, in melodramas like *Little Nell* and *Mrs. Wiggs of the Cabbage Patch*. West then began appearing in burlesque shows, eventually earning the name "the Baby Vamp." She first appeared on Broadway in a musical revue at age fourteen, and for the next few years appeared in other revues and in vaudeville shows. It was at this time that she first began to rewrite the material given to her by others. In 1909 West married Frank Wallace, a song-and-dance man with whom she had appeared in the same vaudeville act. Wallace wanted her to give up her career; she left him and in 1941 paid him a considerable sum to consent to a divorce.

By 1911 West was an established performer on the New York stage, appearing in musical comedies and revues and finally developing her own

Mae West, 1912

men in the cast, was never brought to New York because West feared a second arrest. *The Wicked Age* (1927), West's next Broadway effort, was an exposé of the beauty contests of the 1920s.

Diamond Lil (1928), a Gay Nineties period piece, was West's most successful play; it had a long Broadway run, followed by a lengthy tour, and it was revived by West in 1949 and again in the late 1960s. The success of the play brought West an offer from Paramount studios to appear in their film *Night After Night* (1932), following a strong recommendation from the film's star, George Raft. The movie is set in a thriving speakeasy during Prohibition. Raft, as owner Joe Anton, desperately wants to improve his station in society, and West is Maudie Triplett, the vulgar woman who upsets his plans. West was not pleased with the original screenplay, and she largely rewrote it but received no screen credit. In the script she created what was to become one of her most famous lines: when a hatcheck girl sees Triplett's jewels and exclaims, "Goodness!," Triplett replies, "Goodness had nothing to do with it." West was so identified with this phrase that she used it as the title of her autobiography in 1959.

Following the release of *Night After Night*, Paramount decided to produce a film with West in the title role. She quickly convinced them to film her play *Diamond Lil;* it was released as *She Done Him Wrong* in 1933. Harry Threw and John Bright wrote the screenplay, but West dominated the filming. To convert the play to feature-film length, she suggested the addition of stock characters—the gigolo, the escaped convict, the framed convict, the barfly—and situations from her vaudeville background. She also selected the director, Lowell Sherman, cast the supporting roles, picked then-unknown Cary Grant as her leading man, and made production suggestions that allowed the crew to complete shooting in eighteen days.

She Done Him Wrong has a simple plot. Saloon-keeper Lou (West) gets involved with white slavery, but a police officer (Cary Grant), disguised as a Salvation Army captain, gets her out of trouble and falls in love with her. What makes the film work is its suggestive dialogue (Grant: "You bad girl!" West: "You'll find out."). The oneliners ("Is that a gun in your pocket or are you just glad to see me?") invited censorship, and songs like "Where Has My Easy Rider Gone?" brought calls to strengthen the Hollywood Production Code.

The success of *She Done Him Wrong* led immediately to *I'm No Angel* (1933), West's first credited screenwriting job. The film follows the rise of

vaudeville act. By 1916 she was forging her stage persona; she added a daring dance to her act and dressed in flamboyant gowns sparkling with diamonds. After many years of rewriting the material she performed on stage, West decided she was capable of writing a play. Her first attempt, *Sex* (1926), is about a sailor, a prostitute, and a blackmailer; the courts found it obscene, and West and others responsible for the production were jailed in New York. *The Drag* (1927), subtitled *A Homosexual Comedy Drama in Three Acts*, with forty gay

Tira (West) from carnival dancer and lion tamer to kept woman in a penthouse apartment. Among the men she takes advantage of are Slick Wiley (Ralf Harolde), a professional pickpocket; Ernest Brown (William Davidson), a wealthy suitor whom she steals from his fiancée (Gertrude Michael); and a socialite (Kent Taylor). She finally falls in love with Jack Clayton (Cary Grant), the socialite's naive cousin, and they wed.

Between *I'm No Angel* and *Belle of the Nineties* (1934), an important development in censorship worked to take the edge off West's wit and extravagant sexuality on film. Although the Motion Picture Production Code had been adopted by the industry in 1930, it had proved ineffective. In response to its failures, a committee of Catholic bishops formed the Legion of Decency in 1934, and that same year the Production Code adopted a seal of approval and saw the appointment of a chief censor. Thus, West's films were subject to closer scrutiny than before; many innuendos and ribald scenes were removed from *Belle of the Nineties;* the

Mae West and cameraman Karl Struss during the filming of
Belle of the Nineties

resulting movie is thin on plot and heavy on musical numbers. Singer Ruby Carter (West) is in love with two men—Ace Lamont (John Miljan), a gambler, and Tiger Kid (Roger Pryor), a boxer who ends up working for Ace. Ace and the Kid plot to steal Ruby's jewels. When she discovers their plan, she gets revenge by drugging the Kid before a fight on which Ace has wagered heavily. (At the censors' insistence, a scene was added where Ruby forgives and marries the Kid after Ace's death.)

To many critics, West's films, robbed of their bawdiness, were becoming dull, and her next four films claimed respectively fewer box-office successes. The first of these pictures, *Goin' to Town* (1935), was written by West from a story by Marion Morgan about Cleo Borden (West), a western oil heiress who moves into high society. Some critics thought that West had difficulty separating humor from vindictiveness in her satire of blue bloods; they perceived ill temper in her lampoon of the society women who desired to exclude Cleo Borden from participation in the activities of the Newport aristocracy. *Klondike Annie* (1936), which West adapted from her play *Frisco Kate*, tells of a torch singer (West) who escapes from the police after stabbing her lover (Harold Huber). Putting on the dress of a dead Salvation Army officer, she brings prosperity to a Klondike settlement house by instilling some excitement into the church services. Few critics found credible the character's sudden reformation in the film's climax; most interpreted her conversion to religion as a mockery of the church or an act wrapped in subtle irony. Still, under Raoul Walsh's direction, *Klondike Annie* became one of West's best pictures.

Go West, Young Man (1936) was West's screen adaptation of Lawrence Riley's popular play *Personal Appearance;* Henry Hathaway directed. When her car breaks down in Pennsylvania, film star Mavis Arden (West) falls in love with a local man (Randolph Scott); her agent (Warren William) tries to end the romance because her movie contract forbids her marrying. West's next picture, *Every Day's a Holiday* (1939), was her only movie to lose money. Set in New York's Bowery in 1899, the film is about a con artist, Peaches O'Day (West), who ends up supporting Jim McCarey (Edmund Lowe), an honest police officer, as reform candidate for mayor.

After *Every Day's a Holiday,* West was released from her contract at Paramount. Universal studios invited her to costar with W. C. Fields in *My Little Chickadee* (1940). Fields agreed to the teaming but had already turned down Paramount's script. West

W. C. Fields and Mae West in My Little Chickadee, *the last film for which West received screenwriting credit*

wrote a screen story titled "The Lady and the Bandit," and she and Fields then wrote a screenplay from her story. Although they received equal screen credit and both wrote their own dialogue, West believed that she had contributed more to the script than Fields. Flower Belle Lee (West) is run out of town and meets inept con man Cuthbert J. Twillie (Fields) on the train. Believing him to be wealthy, she enlists the aid of a cardsharp, who poses as a minister and marries them in what Twillie believes to be a real ceremony. When they arrive at the nearest city, she falls in love with the Masked Bandit (Joseph Calleia) and leaves Twillie. The standard characterization that West wrote for herself was not integrated with Fields's character, and *My Little Chickadee* never really works. It was West's final screenplay.

After making one more motion picture, *The Heat's On* (1941), West retired from filmmaking for nearly thirty years. She had devoted much time to a screenplay on Catherine the Great but was never able to find commercial backing for the film; finally she turned it into the play *Catherine Was Great* in 1944. In 1970 she accepted a role in the film version of Gore Vidal's novel *Myra Breckenridge;* she wrote

all of her own dialogue for the film but received no screen credit. In 1979 she starred in *Sextette*, the film version of her play *The Drag*, but she did not write the screenplay. Both pictures were box-office failures, and she never made another film. Mae West died in 1980.

References:

Michael Bayar, *Mae West* (New York: Harcourt Brace Jovanovich, 1975);

Andrew Bergman, *We're in the Money: Depression America and Its Films* (New York: New York University Press, 1971), pp. 49-52, 55-57, 59-60;

Eric Braun, "Doing What Comes Naturally," *Films and Filming*, 17 (October 1970): 27-32; 17 (November 1970): 38-42;

John Mason Brown, *Two on the Aisle: Ten Years of the American Theatre in Performance* (New York: Norton, 1938), pp. 247-248;

Gerald Clarke, "At 84 Mae West is Still Mae West," *Time*, 111 (22 May 1978): 65-66;

Harold Clurman, "Mae West as Diamond Lil," *New Republic*, 120 (21 February 1949): 28;

Frank Condon, "Come Up and Meet Mae West,"

Colliers, 93 (16 June 1934): 26, 42;

Penelope Gilliatt, *Unholy Fools: Wits, Comics, Disturbers of the Peace* (New York: Viking, 1973), pp. 154-156;

Lewis H. Lapham, "Let Me Tell You About Mae West," *Saturday Evening Post*, 237 (14 November 1964): 76-78;

Arthur H. Lewis, *It Was Fun While It Lasted* (New York: Trident Press, 1973);

Arthur Mayer, *Merely Colossal: The Story of the Movies from the Long Chase to the Chaise Lounge* (New York: Simon & Schuster, 1953), pp. 119-123;

Kristina Nordstrom, "Mae West in Venice," *Women and Film*, 1 (1973): 93;

William Troy, "Mae West and the Classic Tradition," *Nation*, 137 (8 November 1933): 548;

Jon Tuska, *The Films of Mae West* (Secaucus, N.J.: Citadel Press, 1973);

Alexander Walker, *The Celluloid Sacrifice: Aspects of Sex in the Movies* (New York: Hawthorn Books, 1966), pp. 64-80;

C. Yurman, "Mae West Talks About the Gay Boys," *Gay*, 24 (20 July 1970): 3.

Calder Willingham
(23 December 1922-   )

Joseph Millichap
Western Kentucky University

See also the Willingham entry in *DLB 2, American Novelists Since World War II*.

MOTION PICTURES: *The Strange One* (Columbia, 1957), story and screenplay, adapted by Willingham from his novel and play *End as a Man*;

Paths of Glory (United Artists, 1957), screenplay by Willingham, Stanley Kubrick, and Jim Thompson;

The Vikings (United Artists, 1958), screenplay;

One-Eyed Jacks (Paramount, 1961), screenplay by Willingham and Guy Trosper;

The Graduate (Embassy, 1967), screenplay by Willingham and Buck Henry;

Little Big Man (National General Pictures, 1970), screenplay;

Thieves Like Us (United Artists, 1974), screenplay by Willingham, Joan Tewkesbury, and Robert Altman.

BOOKS: *End as a Man* (New York: Vanguard, 1947; London: Lehmann, 1952);

Geraldine Bradshaw (New York: Vanguard, 1950; London: Barker, 1964);

The Gates of Hell (New York: Vanguard, 1951; London: Mayflower, 1966);

Reach to the Stars (New York: Vanguard, 1951; London: Barker, 1965);

Calder Willingham

Natural Child (New York: Dial, 1952; London: Mayflower, 1968);

To Eat a Peach (New York: Dial, 1955; London: Mayflower, 1966);

Eternal Fire (New York: Vanguard, 1963; London: Barker, 1963);

Providence Island (New York: Vanguard, 1969; London: Hart-Davis, 1969);

Rambling Rose (New York: Delacorte, 1972; London: Hart-Davis, MacGibbon, 1973);

The Big Nickel (New York: Dial, 1975; London: Hart-Davis, MacGibbon, 1976);

The Building of Venus Four (New York: Woodhill, 1977).

TELEVISION: *Thou Shalt Not Commit Adultery* (NBC, 1978), teleplay by Willingham and Del Reisman.

Like many screenwriters who came to Hollywood with a literary background, Calder Willingham clearly differentiates between the two forms in which he writes—novels and screenplays.

He sees fiction as his "real work," his screenplays as work necessary to support his large family (he has six children). He has said, "I cannot take with genuine seriousness any of the films on which I have worked." Actually Willingham's seven screenplays are mostly admirable efforts, literate and intelligent work for such important films as *Paths of Glory* (1957), *The Graduate* (1967), *Little Big Man* (1970), and *Thieves Like Us* (1974).

Born in Atlanta , Georgia, the son of Eleanor Churchill and Calder Baynard Willingham, a hotel manager, Willingham was raised in the South. He attended the Citadel in South Carolina from 1940 to 1941 and the University of Virginia from 1941 to 1943. He married Helene Rothenberg in 1945, and they had a son, Paul. They were divorced a few years later. He married Jane Marie Bennett in 1953, and they have five children.

His first novel, *End as a Man* (1947), brought Willingham almost immediate success as a writer. The book was set in a military school and drew upon his experiences at the Citadel. Despite critical praise for this early effort, Willingham turned away

Ralph Meeker and Kirk Douglas in Paths of Glory, *a film about honor, valor, and manhood during wartime*

from the realism of *End as a Man* to black humor and expressionistic form in a projected trilogy about the lives of hotel bellmen. Only two volumes, *Geraldine Bradshaw* (1950) and *Reach to the Stars* (1951), were published. A collection of stories and two other novels followed in this black humor mode.

Willingham was brought to Hollywood in 1957 to write the film version of *End as a Man.* Retitled *The Strange One*, the movie was an atmospheric study of the corruption of young men at a military school. The central character, the "strange one," is a cadet (Ben Gazarra) who holds an unexplained influence over the other students, gradually ruining them all.

Stanley Kubrick next hired Willingham to help prepare a script based on German writer Stefan Zweig's story "The Burning Secret." The project fell through and the screenplay was never filmed, but Kubrick kept Willingham in mind and asked him to work in his next film, *Paths of Glory*

(1957). Kubrick, Willingham, and Jim Thompson adapted the movie from Humphrey Cobb's novel, a fact-based account of the execution of three French soldiers for cowardice during the First World War. Willingham's concerns with the definition of manhood surface in this film; the "real men" are not the officers who prattle about honor and glory, but the innocent soldiers, shot just to set an example to the others.

The Vikings (1958) is also concerned with locating manhood, but the film shared little else with Willingham's other efforts. Written from an adaptation by Dale Wasserman of Edison Marshall's novel *The Viking*, Willingham's screenplay reduces a complicated historical novel to a Hollywood action piece, a sort of Western in the Northland. Richard Fleischer directed in conventional action style.

Willingham's next project was a real Western, though hardly a conventional example of the genre. *One-Eyed Jacks* (1961) was adapted from the novel *The Authentic Death of Hendry Jones* by Charles

Anne Bancroft and Dustin Hoffman in The Graduate, *a landmark film of the 1960s*

Neider. Rio (Marlon Brando) and Dad (Karl Malden) are bank robbers in Mexico, where Dad betrays Rio to the *rurales*. Several years later Rio escapes from prison and traces Dad to Monterey, California, where he is now sheriff. Before Rio can take revenge, he falls in love with Dad's pretty stepdaughter (Pina Pelicer) and decides to spare him. Dad reacts fearfully, however, forcing a shootout which only Rio survives. *One-Eyed Jacks* has some exciting moments, which demonstrate that true manhood lies not in vengeance but forgiveness. But the film is severely damaged by its direction; Brando, making his directorial debut, was simply not capable of handling the project. (Stanley Kubrick and Sam Peckinpah had been replaced early on.)

For the next four years, Willingham devoted himself to writing fiction, including *Eternal Fire* (1963), a mock-Southern gothic. He returned to screenwriting in 1967 with *The Graduate*. Buck Henry collaborated on this adaptation of Charles Webb's novel; the script is tighter, funnier, and more telling than its source. In this benchmark film of the 1960s Benjamin Braddock (Dustin Hoffman) graduates from college to return to the empty materialism of his parents' suburban home. He is seduced by Mrs. Robinson (Anne Bancroft), the wife of his father's business partner. Ben tries to escape this meaningless affair and falls in love with the Robinsons' daughter Elaine (Katharine Ross). He resolves his dilemma by rescuing Elaine at the moment before she marries another man.

Braddock's search for the meaning in his life made *The Graduate* ideally suited for the 1960s; Willingham, Henry, Hoffman, Bancroft, and Ross all received Academy Award nominations for their work. The movie was nominated for best picture and Mike Nichols was chosen best director.

In 1970 Willingham adapted *Little Big Man* from Thomas Berger's comic novel; Arthur Penn directed. The film is the story of one man's maturation in the Old West; it follows its protagonist, Jack Crabb (Dustin Hoffman), from his teenaged years through adulthood. He is orphaned, raised by Indians, brought to civilization by white settlers, becomes a gunslinger, and is reunited with the In-dians just before the battle of Little Big Horn. A revisionist history of the West, the story rejects the traditional notions of heroism and courage. The death of Wild Bill Hickok is deglamorized, and George Custer is portrayed as a cruel, virtually insane man. Crabb lives by the Cheyenne definition of "human being"—he is a person at peace with himself, with others, and with his environment. Willingham's script condenses Berger's novel neatly, but the film still seems overlong and suffers from a didacticism which includes indirect references to the Vietnam war.

A young protagonist also discovers his manhood in *Thieves Like Us* (1974), an adaptation of Edward Anderson's novel. (It had been filmed once before, by Nicholas Ray, as *Live by Night* in 1949.) Robert Altman directed and collaborated on the script with Willingham and Joan Tewkesbury. The protagonist is twenty-one-year-old Bowie (Keith Carradine), a country boy sentenced to life in prison for a murder that seems to have been self-defense. He escapes from prison with T-Dub (Bert Remsen) and Chickamaw (John Schuck), and they embark on a series of bank robberies. Bowie finds happiness in his awkward relationship with a simple, sweet girl named Keechie (Shelley Duvall), but his misguided loyalty to T-Dub and Chickamaw leads to his doom. The film is one of Altman's most underrated, a genuine American tragedy told in a clean, understated style. It was Willingham's final screenplay; since 1974 he has devoted himself solely to fiction writing.

Although Calder Willingham's screenplays are all adaptations of novels and frequently written in collaboration, his personal stamp can be seen in the literacy and intelligence of adaptation, the sense of drama, and the consistent concern with themes of maturity and manhood. From his first novel to his most recent, this theme pervades his fiction and, quite naturally, he discovers it in the works he adapted for the screen. Willingham's screenplays may have been primarily intended to underwrite his fiction, but they also provided him the chance to shape disparate materials to fit his vision of the world as an arena in which manhood is painfully won or lost.

Michael Wilson
(1 July 1914-9 April 1978)

Phyllis Z. Singer

MOTION PICTURES: *The Men in Her Life* (Columbia, 1941), screenplay by Wilson, Paul Trivers, and Frederick Kohner;

Border Patrol (United Artists, 1942), screen story and screenplay;

Colt Comrades (United Artists, 1944), screen story and screenplay;

Bar 20 (United Artists, 1944), screen story and screenplay by Wilson, Norman Houston, and Mortimer Grant;

A Place in the Sun (Paramount, 1951), screenplay by Wilson and Harry Brown;

Salt of the Earth (Independent Productions, 1954), screen story and screenplay;

The Sandpiper (M-G-M, 1965), screenplay by Wilson and Dalton Trumbo;

Planet of the Apes (20th Century-Fox, 1968), screenplay by Wilson and Rod Serling;

Che! (20th Century-Fox, 1969), screenplay by Wilson and Sy Bartlett.

OTHER: *Salt of the Earth* (screenplay), in *Salt of the Earth: The Story of a Film*, by Herbert J. Biberman (Boston: Beacon Press, 1965).

Michael Wilson was one of the many Hollywood screenwriters who was denied work and banished from Hollywood in the 1950s because of his supposed Communist beliefs. Wilson himself considered his scripts to be "humanistic" rather than Communistic; he saw himself as a screenwriter who honestly portrayed the human condition and let the viewers infer what they wished. Shortly before his death in 1978 he told *Take One* magazine: "I tend to feel that didactic or agit-prop approach to the whole art form is an incorrect one for progressives. . . . If the aim is primarily to change people, the film artist or creator is better off simply depicting honestly the way things are rather than beating people over the head with his own point of view in a propagandistic way."

Wilson was born in McAlester, Oklahoma. He graduated from the University of California in 1936 and won a grant to study in France in 1937 and 1938. He then taught literature but decided

that, before he could teach properly, he had to learn how to write fiction himself. He published several stories in *Esquire* and *Reader's Digest* in the late 1930s, and these led to his being invited to Hollywood in 1940. Wilson arrived with only scorn for motion pictures, intending to write several scripts, make money, and leave Hollywood to write a novel. Instead, he remained an active screenwriter for nearly thirty years.

His first screenplay was *The Men in Her Life* (1941), adapted from Eleanor Smith's book *Ballerina* (1932). The movie's director, Gregory Ratoff, had already worked with six writers without producing a usable script. Since he was running out of money, he had to find a writer who would accept as little as $100 a week; Wilson accepted the job and wrote his screenplay quickly, completing it only a few hours before shooting was to begin. The final screenplay seemed to reflect the haste in which it was written; the movie was filled with clichéd situations and stock characters. It also suffered in comparison to an earlier French version of Smith's book, *Ballerina* (1938). Circus performer Lina Varsavina (Loretta Young) is made into a ballet dancer by Stanislas Rosing (Conrad Veidt); she gives up her husband and even her baby for her career.

Producer Harry Sherman next engaged Wilson to write three Hopalong Cassidy Westerns: *Border Patrol* (1942), *Colt Comrades* (1944), and *Bar 20* (1944). Wilson's career was interrupted by World War II; he was commissioned a lieutenant in the Marines, serving in Guam, Saipan, and Kwajalein. Upon his return to America, he began writing for 20th Century-Fox. He wrote an uncredited adaptation of *Ali Baba and the Forty Thieves* (1944), one of a series of elaborate fantasy films made by the studio during the 1940s.

Two prestigious assignments followed, but neither was to be fully realized. Wilson wrote a screenplay based on Thomas Wolfe's *Look Homeward, Angel* in 1945; but the screenplay was never produced. Wilson was then asked to work on *It's a Wonderful Life* (1946). The movie had its origins in "The Greatest Gift," a story written by Philip Van Doren Stern, who intended it simply to be a Christ-

Elizabeth Taylor and Montgomery Clift in A Place in the Sun, *adapted from Theodore Dreiser's novel*
An American Tragedy

mas gift for his friends. RKO bought the story and eventually turned it over to Frank Capra. Wilson was one of several authors, along with Clifford Odets and Dalton Trumbo, who worked on the film in its early stages as RKO and Capra tried to find a workable script. However, he received no screen credit, and it is uncertain what contributions he made to the final script, which was attributed to Capra, Frances Goodrich, and Albert Hackett.

A Place in the Sun (1951), adapted from Theodore Dreiser's *An American Tragedy*, finally gave Wilson the chance to write a screenplay in which he could make a social comment. Wilson saw Dreiser's protagonist George Eastman (Montgomery Clift) as a man seduced by luxury. He escapes his life of poverty through a job in a mill, but just when he has the opportunity to become successful from his relationship with socialite Angela Vickers (Elizabeth Taylor), his girlfriend and fellow mill worker Alice (Shelley Winters) informs him she is pregnant. George plans to kill Alice, and when she drowns he is accused of her murder.

There were many arguments between Wilson and director George Stevens when *A Place in the*

Sun was filming. Stevens feared that Wilson's screenplay was too overtly political and the film would be picketed by the American Legion. Eventually Harry Brown was brought in to soften Wilson's work. In particular, Wilson and Stevens disagreed over the film's conclusion, in which George is found guilty of a murder he contemplated but did not commit; Wilson wanted the scene to be an indictment of the American justice system, but Stevens and Brown made it clear that this was an isolated case. When the film was released, some critics felt that it concentrated on the love story and played down Dreiser's social commentary, but Wilson defended the film, calling it an "honest and illuminating statement of the American scene." He and Brown won an Academy Award for their work; Stevens was chosen best director; and the film was nominated for best picture.

In 1951 Wilson was brought before the House Un-American Activities Committee and questioned about his membership in the Communist party. He refused to answer questions, and he was eventually blacklisted and unable to work in Hollywood. Most studios also refused to grant screen credit to anyone with Communist ties, and when Wilson's next movie *Five Fingers* (1952) was released, no screenwriter was credited. It was adapted from L. C. Moyzisch's novel *Operation Cicero*, a spy thriller about British efforts to track Cicero, a German spy who worked as a valet to an English politician. Although Wilson did not intend the film to be a political statement, leftist beliefs can be read into his screenplay. The movie is critical of both Allied and Axis espionage efforts, with one British agent (Michael Rennie) describing himself as "no more than a gossip"; Cicero (James Mason) acts not out of political conviction but simply for money; he is delighted when his wealth makes him the equal, then the superior of a former employer (Danielle Darrieux). At the end, the Germans pay Cicero with counterfeit bills—his riches are worthless. Political comment is subtly presented in the film, which remains foremost a gripping entertainment, well directed by Joseph Mankiewicz, who also worked without credit on the script. The Mystery Writers of America presented Wilson with an Edgar for his screenplay.

Salt of the Earth (1954) was Wilson's first film project after the blacklisting (*Five Fingers*, though released after Wilson was blacklisted, had been filmed before). The movie was conceived as an attempt to allow blacklisted artists to work outside the industry; the blacklist victims working on this film included Wilson; his brother-in-law Paul Jarrico, who produced; director Herbert Biberman; Biberman's wife, actress Gale Sondergaard (who withdrew before shooting began); actor Will Geer; and most of the technical crew. The movie was a fictionalized account of the strike of Mexican American zinc miners against the Empire Zinc Company in Silver City, New Mexico, in 1951 and 1952. The movie was sponsored by the International Union of Mine, Mill and Smelter Workers and made with the cooperation of the striking workers. This project allowed Wilson to spend a month living with the miners and to make subsequent visits to discuss his screenplay with them. He developed a story around two characters: worker Ramon Quintero (Juan Chacon) and his pregnant wife (Rosaura Revueltas), who narrates the film.

Salt of the Earth was plagued with problems both during shooting and after its release. While in production, the movie was attacked in the press; vigilante groups caused violence on the set; and Revueltas was sent back to Mexico by immigration officials. When the film was completed, almost no theater in the United States would show it. It fared better in Europe, playing to large audiences in Rus-

sia and winning the French Academie du Cinema award for best foreign film. Its reputation has also grown in the United States, particularly because of the feminist aspects of the movie: when the workers are prevented from picketing due to a court order, the wives become protestors and the husbands stay at home as housekeepers.

After working on *Salt of the Earth*, Wilson left the United States and went to live in France, where he remained until 1964. With Anatole Litvak he made a film version of Lillian Hellman's *Montserrat*, about the life of Simon Bolivar, but it was never released. Meanwhile, in America, United Artists had filmed Wilson's screenplay for *Friendly Persuasion* (1956). The script had been written in 1947, and Gary Cooper had been selected to star in the film, but Cooper's other commitments delayed production for nearly a decade. The blacklist was in full force by then, and Wilson received no credit for his work. Director William Wyler stated publicly that Jessamyn West had written the script from her own novel, but the film was actually released with no screenwriter credited. It is the story of a Quaker family whose life is disrupted by the Civil War. Son Josh (Anthony Perkins) feels he should join the Army, but his mother (Dorothy McGuire) is strongly opposed to this notion, while the more understanding father (Gary Cooper) tries to find a balance between their strict religious beliefs and the demands of society. The movie's nine-year delay gave it an unexpected timeliness upon its release. Coming shortly after the Korean war, its pleas for a peaceful and moral life took on an added significance. It received an Academy Award nomination for best picture of 1956.

Wilson worked with another blacklisted screenwriter, Carl Foreman, in adapting Pierre Boulle's *The Bridge on the River Kwai* (1957). A British officer is taken prisoner in Malaysia during World War II, and he and his men are ordered by the Japanese to build a bridge across a nearby river. The colonel soon grows obsessed with the building of the bridge and becomes oblivious to the fact that he is helping the Japanese. Because of the blacklist, Wilson and Foreman were denied screen credit, which was given to Boulle, who did not speak or write English. The movie went on to become a great critical and financial success, winning Academy Awards for best picture and best director (David Lean). Wilson and Foreman were unable to claim their best screenplay Oscar. (It was awarded to their widows in 1985.)

In 1959 Wilson wrote a historical epic for Italian director Alberto Lattuada. *La Tempesta (The*

Dorothy McGuire, Anthony Perkins, and Gary Cooper in Friendly Persuasion. *Wilson's name was not included in the screen credits because he was on the Hollywood blacklist.*

Tempest) is a tale of Russia in the time of Catherine the Great. A young guardsman (Geoffrey Horne) is sent to a distant fortress for discipline and falls in love with the Captain's beautiful daughter (Silvana Mangano). Wilson then collaborated with blacklisted director Martin Ritt on *Five Branded Women* (1960), about a group of European women ostracized for consorting with their German lovers during World War II; they decide to join the fight against the Nazis.

David Lean then hired Wilson to work on the screenplay for *Lawrence of Arabia* (1962), based on T. E. Lawrence's *Seven Pillars of Wisdom.* Lawrence was a British intelligence officer during World War I who organized Arabs in a revolt against Turkey. The film romanticized his career, but critics agreed that the enigmatic Lawrence was depicted well, and the movie won an Academy Award for best picture of the year. By this time the blacklist was beginning to end, and an inquiry by the Writers

Guild proved that Wilson had written at least one-third of the script, entitling him to screenplay credit. But Columbia Pictures refused and Robert Bolt received sole credit. Wilson did receive the British Writers Guild Award for his work.

The Sandpiper (1965) was the last variation on a theme that Wilson had explored in *The Men in Her Life, Salt of the Earth, Friendly Persuasion,* and *A Place in the Sun.* He presents a romantically involved couple and examines the differences between what the man and the woman want from the relationship. In *The Sandpiper,* an Episcopalian minister (Richard Burton) has an affair with a free-spirited beachcomber (Elizabeth Taylor). He is overcome by guilt and leaves both his lover and his wife (Eva Marie Saint) to regain his faith. Despite the talent behind the film—Wilson, coauthor Dalton Trumbo, director Vincente Minnelli—it was not a success. Overlong and badly cast, it was one of his most poorly received films.

Kim Hunter, James Daly, Charlton Heston, Woodrow Parfrey, James Whitmore, Maurice Evans, and Roddy McDowall in Planet of the Apes

Wilson next collaborated with Rod Serling on *Planet of the Apes* (1968), adapted from Pierre Boulle's 1963 novel. Four astronauts, traveling two thousand years into the future, land on an unknown planet where humans are unintelligent beasts and society is run by talking apes who capture them. One astronaut (Charlton Heston) escapes from the apes and flees to what the apes have deemed the Forbidden Zone, where he discovers that he is on the planet Earth where a nuclear war has destroyed human civilization. Wilson brought to the material the same romantic slant he had given *Lawrence of Arabia,* and his contributions balanced well against Serling's moralizing. The movie was a great financial success, grossing over fifteen million dollars and inspiring four sequels.

Producer Sy Bartlett offered Wilson the opportunity to work on a film biography of Cuban revolutionary Ernesto "Che" Guevara. Wilson was delighted at the chance to write about the man who, he said, "had captured the imagination of the young people of the world." Shortly after Guevara's

death in 1967, Bartlett had interviewed dozens of people who had known him and formed a screen story based on these interviews. Wilson decided to dramatize the interviews, having his characters appear as participants in the story and as on-camera witnesses describing Guevara to an unseen questioner. Unfortunately the completed film was a shallow, inaccurate account that was met with hostile reviews and indifferent audiences. Wilson later lamented the project's failure but observed: "I should have known better than just to think that one could do an honest picture about Guevara in a stronghold like 20th Century-Fox."

Che! (1969) was Wilson's last screen credit. In the early 1970s, he began work on a script about a Vietnam veteran who becomes an adviser to antiwar activists, but it was never produced. A variety of health problems, including a severe stroke, left him unable to work in the years that followed. Survived by his wife Zelma and their two daughters, Michael Wilson died of a heart attack in California in 1978.

References:
Aljean Harmetz, "Oscars go to writers for 'Kwai,' "
    New York Times, 16 March 1985, p. 11;
Danny Peary, *Cult Movies 2* (New York: Dell, 1983),
    pp. 135-138;
Mitch Tuchman, "Michael Wilson," *Take One*, 6
    (September 1978).

Contributors

Michael Adams...*Syracuse, New York*
Joseph Adamson ....*Santa Monica, California*
Christopher Adcock ....*Los Angeles, California*
Terry L. Andrews ....*Chadwick School*
Joel Bellman...*La Verne, California*
William Boddy...*New York, New York*
Jay Boyer ....*Arizona State University*
Richard Braverman..*Santa Monica, California*
Jonathan Buchsbaum...*New York, New York*
Evan William Cameron ....*Washington State University*
Leslie Clark..*San Francisco, California*
Randall Clark ....*Decatur, Georgia*
James Desmarais...*Venice, California*
John Driscoll...*University of Washington*
Ellen Feldman ....
Alexa Foreman..*Atlanta, Georgia*
Sam Frank..*Van Nuys, California*
John Hagan..*New York, New York*
Michael Hartman ....*Oklahoma State University*
Alan S. Horowitz..*Los Angeles, California*
Eugene L. Huddleston..*Michigan State University*
Edith Hurwitz..*New York, New York*
Bruce Kawin..*University of Colorado*
Tanita C. Kelly ....*Hollywood, California*
Audrey Kupferberg ....*White Plains, New York*
Christopher T. Lee ....*Columbia, South Carolina*
Stephen Lesser ....*Los Angeles, California*
Kevin Mace..*Oklahoma State University*
Richard Macksey ....*Johns Hopkins University*
Linda Malm ....*Mt. Baldy, California*
Gabriel Miller ....*Rutgers University*
Joseph Millichap..*Western Kentucky University*
James Moore ....*Claremont, California*
Joyce Olin ....*Los Angeles, California*
Barton Palmer...*Georgia State University*
Joyce Rheuban ....*Maywood, New Jersey*
Nick Roddick...*London, England*
Barry Sabath..*Urbana, Illinois*
H. Wayne Schuth ....*University of New Orleans*
Roberta Sharp ....*La Verne, California*
Phyllis Z. Singer ....*Bayside, New York*
Thomas Slater ....*Northwest Missouri State University*
Maynard Tereba Smith...*Los Angeles, California*
Botham Stone..*Columbia, South Carolina*
Malvin Wald ....*Sherman Oaks, California*
Dale Winogura ....*Hollywood, California*

Cumulative Index

Dictionary of Literary Biography, Volumes 1-44
Dictionary of Literary Biography Yearbook, 1980-1984
Dictionary of Literary Biography Documentary Series, Volumes 1-4

Cumulative Index

DLB before number: *Dictionary of Literary Biography*, Volumes 1-44
Y before number: *Dictionary of Literary Biography Yearbook*, 1980-1984
DS before number: *Dictionary of Literary Biography Documentary Series*, Volumes 1-4

A

Butler, Samuel 1835-1902 . . . . DLB18

Butterworth, Hezekiah 1839-1905 . . . . DLB42

B. V. (see Thomson, James)

Byatt, A. S. 1936- DLB14

Byles, Mather 1707-1788 . . . . DLB24

Byrd, William II 1674-1744 . . . . DLB24

Byrne, John Keyes (see Leonard, Hugh)

C

Cabell, James Branch 1879-1958 . . . . DLB9

Cable, George Washington 1844-1925 . . . . DLB12

Cahan, Abraham 1860-1951 . . . . DLB9, 25, 28

Cain, George 1943- DLB33

Caldwell, Ben 1937- DLB38

Caldwell, Erskine, 1903- DLB9

Calhoun, John C. 1782-1850 . . . . DLB3

Calisher, Hortense 1911- DLB2

Calmer, Edgar 1907- DLB4

Calverley, C. S. 1831-1884 . . . . DLB35

Calvert, George Henry 1803-1889 . . . . DLB1

Camm, John 1718-1778 . . . . DLB31

Campbell, John 1653-1728 . . . . DLB43

Campbell, John W., Jr. 1910-1971 . . . . DLB8

Campbell, Roy 1901-1957 . . . . DLB20

Cannan, Gilbert 1884-1955 . . . . DLB10

Cannell, Kathleen 1891-1974 . . . . DLB4

Cannell, Skipwith 1887-1957 . . . . DLB45

Cantwell, Robert 1908-1978 . . . . DLB9

Capen, Joseph 1658-1725 . . . . DLB24

Capote, Truman 1924-1984 . . . . DLB2; Y80, 84

Carey, Mathew 1760-1839 . . . . DLB37

Carroll, Gladys Hasty 1904- DLB9

Carroll, John 1735-1815 . . . . DLB37

Carroll, Lewis 1832-1898 . . . . DLB18

Carroll, Paul 1927- DLB16

Carroll, Paul Vincent 1900-1968 . . . . DLB10

Carruth, Hayden 1921- DLB5

Carryl, Charles E. 1841-1920 . . . . DLB42

Carswell, Catherine 1879-1946 . . . . DLB36

Carter, Angela 1940- DLB14

Carter, Henry (see Leslie, Frank)

Carter, Landon 1710-1778 . . . . DLB31

Carter, Lin 1930- Y81

Caruthers, William Alexander 1802-1846 . . . . DLB3

Carver, Jonathan 1710-1780 . . . . DLB31

Carver, Raymond 1938- Y84

Cary, Joyce 1888-1957 . . . . DLB15

Casey, Juanita 1925- DLB14

Casey, Michael 1947- DLB5

Cassady, Carolyn 1923- DLB16

Cassady, Neal 1926-1968 . . . . DLB16

Cassill, R. V. 1919- DLB6

Castlemon, Harry (see Fosdick, Charles Austin)

Caswall, Edward 1814-1878 . . . . DLB32

Cather, Willa 1873-1947 . . . . DLB9; DS1

Catton, Bruce 1899-1978 . . . . DLB17

Causley, Charles 1917- DLB27

Caute, David 1936- DLB14

Challans, Eileen Mary (see Renault, Mary)

Chalmers, George 1742-1825 . . . . DLB30

Chamberlain, Samuel S. 1851-1916 . . . . DLB25

Chamberlin, William Henry 1897-1969 . . . . DLB29

Chambers, Charles Haddon 1860-1921 . . . . DLB10

Chandler, Harry 1864-1944 . . . . DLB29

Channing, Edward 1856-1931 . . . . DLB17

Channing, Edward Tyrrell 1790-1856 . . . . DLB1

Channing, William Ellery 1780-1842 . . . . DLB1

Channing, William Ellery II 1817-1901 . . . . DLB1

Channing, William Henry 1810-1884 . . . . DLB1

Chaplin, Charlie 1889-1977 . . . . DLB44

Chappell, Fred 1936- DLB6

Charles, Gerda 1914- DLB14

Charyn, Jerome 1937- Y83

Chase, Borden 1900-1971 . . . . DLB26

Chase-Riboud, Barbara 1936- DLB33

Chauncy, Charles 1705-1787 . . . . DLB24

Chayefsky, Paddy 1923-1981 . . . . DLB7, 44; Y81

Cheever, Ezekiel 1615-1708 . . . . DLB24

Cheever, John 1912-1982 . . . . DLB2; Y80, 82

D

G

M

P

S

T

Y

Cumulative Index

Z

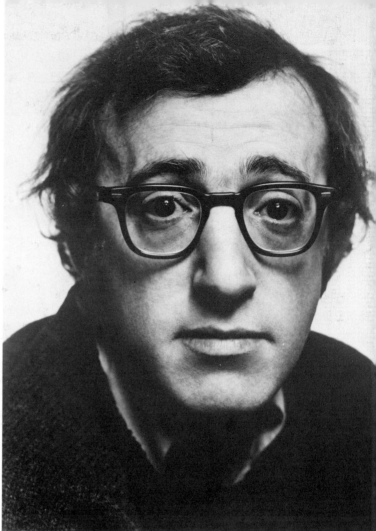